A HISTORY OF THE LAWS OF WAR: VOLUME 1

This unique new work of reference traces the origins of the modern laws of warfare from the earliest times to the present day. Relying on written records from as far back as 2400 BCE, and using sources ranging from the Bible to Security Council Resolutions, the author pieces together the history of a subject which is almost as old as civilisation itself. The author shows that as long as humanity has been waging wars it has also been trying to find ways of legitimising different forms of combatants and regulating the treatment of captives.

This first book on warfare deals with the broad question of whether the patterns of dealing with combatants and captives have changed over the last 5,000 years, and if so, how? In terms of context, the first part of the book is about combatants and those who can 'lawfully' take part in combat. In many regards, this part of the first volume is a series of 'less than ideal' pathways. This is because in an ideal world there would be no combatants because there would be no fighting. Yet as a species we do not live in such a place or even anywhere near it, either historically or in contemporary times. This being so, a second-best alternative has been to attempt to control the size of military forces and, therefore, the bloodshed. This is also not the case by which humanity has worked over the previous centuries. Rather, the clear assumption for thousands of years has been that authorities are allowed to build the size of their armed forces as large as they wish. The restraints that have been applied are in terms of the quality and methods by which combatants are taken. The considerations pertain to questions of biology such as age and sex, geographical considerations such as nationality, and the multiple nuances of informal or formal combatants. These questions have also overlapped with ones of compulsion and whether citizens within a country can be compelled to fight without their consent. Accordingly, for the previous 3,000 years, the question has not been whether there should be a limit on the number of soldiers, but rather who is or is not a lawful combatant. It has rarely been a question of numbers. It has been, and remains, one of type. The second part of this book is about people, typically combatants, captured in battle. It is about what happens to their status as prisoners, about the possibilities of torture, assistance if they are wounded and what happens to their remains should they be killed and their bodies fall into enemy hands. The theme that ties all of these considerations together is that all of the acts befall those who are, to one degree or another, captives of their enemies. As such, they are no longer masters of their own fate.

As a work of reference this first volume, as part of a set of three, is unrivalled, and will be of immense benefit to scholars and practitioners researching and advising on the laws of warfare. It also tells a story which throws fascinating new light on the history of international law and on the history of warfare itself.

A History of the Laws of War: Volume 1

The Customs and Laws of War with Regards to Combatants and Captives

Alexander Gillespie

·HART·
PUBLISHING
OXFORD AND PORTLAND, OREGON
2011

Published in the United Kingdom by Hart Publishing Ltd
16C Worcester Place, Oxford, OX1 2JW
Telephone: +44 (0)1865 517530
Fax: +44 (0)1865 510710
E-mail: mail@hartpub.co.uk
Website: http://www.hartpub.co.uk

Published in North America (US and Canada) by
Hart Publishing
c/o International Specialized Book Services
920 NE 58th Avenue, Suite 300
Portland, OR 97213-3786
USA
Tel: +1 503 287 3093 or toll-free: (1) 800 944 6190
Fax: +1 503 280 8832
E-mail: orders@isbs.com
Website: http://www.isbs.com

British Library Cataloguing in Publication Data
Data Available

ISBN: 978-1-84946-204-4

Typeset by Hope Services, Abingdon
Printed and bound in Great Britain by
TJ International Ltd, Padstow, Cornwall

This book is for my children, Jamie, Conor and Renee,
with the wish that they never have to endure or witness any of the horrors
I have recorded in these pages.

Table of Contents

Treaties and Sources

The 509 BCE Treaty Between Rome and Carthage 509 BC in Lewis, N and Reinhold M (eds) *Roman Civilisation: Records*, Vol 1 (Columbia, Columbia University Press) 72.

The 421 BCE Peace of Nicias in Ferguson, J (ed) (1978) *Political and Social Life in the Great Age of Athens: A Sourcebook* (London, Open University Press) 420–21.

The 241 BCE Peace Treaty Between Rome and Carthage in Lewis, N and Reinhold M (eds) *Roman Civilisation: Records*, Vol 1 (Columbia, Columbia University Press) 153.

The 201 BCE Peace Treaty with Carthage in Lewis, N and Reinhold M (eds) *Roman Civilisation: Records*, Vol 1, 171.

The 200 BCE Treaty Between Crete and Rhodes in Austin, M (ed) (1992) *The Hellenistic World From Alexander to the Roman Conquest: A Collection of Readings* (Cambridge, Cambridge University Press) 93, 95.

The 196 BCE Peace Treaty with Philip V in Lewis, N and Reinhold M (eds) *Roman Civilisation: Records*, Vol 1 (Columbia, Columbia University Press) 174.

The 188 BCE Peace Treaty with Antiochus III of Syria in Lewis, N and Reinhold M (eds) *Roman Civilisation: Records*, Vol 1 (Columbia, Columbia University Press).

The 189 BCE Peace Treaty with the Aetolian League in Lewis, N and Reinhold M (eds) *Roman Civilisation: Records*, Vol 1 (Columbia, Columbia University Press) 178.

The 163 BCE Agreement Between Eumenes I and his Mercenaries in Austin, M (ed) (1992) *The Hellenistic World From Alexander to the Roman Conquest: A Collection of Readings* (Cambridge, Cambridge University Press) 321.

The 271 Treaty With the Vandals in Lewis, N and Reinhold, M (eds) *Roman Civilization: Selected Readings*, Vol II (NYC, Columbia University Press) 437.

The 989 Peace and Truce of God, in Herlihy, D (ed) *The History of Feudalism* (NY, Harper) 286.

The 1250 Treaty in Ghunaimi, M (1968) *The Muslim Conception of International Law* (NYC, Columbia University Press) 49–50.

The 1435 Treaty of Arras in Contamine, P (1984) *War in the Middle Ages* (Oxford, Blackmore) 190.

The 1474 Treaty Between Louis XI and the Swiss 1474 in Laffan, R (ed) (1929) *Select Historical Documents: 800–1492* (NY, Holt) 176.

The 1648 Treaty of Westphalia in Symcox, G (1974) *The Documentary History of Western Civilisation. War, Diplomacy and Imperialism* (NYC, Walker) 41.

The 1657 Treaty of Wehlau in Macartney, C (ed) (1970) *The Habsburg and Hohenzollern Dynasties* (NYC, Harper) 242.

The 1687 Peace of Nijmegen in Reddaway, F (ed) (1930) *Select Documents in European History*, Vol II (London, Methuen) 1492–715, 154.

The 1697 Treaty of Ryswick in Axelrod, A (ed) (2001) *Encyclopedia of Historical Treaties and Alliances*, Vol I (NYC, Facts on File) 59.

The 1714 Rastadt Treaty 1714 in Axelrod, A (ed) (2001) *Encyclopedia of Historical Treaties and Alliances*, Vol I (NYC, Facts on File) 82.

The 1746 Treaty Between Persia and the Ottoman Empire in Hurewitz, T (ed) *Diplomacy in the Near and Middle East: A Documentary Record* (Columbia, NYC University Press) 52.

The 1763 Treaty of Paris in Axelrod, A (ed) (2001) *Encyclopedia of Historical Treaties and Alliances*, Vol I (NYC, Facts on File) 119.

The 1783 Treaty of Paris Between the United States and Great Britain in Axelrod, A (ed) (2001) *Encyclopedia of Historical Treaties and Alliances*, Vol I (NYC, Facts on File) 125.

The 1784 Treaty With the Six Nations in Axelrod, A (ed) (2001) *Encyclopedia of Historical Treaties and Alliances*, Vol I (NYC, Facts on File) 129.

The 1785 Treaty of Amity and Commerce Between His Majesty the King of Prussia, and the United States of America. Full text is available at the Yale Law School 'Avalon Project'. http://avalon.law.yale.edu.

The 1794 Jay Treaty in Bernis, S.F (1962) *Jay's Treaty: A Study in Commerce and Dilpomacy* (New Haven, Yale University Press).

The 1801 Treaty of Luneville in Russell, W (1857) *Russell's History of Modern Europe, Epitomised* (London, Routledge & Co) 536–43.

The 1802 Treaty of Amiens in Axelrod, A (ed) (2001) *Encyclopedia of Historical Treaties and Alliances*, Vol I (NYC, Facts on File) 175.

The 1802 Treaty Between France and the Ottoman Empire in van den Boogert, M.H and Fleet, K (eds) (2003) *The Ottoman capitulations: Text and Context* (Rome, Istituto per l'Oriente CA Nallino) vii, [575]–[727].

The 1803 Treaty Between France and Prussia. Full text available at the Napoleon Series website http://www.napoleon-series.org.

The 1806 Franco–Russian Peace Treaty.

The 1808 Treaty of Tilsit, De Clercq, Traites, II, 270–72, Dodsley, J (1809) *Annual review or A View of the History, Politics, and Literature for the Year 1807* (London, Hardin and Wright & W Wilson) 720–24.

The 1808 Convention of Cintra, Dodsley, J (1809) *Annual Register, or a View of the History, Politics, and Literature, for the Year 1808* (London, Hardin and Wright & W Wilson) 282–84.

The 1808 Treaty Between France and Prussia, Kippis, A et al (1908) *Annual Review or a View of the History, Politics and Literature for the Year 1807* (London, Paternoster Row) 275–76.

The 1809 Treaty of Vienna, Baldwin, Cradock and Joy (1821) *The Annual Register or a View of the History, Politics and Literature for the Year 1809*, Vol 51 (London, TC Hansard) 733–38.

The 1809 Treaty of Schonbrunn in Axelrod, A (ed) (2001) *Encyclopedia of Historical Treaties and Alliances, Vol I* (NYC, Facts on File) 185, 187.

The 1814 Treaty of Fort Jackson, Halbert, H.S and Ball, T.H (1895) *The Creek War of 1813 and 1814* (Tuscaloosa, University of Alabama Press) 282–84.

The 1815 Peace of Paris in Axelrod, A (ed) (2001) *Encyclopedia of Historical Treaties and Alliances*, Vol I (NYC, Facts on File) 189.

The 1820 General Treaty for Supressing Piracy in Hurewitz, T (ed) *Diplomacy in the Near and Middle East: A Documentary Record* (NYC, Columbia UP) 88–89.

The 1841 Quintuple Treaty in Green, D (1866) *Facts and Suggestions, Biographical, Historical, Financial and Political addressed to the People of the United States* (NY, Richardson & Co) 120–23.

The 1842 Treaty of Nanjing Between Great Britain and China in Axelrod, A (ed) (2001) *Encyclopedia of Historical Treaties and Alliances*, Vol I (NYC, Facts on File) 299.

The 1842 Webster-Ashburton Treaty, Eliot, C.W (ed) (1980) *American Historical Documents, 1000–1904* (Danbury, Connecticut; Grolier).

The 1848 Treaty of Guadalupe Hidalgo in Axelrod, A (ed) (2001) *Encyclopedia of Historical Treaties and Alliances*, Vol I (NYC, Facts on File) 222.

The 1856 Treaty of Peace Between Great Britain, Austria, Turkey, France and Russia 1856 in Mowat, R (1918) *The Great European Treaties of the Nineteenth Century* (Oxford, Oxford University Press).

The 1859 Treaty of Peace Between Austria, France and Sardinia in Mowat, R (1918) *The Great European Treaties of the Nineteenth Century* (Oxford, Oxford University Press).

The 1866 Treaty of Peace Between Austria and Prussia in Mowat, R (1918) *The Great European Treaties of the Nineteenth Century* (Oxford, Oxford University Press).

The 1871 Treaty of Peace Between France and Germany in Mowat, R (1918) *The Great European Treaties of the Nineteenth Century* (Oxford, Oxford University Press) 78–85.

The 1895 Treaty of Shimonoseki in Axelrod, A (ed) (2001) *Encyclopedia of Historical Treaties and Alliances*, Vol I (NYC, Facts on File) 316.

The 1896 Treaty of Addis Ababa in Brownlie, I and Burns IR (1979) *African Boundaries: a Legal and Diplomatic Encyclopedia* (London, C Hust & Co) 863–64.

The 1898 Treaty of Peace Between the United States and Spain, Eliot, CW (ed) (1980) *American Historical Documents, 1000–1904* (Danbury, Connecticut; Grolier).

The 1899 Hague Convention. Full texts of the Hague Conventions can be found at Yale Law School 'The Avalon Project' http://avalon.law.yale.edu/subject_menus/lawwar.asp.

The 1902 Treaty of Vereeniging in Axelrod, A (ed) (2001) *Encyclopedia of Historical Treaties and Alliances*, Vol I (NYC, Facts on File) 322.

The 1905 Treaty of Portsmouth in Tyler S (1905) *The Japan–Russia War* (Harriburg, The Minter Company) 564–68.

The 1907 Hague Convention. Full texts of the Hague Conventions can be found at Yale Law School 'The Avalon Project' http://avalon.law.yale.edu/subject_menus/lawwar.asp.

The 1907 Convention Relating to the Conversion of Merchant Ships Into War-Ships in Scott, JB (1909) *Technical Delegate of the United States to the Second Peace Conference at the Hague*, Vol II (Baltimore MD, John Hopkins Press).

The 1918 Treaty of Brest-Litovsk in Axelrod, A (ed) (2001) *Encyclopedia of Historical Treaties and Alliances*, Vol I (NYC, Facts on File) 419.

The 1919 Treaty of Versailles in Axelrod, A (ed) (2001) *Encyclopedia of Historical Treaties and Alliances*, Vol I (NYC, Facts on File) 425.

The 1919 Treaty of St Germain, (1920) No 3 Australian Treaty Series.

The 1920 Treaty of Sevres in Treaties of Peace, 1919–1923, Vol II (New York, Carnegie Endowment for International Peace) 789–945.

The 1921 Treaty of Friendship Between Russia and Turkey in Axelrod, A (ed) *Encyclopedia of Historical Treaties and Alliances*, Vol II (NYC, Facts on File) 514.

The Treaty of Rapallo, in Axelrod, A (ed) *Encyclopedia of Historical Treaties and Alliances*, Vol II (NYC, Facts on File) 570.

The 1930 London Treaty (for the Limitation and Reduction of Naval Armaments), 112 LNTS 65.

The 1935 Agreement Concerning War Graves UNTS No 4711, Vol 326, 170.

The 1937 Nyon Agreement, 181 L.N.T.S. 137 in Hudson, R (ed) (1950) *International Legislation*, Vol VII, 1935–37 (NY, Oceana) 831.

The 1937 Convention for the Prevention and Punishment of Terrorism, in Hudson, R (ed) (1950) *International Legislation*, Vol VII, 1935–37 (NY, Oceana) 862.

The 1949 Geneva Convention (III) Relative to the Treatment of Prisoners of War, Full text is available at Yale Law School 'Avalon Project'. http://avalon.law.yale.edu/subject_menus/lawwar.asp.

The 1963 (Tokyo) Convention On Offences And Certain Other Acts Committed On Board Aircraft in (1970) No 14 *Australian Treaty Series.*

The 1970 Hague Convention For the Supression of Unlawful Seizure of Aircraft, 10 ILM (1971) 133; (1972) No 16 *Australian Treaty Series.*

The 1971 Convention for the Suppression of Unlawful Acts Against the Safety of Civil Aviation 1971, UNTS No 14118, Vol 974, 178–84.

The 1973 United States and the Democratic Republic of Vietnam, Agreement on Ending the War and Restoring Peace in Vietnam and the Protocol on the Return of Captured Military Personnel 12 ILM (1973) 63.

Agreement Granting Independence of Portuguese Guinea 13 ILM (1974) 1244.

The 1979 Convention on the Elimination of All Forms of Discrimination Against Women 19 ILM (1980) 33.

The 1979 International Convention Against the Taking of Hostages, A/C6/34/L23, UNTS, Vol 1316, 205.

The 1991 Agreement on a Comprehensive Political Settlement of the Cambodia Conflict 31 ILM (1992) 183.

The 1991 Agreement Concerning the Sovereignty, Independence, Territorial Integrity and Inviolability, Neutrality and National Unity of Cambodia 31 ILM (1992) 200.

The 1992 Final Peace Agreement in El-Salvador, (A/46/864-S/23501).

The 1992 General Peace Agreement for Mozambique, Protocols IV and VI. Full text available at the United States Institute of Peace http://www.usip.org.

The 1994 Akosombo Agreement (S/1994/1174).

The 1994 Comprehensive Agreement on Human Rights, UNTS No 31370, Vol 1841.

The 1995 Dayton Peace Agreement 33 ILM (1996) 170.

The 1996 Agreement on the Basis for the Legal Integration of the Unidad Revolucionaria Nacional Guatemalteca 36 ILM (1997) 258.

The 1996 Agreement on the Definitive Ceasefire 36 ILM (1997) 274.

The 1996 Agreement on the Strengthening of Civilian Power and on the Role of the Armed Forces in a Democratic Society (A/51/410) (S/1996/853).

The 1996 Agreement on Constitutional Reforms and the Electoral Regime.

The 1997 Terrorist Bombing Convention (A/RES/52/164).

The 1998 Northern Ireland Peace Agreement 37 ILM (1998) 175.

The 1999 Military Technical Agreement Between the International Security Force (KFOR) and the Governments of Federal Republic of Yugoslavia and the Republic of Serbia 38 ILM (1999) 1217.

The 1999 ILO Convention Concerning the Prohibition of the Worst Forms of Child Labour (ILO Convention No 182) 38 ILM (1999) 1207.

The 1999 Interim Agreement for Peace and Self-Government in Kosovo 38 ILM (1999) 1451.

The 2000 Cotonou Agreement with revisions in 2005 and 2010. The full text of the Cotonou Agreement is available at European Commission website. http://ec.europa.eu.

The 2001 Macedonian Framework Agreement, Immigration and Refugee Board of Canada (2003) Macedonia: Implementation of the Framework (Ohrid) Agreement, MCD41727.E.

The 2003 Comprehensive Peace Agreement Between the Government of Liberia and the Liberians United for Reconciliation and Democracy (LURD) and the Movement for Democracy in Liberia (MODEL) and Political Parties. Full text is available as part of the Peace Agreements Digital Collection at the United States Institute of Peace http://www.usip.org.

The 2003 Optional Protocol to the Convention Against Torture and Other Cruel, Inhuman or Degrading Treatment of Punishment. Annex to UNGA Resolution A/RS/57/199 (Jan 9, 2003).

Introduction

1. The Conversation on Sunday Afternoon

THE TOPIC OF this book is the customs and laws of war with regards to combatants and captives. This book is accompanied by two other books, which deal with the customs and laws of war with regards to civilians and weapons. All three of these books began with a discussion I had with my mother over 12 years ago towards the end of the twentieth century, on whether the practices of humanity were better or worse than in the past. Simply put: 'Was humanity making progress or not?' Whilst I argued in the affirmative, my mother argued in the negative. As with many such lunchtime discussions on Sunday afternoons, trying to find robust benchmarks was (and is) very difficult, if not impossible. Although the conversation on this particular Sunday afternoon moved on to other topics, this question of 'progress' caught me.

2. Progress, Utopia and Warfare

There are many philosophical discussions around the idea of 'progress'.[1] These discussions are often linked to various forms of Utopian thinking.[2] I struggle to think of an appropriate figure for how many gallons of ink have been expended in debates on this question, or suggestions of the correct path to Utopia, where the difficulties of the past are bypassed and a bright future awaits humanity. There is no monopoly on these plans, and the libraries are looking rather full on these variations of themes which run for thousands of miles of shelving, from theology to ideology, cross-referenced with a bewildering collection of historical epochs and philosophical musings. These questions have received a great deal of attention since the end of the Cold War, and the triumph of liberal democracies and limited forms of free market capitalism. Despite the attractiveness of such a thesis, this book is *not* about such questions. For me, to answer a question about progress required an examination of a topic somewhat more concrete, and somewhat more difficult. The topic I settled on was warfare, and in particular,

[1] Doren, V (1969) *The Idea of Progress* (NYC, Praeger); Hiderbrand, G (ed) (1949) *The Idea of Progress: A Collection of Readings* (Los Angeles, California University Press); Melzer, A (ed) (1995) *History and the Idea of Progress* (NYC, Cornell University Press); Marx, L (ed) (1996) *Progress: Fact or Illusion* (NYC, Michigan University Press).

[2] Manuel, F (1979) *Utopian Thought in the Western World* (NYC, Harvard University Press); Manuel, F (ed) (1969) *Utopias and Utopian Thought* (NYC, Condor); Buber, M (1949) *Paths in Utopia* (London, Routledge); Mumford, L (1962) *The Story of Utopias* (NYC, Viking); Bernini, M (1950) *Journey Through Utopia* (London, Routledge).

those who fight, those who do not fight but are caught up in the conflict, and the weapons that are utilised. I settled on these three themes by which to measure progress as these, to me, are the most difficult areas to find advancement as when humanity is at the lowest point of its relationships, it is a much more honest test, than studies of when everything is going well.

The other reason I decided to examine the topic of warfare was because the questions humans face in this area are remarkably constant and consistent. The term 'human' in the context of human evolution refers to the genus *Homo*, and the subspecies, *sapiens*, (meaning 'wise man' or 'knowing man'). Anatomically modern humans appear from about 200,000 years ago, and started to move out of Africa between 100,000 to 50,000 years ago. During this process, it appears that our direct ancestors gradually marginalised the 'archaic' homo varieties. It is possible that this 'wise' or 'knowing', species, in combination with natural factors like climate change, systematically drove our closest genetic relatives such as the Neanderthals, to extinction, with the process only ending perhaps 10,000 years ago.[3] Our victorious stone-age ancestors then went on to develop agricultural systems between 8500 and 7000 BCE and civilisations around 3000 BCE, which were leaving written records. This epoch, known as the Bronze Age, is the starting point of this book. The end point of this book is 5000 years later, which is the Nuclear Age. Throughout this period, warfare has been a consistent pattern in human history. I am of the belief that the people who formed these countless generations, although different in terms of technology and social organisation, are essentially the same as their descendants today. Anatomically, and I expect emotionally, the people of the twenty-first century are probably much closer to our historic cousins than we care to admit. This contention is important for this book, as many of the practices examined and questions raised by them allow me to pose the question of whether we, as a species, have progressed over the last 5,000 years when dealing with essentially the same issues, albeit in different historical epochs and with different technologies. That is, the human context on whether to intentionally kill civilians, torture prisoners, or use indiscriminate or unusually cruel weapons in times of war, whether thousands of years ago, or three days ago, is essentially the same.

3. Facts

As I began this project, it quickly became apparent that is was near impossible to answer these questions as there was no cumulative history on all of the acts which I wished to examine. Whilst there are between dozens and thousands of studies on each topic at hand, there was no comprehensive collection of the evidence and facts from which analysis could begin. For example, whilst there is a lot written about the destruction of cultural property in war, most of the work focuses on one particular period. Such a study will typically be about the law, or the particular history of an episode at hand. Rarely will a study look at the way the same issue has been dealt with, in custom and law, over the last 5,000 years, through different ages. This rationale applies to every theme in this book. As such, the collection of this evidence and facts became the foundation of this book. This is an important point, for a large part of my thinking in

[3] Wong, K (2010) 'Twilight of the Neanderthals' in *Selections on Evolution* (NYC, Scientific American) 23–29; Keegan, J (1993) *A History of Warfare* (London, Hutchinson) 116–22.

this book is the Latin principle, *res ipsa loquitur* (the facts speak for themselves). That is, the thematic practices of 5,000 years of warfare should allow the reader to make up their own minds on whether there has been success, or failure, in some of these areas. My interpretations at the end are only the way that I see the evidence. I have no doubt that others will see it differently.

Before I go on, it is necessary to underline two points about 'the facts'. The first concerns the question of numbers. All numbers in this book should be treated with caution. I have tried at all points to give the best figures that are possible, often after looking at examples from multiples sources. Nevertheless, historians and commentators make mistakes for all sorts of reasons, which appear to range from simple mistakes to pure political manipulation. I find this a particularly disturbing part of my studies, as I am of the belief that few matters are more important to citizens, than full and transparent information on matters of warfare. The problem is, this is rarely the case. Governments of all flavours consistently prefer to manipulate the truth to protect themselves, rather than keep their citizens informed of the choices and decisions made in their names.[4]

The second point on 'facts' relates to the sources that are used in this book. The methodology of this book is somewhat complicated. The skeleton on which it is built is treaties. I place a great weight on the bilateral and international instruments of each age, as despite all of the difficulties of different languages and different ages, treaties and/or agreements reflect in the clearest way possible how different nations see a shared problem and shared solution. As the reader will see, I also try to directly quote the applicable law in each instance. For the purpose of this study it is important to show that the governing rules are often much easier to understand (even if unpaletable) than many commentators pretend them to be. As such, at each point, the law on the question has been set out as simply as possible.

In places where there were no treaties, the bones are taken from the practice of key players of the period, which often became custom. In each epoch I have attempted to read and quote the original sources. These have often been supplemented by the best monographs I can find on each epoch. After the Enlightenment, the modern literature is much more plentiful and it is much easier to identify and trace important international events in treaties, custom and literature. This is especially so with events since the beginning of the twentieth century, and more so, since the Second World War. With regard to the later epoch, I have been able to find, read and incorporate, inter alia, every Security Council resolution which is related to the topics at hand. I have done this because the Security Council, in the absence of clear international rules or rulings by the International Court of Justice, is the next best source for obtaining a definitive interpretation on an area.

Although the information on conflicts of the twentieth century is in relative abundance, the same cannot be said for many contemporary conflicts, where reliable sources can be quite patchy, and it is not until a few years have past, that good analysis of an area can be achieved. Of course this is not always the case, as in some instances, some non-governmental sectors provide excellent, up-to-date analysis on a number of contemporary issues. The source I have adopted most frequently in this regard for the conflicts since the 1990s has been Human Rights Watch, which I have found to be most reliable.

[4] Knightley, P (1975) *The First Casualty* (London, Pan) 269.

4. Progress in the Area of Combatants and Captives

This first book on warfare deals with the broad question of whether the patterns of dealing with combatants and captives have changed over the last 5,000 years, and if so, how? In terms of context, the first part of the book is about combatants and those who can 'lawfully' take part in combat. In many regards, this part of the book is a series of 'less than ideal' pathways. This is because in an ideal world there would be no combatants because there would be no fighting. Yet as a species we do not live in such a place or even anywhere near it, either historically or in contemporary times. This being so, a second-best alternative would be to control strictly the size of military forces and, therefore, the bloodshed. This is also not the case by which humanity has worked over the previous centuries. Rather, the clear assumption for thousands of years has been that authorities are allowed to build the size of their armed forces as large as they wish. The restraints that have been applied are in terms of the quality and methods by which combatants are taken. The considerations pertain to questions of biology such as age and sex, geographical considerations such as nationality, and the multiple nuances of informal or formal combatants. These questions have also overlapped with ones of compulsion and whether citizens within a country can be compelled to fight without their consent. Accordingly, for the previous 3,000 years, the question has not been whether there should be a limit on the number of soldiers, but rather who is or is not a lawful combatant. It has rarely been a question of numbers. It has been, and remains, one of type.

The second part of this book is about people, typically combatants, captured in battle. It is about what happens to their status as prisoners, about the possibilities of torture, assistance if they are wounded and what happens to their remains should they fall into enemy hands. The theme that ties all of these considerations together is that all of the acts befall those who are, to one degree or another, captives of their enemies. As such, they are no longer masters of their own fate.

For the purposes of this study, the easiest way to assess whether or not progress had been made was to divide the areas of combatants and captives into seven separate questions, as each of these questions – to me – had a benchmark by which progress could be assessed as there was, in my historically and socially privileged position, a 'right' and 'wrong' answer in each area. The seven questions are:

1. *Can armies be restricted in numbers?* I chose this question because of the contention that military forces are both financially expensive and intrinsically dangerous groups of people to maintain. Moreover, in an ideal world, if conflict must occur, the reduction in the number of people who have to fight appears a good goal.
2. *Who can fight – in terms of age, sex and nationality?* These questions are important because I do not like the idea of children fighting, and I am interested in the question of whether women can fight like men. The question of nationality is about mercenaries. My idealism in this area is that people who are free to sell their military skills to foreign overlords do not necessarily bring stability to peaceful relations.
3. *Can people be forced to fight?* This question is important because being forced to kill other humans appears to me the most extreme form of servitude possible. Progress in this area would reflect freedom of choice, not conscription.

4. *Must the combatants be formal, and identifiable?* This topic demands attention because if combatants look like civilians, civilians will easily become targets. Progress here, is about protecting civilians, not combatants.
5. *What happens to combatants when captured as prisoners of war?* My idealism in this area is that once a soldier has given up their option to fight, that they are no longer an enemy who may be killed without restraint.
6. *Can they be tortured, or helped when wounded?* The progress in this area should be reflected in a movement away from torture (as it seems both pointless and ethically repugnant), whereby prisoners are protected, not exploited. Such protection should also extend to helping them when they are wounded and no longer a threat. To help such captives and show restraint to the way they are treated, to me, appears the core of humanitarian concerns.
7. *And what happens to their remains when dead?* I may have read too much Greek literature, but my benchmark in this area is that when a combatant is dead, they deserve respect, irrespective of what side they fought on. At the point of death, we all become equal.

I

Combatants

1. In an Ideal World

ARMED FORCES ARE full of people who are trained to kill. These forces can represent a threat to both their neighbours and the societies they represent. In an ideal world there would be no armed forces. This would not only save vast amounts of money, it would also make the world much safer. The guarantee to this safety is that there would be perpetual peace and no need to fight. As a second-best alternative, if violence between combatants is required, that should be done at the smallest possible scale, of which single-combat between champions is the ideal.

Single, as opposed to group, combat occurred in a number of primitive societies.[1] It is also recorded in some of the earliest known human records from ancient Sumer (twenty-fourth century BCE). Whilst we are uncertain why single combat occurred in primitive societies, we know, with the aid of written records, that it also occurred at the outset of recorded history because it was a good way to settle disputes between powerful opposing groups, or in this instance, between a ruler and one of his vassals. As a way to settle the conflict, it was suggested by the vassal leaders that, rather than a wholesale resort to arms, a contest between two selected champions could resolve the dispute. Although in practice the armies behind the contestants rarely accepted the outcome and marched happily into slavery if their champion fell, the obviously attractive idea, that only the leaders should fight and thereby resolve the fate of the overall battle (and its outcome), rather than dragging entire armies or populations into conflict, is well-entrenched in the historical records.[2] For example, in the Bible, Goliath suggested that a contest between two champions would be used instead of using two armies. Thus: 'If he be able to fight with me, and to kill me, then we will be your servants, but if I prevail against him, and kill him, then ye shall be our servants and serve us.'[3]

[1] Davie, M (1929) *The Evolution of War* (Boston, Yale University Press) 176–79.

[2] Kramer, S (1981) *History Begins at Sumer* (Philadelphia, University of Pennsylvania Press) 21. Rather than accepting the consequences of Goliath's defeat (slavery), the Philistines fled and had to be run down by the Israelites. Similarly, Menelaos, at the point of victory, had Paris snatched away to safety by Aphrodite, and the fighting amongst the others continued unabated. See the *Illiad* 3.380–82 and 4.445–49.

[3] 1 Samuel 17:9.

Similar practices can be found elsewhere in the Bible,[4] in Ancient Greece,[5] in Rome[6] with the Celts, Vikings and other warriors of the Dark Ages (where it also grew into the practice of settling disputes within society by trial by battle)[7] and by some Byzantine leaders.[8] It was practised, and sometimes offered as an alternative to large-scale conflicts during the early Middle Ages, occasionally during the Crusades, the Hundred Years War, the Renaissance and the Reformation. It also appears to have been cross-cultural. Despite these latter examples, it was rare that the leaders managed to face each other, in substitution for their armies, although they did sometimes collide on the battlefield, such as with Clovis (466–511) the King of the Franks, and Alaric, the King of the Visigoths. The latter met his end at the sharp point of the sword of Clovis in 507. Likewise, the Persian commander, as well as three of his generals, met their end after facing the Byzantine emperor Heraclius (575–674) in single combat before the battle of Nineveh in 627.[9] Although rare in later periods, some leaders continued to issue such king-to-king challenges. For example, when Tamerlane (1370–1405) challenged the leader of Syria, Qara Yusef (1388–1420), to single combat, he argued: 'Why should the world face ruin because of two men?'[10]

In the case of Tamerlane, the challenge was not accepted and tens of thousands of fighting men and non-fighting civilians were swept up and destroyed in the conflict between the two men. All of the epochs until the sixteenth century are similar to this, being punctuated with excuses of why it was not suitable for the leaders to fight their opposing number alone.[11]

2. In the Real World

Since single combat is a practice which has been removed from contemporary history, a second-best approach would be to limit the amount of bloodshed by limiting the overall number of soldiers who could fight as these soldiers can represent a threat to both friends and enemies alike. This necessity to break security forces away from the direct control of leaders, as opposed to the general populace of a country, is also an age-old problem. It

[4] See 2 Samuel 21:18–21; 23:20–21; 1 Chronicles 11: 21–25, 20:4–8. For a discussion of this, see Carrol, R (1995) 'War in the Hebrew Bible' in Rich, J and Shipley (eds) (1993) G *War and Society in the Greek World* (London, Routledge) 22, 36–37; Yadin, Y (1963) *The Art of War in Biblical Lands* (London Weidenfeld) 267.

[5] *The History of Herodotus* trans Rawlson, J (1909) Vol I (London, Dent) 1:82; VanWees, H (2009) *Greek Warfare: Myths and Realitie* (London, Duckworth) 133; Adcock, F (1959) *The Greek and Macedonian Art of War* (California, University of California Press) 4–5.

[6] Livy *The War with Hannibal* in trans De Sekincourt (1972) (London, Penguin) Bks I (23) 7, VII (9) 7, XXIII (26) 4, XXV (18); Ellis, P (1990) *The Celtic Empire* (London, Guild) 19–20, 31, 41, 77; Lendon, J (2005) *Soldiers and Ghosts, A History of Battle in Classical Antiquity* (NYC, Yale University Press) 133–38, 173–76, 186.

[7] Laing, J (2000) *Warriors of the Dark Ages* (London, Sutton) 63, 87, 117; Griffith, P (1995) *The Viking Art of War* (London, Greenhill) 34–35.

[8] Norwich, J (1988) *Byzantium: The Early Centuries* (London, Guild) 297; Contamine, P (1984) *War in the Middle Ages* (Oxford, Blackwell) 41, 261; Norwich, J (1991) *Byzantium. The Apogee* (NYC, Knopf) 234–35.

[9] Wood, H (2008) *The Battle of Hastings* (London, Atlantic) 12, 165; Gillingham, J (1978) *Richard the Lionheart* (London, Weidenfeld) 258; Seward, D (2003) *The Hundred Years War* (London, Robinson) 39–40, 79; Meron, T (1993) *Henry's Wars and Shakespeare's Law* (Oxford, Oxford University Press) 132–41; Arnold, T (2001) *The Renaissance at War* (London, Cassel) 95–96, 142.

[10] Marozzi, J (2005) *Tamerlane: Sword of Islam* (London, Harper) 77.

[11] Rush, P (1964) *The Book of Duels* (London, Harrap) 17, 32–33; Robinson, P (2006) *Military Honour and the Conduct of War* (London, Routledge) 86, 111.

was most aptly displayed in the difference between the Roman Republic and Imperial Rome, as represented by Gnaeus Pompey (106–48 BCE) and Julius Caesar (100–44 BCE). At this point of history, both men worked out that if the military forces were loyal to them, and not the Senate, they could gain control of an empire. Gaius Augustus (63 BCE–14 AD) finished this process in 70 AD when he established a military state with himself as Commander-in-Chief. After that point, the soldier's oath of loyalty was to the Emperor, or as Publius Tacitus (56–117) recorded in 110 AD 'an emperor could be made elsewhere than at Rome'.[12] This process only accelerated as the Roman war-lords increasingly took the provision, control and rewards for the military away from the State, and entrenched them in their own orbit of power (and thus loyalty). This point hit its nadir in 193 AD, when the Praetorian guards announced that the Emperor of the Roman world was to be decided by public auction. The auction was based upon who could offer the largest sums of money to the individual soldiers within the military.[13]

Some 1,900 years after Caesar, the history books are full of versions of military dictatorships, where all of the political power within a country resides with the military. Whilst there are fewer military dictatorships in the twenty-first century than in the past, with only six countries currently classified as such (Burma/Myanmar, Fiji, Guinea, Libya, Niger and North Korea), the twentieth century is replete with examples of the military, rather than civil populations, running countries. This was evident with at least 31 cases in Africa,[14] 21 in the Americas,[15] 16 in Asia[16] and eight in Europe.[17]

[12] Tacitus in trans Wellesley, K (1975) *Histories* (London, Penguin) 1.4. Also, Cook, S (ed) (1966) *The Cambridge Ancient History. The Roman Republic*, 1st edn (Cambridge, Cambridge University Press) 132–37, 293–94, 302–303, 647; Cook, S (ed) (1971) *The Cambridge Ancient History. The Augustan Empire*, 1st edn, Vol X (Cambridge, Cambridge University Press) 218–23, 600, 817–20; Cook, S (ed) (1969) *The Cambridge Ancient History. The Imperial Peace*, 1st edn (Cambridge, Cambridge University Press) 392–99.

[13] Gibbon, E (1926) *The Decline and Fall of the Roman Empire* Vol 1 (London, Methuen) 116–17.

[14] Algeria (1965–78; 1992–94); Benin (1963–64, 1965–68, 1969–70, 1972–75); Burkina Faso (1966–77, 1980–91); Burundi (1966–93, 1996–2003); Central African Republic (1966–79; 1981–91; 2003–05); Chad (1975–79, 1982–93); Comoros (1975–76, 1999–2002); Democratic Republic of the Congo (1965–90); Republic of the Congo (1968–79); Côte d'Ivoire (1999–2000); Egypt (1952–70); Equatorial Guinea (1979–87); Ethiopia (1974–87); The Gambia (1994–96); Ghana (1966–69, 1972–79; 1981–92); Guinea (1984–91; 2008– present); Guinea–Bissau (1980–84; 2003), Lesotho (1986–93), Liberia (1980–84); Libya (1969–present); Madagascar (1972–89); Mali (1968–91); Mauritania (1978–92, 2005–07, 2008–09); Niger (1974–89, 1996–99, 2010–present); Nigeria (1966–79, 1983–89, 1993–98); Rwanda (1973–91), Sierra Leone (1967–68, 1992–96, 1997–98); Somalia (1969–91, local militia rule since 1991); Sudan (1958–64, 1969–86, 1989–2005); Togo (1967–91); and Uganda (1971–79, 1980, 1985–86).

[15] Argentina (1930–32, 1943–46, 1955–58, 1966–73, 1976–83); Bolivia (1828–48, 1861–71, 1876–80, 1930–31, 1936–44, 1951–52, 1964–66, 1969–79, 1980–82); Brazil (1889–94, 1937–45; 1964–85); Chile (1891–96, 1924–25, 1927–31, 1973–90); Colombia (1855–57, 1953–58), Costa Rica (1863–66, 1868–76, 1877–82, 1917–19; 1948–49); Cuba (1933–40; 1952–55), Dominican Republic (1930–61); Ecuador (1876–83; 1937–38; 1963–66; 1972–79); El Salvador (1885–1911, 1931–35, 1944–80); Guatemala (1944–45, 1957–58; 1963–66; 1970–86); Haiti (1950–56; 1986–90), Honduras (1903–07, 1956–57; 1963–71; 1972–82); Mexico (1884–1911); Nicaragua (1937–47, 1950–56, 1967–79); Panama (1968–89); Paraguay (1940–48; 1954–93); Peru (1838–72, 1876–79, 1886–95, 1914–15, 1930–31, 1933–39, 1948–50, 1962–63, 1968–80); Suriname (1980–88); Uruguay (1876–79; 1981–85); and Venezuela (1908–35, 1948–58).

[16] Including Bangladesh (1975–81, 1982–90); Burma (Myanmar) (1958–60, 1962–present); Cambodia (1966–67, 1969–75); Republic of China (1928–75; local militia rule 1912–28); Indonesia (1966–98); Iran (1921–25); Iraq (1949–50; 1952–53; 1958–79); Japan (1936–45); North Korea (1994–present); South Korea (1961–79; 1980–87); Laos (1959–60); Pakistan (1958–71, 1977–88, 1999–2008); Syria (1951–54, 1963–72); Thailand (1933–45, 1946–47, 1948–73, 1976–92, 2006–08); South Vietnam (1963–75); and North Yemen (1962–78).

[17] Including Bulgaria (1934–35, 1944–46); Greece (1922–24, 1925–26, 1936–41, 1967–74); Hungary (1944–45); Poland (1926–35, 1981–83); Portugal (1917–21, 1926–33, 1974–76); Romania (1940–45); Spain (1840–43, 1923–30, 1939–75); Turkey (1960–61, 1970–73, 1980–82).

Of course, not all countries have been the victim of military dictatorships. In some countries, it is the military which allows democratic change to evolve against dictatorships, refusing to enforce the rule of despots. Such examples can reflect the view that – the military is to serve the democracy of its country - rather than the other way around. This approach is well recognised within many Western countries, which were created in the breaking away from non-democratic regimes. In these countries, footnotes to their caution around armed forces (and especially those which are not democratically controlled) can still be seen. For example, the English Bill of Rights of 1689 proclaimed '[t]hat the raising or keeping a standing army within the kingdom in time of peace, unless it be with consent of Parliament, is against law'.[18] The American Declaration of Independence 1776 would add amongst their complaints of the British crown that '[h]e [George III] has kept among us, in times of peace, Standing Armies without the Consent of our legislatures'.[19] The 1789 French Declaration on the Rights of Man and the Citizen supplemented: 'The guarantee of the rights of man and citizens necessitates a public force. This force is, therefore, established for the advantage of all, and not for the private advantage of those to whom it is entrusted.'[20]

In a contemporary context, it has been increasingly, but indirectly recognised at the highest international levels that armed forces which are neither limited nor under the control of a broad type of constitutional power which reflects the will of the people, as opposed to only a few, can be very dangerous and, in many instances, need to be neutralised. For example, the United Nations Security Council recognised in the year 2000 and subsequently that the implementation of the demobilisation and rehabilitation of former combatants, on a case-by-case basis, is an important step in creating peace after there has been conflict either between or within countries.[21] As such, facilitating demobilisation and rehabilitation, if not the complete control over the use of force within a territory, is a common factor in many United Nations' peacekeeping missions.[22] It is also part of a common approach that the Security Council has recommended as an important step to achieving peace in, inter alia, Afghanistan,[23] Angola,[24] Burundi,[25] Cambodia,[26] the Central African Republic,[27] Chad,[28] the Democratic Republic of the

[18] Preamble.

[19] Preamble reprinted in Birley, R (ed) (1944) *Speeches and Documents in American History* Vol I, 1776–1815 (Oxford, Oxford University Press) 1, 4.

[20] Declaration on the Rights of Man and Citizen in Wright, D (ed) (1974) *The French Revolution Documents* (Queensland, University of Queensland Press) 58, 60.

[21] S/RES/1296 (2000, Apr 19).

[22] S/RES/1265 (1999, Sept 17).

[23] S/RES/1536 (2004, Mar 26); S/RES/1589 (2005, Mar 24); S/RES/1624 (2005, Sept 14); S/RES/1662 (2006, Mar 23); S/RES/1419 (2002, June 26).

[24] S/RES/1045 (1996, Feb 8); S/RES/1075 (1996, Oct 11); S/RES/1087 (1996, Dec 11); S/RES/1098 (1997, Feb 27); S/RES/1118 (1997, June 30); S/RES/1118 (1997, June 30); S/RES/1135 (1997, Oct 29); S/RES/1149 (1998, Jan 27); S/RES/1157 (1998, Mar 20); S/RES/1173 (1998, June 12); S/RES/1180 (1998, June 29); S/RES/1087 (1996, Dec 11); S/RES/1102 (1997, Mar 31); S/RES/818 (1993, Apr 14); S/RES/850 (1993, July 9); S/RES/863 (1993, Sept 13); S/RES/747 (1992, Mar 24); S/RES/785 (1992, Oct 30); S/RES/793 (1992, Nov 30); S/RES/804 (1993, Jan 29); S/RES/1008 (1995, Aug 7); S/RES/1055 (1996, May 8); S/RES/1064 (1996, July 11).

[25] S/RES/1545 (2004, May 21).

[26] S/RES/745 (1992, Feb 28).

[27] S/RES/1182 (1998, July 14).

[28] S/RES/1778 (2007, Sept 25).

Congo,[29] Cote d'Ivoire,[30] Cyprus,[31] East Timor,[32] El Salvador,[33] Georgia,[34] Guinea-Bissau,[35] Haiti,[36] Iraq,[37] Lebanon,[38] Liberia,[39] Mozambique,[40] Nicaragua[41] and Sierra Leone.[42]

Supplementary peace agreements which have limited the size of national militaries and sought to ensure that they are both democratised and made subject to fundamental human rights considerations, can be seen with the treaties which ended the conflicts within, inter alia, Angola,[43] Bosnia,[44] Cambodia, Columbia,[45] El Salvador,[46] Guatemala,[47] Kosovo,[48] Liberia,[49] Macedonia,[50] Mozambique[51] and the Philippines,[52] Likewise, in Northern Ireland, an important part of the peace process was '[t]he

[29] S/RES/1592 (2005, Mar 30); S/RES/1376 (2001, Nov 9); S/RES/1417 (2002, June 14); S/RES/1445 (2002, Dec 4); S/RES/1653 (2006, Jan 7); S/RES/1663 (2006, Mar 24); S/RES/1522 (2004, Jan 15); S/RES/1565 (2004, Oct 1); S/RES/1621 (2005, Sept 6).

[30] S/RES/1528 (2004, Feb 27); S/RES/1609 (2005, June 24); S/RES/1633 (2005, Oct 21); / RES/1739 (2007, Jan 10).

[31] S/RES/789 (1992, Nov 25); S/RES/831 (1993, May 27); S/RES/927 (1994, June 15); S/RES/1000 (1995, June 23); S/RES/1032 (1995, Dec 19); S/RES/1089 (1996, Dec 13); S/RES/1178 (1998, June 29); S/RES/1217 (1998, Dec 22); S/RES/1251 (1999, June 29); S/RES/1218 (1998, Dec 22); S/RES/1528 (2004, Feb 27); S/RES/1603 (2005, June 3); S/RES/1609 (2005, June 24); S/RES/1633 (2005, Oct 21); S/RES/1739 (2007, Jan 10); S/RES/1795 (2008, Jan 15).

[32] S/RES/1246 (1999, June 11); S/RES/1473 (2003); S/RES/1543 (2004, May 14); S/RES/1599 (2005, Apr 28); S/RES/1704 (2006, Aug 25).

[33] S/RES/888 (1993, Nov 30); S/RES/920 (1994, May 26).

[34] S/RES/1138 (1997, Nov 14); S/RES/1494 (2003, July 30); S/RES/1582 (2005, Jan 28).

[35] S/RES/1233 (1999, Apr 6).

[36] S/RES/1542 (2004, Apr 30); S/RES/1702 (2006, Aug 15); S/RES/1743 (2007, Feb 15); S/RES/1840 (2008, Oct 14).

[37] S/RES/1511 (2003, Oct 16); S/RES/1546 (2004, June 8).

[38] S/RES/1559 (2004, Sept 2); S/RES/1583 (2005, Jan 28); S/RES/1614 (2005, July 26); S/RES/1655 (2006, Jan 31); S/RES/1701 (2006, Aug 11).

[39] S/RES/972 (1995, Jan 13); S/RES/1014 (1995, Sept 15) S/RES/1041 (1996, Jan 29); S/RES/1509 (2003, Sept 19); S/RES/1607 (2005, June 21); S/RES/1626 (2005, Sept 19); S/RES/1777 (2007, Sept 20); S/RES/1818 (2008, June 13).

[40] S/RES/818 (1993, Apr 14); S/RES/850 (1993, July 9); S/RES/863 (1993, Sept 13); S/RES/882 (1993, Nov 5); S/RES/898 (1994, Feb 23); S/RES/916 (1994, May 6).

[41] S/RES/ 654 (1990, May 4); S/RES/ 656 (1990, June 8).

[42] S/RES/1181 (1998, July 13); S/RES/1260 (1999, Aug 11); S/RES/1270 (1999, Oct 22); S/RES/1289 (2000, Feb 7); S/RES/1370 (2001, Sept 18); S/RES/1470 (28 March 2003) S/RES/1562 (2004, Sept 17).

[43] Lusaka Protocol 1994, Annexes 3 and 4.

[44] Dayton Peace Agreement 1995, Art II, Annex 1A.

[45] Plan for a Peace Process in Columbia. Source: Colombia. President. Plan Colombia: Plan for Peace, Prosperity, and the Strengthening of the State [Bogota], Colombia: Presidency of the Republic, 1999. Note, Human Rights Watch (2005) *Colombia: Letting Paramilitaries Off the Hook* (NYC, HRW); Human Rights Watch (2005) *Columbia's Demobilisation of Paramilitary Groups* (NYC, HRW) 7–14.

[46] Final Peace Agreement in El-Salvador 1992, Ch I, Arts 4, 8, 9 and 10.

[47] Agreement on the Basis for the Legal Integration of the Unidad Revolucionaria Nacional Guatemalteca 1996; Agreement on the Definitive Ceasefire 1996, Arts 3–14, 17–21, 27–31; Agreement on the Strengthening of Civilian Power and on the Role of the Armed Forces in a Democratic Society 1996, Arts 37–45; Agreement on Constitutional Reforms and the Electoral Regime 1996, Arts 20–27.

[48] Military Technical Agreement Between the International Security Force (KFOR) and the Governments of Federal Republic of Yugoslavia and the Republic of Serbia 1999.

[49] Cotonou Agreement, Art 8; Akosombo Agreement, Art 9; Comprehensive Peace Agreement In Liberia, Arts 6 and 7.

[50] Macedonian Framework Agreement 2001, Art 12.

[51] General Peace Agreement for Mozambique 1992, Protocols IV and VI.

[52] See www.usip.org/publications/peace-agreements-philippines.

reduction of the numbers and role of the Armed Forces deployed in Northern Ireland to levels compatible with a normal peaceful society'.[53]

When the question becomes one of limiting the size of armies because of their threat to regional or international security, examples are harder to find. This is despite some very clear advocacy from Immanuel Kant (1724–1804). Kant, in laying out his blueprint for a universal and perpetual peace argued:

> Standing armies shall be gradually abolished. For they constantly threaten other nations with war by giving the appearance that they are prepared for it, which goads nations into competing with one another in the number of men under arms, and this practice knows no bounds. . . . Standing armies are the cause of wars of aggression that are intended to end burdensome expenditures. Moreover, paying men to kill or be killed appears to use them as mere machines and tools in the hands of another (the nation), which is inconsistent with the rights of humanity.[54]

Kant's proposal has consistently failed to be taken seriously. This is unlike the more common option in this area where armed forces of one nation are reduced as a consequence of losing a war and having a peace treaty imposed upon them. The earliest example I can find of this was the Peace Treaty of Philip V of Macedonia (238–179 BCE) in 196 BCE, by which Philip was restricted by the Romans to having an army of no more than 5,000 men.[55] This idea, that the victor was to set the size limit of the defeated enemy as part of a peace treaty, followed through the subsequent treaties, with particularly good examples during the Napoleonic wars. For example, by the Treaty of Paris of 1808, Napoleon imposed an overall limit of 42,000 men on the Prussian army, and forbade them from raising a civil guard. Following the Napoleonic wars, France was limited to an army of 150,000 men.[56] Similarly, after the First World War the Treaty of Versailles limited Germany to an army of 100,000 men. The 100,000 men limit was also the size that the Germans imposed upon the defeated French after the Armistice of June 1940.[57]

Beyond these examples of limits being placed upon the number of people in armed forces as a method to hold down the defeated, the exemplars of history are remarkably few. This is unlike the numerous arms' control treaties whereby the number of weapons has been restricted by mutual agreement. With regards to soldiers, there are very few examples whereby equals have agreed to reduce or control the size (or quality) of their armed forces. Examples which called for the general 'disbandment and discharge' of military forces (beyond what was necessary for national security), like that from the 1648 Peace of Westphalia,[58] and the soft promises that accompanied the end of the Nine Years War (1688–97) are rare (and were not honoured).[59] In a more contemporary context, a

[53] Northern Ireland Peace Agreement 1998, s 8.

[54] Kant, I (1795) 'To Perpetual Peace: A Philosophical Sketch' in Humphrey, T (ed) (1983) *Immanuel Kant. Perpetual Peace and Other Essays* (NYC, Hackett) 107, 108.

[55] Peace Treaty with Philip V 196 BCE in Lewis, N and Reinhold, M (eds) (1951) *Roman Civilization: Selected Readings* (NYC, Columbia University Press) 195.

[56] The Peace of Paris 1815, Art V. Note also the 1803 and 1808 Treaties between France and Prussia, the Treaty of Vienna 1809 and the Frankfort Declaration 1813.

[57] The Treaty of Versailles, Arts 159–62, 183 and 199; the Treaty of St Germain 1919, Art 118; the Treaty of Brest-Litovsk 1918, Art V; the Treaty of Sevres, Arts 181 and 182.

[58] Arts LIV, CXVI and CXVIII.

[59] Bromley, J (1970) *The New Cambridge Modern History. The Rise of Great Britain and Russia*, Vol VI (Cambridge, Cambridge University Press) 382–83.

few similar, isolated, examples exist, such as with the Convention Regarding Central America 1923, through which the five Central American states agreed that except in cases of civil war or impending invasion by another state, their standing armies and national guards would not exceed certain, rather low, levels. These levels were 5,200 for Guatemala, 4,200 for El Salvador and between 2,000 and 2,500 each, for Costa Rica, Honduras and Nicaragua. However, this Central American example is very rare within regional or international contexts, whereby the typical reaction to mutual and cooperative reductions in the size of armed forces has been unsuccessful. The one time that the idea was clearly advocated (by the Russians) at the 1899 Hague Conference, it was clearly rejected. Further attempts in the 1950s as part of the all-encompassing disarmament discussions to limit the amount of manpower in armed forces, spurred on by recommendations of the United Nations General Assembly, of all the major belligerents (with around one million men for the United States, the Soviet Union and China, and 650,000 for France and the United Kingdom) all came to nothing.[60]

3. Building Armed Forces

Despite all of these examples where the Security Council, or countries by themselves, have come to restrict armed forces after conflict as a way to build peace within a society, the fact is that that this overall questioning of the size and amounts of combatants – especially between countries – is very rare. Rather, the clear assumption for thousands of years has been that authorities are allowed to build their armed forces to as large a size as they wish. The restraints that have been applied are in terms of the quality and methods by which combatants are taken. The considerations pertain to biological considerations such as age and sex, geographical considerations such as nationality, and the multiple nuances of informal or formal combatants. These questions have overlapped with ones of compulsion and whether citizens within a country can be compelled to fight without their consent. Accordingly, for the previous 3,000 years, the question has not been whether there should be a limit on the number of soldiers, but rather who is or is not a lawful combatant. It has rarely been a question of numbers. It has been, and remains, one of type.

4. The First Armed Forces

In primitive societies, the 'all-volunteer' forces reflected a far greater mobilisation than most modern States, with most, if not all males, being involved in the conflicts. In addition, women often acted in support in times of combat and a number of examples exist where women were witnessed partaking in combat as equals of men. That is, from the earliest points that can be examined, warriors were not always men.[61]

[60] UNGA Resolution (1946) 41(I) Principles Governing the General Regulation and Reduction of Armaments; Goldblat, J (2003) *Arms Control* (London, Sage) 41–46, 233; Vaghts, D (2000) 'The Hague Conferences and Arms Control' 94 *American Journal of International Law* 31, 34.

[61] Keeley, L (1996) *War Before Civilisation* (Oxford, Oxford University Press) 34, 35; Davie, M (1929) *The Evolution of War* (Boston, Yale University Press) 30–45.

The first armies post-3000 BCE were probably conscripted. By the time of Sargon (2300 BCE) there is evidence that a system of recruitment through an early form of feudalism, with military service linked to landholding, was in practice. This system gave Sargon 5,400 troops at his disposal. One temple alone in the city of Lagash furnished 500 to 600 men from its tenants for the military levy. Failure to turn up to serve could result in execution, and attempts to avoid service by sending substitutes were severely dealt with, with the avoider being put to death and the substitute inheriting all of their property.[62] Mercenaries were probably involved, at some level or other, in these early States, being noted in various epochs, at least as early as 2200 BCE. The word 'mercenary' comes from the word mercer meaning to buy and sell. The role of men who bought and sold military skills in these early epochs is unknown, although the earliest records of mercenaries record them as being unreliable and dangerous 'locust swarms [which] covered the land'.[63] This early epoch was also the first to record assassination. Assassination is political murder. Assassinations can provoke wars, bring on revolutions and cause seismic shifts in national, regional and/or international power. The essence of the act of assassination as a method of informal warfare is treachery via unexpected attack due to the disguise of the assassin, in both methods and/or physical appearance. Around 2300 BCE, Sargon lost both of his sons to this practice.[64]

By 1400 BCE, the Egyptians had a form of conscription through which every temple was obliged, when called upon, to send to the army of the Pharaoh one man in 10 from its dependents. The emphasis was upon men; that is, whilst the Egyptians may have encountered some female cavalry fighting against them in the period of Ramses II (1303–1203 BCE), they themselves did not utilise female fighters. The records suggest that the standard required for entry into the army was, in addition to being male, a minimum height of one metre. Accordingly, boys as young as 10 could be taken into the army. The army itself appears to have been largely standardised. At the first ever recorded battle in history, at Megiddo in 1479 BCE, the Egyptian soldiers were identifiable by their brightly coloured shields which were painted according to which division they were in.[65] The Egyptians also appear to be the first civilisation where there were clear records of an establishment keeping individuals of foreign descent, whom they had branded, in their army. The Egyptians were also the first civilisation to leave records detailing dealings with pirates. The English word pirate is derived through the Latin *pirata*, which is explained as one who makes or attacks ships. Such 'sea raiders' were a problem for both Ramses II and Ramses III (1198–1167), although variations

[62] Kramer, S (1963) *The Sumerians. Their History, Culture and Character* (Chicago, University of Chicago Press) 260; Dawson, D (2001) *The First Armies* (London, Cassell) 89, 94; Postgate, J (1996) *Early Mesopotamia: Society and Economy and the Dawn of History* (London, Routledge) 242. For the subsequent codification of the rules in the early legal systems, see VerSteeg, R (1999) *Early Mesopotamian Law* (Carolina, Carolina Academic Press) 122; Edwards, I (ed) (1971) *The Cambridge Ancient History. Early History of the Middle East*, 3rd edn, Vol 1(2) (Cambridge, Cambridge University Press) 121.

[63] See Cooper, J.S (1983) *The Curse of Agade* (Chicago, University of Chicago Press) 58, line 155–58. Also, Klein, J (1981) *The Royal Hymns of Shulgi King of Ur* (University of Philadelphia) 131; Edwards, I (ed) (1971) *The Cambridge Ancient History. Early History of the Middle East*, 3rd edn, Vol 1(2) (Cambridge, Cambridge University Press) 430; Edwards, I (ed) (1975) *The Cambridge Ancient History. History of the Middle East and Aegean Region 1380–1000 BCE*, Vol II(2), 3rd edn (Cambridge, Cambridge University Press) 509.

[64] Dawson, D (2001) *The First Armies* (London, Cassell) 100; Fetherlin, G (2001) *The Book of Assassins* (London, Wiley) 2–8.

[65] Janssen, R (1990) *Growing Up in Ancient Egypt* (London, Rubicon) 103–106; Ferrill, A (1988) *The Origins of War* (London, Thames & Hudson) 46–47; Dawson, D (2001) The *First Armies* (London, Cassel) 150.

and records of 'lawless robbers' operating within State authority go back 1370 BCE. Finally, the Egyptians left the first records pertaining to spies, which were captured and tortured before the battle of Kadesh (c 1274 BCE).[66]

The Assyrian Empire appears to have maintained the first large-scale standing army where, in a basically feudal system, landholding was given in exchange for military service. The Hittites did the same. Both civilisations also had a penchant for using foreign soldiers with specialised military skills, such as those who could man chariots. However, the Hittites were to record the difficulties that such foreign soldiers may represent, recording in 1400 BCE that there was 'no silver left in the land' due to the cost of paying for foreign soldiers. The other point of originality for the Hittite civilisation is that theirs was the first to clearly record reference to guerrilla-type warfare in the fifteenth century BCE. In this, the Hittite King Mursilis (ruled, 1620–1590 BCE) referred to attacks on his forces by non-conventional soldiers operating at night.[67]

The Hebrews maintained forms of obligation to perform military service for most males from a young age. Exactly how old David was when he slew Goliath is a matter of conjecture, although he may well have been under 18. Female warriors are not notable with this civilisation, although the Bible does involve stories of female leaders in times of conflict, such as Deborah, who was called upon by the Israelites to guide them in their war against the Canaanites. The authorities of David and Solomon were also known to utilise mercenaries.[68] the Bible also contains stories of guerrilla-type warfare. One of the best illustrations is the story of Judas Maccabeus, who led a revolt in Palestine against the Syrians from 166 BCE until his death six years later. As described in the Old Testament's book of Daniel and in two books of the Maccabees in the Apocrypha, the Maccabean forces ambushed the Syrians, stole their weapons, visited local villages secretly at night to rally support and slowly forced the Syrians into fortified garrisons from which they made the occasional foray. It was from this growing strength that Judas sent ambassadors to Rome to form a treaty of defensive alliance against the Syrians. The ancient Israelites were also known to have an effective awareness of the value of spies. Indeed, whilst Joseph was accusing his brothers of being spies, Moses was quick to send out spies to 'bring back a report about the route we are to take' to the land of Canaan. Joshua also utilised spies and Delilah was the first recorded female secret agent in history.[69]

What was most notably different about the Hebrew laws on building armies from their predecessors was not that the Israelites found the commandment 'Thou Shalt Not Kill' so easy to circumvent,[70] but that they contained exceptions whereby certain men could be excused from military service. Thus, although general levies from individual tribes appears the early practice, as the rules solidified, exceptions were built in

[66] Breasted, H *The Ancient Records of Egypt* Vol III (Chicago, University of Chicago Press) ss 580 and 617; Edwards, I (ed) (1975) *The Cambridge Ancient History. History of the Middle East and Aegean Region 1380–1000 BCE*, 3rd edn, Vol II (2) (Cambridge, Cambridge University Press) 99.

[67] Dawson, D (2001) *The First Armies* (London, Cassell) 90, 175, 187; Kelle, B (2007) *Ancient Israel at War* (Oxford, Osprey) 23, 111, 188. For the reprinted section of Hittite Laws, see McNeill, W (ed) (1968) *Readings in World History: The Ancient Near East*, Vol II (New York, Oxford University Press) 199.

[68] Yadin, Y (1963) *The Art of War in Biblical Lands* (London, Weidenfeld) 260, 273, 275–78; Ferrill, A (1988) *The Origins of War* (London, Thames & Hudson) 63. Note Judges 4:8–9.

[69] Joshua 2:2; 2:8–10; 7:2–5; Judges 1:23 and 16:5; 1 Maccabees 8.;

[70] It does not say 'except in self-defence, or when necessary'. Note also the dictum in the Book of Leviticus, 'Love your neighbour as yourself'. See Exodus 20:13 and Leviticus 19:18.

for those that had built a new home and not dedicated it, planted a vineyard and not eaten of it, betrothed a wife and not 'taken' her or where the man was 'fearful and fainthearted'. If this was so, it was mandated to 'let him go and return unto his house, lest his brethren's heart faint as well as his heart'.[71]

The Persians, with a system based on imperial conscription applied in all the satrapies, could raise an army of around 300,000 men. These men were divided into divisions, each dressed in their own distinctive colour, with troops marching in sashes of red, blue, yellow and purple. The Persians also maintained an extensive network of informal combatants as spies.[72]

For the Spartans, there were no debates about conscription or who would serve in the military. Every male citizen was a soldier, poor and wealthy alike, and all males were trained as such between the ages of seven and 60, although the Spartan boys rarely saw combat before the age of 18. Phillip V of Macedon (238–179 BCE) in his grinding war with the Romans, ended up enlisting all boys from the age of 16 and above into his armies. The Athenians did not assume that all citizens were soldiers, although they could become so via conscription. Athenian armies could be conscripted via one of two methods. At the height of the Peloponnesian War, Athenian generals posted the names of eligible citizens on 10 lists known as *katalogoi*. In earlier times, service in the army of Athens was required of all men who could pay for their own weapons and armour. By the fourth century, the government began to supply weapons, thus effectively eliminating exemptions from military service for the inability to provide one's own weapons. In this setting, all men between the ages of 18 and 60 appear to have been enlisted and, depending on the size of the conflict, may have been obliged to serve. The general levy for an Athenian incursion into Boeotia in 424 BCE involved citizens from all classes, resident foreigners, slaves and any members of allied States who happened to be in the city – in short, just about all of the available manpower between 'the youngest and the oldest'.[73] Athens would also press foreigners into their triremes when required. The second method of conscription involved potential soldiers being sorted by age group, and men between certain ages being called up to do duty periodically. Only Thebes, which kept the renowned Sacred Band (the 300 hoplites organised in pairs of lovers) kept a military unit permanently under arms and trained at the public expense. When called out, the lists of those obliged to serve were posted next to the lists of those who had evaded the draft. To avoid service was seen as distasteful in Ancient Greece, as the burden of defending the State was believed to fall evenly on all citizens. Accordingly, accusations that some sections of society were bearing a disproportionate share of military service were taken very seriously.[74]

[71] Deuteronomy 20:8. The other exceptions are contained in 20:4–7. For a discussion of this, see Walzer, M (1996) 'War and Peace in the Jewish Tradition' in Nardin, T (ed) *The Ethics of War and Peace* (New Jersey, Princeton University Press) 95–96, 103–105; Edwards, I (ed) (1975) *The Cambridge Ancient History: History of the Middle East and Aegean Region 1380–1000 BCE*, 3rd edn, Vol II (2) (Cambridge, Cambridge University Press) 570, 573–74.

[72] Bury, J (ed) (1969) *The Cambridge Ancient History. The Persian Empire and the West*, 1st edn (Cambridge, Cambridge University Press) 19–21, 190–91.

[73] Bury, J (ed) (1969) *The Cambridge Ancient History. Athens*, Vol V (Cambridge, Cambridge University Press) 78–83; Cook, S (ed) (1970) *The Cambridge Ancient History. Rome and the Mediterranean*, Vol VIII (Cambridge, Cambridge University Press) 174, 596–98.

[74] van Wees, H (2009) *Greek Warfare: Myths and Reality* (London, Duckworth) 45–46, 93–94, 102–103; Straus, B (2005) *Salamis* (NYC, Arrow) 83; Bury, J (ed) (1969) *The Cambridge Ancient History. Macedon*, Vol VI (Cambridge, Cambridge University Press) 77.

In terms of identification, the warriors of the Greek epoch were highly identifiable and largely standardised in what they wore (in terms of having the same types of equipment, rather than it all being made by the same manufacturer). This was because each man, as a general rule, was responsible for his own equipment and the outfits tended to reflect their social status. Fundamentally, it was possible to distinguish the warriors from the non-combatants. Alexander's armies had distinctive armour and some sections, such as the Royal Couriers, had matching uniforms. However, instances were recorded when Greek soldiers were dressed as Persians, as a way to secretly enter into their camps and attack them.[75] Such tactics were not viewed favourably by most Greeks. In this regard, the Greeks proclaimed a high value upon combat without trickery. A 'fair and open' battle, that is, a battle without trickery or deceit, was the ideal of Greek battle. Hector, speaking in the *Iliad* would set this standard when he was facing an opponent who invited him to strike whilst what he was not looking. Hector replied, 'yet great as you are I would not strike you by stealth, watching from my chance, but openly'.[76]

Herodotus (484–425 BCE) records, and modern archaeology supports, fighting females in a number of contexts, of whom the Amazons are the most well known. He quoted other examples of women leaders who managed to display cruelties, such as rebels being impaled on stakes and the breasts of their women cut off, upon enemies which were consistent with the worst examples of the age. There were dozens of warrior queens who directed armies between 1700 and 500 BCE. Artemisia, queen of Halicarnassus (today Bodrum, Turkey) commanded a ship in the thick of combat at Salamis in 480 BCE, whilst Alexander the Great (356–323 BCE) came upon fighting females, with at least one instance recorded where women took the place of the men that had fallen. Despite such examples, the Greeks did not appreciate women fighting, or as Hector said 'the men must see to the fighting'.[77] Aristophanes (446–386 BCE) concurred 'war is care and the business of men'.[78] However, there are a number of examples of women being directly involved in defensive work in sieges 'with a courage beyond their sex' in throwing tiles from rooftops.[79] Likewise, in 272 BCE, when Pyrrhus (319–272 BCE) marched on Sparta, rather than leave the men to defend the city, the women stayed and helped dig a trench to help successfully defend the city. Plutarch (46–120 BCE) recorded how 'the women too were in the thick of the action, handing the men arrows and javelins, bringing food and drink whenever they needed and carrying the wounded'.[80] Such actions were not unexpected, given that, as early as the seventh century BCE, the great Spartan king, Lycurgus (800–730 BCE) formally encouraged Spartan women to excel at javelin throwing, running, boxing and wrestling.[81]

[75] Thucydides 6.31.3; Durschmied, E (2002) *From Armageddon to the Fall of Rome* (London, Hodder) 20, 21, 71, 119; Bury, J (ed) (1969) *The Cambridge Ancient History. Athens* Vol V (Cambridge, Cambridge University Press) 54.

[76] Homer in trans Knox, B (1999), The *Iliad* (Penguin, London) Section 7.232. Note also Lendon, J (2005) *Soldiers and Ghosts, A History of Battle in Classical Antiquity* (NYC, Yale University Press) 22–28, 41.

[77] *Iliad* 6.492.

[78] Aristophanes, *Lysistrata* reprinted in Botsford, G (ed) (1929) *Hellenic Civilisation: Records of Civilisation* (Columbia University Press) 342.

[79] Thucydides 2.4; 3.74.

[80] Plutarch in trans Dryden, G (1920), *Roman Lives* (Boston, Harvard University Press,) 417–19.

[81] *The History of Herodotus* trans Rawlson, J (1909), Vol I (London, Dent) 4:110–14, 4: 202; McCrindle, J (1896) *The Invasion of India by Alexander the Great*, 1969 edn (New York, Barnes) 270; Holmes, B 'Women Warriors Come Back from the Grave' *New Scientist* (8 Feb 1997) 17; Strauss, B (2005) *Salamis* (NYC, Arrow) 2.

It was Homer, writing around 850 BCE, who called foreign soldiers serving overlords from another country *epikouroi*. This was an all-encompassing label for men who could have been sent by allied States, come voluntarily, or come for wages. He called the last group *misthophoroi*, or what is today known as 'mercenaries'. These men had a very long history in Greek society, with Homer speaking of such men at Troy, mixed with volunteers and allies, in a way which often makes it very difficult to disentangle differences between national forces, supplementary foreign forces agreed by alliance, and foreign fighters/pirates who joined one side or the other, independently. Homeric literature talks at length about men without sovereign allegiances preying upon others on both land and sea, joining campaigns or fighting independently. The *Odyssey*, which may be read, in part, as a romantic story of piracy, along with the commentaries of the period and subsequently, suggests that piracy, far from frowned upon was actually part of a long-standing tradition, although he also noted that sometimes such men were prone to inflicting indiscriminate cruelties upon local populations.[82]

Herodotus referred to 'hired men' of Greek origin fighting in the wars of many foreign powers. The Egyptian army which defeated and killed Josiah in 609 BCE appears to have included Greek mercenaries, whilst the emergent city States of the sixth century BCE, were quick to utilise foreign soldiers who were willing to sell their skills.[83] Such soldiering was exemplified by Xenophon (430–354 BCE), who told the story of his leadership of the 13,000 Greek warriors in the service of Cyrus of Persia, who served not out of the desire for money but for adventure and to escape the boredom of their everyday lives.[84] By the time the Spartan hegemony collapsed in 371 BCE, Greece had become so fragmented that committed allies were almost impossible to find, and from then on, mercenaries feature in almost all of the Greek wars. This utilisation was often assisted with promises from the mercenaries that they would be loyal, and never, ever, turn against their paymaster. For example, the Agreement between Eumenes I and his mercenaries of 163 BCE recorded:

> I swear by Zeus, the Earth, the Sun, Poseidon, [etc] . . . and all the gods and goddesses . . . that I shall not conspire against Eumenes nor shall I bear arms against him, nor shall I desert him, but I shall fight for him and his interests and sacrifice my life for him.[85]

Even Alexander came to use non-Greeks in his forces, including at least 4,700 mercenaries in his armies when he invaded Persia. He was known to be lenient to these men if they were fighting against him, on condition that they joined his forces. The exception to this was with Greek mercenaries fighting against him, who were all executed when captured. This was a practice which had earlier been utilised by Dionysius I (432–367 BCE) who crucified all the Greek mercenaries he captured fighting against

[82] See Homer in trans Rieu, E (1984) *The Odyssey* (Penguin, London). For similar commentary within the *Iliad*, see sections 4.438, 10.420 and 17.222–6; Strauss, B (2006) *The Trojan War* (NYC, Simon & Schuster) 59–61, 88–89; Edwards, I (ed) (1975) *The Cambridge Ancient History. History of the Middle East and Aegean Region 1380–1000 BC*, 3rd edn, Vol II (2) (Cambridge, Cambridge University Press) 204; Bury, J (ed) (1965) *The Cambridge Ancient History. The Assyrian Empire*, 1st edn, Vol III (Cambridge, Cambridge University Press) 290–92.

[83] Herodotus 1.61.4; Bury, J (ed) (1969) *The Cambridge Ancient History. The Persian Empire and the West*, 1st edn (Cambridge, Cambridge University Press) 81.

[84] Anabasis in trans Dakyns, H (1890) *The Works of Xenophon*, Vol 1 (London, Macmillan) 80–85.

[85] Agreement Between Eumenes I and his Mercenaries in Austin, M (ed) (1992) *The Hellenistic World From Alexander to the Roman Conquest: A Collection of Readings* (Cambridge, Cambridge University Press) 321.

him. Although the mercenaries in the service of Alexander were loyal during his lifetime, when he died, they were at the forefront of leading uprisings in the newly founded empire. Similarly, mercenaries without pay showed themselves to be very unreliable in the siege of Corcyra in 374 BCE.[86] With such precedents, commentators of the age were becoming increasingly aware that mercenaries were becoming 'a common terror and a growing danger to us all' as they congregated in large numbers and were only relatively stable when there was warfare for which they were employed. Isocrates (436–338 BCE) who may have been the first to critically warn against mercenaries, argued in his essay *On the Peace* in 355 BCE, that Athens should abandon all claims to her maritime empire, and free herself from the evils attendant upon the employment of unreliable and dangerous mercenary armies. Aeneas Tacticus writing around the fourth century BCE, would supplement these views and pointed out that 'nothing is more dangerous than an unpaid mercenary'.[87]

Although the practice of utilising foreign forces for military purposes may have become acceptable, the practice of piracy whereby the freelancers were answerable to no authority but themselves was not. In this regard, Minoan Crete (2700–1400 BCE) may have been the first civilised State that had to deal with the evils of piracy and protect its seaborne commerce. By the time of the Peloponnesian War, the Spartans were known to keep garrisons on certain islands to prevent their occupation from pirates and to give security to merchant vessels passing by. The Athenians also attempted to keep brigandry from the eastern Mediterranean from 480 to 200 BCE, dealing with them 'in a manner that befitted their villainy'.[88] In time, these attempts became bilateral. In this regard, the first international agreements to suppress piracy can be traced to the end of the Amphissean War, when Philip II of Macedon (382–336) stipulated that Athens and Macedon would unite in the suppression of piracy to protect a freedom of the seas. Just over one hundred years later, the agreement between Rhodes and Crete around 200 BCE had both States agree that they would not allow pirates to seek shelter or assistance and they would both 'take part in operations by land and by sea with all possible strength' against this collective enemy.[89]

5. Rome

During the sixth century BCE, a citizen army evolved in Rome. In its earliest form, this was a militia, with citizen conscripts serving for a campaign and then returning home. Polybius (230–120 BCE) recorded this process as one where:

[86] Bury, J (ed) (1969) *The Cambridge Ancient History. Macedon*, Vol VI (Cambridge, Cambridge University Press) 77 368; Barker, E (1959) *From Alexander to Constantine: Passages and Documents Illustrating the History of Social and Political Ideas* (Oxford, Oxford University Press) 4–5; McCrindle, J (1896) *The Invasion of India by Alexander the Great*, 1969 edn (New York, Barnes) 36.

[87] Aeneas Tacticus *How to Survive Under Siege* (Oxford, Clarendon) 10.19 and 10.20; Bury, J (ed) (1969) *The Cambridge Ancient History. Athens*, Vol V (Cambridge, Cambridge University Press) 153–54; Bury, J (ed) *The Cambridge Ancient History. Macedon*, Vol VI (Cambridge, Cambridge University Press) 122; Ellis, P (1990) *The Celtic Empire* (1969) (London, Guild) 112–16.

[88] Thucydides IV, 53; Ormerod, H (1987) *Piracy in the Ancient World* (NYC, Dorset) 55–56, 100–38.

[89] Treaty Between Crete and Rhodes in Austin, M (ed) (1992) T*he Hellenistic World From Alexander to the Roman Conquest: A Collection of Readings* (Cambridge, Cambridge University Press) 93, 95; Bury, J (ed) (1969) *The Cambridge Ancient History. Macedon*, Vol VI (Cambridge, Cambridge University Press) 265.

> The consols, when they are about to enrol soldiers, announce at a meeting of the popular assembly the day on which all Roman citizens of military age must present themselves, and they do this annually.[90]

The Latin word for this call, *Legio*, translates literally as 'conscription' and is the root of the word 'legion'. In the late Republican period, of 225 legions, approximately 17 per cent of all adult male citizens were in the army. In 213 BCE, at the height of the war with Hannibal (248–182 BCE), the figure was 29 per cent. By the first century BCE, the Roman legions had evolved into a professional army of career soldiers recruited from the poor and equipped by the State. Soldiers and officers in the Roman army enjoyed long careers, with Augustus setting the term of military service at 20 years. The Byzantines operated a similar system, with the assumption that all free male citizens under the age of 40 had an obligation to serve in the army. Specifically, Emperor Maurice (539–602) would explain 'we wish that every young Roman of free condition should learn the use of the bow, and be constantly provided with that weapon and with two javelins'[91]

The Roman restrictions on joining the army, like the Egyptian one, was generally not based on age, but height, with a minimum height of between 1.63 and 1.8 metres (the latter being six feet). In the period of the Republic, this changed and 17 was recognised as the minimum age of enlistment. However, in times of shortage, as in the wars with Hannibal, the age could be lowered to 16. These men were all uniformed in a very similar way, and apart from when they were fighting each other in the civil war and were indistinguishable to each other; as a rule, they were clearly distinct from the general populace.[92]

With regards to women, the Roman view was that their place was at home and not in the front line. In practice, it was likely that in a number of instances the women who were following the legions were caught up in the fighting. The Romans were also familiar with fighting women, as they appear to have been an established part of the Gladiator system. However, the Romans did not approve of having women fighters in their armed forces, although they were clearly familiar with such practices being operated by some of their enemies. Tacitus noted:

> It stands on record that armies wavering on the point of collapse have been restored by the women. They have pleaded heroically with their men, thrusting their bosoms before them and forcing [the men] to realise the imminent prospect of their enslavement – a fate they fear more desperately for their women than themselves.[93]

The wives of the Celts were described as being impressive in combat. Caesar recorded that often, although not in the forefront of the conflict, Germanic woman were the ones who collectively decided on whether their men would fight or not. Female battle

[90] Polybius in trans Paton W, R (1992) *Histories V* (Cambridge, Harvard University Press), xix.

[91] The Edict of Maurice Reprinted in Geanakoplos, D (ed) (1984) *Byzantium: Church, Society and Civilisation Seen Through Contemporary Eyes* (Chicago, University of Chicago Press) 98. See also Hussey, J (ed) (1967) *The Cambridge Medieval History. The Byzantine Empire*, Vol IV (II) (Cambridge, Cambridge University Press) 35–36.

[92] Hopkins, M (1978) *Conquerors and Slaves* (Oxford, Oxford University Press) 31–35; Goldsworthy, A (1998) *The Roman Army at War 100 BCE–AD 200* (Oxford, Oxford University Press) 28–29; Elton, H (1997) *Warfare in Roman Europe* (Oxford, Oxford University Press) 154; Tacitus in trans Wellesley, K (1975). *The Histories* (Cambridge, Harvard University Press) (London, Penguin) 158; Cook, S (ed) (1966) *The Cambridge Ancient History. The Roman Republic*, 1st edn (Cambridge, Cambridge University Press) 62.

[93] *Tacitus on Britain and Germany* trans Mattingly, H (1951) (London, Penguin) 107.

leaders were also not unusual in this epoch, such as Boudica (ruled, AD 60) and Cleopatra (69–30 BCE). These two female leaders were unlike Zenobia (240–274), the queen of Syria, who not only made military decisions but also fought with her soldiers until her forces were defeated by the Romans and she was captured, brought back to Rome in gold chains, and executed.[94]

By the time of the Empire, the two main sources of recruits for the military were volunteers and conscripts. First, the sons of soldiers were required to enlist, in both the Western and Byzantine Empires. For example, the Edict of Emperor Valens (328–378) stipulated:

> Your authority shall announce to all veterans whatsoever that if any of them should not, of his own free will, offer his son who is entirely worthy of the honour of bearing arms to the imperial service for which the veteran himself has toiled, he shall be involved in the toils of Our law.[95]

Secondly, annual levies were taken. Supplementary levies could be called for at necessary times. The annual conscription of troops, enforced upon landowners either alone or in groups according to the value of their estates, required them to provide a man from their lands or from merchants. However, it appears that after the third century, the obligation to serve could be commuted in both the Roman and Byzantine sectors by a payment.[96] Although conscription was clearly effective in making Rome the superpower of its day, in periods of stress, it was often a deeply unpopular tactic, such as when Hannibal was rampaging through Italy, destroying fresh legions with relative ease. Accordingly, whilst seeking to win over allies, one of the promises Hannibal made was that unlike the Romans, there would be no conscription for his armed forces. Despite conscription becoming a defining feature of this period, the Romans did not change their approach, and retained their traditional rules whereby only the weak or infirm, slaves or inhabitants of workhouses were not expected to serve. At various times, Jews were also excluded from service. By the third century, the Romans practice whilst retaining the fundamental principle of the universal obligation to serve in the armed forces, was modified by the introduction of a levy. The levy affected the sons of soldiers, who were subject to a hereditary obligation to serve and men who were not attached to a particular piece of land or had obligations to the State. An indirect levy also applied to landowners to provide at least one recruit when required. However, as the difficulties of getting recruits increased, some of the emperors appear to have accepted requests to commute the provision of recruits with money.[97] What the emperors would not accept as a justification not to serve in the

[94] Webster, G (1978) *Boudica: The British Revolt Against Rome AD 60* (London, Anchor Press) 97–99; Jones, T (2006) *Barbarians: An Alternative Roman History* (London, BBCE Books) 206; Meijer, F (2004) *The Gladiators* (Dunne, NYC) 76–79; Wells, P (2003) *The Battle That Stopped Rome* (NYC, Norton) 99; Aeneas Tactius 3.6; *Caesar's War Commentaries* (1955) in trans Warrington, J (London, Dent) 27.

[95] The Edict of Valens. Reprinted in Geanakoplos, D (ed) (1984) *Byzantium: Church, Society and Civilisation Seen Through Contemporary Eyes* (Chicago, University of Chicago Press) 97.

[96] Norwich, J (1988) *Byzantium: The Early Centuries* (Guild, London) 330; Contamine, P (1984) *War in the Middle Ages* (Oxford, Blackwell) 7; Elton, H (1997) *Warfare in Roman Europe* (Oxford, Oxford University Press) 128–30; Hussey, J (ed) (1967) *The Cambridge Medieval History. The Byzantine Empire*, Vol IV (II) (Cambridge, Cambridge University Press) 41–43.

[97] Elton, H (1997) *Warfare in Roman Europe* (Oxford, Oxford University Press) 153–54; Cook, S (ed) (1970) *The Cambridge Ancient History. Rome and the Mediterranean* Vol VIII (Cambridge, Cambridge University Press) 55–56. Cook, S (ed) (1966) *The Cambridge Ancient History. The Roman Republic*, 1st edn (Cambridge, Cambridge University Press) 132–37; Cook, S (ed) , (1971) *The Cambridge Ancient History. The Augustan Empire*, 1st edn,

armed forces were considerations of conscience. This was a particular problem which appeared with the advent of Christianity and the language of the *New Testament*. In this regard, aside from some relatively ambiguous text, the central portion of the Sermon on the Mount appears relatively clear. Thus:

> Ye have heard that it hath been said, An eye for an eye, and a tooth for a tooth, But I say unto you, That ye resist not evil: but whosoever shall smite thee on thy right cheek, turn to him the other also . . . Love your enemies, bless them that curse you, do good to them that hate you, and pray for them which despitefully use you, and persecute you.[98]

Additional text suggests that all those 'that take the sword, shall perish with the sword' and the call to 'beat their swords into ploughshares' created great turmoil for some Christians in Rome.[99] This was particularly so for the early theologians such as Ignatius (c 50–98), Tertullian (160–220) and Origen (185–254) who all took the command to love your enemy in a literal manner and ended up at points very close to non-violent resistance.[100] From such scholarship, a number of Christians, of whom a young man called Maximilianus appears to have been the first (in 298), went on to throw away their arms and 'choose to serve Christ, rather than the Emperor'. The conscientious objection of Maximilianus was met with court martial and execution. When the death sentence was passed, the court secretary, Cassian protested that the sentence was unjust and that he too was a Christian. He also was arrested, tried and executed. It was, in part, due to such instances that the last great persecutions against the Christians from the middle of the third to the beginning of the fourth century occurred, as it was feared that Christians could not be relied upon as soldiers. Although the early Church attempted to control this situation (by suggesting times when conscientious objection may not be acceptable), a number of soldiers continued to drop their weapons and refused to fight. These acts, which led to the swift and violent reply of the Roman State, were only countered when the heavyweight church doctors of Ambrose (339–397) and Augustine (354–430) came to link Christianity, citizenship and patriotism.[101] These links were strengthened by the insecurity of the times Augustine existed in, which led to his death during a siege of the Vandals in 430. Against such considerations, Augustine argued that the teachings of Christ were not contrary to the Roman Empire and that it was possible to serve both the military and God, arguing that Christ did not tell soldiers to throw their weapons away, but to serve with integrity.[102] Accordingly, conscientious objection on the grounds of interpretations of Christianity was not acceptable to the ruling status quo of Christian leaders.

Vol X (Cambridge, Cambridge University Press) 366–69; Cook, S (ed) (1969) *The Cambridge Ancient History. The Imperial Crisis*, Vol XII (Cambridge, Cambridge University Press) 366–397; Gwatkin, H (ed) (1957) *The Cambridge Medieval History. The Christian Roman Empire*, 1st edn, Vol I (Cambridge, Cambridge University Press) 44–45.

[98] Matthew 5:38–48. For the ambiguous text, see Luke 3:14; Matthew 8:5–13; Romans 13: 1–4; 1 Timothy 2:1–2; 1 Peter 2:13–17.

[99] Matthew 26:52 and Isaiah 2:4.

[100] Cahill, L (1994) *Love Your Enemies: Pacifism and Just War Theory* (NYC, Cahill) 41–55.

[101] Eppstein, J (1935) *The Catholic Tradition of the Law of Nation* (NYC, Burns) 4–11, 14–15 17–20, 31, 32–35; Ayerst, D (ed) *Records of Christianity*, Vol I (London, Blackwell) 131; Finucane, R (2004) *Soldiers of the Faith* (London, Phoenix) 12; Cahill, L (1994) *Love Your Enemies: Pacifism and Just War Theory* (NYC, Cahill) 58–63.

[102] *Augustine: Political Writings* (1994) trans Tkacs, M (NYC, Hackett) xiii, 189, 204, 209, 219.

The Roman army was built upon the ideal of soldiers being upright warriors who kept their word and fought openly without recourse to deceit, treachery or perfidy – such as the wooden horse at Troy. History has it that when Roman commanders who achieved success with 'novel' tactics had to report back to the Senate, they were sometimes rebuked for their 'new and too-clever wisdom'. In one instance, the commander was told: 'Our ancestors did not wage war by ambush or night battle, nor by pretended flight and surprise return catch the enemy off guard, so that they could glory in craftiness rather than real virtus'.[103] Hannibal's 'un-Roman' conduct, due to the mercenary content of the soldiers (he had at least 20,000 when he invaded Italy, although this may have been much higher at the outset) who wore a mixture of colours and dress, was frowned upon. In this regard, the expression of the Romans can only be guessed at when facing some of the Barbarian tribes, especially the Celts, who preferred to fight naked, relying on the magic of woad-painted symbols on their bodies.[104] The only fighters that the Romans disliked with greater intensity were informal soldiers who were not under any sovereign command structure, namely pirates. In this regard, as piracy grew as Rome destroyed previously powerful entities which had kept pirates at bay, such as Carthage and Corinth, the Romans had to devote considerable resources, such as the 100,000 men and 270 ships given to Pompey, to defeat the pirates who quickly proliferated and threatened to, or did, overrun about 400 settlements. Accordingly, it fell to Rome to sweep the waters clean of fighters who were believed to deserve neither mercy nor restraint.[105]

In the eyes of the Romans, barely one step above the pirates were what are currently known in popular culture as 'guerrillas'. The works of Polybius Frontinus (40–103), Plutarch (46–120), Appian (95–165) and Tacitus (56–117) all catalogue a succession of guerrilla-type campaigns that the Romans encountered as they expanded their empire. Julius Caesar was quick to condemn the army of Vercingetorix (82–46 BCE) in Gaul as 'vagabonds and robbers' because it contained a large informal element. In ancient Israel the irregular elements took to hiding amongst the civilians and the occupying force of the Romans. The group currently identified as the Zealots terrorised the occupying Romans from 48 AD. At the time they were known as *sicarii* – a generic Latin term derived from *sicarius* – 'daggerman'. Concealing their short daggers under their clothes, they moved freely among the general population, striking down prominent collaborators, or kidnapping them for hostage exchanges with the Romans. They killed both Romans and Jews, including the High Priest Jonathan, arguing that assassination was justifiable as they were fighting terror with terror.[106]

[103] Livy 3.42.4; 3.60.8; 37.32.5. Note also Lendon, J (2005) *Soldiers and Ghosts, A History of Battle in Classical Antiquity* (NYC, Yale University Press) 194; Virgil trans Jackson Knight, WF (1956). *The Aeneid* (Harmondsworth, Penguin) 9.142–44.

[104] Goldsworthy, A (2003) *The Fall of Carthage* (London, Cassell) 32–34, 208; Webster, G (1978) *Boudica: The British Revolt Against Rome AD60* (London, Anchor Press) 74–75; Ellis, P (1990) *The Celtic Empire* (London, Guild) 38.

[105] Austin, M (ed) (1992) *The Hellenistic World From Alexander to the Roman Conquest: A Collection of Readings* (Cambridge, Cambridge University Press) 282–83; Cook, S (ed) (1966) *The Cambridge Ancient History. The Roman Republic*, Vol IX (Cambridge, Cambridge University Press) 372–75.

[106] Chaliand, G (2007) *The History of Terrorism* (California, University of California Press) 55–59; Ellis, J (1995) *From the Barrel of a Gun: A History of Guerrilla Warfare* (London, Greenhill) 18, 21–22; Cook, S (ed) (1971) *The Cambridge Ancient History. The Augustan Empire*, 1st edn, Vol X (Cambridge, Cambridge University Press) 859–61.

The Romans took their views on integrity to such an extent that, unlike their enemies who made active use of spies, espionage and assassination, such informal methods of warfare were poorly viewed.[107] Although they would exploit or mutilate any captured foreign spies operating against Rome, they showed a haughty contempt for practices which were equated with deception and secrecy, seeing these as tactics that only those who were weak or without honour would adopt. Julius Caesar, perhaps to his own detriment, repeatedly refused to establish a secret service.[108]

The final source of manpower for the Roman army was foreigners. During the reign of Augustus (27 BCE–14 AD) 68 per cent of legionnaires were of Italian origin but by the end of the second century AD, as little as 2 per cent of the legionnaires were of Italian origin. The Romans, especially in the period of the Republic where citizenship and military service were closely linked, did not like the idea of providing or utilising former prisoners of war or mercenaries. Key military scholars like Vegetius clearly recommended, perhaps in the fourth century AD, that it was better for Roman rulers to train their own subjects 'than to take and retain under his great fusion of strange soldiers that he knoweth not'.[109] To Vegetius, the risks were not just military, but also social due to the fear that the State could lose its own identity and fighting spirit. The Romans were also highly aware that the employment of mercenaries could alter the balance of power in some countries. Accordingly, in the early years of the Republic, they attempted to stop their former enemies from utilising mercenaries, and in this regard, led the first international treaty to deal with, inter alia, mercenaries. Specifically, under the Peace Treaty with Antiochus III of Syria in 188 BCE, the king agreed he would 'not have the right to hire mercenary troops from those nations which are under Roman rule, nor even to accept volunteers there-from'.[110]

Despite these positions against the employment of mercenaries or non-Roman soldiers, if circumstances demanded it, they would be employed. This became a clear pattern when Rome became an Empire, the military needs of the Empire increased, and the desire of the Italians to fight decreased. Accordingly, they were forced to look to alternative sources of manpower. The sources they found managed, on paper, to allow peace deals to be made and also deal with the problem of a shortage of manpower via the employment of 'auxiliaries' or *laeti*, who were to keep their national standards, yet receive money to fight for Rome. For example, the Treaty of Peace with the Vandals in 271 obliged the Vandals to provide 2,000 horsemen to serve with the Romans. When the tribes of Germany were finally subdued in 278, part of the peace treaty involved the obligation of supplying to the Roman army 16,000 recruits, the bravest and most robust of their youth. Likewise, the treaty of 382 with the Huns required them to defend various frontiers, in exchange for an annual sum of money. The Byzantinian Empire would follow suit. For example, Justinian (483–565) in 534,

[107] But note the story of Gaius Mucius who, having obtained the consent of the Senate, exited besieged Rome, with a hidden dagger concealed in his robe. He then managed to mix with the Etruscan soldiers (so he was clearly not recognised as a military man) and then attempted to stab the Tarquin king, but by mistake killed his paymaster instead. This act was regarded so highly by the king, that he demanded that he be treated like a soldier, and not an assassin, and allowed him to return to Rome free. See Livy *History of Rome* 2.12.1–13.5.

[108] Singer, K (1953) *Spies and Traitors* (London, Allen) 72–75.

[109] Vegetius *The Epitome of Military Science* Milner, P (trans) (Liverpool, Liverpool University Press) 26.

[110] Peace Treaty With Antiochus III of Syria 188 BCE in Lewis, N and Reinhold, M (eds) (1951) *Roman Civilization: Selected Readings* (NYC, Columbia University Press) 195.

rather than kill or sell most of the prisoners taken in his wars against the Vandals in North Africa, had them transferred into five imperial regiments and marched off to the Persian front, to fight for their new emperor.[111]

The only difficulty, and the Romans were well aware of this problem, was that mercenaries or soldiers of foreign lands could turn on their paymasters. The Romans were well aware that mercenaries in the pay of Carthage, whilst stationed in Sardinia, had turned against their paymasters and tried to sell Sardinia to Rome. They also witnessed in their war with Cleopatra VII (69 BCE–30 AD) how her mercenary forces swapped sides in her hour of need.[112] Despite knowledge of these precedents, the very same thing would happened to Rome, when Alaric (370–410) and his Goths turned on their Roman paymaster when their payment of 4,000 pounds of gold was late. Attila the Hun (406–453), who was also previously an employee of Rome, later did exactly the same.[113]

6. The Dark Ages

The Dark Ages are punctuated by three types of belligerents. First, the Byzantine Empire attempted to carry on the traditions of the Roman Empire with large-scale conscription, although in some areas they were heightened. For example, the Byzantines adopted an age requirement of 18 years and a height requirement of about five feet and six inches. However, unlike their Roman cousins, they developed a remarkable system of espionage and were, at the beginning, selective in their use of mercenaries. For example, as part of a peace settlement in 522, they agreed not to conscript Gothic forces into the Byzantine armies. However, this approach was short-lived, and the Imperial army, in Justinian's time, was essentially made up of mercenaries from East and West: Huns, Gepids, Heruls, Vandals, Goths, Lombards, Antae, Slavs, Persians, Armenians, Arabs from Syria and Moors from Africa. Over 50,000 of such men were in the service of the Byzantine Empire in the middle of the tenth century. The Byzantines were not, however, ignorant to the risks these men posed. Their emperor Leo IV (866–912) had earlier warned:

> If you are using foreign troops, it is prudent that they be fewer in number than your own, especially if you are defending your country, for if they are more numerous, they may

[111] 'Treaty With the Vandals 271 AD' in Lewis, N and Reinhold, M (eds) *Roman Civilization: Selected Readings*, Vol II (NYC, Columbia University Press) 437-; Barbero, A (2005) *The Day of the Barbarian.* (London, Atlantic) 137–39; Gwatkin, H (ed) (1957) *The Cambridge Medieval History. The Christian Roman Empire* Vol I (Cambridge, Cambridge University Press) 253–55; Elton, H (1997) *Warfare in Roman Europe* (Oxford, Oxford University Press) 91–94, 126–27, 135; Sampson, G (2008) *The Defeat of Rome in the East* (Philadelphia, Casemate) 27; Jones, T (2006) *Barbarians: An Alternative Roman History* (London, BBC Books) 82.

[112] Elton, H (1997) *Warfare in Roman Europe* (Oxford, Oxford University Press) 129–30, 135, 197–98; Goldsworthy, A (1998) *The Roman Army at War 100 BCE–AD 200* (Oxford, Oxford University Press) 18–19, 71–73; Laing, J (2000) *Warriors of the Dark Age* (London, Sutton) 53; Man, J (2005) *Attila the Hun* (London, Bantam) 17–20; Cook, S (ed) (1971) *The Cambridge Ancient History. The Augustan Empire*, 1st edn, Vol X (Cambridge, Cambridge University Press) 104–109; Cook, S (ed) (1969) *The Cambridge Ancient History. The Imperial Peace*, 1st edn (Cambridge, Cambridge University Press) 131–34.

[113] Gibbon, E (1926 edn) *The Decline and Fall of the Roman Empire*, Vol III (London, Methuen) 253, 302–303; Cook, S (ed) (1969) *The Cambridge Ancient History. The Imperial Crisis*, 1st edn, Vol XII (Cambridge, Cambridge University Press) 218–20, 379.

> seize it for themselves. Those who sell their service for money may allow themselves to be corrupted by a larger sum to turn against you.[114]

In time to come, this warning would come true, as mercenaries in the pay of the Byzantine Empire would either swap side, attempt to set up independent States within Byzantine territory, or quickly retreat when they feared a dead end for themselves.[115]

The second type of belligerents that occupied the Dark Ages were informal in most things. Warriors of the Dark Age were not usually susceptible to organised warfare. The original definition of the word 'Viking' was a pirate who attacked law-abiding boats on the high seas. Such men did not merely ravage coastal communities, but intercepted trade, and captured or killed seamen for their wealth. The culture was one in which military theory and deception were closely linked. Indeed, Odin, the Viking God of war, was also, inter alia, the God of deceit and trickery, and cheating was a key part of the Viking theory of war. There was no standardisation of weapons or uniforms in this period, with each man being responsible for providing his own hardware. They were also notorious freebooters, selling their military services to, inter alia, the English, Italians and even the Byzantine emperors. However, in all instances the Vikings showed they were not only mercenaries, but also spectacular opportunists. For example, with the Vikings in England, it appears that the very first of these people were invited in as hired military help, but that after their contract ended, in defiance of their terms they decided to stay and impose themselves on the local populations. In other instances, as with the Byzantine Emperors such as with Basil II (958–1025), they ultimately became the kingmakers.[116]

In western Europe during this epoch, it appears that every free man, with the possible exception of some religious leaders like Druids, was considered to be warriors. History is remarkably silent about female Goths, Huns or Vandals in fighting mode, although in some pagan cemeteries, the women were buried with weaponry. As such, it appears that warfare was largely a male occupation and as soon as males were old and strong enough (which was 12 years old in the case of the Vikings) they were obliged to obey the military summons and serve. Statistics suggest that up to 25 per cent of many of these societies could be fielded when required.[117] With the Visigoths, it was an offence for army officers 'not to compel' recruits to leave their homes and join the army as they were obliged.[118] The laws of Aistulf of the Lombards (750) linked military obligations to wealth, although even slaves could be included in military service if necessary. Fifty years later, distinctions began to appear between free men whose obligations were limited and vassals who were maintained either directly or indirectly

[114] Leo VI in Chaliand, G (ed) *The Art of War in World History* (California, California University Press) 375; Haldon, J (2002) *Byzantium at War* (London, Osprey) 61; Norwich, J (1988) *Byzantium: The Early Centuries* (London, Guild) 253, 293; Norwich, J (1991) *Byzantium: The Apogee* (NYC, Knopf) 175–77; Gwatkin, H (ed) (1957) *The Cambridge Medieval History. The Rise of the Saracens* Vol II (Cambridge, Cambridge University Press) 10–11.

[115] Norwich, J (1991) *Byzantium: The Apogee* (NYC, Knopf) 349–54, 359–60; Norwich, J (1995) *Byzantium: The Decline and Fall* (London, Penguin) 2–3, 13–21.

[116] Griffith, P (1995) *The Viking Art of War* (London, Greenhill) 60–62, 78, 106–109; Laing, J (2000) *Warriors of the Dark Ages* (London, Sutton) 92; Haldon, J (2002) *Byzantium at War* (London, Osprey) 44–45, 51; Urban, W (2006) *Medieval Mercenaries* (London, Greenhill) 40, 52; Laffin, J (1966) *Boys in Battle* (Toronto, Schuman) 22.

[117] Laing, J (2000) *Warriors of the Dark Ages* (London, Sutton) 115; Webster, G (1978) *Boudica: The British Revolt Against Rome AD 60* (London, Anchor Press) 64; Elton, H (1997) *Warfare in Roman Europe* (Oxford, Oxford University Press) 73.

[118] The Visigoth Law Code, Bk IX, s I.

by the king, and had very strict duties. Obligations and expectations proceeded down a long list of free peoples, from those just below the king, to those just above the serfs. The exception to this approach of obligatory military service appeared in the middle of the seventh century, when some legal codes, such as that of Rothari in 643, allowed someone to avoid military service in exchange for a heavy fine. It appears that some leaders from this period preferred the idea of cash, as opposed to service, as they could then purchase exactly what they wanted.[119]

The third source of belligerent to emerge out of the Dark Ages, were those under the banner of Islam, which utilised many of the same processes as its Byzantine neighbour. For example, the Quran was clear that when required 'fighting is obligatory for you, much as you dislike it'.[120] Unless someone was disabled, sick or an instructor of religion, they were to be 'punished sternly' if they refused to fight.[121] This was not surprising given that, although Mohammed (570–632) had a vision to create a perfect society which would enforce a complete ban on violence, until that point was reached, violence may be necessary. As such, there are many passages in the Quran which allow war, whilst Mohammed himself is believed to have fought in 19 campaigns. Of interest, although women were not expected to be at the forefront of such conflicts, female warriors were recorded as notable opposition in the early conflicts of Islam. For example, the battle queen Hind al-Hunud met her enemy, Mohammed, in battle in the seventh century AD. Far more than a symbol of the warrior spirit in this encounter, Hind is chronicled as 'brandishing a broadsword with great gusto'.[122]

One notable feature of military practice under some branches of Islam, which was evident almost from its inception, was the use of informal warriors and the practice of assassination. For example, Caliph Ali (598–661) who was murdered with a poisoned dagger to the head, was the third of the Mohammed's four successors to be assassinated.[123] By the twelfth century such practices had become perfected by what has come to be known as the Order of the Assassins, who operated throughout the Middle East. This group was an extreme Shi'ite organisation, who brought havoc to the region for over 150 years. Their targets were typically killed by knife as they disdained the use of poison, seeing themselves as soldiers rather than 'harem murderers'. Their preparation was immaculate with some deep cover agents slowly infiltrating the households of targets over long periods of time to lure them into a false sense of security. Their targets were carefully chosen with the aim of destabilising and ultimately overthrowing the established and ruling Sunni orthodoxy. Hundreds of prominent figures, Muslim and Christian, fell to the Assassins' knives, before the Mongolians had the sect destroyed.[124]

[119] Contamine, P (1984) *War in the Middle Ages* (Oxford, Blackwell) 17, 19, 25; Prestwich, M (1995) *Armies and Warfare in the Middle Ages* (New Haven, Yale University Press) 42–43; Gwatkin, H (ed) (1957) *The Cambridge Medieval History. The Rise of the Saracens*, Vol II (Cambridge, Cambridge University Press) 666–67.

[120] Quran 2:216.

[121] 9:38, 9:83. Note also 9:87, 9:93, 9:122, 9:87.

[122] Kurlansky, M (2006) *Non-Violence: The History of a Dangerous Idea* (London, Cape) 34–35; Jones, D (2000) *Women Warriors: A History* (NYC, Brassey's) 13; Marozzi, J (2005) *Tamerlane: Sword of Islam* (London, Harper) 103, 195; Gibbon, E (1926) *The Decline and Fall of the Roman Empire*, Vol V, 2nd edn (London, Methuen) 451–52.

[123] See Foss, C 'Islam's First Terrorists' *History Today* (12 Dec 2007).

[124] Lewis, B (1967) *The Assassins: A Radical Sect in Islam* (London, Macmillan); Runciman, S (1954) *A History of the Crusades*, Vol 2 (Cambridge, Cambridge University Press) 120, 407; Maalouf, A (2006) *The Crusades Through Arab Eyes* (Paris, Sagi) 104–105, 182–83; Turnbull, S (2003) *Genghis Khan and the Mongol Conquests* (London, Osprey) 56–57.

7. The Feudal Age

The Feudal Age saw a continuation of practices which led to the creation of large, compulsory, armed forces. Feudalism invoked a structure where everyone was obliged to furnish certain duties as part of their homage and loyalty to their overlord. One of the most typical of these was the provision of a certain number of knights or other soldiers. As such, by its very structure, feudalism produced an excessive number of men who, on average, appear to have been liable between the ages of 14 and 60, with the starting age differing in each area and epoch. However, it should be noted that the age at which they could go into combat was different from the age when they started to learn how to fight. For example, mandatory training for all boys in England in the use of the longbow in 1363 began at seven years of age. However, even if these boys quickly acquired the necessary skills, it was unlikely that they could go into actual combat until their teenage years or later. For example, from 1167 the Oath of the Lombard League had military service starting at the age of 14, whilst in Venice the age of service was 20 in 1338. Similarly, a youth could not enter the orders of the Crusaders until 16 and even then, they could not serve in the Middle East until reaching the age of 20. The usual age for a young man to be able to become a knight was 21. Nevertheless, with Europe, sometimes boys were knighted much younger and the benchmark of age by which boys went into battle was often much less. For example, in 1346, the Black Prince (1330–76) was only 16 when he led the right wing for his father, Edward III, at the battle of Crecy. Jean Froissart (1337–1405) suggested that every knight or squire between the ages of 15 and 60 was called up in Amiens and other testimony suggests some knights first took to the field at the age of 14, whilst the men at arms who wore mail and carried lance, sword, dagger and shield, may have started training as early as 10, although in practice, a boy was only meant to be allowed to train as a squire, from the age of 14 and above. The Mongolians took boys into service from the age of 15.[125]

In this age of chivalry, it was expected that women would not be combatants. However, in practice, there is a rich history of female combatants fighting during situations of siege, such as the woman who operated the siege machine at the siege of Toulouse which killed Simon de Montfort, leader of the Albigensian Crusade, in 1218. During the Crusades in the Middle East, women fought in the Frankish armies and historical records recount women riding to war on horseback as knights would, carrying weapons. In the Third Crusade, it was only when the dead warriors were stripped of their armour after one particular battle, was it apparent that three of the Crusaders were women. Despite such precedents it is Joan of Arc (1412–31) who is the exemplar of the female warrior of the Middle Ages.[126]

[125] Oath of the Lombard League 1167 in Laffan, R (ed) (1929) *Select Historical Documents: 800–1492* (NY, Holt) 94; Contamine, P (1984) *War in the Middle Ages* (Oxford, Blackmore) 84, 153, 155, 270; Prestwich, M (1995) *Armies and Warfare in the Middle Age* (Yale University Press) 55; Seward, D (1974) *The Monks of War* (Herts, Penguin) 1198; Laffin, J (1966) *Boys in Battle* (Schuman, Toronto) 27; Man, G (2004) *Genghis Khan* (London, Bantham) 123; Runciman, S (1954) *A History of the Crusades*, Vol 3 (Cambridge, Cambridge University Press) 241; Tanner, J (ed) (1957) *The Cambridge Medieval History. Victory of the Papacy*, Vol VI (Cambridge, Cambridge University Press) 802, 805, 807.

[126] Lucie-Smith, E (1976) *Joan of Arc* (London, Penguin); Finucane, R (2004) *Soldiers of the Faith* (London, Phoenix) 177; Contamine, P (1984) *War in the Middle Ages* (Oxford, Blackmore) 241–42; Runciman, S (1965)

Within the feudal system obligations existed for all men who were not knights to perform non-knightly or non-military support. Duties included, inter alia, looking after the royal hawks, rearing royal puppies, even counting the King's chess men and putting them back in the box after a game. Among historians, perhaps the most celebrated is that attached to the manor of Hemingstoke in Suffolk, whose tenant was to leap, whistle and fart to the King's amusement every Christmas Day. Sometimes the obligation was specified in detailed contracts, such as the provision of castle garrisons. For example, in 1301 John Kingston agreed to hold Edinburgh castle with a force of 30 men-at-arms, and 54 foot and ancillary soldiers for £220 per year. Other feudal obligations were more straightforward in terms of the provision of men armed for campaigns. This type of service, which may have also been a pre-Norman obligation, was unpaid and typically lasted 40 days. To assist this process, the overlords would specify what weaponry each man was expected to possess through the issue of various Assizes of Arms. For example, the Assize of Henry II (1133–89) in 1181 specified:

> Let every holder of a knight's fee have a hauberk, a helmet, and a shield and a lance. And let every knight have as many hauberks, helmets, shields, and lances, as he has knight's fees in his demnesne. Also let every free layman, who hold chattels or rent to the value of 16 marks, have a hauberk, a helmet, a shield and a lance[127]

For campaigns that were not defensive in nature, it was a clear possibility that a knight could opt to pay a sum to avoid such service if he so desired. This right to pay for substitution was written into the English Magna Carta in 1215.[128] Nevertheless, the expectation to serve in campaigns of the overlord, not related to self-defence, but according to capacity was a strong one and most knights appeared willing to serve.[129] However, instances are recorded where knights offered excuses (poverty, ill health and so on) for why they could not join a overlord's campaigns. These excuses were in accordance with the codes of the period. For example, the Norman Code of 1258 stipulated:

> No-one who owes this service may by any manner excuse himself from service in the army of the prince, unless by the evident impairment of his own body, and then he is bound to send a substitute who can perform for him the service which he owes.[130]

If the excuses were not held to be valid, or if the person simply refused to fight, they could be fined and/or lose their land.[131] From such scenarios, Henry II is often recognised as introducing the principle of scutage (meaning 'shield money'). By this means it was possible to employ others who would already be trained, equipped, and willing to fight.[132] Overlords liked scutage as they could hire strong, healthy, well-equipped men, without the worry of the politics behind them.[133]

The Fall of Constantinople 1453 (Cambridge, Cambridge University Press) 133; Seward, D (1974) *The Monks of War* (Herts, Penguin) 250.

[127] Baker, D (1966) *The Early Middle Ages: Portraits and Documents* (London, Hutchinson) 106; Contamine, P (1984) *War in the Middle Ages* (Oxford, Blackmore) 67, 89; Warner, P (2004) *Sieges of the Middle Ages* (Yorkshire, Pen and Sword) 153; Prestwich, M (1995) *Armies and Warfare in the Middle Ages* (New Haven, Yale University Press) 44–45, 91; Gravett, C (1990) *Medieval Siege Warfare* (London, Osprey) 13, 15.

[128] See Arts 12 and 29 of the Magna Carta.

[129] Prestwich, M (1995) *Armies and Warfare in the Middle Ages* (New Haven, Yale University Press) 77.

[130] The Norman Code in Herlihy, D (ed) *The History of Feudalism* (NYC, Harper) 179.

[131] Prestwich, M (1995) *Armies and Warfare in the Middle Ages* (New Haven, Yale University Press) 55, 58, 68.

[132] Warner, P (2004) *Sieges of the Middle Ages* (Yorkshire, Pen and Sword) 113.

[133] Urban, W (2006) *Medieval Mercenaries* (London, Greenhill) 38; Nusbacher, A (2005) *1314: Bannockburn* (Tempus, Gloucestershire) 71–72.

It was a different situation with regard to conflicts of self-defence. In these times, all men, including those in prison 'except paralytics, the dumb and the blind'[134] could expect to be compelled to serve in the fyrd in the interests of self-preservation, irrespective of the niceties of feudal service. With these general mobilisations, the entire adult male population could be brought to arms. For example, the Laws of William I declared that all free men had a duty of fealty to the king and to defend his land and honours against enemies and foreigners. Very similar obligations upon all citizens to defend their homeland in cases of self-defence can be found within, inter alia, the Oath of the Lombard League of 1167, the Golden Bull of 1222, the Norman Code of 1258 and in the assertions of various monarchs.[135] The only men who could not be pressed into service were clerics and monks, and these men were meant to refrain from carrying weapons or being involved in combat within both the Eastern and Western Christian Empires. Thus, at Verdun-sur-le-Doubs in 1016, the nobility swore not to impress clerics into their forces.[136] The Peace and Truce of God, from the Council of Toulouges from 989 added that it was 'forbidden that any one attack the clergy, who do not bear arms'.[137] These views were replicated thereafter by key scholars such as Thomas Aquinas (1225–74) who argued 'it is altogether unlawful for clerics to fight, because war is directed at the shedding of blood'.[138] Despite such thinking, this rule was often bent or broken by theologians in Western and Eastern Europe, as well as those accompanying the Crusades in the Middle East, who found that the perfect counterweight to the Testaments in one hand was a battleaxe in the other.[139] Although the Christian leaders had the right not to be taken into the armed forces, the same right did not extend to pilgrims of less importance, who remained eligible for service, even with a conscientious belief against fighting in wars.[140]

One of the by-products of the age of feudalism was the unprecedented creation of an international flow of soldiers of fortune, with soldiers fighting for any number of commanders. For example, when the rebellion in England was over, the Flemish soldiers in the service of England moved into the service of Frederick Barbarossa (1122–90), to campaign in Italy. However, when war broke out between Richard I (1157–99) and Phillip II of France (1165–1223), new opportunities caused movement

[134] Oath of the Lombard League 1167 in Laffan, R (ed) (1929) *Select Historical Documents: 800–1492* (NY, Holt) 94; Prestwich, M (1995) *Armies and Warfare in the Middle Ages* (New Haven, Yale University Press) 67, 119–21, 123, 126; Contamine, P (1984) *War in the Middle Ages* (Oxford, Blackmore) 38, 84; Morillo, S (1994) *Warfare Under the Anglo-Norman Kings* (Suffolk, Boydell) 20, 24, 48; Baker, D (1966) *The Early Middle Ages: Portraits and Documents* (London, Hutchinson) 100, 103–105.

[135] The Norman Code of 1258 in Herlihy, D (ed) *The History of Feudalism* (NY, Harper) 179; Oath of the Lombard League 1167 in Laffan, R (ed) (1929) *Select Historical Documents: 800–1492* (NY, Holt) 94; Golden Bull of Hungary 1222, see Laffan at 120.

[136] Runciman, S (1954) *A History of the Crusades*, Vol 1 (Cambridge, Cambridge University Press) 85.

[137] The Peace and Truce of God (989), Art 3 reprinted in Herlihy, D (ed) *The History of Feudalism* (NY, Harper) 286.

[138] Aquinas noted in Finucane, R (2004) *Soldiers of the Faith* (London, Phoenix) 71.

[139] Seward, D (1974) *The Monks of War* (Penguin, Herts); Contamine, P (1984) *War in the Middle Ages* (Oxford, Blackmore) 19, 39, 86, 223, 241, 266, 268–70, 277; Prestwich, M (1995) *Armies and Warfare in the Middle Ages* (New Haven, Yale University Press) 169–71; Contamine, P (1984) *War in the Middle Ages* (Oxford, Blackwell); Haldon, J (2002) *Byzantium at War* (London, Osprey) 61; Finucane, R (2004) *Soldiers of the Faith* (London, Phoenix) 120. McGlynn, S (2008) *By Sword and Fire: Cruelty and Atrocity in Medieval Warfare* (London, Weidenfeld) 68; Meron, T (1993) *Henry's Wars and Shakespeare's Laws* (Oxford, Oxford University Press) 90–91, 98–103.

[140] Seward, D (2003) *The Hundred Years War* (London, Robinson) 135; Kurlansky, M (2006) *Non-Violence: The History of a Dangerous Idea* (London, Cape) 50–51.

yet again to their new French employer. More often than not, these soldiers of fortune were supplementing existing national forces, although sometimes, as with the force assembled by Pope Alexander III (1100–81) in 1159, they were (and remain to this day) independent of the local politics. Groups of soldiers were also exchanged between various feudal authorities. For example, in 1101, Henry I (1068–1135) entered into an arrangement with the Count of Flanders who promised to provide him with 1,000 knights. Likewise, under the terms of the agreement of Henry II's penance for the death of Thomas Becket (1118–70), Henry was obliged to hire 200 knights to serve with the Templars in the Middle East. Often the men who made up these quotas were 'swords of hire', solicited by various authorities in payment for associated feudal obligations and onsold. This point is important as, unlike feudal soldiers who gave service by virtue of feudal relationships between the land and their overlord, the mercenary gave service for money, although in time, they could move back into the feudal context. For example, Gerard of Ridefort (d 1189), the later Master of the Temple, originally went to the Holy Land as a hired sword. Ridefort's entry into the Middle East was like that of thousands of others, who were brought with the pay packet of Crusading kings or the Latin Kingdoms or outposts which were established.[141]

Despite the widespread utilisation of soldiers of fortune, it was clearly evident by the time of the early Middle Ages that the system had two major faults. The first major difficulty was their association with cruelty and warfare without restraint practiced on non-combatants. This was a pattern that was repeatedly noted from the eleventh to the fifteenth century, but especially with the so-called 'Free Companies' that roamed France unrestrained after the peace of 1360, in search of sustenance, booty and pleasure. The pirates of the period, who were known to infest the waters of the Baltic shared exactly the same reputation, going so far as to burn and plunder Bergen in 1387.[142]

The second major difficulty with mercenaries from this period was that the only loyalty the soldiers of fortune recognised was that to the highest bidder. As such, they were known not to fulfill their duties (especially if not paid) or to change sides when a former employer was outbid. For example, Edward III almost lost his hard-fought for Calais in the Hundred Years' War after the mercenary company who were guarding it offered to sell it to the French. A number of instances of this period are recorded of mercenaries swapping sides or attempting to usurp all power whilst campaigning in, inter alia, the Northern Crusade, the wars of the Byzantine Empire, and the Hundred Years' War and its aftermath. For example, following the first peace treaty of 1360 in the Hundred Years' War, the White Company under the command of John Hawkwood (1320–94), previously in the pay of England, moved to Italy to fight the Visconti, then

[141] Prestwich, M (1995) *Armies and Warfare in the Middle Ages* (New Haven, Yale University Press) 148–150; France, J (1999) *Western Warfare In the Age of the Crusades* (London, University College London Press) 3, 28, 60–61; Morillo, S (1994) *Warfare Under the Anglo-Norman Kings* (Suffolk, Boydell) 11, 50–55, 114; Gravett, C (1990) *Medieval Siege Warfare* (London, Osprey) 12–13; Finucane, R (2004) *Soldiers of the Faith* (London, Phoenix) 11, 61, 211; Urban, W (2006) *Medieval Mercenaries* (London, Greenhill) 40–49; Gillingam, R (1978) *Richard the Lionheart* (London, Weidenfeld) 100–101.

[142] Prestwich, M (1995) *Armies and Warfare in the Middle Ages* (New Haven, Yale University Press) 148; Contamine, P (1984) *War in the Middle Ages* (Oxford, Blackmore) 243; Seward, D (2003) *The Hundred Years War* (London, Robinson) 104–12, 194; Meron, T (1993) *Henry's Wars and Shakespeare's Laws* (Oxford, Oxford University Press) 18; Urban, W (2006) *Medieval Mercenaries* (London, Greenhill) 106–107; Tanner J (ed) (1957) *The Cambridge Medieval History. Decline of Empire and Papacy*, Vol VII (Cambridge, Cambridge University Press) 222–24.

went into the Visconti employ, then switched side again, only, in 1363, to fight for Pisa against Florence. When his pay was cut by a displeased Visconti, Hawkwood went to fight for the Pope. At one point, Hawkwood met two friars who wished him peace. According to legend, he responded 'May God take away your alms. Do you not know that I live by war and that peace would be my undoing'.[143]

Such practices were far from unknown for the mercenary condottieri selling their skills throughout Italy, such as Pandolfo Malatesta (1417–68), Ottobuono Terzo (d 1409) and Gabrino Fondulo (d 1415), who all swapped sides, respectively, at the battles of Brescia, Cremona and Parma.[144]

There are also records of Muslims fighting in the service of the Christians during the Crusades and Christians fighting in the service of Muslims. These men ranged from the Barbary pirate Barbarossa (1478–1546) through to the Christian engineer who pledged himself to the Mehmed II (1432–81) who, with a salary four times greater than that offered by his Christian colleagues, provided and fired a weapon that could shoot a cannon ball which would travel a mile and then bury itself six feet deep in the earth. This weapon brought down the walls of Constantinople, and the Byzantine Empire with them.[145]

From the Middle Ages onwards, there was a clear attempt to limit the use of mercenaries. These attempts were particularly strong with the Church, which was trying to control the use of force and had contempt for the arming of anything other than legitimate forces with legitimate soldiers. This was most evident with the Lateran Council of 1179, which excommunicated mercenaries and their employers, explicitly associating them with heresy and uncontrolled mobs. In 1215, Innocent III went further, specifically condemning all Christians who were willing to help Islamic forces. Similarly, as Europe began to solidify into early nation States, the expulsion of foreign forces became a recognised building block to peace. This was evident in the mid-1160s when Louis VII (1120–80) and Barbarossa agreed to expel all mercenaries from parts of their dominions. Similarly, the settlement of the Albigensian Crusade in France with the 1228 Treaty of Meaux involved the expulsion of all mercenaries from the province. Likewise, in England the removal of foreign mercenaries from the Low Countries, South Wales and Ireland, who Henry II had employed, but who had 'infested the lands' was agreed.[146] Accordingly, Article 51 of the Magna Carta specified that

143 Urban, W (2006) *Medieval Mercenaries* (London, Greenhill) 80; Arnold, T (2001) *The Renaissance at War* (London, Cassel) 155; Prestwich, M (1995) *Armies and Warfare in the Middle Ages* (New Have, Yale University Press) 152; Previte, C (ed) (1966) *The Cambridge Medieval History. The Close of the Middle Ages*, Vol VIII (Cambridge, Cambridge University Press) 208–209, 658–59.

144 Keegan, J (1993) *A History of Warfare* (London, Hutchinson) 230–32.

145 France, J (1999) *Western Warfare in the Age of the Crusades 1000–1300* (London, University College London Press) 28, 60; Urban, W (2006) *Medieval Mercenaries* (London, Greenhill) 44; Arnold, T (2001) *The Renaissance at War* (London, Cassell) 59, 111; Seward, D (1974) *The Monks of War* (Herts, Penguin) 128, 238; Runciman, S (1965) *The Fall of Constantinople 1453* (Cambridge, Cambridge University Press) 5, 32, 78, 134; Haldon, J (2002) *Byzantium at War* (London, Osprey) 88; Prestwich, M (1995) *Armies and Warfare in the Middle Ages* (New Haven, Yale University Press) 87, 109, 148; Seward, D (2003) *The Hundred Years War* (London, Robinson) 72.

146 Baker, D (1966) *The Early Middle Ages: Portraits and Documents* (London, Hutchinson) 139; Morillo, S (1994) *Warfare Under the Anglo-Norman Kings* (Boydell, Suffolk) 178; France, J (1999) *Western Warfare in the Age of the Crusades 1000–1300* (London, University College London Press) 61–62, 70–74; Prestwich, M (1995) *Armies and Warfare in the Middle Ages* (New Haven, Yale University Press) 152–53; Contamine, P (1984) *War in the Middle Ages* (Oxford, Blackmore) 147; Madaule, J (1967) *The Albigensian Crusade* (London, Burns) 92; Innocent III's Proclamation of 1215 is reprinted in Laffan, R (ed) (1929) *Select Historical Documents: 800–1492* (NY, Holt) 67.

'Immediately after the reestablishment of peace we will remove from the kingdom all foreign born soldiers, cross-bow men, sergeants, and mercenaries who have come with horses and arms for the injury of the realm'.[147]

In the centuries that followed, it became increasingly common for national leaders to abolish forms of independent military powers which were loosely connected to them. As such, Edward III banned Free Companies in 1361, the Pope excommunicated them in 1362, and Charles VII gave them the option of joining his national army or being declared outlaws in 1439. These acts led to the formation of what eventually became regular armies, which could only be raised or led with express permission of the sovereign. Failure to have such permission meant that they could be seen as waging war illegally and therefore without any of the rights or privileges that would otherwise accompany them like the right to pillage.[148]

The formation of national armies was a slow process. This was evidenced by two factors. First, the nature of warfare was often far from formal, with informal insurgencies being recorded in many of the forests and hinterlands of large parts of Europe, ranging from the mythical figures of Robin Hood and William Tell through to the Welsh insurgents like Giraldius Cambrensis (1146–1223) who devised a method of warfare which stressed the avoidance of open engagements, preferring to fight at night or by ambush.[149] Second, even the national armies had difficulties distinguishing themselves because there was no standard kit for allied combatants. Although coats of arms and the advent of heraldry helped identify different individuals on a field, there was often very little linking the physical identity of the combatants, which tended to turn battles into uncontrolled melees as friend and foe could not always be distinguished. This only began to really change with the Crusades, when the Franks, as a symbol of their unity, wore crosses sewn onto the shoulder of their surcoat. In time, different Christian nations took different colours. Originally, the French would wear red crosses (which later changed to white), whilst those from England had white crosses (later changed to red), and those from Flanders wore green crosses. The Hospitallers, owing direct obedience to the Pope, were given a uniform of a white cross on a black background. Innocent III (1160–1216) assigned the uniform of a white tunic with a black cross to the Teutonic Knights in 1199 (the basis of the Iron Cross medal). Islamic armies also created uniforms. This was particularly so for the ghazi (the equivalent of a Christian knight) who utilised distinctive insignia. The Janissaries wore a uniform of green and yellow cloaks over their chain mail with white ostrich plumes and tassels hanging from high white mitres. National uniforms, with multiple variations, often designed by each field commander for some of their combatants proliferated thereafter, helping distinguish combatants on the field, although both sides took turns disguising themselves in each others' uniforms.[150] Sometimes the modes of distinction were

[147] The Magna Carta in Herlihy, D (ed) *The History of Feudalism* (NY, Harper,) 266. See also Tanner, J (ed) (1957) *The Cambridge Medieval History. Victory of the Papacy*, Vol VI (Cambridge, Cambridge University Press) 250, 253.

[148] Keen, M (1965) *The Laws of War in the Late Middle Ages* (London, Routledge) 96–97; Meron, T (1993) *Henry's Wars and Shakespeare's Laws* (Oxford, Oxford University Press) 124–29; Previte, C (ed) (1966) *The Cambridge Medieval History. The Close of the Middle Ages*, Vol VIII (Cambridge, Cambridge University Press) 254–58.

[149] Corbett, R (1986) *Guerrilla Warfare* (London, Orbis) 10.

[150] Kirsch, J (2004) *God Against Gods* (NYC, Viking) 143; Seward, D (1974) *The Monks of War* (Herts, Penguin) 19, 99, 327; Runciman, S (1954) *A History of the Crusades* (Cambridge, Cambridge University Press) Vol 1, 109, Vol 2, 44 and 157; Seward, D (2003) *The Hundred Years War* (London, Robinson) 53;

specified in treaty. For example, the 1435 Treaty of Arras stipulated that the duke of Burgundy and his subjects had the cross of St Andrew as an emblem, and were not to be forced to wear anything else while under the authority of the King. A few decades later, Charles the Bold (1433–77) implemented a strict system of uniforms and numbering units, in a way which reflected what was to become a national army. However, this was not wholly successful, and when he fell on the field in 1477 at the battle of Nancy, he was killed by plunderers who did not recognise his insignia, which should have told them of the economic value in keeping him alive.[151]

8. The Renaissance and Reformation

Some scholars such as Francis Bacon (1561–1626) condemned standing armies because it was a terrible mistake to put weapons in the hands of the 'common people'. Adam Smith (1723–90) added standing armies were too much of a burden on civilised people. Despite such concerns, the movement towards permanent armed forces under a centralised and disciplined command structure was a key feature of Europe from the fifteenth century onwards. For example, in 1421 Venice would declare it was their policy to always 'have men of worth in our service both in peace and war'.[152] However, obtaining enough men to make up the armies of sovereigns who increasingly demanded armed forces of ever-bigger sizes was a difficult task. Accordingly new methods had to be created, such as that in Sweden in 1554 by which the sovereign required every 10 peasants to provide and equip one soldier. Alternately, the Ottoman Empire maintained a standing army of Janissaries (literally 'new troops') which were recruited via a tax every five years on the sons of Christians and rural households. However, such methods were often not sufficient in terms of supply, and by the end of the sixteenth century countries had to develop additional methods which brought in even greater numbers. The Netherlands required all males to register for the militia towards the end of the sixteenth century and by 1600 registration was accompanied by universal military training. This process accelerated throughout Europe during the Thirty Years' War and thereafter as sovereigns took an increasing dislike to mercenaries and viewed strong national defence forces, which could be quickly augmented with all available manpower, with affection. By such approaches, Spain managed to grow her army from 20,000 men in the 1470s to over 300,000 in the 1630s. Other countries followed suit, with a variety of other methods to supplement the growing the forces. For example, in France in 1688, the *milices* was formed. This involved the drawing of lot from a list of all local men in a parish, and those selected serving for two years. These men were to be equipped and paid by the parishes of certain regions (who trained and exercised every Sunday and public holiday when not in times of war) under the command of paid officers drawn from the local nobility.

Runciman, S (1965) *The Fall of Constantinople 1453* (Cambridge, Cambridge University Press) 26, 36; Finucane, R (2004) *Soldiers of the Faith* (London, Phoenix) 42, 86; Arnold, T (2001) *The Renaissance at War* (London, Cassell) 68; Prestwich, M (1995) *Armies and Warfare in the Middle Ages* (New Haven, Yale University Press) 141, 298; Nusbacher, A (2005) *1314; Bannockburn* (Gloucestershire, Tempus) 94, 100; Gravett, C (1990) *Medieval Siege Warfare* (London, Osprey) 26.

[151] Treaty of Arras in Contamine, P (1984) *War in the Middle Ages* (Oxford, Blackmore) 190; Urban, W (2006) *Medieval Mercenaries* (London, Greenhill) 219, 225.

[152] Contamine, P (1984) *War in the Middle Ages* (Oxford, Blackmore) 172.

The problem was that those who volunteered were the poor and 'good-for-nothings' whose families no longer wanted them. The bulk of the army, on the other hand, was still obtained by what amounted to press-gang methods. Thus, the typical manner of recruiting, prior to the French Revolution, was that a sovereign contracted with an officer or civilian to raise a regiment, giving him a 'beating order' (as in a drum, not a thump) that made his enlisting legal. The contractor was given bounty money for each recruit, who was often signed up for life. The goal was that people volunteered to fight, no matter how disingenuous such enticements may have been. Theoretically, recruits signed on of their own free will. In practice, poverty was a key reason for why men joined armed forces. In addition, recruiting officers used cunning devices to ensnare simple souls by false promises and convivial drinking. Failing all else, they seized hold of whom they could. When such ad hoc systems quickly failed to meet the expectations of the sovereigns of the period, the entire basis for obtaining soldiers began to change. Thus, Louis XIV (1638–1715) introduced universal conscription after 1688, whilst Philip V of Spain (1683–1746) decreed in 1704 that military service was obligatory for all males between the ages of 20 and 50, unless the male was one who could be excused, such as noblemen. Sweden and the Hanoverian lands followed suit.[153]

There was no universally agreed age for males coming into the armed forces in this period, and the ages ranged from seven for boys taken to join the Janissaries in the Ottoman Empire through to 18, which Machiavelli argued should be the age of entry into the armed forces. Some countries, like Sweden, initially agreed with the age of 18, although they later dropped it to 15 in the Thirty Years' War when manpower was scarce. Sixteen was a not uncommon age in the English Civil War, although many boys started training at 15. Pope Pius V (1504–72) ordered that his men were 'not to enrol any beardless boy' in 1565 in his war with the Ottomans.[154]

Warfare was a primarily male occupation, although there were a series of notable female leaders in times of war, such as Isabella of Spain (1451–1504) and Elizabeth I (1533–1603). In addition, during actual conflict, female warriors appeared in various struggles. These ranged from female pirates such as Grace O'Malley (1530–1603) through to more conventional belligerents, as in the English Civil War where women warriors were found on both sides. Amongst others, Lady Ann Cunningham (d 1646), with daggers in her belt and pistols attached to her belt, rode at the head of a troop of mixed cavalry fighters.[155]

It was, of course, a little easier for either boys or women to disguise themselves in this period amongst fighting men, for although standardised military dress had not yet arrived, it was getting closer. Some armed forces, such as the Swiss and the Spanish, particularly disdained any appearance of a uniform, preferring to express their individuality in lashings of colour, folds and expensive bills from their tailors. If certain units looked alike, it was because of the whim of a wealthy captain or nobleman, or

[153] Elton, G. (ed)(1968) *The New Cambridge Modern History: The Reformation*, Vol II (Cambridge, Cambridge University Press) 488–91; Bromley, J (1970) *The New Cambridge Modern History. The Rise of Great Britain and Russia*, Vol VI (Cambridge, Cambridge University Press) 224, 326, 367, 764, 767, 770.

[154] Arnold, T (2001) *The Renaissance at War* (London, Cassell) 116; Bradford, E (1962) *The Great Siege* (London, Reprint Society) 85; Childs, J (2001) *Warfare in the 17th Century* (London, Cassell) 47, 94, 126; Contamine, P (1984) *War in the Middle Ages* (Oxford, Blackmore) 169, 249; Cohen, E (1985) *Citizens and Soldiers: The Dilemmas of Military Service* (Ithaca, Cornell University Press) 120; Capponi, N (2006) *Victory of the West. The Battle of Lepanto* (London, Macmillan) 213; Laffin, J (1966) *Boys in Battle* (Toronto, Schuman) 36.

[155] Jones, D (2000) *Women Warriors. A History* (NYC, Brassey's) 68–74.

because of the bulk purchase of a particular cloth by an army contractor. This very ad hoc nature of appearance appears to have been similar to the way pirates came to dress, for like most seamen of the period, they liked to wear short jackets over checked shirts, and either long canvas trousers or 'petticoat' breeches which somewhat resembled culottes. In addition, they frequently wore red waistcoats and tied a scarf or handkerchief loosely around their necks. Exotic clothes stolen from captured ships were usually part of the mix. And of course, a good captain was poorly dressed if he did not have a parrot on his shoulder. Matching uniforms during the sixteenth century were unusual for any forces except royal bodyguards and elite units. This started to change as different localities started to dress all of their armed men in matching uniforms. Such uniformity grew particularly out of the Thirty Years' War. For example, in 1632 Albrecht Wallenstein (1583–1634), stipulated that all soldiers in the Austrian and Spanish armies must wear a red sash or red feather in their hats, whilst Gustavus Adolphus (1594–1632) commanded regiments that were known by the various colours they had attempted to incorporate in their dress. By 1644, red was the chosen colour of England's New Model Army, with different regiments having different linings.[156]

This concentration upon centralised State-based forces was buttressed by a sustained attack on non-State informal forces. This was especially so in the face of pirates. In this regard, although some States, such as England, had legislation mandating the death penalty for all pirates as early as 1536, some pirate groupings, such as the Mediterranean Corsairs and the Madagascar Pirates, had became so powerful that they almost became independent nations. It is suggested that the Corsairs, who were a kind of Muslim privateer (as the various rulers took a share of the profits) preyed on European vessels in two periods, between 829 and 1400, and again between 1600 and the early 1640s. In the second instance, they seized more than 800 English, Scottish, Welsh and Irish trading vessels operating in the Atlantic and Mediterranean. Over the period 1617–25 same 200 Dutch ships were also taken by these pirates. In addition to the vessels and their cargos, people were also taken and enslaved. In this regard, over the course of the seventeenth and eighteenth centuries, probably 20,000 or more British subjects were seized and made slaves by these pirates, as were at least 15,000 Spanish subjects. In the case of the so-called 'Madagascar pirates', a type of 'pirate republic' flourished in the West Indies around 1715, and was only brought to boot when the option of amnesty (for the small price of 121 barrels of gold) seemed preferable to the fate suffered by notables such as Edward Teach (1680–1718), or Blackbeard as he was more popularly known, who was taken down for the price of £100 for his head, and £20 for each of his shipmates. These men were in the company of 26 other pirate captains of the period and hundreds of their men who met their end via a length of rope on a British yardarm. Estimates suggest that in the period 1716–26 alone, probably between 500 and 600 Anglo-American pirates met their end in this manner.[157] However, throughout this

[156] Parker, G (1997) *The Thirty Years' War* (London, Routledge) 171; Cordingly, D (2006) *Under the Black Flag* (NYC, Random) 11–12; Hanson, N (2003) *The Confident Hope of a Miracle. The True Story of the Spanish Armada* (London, Corgi) 336; Anderson, M (1998) *War and Society in Europe of the Old Regime* (London, Sutton) 62; Childs, J (2001) *Warfare in the Seventeenth Century* (London, Cassell) 103; Cooper, J (ed) (1970) *The New Cambridge Modern History. The Decline of Spain and the Thirty Year War* (Cambridge, Cambridge University Press) 207.

[157] Thomson, J (1994) *Mercenaries, Pirates and Sovereigns* (NJ, Princeton University Press) 50–53, 109, 113; Earle, P (2004) *The Pirate Wars* (London, Methuen) 42–43, 122–26, 165, 189, 194–95, 207; Cooley, L (2002) *Captives: Britain, Empire and the World 1600–1850* (London, Cape) 43–45.

period, it was not only pirates who were denied any form of standing in the laws of war. The same lack of standing also accompanied informal military types. For example, during the war in the Spanish Netherlands, it was stipulated that for those involved in the fight against Spain, they could not be given prisoner of war status unless members of a 'party', at least 25 in number and under the command of an officer.[158]

Despite such attacks on non-formal actors not clearly aligned to a State or identifiable in their acts, it would be a mistake to assume that this was a clear-cut area, as a number of sovereigns, whilst condemning informal combatants on one hand, were quick to use them with the other. This was not particuarly surprising when key scholars of the period, such as Thomas More (1478–1535) spoke strongly in favour of using informal combatants such as assassins in times of conflict.[159] One step further towards even greater informal warfare was the proliferation of State-sponsored piracy, or privateers.

Modern State-sponsored terrorism can be traced to the Dutch Revolt and the rise of the Netherlands. Whilst the Dutch were trying to lift the bar in terms of formal warfare, the Spanish were trying to lower it, with their active employment of disguised assassins who intended to kill Elizabeth I, and succeeded in dispatching William of Orange (1533–84), the first head of State assassinated with a handgun. Such acts of assassination were joined in 1605 by the attempt of Guido (Guy) Fawkes (1570–1606) and his accomplices to blow up the British House of Lords. The 36 barrels of gunpowder that they had obtained contained 3,600 pounds of gunpowder. Had this exploded, the death of the King and the Royal Family would have been assured. So too would have been the deaths of many innocent bystanders as the House of Lords turned to rubble. Although there is evidence that the plotters were anguished over the killing of the innocent, they recognised this as a 'cruel necessity' which was eclipsed by the justice of their act.[160]

Modern-State based piracy in the guise of privateers can be traced to the early Middle Ages. The point about State control of these forces is critical, as it was this control that distinguished pirates, which were illegal, from privateers, which were not – even though they acted substantively the same. Privateers were vessels belonging to private individuals but sailing under a commission of war issued by the State, empowering them to carry on all forms of hostility which were permissible at sea by the usages of war. It was the authorisation of the sovereign, not the personal desires of the ship's captain, that legitimised attacks and capture upon specific classes of foreign vessels. This authorisation was contained in what was known as a Letter of Marque. This was an impressive looking certificate written in ponderous legal phrases and decorated with elaborate pen and ink flourish, which provided the licence under which the privateer operated. To ensure privateers remained under State control, they had particular requirements. First, they had report to their local admiralty offices and turn over any prizes they captured to the authorities when they returned from voyages. The rewards would be distributed between the sovereign and the privateer. For example, in 1243, Henry III (1207–72) issued a commission which provided that the King would receive

[158] Anderson, M (1998) *War and Society in Europe of the Old Regime* (London, Sutton) 17–19, 50; Childs, J (2001) *Warfare in the Seventeenth Century* (London, Cassell) 86, 89.

[159] More, T & Logan, G (ed) (1975) *Utopia* (Cambridge, Cambridge University Press) 205–206.

[160] Fraser, A (1996) *The Gunpowder Plot* (London, BCA) 106, 121, 284; Jardine, L (2005) *The Awful End of Prince William the Silent. The First Assassination of a Head of State With a Handgun* (London, Harper) 112, 17–32.

half the proceeds of whatever prizes were captured. This arrangement allowed many sovereigns to neglect building a substantial navy for the next few hundred years, yet share in the booty taken from the vessels of other countries.[161] Second, privateers had to fly under the sovereign's flag; that is, although it was possible for both privateers and conventional ships of war to utilise ruses such as flying under other flags to be able to get close to the prey, before the attack began (even if this was for a very short time period) they had to fly under the correct flag or show 'one's true colours'.[162] This was different from pirates who, despite their legendary flags depicting skulls and cross-bones, never felt obliged to show their true colours until they wanted to. Consequently, and of greatest significance, captured privateers were in principle meant to have the right of surrender (even if they ended up as galley slaves) whilst the pirate would be hung.[163]

Although privateers were known in Antiquity, it was not until the Middle Ages that the practice became entrenched. Despite the risks that giving military licences to private men represented, such as acting without restraint or going feral (as Captain Kidd later did, deciding it was more fun to be a pirate than a privateer), the practice of issuing Letters of Marque was particularly popular with both Henry VIII (1491–1547) and Elizabeth I (1533–1603), as both realised they could harass their enemies and profit from the exercise at relatively little cost to their treasury. The so-called Elizabethan Sea Dogs, of which Francis Drake (1540–96) and Walter Raleigh (1552–1618) were at the forefront, are the most prominent examples of this practice at work, which saw at least 100 privateering voyages leaving England each year in the early 1590s. Whilst these men were not the 'enemies of mankind' as pirates were meant to be, they were certainly the enemies of the Portuguese, Venetians and the French. They were also, in the case of Drake, sufficient cause for war to be declared on Elizabeth and the fated Spanish Armada launched. In the three years following the Armada (1589–91) they took at least 299 prizes, which equated to the government's annual revenue, and well over £100,000 thereafter. Privateers based in Ireland between 1642 and 1650 may have taken as many as 1,900 vessels, whilst during the war of the League of Augsburg (1688–97), Britain lost about 4,200 ships to privateers flying under the French flag. These French privateers captured both ships and areas on behalf of the Crown. For example, the French capture of Cartagena in 1697 was planned by a privateering company in which Louis XIV had a share and the French navy contributed 10 ships to the overall flotilla made up of vessels provided by private individuals.[164]

[161] Marsden, R (1915) *The Law and Customs of the Sea* (London, Navy Records Society I) 116; Ormerod, H (1987) *Piracy in the Ancient World* (NYC, Dorset Press) 61, 117; Symcox, G (1974) *War, Diplomacy and Imperialism* (NYC, Walker) 243; Previte, C (ed) (1966) *The Cambridge Medieval History. The Close of the Middle Ages*, Vol VIII (Cambridge, Cambridge University Press) 364–65.

[162] Hobbes, N (2003) *Essential Militaria* (London, Atlantic) 158.

[163] Latimer, J (2003) *Deception in War* (London, Murray) 162; Earle, P (2004) *The Pirate Wars* (London, Methuen) 51, 174; Cordingly, D (2006) *Under the Black Flag* (NYC, Random,) 106, 114.

[164] Keen, M (1965) *The Laws of War in the Late Middle Ages* (London, Routledge) 218–38; Thomson, J (1994) *Mercenaries, Pirates and Sovereigns* (NJ, Princeton University Press) 22, 43; Andrews, K (1964) *Elizabethan Privateering* (Cambridge, Cambridge University Press) 12, 17–20, 35–39, 58, 61; Hanson, N (2003) *The Confident Hope of a Miracle. The True Story of the Spanish Armada* (London, Corgi) 96, 108; Parker, G (2002) *Empire, War and Faith in Early Modern Europe* (London, Penguin) 87, 190; Cordingly, D (2006) *Under the Black Flag* (NYC, Random) 37, 42–55; Bromley, J (1970) *The New Cambridge Modern History. The Rise of Great Britain and Russia*, Vol VI (Cambridge, Cambridge University Press) 355–56.

The other method by which sovereigns acquired troops that were not taken directly from their own territories was via the utilisation of foreign soldiers. The difference from the feudal period is that by the time of the Reformation and thereafter, it became increasingly possible to bring in foreign soldiers by treaty arrangements between sovereigns, as opposed to individuals in search of the highest bidder. For example, the 1474 Treaty between the Swiss and Louis XI (1423–83) contained a commitment by Swiss soldiers to serve in the campaigns of Louis and the financial rates he would pay them. A later treaty of 1516 contained the promise that the Swiss would never war against France (after they had earlier turned against him in 1503), and the king of France was authorised to enlist up to 16,000 men – for defence only – in return for valuable economic preferences. Finally, in 1522, Switzerland agreed to have done with mercenary war. France, Germany and then England attempted to follow suit, trying to stop their own volunteers from joining foreign adventures. However, such actions were largely without success as large-scale armies came to include very diverse volunteers from any number of countries. For example, among the 25,000 troops on the Catholic side at Moncourtour (1569) 4,000 were Italian, 3,000 were German and – despite their earlier attempts at self restraint, 6,000 were Swiss. The army which Portugal invaded North Africa with in 1578 contained men from Portugal, Spain, Germany and the Walloon Region, and Papal troops under an English commander. Scots were found in the guard of the rulers of Poland, and Englishmen fought on both sides in the Netherlands (and sometimes changed from one side to the other).[165]

Thousands of Saxon soldiers were brought to fight for the York cause in the War of the Roses, whilst thousands of others would travel under the flag of Spain to the New World. Similarly, Elizabeth I would consent to over 6,000 'volunteers' going to fight in the Netherlands against the Spanish. In turn, Spanish and Italian mercenaries were landed in Ireland in 1580. Such practices of having substantial standing foreign elements in national armies, such as the Irish and Scottish regiments in the French army (which can be traced back to 1420), which was 25 per cent foreign, grew during the seventeenth and eighteenth centuries. During the Thirty Years' War, traditional mercenaries offering service because of money, not treaty obligations, proliferated. In the different German armies alone, there were close to 1,500 'military enterprise' commanders who owned their own regiments, if not armies, made up of a polyglot of nationalities, which could be offered for lease to interested princes. The Netherlands continuously used regiments of English, Scottish, French, German and Walloon troops in their service. Spain fought her wars mainly with Italians, Burgundians, Walloons, Germans and Swiss. German mercenary calvary and infantry were important in the French religious wars. Foreign soldiers fought for both sides in the English Civil War, with Charles making great use of French soldiers. By 1677, although the percentages were declining, at least one eighth of the French army was made up of Dutch, Danish, English and Hessian soldiers.[166] Such practices of recruiting mercenaries continued

[165] Treaty Between Louis XI and the Swiss 1474 in Laffan, R (ed) (1929) *Select Historical Documents: 800–1492* (NY, Holt) 176; Potter, G (ed) (1967) *The New Cambridge Modern History. The Renaissance*, Vol 1 (Cambridge, Cambridge University Press) 207–208, 263; Elton, G (ed) (1968) *The New Cambridge Modern History: The Reformation*, Vol II (Cambridge, Cambridge University Press) 100; Wernham, R (ed) (1968) *The New Cambridge Modern History. The Counter Reformation*, Vol III (Cambridge, Cambridge University Press) 181–82, 201.

[166] Arnold, T (2001) *The Renaissance at War* (London, Cassell) 63; Wood, M (2000) *Conquistadors* (London, BBC) 108; Hanson, N (2003) *The Confident Hope of a Miracle. The True Story of the Spanish Armada* (London,

throughout this period, despite their continuing problems of economic cost, unreliability and their potential for cruelty towards either civilians or opposing combatants. In this regard, the failure of Swiss mercenaries to fight in 1500 at the battle of Novara (when they discovered that fellow Swiss were employed by both sides) is notable. So too was the sacking of Antwerp in 1576 as it was done by the troops who were paid to defend it. Throughout this period, the possibility of paid foreigners swapping sides was not seen as a matter of embarrassment for the men involved.[167] Nevertheless, aside from the traditional practice of killing captured mercenaries who were fighting against their own nationality, there were no major reactions to the utilisation of foreign soldiers in national forces in this period. The exception to this was in only a few instances of theory and practice. In practice, after the English Civil War some of the core charges for which Charles I (1600–49) lost his head, were, inter alia, wrongfully seeking military assistance from opposing powers in France, Ireland and Scotland.[168] In theory, Machiavelli warned:

> Mercenary and auxillary arms are useless and dangerous; and if one keeps his state founded on mercenary arms, one will never be firm or secure; for they are disunited, ambitious, without discipline, unfaithful; bold among friends, among enemies cowardly; no fear of God, no faith with men; ruin is postponed only as long as attack is postponed; and in peace you are despoiled by them, in war by the enemy. The cause of this is that they have no love nor cause to keep them in the field other than a small stipend, which is not sufficient to make them want to die for you.[169]

Thomas More added that such men:

> Take sides on such terms that if someone, even the enemy, offers them more money tomorrow, they will take his part; and the day after tomorrow, if a trifle more is offered to bring them back, they return to their first employers.

However, unlike Machiavelli, More did not argue against their utilisation, preferring to see them as a regrettable necessity. As such, he simply underlined his primary rule in this area, that if mercenaries are required ensure that the employer is not outbid by others, or the mercenaries will change side.[170]

Where Machiavelli was successful was in forcing leaders to realise that their military forces were best served by their own citizens. This resulted in a surge in compulsion into armed forces. Unsurprisingly, this was also accompanied by a surge in resistance to being forced into the armed forces. The resistance, on an ad hoc basis, was evident from Spain to Russia, where the leaders were often forced to make promises that they would either relax or create exceptions to universal conscription. Such political unrest was joined by a

Corgi) 214; Anderson, M (1998) *War and Society in Europe of the Old Regime* (London, Sutton) 24, 47, 52; Cooper, J (ed) (1970) *The New Cambridge Modern History. The Decline of Spain and the Thirty Year War* (Cambridge, Cambridge University Press) 217; Bromley, J (1970) *The New Cambridge Modern History. The Rise of Great Britain and Russia*, Vol VI (Cambridge, Cambridge University Press) 742; Childs, J (2001) *Warfare in the Seventeenth Century* (London, Cassell) 34, 66. Downing, T (1991) *Civil War* (London, Gardner) 73.

167 Arnold, T (2001) *The Renaissance at War* (London, Cassell) 59; Childs, J (2001) *Warfare in the Seventeenth Century* (London, Cassell) 35–38; Prestwich, M (1995) *Armies and Warfare in the Middle Ages* (New Haven, Yale University Press) 156; Potter, G (ed) (1969) *The New Cambridge Modern History. The Renaissance*, Vol 1 (Cambridge, Cambridge University Press) 357.

168 Robertson, G (2006) *The Tyrannicide Brief* (London, Vintage) 65, 117, 174.

169 Machiavelli, N (1985) *The Prince* in trans Mansfield, T (Chicago, Chicago University Press) 67–68.

170 More, T & Logan, G (ed) (1975) *Utopia* (Cambridge, Cambridge University Press) 209–10.

growing chorus of ethical unrest with the development of conscientious objectors who refused to serve in military forces on religious grounds. For example, Francisco Vitoria (1492–1546), building on the earlier arguments of Aquinas that a man is only obliged to obey a secular prince if the order is just, argued: 'If their conscience tells subjects that the war is unjust, they must not go to war, even if their conscience is wrong, for whatsoever is not of faith, is sin.'[171] Thomas More broadly concurred, that in an ideal society 'no-one is forced to fight abroad against his will'.[172]

Whilst More did not hold the same rule for situations of national defence (of which compulsion was possible), other Christians came to draw no distinction between offensive and defensive wars. The Anabaptists who arose in Switzerland as part of the Protestant Reformation adopted a similar approach, refusing to fight against either Christians or Muslims.[173] Whilst Martin Luther (1483–1546) argued 'the sword is indispensable for the whole world, to preserve peace, punish sin and restrain the wicked',[174] the Anabaptists (or Mennonites or Dunkers as they came to be known elsewhere) adopted a different interpretation, and argued for a complete ban on all violence, although they were willing to do non-combative work in exchange for active service. Although their original leader Ulrich Zwingli (1484–1531) would distance himself from such suggestions (and argue they should all 'be drowned without mercy' for their heresy),[175] their philosophy was persuasive and quickly spread throughout Europe. As such, by 1572, the emerging Dutch State was willing to formally create an exception for them from military service on condition that they were willing to either do non-combative work or pay for a substitute to go into the military.[176] These issues were of such an importance in this age that even Hugo Grotius (1583–1645) dedicated a chapter to them in his work of *The Rights of War and Peace*. He recognised that the right of Christians to object was as valid as the right to demand compliance with the military needs of the State.[177] Such 'rights' were demonstrated soon after by the Quakers who provoked anger by refusing to take any oaths or even to tip their hats as a sign of respect. Nevertheless, they were largely protected by Oliver Cromwell (1599–1658) who was willing to make an exception for these men on grounds of religious conscience. However, Cromwell would not make an exception for the English Levellers who were possibly the first group, ever, to argue against being forced into the military on grounds of political conscience. The spokesman for the Levellers, Richard Overton (1559–1664), argued against Cromwell as he pressed men into his New Model Army in Ireland:

> We entreat you to consider what difference there is between binding a man to an oar as a galley-slave in Turkey, and pressing of men to serve in your war. To surprise a man . . . force

[171] Vitoria in Pagden, A (ed) *Vitoria: Political Writings* (Cambridge, Cambridge University Press) 308, 312; Baumgarth, W (ed) *Saint Thomas Aquinas. On Law, Morality and Politics* (NYC, Hackett) 246.

[172] More, T & Logan, G (ed) (1975) *Utopia* (Cambridge, Cambridge University Press) 210.

[173] See 'Anabaptism' in Elton, G (ed) (1968) *Renaissance and Reformation* (Cambridge, Cambridge University Press)169–70.

[174] Hopel, H (ed) *Luther and Calvin on Secular Authority* (Cambridge, Cambridge University Press) 13. But note the entire chapter, 3–22.

[175] Zwingli in Reddaway, F (1930) (ed) *Select Documents in European History* Vol II, 1492–715 (London, Methuen) 66.

[176] Anderson, M (1998) *War and Society in Europe of the Old Regime* (London, Sutton) 20, 115; Kurlansky, M (2006) *Non-Violence: The History of a Dangerous Idea* (London, Cape) 52–55; Brock, P (2006) *Against the Draft* (Toronto, University of Toronto Press) 18–19, 47.

[177] Grotius, H (1625) *The Rights of War and Peace*, edn 1901 (London, Dunne) 39–54.

> him from his calling where he lived comfortably from a good trade, from his dear parents, wife or children, against inclination and disposition to fight for a cause he understands not and in company of such as he has no comfort to be withal, for pay that will scarce give him sustenance – and if he live, to return to a lost trade, or beggary, or not much better; if any tyranny or cruelty exceed this, it must be worse than that of a Turkish galley-slave.[178]

Although the arguments of the Levellers came to nothing as their dissent was crushed, the arguments of the Quakers came to gain ground. By the 1650s their position was clear. At the end of the 1660s, they presented a testimony to King Charles II:

> All bloody principle and practices we . . . do utterly deny . . . with all outward wars and strife, and fightings with outward weapons . . . The Spirit of Christ . . . will never move us to fight and war any man with outward weapons, neither for the Kingdom of Christ, nor for the kingdoms of this world . . . So we, whom the Lord hath called into the obedience of the Truth, have denied all wars and fightings, and cannot again any more learn it . . . our swords are broken into ploughshares, and spears into pruning hooks.[179]

Quakers would not serve, pay fines (although some came to relent on this) or pay for substitutes in their refusal to perform military service. The first recorded American conscientious objector, Richard Keene, was a Quaker, who refused to participate in the Maryland militia in 1656. By 1658, four Quakers had been executed, but their influence continued to grow, with William Penn (1644–1718) converting to Quakerism in 1667. Under the leadership of Penn they issued their solemn declaration promising never 'to fight and war against any man with outward weapons'.[180]

9. The Enlightenment

A. Boys, Women and Men

In theory the emphasis of this period was upon men, not boys; nevertheless, 'cabin boys' or 'powder monkeys' (a particularly dangerous job involving the ferrying of gunpowder) were notable in this period. By the rule of 1731 the age of entry for any captain's servants was fixed at 13, unless the son of an officer, when the minimum age was 11. By the end of the eighteenth century, the official rule was that the minimum age to serve on a warship was the age of 12, although there are many cases before the Crimean War of a boys name being entered on a ship's book below that age (with some being as young as nine) in order to gain seniority. A single large man-of-war could contain up to 50 such boys, whilst some 8 per cent of the overall British navy (in 1814) was made up of boys. On land, aside from 'drummer boys', the more common age that boys entered into service was 16. This was the adopted age at the beginning of the French Revolution, and at the end of the Napoleonic period when manpower supplies were dwindling, the age for combat was dropped back from 18 to 16. This was despite Napoleon's reservations about the youth of this age. However, examples of boys as young as 15 seeing combat also exist. This was recorded during the American

178 Overton in Sharp, A (1998) *The English Levellers* (Cambridge, Cambridge University Press) 47–48.

179 Noted in Brock, P (2006) *Against the Draft* (Toronto, University of Toronto Press) 53.

180 Kurlansky, M (2006) *Non-Violence: The History of a Dangerous Idea* (London, Cape) 56, 59, 65; Bell, D (2007) *The First Total War: Napoleon's Europe and the Birth of Modern Warfare* (London, Bloomsbury) 53, 59–62; Brock, P (2006) *Against the Draft* (Toronto, University of Toronto Press) 92–93.

War of Independence and elsewhere. Andrew Fitzgibbon (1845–83), at the age of 15, was the youngest person ever to win a Victoria Cross in the Second China War in 1860 Around the same period in Latin America, Simon Bolivar (1758–1806) ordered the enlistment of all males, down to the age of 14, whilst in the conflict between the United States and Mexico between 1846 and 1848, Mexican defenders were known to utilise boys as young as 10.[181]

This epoch saw female pirates on the high seas, such as Mary Read (d 1721), Ann Bonny (1702–82) and the so-called 'Mrs Cheng', a former prostitute from Canton who oversaw around 40,000 pirates with some 400 junks operating in the South China Sea. Female warriors were also engaged in the American War of Independence, and again in their 1812 war with England. At least 40 women soldiers fought for the Republic during the French Revolution before they were ordered from the ranks. Notable female warriors, such as Charlotte Corday (1768–93) – the woman who assassinated John-Paul Marat (1743–1793)– fought against the Revolution. Female combatants who were also particularly notable appear in the Spanish theatre of the Napoleonic wars. Whilst some acted as spies, others such as Augustina Zaragoza (1786–1857) led a garrison of 220 against 12,000 French soldiers, and assisted at the front lines and during the sieges. Despite these European examples, nothing of this period could match that of the forces of the Dahomey kingdom in West Africa, which by 1850 had over 5,000 female soldiers in the army.[182]

B. Conscription and Impressment

The Continental Army of the American Revolution was made up largely of state miltias of volunteers who were complemented by men who had been enticed to enlist by incentives of land and cash. However, George Washington (1732–99) soon discovered that he did not have enough soldiers. He was not in favour of unregulated miltias and was of the belief that 'a primary position and the basis or our [democratic] system, that every citizen who enjoys the protection of a free government owes not only a proportion of his property, but even his personal service to the defence of it'.[183]

The core of this thinking, which retains a resonance in all democracies, is that if everyone has the same benefits of an egalitarian society, then everyone should also share the same risks to defend what they all value. Accordingly, when Washington was president he sought to improve the countries military posture by signing into law, in 1792, the

[181] Black, J (1994) *European Warfare 1600–1815* (New Haven, Yale University Press) 222–23; Fowler, W (2005) *Empires at War* (NYC, Walker) 65; Clayton, T (2004) *Trafalgar: The Men, the Battle, the Storm* (London, Hodder) 43, 67; Scheina, R (2003) *Latin America's Wars: The Age of the Caudillo, 1791–1899* (Washington, Brassey's) 36, 195; McCullough, D (2005) *1776. America and Britain at War* (London, Penguin) 138; Griffith, P (1998) *The Art of War of Revolutionary France: 1789–1902* (Greenhill, London) 82; Luvaas, J (1999) *Napoleon on the Art of War* (NYC, Free Press) 2–3; Rothenberg, G (2000) *The Napoleonic Wars* (London, Cassell) 182; Ponting, C (2005) *The Crimean War: The Truth Behind the Myth* (London, Pimlico) 22; Hernon, I (2007) *Britain's Forgotten Wars. Colonial Campaigns in the 19th Century* (London, Sutton) 381.

[182] Rothenberg, G (1980) *The Age of Warfare in the Age of Napoleon* (Bloomington, Indiana University Press) 88; Andress, D (2007) *The Terror: Civil War in the French Revolution* (NYC, Brown) 158; Cordingly, D (2006) *Under the Black Flag* (NYC, Random) 5–6, 56–66, 71–78; Black, J (1999) *Warfare in the Eighteenth Century* (London, Cassell) 170–71.

[183] Washington in Tracy, J (2006) *The Military Draft Handbook* (San Francisco, Manic Press) 16; Cohen, E (1985) *Citizens and Soldiers: The Dilemmas of Military Service* (Ithaca, Cornell University Press) 127.

National Conscription Act, which stated that 'every able-bodied white male citizen of the age of 18 years and under the age of 45 be enrolled in the militia'.[184] However, this was not an easily agreed principle and whilst the American Constitution of 1789 gave Congress the 'power to raise and support armies' the question of mandatory service was neither mentioned nor prohibited. The trend of the early years of the nineteenth century was that proposals for mass conscription by presidents John Adams (1735–1826), James Madison (1751–1836) and Thomas Jefferson (1743–1826) were without success, as Congress consistently erred on the side of volunteering as opposed to compulsion in times of war. Specifically, forced military service was seen to represent the most extreme demand a community could impose on its members – the requirements that they kill and/or die on its behalf. Additional concerns ranged from those of extreme conformity through to the loss of free choice or individual identity. Such situations were usually seen as quickly creeping towards the totalitarianism that democracies often have to oppose. Accordingly, the government had to revert to enticements of land and cash (which was classified as 'bounties') for enlistment for its major conflicts.[185] In addition, the Americans were, from the outset of their claim for independence, swift to protect the rights of religious pacifists who were not to be prosecuted for refusing war service, as long as they paid their taxes to support the war, including an annual fine. For example, the Virginia Convention held before the ratification of the American Constitution proposed that the Bill of Rights should (although it did not eventuate) include the statement that 'any person religiously scrupulous of bearing arms ought to be exempted, upon payment of an equivalent to employ another to bear arms in his stead'.[186]

The intellectuals of the French Revolution, such as Jacques Brissot (1754–93) and Maximilien Robspierre (1758–94), like their American counterparts, defended the rights of Quakers and Anabaptists or Mennonites to avoid military service if they were willing to either do non-military support work, pay a fine or pay for a substitute to serve. Although some wealthy men managed to utilise substitutes to escape service, on the whole, France became a system of universal conscription. The roots of the French system can be traced to Maurice de Saxe (1696–1750) who argued:

> Would it not be better to prescribe by law that every man, whatever his condition in life, should be obliged to serve his prince and his country for five years. This law could not be objected to because it is natural and just that all citizens should occupy themselves with the defence of the nation. No inconvenience could result if they were chosen between the ages of twenty and thirty . . . this method of raising troops would provide an inexhaustible reservoir of fine recruits who would not be subject to desertion . . . It is essential to make no distinctions, to be immovable on this point, and to enforce the law particularly on the nobles and the rich. Then, no one will complain.[187]

This view was very influential in French thinking, with Jacques Count de Guibert (1743–93), Denis Diderot (1713–84) and even Jean Jacques Rousseau (1712–88) all

[184] Haskew, M 'To Field An Army' *Military Heritage* (Feb 2008) 52, 54.

[185] Tracy, J (2006) *The Military Draft Handbook* (San Francisco, Manic Press) 16; Boatner, M (1969) *The Encyclopaedia of the American Revolution* (NYC, McKay) 842–43, 923; Cohen, E (1985) *Citizens and Soldiers: The Dilemmas of Military Service* (Ithaca, Cornell University Press) 33–34, 148, 923. Haskew, M (2008) 'To Field An Army' *Military Heritage* (Feb 2008) 52, 54.

[186] Cohen, E (1985) *Citizens and Soldiers: The Dilemmas of Military Service* (Ithaca, Cornell University Press) 123; Kurlansky, M (2006) *Non-Violence: The History of a Dangerous Idea* (London, Cape) 76.

[187] Saxe in Chaliand, G (ed) (1994) *The Art of War in World History* (California, University of California Press) 581, 582.

adopting this principle, with the addition being that it was citizens, not subjects, who were to make up the military forces of the future. Thus, Rousseau could proclaim 'every citizen should be a soldier by duty'.[188] From such thinking, on 23 August 1793, the Mass Conscription Order, despite being a lightning rod for the opposing French forces, was passed by the French National Convention. Following on from the Constitution of 1793 which stated 'All Frenchmen shall be soldiers; they shall be trained in the use of arms', the *levee en masse* added:

> From this moment, until our enemies have been driven from the soil of the Republic, the whole French people is in permanent requisition for army service. Young men shall go into battle; married men shall forge arms and transport supplies; women shall make tents and clothing and serve in hospitals; children shall turn old linen into lint and old men shall have themselves taken to public places to arouse the courage of the warriors and hatred of kings, and to encourage the unity of the Republic . . . No-one may be replaced by a substitute in the service for which he is requisitioned.[189]

In 1798 the Assembly rationalised the rules of recruitment which were, by this stage, already in force, although these rules were not finally codified until 1811. Military service was legally due from all Frenchmen between the ages of 20 and 25. But there were limits upon universality even within these ages. First, the law expressly exempted many groups from military service: married men, men with dependents (whether married or not) and later, priests. In addition, until the last critical years of the Empire, it was standard to only call up a proportion of those named on the lists. Finally, it was possible (from 1802 forwards) for those chosen to find a substitute or replacement. Despite these exceptions, the *levee en masse* were so successful that the French army grew exponentially. For example, the French army grew from 50,000 in 1550 to 77,000 in the eighteenth century to 700,000 during the Revolution (1789–99). Napoleon would go on to command more than 100,000 men in seven of his battles, and take over 400,000 soldiers into Russia. To achieve such numbers, in addition to large numbers of volunteers, he also drafted nearly 2,500,000 men by 1813. Note however, that this amount of conscription was well under 50 per cent of the men whose names appeared on the lists of those eligible for military service.[190]

On the question of universal conscription for all men of fighting age, France was followed by Sweden in 1812, Prussia and Norway in 1814, Spain in 1831 and Denmark in 1849. The results of such practices were often impressive. For example, following the adoption of conscription in Prussia, by 1813, nearly 6 per cent of the population – or 300,000 men – was under arms. This was a force which was nearly twice as large

[188] Rousseau, in Cohen, E (1985) *Citizens and Soldiers: The Dilemmas of Military Service* (Ithaca, Cornell University Press) 17; Bell, D (2007) *The First Total War: Napoleon's Europe and the Birth of Modern Warfare* (London, Bloomsbury) 79; Brock, P (2006) *Against the Draft* (Toronto, University of Toronto Press) 70–79; Cohen, E (1985) *Citizens and Soldiers: The Dilemmas of Military Service* (Ithaca, Cornell University Press) 55; Rothenberg, G (1980) *The Age of Warfare in the Age of Napoleon* (Bloomington, Indiana University Press) 101; Mason, J (ed) *Diderot. Political Writings* (Cambridge, Cambridge University Press) 153; Symcox, G (1974) *War, Diplomacy and Imperialism* (NYC, Walker) 176–79.

[189] Arts 1 and 7 of the Levee en Masse in Wright, D (ed) *The French Revolution Documents* (Queensland, University of Queensland Press) 181–83. See also Andress, D (2007) *The Terror: Civil War in the French Revolution* (NYC, Brown) 202; Griffith, P (1998) *The Art of War of Revolutionary France: 1789–1902* (London, Greenhill) 30.

[190] Cohen, E (1985) *Citizens and Soldiers: The Dilemmas of Military Service* (Ithaca, Cornell University Press) 52.

as the standing army of Frederick the Great (1712–86). Only a few countries such as Austria and Britain refused to instigate such measures, preferring other methods to build their armed forces when volunteers were not sufficient. The most notable of these was via impressments. Impressments could target any area of society. English Press Acts allowed for the forcible recruitment of debtors, vagrants and other marginal members of society throughout the seventeenth and eighteenth centuries. The pressing was often done by unscrupulous men who stood to profit by obtaining all the recruits they could muster my fair means or foul. False promises, trickery of many kinds, and even acts close to kidnapping were utilised in such times. Alternately, if more specialised forces were required, such as sailors, armed seamen would descend on ports and ships and literally carry off men of their own nationality, and anyone else they could persuade to serve, for military service. The legal aspect of press-gangs, which were clearly recognised as inhumane, inefficient and disliked equally by officers and men, was justified by Lord Mansfield (1705–93) due to the fact that there was no alternative. Specifically, impressment was 'founded upon immemorial useage allowed for ages. It can have no power to stand upon, nor can it be vindicated or justified by any reason except the safety of the State'.[191] Accordingly, France, Spain – and especially England – all used this method to man their own navies whilst depleting that of their enemies. The impressments, or imprisonment of foreign sailors found on the high sea was well described by Napoleon's Berlin Decree of 1806, which classified this British practice as against 'the system of international law universally observed by all civilized nations', and which he used as a justification for his attempted blockade of the British Isles.[192]

Although this practice helped underpin British mastery of the oceans (especially during its conflicts with France), it was the cause of great consternation between countries, as sailors of foreign nationalities got caught up with the overzealous impressments of seamen of British nationality serving with other countries, such as the 50,000 to 100,000 serving with American merchant vessels. In an attempt to stem this problem, both Britain and the United States agreed by treaty in 1794 that the two nations would 'not . . . endeavour to enlist in their military service, any of the subjects or citizens of the other party'.[193] However, Britain impressed over 6,000 American seamen (despite releasing 273 of such men between 1803 and 1805, out of 1,500 official American requests) in the early part of the following century in an attempt to keep the Royal Navy fully manned in their fight against Napoleon. The result of this practice was a declaration of war by the United States against Britain, for as James Madison explained:

> British cruisers have been in the continued practice of violating the American flag on the great highway of nations, and of seizing and carrying off persons sailing under it, not in the exercise of a belligerent right founded on the law of nations against an enemy, but of a municipal prerogative over British subjects. British jurisdiction is thus extended to neutral vessels in a situation where no laws can operate but the law of nations and the laws of a

[191] Mansfield, noted in Goodwin, A (ed) (1968) *The New Cambridge Modern History: The American and French Revolutions*, Vol VIII (Cambridge, Cambridge University Press) 177.

[192] Bell, D (2007) *The First Total War: Napoleon's Europe and the Birth of Modern Warfare* (London, Bloomsbury) 253; Anderson, M (1998) *War and Society in Europe of the Old Regime* (London, Sutton) 120–27; Parker, G (1997) *The Thirty Years' War* (London, Routledge) 173.

[193] Jay's Treaty1794, Art XXI.

> country to which the vessels belong . . . the practice . . . far from affecting British subjects alone . . . [has entrapped] . . . thousands of American citizens . . . [these men] . . . have been dragged on board ships of war of a foreign nation and exposed, under the severities of their discipline . . . to risk their lives in the battles of their oppressors.[194]

Despite this practice being a large part of the cause of the war of 1812, this issue was not resolved in the 1814 Treaty of Ghent which brought back peace between Britain and the United States. However, no renunciation of the practice of impressing men at sea was achieved as no British government could renounce this method to gain manpower for the navy. Indeed, it was not until the 1870s that the need for impressment for Britain's navy finally disappeared. It only disappeared when the demands for large numbers of men were less, the pay was more attractive and the harsh discipline that was necessary to make men too scared to abscond, was finally 'suspended'. At this point, volunteers came to replace men who had been previously been coerced into the navy.[195]

C. Foreign Forces and Mercenaries

The other area that Britain profited from in terms of manpower was its utilisation of foreign soldiers. Independent mercenaries were a common feature of the mercantile companies that proliferated from the seventeenth century, as well as within formal armies, as with the army of Frederick the Great who, despite attempts to use men of his own cantons ended up with up to 66 per cent of 'his' men being of foreign nationality. These men often included prisoners of war that Frederick's armies had captured who were then forced to fight against their own countrymen. As the Enlightenment expanded, some European countries began to respond favourably to such (and other) arguments and moved towards systems whereby men of a given nationality would not be allowed to fight for another country unless there was an express agreement between the countries. However, despite such attempts as the 1819 Enlistment Act of Britain, thousands of English (and other European) soldiers migrated in search of both adventure and money. Thousands who fought in the Napoleonic wars, but were subsequently left without an employer when the conflicts ended, went to fight in the wars of independence in Greece and Latin America. Initially such men fought under the flag of Simon Bolivar, despite the protestations of the Spanish authorities. Soon after, over 1,200 English, Irish and American seamen flocked to fight in the Brazilian war of Independence (1825–28), although many of these men later mutinied in 1828 due to numerous grievances. Amongst others, British, French, American and Italian mercenaries would continue to find paymasters in the region or come to act as independent filibusterers (of which there were thousands), in search of territory they could claim as their own (in northern Mexico, Cuba and Central America) between 1819 and 1860. Hundreds of European adventurers also opted to fight for Brazil in the war of the

[194] Madison in Birley, R (ed) (1944) *Speeches and Documents in American History*, Vol I, 1776–1815 (Oxford, Oxford University Press) 274, 275; Bury, J (ed) (1964) *The New Cambridge Modern History: The Zenith of European Power*, Vol X (Cambridge, Cambridge University Press) 294–99.

[195] Hickey, D (1995) *The War of 1812* (Chicago, University Press Illinois) 11, 17, 284; Lambert, A (2002) *War at Sea in the Age of Sail* (London, Cassell) 50; Clayton, T (2004) *Trafalgar: The Men, the Battle, the Storm* (London, Hodder) 38–43; Thomson, J (1994) *Mercenaries, Pirates and Sovereigns* (NJ, Princeton University Press) 31.

Triple Alliance between 1864 and 1870. Soldiers of fortune from Europe and the Americas flocked to Cuba between 1868 and 1898 to join the revolutionary forces against Spain.[196] Such practices were increasingly frowned upon by countries like France, Britain and the United States, who all took legislative steps to prevent their own citizens serving in the armies of others. However some countries such as France were ambivalent on this point, as volunteers had earlier crowded to their revolutionary cause and they bloated with captured men willing to change sides, although this was not formalised into the French Foreign Legion until 1831.

Other countries preferred to hire entire military units of foreigners, as opposed to wandering individuals.[197] England, under the leadership of the Hanoverian George III (1738–1820), hired entire units (culminating in about 28,000 men) from the Hessians during the Napoleonic wars. The British had done the same throughout the eighteenth century using, inter alia, at least 6,000 Hessian troops to defeat Bonnie Prince Charlie in 1745. The last army of foreigners raised to fight a war under the British flag was in 1854, when the British crown hired 16,500 German, Italian and Swiss mercenaries for the Crimean War. Before this, during the American War of Independence, over half of the 'British' forces were non-British, of which the Hessians were most dominant. It was initially argued by the Americans (forgetting their own French volunteers) that troops so utilised should not be given prisoner of war status. The use of non-British soldiers in British uniforms was one of the reasons recorded by the Americans in their Declaration of Independence for why they wished to divorce themselves from England. Specifically:

> [A]t this Time, [he is] transporting large Armies of foreign Mercenaries to complete the Works of Death, Desolation, and Tyranny, already begun with circumstances of Cruelty and Perfidy, scarcely paralleled in the most barbarous Ages, and totally unworthy the Head of a civilized Nation.[198]

Accordingly, when the Treaty of Paris of 1783, which ended the American War of Independence, was concluded, all troops in British uniform were to be evacuated 'with all convenient speed'[199] from the country. In some regards, the Europeans began to learn from such experiences, as some of the key scholars of the age, such as Immanuel Kant came to argue that 'the hiring out of troops of one nation to another for use

[196] Scheina, R (2003) *Latin America's Wars: The Age of the Caudillo, 1791–1899* (Washington, Brassey's) 34–38, 95, 104, 120–21, 141, 143–44, 205–33, 319, 353.

[197] Bell, D (2007) *The First Total War: Napoleon's Europe and the Birth of Modern Warfare* (London, Bloomsbury) 45, 263; Rothenberg, G (2000) *The Napoleonic Wars* (London, Cassell) 51, 112; Esdaile, C (2003) *The Peninsular War* (London, Penguin) 113–16; Griffith, P (1998) *The Art of War of Revolutionary France: 1789–1902* (Greenhill, London) 57; Luvaas, J (1999) *Napoleon on the Art of War* (NYC, Free Press) 8; Thomson, J (1994) *Mercenaries, Pirates and Sovereigns* (NJ, Princeton University Press) 33–39, 35–39, 60–67, 97–106; Black, J (1994) *European Warfare 1600–1815* (New Haven, Yale University Press) 223; Symcox, G (1974) *War, Diplomacy and Imperialism* (NYC, Walker) 117–25; Marston, D (2001) *The Seven Years' War* (London, Osprey) 20; Luvaas, J (1999) *Frederick the Great on the Art of War* (NYC, De Capo) 57–59, 72–73.

[198] The quote is from the preamble of the Declaration of Independence in Birley, R (ed) (1944) *Speeches and Documents in American History*, Vol I, 1776–1815 (Oxford, Oxford University Press) 1, 5. For further commentary on this question from this period, see McCullough, D (2005) *1776. America and Britain at War* (London, Penguin) 10, 241, 244; Boatner, M (1969) *The Encyclopaedia of the American Revolution* (NYC, McKay,) 425; Duffy, C (2003) *The '45* (London, Cassell) 131, 213; Bell, D (2007) *The First Total War: Napoleon's Europe and the Birth of Modern Warfare* (London, Bloomsbury) 23; Thomson, J (1994) *Mercenaries, Pirates and Sovereigns* (NJ, Princeton University Press) 29, 88.

[199] Peace Treaty of 1783, Art 7.

against an enemy not common to both of them . . . [must be prohibited], for by this practice subjects are used and wasted as mere objects to be manipulated at will.'[200]

D. Formal and Informal Combatants

Although such fighting men throughout this epoch may have been from many locations, by the end of the seventeenth century, all of the primary belligerents of the age put great stock in having their armed forces fully and consistently uniformed. This distinguished them from their enemies and civilians alike. The military uniform had other complementary functions such as promoting obedience, comradeship and a display of strength. It was also highly symbolic that the struggle was legitimate and the soldiers were formal, under control and not brigands.[201] Brigands could expect no quarter during a conflict, and possibly, no rights of pardon after a war. For example, the 1652 Act of Settlement, which ended the conflict in Ireland with England, stipulated that the pardon being offered would not apply to anybody who killed Parliamentary troops when not '[p]ublically entertained and maintained in arms as an officer of private soldiers under the command and pay of the Irish against the English'.[202]

Such ideas were highly influential on emerging regimes, such as the United States of America, which were seeking to represent themselves as legitimate authorities. Thus, one of the first acts of George Washington was to issue uniform dress of red-trimmed blue coats, white waistcoats, buckskin breeches and white woollen stockings for all of his soldiers, and replace the motley collection of outfits that they had begun the war with. This also helped stop the practices of some Hessian troops who refused to take prisoners because the American rebels 'had no uniforms, but only torn blouses of all colors'.[203] Similarly, when James Aitken (1752–77), who wandered the English country in disguise setting fire to British dockyards in support of the American Revolution, was caught, he found his conclusion at the end of a yardarm.[204]

This idea of the identification of combatants, as distinct from civilians, continued with the French Revolution where the forces arraigned against the revolutionaries, despite not having uniforms, opted to wear either squares of white cloth adorned with a red heart and a cross or vivid red handkerchiefs (around their head, neck or waist) as a way to distinguish themselves from the other side and from common criminals. From such beginnings, the French went on to develop highly uniformed armed forces, and apart from the landing of the *Legion Noire* of 1,224 men in England in 1797, disguised in British uniforms, they generally seem to have shown a respect for its importance.[205]

[200] Kant, I (1795) 'To Perpetual Peace: A Philosophical Sketch' in Humphrey, T (ed) (1983) *Immanuel Kant. Perpetual Peace and Other Essays* (NYC, Hackett) 107, 108.

[201] Fuller, J (1972) *The Conduct of War 1789–1961* (London, Methuen) 20; Black, J (1994) *European Warfare 1600–1815* (New Haven, Yale University Press) 115.

[202] O'Siochru, M (2008) *God's Executioner: Oliver Cromwell and the Conquest of Ireland* (London, Faber) 228. For the Irish, non-formal combatants, see 192–220.

[203] McCullough, D (2005) *1776. America and Britain at War* (London, Penguin) 12, 33, 69, 149, 181; Boatner, M (1969) *The Encyclopaedia of the American Revolution* (NYC, McKay) 1131; Higginbotham, D (1984) 'Reflections on the War of Independence: Guerrilla Warfare' in Hoffman, R (ed) *Arms and Independence: The Military Character of the American Revolution* (Virginia, Virginia University Press) 12.

[204] Warner, J 'Britain's First Terrorist' *BBC History* (March 2005) 22–27.

[205] Latimer, J (2003) *Deception in War* (London, Murray) 20–23; Bell, D (2007) *The First Total War: Napoleon's Europe and the Birth of Modern Warfare* (London, Bloomsbury) 166; Andress, D (2007) *The Terror: Civil War in the French Revolution* (NYC, Brown) 246.

The importance of uniforms, and their link to an organised and authorised military force, was most clearly demonstrated with warfare that gave birth to the word 'guerrilla'. This term evolved from Napoleon's campaign in Spain between 1808 and 1813 and meant 'little war'. The concept acknowledges a conflict between armed civilians and a powerful nation State army, either foreign or domestic, and uses tactics such as ambush, sabotage and mobility in attacking vulnerable targets in enemy territory. The key point is that the belligerents, who are the 'armed civilians', are not in uniform and dress to blend in with non-combatants. This practice, although linked to the Napoleonic wars, was clearly evident decades before this point, such as during the wars of Louis XIV (1638–1715) when non-military peasants in occupied lands were beginning to resist – out of uniform, but in possession of military weapons. The response, such as when the French crushed the uprising in Corsica between 1768 and 1769, was that everyone they found carrying a gun who was not in a uniform was executed. This approach was directly mirrored in the wars of the French Revolution and Napoleon. From the outset, the French authorities were harsh on civilians, as opposed to formal armies, who attempted to stand against them. The Republican general Francois Salomon put the matter clearly in its own civil war in 1793 'Since this is a war of brigands, we must become brigands ourselves. We must, for a time, forget all military rules.'[206] Additional orders stated '[a]ll brigands taken under arms, or convicted of having taken them up, are to be run through with bayonets'.[207]

Once the revolution began to spill over boundaries, the opponents of the French were to adopt the same rules. For example, the Spanish general Ricardo Carillo wrote to his French counterpart as his forces crossed the Pyrenees in 1793 and warned:

> [A]ny peasant or bourgeois who is found to have arms upon his person, or hidden in his premises, and above all if he used the same against my troops or any village which I have occupied . . . if he is not serving in some unit or wearing a uniform, badges and equipment . . . I shall hang him immediately, and I shall be justified in doing so.[208]

Although Napoleon was willing to cut some slack for civilians serving in properly constituted bodies, he was ruthless in his dealings with the partisans or guerrillas who waged war independently and demonstrated little respect for the limits expected in warfare of the period, such as the taking of prisoners of war or respect for civilians. He proclaimed:

> Generals marching against villages must take all the necessary force of repression against all those found with arms on their person, such as setting fire to them and having them shot. All the priests, the nobles that have remained in the rebel communes shall be arrested as hostages and sent to France . . . All villages who sound the tocsin as warning shall be burnt on the spot.[209]

Despite such promises and actions, guerrillas were rarely deterred and informal combatants proliferated around Napoleon as he attempted to subdue entire countries. From a military perspective, theorists like Denis Davydov (1784–1839) argued that:

[206] Bell, D (2007) *The First Total War: Napoleon's Europe and the Birth of Modern Warfare* (London, Bloomsbury) 170.

[207] Andress, D (2007) *The Terror: Civil War in the French Revolution* (NYC, Brown) 249.

[208] Carillo in Glover, M (1982) *The Velvet Glove. The Decline and Fall of Moderation in War* (London, Hodder) 49. See also Lynn, J (2002) *The French Wars 1667–1714* (London, Osprey) 82–83; Black, J (1994) *European Warfare 1600–1815* (New Haven, Yale University Press) 155.

[209] Napoleon in Nabulsi, K (2005) *Traditions of War* (Oxford, Oxford University Press) 59.

> Guerrilla warfare stops up the source of the [enemy] army's strength and continuing existence and put it at the mercy of the guerrillas' own army while the enemy army is weakened, hungry . . . and deprived of the saving bonds of authority . . . the greater the distance separating the battlefield and the reserve field becomes, the most effective guerrilla warfare can be.[210]

From such teachings, insurgents proliferated throughout many of the countries Napoleon sought to occupy. This was particularly so in Russia, Italy and Spain. The conflict in Calabria, part of the Kingdom of Naples, cost Napoleon over 20,000 men. The same methods cost him over five times this amount in his retreat from Russia. Similar figures can be adduced for his war in Spain, from which the so-called 'Junta of Seville' of 1808 called upon 'all Spaniards' to fight the French as either uniformed or irregular combatants. In the latter instance, although both Spanish and British authorities increasingly tried to regularise the informal troops, placing them in uniforms and under order, the French were clear that when in Spain, if they captured insurgents who were not wearing uniforms, they would execute them. Only the fear of reciprocal action taken against French prisoners held by the guerrillas sometimes slowed the enthusiasm for this policy. When the Allies invaded France in 1814 and faced French guerrillas, they followed the example of Napoleon, whereby unauthorised and non-uniformed groups of combatants captured were executed, or, if not found, reprisals placed upon the places where they were believed to have originated.[211]

This strictness of policy was not wholly surprising given the lengths that the British had gone to to avoid anything but strictly formal war. That is, English ministers even went so far as to specifically warn Napoleon that there were plans to assassinate him by men in the pay of England.[212] This type of view was in complete accordance with the suggestion of Immanuel Kant that during war assassins should not be employed because such acts of hostility make mutual confidence in the subsequent peace impossible.[213]

Despite the near uniformity of agreement among the major actors of the period that warfare carried out by non-uniformed irregular bands was not permissible and would be met with strict and heavy consequences, the attraction of this type of warfare continued to grow. Indeed, guerrilla-type warfare was part and parcel of the conflicts in the Greek War of Independence, the Carlist War in Spain, and in a number of colonial adventures within, inter alia, Afghanistan, Burma, large parts of Africa, India and New Zealand. Irregular armies were also very common in the conflicts of Latin America throughout the nineteenth century, appearing in the wars of Simon Bolivar, the war for Mexican Independence (1810–29), and in the second half of the nine-

[210] Davydov in Chaliand, G (ed) *The Art of War in World History* (California, California University Press) 653, 655.

[211] Nabulsi, K (2005) *Traditions of War* (Oxford, Oxford University Press) 52–55; Best, G (1980) *Humanity in Warfare* (London, Weidenfeld) 119; Esdaile, C (2003) *The Peninsular War* (London, Penguin) 39–40, 194–95, 254; Glover, M (1982) *The Velvet Glove. The Decline and Fall of Moderation in War* (London, Hodder) 51–53; Bell, D (2007) *The First Total War: Napoleon's Europe and the Birth of Modern Warfare* (London, Bloomsbury) 271, 285–86; Rothenberg, G (1980) *The Age of Warfare in the Age of Napoleon* (Bloomington, Indiana University Press) 89.

[212] Clayton, T (2004) *Trafalgar: The Men, the Battle, the Storm* (London, Hodder) 23.

[213] Kant, I (1795) 'To Perpetual Peace: A Philosophical Sketch' in Humphrey, T (ed) (1983) *Immanuel Kant. Perpetual Peace and Other Essays* (NYC, Hackett) 107, 109.

teenth century, the insurgencies against the Latin American authorities in Bolivia, Columbia, Mexico, Haiti and Cuba.[214] Giuseppe Mazzini (1805–72) would argue during the wars of Italian unification that:

> Insurrection – by means of guerrilla bands – is the true method of warfare for all nations desirous of emancipating themselves from a foreign yolk . . . Guerrilla warfare causes minds to adapt themselves to independence and to an active and heroic life, it makes nations great . . . [it is] invincible and indestructible.[215]

E. Pirates and Privateers

In addition to bringing national armies under greater State control, the leading countries of the period were also determined to confront the problem of military forces, namely pirates, which were not under State control via bilateral and multilateral treaties. One of the first of these was the 1794 Treaty of Amity, Commerce and Navigation between the United States and Britain (Jay's Treaty) by which both Parties agreed to:

> [R]efuse to receive any pirates into any of their ports, havens or towns, or permit any of their inhabitants to receive, protect, harbor, conceal or assist them in any manner, but will bring to punishment all such inhabitants as shall be guilty of such acts or offences. And all their ships, with the goods or merchandizes taken by them and brought into the port of either of the said parties shall be seized . . . even in case such effects should have passed into other hands by sale, if it be proved that the buyers knew or had good reason to believe or suspect that they had been piratically taken.[216]

Bilateral cooperation was also replicated in the 1802 Treaty Between France and the Ottoman Empire. This treaty followed Napoleon's earlier capture of Malta in 1798, when he freed 2,000 Muslims who were held as slaves and terminated the commissions of the (Christian) Corsairs who were still active.[217] After the Napoleonic wars, the 1814 Congress of Vienna and the 1818 Congress of Aix-la-Chapelle both saw proposals for multi-national forces to be sent to deal with the Barbary Corsairs. This followed over 150 years of earlier European attempts to either fight or buy off the Barbary pirates. Although nothing came of the 1814 and 1818 proposals, in the same period, the United States in its first conflict outside its own territory, declared war on the places which were safe havens for the pirates around Algiers who were targeting, inter alia, vessels flagged to the United States. Sixteen years later in 1830 France invaded Algeria, in part because of the remaining problem of pirates, whilst in 1842 with the Webster–Ashburton Treaty, the United States and Britain agreed to maintain two squadrons for the suppression of slavery and its closely-related cousin piracy.[218]

[214] Scheina, R (2003) *Latin America's Wars: The Age of the Caudillo, 1791–1899* (Washington, Brassey's) 35, 80, 264, 275, 286, 302, 361.

[215] Mazzini in Nabulsi, K (2005) *Traditions of War* (Oxford, Oxford University Press) 235.

[216] Jay's Treaty 1794, Art XX.

[217] The Parties agreed to cooperate to 'with common consent take vigorous measures to cleanse the seas, which the ships of both states navigate, from all kinds of pirates' in Wilks, R (1840) *A View of the History, Politics, and Literature for the Year 1802*, Vol 14 (London, Wilks) 34.

[218] See Art 8 of the 1842 Webster-Ashburton Treaty. Also, Lambert, F (2005) *The Barbary Wars* (NYC, Hill) 45, 55, 61, 71, 73–75, 77, 80–84, 129, 140, 190–95; Fails, N 'The Conquest of Algiers' *History Today* (Oct 2005) 44–48.

Even greater achievements were made with the decision to end privateering, but this did not occur until the middle of the nineteenth century. This was a great achievement because in the eighteenth century privateering had been a lucrative pastime for many nations. During the War of Spanish Succession of 1701–13, British and American privateers seized more than 2,000 Spanish vessels. French privateers are believed to have caught the same number of British ships. French privateers were also used to transport the troops of Bonnie Prince Charlie in 1745, rather than the French navy, so that the French crown could distance itself from the expedition if it should go sour. Later in the century, during the American War of Independence, Letters of Marque issued from the 13 colonies in rebellion resulted in at least 1,151 private American vessels going to sea between 1775 and 1783 and capturing some 3,386 British vessels, including 16 men of war. With such successes, it was not surprising that the ability to issue Letters of Marque was later a right given (and remains) to the Congress of the United States in their Articles of Confederation of 1777.[219] Around the same period, between 1793 and 1795, French privateers brought in 2,099 ships as prizes, and in the war with Britain between 1812 and 1815, whilst the American navy ships took 165 British prizes, American privateers took 1,344.[220] Some 57 privateers of multiple nationalities were commissioned by Uruguay during her war against Brazil between 1825 and 1828, and these vessels captured 405 prizes. Privateers were also utilised by Peru in its war with Chile and later (in 1845) by Haiti in the war of independence of Dominica.[221]

Despite these practices, by the end of the eighteenth century, in a clear attempt to show that all military forces were fully under State control, the principal actors of the period first attempted to regulate privateering in various treaties, such as in the 1794 Treaty of Amity, Commerce and Navigation between the United States and Britain (Jay's Treaty)[222] noted above, and then completely prohibited it. The second step occurred after the principal actors increasingly stopped issuing Letters of Marque. These attempts were formalised in 1856 at the end of the Crimean War after Russia had attempted to re-instigate the practice of issuing Letters of Marque. The 1856 Declaration of Paris was the first multilateral law of war treaty which sought to create a uniform doctrine of maritime law in times of war. Through this it was agreed in unequivocal terms that 'privateering is, and remains abolished'.[223]

[219] See Art IX of the Articles of Confederations 1777 in Birley, R (ed) (1944) *Speeches and Documents in American History*, Vol I, 1776–1815 (Oxford, Oxford University Press) 11; Goodwin, A (ed) (1968) *The New Cambridge Modern History: The American and French Revolutions*, Vol VIII (Cambridge, Cambridge University Press) 188.

[220] Boatner, M (1969) *The Encyclopaedia of the American Revolution* (NYC, McKay) 897; Thomson, J (1994) *Mercenaries, Pirates and Sovereigns* (NJ, Princeton University Press) 25; Cooley, L (2002) *Captives: Britain, Empire and the World 16001850* (London, Cape) 46; Duffy, C (2003) *The '45* (London, Cassell) 207.

[221] Scheina, R (2003) *Latin America's Wars: The Age of the Caudillo, 1791–1899* (Washington, Brassey's) 101–102, 137–38, 345; Anderson, M (1998) *War and Society in Europe of the Old Regime* (London, Sutton) 57.

[222] Jay's Treaty, Arts XIX, XXI, XXII and XXIV.

[223] Baumgart, W (1981) *The Peace of Paris 1856* (Oxford, ABC) 164–68.

10. Between 1860 and 1945

A. Conscription

After 1850, conscription of all men into the armed forces was the common pattern of most modern States. This was despite the forceful criticism of philosophers and political theorists. Of the former, Frederick Nietzsche (1844–1900) argued that:

> The great disadvantage of the conscript armies much extolled nowadays is the quandering of men of the highest civilisation they involve; it is only by the grace of circumstance that they exist at all – how thrifty and cautious we ought to be with them.[224]

Of the latter, a number of emerging Marxist leaders, like Fredrich Engels (1820–95), despite being attracted to the revolutionary potential of large conscript armies for the spreading of communism, came out against the mass enlistment of men to fight for certain wars.[225] From such arguments, a number of prominent conscientious objectors argued for their right to be excluded from military service on political – not religious- grounds. The extent that these arguments gained traction depended upon the countries being examined. Whilst some countries agreed that exceptions may be possible, others did not. For example, the 1871 Constitution of the German Empire stipulated that 'every German is liable to military service and cannot have that service performed by a substitute'.[226] Conversely, the principle of substitution was accepted by both sides in the American Civil War, who implemented near universal conscription, of which drafted men made up 5 per cent of Northern and 30 per cent of Southern armies. Substitution avoided the issue of why men did want to fight, provided they ensured that a substitute served in their place. This allowed for those who were financially able to avoid the draft, either through paying $300 for an exemption or by hiring a substitute. This meant the conflict became known as 'a rich man's war and a poor man's fight'. One riot about conscription and the inability of poor people to buy substitutes in New York resulted in the deaths of upwards of 1,200 people and $5m worth of economic damage. Despite the disturbances, the policy of substitution remained, and in the North, some 87,000 men – including those who were, inter alia, Seventh Day Adventists, Quakers, Mennonites, Amish and Dunkers (later known as the Church of the Brethren) paid commutation and over 118,000 substitutes were raised. Nevertheless, such exchanges did not always go smoothly, especially in the South, where those who sought to avoid active service were often subjected to abuse, torture or even death.[227]

General conscription existed among all the major warring powers from 1914 to 1918, although Britain did not come to this position until 1916 when manpower supplied by voluntary means failed to fill the widening gaps caused by the exponential

[224] Nietzsche, F *Human, All Too Human* in trans Hollingdale, R (1969) (Cambridge, Cambridge University Press) 162–63.

[225] Gallie, W (1978) *Philosophers of Peace and War* (Cambridge, Cambridge University Press) 69, 83–84, 94.

[226] The Constitution of the German Empire 1871, Art XVII in Mowat, R (1918) *The Great European Treaties of the Nineteenth Century* (Oxford, Oxford University Press) 305.

[227] Kurlansky, M (2006) *Non-Violence: The History of a Dangerous Idea* (London, Cape) 103; Tracy, J (2006) *The Military Draft Handbook* (San Francisco, Manic Press) 17; Cohen, E (1985) *Citizens and Soldiers: The Dilemmas of Military Service* (Ithaca, Cornell University Press) 138, 143; Stout, H (2006) *Upon the Altar of the Nation: A Moral History of the Civil War* (NYC, Viking) 245.

death tolls emerging from the trenches. By the end of this war, of the 5.7 million who served for Britain, no fewer than 2.5 million did so voluntarily. The need for men was so great that by early 1918 the British Parliament had extended the auspice of who could be conscripted to include clergymen – although this was eventually withdrawn for fear of another Irish rebellion if priests were taken in as combatants. The Congress of the United States passed the Selective Service Act in the middle of 1917, which led to the registration of 24 million men, of whom 2.8 million were taken for military service by the end of the conflict.[228] Such compulsion was the subject of strong protests in, inter alia, Ireland (especially after the 1916 Easter Uprising), Russia, New Zealand, Canada and parts of the United States, where their Supreme Court concluded that in times of war citizens did not have the right to argue that conscription was the same as involuntary servitude.[229]

Each country had its own way of dealing with conscientious objectors. With both Germany and Russia, religious objectors such Mennonites and Seventh Day Adventists were often in the military, but typically placed in non-combatant positions such as medics. Those who refused any form of military service were imprisoned or hospitalised. With the United States, 64,700 men sought conscientious objector status. Of the 20,900 whose status was denied and who were drafted into the army, about 25 per cent refused any sort of military service.[230] In Britain, some 16,500 men objected to conscription. The foremost option for these men was the Non-Combatant Corps. Service in this Corps was open to any objector, religious or secular, who was considered to be sincere. The work ranged from anything that involved the non-handling of weapons, such as building, through to the hugely respected stretcher bearers in the front lines (as part of the 1,200 who did medic-related work). Some 7,000 men agreed to undertake non-combative military service. A further 3,000 were placed in labour camps, where they remained until the middle of 1919, released with a decade-long disenfranchisement. Around 1,500 men refused, or continued to refuse, to serve or help in any capacity. Many of them were transferred to military camps anyway, where they would become subject to military law. Some of these men were transferred from as far away as New Zealand to France, where there were, apparently, plans to execute them. However, these plans were overruled.[231]

After the First World War, the question of conscription arose in an international context in three settings. First, it was decided that a person, even if they had double nationality, could choose to fight for only one country.[232] Secondly, it was agreed in

[228] Tucker, S (1996) *The European Powers in the First World War* (New York, Garland) 313; Haskew, M 'To Field An Army' *Military Heritage* (Feb 2008) 52, 54; Stearn, T 'The Case for Conscription' *History Today* (Apr 2008) 16–22.

[229] *Schenck v United States* 249 US 47 (1919).

[230] Mawdsley, E (2000) *The Russian Civil War* (Edinburgh, Birlinn) 150; Kramer, A (2007) *Dynamic of Destruction: Culture and Mass Killing in the First World War* (Oxford, Oxford University Press) 278; Townshend, C (2006) *Easter 1916. The Irish Rebellion* (London, Penguin) 77, 143; Tracy, J (2006) *The Military Draft Handbook* (San Francisco, Manic Press) 21; Brock, P (2006) *Against the Draft* (Toronto, University of Toronto Press) 201–18, 280–90, 308.

[231] Holmes, R (1999) *The Oxford Companion to Military History* (Oxford, Oxford University Press) 225; Goodall, F (1997) *A Question of Conscience: Conscientious Objection in the Two World Wars* (London, Sutton) 15, 19, 26, 27, 62, 70; McGibbon, I (2000) *The Oxford Companion to New Zealand Military History* (Oxford, Oxford University Press) 116; Kurlansky, M (2006) *Non-Violence: The History of a Dangerous Idea* (London, Cape) 120.

[232] Protocol Relating to Military Obligations in Certain Cases of Double Nationality in Hudson, R (ed) (1950) *International Legislation*, Vol V, 1929–31 (NY, Oceana) 374.

1932 that whilst forced or compulsory labour was outlawed, the term 'forced or compulsory labour' did not include 'any work or service exacted in virtue of compulsory military service laws for work of a purely military character'.[233] Therefore, conscription was not seen as illegal per se, nor as something restricted in international law. Finally, the losers of the First World War, notably Turkey and Germany, had their compulsory military service systems abolished in the treaties of Versailles and Sevres.[234]

As such, up until the point of 1935, the German army grew only by voluntary enlistment. Post-1935, as Hitler multiplied the army by five times the limit imposed on it at Versailles, it grew by mass conscription. The army's elite divisions (airborne and armoured) consisted of volunteers. Hitler, who himself may have originally sought to avoid conscription in Austria before the First World War, only adopted conscription as a bargaining chip against France. His generals preferred voluntary enlistment and felt they could meet their numbers by this method. This was not to suggest that the Nazis were tolerant of pacifists, which Hitler and the Nazi hierarchy vehemently disliked. When conscription was introduced, the only groups to be excluded from serving were Jews. Anyone else who refused to participate, such as Jehovah's Witnesses, ended up in either mental hospitals, concentration camps (at least 10,000 people with one in four dying) or being executed (at least 300).[235]

The Soviets ended up with a position very similar to the Fascists on the question of conscription. From the outset of the end of 1917, the Soviet leadership was keen 'to train systematically and comprehensively in military matters and military operations the entire adult population of both sexes'.[236] Originally, the Soviets were lenient in accepting conscientious objectors, both religious and otherwise, as exemplified by the followers of Leo Tolstoy (1828–1910).[237] The Soviets initially adopted this tolerance because it distinguished them from the Tsar who reflected no such consideration. Accordingly, Vladimir Lenin (1870–1924) attempted to facilitate objectors into medical units. However, with the death of Lenin, Joseph Stalin (1878–1953) decided to censure pacifist organisations, with most of those objecting, especially Mennonites, being swept into labour battalions. By the end of the Second World War, after some 30 million men and women had been conscripted into the ranks of the Red Army, the Soviet authorities could claim they had no applications for conscientious objection.[238]

The British Parliament passed the Conscription Act in 1939 and called up all males aged between 18 and 41 for military service. Although the British had some difficulties with objectors, ranging from Oswald Mosley (1896–1980) through to Mohandus Gandhi (1869–1948), they had learnt from their First World War experiences. Some 60,000 men and women registered to be conscientious objectors. Approximately 3,000 individuals were granted unconditional exemption, whilst 5,000 were prosecuted, most of whom were imprisoned. The rest were formed into units that could help the war

[233] (ILO No 29), 39 UNTS 55 in Hudson, R (ed) (1950) *International Legislation*, Vol V (NY, Oceana) 1929–31. 609. See Art 2.

[234] Versailles, Arts 173–178 and 194; Sevres, Art 165.

[235] Laqueur, W (ed) (2001) *The Holocaust Encyclopaedia* (New Haven, Yale University Press) 348–50; Tucker, S (1996) *The European Powers in the First World War* (New York, Garland) 345; Cohen, E (1985) *Citizens and Soldiers: The Dilemmas of Military Service* (Ithaca, Cornell University Press) 78, 84; Baker, N (2008) *Human Smoke* (London, Simon & Schuster) 37–38; Kershaw, I (2008) *Hitler* (London, Allen) 45–46.

[236] Mawdsley, E (2000) *The Russian Civil War* (Edinburgh, Birlinn) 37, 61–63; Bullock, D (2008) *The Russian Civil War* (London, Osprey) 32–33.

[237] Gallie, W (1978) *Philosophers of Peace and War* (Cambridge, Cambridge University Press) 101–32.

[238] Brock, P (2006) *Against the Draft* (Toronto, University of Toronto Press) 165, 345–53.

effort, which ranged from agriculture to helping with the fire service during the Blitz. The Non-Combatant Corps was re-established and 6,766 individuals joined them. Of these, 456 men volunteered for bomb disposal work, whilst many others went on to become medics. One hundred and fifty objectors made up one third of the parachute field ambulance for D-Day.[239] Similarly, in the United States which implemented conscription from the middle of 1940, all men between the ages of 18 and 35 had to register for military service. Over the course of the conflict some 10 million men were inducted into the military forces. Of this number, 72,000 filed claims to be considered conscientious objectors and 25,000 of these men entered into non-combatant positions such as medics, and another 12,000 went to civilian work camps performing alternative duties in mental and medical hospitals, factories and conservation camps. Approximately 20,000 had their claims rejected and 6,000 (most of whom were Jehovah's Witnesses) who refused to do anything went to jail.[240]

B. Physical Considerations

Mass conscription, as required, was the entrenched pattern of most countries during the latter half of the nineteenth century. Thus, when not at war, only a certain number of men were taken by ballot for training, but when at war, all men between certain ages such as 21 and 40 (as with the French call up during 1870 against Prussia) could be taken.[241] Once more, the emphasis was upon men, not women. This was despite the fact that female combatants were notable in the American Civil War where at least 400 women fought, during the Paris commune where there was a dedicated battalion of women, and in some of the indigenous forces opposing the colonial armies in Africa.[242] The only recognition of the possibility of female combatants from this era came from the 1863 Lieber Code, which recognised 'the law of war, like the criminal law regarding other offenses, makes no difference on account of the difference of sexes, concerning the spy, the war-traitor, or the war-rebel.'[243]

In the First World War, approximately 80,000 women served in the three British women's forces and over 30,000 female nurses accompanied the American forces to Europe. However, very few of these women saw combat. That was unlike in Russia, when some shock battalions of female soldiers were created in 1917, such as the 'Women's Battalion of Death' which were intended to shame the men into fighting, as opposed to deserting (whereas in fact it produced the opposite effect, with the male

[239] Holmes, R (1999) *The Oxford Companion to Military History* (Oxford, Oxford University Press) 225; Goodall, F (1997) *A Question of Conscience: Conscientious Objection in the Two World Wars* (London, Sutton) 117, 146–50, 171, 181; Brock, P (2006) *Against the Draft* (University of Toronto Press) 400–10; Nichol, J and Rennell, T (2009) *Medic* (London, Penguin) 119; Baker, N (2008) *Human Smoke* (London, Simon & Schuster) 269, 329; Kurlansky, M (2006) *Non-Violence: The History of a Dangerous Idea* (London, Cape) 9.

[240] Littleton, M (2005) *DOC* (Minnesota, Zennith) 79–89; Tracy, J (2006) *The Military Draft Handbook* (San Francisco, Manic Press) 23–25; Cohen, E (1985) *Citizens and Soldiers: The Dilemmas of Military Service* (Ithaca, Cornell University Press) 165; Kurlansky, M (2006) *Non-Violence: The History of a Dangerous Idea* (London, Cape) 132; Baker, N (2008) *Human Smoke* (London, Simon & Schuster) 208.

[241] Howard, M (2002) *The Franco-Prussian War* (London, Routledge) 13–15, 244.

[242] Horne, A (2004) *The Terrible Year: The Paris Commune, 1871* (Phoénix, London) 126; Kiernan, V (1998) *Colonial Empires and Armies* (London, Sutton) 87; Walker, J 'Private Cashier Was a Woman' *Military Heritage* (Aug 2008) 46.

[243] Lieber Code, Art 102.

soldiers seeing it as an act of sheer desperation). Female combatants were also notable in the civil wars that followed. Women battalions served at the front for the revolutionaries at the outset of the Russian Civil War before they were disbanded at the end of 1917, after which point they were relegated to positions ranging from administration to torturers. Female fighters were notable in the Anglo-Irish war, with a female Irish volunteer from the General Post Office in Dublin in 1916 being noteworthy, as she was the one sent forward with the flag of surrender. However, such actions became increasingly rare and women in this war, the subsequent civil war, and then the terrorist struggle with Britain in Northern Ireland becoming relegated to strictly auxiliary roles and doing very little of the actual fighting. Similarly, with the Spanish Civil War, at the outset there were up to 1,000 females fighting at the front and several thousand under arms in the rear areas. A woman's battalion took part in the defence of Madrid. However, by 1938, all of the women fighters had been moved to strictly auxiliary positions.[244] Despite the somewhat restrained approaches on the question of women fighters by some revolutionary conflicts, it was in this period that international law first recognised that females could be lawful combatants. This was done in an indirect type of manner, as it was recognised in the 1929 Convention on Prisoners of War that, assuming they fulfilled the criteria as a lawful combatant, they '[a]re entitled to respect for their persons and honour. Women shall be treated with all consideration due to their sex.'[245]

In the Second World War, due to a shortage of manpower, in late 1941 the British government introduced conscription for women into the supporting functions for the military forces and civil needs. The proportion of British women in the armed forces reached a high point of 9.2 per cent (449,100) at the end of 1943. The work of these women ranged from intensive work in munitions factories through to ferrying the combat aircraft all over Britain and the United States. Some 60,000 women worked on anti-aircraft defences, sighting (not firing) the guns in Britain. Thousands also worked as spies and resistance workers, with estimates suggesting that as many as 35,000 women were partisans in Italy alone. Britain sent at least 50 female agents into occupied France as skilled combatants. Japan and German both used hundreds of thousands of women in supporting roles. In Germany, more than a million females worked in arms factories, whilst a further 300,000 served as army reservists, with 20,000 in the navy and 130,000 in the air force. Over 15,000 women staffed the searchlight batteries, and although they were not meant to, some also worked the anti-aircraft guns. A number also worked in concentration camps and became directly involved in the Holocaust. Iron Cross (first class) holder Hanna Reitsch (1912–79) was not only a test pilot, she was also one of the last pilots to fly into Berlin when it was under siege. The Soviet Union fielded an estimated one million women who took part in the actual fighting, including 800,000 in the armed forces and 200,000 in resistance movements. Some 2,000 would be assigned to sniping, of which only 500 would survive the war.

[244] Beevor, A (1982) *The Spanish Civil War* (London, Cassell) 128–29; Bullock, D (2008) *The Russian Civil War* (London, Osprey) 110–13; Tucker, S (1996) *The European Powers in the First World War* (New York, Garland) 313; Moloney, E (2002) *A Secret History of the IRA* (London, Penguin) 55; Greenwood, J (2005) *Medics at War: Military Medicine from Colonial Times to the 21st Century* (Annapolis, Naval Institute Press) 67.

[245] 1929, Art 3. For a discussion of this and WWII, see Krill, F (1994) 'The Protection of Women In International Humanitarian Law' *International Review of the Red Cross* 249: 337–63.

Lyudmila Pavlichenko (1917–74) was credited with killing 309 Germans, including 39 of their snipers. Any female Red Army soldiers captured were immediately shot, since front-line armed women flew in the face of German notions of military propriety. The fact that they were snipers did not help. All-female Soviet aviation regiments, as both fighters and bombers, saw battle against the Germans. More than a thousand Soviet women flew a combined total of 30,000 combat sorties, producing at least 30 Heroes of the Soviet Union. More than 50 such pilots were killed in action. They also served in multiple other functions from manning anti-aircraft guns through to digging trenches in the front lines.[246]

With regards to considerations of age, although military cadetships from the age of 12 were introduced in some colonies during the First World War, the minimum age for recruitment was 18 to be inducted in England and 19 for overseas service. Nevertheless, boys of 17, 16, 15, 14 and even 13 seem to have made it into the front lines before recruitment regimes were made more robust. This was not unusual given that the military had a number of routes by which boys could enter into the services. For example, around 1900, boys were allowed to enter into the navy as cadets at the age of 12 and a half, before going to sea as midshipmen at the age of 16. The youngest soldier to die was Horace Iles (1900–16), whilst Tom Ricketts (1901–67) was only 17 when he won the Victoria Cross.[247]

In the Second World War, one estimate suggests that as many as 25,000 children aged between six and 16 marched with the Soviet army at various stages. A number of these may have fought. In rare instances, soldiers as young as 14 fought in the defence of Stalingrad. This situation was unlike that with Germany and its Hitler Youth. Hitler stated he wanted 'a youth, a cruel, unflinching youth, as hard as steel – Krupp steel'.[248] The Hitler Youth began at the age of 10. By 1939, a membership of almost nine million was achieved. Before the war degenerated and the boys had to fight, from the time they joined they were all integrated in some way or other into the war economy (from helping harvesting to fire-fighting). In 1942, 15 and 16-year-olds were conscripted to 'man' the flak, although by the end of the war, some as young as 11 were doing this job in ever-increasing attempts to release men to serve at the front lines. Although there were some objections to this process in 1943, the SS-Panzer-Division *Hitlerjugend*, was formed. The division was made up of a majority of cadre drawn from Hitler Youth boys and aged between 16 and 18. Twenty per cent of this division were killed in combat whilst a further 40 per cent were wounded or went missing. By 1945, the *Volkssturm*, despite having theoretical limits of 16 years of age, was commonly drafting 12-year-old Hitler Youth members into its ranks. Hitler labelled some of these boys, who had

[246] Goldstein, J (2001) *War and Gender* (Cambridge, Cambridge University Press) 78, 130–57; Bourke, J (2000) *An Intimate History of Killing* (London, Granta) 310–16, 328–35; Goodpaster, A (2008) *Flying For Her Country: The American and Soviet Military Pilots of World War II* (Connecticut, Westport); Beevor, A (1998) *Stalingrad* (London, Penguin) 158; Jones, M (2009) *Leningrad: State of Siege* (London, Murray) 83–84; Butler, R (1986) *Hitler's Young Tigers* (London, Sheridan) 4, 94–95; Goodall, F (1997) *A Question of Conscience: Conscientious Objection in the Two World Wars* (London, Sutton) 107; Whittel, G 'When Women Flew Spitfires' *BBC History* (Nov 2007) 26–30; Vandiver, F (2003) *1001 Things Everyone Should Know About World War II* (NYC, Broadway) 163.

[247] Hanson, N (2005) *The Unknown Soldier* (London, Doubleday) 24, 239; Costello, H 'Too Young to Die' *BBC History* (Nov 2004) 66; Hill, R (2000) *War at Sea in the Ironclad Age* (London, Cassell) 86–87.

[248] Butler, R (1986) *Hitler's Young Tigers* (London, Sheridan) 188.

an average age of 14 and were given Panzerfaust to strap to the handlebars of their pushbikes, as 'tank-destroyer divisions' in the defence of Berlin.[249]

C. Soldiers of Foreign Lands

Although the question of mercenaries was not resolved between 1860 and 1945, international law did dabble in this area. This process began with the Lieber Code, which prohibited the earlier practice of 'forcing' citizens of an occupied country 'into the service of the victorious government',[250] with the exception of 'pressing them into being guides, if such guides cannot be obtained from elsewhere'.[251] The Code added: 'Citizens who accompany an army for whatever purpose, such as sutlers, editors, or reporters of journals, or contractors, if captured, may be made prisoners of war, and be detained as such.'[252]

The 1874 Project of an International Declaration concerning the Laws and Customs of War clarified the principle at play here. Namely, the population of an occupied territory cannot be forced to take part in military operations against its own country.[253] However, the 1874 Declaration also reiterated that contractors, *et al.*, if in possession of a permit issued by the competent authority and of a certificate of identity could be considered as prisoners of war.[254] These principles about not compelling citizens of occupied places to take part in the operations of war directed against their own country were reiterated in the Hague instruments of 1899 and 1907.[255] So too was the exception for authorised individuals 'who follow an army without directly belonging to it'.[256] The only other step that occurred in this period was from Hague Convention V from 1907, Respecting the Rights and Duties of Neutral Powers and Persons in Case of War on Land. This stipulated in Article 4 that a core part of being neutral meant '[c]orps of combatants cannot be formed nor recruiting agencies opened on the territory of a neutral Power to assist the belligerents'.

This point was important, as it was this approach of 'neutrality' that was adopted, rather than the proposal by the German government at the 1907 conference for a total ban on the service of foreigners in national militias. The German proposal was seen as too radical and the Parties merely opted to require neutral states to prevent commercial recruiting within their territories.[257] In addition, and of great importance, the 1899 and 1907 reiterations of the rule of what makes a formal combatant (identification, command structure, follows the rules of war and carries their arms openly) did not give consideration to issues such as nationality or motivation for fighting in the armies of choice.

249 Beevor, A (2002) *Berlin: The Downfall 1945* (London, Penguin) 280–81, 338; Butler, R (1986) *Hitler's Young Tigers* (London, Sheridan) 108–10, 124, 159, 169; Merridale, C (2005) *Ivan's War: The Red Army 1939–45* (London, Faber) 216; Rees, L (1999) *War of the Century: When Hitler Fought Stalin* (London, BBC) 160; Taylor, F (2005) *Dresden: Tuesday 13 Feb 1945* (Edinburgh, Bloomsbury) 233; Neillands, R (2002) *The Bomber War* (London, Murray) 139; Davidson, E (1966) *The Trial of the Germans: 22 Defendants at Nuremberg* (NY, Macmillan) 239, 295–304.

250 Lieber Code, Art 33.

251 Lieber Code, Arts 93 and 94.

252 Lieber Code, Art 50.

253 Declaration 1874, Art 36.

254 Declaration 1874, Art 34. A similar point can be traced to Art 50 of the Lieber Code.

255 1899, Art 23(h). Note also Arts 44 and 45 of both the 1899 and 1907 instruments.

256 Hague IV 1907, Art 13.

257 See Cockayne, J (2006) 'The Reorganisation of Legitimate Violence' 88 (863) *IRRC* 459, 474.

These decisions of 1899 and 1907 helped facilitate a free-flow of foreign individuals that became part and parcel of the practice of warfare in the coming decades. For example, in the First World War, before the Americans entered the conflict, American pilots enlisted to fight for both France and Germany. Although Germany objected to this alleged breach of neutrality, it was ensured in both instances that the uniforms, planes, commanders and even colleagues were of one of the primary belligerents. Before this question could be discussed further, the Russian Revolution began and foreign volunteers flocked to help both sides, with the Soviets receiving an influx of at least 50,000 'internationalists'.[258] Even with this conflict, the question was not directly examined. That is, the sixth point of the '14 Points' from Woodrow Wilson (1856–1924) that were used as the basis of negotiating an end to the First World War, called for an 'evacuation of Russian territory'. The context for this was the evacuation by the so-called White Armies, not the volunteers who had gone to help the Soviets. A further acceptance of the possibility of foreign volunteers occurred, again in the 1929 Prisoner of War Convention, which reiterated the earlier principle that non-military associated peoples 'can produce a certificate from the military authorities of the army they were accompanying' to give them prisoner of war status.[259] The only small addition in this area was with the Treaty of Versailles which forbade Germany from allowing any of her nationals to join foreign forces, with the exception of the French Foreign Legion.[260] Accordingly, without any form of international restraints, when the Spanish Civil War broke out in the middle of 1936, foreign troops flooded into Spain to help both sides. On the side of the Republic, in addition to some 4,000 Soviet advisors, some 35,000 volunteers from over 53 countries came to join the 'International Brigades'. On the other side, almost 50,000 Italian, 12,000 German and 8,000 Portuguese 'volunteers' came to serve Francisco Franco (1892–1975). By the time the international community had agreed that this flow of foreign fighters should be stopped because it was only fuelling the conflict, it was not only too late, but Franco also turned a blind eye to his commitments to stop allowing such volunteers.[261]

Following such patterns, the Second World War also saw large-scale movements of foreign private individuals going to fight for their favoured causes. Notable amongst these men from the Allied side were the Eagle Squadrons and Flying Tigers, both consisting of American volunteers and fighting for either Britain or China. Volunteers from Czechoslovakia, Poland and France who continued to serve with Britain after their countries had capitulated also supplemented the Allies. The German view of these people could be quite harsh. For example, in the Franco-German Armistice of June 1940, the Germans warned:

> The French Government will forbid French subjects from fighting against the Reich in the armies of the countries which are still at war with the latter. French subjects who do not conform to this law will be treated by German troops as francs-tireurs.[262]

[258] Bullock, D (2008) *The Russian Civil War* (London, Osprey) 35, 75, 90–91, 92–94, 97–98.

[259] Art 81.

[260] Art 179.

[261] Othen, C (2008) *Franco's International Brigades* (Wiltshire, Reportage) 9–11; Beevor, A (1982) *The Spanish Civil War* (London, Cassell) 178–81, 212–13, 353.

[262] The 1940 Franco-German Armistice Art 9, in Thomson, D (ed) (1969) *France: Empire and Republic, 1850–1940* (NYC, Harper). Note, the Germans did not enforce this following De Gaulle's promise that the Free French forces would abide by the Geneva Conventions.

The Germans took a similar view of Czechs who had been brought into the Reich, and Jews who had fled it, both of whom they presumed to be traitors. However, as with the French captured in Allied uniforms, their practice was that if they were captured wearing a uniform they were entitled to become a prisoner of war of the country they were fighting for. This, however, was not always clear cut. For example, following the defection of Italy from the Axis in 1943, over 200,000 Italian soldiers were taken prisoner by the Germans. However, the Germans refused to allow the ICRC to visit these men, referring all questions about them to the neo-Fascist Italian government, still resident in Northern Italy. Following through, the Germans classified these Italian prisoners as 'Italian Military Internees' and refused to give them the benefits of the 1929 Convention, as they were not lawful Italian combatants.[263]

The German tolerance towards foreign volunteers fighting for legitimate sovereign opponents was not surprising, given that they also supplemented their fighting forces with vast amounts of foreign volunteers. Many of these came from allied fascist countries, where the obligations between volunteers and national levies were never entirely clear. This was especially so with operations like those in the Soviet Union that saw on the eve of the invasion the German forces being supplemented by 600,000 Croats, Finns, Romanians, Hungarians, Italians, Slovaks and Spaniards. Denmark, the Netherlands, Belgium and Norway added another 117,000 men. Following the invasion Latvians, Lithuanians, Karelian Finns, Estonians and men from Byelorussia also flocked to join German associated units. As many as 250,000 Soviet citizens may have served in the Waffen SS alone. However, attempts by the Germans to raise English, Irish, and even Indian volunteers from disgruntled prisoners came to little, with around only 60 British or Commonwealth nationals fighting for the Nazis under the 'British Free Corps'. Nevertheless, other foreigners served in large numbers. Of the 47 Waffen SS divisions, 20 were formed wholly or partly out of non-German recruits and towards the end of the war there were more non-Germans than Germans fighting in the SS as the Reich crumbled. Over 1,000 French fascists went to fight (and die) in the ruins of Berlin.[264]

D. Informal and Formal Combatants

The last serious attempt to use privateers was in the American Civil War, when Confederate President Jefferson Davis (1808–89) invited ordinary citizens to become privateers via his Letters of Marquee. Davis justified this, in part, by the fact that the United States had not signed the 1856 Declaration. Some individuals who took up this offer, like Raphael Semmes (1809–77), managed to take (and generally burn) over 40 Union prizes, whilst causing no loss of life. When Abraham Lincoln (1809–65) was made aware of such Confederate efforts to employ privateers, he publically adhered to

[263] Durand, A (1984) *A History of the International Committee of the Red Cross: From Sarajevo to Hiroshima* (Geneva, Dunant Institute) 434–35. Ford, D (2007) *Flying Tigers: Claire Chennault and His American Volunteers, 1941–1942* (Washington, HarperCollins) 24, 29, 71; Gilbert, A (2006) *POW: Allied Prisoners in Europe* (London, Murray) 203, 213–15.

[264] Beevor, A (2002) *Berlin: The Downfall 1945* (London, Penguin) 292–93, 322; Weale, A (1994) *Renegades: Hitler's Englishmen* (London, Weidenfeld) 17, 24–34; Thomas, N (1983) *Partisan Warfare 194–45* (London, Osprey) 13–17; Gilbert, A (2006) *POW: Allied Prisoners in Europe* (London, Murray) 249; MacArthur, B (2005) *Surviving the Sword: Prisoners of the Japanese* (London, Time) 29; Ferguson, N (2006) *The War of the World* (London, Allen Lane) 458–59.

the Declaration. Thereafter, when Confederate-employed privateers were captured, Lincoln expressed his intention to try them as pirates and execute them if found guilty. However, fearing reprisals against prisoners from the Union held in the South, he did not pursue this idea of executions. Nevertheless, when the war was concluded under the auspice of Andrew Johnson (1808–75) 'all persons who have been engaged in the destruction of the commerce of the United States on the High Seas' were explicitly excluded from the Act of pardon and amnesty.[265]

The American Civil War was also notable for the way in which informal combatants were dealt with. These dealings ranged from the prohibition of assassination (although the death of Abraham Lincoln suggested this rule was far from universal)[266] through to the prohibition of guerrilla-type warfare and the treatment of spies. This was notable, as during this conflict, a number of informal units from the South had decided not to wear uniforms so as to take advantage of the conditions around them and went marauding. To facilitate such activities, the Confederacy authorised the Partisan Ranger Act of 1862 which allowed the (Southern) President 'to commission such officers as he may deem proper with authority to form bands of partisan rangers, in companies, battalions, or regiments, to be composed of such members as the President may approve'. The problem was that, although some good soldiers and practices came from this, any good work was eclipsed by some of the bad soldiers, who were often impossible to distinguish from common criminals in the way they came to attack civilians on the opposing side. One group, which was led by William Quantrill (1837–1865), entered the town of Lawrence, Kansas and killed 150 men and boys in an act of senseless violence. This attack led to Confederate President Davis repealing the Ranger Act, despite the military advantages that were offered to a side that was being systematically destroyed.[267]

The Union side fought against such men out of uniform without restraint. The basis of their reasoning was contained in the Lieber Code. This stated, in Article 82 that combatants who were not part and portion of the organised hostile army, and who intermittingly returned home with the 'semblance of peaceful pursuits' and 'divest themselves of the character or appearance of soldiers' were not entitled to prisoner of war status and could be treated summarily as highway robbers or pirates. Article 83 stipulated that enemy scouts – if disguised in enemy uniform and found behind the lines – would be treated as spies and suffer death, whilst Article 84 promised a similar fate awaited 'armed prowlers' or 'persons who steal within the lines of the hostile army for the purpose of robbing, killing, or of destroying bridges, roads or canals, or of robbing or destroying the mail, or of cutting the telegraph wires'. It was added that captured spies may also be executed.[268] This was because whilst:

[265] The 1865 Proclamation of Amnesty and Pardon in Axelrod, A (ed) (2001) *Encyclopaedia of Historical Treaties and Alliances*, Vol I (NYC, Facts on File) 273; Harris, B (1997) *The Navy Times Book of Submarines. A Political, Social and Military History* (NYC, Berkley) 79, 81; Hill, R (2000) *War at Sea in the Ironclad Age* (London, Cassell) 125–28.

[266] The Lieber Code, which was only code of standing to ever address assassination, added that 'civilized nations look with horror upon offers of rewards for the assassination of enemies as relapses into barbarism', Art 148. See also, Fetherlin, G (2001) *The Book of Assassins* (London, Wiley) 64–65.

[267] Stout, H (2006) *Upon the Altar of the Nation: A Moral History of the Civil War* (NYC, Viking) 58, 261; Mackey, R (2004) *The UnCivil War: Irregular Warfare in the Upper South, 1861–1865* (Oklahoma, Oklahoma University Press) 29, 36, 57–59.

[268] A spy was defined as 'a person who secretly, in disguise or under false pretence, seeks information with the intention of communicating it to the enemy'. See Arts 85 and 89 of the Lieber Code.

> [D]eception in war is admitted as a just and necessary means of hostility . . . the common law of war allows even capital punishment for clandestine or treacherous attempts to injure an enemy, because they are so dangerous, and it is difficult to guard against them.[269]

With this code, the already established practice of shooting all 'outlaws' when captured, was codified. A number of the 'outlaws' that were captured were executed by the men of George Custer (1839–76). The 'outlaws' responded in kind, executing all Union prisoners they possessed.[270]

A very similar process was adopted in some of the European wars of the same period. For example, during its war with Austria in 1866, the Prussian forces discovered they were being sniped at by civilians, or what they called *franc-tireurs* – literally, 'free shooters'. Faced with this, Helmuth von Moltke (1800–91), the Prussian Field Marshall, stipulated that 'franc-tireurs are not soldiers and thus are subject to . . . the laws of war and to death'.[271] This rule followed directly into the Prussian conflict with France in 1870–71. This was especially after the French authorities advised their commanders to use their mobile forces as partisans 'whose role is less to fight than to harass the enemy . . . to obstruct him in his requisitions . . . to capture convoys, cut roads and railways, and destroy bridges'. The idea was to make France 'into one great guerrilla'.[272] The Prussians responded by executing all men who were captured and suspected of being involved in the hostilities if they were not in uniform and could not produce an individual certificate from the French Government to show that they were authorised by the State. They had no right to be made a prisoner of war as it was impossible to distinguish them from non-combatants. When Otto von Bismarck (1815–98), the Chancellor of the new German empire, was confronted with the argument by the French that their franc-tireurs were only following the practice of Prussian irregulars in their warfare against Napoleon, he replied 'true, and we can still see the trees on which you hanged them'.[273]

Following directly on from the American Civil War and the Franco-Prussian conflict, the majority of notable countries at the time agreed that war should be a matter for full-time soldiers, and not part-time civilians.[274] The first clear recognition of this occurred with the 1874 Project of an International Declaration concerning the Laws and Customs of War which concluded that, aside the times when a population rises *en mass* before being occupied,[275] the laws, rights, and duties of war apply not only to armies, but also to militia and volunteer corps fulfilling the following conditions:

[269] Lieber Code, Art 101.

[270] Beckett, I (2001) *Modern Insurgencies and Counter Insurgencies* (London, Routledge) 30–31.

[271] Hull, I (2005) *Absolute Destruction: Military Culture and the Practices of War in Imperial Germany* (Ithaca, Cornell University Press) 118–21.

[272] Howard, M (2002) *The Franco-Prussian War* (London, Routledge) 249–51.

[273] Bismarck noted in Glover, M (1982) *The Velvet Glove. The Decline and Fall of Moderation in War* (London, Hodder) 55; Howard, M (2002) *The Franco-Prussian War* (London, Routledge) 3, 78, 97; Best, G (1980) *Humanity in Warfare* (London, Weidenfeld) 191, 194–95.

[274] Moorehead, C (1998) *Dunant's Dream: War, Switzerland and the History of the Red Cross* (NYC, Carroll & Graf) 124.

[275] 'The population of a territory which has not been occupied, who, on the approach of the enemy, spontaneously take up arms to resist the invading troops without having had time to organize themselves in accordance with Art 9, shall be regarded as belligerents if they respect the laws and customs of war.' See Art 10 of the 1874 Declaration. This rule was reiterated in 1899 (Art 1), 1907 (Arts 1 and 2), 1929 (Art 1) and 1949 (Art 4).

1. That they be commanded by a person responsible for his subordinates;
2. That they have a fixed distinctive emblem recognisable at a distance;
3. That they carry arms openly; and
4. That they conduct their operations in accordance with the laws and customs of war.[276]

It was also agreed that the population of a territory which has not been occupied, who, on the approach of the enemy, spontaneously takes up arms to resist the invading troops without having had time to organise themselves in accordance with the above considerations, would be regarded as belligerents if they respected the laws and customs of war.[277] However, those who acted independently of such a *levee en mass*, or operated as spies by 'wearing a disguise' and 'not carrying this mission out in the open' could not be considered as lawful soldiers.[278] At a minimum, even these captured fighters were to be treated 'humanely' and given a fair trial to consider their guilt.[279] However, the underlying conclusion that it was permissible to execute spies was clear. This was not to suggest that States could not use non-formal members such as spies or guerrillas in their armed forces, only that they would not be granted prisoner of war status if captured. This approach was clearly applied in 1899, which was a conspicuous year for informal warfare and international law. In terms of warfare, both the British and the Americans were involved in large-scale counter-insurgency operations. The Americans, in their war in Philippines between 1899 and 1902, adopted exactly the same approach at the Prussians in combating the irregular troops who fought against them. All of those who were caught with arms but were not in uniform were treated like 'highway robbers or pirates' and all of such individuals over the age of 10 were executed.[280] Although the British did not adopt such direct methods in their wars with the Boers in 1881 and 1899–1902, the anti-guerilla strategy adopted by the British involved the formation of large-scale concentration camps and viscous forms of scorched earth designed to directly impact upon the non-combatants who supported the guerrillas.

Against this background, the principles of 1874 were reiterated in the 1899[281] and 1907[282] Hague Conventions which stipulated that the laws, rights, and duties of war apply not only to armies, but also to militia and volunteer corps, if they fulfilled the 1874 considerations of being commanded by a person responsible for his subordinates; having a fixed distinctive emblem recognisable at a distance; carrying their arms openly; and conducting their operations in accordance with the laws and customs of war. To give greater clarity, with regards to spies it was added that 'soldiers not in disguise who have penetrated into the zone of operations of a hostile army to obtain information are not considered spies'.[283] The result of the 1899 and 1907 Conventions was that, despite the fact that a number of key countries were directly involved in

[276] 1874 Declaration, Art 9.

[277] 1874 Declaration, Art 10.

[278] 'A person can only be considered a spy when acting clandestinely or on false pretences he obtains or endeavours to obtain information in the districts occupied by the enemy, with the intention of communicating it to the hostile party'. See Art 19 from the 1874 Declaration. Also Arts 20, 21 and 22.

[279] Hague 1899, Arts 30 and 31; Oxford 1913 Naval Rules, Art 66; Geneva IV, Art 5. Also, Protocol I, Art 46(4).

[280] Boot, M (2002) *The Savage Wars of Peace: Small Wars and the Rise of American Power* (NYC, Basic) 116, 120, 122.

[281] Hague 1899, Land Warfare, Art 1. The point about spontaneous uprising is found in Art 2.

[282] Hague 1907, Land Warfare, Art 1. Note also Art 2.

[283] Hague 1899, Art 29.

warfare with irregular combatants, very little was changed to give such individuals additional status and protections. The only change that did occur was the so-called 'Martens clause' which was introduced into the preamble to the 1899 Hague Convention on the Laws and Customs of War on Land. The clause, which appears in a slightly modified form in the 1907 Hague Convention, was introduced as a compromise wording for the dispute between the Great Powers who considered *franc-tireurs* to be unlawful combatants and therefore subject to execution on capture, and smaller States who maintained that they should be considered lawful combatants. The clause stated:

> Until a more complete code of the laws of war is issued, the High Contracting Parties think it right to declare that in cases not included in the Regulations adopted by them, populations and belligerents remain under the protection and empire of the principles of international law, as they result from the usages established between civilized nations, from the laws of humanity and the requirements of the public conscience.[284]

Despite the humanitarian appeal of the Martens Clause, as the major belligerents went into the First World War, it was clear that both Britain and Germany were going to stick to the letter of the 1899 and 1907 Conventions on the requirements of combatants to meet certain formal standards if they wished to be eligible for prisoner of war status. As the 1914 War Book of the German General Staff explained:

> The organisation of irregulars in military bands and their subjection to a responsible leader are not by themselves sufficient to enable one to grant them the status of belligerents, even more important than these is the necessity of being able to recognise them as such [at a distance] and of them carrying their arms openly. The soldier must know who he has against him as an active opponent, he must be protected against treacherous killing.[285]

In all, this rule was largely followed and most of the conflict was conducted by uniformed soldiers. By the end of the nineteenth century, it was unheard of to suggest that professional combatants would not be in full uniform at the time of battle. The only remaining questions at this point were over what to wear. Thus, light grey and khaki uniforms came to eclipse the fashionable splendour of earlier generations. The last war fought by the British in their famous Red Coats was the Zulu war of 1879, and although many French soldiers turned up at the front in 1914 wearing their peacetime uniforms of blue tunics and red trousers, these, like the preposterous *pickelhaube* helmet of the Germans, were quickly relegated to history. Even the Soviet revolutionaries of 1917 would attempt to distinguish themselves in combat before they were given proper uniforms by wearing red ribbons or other Soviet insignia, such as relatively large red stars.[286]

In the period of the First World War, the exception to soldiers involved with land warfare wearing uniforms was seen with Thomas Lawrence (Lawrence of Arabia, 1888–1935) who was the exemplar of guerrilla warfare, in allowing his soldiers to appear as non-uniformed combatants, or as he explained 'to contain the enemy by the silent threat of a vast unknown desert, not disclosing themselves till the moment of

[284] Preamble, Hague II 1899.

[285] Grossgeneralstab (1915) *War Book of the German General Staff* trans Morgan, T (2005) (Pennsylvania, Stackpole Books) 12–13.

[286] Latimer, J (2003) *Deception in War* (London, Murray) 55–56; Hanson, N (2005) *The Unknown Soldier* (London, Doubleday) 10; Mawdsley, E (2000) *The Russian Civil War* (Edinburgh, Birlinn) 185.

attack'.[287] Although this type of irregular warfare against the old Turkish State was not that unique, what was unique was that the new Turkish State responded in kind a few years later and used its own irregulars to achieve policies that no respectable government could publically sanction. That is, Turkish irregulars engaged in mass murder, rape and pillage of the non-Muslim communities on the Levantine coast of Turkey in 1922, in an attempt to ethnically cleanse – for the benefit of the State – the area for the new Turkish state.[288] These early officially condoned 'pro-government non-State armed groups' can be contrasted with the second development in this area, which was seen with the uprising and subsequent civil war in Ireland where non-uniformed insurgents, who were not authorised, gave battle to conventional armed forces. The same pattern was followed in Latin America during, inter alia, the Mexican Revolution of 1910–20, the conflict in the Dominican Republic between 1916 and 1924 and the conflict in Nicaragua between 1927 and 1933. These were all the forerunners of most of the guerillas wars in the later the twentieth and twenty-first centuries.[289]

With regards to war at sea, the issue of identification was the subject of prolonged dispute. The root of the problem was that the Oxford Manual on the Laws of Naval War in 1913 stipulated that whilst 'ruses of war are considered permissible . . . methods, which involve treachery are forbidden'. In this context, treachery involved, inter alia, making improper uses of a flag of truce, false flags or insignia, of whatever kind, especially those of the enemy, as well as of the distinctive badges of the medical corps.[290] Whilst sailing very close to the wind, both the British and the Germans in both the First and Second World War would utilise warships disguised as merchant ships. In theory, this act of converting vessels was quite permissible, and even facilitated through the 1907 Convention Relating to the Conversion of Merchant Ships into War-Ships. However, to do so, such converted vessels were meant to bear the external marks which distinguished the war-ships of their nationality.[291] In addition, it was stipulated that a belligerent who converted a merchant ship into a war-ship 'must, as soon as possible, announce such conversion in the list of war-ships'.[292] Both Britain and Germany quickly forgot these obligations. The British forgot with their creation of at least 225 'Q-ships'. Q-ships were vessels that were disguised as merchant vessels but were in fact heavily armed. The aim of the Q-ships was to lure the enemy to within point blank range of their hidden guns, before raising the Royal Ensign at the last minute and opening fire. This was unlike situations where captains of merchant ships, who were not navy personnel, attempted to attack German submarines by ramming them, who were subsequently executed by the Germans when they were caught, as *franc-tireurs*. The German equivalent of Q-ships was their Armed Merchant Raiders, which were heavily armed vessels, disguised as foreign merchant ships, who waited for their Allied prey to draw close, and then hoisted the German ensign at the last minute before attacking them. One German ship – *the Wolf* – sailed the globe from Germany to South Africa and then to New Zealand capturing 14 ships and sinking 280,000 tons

[287] Lawrence in Chaliand, G (ed) *The Art of War in World History* (California, California University Press) 885.

[288] Milton, G (2008) *Paradise Lost. Smyrna 1922: The Destruction of Islam's City of Tolerance* (London, Sceptre) 49–51, 168–69, 198–99, 202, 215, 229, 271, 275.

[289] Scheina, R (2003) *Latin America's War. The Age of the Professional Soldier, 1900–2001*, Vol II (NYC, Brassey's) 13–14, 51, 55.

[290] Oxford Manual, Art 15.

[291] Convention Relating to the Conversion of Merchant Ships into War-Ships 1907, Art 2.

[292] Convention Relating to the Conversion of Merchant Ships into War-Ships 1907, Art 6.

f shipping on the journey.[293] The Allies continued to use similar ruses in the Second Vorld War, whilst Germany continued to utilise Armed Merchant Raiders. In the later nstance, whilst always hoisting the Kriegsmarine ensign before opening fire, the Armed Merchants managed to snare a surprising amount of prey. For example, the *Atlantis* sunk (with chivalry) 22 Allied freighters and the *Kormoran* managed to sink the Australian Cruiser *Sydney* on which all 645 hands perished.[294]

Where the Second World War was significantly different from the First was with regards to the proliferation of informal combatants. This was despite the fact that the same rules applied about who was a lawful combatant, as defined in the 1899 and 1907 Hague Conventions, and reconfirmed in 1929 with the Prisoner of War Convention.[295] Thus, despite the fact that guerrillas or partisans could not claim prisoner of war rights, over one million men and women acted as informal combatants in World War Two. The forerunner to this type of conflict occurred in Ireland in both the Anglo-Irish war and the following Irish Civil War, when the Irish Republican Army opted for a policy of guerrilla tactics over open combat, in which the rebels 'mixed with peaceful citizens'.[296] In the Anglo-Irish war, although hundreds of civilians were killed in conflict, the preferred target was Irish police officers (of which 513 were killed and 682 were wounded between 1918 and 1922). Most of these men were not at work at the time they were attacked. In addition, the execution of spies was remarkably common. The only problem was that many of the people executed were innocent. For example, in County Cork, of 122 people executed by the IRA between 1919 and 1923, subsequent records showed only 38 were actually passing over information.[297]

Within the 1916 Uprising some 3,430 men and 79 women informal combatants were arrested on charges related to killing, of which 90 were convicted and sentenced to death on grounds of murder, treason and assisting the enemy. All but 15 of these men had their sentences commuted. Despite gaining both domestic and international support for an independent Ireland, with even the United States Senate urging clemency from Britain 'in the treatment of [the 15] Irish political prisoners', the British followed through with their sentences.[298] The same process was repeated with the Irish Civil War when the Republicans resorted, once more, to guerilla types of conflict. The guerrilla activities of the Republicans, labeled 'irregulars' by the newly-minted National Government of Ireland, initially achieved a modest degree of success. However, this situation quickly turned as over 12,000 Republicans were placed in jail and a number of them were executed for either the crimes they committed, such as targeting cabinet ministers, or as reprisals, which were either official or unofficial in implementation.[299]

[293] Tucker, S (1996) *The European Powers in the First World War* (New York, Garland) 290; Harris, B (1997) *The Navy Times Book of Submarines. A Political, Social and Military History* (NYC, Berkley) 203; Bridgland, T (1999) *Sea Killers In Disguise* (Yorkshire, Pen and Sword) xi, 17–19, 29, 73, 150.

[294] Latimer, J (2003) *Deception in War* (London, Murray) 167–68; Dorrian, J (2006) *Saint-Nazaire: Operation Chariot – 1942: Battleground French Coast* (London, Pen and Sword) 76, 79.

[295] 1929, Art 1.

[296] Townshend, C (2006) *Easter 1916. The Irish Rebellion* (London, Penguin) 98, 270.

[297] Cottrell, P ((2006) *The Anglo-Irish War. The Troubles of 1913–1922* (London, Osprey) 70.

[298] Cottrell, P (2006) *The Anglo-Irish War. The Troubles of 1913–1922* (London, Osprey) 20, 44, 52, 54; Townshend, C (2006) *Easter 1916. The Irish Rebellion* (London, Penguin) 279, 287, 312.

[299] Hopkinson, M (2004) *Green Against Green. The Irish Civil War* (Dublin, Gill) 12, 172–73, 180, 190–91, 236, 240–41, 274; Breadun, D 'Free State Account of Controversial Deaths in 1923' *The Irish Times* (31 Dec 2008) 8–9.

Eighteen years later, the Second World began. In this conflict, over one million people operated behind German lines, fighting the occupiers – and often each other – in the occupied Soviet Union, Yugoslavia (with 390,00), France (with 350,000), Italy and Greece. Tens of thousands existed in other occupied places as well. Such forces provided vast amounts of support to the Allied war effort. This ranged from the 33,000 Allied soldiers that were smuggled through France back to Britain through to the 9,644 bridges, 21,376 trains and 4,538 armored fighting vehicles that were destroyed behind German lines in the Soviet Union. Aside the killing of Axis enemies in open and concealed confrontations, the informal fighters were also known to execute large numbers of captured prisoners and even more collaborators. In France, somewhere between 10,000 and 100,000 people were killed after the Germans had been forced out, as revenge, retribution, vengeance and opportunity all came into line for those on the winning side. Acts of vengeance at the end of the war were also recorded in, inter alia, Belgium, Greece and Italy. In the latter instance, between 15,000 and 30,000 Italian fascists and those who collaborated with the enemy were killed by the Partisans in the North of Italy.[300]

The response by the German forces to those in the resistance or to partisans was short and sharp. This became evident almost as soon as the war started. Thus, on 4 September 1939, the German Eighth Army decreed that civilians who were suspected of having shot at German troops, or were inside buildings from which shots had been fired, or who had weapons at home, were to be summarily shot, without any legal proceedings. With such a background, by the end of October 1939, the Wehrmacht had executed at least 16,000, and possibly as many as 27,000 Poles allegedly found with weapons whilst not in uniform. Similar policies were followed when the Germans occupied other countries. For example, the Ninth (of Ten) Commandments of the Parachutist each had sewn on the inside of their packs stated 'Against an open foe fight with chivalry, but to a guerilla extend no quarter'.[301] In the Soviet theatre, Hitler explicitly forbade the taking of partisans as prisoners of war because they were involved in 'a struggle of total annihilation of one side or the other'.[302] Accordingly, he ordered the shooting of all partisans and all Russians suspected of being so (such as by having close cropped hair) whether they were fighting or escaping. Orders also went out classifying those caught west of the Berezina River as partisans, who should be shot, even if in uniform. Albert Kesselring (1885–1960) would add:

> The fight against the partisans must be carried out with all means at our disposal and with utmost severity. I will protect any commander who exceeds our usual restraint in the choice of severity of methods he adopts against partisans.[303]

[300] Holland, J (2008) *Italy's Sorrow: A Year of War, 1944–1945* (London, St Martin's) 528; Jurado, C (1985) *Resistance Warfare* (London, Osprey) 12, 18, 24; Schoenbrum, D (1980) *Soldiers of the Night. The Story of the French Resistance* (NYC, Dutton) 321–24; de Zayas, A (1989) *The Wehrmacht War Crimes Bureau, 1939–1945* (Nebraska, Nebraska University Press) 151; Beevor, A (2009) *D-Day. The Battle for Normandy* (London, Viking) 448; Viven, R (2006) *The Unfree French: Life Under Occupation* (London, Penguin) 340–41; Thomas, N (1983) *Partisan Warfare 1941–45* (London, Osprey) 19–20, 24–25; Holland, J (2008) *Italy's Sorrow: A Year of War, 1944–1945* (London, St Martin's) 124, 264, 37; Rees, L (1999) *War of the Century: When Hitler Fought Stalin* (London, BBC) 108.

[301] Clark, A (2001) *The Fall of Crete* (London, Cassell) 54, 83; Burleigh, M (2010) *Moral Combat. A History of World War II* (London, Harper) 126.

[302] Rees, L (1999) *War of the Century: When Hitler Fought Stalin* (London, BBC) 116.

[303] Kesselring, in Gellately, R (2007) *The Nuremberg Interviews* (London, Pimlico) 327.

Such orders were supplemented by Hitler's Night and Fog Decree, whereby suspected irregulars would vanish without a trace into the night and fog. This guaranteed the secret transfer to concentration camps (or instant death) of all such peoples if they were resident in occupied countries that did not have the death penalty. Even in Western Europe as late as the middle of 1944, the German Army commander of this theatre could declare '[p]ersons taking part in movements of rebellion directed against the rear of the forces of the occupying Power, have no right whatever to the protection which may be claimed by regular combatants'.[304] Collectively, tens of thousands of resistance or partisan fighters were killed by such methods, with over 30,000 French resistance fighters alone killed in the conflict.[305]

Despite the strict nature of the above examples, it should be noted that as the Second World War neared its end, the Germans ended their rigidity on refusing to allow irregular forces to be taken as prisoners and verbally notified the International Committee of the Red Cross (ICRC) that they would regard as lawful combatants all but Soviet partisans who met the requirements of the Hague Conventions. This act was done, largely, to stop the ongoing execution of captured German soldiers by the informal forces. Although, the ICRC could not persuade the Germans to declare this policy publically, this policy was utilised in a number of places. For example, Field Marshal Maximilian von Weichs (1881–1954), the German commander in the Western Balkans, ordered the partisans in that area of war to be known as lawful combatants from late 1944 on the ground from that 'the armament, size, organisation and operation of the partisan units justified . . . considering them as an enemy on the same plane with the regular forces of other nations with which the Reich was at war'.[306]

Similarly, with the Warsaw Uprising in 1944, although all of the resistance fighters tried to distinguish themselves with a red and white armband but Hitler originally ordered no prisoners to be taken – the negotiated surrender of the 9,000 members of the Polish Home Army required the German authorities to recognise the insurgents as lawful combatants and therefore as eligible for prisoner of war status.[307] In Paris – but not elsewhere in occupied France – General Dietricht Von Cholitz (1894–1966), whilst awaiting the Allied forces to liberate Paris (and despite his orders) agreed that he would recognise the resistance fighters as regular troops, and if captured, they would be treated as prisoners of war. In return, the Resistance (at least, the non-Communist part) agreed to wear the red, white and blue brassards with the initials FFI embroidered onto them to help distinguish themselves and not to attack any German strongpoints in the city. Likewise, the Germans themselves came to adopt similar tactics when they became worried about the capture of the boys arming the flak batteries and their being treated as partisans by advancing Soviet armies. Accordingly, they issued each of

[304] Western Europe Order in Kalshoven, F (2005) *Belligerent Reprisals* (Leiden, Nijhoff) 194.

[305] Glover, M (1982) *The Velvet Glove. The Decline and Fall of Moderation in War* (London, Hodder) 65; Beevor, A (1998) *Stalingrad* (London, Penguin) 54, 55; Thomas, N (1983) *Partisan Warfare 1941–45* (London, Osprey) 10; Bartov, O (1991) *Hitler's Army: Soldiers, Nazis and War* (NY, Oxford University Press) 86; Megargee, G (2007) *War of Annihilation: Combat and Genocide on the Eastern Front, 1941* (Boulder, Rowman) 16; Beevor, A (2009) *D-Day. The Battle for Normandy* (London, Viking) 146, 445.

[306] Best, G (1980) *Humanity in Warfare* (London, Weidenfeld) 239–40.

[307] Olson, L (2003) *For Your Freedom and Ours* (London, Heineman) 321, 327, 350; Davies, N (2003) *Rising '44: The Battle for Warsaw* (London, Pan) 247, 249, 278, 357.

them with insignia armbands and a note which explained that, if they were captured, they were to be treated as if in the German Army.[308]

The other types of informal combatants of note in both the First and Second World Wars were spies. In the latter instance, Winston Churchill (1874–1965) created the Special Operations Executive with the task of 'setting Europe ablaze', of which some 7,500 agents were sent into occupied Western Europe and 4,000 into Italy and the Balkans.[309] When the spies were captured, all of the belligerents, with the exception of the United States, exercised the right to execute them. The United States did not execute the spies, as they were captured in the United States in German uniforms. However, American guerrillas operating behind Japanese lines in the occupied Philippines concluded that the strict laws of war could not be applied if they were to survive and 'informers and spies' had to be 'destroyed'.[310] The Japanese and the British also both executed spies, with the latter dispatching 16 captured spies during the conflict; one of them, Josef Jakobs (1898–1941), being the last person ever to be executed at the Tower of London. The Germans did the same. Thus, when caught, Allied spies could be executed outright or sent to concentration camps. For example, 37 Special Operation operatives were sent to Buchenwald in 1944, where 17 were hanged. Alternately, captured spies could 'disappear'. At least 52 British spies, including 12 women, were unaccounted for after the end of the war.[311]

E. The Rise of the Non-formal Belligerents in Times of Peace

As States were trying to formalise the enemies they faced outside their national boundaries, enemies willing to use extreme violence were proliferating within them. Problems in this area began to appear after the Napoleonic wars, such as when French republicans attempted to assassinate Louis-Philippe (1773–1850) in 1835 with a gun which had 25 barrels. This weapon managed to kill 14 innocent bystanders, but not the king (who went on to survive a further seven assassination attempts on his life). Such acts were attractive to many non-formal belligerents operating within, and against, citizens of their own country. The new creed which was influential at this period was anarchism and the writings of Mikhail Bakunin (1814–1876). Bukunin argued:

> Let us put our trust in the eternal spirit which destroys and annihilates only because it is the unsearchable and eternally creative source of all life. The urge to destroy is also a creative

[308] Schoenbrum, D (1980) *Soldiers of the Night. The Story of the French Resistance* (NYC, Dutton) 454; Beevor, A (2009) *D-Day. The Battle for Normandy* (London, Viking) 488; de Zayas, A (1989) *The Wehrmacht War Crimes Bureau, 1939–1945* (Nebraska, Nebraska University Press) 151, 153; Neillands, R (2002) *The Bomber War* (London, Murray) 140.

[309] Churchill in Jurado, C (1985) *Resistance Warfare* (London, Osprey) 7; Farrington, K (2003) *World War II War Crimes and Espionage* (Leicester, Abbeydale) 17; Koss, P (2004) *The Encyclopaedia of World War II Spies* (Boston, Yale University Press); Seligmann, M (2006) *Spies in Uniform: British Military and Naval Intelligence on the Eve of the First World War* (Oxford, Oxford University Press).

[310] Best, G (1980) *Humanity in Warfare* (London, Weidenfeld) 241.

[311] Crowdy, T (2006) *The Enemy Within. A History of Espionage* (London, Osprey) 153, 250, 290–91; Maga, T (2000) *Judgment at Tokyo* (Kentucky, Kentucky University Press) 114–19; Bailey, F (2009) *Forgotten Voices of the Secret War* (London, Ebury) 98, 144, 156, 162–63, 176, 196, 220, 224, 228, 299–302; Whitlock, F 'Horrific Discovery' *WWII History* (Nov 2008) 49, 54; Helm, S 'The Lost Secret Agents' *BBC History* (July 2005) 35–40; Gilbert, A (2006) *POW: Allied Prisoners in Europe* (London, Murray) 20–21, 88–89; Owen, F (1960) *The Fall of Singapore* (London, Penguin) 115.

> urge . . . the revolutionary is a man under a vow. He ought to occupy himself entirely with one exclusive interest, with one thought and one passion: the Revolution . . . He has only one aim, one science: destruction . . . Between him and society there is war to the death, incessant, irreconcilable . . . he must make a list of all those who are condemned to death, and expedite their sentence.[312]

The result of such interest and the willingness of disguised individuals to take violence into their own hands as a method of challenging the status quo was a rapid upsurge in attempts of assassination and public bombings. These efforts swept Europe during the 1880s with over 60 civilian deaths caused by bombs going off in public places, such as in restaurants in France in 1882, 1893 and 1894. Across the channel, the Fenians brought havoc to London in the same period with bullets against notable individuals and bombs in Big Ben, London Bridge, the London Underground and city gasworks, all designed to create mass panic. Russia was also convulsed by a series of bombings and assassination attempts, which finally succeeded in the killing of Alexander II (1818–81). These acts were supplemented by assassinations of other heads of State, royalty or captains of industry. President Marie Carnot of France (1837–94), Antonia del Canovas, the Prime Minister of Spain (1828–97), the Empress Elisabeth of Austria-Hungary (1837–98) and King Umberto of Italy (1844–1900) all met their end through the acts of anarchist assassins. In a number of these instances, innocent bystanders were killed in the blast. In 1893, a bomb was thrown into a crowd of opera-goers in Barcelona; for the first time, a class of non-combatants was the explicit target and over 20 people met their death.[313]

All of these multifarious acts of violence achieved nothing beyond the individual tragedies of those people killed or maimed. They had little significant impact on the domestic or international politics of any of the countries concerned, and certainly did not collapse the social orders that they raged against. They did, however, act as the catalyst from which an international response began to emerge. Due to such actions, national police forces started to cooperate in Europe as early as 1893. Five years later, the government of Italy organised a conference for the Social Defense Against Anarchists. This was attended by official delegates from 21 European countries. These countries agreed in principle to strictly control and share information on organisations and individuals involved in anarchism (defined as any act 'having as its aim the destruction, through violent means, of all social organization') and to extradite anarchists involved in cross-border assassination attempts. These measures had limited success, as Britain and Belgium insisted that anarchist violence could be adequately contained by existing domestic laws. However, following the assassination of American President William McKinley (1843–1901), a further international conference on anarchism was held in 1904 in Russia. This resulted in the Secret Protocol for the International War on Anarchism. Although this was agreed by nine countries, France, Britain and the United States refused to sign it, sceptical at the degrees of intrusion that were being sought and how effective it would be. In this regard, they were proved partly correct as the practice of bomb throwing did not end, but accelerated around Europe with

[312] Bakunin reprinted in Woodstock, G (1986) *Anarchism, A History of Libertarian Ideas and Movements* (London, Pelican) 125, 143–44.

[313] Rapport, M (2009) *1848: Year of Revolution* (London, Abacus) 26; Chaliand, G (2007) *The History of Terrorism* (London, University of California Press) 118–21, 125–31; Burleigh, M (2008) *Blood and Rage. A Cultural History of Terrorism* (London, Harper) 14–18, 60–61.

literally thousands of bombs being exploded across Europe. Some of these, such as such as the 1906 attempt on King Alfonso XIII of Spain (1886–1941) killed 24 innocent people by mistake. In the same year, three Russian terrorists attempting to kill their Prime Minister became the first suicide bombers in history, each detonating their 16 pound bomb they held in their hands, killing themselves and 27 others (but not the Prime Minister), including women, children and the elderly. These deaths were part of a pattern between 1900 and 1913 where no fewer than 40 heads of State, politicians and diplomats were murdered, including four kings, six prime ministers and three presidents. In the Balkans two kings, one queen, two prime ministers and the commander-in-chief of the Turkish army were all assassinated.[314] However, all of the above examples are but footnotes to the bullets belonging to Gavrilo Princip (1894–1918) that killed Austrian Archduke Franz Ferdinand (1863–1914) and his pregnant wife Sophie (1868–1914) in Sarajevo on 28 June 1914. These bullets sparked a war that would leave over 10 million dead. Up until the point of Princip's execution in 1918 (he could not be executed earlier because he was a minor) he refused to plead guilty because he continued to believe that the assassination he had completed, irrespective of its consequences, was a just act.[315] Such thinking continued in the 1920s and 1930s, as civilians became the collateral damage or the direct target of bombing campaigns that occurred outside of the time of formal conflicts. For example, in 1925 Bulgarian communists blew up the roof of the Saint Nedelya Church in Sofia. One hundred and fifty people, mainly from the country's political and military elite, were killed in the attack and around 500 were injured. This bomb attack, notable for its size, was accompanied by another notable attack in 1933 in the United States when a Boeing 247 was destroyed in flight by a bomb, killing all seven people on board. The following year, King Alexander I of Yugoslavia (1888–1934) was assassinated.[316]

With such bombs and bullets punctuating the decades in countries at peace following the First World War, which in itself was caused by such acts, the French government submitted to the League of Nations a memorandum for an agreement with a view to the suppression of terrorism. The League of Nations then drafted the Convention for the Prevention and Punishment of Terrorism. This Convention, which focused on State-sponsored terrorism, was the first and only instrument of international law which attempted to deal with terrorism in a generic manner. Terrorism was defined as '[c]riminal acts directed against a State and intended or calculated to create a state of terror in the minds of particular persons, or groups of persons or the general public'.[317] The Convention was built around:

> [T]he principle of international law in virtue of which it is the duty of every State to refrain from any act designed to encourage terrorist activities directed against another State and to prevent the acts in which such activities take shape.[318]

[314] Carr, M 'Cloaks, Daggers and Dynamite' *History Today* (Dec 2008) 29–31; Adams, J (2005) 'Anarchists in the UK' *BBC History* June 34–35.

[315] Fetherlin, G (2001) *The Book of Assassins* (London, Wiley) 304–305; Ferguson, N (2006) *The War of the World* (London, Allen Lane) 72–78.

[316] Read, A 'Reds Under the Bed' *History Today* (Apr 2008) 50–54.

[317] Convention for the Prevention and Punishment of Terrorism 1937 in Hudson, R (ed) (1950) *International Legislation*, Vol VII, 1935–37 (NY, Oceana) 862, Art 2.

[318] Convention for the Prevention and Punishment of Terrorism, Art 1.

The Parties to the Convention were meant to make illegal acts directed against another State 'constituting an act of terrorism' by either 'directly doing or assisting, killing or causing injury to Heads of State or their families, killing or causing injury to people charged with public functions'. This goal was added to with prevention of 'the willful destruction of public property or any willful act calculated to endanger the lives or members of the public'.[319] Despite these very basic goals, the Convention never entered into force.

11. From the Cold War to the Twenty-first Century

A. Age

After the shooting had stopped in the Second World War, it became apparent that some of the most obvious victims of the conflict were children. The idea of a specific convention on the protection of children in times of war had been mooted during the 1930s, but never eventuated. Whether it would have slowed the inflictions upon children between 1939 and 1945 is a matter of conjecture. What is not a matter of conjecture is that children, as in individuals under the age of 18, were intentionally killed in concentration camps, and were the victims of collateral damage and reprisals. They were abducted in the hundreds of thousands and taken to the Reich, with some 33,000 'foundlings', picked up on the roadside or lifted from the bodies of dead parents, to which they were clinging in 1945.[320] The initial response to such problems, following some interest in the topic at the Nuremberg Trials,[321] was the Fourth Geneva Convention of 1949 Relative to the Protection of Civilians in Time of War. Amongst multiple other concerns, this established a large collection of rules for the protection of children during times of conflict, ranging from feeding them to trying to keep them with their families.[322] These rules were later supplemented by the human rights applicable to children that were confirmed in the International Covenant on Civil and Political Rights[323] and the International Covenant on Economic, Social and Cultural Rights.[324] These generic documents on human rights were then added to by the United Nations Declaration on Children[325] and the United Nations Convention on the Rights of the Child.[326] The singling out of children for special protection in times of armed conflict was clearly done by the United Nations General Assembly in 1974 because

[319] Convention for the Prevention and Punishment of Terrorism, Art 2.

[320] Moorehead, C (1998) *Dunant's Dream: War, Switzerland and the History of the Red Cross* (NYC, Carroll & Graf) 513, 523; Durand, A (1984) *A History of the International Committee of the Red Cross: From Sarajevo to Hiroshima* (Geneva, Dunant Institute) 162–66; Davies, N (2003) *Rising '44: The Battle for Warsaw* (London, Pan) 95; Bourke, J 'Under Fire: Civilians In the World of Total War' *BBC History* (Nov 2001) 35–40.

[321] Law Reports of Trials of War Criminals: United Nations War Crimes Commission (1946) Trial of Heinrich Gerike, Case No 42, Vol VII (London, HMSO) 75.

[322] 1949 Convention, Civilians, Arts 24, 50, 68, 78, 82, 89 and 94.

[323] GA Res 2200A (XXI), 21 UN GAOR Supp (No 16) at 52; UN Doc A/6316 (1966); 999 UNTS 171, Art 24.

[324] GA Res 2200A (XXI), 21 UN GAOR Supp (No 16) at 49, UN Doc A/6316 (1966), 993 UNTS 3, Arts 10 and 13.

[325] Declaration of the Rights of the Child, GA Res 1386 (XIV) 14; GAOR Supp (No 16) at 19, UN Doc A/4354 (1959).

[326] GA Res 44/25, Annex, 44 UN GAOR Supp (No 49) at 167, UN Doc A/44/49 (1989).

they were/are 'the most vulnerable members of the population'.[327] The 1977 Additional Protocols to the Geneva Conventions added to this, stating that children 'shall be the object of special respect . . . [and be] provide[d] with the care and aid they require'.[328] From this goal, a number of additional considerations were agreed to protect children in times of conflict. Although the international law surrounding children is much more robust than in the past, the problems of children who are lost, stolen, killed as collateral damage or directly targeted (as with the hostage-taking of the Beslan school in 2004) in times of conflict are still omnipresent.[329]

In addition to all of the above concerns, children have also been recruited or utilised in the armed forces. The use of children in armed forces, trained to kill or be killed, is an unmitigated evil. To kill your own young is also a symptom of madness. Even if the children in these conflicts do survive, they are often abused through the processes, and can have great difficulty reintegrating into society as functioning adults for any number of reasons. This is not surprising given the violence they have had done to them, and have committed and witnessed.[330] However, despite these huge costs upon human young, the practice of utilising them for warfare, as seen above, is deeply entrenched. The first clear step to try to prevent this one particular evil occurred at the 1974–77 Diplomatic Conference on the Reaffirmation and Development of International Humanitarian Law in Armed Conflict, when Brazil proposed the prohibition on the recruitment of persons under the age of 18 into the armed forces. Although the negotiation process saw the age lowered to 15, not the 18 proposed by Brazil, the signatories to the 1977 Protocols finally placed some limits in this area.[331] Protocol I stated that the Parties to the regime would:

> [T]ake all feasible measures in order that children who have not attained the age of fifteen years do not take a direct part in hostilities and, in particular, they shall refrain from recruiting them into their armed forces. In recruiting among those persons who have attained the age of fifteen years but who have not attained the age of eighteen years the Parties to the conflict shall endeavour to give priority to those who are oldest.[332]

The 1977 Protocol added that children who are made prisoners of war because they were actively engaged in the conflict were still to be given special protection, such as separate quarters. Moreover, the death penalty for an offence related to the armed conflict shall not be executed on persons who had not attained the age of 18 years at the time the offence was committed.[333]

Some of the large countries like China and the United States were receptive to such objectives, and were already raising the age by which children could see combat. For

[327] UNGA Res 3318 (XXIX) Declaration on the Protection of Women and Children in Emergency and Armed Conflict.

[328] 1977, Protocol 1, Art 77. See also Arts 74 and 77. Note Arts 4 and 6 in Protocol II.

[329] Red Cross (2001) 'Children and War' *IRRC* 844: 1163–73; Merkelbach, M (2000) 'Reuniting Children Separated From Their Families After the Rwandan Crisis' *IRRC* 838: 351–67; Platner, D (1984) 'Protection of Children in International Humanitarian Law' *IRRC* 240: 140–52; McAllister, J 'Defenceless Targets' *TIME* (13 Sept 2004) 10–19.

[330] Boothby, N (2000) 'Children of the Gun' *Scientific American*, June 40–45; Aldhous, P 'Child Soldiers Adapt to Life After War' *New Scientist* (10 May 2008) 6–7; Schoomeyer, J (2006) 'Lost Boys Found' *Bulletin of the Atomic Scientists* May 11; Anon 'Liberia's Neglected Victims' *New Scientist* (16 Aug 2008) 4.

[331] See Protocol II, Art 4(3)(c).

[332] 1977, Protocol 1, Art 77(2). For commentary, see Dutli, M (1990) 'Captured Child Soldiers' *IRRC* 278: 421–34.

[333] 1977, Protocol 1, Art 77(3).

example, whilst Mao-Tse Tung (1893–1976) would not allow anyone under the age of 16 to be involved in combat, the Americans would progressively move away from situations that saw 17-year-olds in the Korean War, to the average age of an American soldier in Vietnam being 24.[334] These approaches were somewhat unique compared to that adopted by belligerents in other conflicts. For example, the Kymer Rouge started taking children into his armed forces in Cambodia between the ages of eight and nine.[335] Simultaneously, during the Indonesian occupation of East Timor, all sides to the conflict utilised children from the age of 10 up. Meanwhile, during the Iran–Iraq war, Iran came to make great use of a 'youth volunteer force' for boys aged over 12, for everything from clearing minefields by running through them to being taught to ride forward on their push-bikes and throw grenades. In the same time period, the government forces in Ethiopia were raiding football stadiums and taking boys over the age of 14 directly into the military.[336] Unfortunately, the last decade of the twentieth and the first of the twenty-first centuries followed in exactly the same manner, with belligerents taking children under the age of 15 and making them fight within, amongst others Afghanistan,[337] Angola,[338] Burma,[339] Burundi,[340] Columbia,[341] Chad,[342] Liberia, Nepal,[343] Rwanda,[344] Sri Lanka,[345] Sudan,[346] Sierra Leone[347] (80 per cent of the rebels were aged between seven and 14) and Uganda.[348] In some conflicts, such as in Liberia, perhaps as many as 60 per cent of the combatants in some factions were under 18, with some as young as seven years of age.[349] In the Middle East, suicide bombers were being delivered to their fate at

334 Chinnery, P (2000) *Korean Atrocity. Forgotten War Crimes 1950–1953* (Naval Institute Press, Maryland) 11; Mao Tse Tung (2005) *On Guerrilla Warfare* (Dover, NYC) 80.

335 Courtois, S et al. (1999) *The Black Book of Communism. Crimes, Terror, Repression* (Massachusetts, Harvard University Press) 620, 621.

336 Commission for Reception, Truth and Reconciliation Timor-Leste (2005) *Chega!* (CRTP, Faber) 124–40; The Executive Summary for this report is found at http://www.etan.org/etanpdf/2006/CAVR/Chega!-Report-Executive-Summary.pdf See also Karsh, E (2002) *The Iran-Iraq War* (London, Osprey) 62–63; Fisk, R (2006) *The Great War for Civilisation: The Conquest of the Middle East* (London, Harper) 248.

337 Human Rights Watch (2002) *Child Soldiers and the West Asian Crisis* (NYC, HRW).

338 Human Rights Watch (1994) *Arms Trade and Violations of the Laws of War Since the 1992 Elections* (NYC, HRW) 112, 150–53; Human Rights Watch (2003) *Forgotten Fighters: Child Soldiers in Angola* (NYC, HRW) 7–19.

339 Human Rights Watch (2007) *Sold to be Soldiers: Child Soldiers in Burma* (NYC, HRW) 1–3, 4–9; Human Rights Watch (2002) *'My Gun Was As Tall As Me': Child Soldiers in Burma* (NYC, HRW) 4–13.

340 Human Rights Watch (2006) *Child Soldiers in Burundi* (NYC, HRW) 3–13.

341 Human Rights Watch (1998) *Columbia and International Humanitarian Law* (NYC, HRW) 5–6; Human Rights Watch (1994) *Generation Under Fire: Children and Violence in Columbia* (NYC, HRW); Human Rights Watch (2001) *Columbia: Beyond Negotiation: International Humanitarian Law and its Application to the Conduct of the FARC* (NYC, HRW) 15–18; Human Rights Watch (2003) *You'll Learn Not to Cry: Child Combatants in Columbia* (NYC, HRW) 11–26.

342 Human Rights Watch (2007) *Child Soldiers in the Chad Conflict* (NYC, HRW) 14–19.

343 Human Rights Watch (2006) *Children in the Ranks: The Maoist Use of Child Soldiers in Nepal* (NYC, HRW) 7–10, 14–20.

344 Human Rights Watch (2001) *Reluctant Recruits* (NYC, HRW).

345 Human Rights Watch (2006) *Complicit in Crime: Abduction and Child Recruitment* (NYC, HRW) 2–8, 12–19, 23–26; Human Rights Watch (2004) *Living in Fear: Child Soldiers and the Tamil Tigers* (NYC, HRW) 12–18.

346 Human Rights Watch (1994) *Sudan: The Lost Boys* (NYC, HRW).

347 Human Rights Watch (1998) *Sierra Leone: Atrocities Against Civilians* (NYC, HRW) 43–48.

348 Human Rights Watch (1997) *The Scars of Death: Children Abducted by the Lord's Resistance Army in Uganda* (NYC, HRW); Human Rights Watch (2003) *Stolen Children: Abduction and Recruitment in Northern Uganda* (NYC, HRW) 11–35.

349 Human Rights Watch (2004) *How to Fight, How to Kill: Child Soldiers in Liberia* (NYC, HRW); Human Rights Watch (1994) *Easy Prey: Child Soldiers in Liberia* (NYC, HRW); Human Rights Watch (2002) *Back to the Brink; War Crimes By The Liberian Government and Rebels* (NYC, HRW) 28–38.

the age of 16, whilst insurgents of similar ages were being captured and taken to Guantanamo Bay.[350] Collectively, it was estimated that by the end of the 1990s, there were 300,000 children under the age of 15 carrying weapons. These numbers declined during the early part of the next decade, although by 2008, child soldiers were still identified as fighting in 17 conflicts (down from 27 in 2004).[351]

Against this background, in a remarkably clear move, the Security Council has come to condemn consistently '[t]he . . . inhumane and abhorrent . . . practice of recruiting, training and deploying children for combat'.[352] This condemnation was most clear in 1999 when they explicitly condemned the recruitment and use of children in armed conflict as a clear violation of international law and went on to call all Parties involved in armed conflict to include provisions in their peace agreements for the disarmament, demobilisation and reintegration of child combatants wherever possible.[353] Failure to do so, and the continued use of child soldiers, has meant that the Security Council directly criticised warring factions in the late 1990s in Liberia[354]and Sierra Leone.[355] In the new century, similar criticism was again levelled at Liberia,[356] Côte d'I'voire,[357] Burundi[358] and repeatedly with the Congo.[359]

The Security Council's concerns have been bolstered by the International Criminal Court which has come to recognise as a war crime, for both internal and international conflicts, conscripting and enlisting children under the age of 15 for active participation in hostilities.[360] In 1999, the forced or compulsory recruitment of youths under the age of 18 for use in armed conflict was recognised by the International Labour Organization as one of the worst forms of child labour.[361] The Optional Protocol to the Convention on the Rights of the Child went one step further, moving the age limit for the recruitment of soldiers, voluntary or otherwise, to the age of 18, with those under the age of 18 not being allowed to be engaged in hostilities.[362] The Security Council has endorsed this instrument,[363] and has subsequently threatened to consider the utilisation of arms embargos against those countries which have failed to stop their utilisation of child soldiers.[364]

International criminal law has also come to focus on the problem of child soldiers, with defendants such as Sam Hinga Norman (1940–2007) being found guilty of such practices by the Special Court for Sierra Leone. Conviction on this ground, was later

[350] Carrel, S 'Child Prisoners in Guantanamo Bay' *New Zealand Herald* (29 May 2006) B2; Associated Press 'Father Blames Al Aqsa For Boys Deadly Quest' *New Zealand Herald* (5 Nov 2003) B2.

[351] Human Rights Watch/Coalition Against the Use of Child Soldiers (2008) *Global Report* (NYC, HRW) 9–15.

[352] S/RES/1071 (1996, Aug 30).

[353] S/RES/1261 (1999, Aug 30); S/RES/1314 (2000, Aug 11); S/RES/1366 (2001, Aug 30).

[354] S/RES/1083 (1996, Nov 27).

[355] S/RES/1231 (1999, Mar 11); S/RES/1346 (2001, Mar 30).

[356] S/RES/1478 (2003); S/RES/1509 (2003, Sept 19).

[357] S/RES/1479 (2003).

[358] S/RES/1791 (2007) Dec 19.

[359] S/RES/1332 (2000, Dec 14) S/RES/1341 (2001, Feb 22) S/RES/1355 (2001, June 15); S/RES/1445 (2002, Dec 4); S/RES/1468 (2003); S/RES/1493 (2003, July 28); S/RES/1698 (2006, July 31); S/RES/1804 (2008, Mar 13).

[360] ICC 8 b (xxvi) and 8 e (vii); S/RES/1460 (2003).

[361] ILO, Convention Concerning the Prohibition of the Worst Forms of Child Labour, ILO Convention No 182, Art 3.

[362] 39 ILM (2000) 1285. See Arts 3 and 4.

[363] S/RES/1314 (2000, Aug 11); S/RES/1379 (2001, Nov 20).

[364] S/RES/1539 (2004) Apr 22; S/RES/1612 (2005) July 26.

supplemented with the cases of Allieu Kondewa (b 1950), Alex Tamba Brima (b 1971) and Santigie Borbor Kanu (b 1965).[365] Similarly, the very first case at the International Criminal Court came to focus on the utilisation of child soldiers by Thomas Lubanga (b 1960) in the Democratic Republic of the Congo.[366] Lubanga has been accompanied by other belligerent leaders in the Congo accused of the same crime, namely, Germain Katanga (b 1978), Mathieu Ngudjolo Chui (b 1970–)[367] and Bosco Ntaganda (b 1973).[368] The same crimes have also been alleged with a number of members of the Lord's Resistance Army, operating in and from Uganda such as Joseph Koni (b 1961) Vincent Otti (1946–2007), Okot Odhiambo and Dominic Ongwen.[369]

B. Sex

After the Second World War, when the international community gathered at Geneva to re-evaluate the laws of war, it was again indirectly agreed that women could be combatants, as they were given special consideration within the Convention on Prisoners. 'women . . . shall in all cases benefit by treatment as favourable as that granted to men'.[370] It was later elsewhere specifically recognised that the 'maximum participation of women on equal terms with men in all fields'[371] was a noble international goal.

That recognition was timely in that, although armed forces of the twenty-first century are approximately 97 per cent male, as the decades after 1945 unfolded it became increasingly apparent that women could perform most of the same functions as men in the military with the same levels of skill. This has been evident with regards to excellent commanders in times of military conflict, such as Golda Meir (1898–1978), Indira Gandhi (1917–84) and Margaret Thatcher (b 1925), and also with excellent fighters, who have been increasingly engaged in conflicts. For example, approximately, one fifth of the soldiers who fought in the Greek civil war between 1943 and 1947 were females. By the middle of 1948, the 6,000 member defence squads for what became Israel included some 1,200 women with five women leading combat units – before they were excluded from combat in 1949. Thousands of women fighters were also utilised by the Vietcong.[372] In the decade that followed, female insurgents became increasingly notable in conflicts which spanned the globe. Women comprised 30 per cent of the insurgents in Nicaragua in 1976, 33 per cent of the Tamil tigers in Sri Lanka, and 100 per cent in some terror-based units, such as with the 'Black Widows' of the Chechen war.[373]

[365] The Sam Ninga Norman case reprinted in 43 ILM (2004) 1129. For the crime, see Art 4(c) of the Special Court. Also, Coker, C (2001) *Humane Warfare* (London, Routledge) 123.

[366] ICC–01/04–01/06.

[367] ICC–01/04–01/07.

[368] ICC–01/04–02/06.

[369] ICC–02/04–01/05.

[370] 1949, Art 14. See also Art 25.

[371] Convention on the Elimination of All Forms of Discrimination Against Women 1979, Preamble.

[372] Jones, D (2000) *Women Warriors. A History* (NYC, Brassey's) 130, 131, Lindsey, C (2001) 'Women and War' *IRC* 83: 505, 506; Tucker, S (1998) *The Encyclopaedia of the Vietnam War* (Oxford, Oxford University Press) 488–89.

[373] Lindsey, C (2000) 'Women and War' *IRRC* 839: 561–79; Gilligan, E (2010) *Terror in Chechnya* (New Jersey, Princeton University Press) 132–33; Bloom, M (2005) 'Mother, Daughter, Sister, Bomber' *Bulletin of Atomic Scientists* Nov 54–60; Moran, D (2001) *Wars of National Liberation* (London, Cassell) 107; Jones, D (2000) *Women Warriors. A History* (NYC, Brassey's) 103; Goldstein, J (2001) *War and Gender* (Cambridge, Cambridge University Press) 80, 83–87, 106.

With regards to more conventional forces, the American record in this area is notable, with up to 21,000 females being deployed to assist military operations in non-combat roles. By the turn of the century, nearly 200,000 women were serving in the United States military (14 per cent of the total force), of which some had seen combat since 1990 when female pilots were first authorised to fly combat missions. This approach is consistent with some European practices. For example, when Srebrenica fell to the Bosnian Serbs in 1995, one of the few sorties flown against those overrunning the safe area, was by a female Dutch pilot. Others, like Britain, have gone on to allow female medics into combat zones.[374]

C. Conscription

The question of conscription was dealt with at Nuremberg. First, Robert Wagner (1895–1946)[375] was found guilty at Nuremberg of, inter alia, forcing the French nationals of the Alsace region to join the German army and effectively fight against their own country. Likewise, in the case of Wilheim List (1880–1971),[376] the forced conscription of Italian nationals after Italy had surrendered to the Allies but was still occupied in part by Germans was seen as a clear violation of international law. This rule, that an Occupying power may not compel, pressure or even propagandise protected persons to serve in its armed or auxiliary forces, was reiterated in the Fourth Geneva Convention of 1949.[377] This approach was later noted by the United Nations General Assembly when dealing with South Africa in Namibia, whilst the principle was later reiterated within the Statute for the International Criminal Court.[378]

Beyond this one area where conscription cannot be practiced, no right to object to conscription was then, or has been subsequently agreed to by the international community. Thus, although the right to 'conscience' was dealt with by the United Nations General Assembly in Article 18 of the 1948 Universal Declaration of Human Rights, there was no explicit linkage to a right to conscientious objection. Moreover, when this question was examined with the 1966 International Covenant on Civil and Political Rights of 1966, 'the right to freedom of thought, conscience and religion' was 'subject . . . to such limitations as are prescribed by law and are necessary to protect public safety, order, health, or morals or the fundamental rights and freedoms of others'. Some States argued that such limitations permitted them to recognise conscientious objection during time of war as a threat to public safety.

Thus, despite repeated entreaties that 'the right to refuse to kill' should be considered a fundamental right, no countries have recognised this as a matter of international standing. As such, the matter remains for each country to resolve, with some, like China, rejecting conscription and relying upon an all-volunteer force, whilst others

[374] Honig, J (1997) *Srebrenica: Record of a War Crime* (London, Penguin) 25; Goldstein, J (2001) *War and Gender* (Cambridge, Cambridge University Press) 10–11; Nichol, J and Rennell, T (2009) *Medic* (London, Penguin) 279–98; Goldstein, J (2001) *War and Gender* (Cambridge, Cambridge University Press) 86–87; Glasser, R (2006) *Wounded* (NYC, Braziller) 70–71; Bin, A (1998) *Desert Storm. A Forgotten War* (Westport, Prager) 250.

[375] UN War Crimes Commission (1948) Law Reports of the Trials of War Criminals The Trial of Robert Wagner Case No 13, Vol III (London, HMSO) 1.

[376] UN War Crimes Commission (1949) Law Reports of the Trials of War Criminals (1949) The Trial of Wilhelm List, Case No 47, Vol VIII, 38.

[377] Convention, Civilians 1949, Art 51.

[378] ICC, Arts 8(v) and 8.b(xv). UNGA Res 43/26 Question of Namibia (1988).

would utilise it periodically, as required by various military needs, such as with the United States in Korea and especially in Vietnam.[379]

In the Korean conflict about 1.5 per cent of those drafted claimed conscientious objection status (of which some 7,777 men were registered with the Selective Service as conscientious objectors in 1952).[380] With the Vietnam War (where some 1,857,304 men were taken into service), 170,000 men were recognised by military boards as conscientious objectors who ended up doing non-combatant military service (including being medics) or civilian work in the national interest. A further 100,000 took some form of alternative service such as working in low-paying public service work like hospitals. An approximate 570,000 men evaded the draft illegally. Among draft evaders, 8,800 were caught and convicted, with 4,000 sent to prison. In addition, legal exemptions of deferments were given to 15.4 million men. There were undergraduate deferments for college and graduate school deferments. There were also deferments for enlistment in the National Guard and Reserve units. Accordingly, many sought to avoid being sent to Vietnam by joining the National Guard or some component of the Reserves. The 147th Fighter Group of the Texas Air National Guard was notorious. Its privileged roll included future president George W Bush (b 1946), seven members of the Dallas Cowboys football team and the sons of three State senators. These cumulative measures became so unpopular that the day after signing the Paris Accords in 1973 which ended American involvement in Vietnam, Richard Nixon (1913–94) ended the draft and inaugurated the all-volunteer military. Subsequent presidents in 1974 and 1977 had to go further and issue amnesties to the men who had avoided being conscripted. Despite these problems, the United States has retained its basic system, and although it has not been necessary to draft troops into combat, the obligation of all men between the ages of 18 and 26 to be registered for Selective Service has stayed in place.[381]

Elsewhere, from the mid 1970s onwards, forced conscription and resulting human rights abuses, was recognised as a serious problem in Argentina[382] and Cambodia,[383] in the war by the Mujahedeen against the Soviets in Afghanistan during the 1980s,[384] and throughout (and after) the 1990s with Ethiopia,[385] Liberia.[386] Mozambique[387] and

[379] Brock, P (2006) *Against the Draft* (Toronto, University of Toronto Press) 78; Cohen, E (1985) *Citizens and Soldiers: The Dilemmas of Military Service* (Ithaca, Cornell University Press) 26. Mao Tse Tung (2005) *On Guerrilla Warfare* (Dover, NYC) 86.

[380] Cohen, E (1985) *Citizens and Soldiers: The Dilemmas of Military Service* (Ithaca, Cornell University Press) 104, 105. Tracy, J (2006) *The Military Draft Handbook* (San Francisco, Manic Press) 29; Haskew, M 'To Field An Army. *Military Heritage* (Feb 2008) 52, 54.

[381] Tracy, J (2006) *The Military Draft Handbook* (San Francisco, Manic Press) 30; Cohen, E (1985) *Citizens and Soldiers: The Dilemmas of Military Service* (Ithaca, Cornell University Press) 108; Tucker, S (1998) *The Encyclopaedia of the Vietnam War* (Oxford, Oxford University Press) 82; Haskew, M 'To Field An Army' *Military Heritage* (Feb 2008) 52, 54. Note the two Supreme Court cases in this area, *Gillette v United States* 401 US 437 and *USA v Sisson* in 8 ILM (1969) 1248–59.

[382] The National Commission of Argentina on Disappeared People (1986) *Nuncas Mas* (London, Faber) 355–60.

[383] Rummel, R (1996) *Death by Government* (London, Transaction) 174.

[384] Human Rights Watch (1988) *Violations of the Laws of War in Afghanistan By All Parties to the Conflict* (NYC, HRW) 57–62; Human Rights Watch (1991) *The Forgotten War* (NYC, HRW) 2.

[385] Human Rights Watch (1991) *Evil Days: Thirty Years of War and Famine in Ethiopia* (NYC, HRW) 5.

[386] Human Rights Watch (1990) *Liberia: A Human Rights Disaster* (NYC, HRW) 6–9; Human Rights Watch (2002) *Back to the Brink; War Crimes By The Liberian Government and Rebels* (NYC, HRW) 13–28.

[387] Human Rights Watch (1992) *Conspicuous Destruction: War, Famine and the Reform Process in Mozambique* (NYC, HRW) 85–101.

Sierra Leone.[388] It was a problem in the wars of the former Yugoslavia[389] and has remained a clear problem in Russia, where young men go to great lengths to avoid it, with resulting social problems from trying to force them to comply.[390] In some instances, such as with Angola[391] and Sierra Leone,[392] the Security Council had demanded that conscription be stopped. Meanwhile in other areas, such as where peace has been brought to a country, the peace treaties, such as in Mozambique,[393] and Guatemala[394] have completely done away with conscription; or, as in the case of El-Salvador, the importance of having an equitable and fairly shared system of universal service was agreed in the final peace treaty.[395]

D. Soldiers of Foreign Lands

Following the Second World War, whilst there was a reiteration of the established rule of what makes a formal combatant (identification, command structure, follows the rules of war and carries their arms openly), there was no consideration given to issues such as nationality or motivation for fighting in the armies of choice. Moreover, the 1949 Convention on Prisoners of War reiterated the general rule that the following people could also be classified as prisoners of war:

> Persons who accompany the armed forces without actually being members thereof, such as civilian members of military aircraft crews, war correspondents, supply contractors, members of labour units or of services responsible for the welfare of the armed forces, provided that they have received authorization from the armed forces which they accompany, who shall provide them for that purpose with an identity card similar to the annexed model.[396]

Thus, the possibility of allowing other than strictly military personnel on or near the battlefield was retained. At the same time, the question of mercenaries was not examined. This was not a large surprise, as apart from the instance of China who argued that the Chinese soldiers fighting for North Korea were only 'volunteers', the issue was not of great magnitude during the 1950s, although it was beginning to appear in Latin America as groups like the 'Caribbean Legion' (who were essentially foreign soldiers of a left leaning) and the 'Foreign Legion' (which was made up of right-wing volunteers who had previously fought for the Axis and still wanted to fight communism) began to appear in Latin America.[397]

In the 1960s, the problem appeared in great force as the war in the Congo erupted and the Security Council (and the General Assembly) of the United Nations called for the withdrawal and evacuation of all Belgian forces and all 'other foreign military and

[388] Human Rights Watch (1998) *Sierra Leone: Atrocities Against Civilians* (NYC, HRW) 32–39.
[389] Glenny, M (1996) *The Fall of Yugoslavia* (London, Penguin) 20, 131
[390] Human Rights Watch (2002) *Conscription Through Detention in Russia's Armed Forces* (NYC, HRW); Human Rights Watch (2004) *The Wrongs of Passage* (NYC, HRW).
[391] S/RES/1190 (1998, Aug 13).
[392] S/RES/1346 (2001, Mar 30).
[393] General Peace Agreement for Mozambique 1992, Protocol IV: I.
[394] Comprehensive Agreement on Human Rights, 1994, s VI; Agreement on the Strengthening of Civilian Power and on the Role of the Armed Forces in a Democratic Society 1996, Art 43.
[395] Final Peace Agreement in El-Salvador 1992, Ch I, Art 11.
[396] Art 4(4).
[397] Scheina, R (2003) *Latin America's War. The Age of the Professional Soldier, 1900–2001*, Vol II (NYC, Brassey's) 239–40.

paramilitary personnel and political advisers not under the United Nations command, and mercenaries'.[398] These calls, especially as the mercenaries started fighting soldiers fighting under the flag of the United Nations directly, were reiterated throughout the 1960s, and were often especially targeted at Belgium.[399] From the end of this conflict around 1968, the mercenaries appear to have become involved in the Nigerian Civil War (1967–70) via their provision of 'security services'. These services, as with their time in the Congo, were used to both good and bad effect upon civilians and sovereignty, sometimes supporting democratically elected governments, and sometimes being employed to undermine them.[400] By the early 1970s, when mercenaries were being increasingly linked to the support of corrupt or apartheid led regimes, they were being classified in the United Nations General Assembly as 'criminals'.[401] This approach, followed through in Africa, where mercenaries continued to appear throughout the 1970s, and especially after former troops in the pay of one government, such as Portugal, were specifically forced to leave countries when peace agreements were concluded.[402] Such men often became soldiers of fortune and when captured, as in Angola, they were persecuted under national laws as criminals and the charge sheets made no mention of the word 'mercenary'.[403]

By 1977, this situation was beginning to change when two instruments attempted to deal with the problem in the same year. The first, Protocol I to the Geneva Convention, defined a mercenary as any person who fulfils all of six conditions. The six conditions are that: they are specially recruited locally or abroad in order to fight in an armed conflict; they take a direct part in the hostilities; they are motivated to take part in the hostilities essentially by the desire for private gain (which is substantially in excess of that promised or paid to combatants of similar ranks and functions in the armed forces of that Party); they are neither a citizen of the Party to the conflict, nor a member of the armed forces of a Party to the conflict; and they have not been sent by a State which is not a Party to the conflict on official duty as a member of its armed forces.[404] The core of these is that they are significantly motivated by financial reward, are foreign and are not a member of a State Party to the conflict. The consequence of fulfilling these six conditions is that 'a mercenary shall not have the right to be a combatant or a prisoner of war'.[405] Of note, the 1977 Protocol I did not prohibit mercenaries, it just denied them prisoner of war status if captured. This was unlike the 1977 Convention on the Elimination of Mercenarism in Africa. Although this utilised most

[398] S/RES/161 (1961, Feb 21); UNGA Resolution (1961) 1599 (XV) The Situation in the Republic of the Congo.

[399] UNSCR Res 143 (1960, July 14); S/RES/145 (1960, July 22); S/RES/146 (1960, Aug 9); S/RES/169 (1961, Nov 24); Secretary General. Implementation of the Plan of National Reconciliation in the Congo 2 ILM (1963) 303; S/RES/199 (1964, Dec 30); S/RES/ 169 (1961, Nov 24); S/RES/199 (1964, Dec 30); S/RES/ 226 (1966, Oct 14); S/RES/241 (1967, Nov 15).

[400] Geraghty, T (2007) *Guns For Hire* (London, Portrait) 39–54.

[401] See UNGA Res 3103 (XXVIII) Basic Principles of the Legal Status of Combatants Struggling Against Colonial and Alien Domination and Racist Regimes (1973) Para 5.

[402] See, eg, the Agreement Granting Independence of Portuguese Guinea 13 ILM (1974) 1244 and Protocol of the Accord Between the Portuguese Government and the Liberation Movement of Sao Tome 13 ILM (1974): 1467, Art 13.1.

[403] Hoover, M (1977) 'The Laws of War and the Angolan Trial of Mercenaries' *Case Western Reserve Journal of International Law* 9 (2) 323–406. For the rise of mercenaries in Africa after the 1980s, see Turner, J (1998) *Continent Ablaze: The Insurgency Wars in Africa* (Cassell, London) 88–89, 95–96, 153, 228–29.

[404] Art 47(2).

[405] Art 47(1).

of the same criteria as Protocol I (but did not require private gain 'substantially in excess' of what the other soldiers were getting) this convention sought to criminalise the people involved in this activity, with an emphasis upon co-operation, prosecutions and/or extradition.[406] It also went further in recommending the 'severest penalties . . . including capital punishment'[407] for the offences it encompassed.

Despite these first international and regional laws attempting to control mercenaries, they remained a clear problem. Indeed, in the very same year (1977) the international community first attempted to address this issue, mercenaries attempted to overthrow Benin and four years later, in 1981, the Seychelles, both of which were a direct concern to the Security Council.[408] Similarly, the Security Council was clear that peace in Zimbabwe would only be possible if the mercenaries were removed from the country.[409] Despite these growing concerns, mercenary activity continued to be found where large-scale conflicts were occurring. As such, during the 1980s, they were particularly notable in conflicts all over the world, although it was not always clear if the foreign fighters were mercenaries when taking into account the new definition. For example, with the Soviet war in Afghanistan, at least 25,000 Arab 'volunteers' went to fight (including Osama bin Laden, 1957–2011) and were financially supported (at around US$300 per month, per soldier) and trained by nations that wanted to punish the Soviet Union.[410] In other conflicts, such as those in central America, in south west Africa and around Angola, the foreign fighters employed to fight communists were more a loose connection of 'British and American fantasists, amateurs, bank robbers, psychopaths, plus a handful of idealists' who came to act with very few restraints in their conflict of occupation. Accordingly, in the case of Angola it was no surprise that their removal, along with the foreign soldiers from both Cuba (who had provided tens of thousands of soldiers to fight in Africa, in addition to thousands of men who were provided independently, through the operations of at least 80 companies providing military services) and South Africa, was a prerequisite for peace.[411]

At the end of the 1980s, the international community responded with the first dedicated global instrument on this topic, the 1989 International Convention against the Recruitment, Use, Financing and Training of Mercenaries.[412] This Convention reiterated the criteria from Protocol I, and added points that a mercenary is a person involved in a concerted act of violence aimed at overthrowing a Government or other-

[406] Arts 8–10.

[407] Arts 3 and 7.

[408] S/RES/405 (1977, Apr 14); S/RES/ 507 (1982, May 28); S/RES/ 496 (1981, Dec 15); S/RES/507 (1982, May 28); S/RES/496 (1981, Dec 15).

[409] S/RES/460 (1979, Dec 21).

[410] Geraghty, T (2007) *Guns For Hire* (London, Portrait) 127–38; Fisk, R (2006) *The Great War for Civilisation: The Conquest of the Middle East* (London, Harper) 109.

[411] See the 1988 Agreement Among the People's Republic of Angola, the Republic of Cuba and the Republic of South Africa. See also the 1988 Agreement Between the Government of the Republic of Cuba and the Government for the People's Republic of Angola for the Conclusions of the Internationalist Mission of the Cuban Military Contingent 28 ILM (1989) 950. Also, S/RES/ 581 (1986, Feb 13). And, 1994 Lusaka Protocol, Annex 3. Also, S/RES/1008 (1995, Aug 7). For commentary on the period, see Singer, P (2008) *Corporate Warriors* (London, Cornell University Press) 10–11, 109–10, Geraghty, T (2007) *Guns For Hire* (Portrait, London) 61, 65–67, 140–52; Turner, J (1998) *Continent Ablaze: The Insurgency Wars in Africa* (London, Cassell) 53–54, 87–88, 100, 114–16.

[412] A/RES/44/34. Also, 29 ILM (1990) 89.

wise undermining the constitutional order or territorial integrity of a State.[413] This was an important addition, as it effectively meant that mercenaries could only be those involved in overthrowing, not supporting, a State. Such acts were to be considered as offences of grave concern to all States and any person committing any of these offences should be either prosecuted or extradited. It was agreed that the signatories to the Convention would not recruit, use, finance or train mercenaries and would prohibit and punish such activities.[414] Seeking to establish jurisdiction over the people concerned and cooperating with other Parties was expected. Extradition of such persons was to be facilitated, as was the sharing of information. If extradition was not possible, the obligation to prosecute was deemed even greater.[415] Nevertheless, the Convention went to some lengths to ensure that any persons taken into custody were accorded due process and the interested State Parties notified and allowed visits by the ICRC.[416] It did not suggest they were to be accorded a protected status like that given to prisoners of war. On this question, the 1989 Convention was clear that it was explicitly, '[w]ithout prejudice to law of armed conflict and international humanitarian law, including the provisions relating to the status of combatant or of prisoner of war'.[417]

Despite what appeared to be an emerging consensus on such issues, the 1990s, and although having strong support from the General Assembly of the United Nations, witnessed only a very limited uptake of signatories to the 1989 Convention (and some countries like the United States are not signatories to Protocol I either); and an extreme proliferation of multiple types of non-authorised foreign soldiers wandering from battlefield to battlefield in search of engagement.[418] This situation became so uncertain that when the International Criminal Court was created in 1998, it was not given jurisdiction over mercenaries or related crimes, as there was no clear consensus on the definition, scale or best way to handle this emerging problem.

The lack of consensus over the status of foreign fighters, coincided with a surplus in the supply of military trained personnel, and strong demands for their services, as governments (and non-governmental groups) have increasingly sought specialised military knowledge and its application. In other instances, commanders are simply looking for non-specialised volunteers. For example, insurgents like Osama bin Laden, after leading an army of thousands of foreign 'volunteers' in Afghanistan against the Soviet Union, went on to lead thousands of other such people in the conflicts against the United Nations in Afghanistan, and the American-lead coalition in Iraq. That is, approximately 3,000 non-Iraqi Muslim freelance fighters, including about 150 British volunteers, joined the insurrection in Iraq, with many signing up to Al-Qaeda's own foreign legion, of which the Security Council demanded that such 'foreign elements' exit the country.[419] Hundreds, if not thousands more, moved between Afghanistan,

[413] Art 1(2).

[414] Arts 5 and 6.

[415] Arts 7–9, 12, 13, 14 and 15.

[416] Arts 10 and 11.

[417] Art 16.

[418] UNGA Resolution (2010) 64/151 Use of Mercenaries as a Means of Violating Human Rights and Impeding . . . Self Determination. Also, amongst other iterations, 63/164 (2009); 58/162 (2004); 46/98 (1991).

[419] S/RES/1637 (2005, Nov 11), Annex I.

Algeria, Chechnya, Sudan, Somalia and Yemen. An estimated 7,620 Islamic militants from Somalia alone went to fight in Lebanon against Israel in 2006.[420]

Such fighters can be the antithesis of any attempt to find peace in warring countries. As such, the removal of such fighters has been repeatedly recognised as a key part of the peace settlements in, inter alia, Afghanistan,[421] Cambodia,[422] Côte d'Ivoire,[423] Guinea-Bissau,[424] Liberia,[425] Mozambique,[426] Somalia[427] and Sierra Leone.[428] In the case of the Democratic Republic of the Congo[429] and the surrounding Great Lakes region of Africa, the withdrawal of all 'external forces, including mercenaries' has been clearly called for by the Security Council.[430] These calls have been particularly pertinent, as despite the regional attempts in Africa to control mercenaries, these people have continued to proliferate in this region throughout the 1990s and the first decade of the new century.[431]

Mercenaries of all descriptions were a problem in the former Yugoslavia. These ranged from the 'weekend mercenaries' who would go across borders and join the conflict for a few days before returning home, those in so-called 'private armies' who fought for paymasters (and managed to swap sides on occasion), through to Muslim combatants who came from all over the world to help fight, for religion rather than money.[432] Accordingly, it was no surprise that the peace agreements for the former Yugoslavia, including Kosovo,[433] required the withdrawal of all forces which were 'not of local origin . . . including individual advisors, freedom fighters, trainers, volunteers, and personnel from neighbouring and other States'.[434]

[420] Coll, S (2005) *Ghost Wars* (London, Penguin) 155, 201; Harclerode, P (2002) *Fighting Dirty* (London, Cassell) 574–75; Rutherford, K (2008) *Humanitarianism Under Fire: The US and UN in Somalia* (Virginia, Kumarian) 145, 190; Geraghty, T (2007) *Guns For Hire* (London, Portrait) 62.

[421] S/RES/1193 (1998, Aug 28).

[422] Agreement on a Comprehensive Political Settlement of the Cambodia Conflict 1991, Art 8. See also the 1991 Agreement Concerning the Sovereignty, Independence, Territorial Integrity and Inviolability, Neutrality and National Unity of Cambodia. For Security Council comments, see S/RES/766 (1992, July 21); S/RES/810 (1993, Mar 8). Note also the UNGA Resolution (1989) 44/22 The Situation in Kampuchea.

[423] S/RES/1633 (2005, Oct 21); S/RES/1479 (2003); S/RES/1584 (2005, Feb 1).

[424] S/RES/1233 (1999, Apr 6).

[425] S/RES/1626 (2005, Sept 19).

[426] General Peace Agreement for Mozambique 1992, Protocols IV, VI.

[427] S/RES/1725 (2006) Dec 6; S/RES/1801 (2008, Feb 20).

[428] S/RES/1231 (1999, Mar 11); S/RES/1343 (2001, Mar 7); S/RES/1408 (2002, May 6); S/RES/1610 (2005, June 30).

[429] Memorandum of Understanding Between the Governments of the Republic of the Congo and Rwanda on the Withdrawal of Troops 41 ILM (2002) 1053. For Security Council comments, see S/RES/1230 (1999, Feb 26); S/RES/1304 (2000, June 16); S/RES/1341 (2001, Feb 22); S/RES/1355 (2001, June 15); S/RES/1376 (2001, Nov 9); S/RES/1417 (2002, June 14); S/RES/1445 (2002, Dec 4); S/RES/1234 (1999, Apr 9); S/RES/1456 (2003); S/RES/1468 (2003); S/RES/1565 (2004, Oct 1); S/RES/1592 (2005, Mar 30); S/RES/1756 (2007, May 15); S/RES/1804 (2008, Mar 13); S/RES/1794 (2007, Dec 21); S/RES/1856 (2008, Dec 22).

[430] S/RES/1097 (1997, Feb 18); S/RES/1663 (2006) Mar 24; Human Rights Watch (2005) *Youth, Poverty and Blood* (NYC, HRW) 7, 21–29, 37–40.

[431] Prunier, G (2009) *Africa's World War* (Oxford, Oxford University Press) 128–31, 185–86, 194, 210.

[432] Commission on Human Rights (2003) *Report of the Special Rapporteur on Mercenaries* E/CN4/2004/15, Para 28; Commission on Human Rights (2002) *Report of the Special Rapporteur on Mercenaries* E/CN4/2003/16, Para 25; Finlan, A (2004) *The Collapse of Yugoslavia 1991–1999* (London, Osprey) 27.

[433] Interim Agreement for Peace and Self-Government in Kosovo 1999, Ch 7.

[434] Dayton Peace Agreement 1995, Art II, Annex 1A: 3. Also, 1994 Washington Agreement, s VI. For Security Council comments on aspects of this problem, see S/RES/752 (1992, May 15); S/RES 757 (1992, May 30); S/RES/762 (1992, June 30); S/RES/787 (1992, Nov 16); S/RES/802 (1993, Jan 25); S/RES/787 (1992, Nov 16).

The Dayton Peace Accord was not talking about the advisors, trainers and consultants who were providing assistance to the United Nations or NATO-led forces. Rather, it was only referring to those providing such assistance to any of the belligerents who were signatories to the peace treaty. This is an important point, because by this time one in every 10 of such people was a civilian under contract. This figure had grown rapidly since the first Gulf War in 1991, when it was one in 50. By the new century, 'private contractors' were ubiquitous. These people, floating under the label 'contractor', had developed a certain legitimacy to be on a battlefield via the 1899, 1907, 1929 and 1949 conventions, and appeared on at least 50 battlefields from Chechnya to Iraq. More often than not, these soldiers were employed at the behest of a sovereign State, and rarely for United Nations' operations such as peacekeeping, where, if tightly controlled, they may have some merit. At other times, these soldiers have been employed by insurgent groups and/or criminal gangs, such as in Mexico and Columbia, where drug cartels have been schooled (and supported) in military tactics and counter-surveillance tactics.[435]

Companies within the United States and the United Kingdom are responsible for the provision of more than 70 per cent of private military services in the very lucrative world market. However, large amounts of private military services are also provided by companies in countries like Russia, which have been active in Chechyna, Azerbaijan, Armenia and Kazakhstan. In this regard, an estimated 30,000 Russian mercenaries are believed to have fought in the various wars of the former Soviet Union, and more than 2,000 Russians fought in the former Yugoslavia. In the western realm of influence, in 2008, the estimated economic value of contracts going to 'private contractors' in Iraq and Afghanistan alone was between US$20 and US$100 billion per year, with former special services soldiers, in some instances, being able to earn thousands of dollars per day. In 2008, in Iraq, the number of 'private contractors' fulfilling a number of military and quasi-military tasks varied according to different sources and the manner in which they were counted. The figures range between 20,000 and 130,000 persons, operating through at least 28 private security firms. Most estimates agree on a figure of between 20,000 and 50,000 foreign armed 'private contractors' – compared to an estimated 157,000 American troops at the peak of their occupation. In Afghanistan, the figure of non-official military, non-Afghani contractors is around 8,000, with around 4,000 of these being 'security' focused. The death rate for security contractors in Iraq passed 1,000 in the middle of 2007. A further 13,000 have been wounded.[436] These contractors have come to play a vital role in the American effort in these countries, or as the United States Under-Secretary of State for Management,

[435] Human Rights Council (2009) 'Report of the Working Group on Mercenaries' A/HRC/10/14, Paras 38–74; Human Rights Council (2008) 'Report of the Working Group on Mercenaries' A/HRC/7/7, Paras 27 and 38; Commission on Human Rights (2004) 'Report of the Special Rapporteur on Mercenaries' E/CN4/2005/14, Para 55; Commission on Human Rights (1999) 'Report of the Special Rapporteur on Mercenaries' E/CN4/1999/11, Para 80; Commission on Human Rights (2003) 'Report of the Special Rapporteur on Mercenaries' E/CN4/2004/15, Paras 43–47; Commission on Human Rights (2002) 'Report of the Special Rapporteur on Mercenaries' E/CN4/2003/16 Para 19; Geraghty, T (2007) *Guns For Hire* (London, Portrait) 139, 156–58, 248; Clapham, A (2006) 'Human Rights Obligations of Non-State Actors in Conflict Situations' 88(863) *IRRC* 491; Cameron, L (2006) 'Private Military Companies: Their Status Under International Humanitarian Law' 88 (863) *IRRC* 573, 582; Fallah, K (2006) 'The Legal Status of Mercenaries in Armed Conflict' 88 (863) *IRRC* 599. Singer, P (2008) *Corporate Warriors* (London, Cornell University Press) 14–17, 43.

[436] Human Rights Council (2008) *Report of the Working Group on Mercenaries* A/HRC/7/7, Para 30; Singer, P (2008) *Corporate Warriors* (London, Cornell University Press) 12–13, 37.

Patrick Kennedy (b 1949) explained 'we cannot operate without private security firms in Iraq. If the contractors were removed, we would have to leave Iraq.'[437]

Due to such an importance, the United States administration went to great lengths to attempt to regulate the contractors themselves, rather than having them dealt with domestically by Iraqi authorities. This proved increasing problematic in the last years of the decade when some of these contractors were involved in the deaths of civilians and could not be prosecuted by Iraqi authorities. As such, when the response of the American authorities was felt to be inadequate, the Iraqi authorities did the only thing they could and demanded that the employees of the particular security contractor involved leave the country.[438]

E. Formal and Informal Combatants

The question of formal and informal combatants did not advance far directly after the Second World War. In France alone, some 2,200 German soldiers who had given orders to shoot partisans were tried. The principles by which such men were judged were broadly given out at the Nuremberg trials, such as that of Gerhard Flesch (1909–48). Flesch, who was found guilty of the murder and torture of Norwegian resistance fighters, was convicted due to the following two considerations. First, it was held that 'when such acts of sabotage were carried out by soldiers in uniform, they did not constitute a breach of international law'.[439] Secondly, even if such acts were carried out by soldiers not in uniform, they still had some rights, such as the right to a fair trial to determine their status.[440] It was added in the Bruns case that 'they had no rights as soldiers as long as they did not appear in uniform, they did not bear marks of distinction and did not carry their arms openly. They could, therefore, be shot when caught.'[441]

However, if they wore distinguishing marks such as a tricolour armband and/or army fatigues, carried their arms openly, were clearly well organised and coordinated, followed the laws of war and clearly held territory, then it was arguable that they may have been classified as lawful combatants with the same rights as prisoners of war if captured.[442] In addition, failure to meet these criteria did not lead to the conclusion that such irregulars had no rights at all. Both the Nuremberg[443] and Tokyo[444] war

[437] Kennedy noted in 'Verbatim' *TIME* (22 May 2008) 10.

[438] Human Rights Council (2008) Report of the Working Group on Mercenaries A/HRC/7/7, Paras 34, 45, 46 and 47; AP 'Private Security Operatives Ordered to Leave Country' *New Zealand Herald* (12 Feb 2010) A16; Risen, J 'End of Immunity Worries US Contractors in Iraq' *NY Times* (1 Dec 2008) A14; Reuters 'Blackwater News Angers Citizens' *New Zealand Herald* (7 April 2008) B2.

[439] Law Reports of Trials of War Criminals: United Nations War Crimes Commission (1948) Trial of Ernst Flesch, Case No 36, Vol VI (London, HMSO) 115.

[440] Law Reports of Trials of War Criminals: United Nations War Crimes Commission (1948) Trial of Ernst Flesch, Case No 36, Vol VI (London, HMSO) 111.

[441] Law Reports of Trials of War Criminals: United Nations War Crimes Commission. Trial of Richard Bruns, Case No 12, Vol III (London, HMSO).

[442] UN War Crimes Commission, Law Reports of the Trials of War Criminals (1949) The Trial of Carl Bauer, Case No 45, Vol VIII (London, HMSO) 1.

[443] UN War Crimes Commission, Law Reports of the Trials of War Criminals (1948) The Trial of Oscar Hans, Case No 34, Vol VI (London, HMSO) 83.

[444] UN War Crimes Commission, Law Reports of the Trials of War Criminals (1948) The Trial of Shigeru Ohashi, Case No 26, Vol V (London, HMSO) 1.

crimes tribunals emphasised that those suspected of being partisans or resistance had some basic rights like not being tortured and that they could not be summarily executed, and must be given a fair trial first to determine their status.[445]

Following directly on from Nuremberg, the international community assembled in Geneva to renew and update the laws of war. In this regard, it is notable that despite the fact that informal soldiers played such a significant part in the Second World War, the law that evolved afterwards did not change dramatically to accommodate them. Some countries, like the United Kingdom, did not want it to advance at all. However, following prolonged debate, the Third Geneva Convention on Prisoners of War came to recognise that a new type of combatant could be granted prisoner of war status if captured. These were 'members of other militias and members of other volunteer corps, including those of organized resistance movements, belonging to a Party to the conflict and operating in or outside their own territory, even if this territory is occupied, provided that such militias or volunteer corps, including such organized resistance movements, fulfil the following conditions'.[446]

Although this was a clear stop to the efforts of the French Resistance, if members of the militia or other volunteer corps, including organised resistance movements, wanted prisoners of war rights, they still had to fulfil the traditional conditions of being commanded by a person responsible for his subordinates; having a fixed distinctive sign recognisable at a distance; carrying arms openly and conducting their operations in accordance with the laws and customs of war.[447] Even if the irregulars failed to satisfy these considerations they were still entitled to 'enjoy the protection of the present Convention until such time as their status has been determined by a competent tribunal'.[448] If a finding was made that they were not lawful combatants, their fate was in the hands of their captors. In such situations, when dealing people like spies, their fate could be dire. That is, although the 1949 Convention (IV) Relative to the Protection of Civilian Persons in Time of War, placed vast amounts of new restraints on occupying forces, an exception was clearly made for civilians involved in spying. Specifically, Article 68 stipulated that the death penalty could be applied 'in cases where the person is guilty of espionage'.[449]

Despite the fact that the laws of war on this question were not effectively changed, the use of irregular forces continued to increase exponentially. They were especially attractive to peoples who were, according to Mao 'inferior in arms' and fighting 'a more powerful aggressor nation'.[450] Following through, insurgency warfare was recorded in the conflicts of, amongst others, Angola, Bolivia, Borneo, China, Columbia, the Congo, Costa Rica, Cuba, Cyprus, East Timor, El Salvador, Greece, Guatemala, Hungary, Lebanon, Malaysia, Mozambique, Nicaragua, Nigeria, Pakistan, Paraguay, the Philippines,

[445] UN War Crimes Commission, Law Reports of the Trials of War Criminals (1949) The Trial of Nickolaus Von Falkenhorst, Case No 61, Vol XI (London, HMSO) 28–29; Law Reports of Trials of War Criminals: United Nations War Crimes Commission (1945) The Almelo Trial, Case No 3, Vol I (London, HMSO) 35; Law Reports of Trials of War Criminals: United Nations War Crimes Commission, Trial of Richard Bruns, Case No 12, (London, HMSO) Also, the Trial of Eitaro Shinohara (1948) Case No 27, Vol V (London, HMSO) 33.

[446] Geneva III, Art IV(2).

[447] Geneva III, Art IV (2)(a)–(d) Also, Best, G (1980) *Humanity in Warfare* (London, Weidenfeld) 298; Best, G (2002) *War and Law Since 1945* (Oxford, Oxford University Press) 130–31.

[448] Geneva III, Art V.

[449] See also Convention on Civilians 1949, Art 5.

[450] Mao Tse Tung (2005) *On Guerrilla Warfare* (NYC, Dover).

Rhodesia, Sri Lanka, Sudan, and Venezuela. Some instances, as discussed below, are particularly instructive for in these conflicts the insurgent that Mao labeled a guerrilla stopped 'mov[ing] among the people as a fish swims in the sea' and became closer to a shark, preferring to attack the very non-combatants they hid within. This was especially so if the non-combatants were not on 'their' side. The difficulty this presented is that at this point the nomenclature between the guerrilla and the terrorist is hard to disentangle. In an ideal world, there would be strong lines demarcating the differences between guerrillas and terrorists. In theory, guerrillas try to operate as military units, sometimes in uniform, attacking enemy military forces and seizing and holding territory while also exercising some form of sovereignty or control over a defined area and its population. Terrorists, however, rarely function in the open as armed units, do not wear uniforms, do not attempt generally to capture or control territory, and usually seek to avoid engaging enemy military forces. Guerrillas are meant to be highly disciplined and do not target civilian populations. According to Lenin 'evil does not exist in guerrilla warfare but only in the unorganised and undisciplined activities that are anarchism'.[451] Likewise, Mao was clear that 'vagabonds and vicious people must not be accepted for service' as guerrillas. Moreover, guerrillas must not steal, be selfish or unjust, and must be courteous and honest. This is because 'it is only undisciplined troops who make the people their enemies and who, like the fish out of its native element, cannot live'.[452] Fundamentally, Mao recognised that his revolution required the support of the peasants, and men who were without scruples, were unkind, or even unhelpful towards poor peasants would directly hurt his campaign. Che Guevara (1928–67) added to this thinking by arguing that it is the support of the people that makes them different from 'gangs of bandits'.[453] However, even if they were different to gangs of bandits, they were not synonymous with lawful combatants who had the right to prisoner of war status, as testified by the execution of Guevara in Bolivia in 1967.

In theory, guerrillas are not terrorists because they have standards. Conversely, terrorists wage war by their own standards, not those of anyone else and often have little regard to other people, armed or not. This means that terrorists are rarely driven by goals of self-aggrandisement, fiscal or social gain. This is a defining characteristic which explains why terrorists are often not like common criminals. When a criminal employs violence as a means to obtain money, acquire material goods or to kill or injure, they are acting primarily for personal motivations which are typically selfish. Conversely, the fundamental aim of the terrorist is publicity and changing governmental policies. Criminals rarely seek to change governmental or social policies but this is often the primary goal of the terrorist. Ironically, the terrorist is fundamentally an altruist (or at least, a violent intellectual) as he or she believes they are serving a good cause for a wider cause or community. Of course, any insurgent, guerrilla or otherwise, may share exactly the same goal. The problem this causes is, quite simply, the overlap between guerrillas and terrorists, who can both act clandestinely and are both prone to the use of tactics which are identified as crimes of war or crimes against humanity, makes any attempt at distinction ridiculous.[454] That is, between 1945 and 1977 irregular forces, most of which would have

[451] Lenin, noted in Mao Tse Tung (2005) *On Guerrilla Warfare* (NYC, Dover) 46.

[452] Mao Tse Tung (2005) *On Guerrilla Warfare* (NYC, Dover) 87, 92–93.

[453] Deutschmann, D (ed) (1987) *Che Guevara and the Cuban Revolution* (Sydney, Pathfinder) 78.

[454] Chaliand, G (2007) *The History of Terrorism* (Berkeley, University of California Press) 24–31; Hoffman, B (1998) *Inside Terrorism* (London, Indigo) 14; Whittaker, D (ed) (2001) *The Terrorism Reader* (London, Routledge) 4–13, 18; Carr, C (2002) *The Lessons of Terror: A History of Warfare Against Civilians* (NY, Little) 122; Gasser, H (2002) 'Acts of Terror, Terrorism and International Humanitarian Law' *IRRC* 847, 547, 553;

failed the tests of the Third Geneva Convention with regards to being identifiable and distinguished from civilian populations, also operated outside the requirements of having to comply with the laws of war as they were recognised in 1949. This was especially so with regards to Article 33 of the 1949 Convention (IV) Relative to the Protection of Civilian Persons in Time of War which explicitly prohibited collective penalties, reprisals and all measures of intimidation or of terrorism against civilians. It was clearly added '[a]ll measures of intimidation or of terrorism are prohibited.'

Despite this very simple rule that the use of terror against civilians was prohibited, the converse often became the practice in the coming decades with warfare including other than formal combatants. This problem became evident directly after the Second World War in what became Israel, when two irregular Jewish groups, Stern and Irgun, inter alia, blew up hotels which housed British targets but still caused large-scale collateral damage, massacred hundreds of local unarmed Arab civilians, executed captured British soldiers as reprisals, and assassinated the United Nations envoy (Count Folke Bernadotte 1895–1948) and associated staff.[455] In decades to come, a number of forces aligned against Israel would come to utilise a very similar logic as they would shoot rockets, indiscriminately, into civilian areas. This choice of target was decided because it was suggested that all Israeli people are legitimate targets as many of them are in the military and, even if they are not, they are on occupied lands and have lost their right to civilian status.[456] Similarly, Osama bin Laden justified the deaths of 'women and children' whom he later denied were 'innocents' (due to their complicity with the American regime) as a type of reprisal by his assertion that American-led forces and their allies kill many more Muslim non-combatants than him. Moreover, 'American people are not exonerated from their responsibilities . . . to kill the American and their allies – civilian and military – is an individual duty incumbent upon every Muslim'. Only after 9/11 did he suggest that 'the balance of terror has evened out between the Muslims and the Americans.'[457]

After the initial examples in the Middle East, such practices quickly accelerated in other hotspots, such as Algeria, which became engulfed in a civil war in the late 1950s and early 1960s. That is, by the second half of 1961 it was estimated that there was an average of 3,000 acts of terror per month, as executions, torture, reprisals, assassinations and bombs attacks against civilians, in both France and Algeria, became the norm and civilians became the primary, not the supplemental, target.[458]

Post, J (1998) '*Terrorist Behaviour as a Product of Psychological Forces*' in Reich, W (ed) *The Origins of Terrorism* (Baltimore, John Hopkins University Press) 25–38. Crenshaw, M (1981) 'The Causes of Terrorism' *Comparative Politics* July 381–85. Jenkins, B (1986) 'Defence Against Terrorism' *Political Science Quarterly* 101, 779–90; Gurr, N (2000) *The New Face of Terrorism* (London, Taurus) 86, 88, 114–17, 119, 163–94.

455 Fisk, R (2006) *The Great War for Civilisation: The Conquest of the Middle East* (London, Harper) 453–59; Sinclair, A (2003) *An Anatomy of Terror* (London, Macmillan) 278–81. For the Security Council concerns on the assassination, see S/RES/72 (1949, Aug 11); Moorehead, C (1998) *Dunant's Dream: War, Switzerland and the History of the Red Cross* (NYC, Carroll & Graf) 565.

456 Fisk, R (2006) *The Great War for Civilisation: The Conquest of the Middle East* (London, Harper) 589.

457 Lawrence, B (ed) *Messages to the World: The Statements of Osama Bin Laden* (London, Verso) 40, 47. 51, 61, 106–107, 114, 119, 140–41, 162–67. Also, Slim, H (2008) *Killing Civilians* (NYC, Columbia University Press) 172–74. Coll, S (2005) *Ghost Wars* (London, Penguin) 279–80; Karsh, E (2006) *Islamic Imperialism. A History* (NYC, Yale University Press,) 222–28; Associated Press 'We Don't Kill Innocents' *New Zealand Herald* (4 April 2008) B.2.

458 Horne, A (2006) A *Savage War of Peace: Algeria 1954–1962* (NYC, New York Review of Books) 84, 86, 88, 93–94, 115, 119, 121, 135, 185–86, 192, 209–10, 441, 470, 486, 503, 534; Harclerode, P (2002) *Fighting Dirty* (London, Cassell) 223, 230–33, 243, 262; Fisk, R (2006) *The Great War for Civilisation: The Conquest of the Middle East* (London, Harper) 665–75.

The novelty of the Algerian situation was not that insurgents would target civilians, but that acts of terror were being perpetuated by both non-governmental insurgents and insurgents linked to the State. In theory, this presents a problem as the assumption is that all insurgents, guerrillas or terrorists, are non-governmental. However, in practice, in multiple domestic contexts, the creation of bodies which practiced terror upon civilians or opponents to governing regimes became entrenched after the Second World War as pro-government non-State armed groups – the euphemism for what is known as 'death squads' proliferated. The difference between pro-government non-State armed groups and other forms of State-based terror, as manifested in both the French and Russian Revolutions, is that the pro-government groups are clandestine and usually paramilitary irregular organisations operating without uniforms or other forms of identification. These groups carry out extrajudicial executions and other violent acts such as torture, rape, bombing and so on against clearly defined individuals or groups of people. They operate with the overt support, complicity, or acquiescence of governments or at least parts of it. As such, they are authorised and are not vigilantes (although there is often an overlap), nor are they individual assassins targeting one or two people. The importance of being linked to the authorities but not explicitly approved by them is that it allows the real authorities to possess 'deniability' over acts which they want done which are outside the rule of law and would otherwise be considered illegal in national, if not international, law. Accordingly, death squads are particuarly attractive options in times of civil war, when the boundaries between what is lawful and what is not often get blurred and formal State control of belligerents is hard to define. In such situations, para-military groups quickly proliferate. For example, Serbia had at least 84 separate paramilitary formations by 1994 operating in conjunction with the formal armed forces.[459]

It is by such methods of informal combatants being linked to State forces that many governments have sought to fight in recent decades. This has especially been the case in civil wars. The results have been high death rates for insurgents and associated civilians in conflicts which have spilled into civil war without restraint in the decades following the Second World War, and into the first decade of the twenty-first century. The conflicts of note include, amongst others, Angola,[460] Argentina,[461] Chile,[462] Columbia,[463] Indonesia,[464]

[459] Glenny, M (1996) *The Fall of Yugoslavia* (London, Penguin) 101, 104, 111, 184–85, 204.

[460] Turner, J (1998) *Continent Ablaze: The Insurgency Wars in Africa* (London, Cassell) 116–17, 121.

[461] Scheina, R (2003) *Latin America's War. The Age of the Professional Soldier, 1900–2001*, Vol II (NYC, Brassey's) 298–99.

[462] Inter-American Commission on Human Rights: Report on the Status of Human Rights in Chile 14 ILM (1975) 115; Human Rights Watch (2003) *The Discreet Path to Justice? Chile, Thirty Years After the Military Coup* (NYC, HRW).

[463] Human Rights Watch (2010) *Paramilitary Heirs* (NYC, HRW) 2–9, 14–23, 25–29; Human Rights Watch (2002) *Columbia* (NYC, HRW) 7–19; Human Rights Watch (2001) *The Sixth Division: Military Paramilitary Ties in US Policy in Columbia* (NYC, HRW); Human Rights Watch (2001) *Columbia: Beyond Negotiation: International Humanitarian Law and its Application to the Conduct of the FARC* (NYC, HRW) 9–14; *Human Rights Watch (1998) Columbia and International Humanitarian Law* (NYC, HRW) 5–9; Human Rights Watch (1994) *State of War: Political Violence and Counterinsurgency in Columbia* (NYC, HRW).

[464] Totten, S (2004) *Century of Genocide* (London, Routledge) 233–37, 277–78.

Nicaragua,[465] Peru,[466] Rwanda,[467] Somalia,[468] Spain[469] South Africa,[470] and Uganda.[471] In some cases, such as with Guatemala, this meant that over 93 per cent of violations of human rights and/or humanitarian law were attributable to the State or State aligned forces (with the 'Civil Patrols' being directly accountable for 18 per cent of the atrocities). Similar figures appeared with El Salvador, with the insurgents only be credited by their Truth Commission for about 5 per cent of all of the atrocities registered, with the rest going to forces of the State (of which Civil Defence and Death Squads being attributed 20 per cent and 10 per cent respectively).[472]

In one instance, the death squads, such as those shared between Argentina, Bolivia, Brazil, Chile, Paraguay and Uruguay became international with what became known as Operation Condor. This group managed to secretly trade and torture suspected opponents, and assassinated political opponents in a number of countries including the former Chilean Foreign Minister Orlando Letelier (1932–76) by detonating a car bomb in downtown Washington.[473] These groups act outside the rule of law either nationally or internationally. Accordingly, peace within the societies that they operate in is only possible when there is, in the words of the Northern Ireland Peace Agreement, a 'total [and verified] disarmament of all paramilitary organizations',[474] or as with the peace in Guatemala, a commitment by the Government that there would be no illegal security forces or 'clandestine security machinery' bearing arms.[475]

Before peace can be reached in these countries, the difficulty is, and was, that such violence against non-combatants rarely makes opponents cower, but more than likely helps them adopt the same regressive approach, with civilians, not combatants, becoming the primary target of operations. Such practices do not, as the International Court of Justice politely suggested in 1984 with regard to the United States support for the Contra insurgents in Nicaragua, 'ensure respect' for the goals of the 1949 Geneva Conventions.[476] This, of course, is an understatement as for many insurgent groups, from Columbia to Iraq between 1980 and the twenty-first century, civilians have been come the prize target.[477] This became evident in the wars in Central and South

[465] Scheina, R (2003) *Latin America's War: The Age of the Professional Soldier, 1900–2001*, Vol II (NYC, Brassey's) 282–83, 351.

[466] The Peruvian Truth and Reconciliation Commission (2003) *Final Report* (Lima). 39–51; Strong, S (1992) *Shining Path* (NYC, Fontana) 104–107, 137–43.

[467] Totten, S (2004) *Century of Genocide* (London, Routledge) 400–401.

[468] Turner, J (1998) *Continent Ablaze: The Insurgency Wars in Africa* (London, Cassell) 192–95.

[469] Burleigh, M (2008) *Blood and Rage. A Cultural History of Terrorism* (London, Harper) 278–80, 284.

[470] Truth and Reconciliation Commission (2003) *South Africa Report* (TRC, Cape Town) 720–25.

[471] Campbell, B (2000) *Death Squads in Global Perspective* (London, St Martin's) 1–17.

[472] Historical Clarification Commission (1999) *The Guatemala Memory of Silence* (Guatemala) 82, 92–94; Report of the United Nations Truth Commission on El Salvador, S/25500 (1 April 1993) 54–92, 127–53.

[473] Dinges, J (2005) *The Condor Years* (NYC, New Press) 1, 4–7, 46, 77, 111, 131–32, 153, 174, 182–83, 191; Hitchens, C (2001) *The Trial of Henry Kissinger* (Melbourne, Text) 68–69.

[474] The Northern Ireland Peace Agreement 1998, s 7.

[475] Comprehensive Agreement on Human Rights 1994, s IV. Also, the Agreement on the Strengthening of Civilian Power and on the Role of the Armed Forces in a Democratic Society 1996, Art 60. See also the examples for, inter alia, Kosovo (S/RES/1244 (1999, June 10), S/RES/1345 (2001, Mar 21) and the General Peace Agreement for Mozambique 1992, Protocol IV, s III.

[476] Case concerning the Military and Paramilitary Activities in and Against Nicaragua (*Nicaragua v United States of America* ICJ (1986), para 255 and 129–30.

[477] Human Rights Watch (2006) *The Human Cost: The Consequences of Insurgent Attacks in Afghanistan* (NYC, HRW) 2–12, 7–101; Human Rights Watch (2006) *A Face and a Name: Civilian Victims of Insurgent Groups* (NYC, HRW) 17–23, 34–38, 42, 51–69; Human Rights Watch (2001) *Columbia: Beyond Negotiation: International Humanitarian Law and its Application to the Conduct of the FARC* (NYC, HRW) 11–13; Lacayo, J (2000)

America, as civilians became continually targeted in the wars of, amongst others, Columbia, El Salvadaor, Guatemala and Peru.[478] In all of these conflicts, the intentional killing of civilians was an established part of the warfare of both the government forces and the insurgents. The differences, as various truth commissions have come to ascertain is (as noted above) in the percentages of responsibility. Thus, whilst State lead forces were responsible for the majority of extra-judicial killings, disappearances and torture in Guatemala and El Salvador, the same has not been concluded for Peru. This was not surprising as the Shining Path operated in Peru viewing as legitimate targets 'all vestiges of bureaucratic capitalism', which included bombing everything from shops to churches to fast food restaurants, in which nearly 30,000 civilians would die.[479]

F. The Lines Blur on the Question of Identification

The war in Vietnam was the defining conflict before which the issue of identification of combatants was again examined by the international community in 1977. This conflict was particularly messy. From the early 1950s, the Viet Minh had learnt in their fight with the French the value of disguising their combatants as civilians. They had also learnt to link guerrilla warfare against French soldiers with terrorism against non-combatants. Although the American forces came to use some informal insurgents in their combat in Vietnam (and the Southern Vietnamese government employed its own death squads), this was an art of warfare perfected by the Viet Cong. As such, their use of 'part time' combatants disguised as civilians who inflicted terror upon non-combatants became entrenched. Sometimes the terror was selective, so that its victims could be explained away by communist propaganda as collaborators, exploiters or criminals. At other times, the terror was indiscriminate, via the explosion of bombs in public places, so as to create a climate of insecurity and undermine assertions that the populace was safe.[480] The United States correctly pointed out that many of these insurgents relied 'heavily on disguise and disregard[ed] generally accepted principles of warfare'.[481] This meant that American forces were often at a disadvantage. Indeed, the ground forces of the United States only had the initiative in 14 per cent of engagements. The United States and the ICRC emphasised the fact that it was only those captured 'wearing uniform or bearing an emblem clearly indicating his membership of the armed forces' who had a right to be made a prisoner of war.[482] Although the Americans unlike their South Vietnamese allies did not execute such captives, allowed

'International Humanitarian Law and Irregular Warfare: Lessons Learnt in Latin America' *IRRC* 840 941–51.

[478] Scheina, R (2003) *Latin America's War. The Age of the Professional Soldier, 1900–2001*, Vol II (NYC, Brassey's) 190, 214–20.

[479] The Peruvian Truth and Reconciliation Commission (2003) *Final Report* (Lima) 13, 18; Strong, S (1992) *Shining Path* (NYC, Fontana) 103, 164, 217–21.

[480] Corbett, R (1986) *Guerrilla Warfare* (London, Orbis) 59, 96–98, 104–10; Beckett, I (2001) *Modern Insurgencies and Counter-Insurgencies* (London Routledge) 81; Harclerode, P (2002) *Fighting Dirty* (London, Cassel) 467.

[481] Reply of the United States to the Letter of the International Committee of the Red Cross 4 ILM (1965) 1171.

[482] Letter of the International Committee of the Red Cross 4 ILM (1965) 1171. The figure of 14% is from Bourke, J (2000) *An Intimate History of Killing* (London, Granta) 203.

ICRC visits to them and treated them humanely before exchanging them for American captives in 1973, they were clearly within their rights to execute the captives captured out of uniform.[483]

Despite this leniency which the United States was not obliged to follow, when the question came up in international organisations in the 1970s, it was clear that a change in emphasis was occurring. For example, in 1970, the United Nations General Assembly voted that 'all freedom fighters under detention shall be treated in accordance with the relevant provisions of the [1949] Geneva Convention Relative to the Treatment of Prisoners of War'.[484] A very similar suggestion was reiterated in 1973, in an attempt to give those fighting against 'colonial' or 'racist' regimes combatant status during conflicts and prisoner of war status if captured. This was particuarly so with Portugal, of whom the General Assembly demanded that they 'treat the freedom fighters of Angola and Mozambique captured during the struggle as prisoners of war in accordance with the principles of the [1949] Geneva Convention relative to the Treatment of Prisoners of War'.[485] This clear change of emphasis manifested itself in the Additional Protocol to the Geneva Conventions of 1977. In particular, it was agreed that whilst all combatants were obliged to comply with the rules of international law applicable in armed conflict, violations of these rules should not automatically deprive a combatant of their right to be a legitimate combatant or prisoner of war if captured.[486] The broad approach was that those who were allowed to legitimately partake in combat were:

> The armed forces of a Party to a conflict consisting of all organized armed forces, groups and units which are under a command responsible to that Party for the conduct or its subordinates, even if that Party is represented by a government or an authority not recognized by an adverse Party. Such armed forces shall be subject to an internal disciplinary system which, inter alia, shall enforce compliance with the rules of international law applicable in armed conflict.[487]

Thus, any such combatant who falls into the power of an adverse Party shall be a prisoner of war.[488] The important difference from the earlier Hague and Geneva Conventions was that in 1977 it was agreed that, although combatants are obliged to distinguish themselves from the civilian population (and feigning of civilian, non-combatant status was recognised as an act of perfidy),[489] 'there are situations in armed conflicts where, owing to the nature of the hostilities an armed combatant cannot so distinguish himself'.[490] Nevertheless, they were still meant to distinguish themselves from civilians at the time of an attack by carrying their arms openly and having a distinctive sign.[491] Failure to do so meant they could not be considered prisoners of

[483] Forsythe, D (2005) *The Humanitarians: The International Committee of the Red Cross* (Cambridge, Cambridge University Press) 77. Note also the Reply of the Republic of Vietnam to the Letter of the International Committee of the Red Cross 4 ILM (1965) 1171.

[484] UNGA Res 2621 (XXV) Programme of Action for the Full Implementation of the Declaration on the Granting of Independence to Colonial Countries and Peoples (1970).

[485] See UNGA Res 3103 (XXVIII) Basic Principles of the Legal Status of Combatants Struggling Against Colonial and Alien Domination and Racist Regimes (1973); UNGA Res 3113 (XXVIII) Questions of Territories Under Portuguese Administration (1973).

[486] 1977, Protocol 1. See Arts 4 and 44(2).

[487] 1977, Protocol 1, Art 43.

[488] 1977, Protocol 1, Art 44

[489] 1977, Protocol 1, Art 44 (3)(b) which links into Art 37(1)(c) which prohibited perfidy.

[490] 1977, Protocol 1, Art 44(3).

[491] 1977, Protocol 1, Art 44(3).

war.[492] Consequently, the Protocol relaxed the obligation to wear a distinctive sign at all times and sufficed those engaged in warfare only to distinguish themselves from the civilian population during military engagements and immediately before launching an attack.[493] Despite the fact that the combatant had to distinguish themselves at the time of the combat, the fact that they did not have to before and after the combat meant that the United States would not sign Additional Protocol I. This was:

> [B]ecause it would give a special status to wars of 'national liberation' – an ill defined concept expressed in vague, subjective, politicized terminology [and it] would grant combatant status to irregular forces, even if they do not satisfy the traditional requirements to distinguish themselves from the civilian population and otherwise comply with the laws of war.[494]

Although the United States was involved in other conflicts before 2001, it was with the war in Afghanistan that the consequences of their earlier refusal to accept Protocol I of 1972 was clearly displayed when large numbers of people were captured without uniforms, insignia or obvious command structures. The United States explained:

> Under Article 4 of the Geneva Convention . . . Taliban detainees are not entitled to Prisoner of War status . . . The Taliban have not effectively distinguished themselves from the civilian population of Afghanistan. Moreover, they have not conducted their operations in accordance with the laws and customs of war . . . Al Qaeda is an international terrorist group and cannot be considered a state Party to the Geneva Convention. Its members, therefore, are not covered by the Geneva Convention.[495]

Although George W Bush promised to treat the detainees 'humanely', he added that they would be tried and if they were found to have committed any offences they could 'be punish[ed] in accordance with the penalties provided under applicable law, including life imprisonment or death'.[496] The strict Special Military Tribunals, which were of direct interest to other countries involved in similar conflicts,[497] were separated from many basic due process rights (such as allowance of hearsay evidence, limited rights for challenging evidence, limited choice of legal representation and verdicts not needing to be unanimous), under which hundreds of captured insurgent from both Afghanistan and Iraq were expected to be tried. In doing so, it was suggested that 'different rules have to apply' and that Geneva Convention III on Prisoners of War was 'obsolete' in the so-called 'war on terror' as the detainees were fundamentally not lawful combatants.[498] However, before this process could get fully underway, and despite the hopes of the Bush administration that the base at Guantanamo Bay was outside

[492] 1977, Protocol 1, Art 44(4) and 44(5).

[493] See Preux, J (1997) 'The Protocol's Additional to the Geneva Conventions' *IRRC* 320 473–82.

[494] Message from the President Transmitting Protocol II Additional to the Geneva Conventions 26 ILM (1987) 561.

[495] US Statement on Taliban Detainees in Response of the United States to Request for Precautionary Measures 41 ILM (2002) 1015.

[496] The Presidential Military Order on the Detention, Treatment and Trial of Certain Non-Citizens in the War Against Terrorism 41 ILM (2002) 252. Also, Executive Order on Common Article 3 of the Geneva Conventions 46 ILM (2007) 978.

[497] For this discussion in Israel, see *Anonymous v The State of Israel* 47 ILM (2008) 766. See also Human Rights Watch (2004) *Undue Process: Terrorism Trials in Southern Chile* (NYC, HRW) 7–19.

[498] Anon 'Easier to Open than Close' *Economist* (26 May 2007) 33; Rose, D (2004) *Guantanamo* (London, Faber) 9–11, 28–29, 32–33; Reuters (2004) 'Rumsfeld Defends Detention Policy' *New Sunday Times* A17; Tyrangiel, J 'And Justice For . . .' *TIME* (26 Nov 2001) 52–54; Human Rights Watch (2002) Presumption of Guilt: Human Rights Abuses of Post September 11 Detainees (NYC, HRW) 7–26; Human Rights Watch (2004) *Neither Just Nor Effective: Indefinite Detention Without Trial in the United Kingdom* (NYC, HRW).

the auspice of the American legal system, a number of challenges quickly presented themselves. The most fundamental of these pertained to Article 5 of Geneva Convention III which stipulated:

> Should any doubt arise as to whether persons, having committed a belligerent act and having fallen into the hands of the enemy, belong to any of the categories enumerated [in Article 4,] such persons shall enjoy the protection of the present Convention until such time as their status has been determined by a competent tribunal.[499]

From this obligation, a succession of human rights authorities suggested, and detainees at Guantanamo Bay demanded, that their status – as if they really were prisoners of war or not held in accordance with Geneva Convention III – must first be determined before the prosecutions could proceed.[500] The United States Supreme Court agreed with this contention. In essence, the principle of *habeas corpus* was applied and therefore the detainees could not just be assumed to be 'unlawful combatants'.[501] The ruling had the practical effect of suspending all military commissions at Guantanamo Bay until a reconstituted military commission could be expressly authorised by an Act of Congress to make sure the prisoners' status could be could be correctly determined.[502] Although the Bush Administration complied with the obligations imposed on it by the Supreme Court and established a new set of Commissions by which prosecutors could still ask for the death penalty, only a few relatively inconsequential detainees were prosecuted, such as Osama bin Laden's driver, Salim Hamden (b 1970), who was given five years' detention for carrying around missiles in Afghanistan.[503] Before more prosecutions could be made, President Barrack Obama (b 1961) required the Guantanamo Bay detention facility and all other places of CIA detention to be closed as 'as soon as possible'. He then tasked the government with developing policies for the detention, trial, transfer or release of persons captured in armed conflicts or as suspected terrorists. As of the end of 2009, more than 220 detainees at Guantanamo Bay were awaiting the outcomes of this process.[504]

[499] Note, this right is elaborated upon in Art 45 of Protocol I – to which the United States is not a Party. For discussion, see Naqvi, Y (2002) 'Doubtful Prisoner of War Status' *IRRC* 847 571–95.

[500] Commission on Human Rights (2006) Situation of Detainees at Guantanamo Bay 45 ILM 716; Inter-American Commission on Human Rights (2006) 'Reiteration and Amplification of Precautionary Measures and Requests for Additional Information on the Detainees at Guantanamo Bay' 45 ILM 671. In addition to Art IV of Geneva Convention III, these groups also emphasised Arts 9 and 14 of the ICCPR. See Zayas, A (2005) 'Human Rights and Indefinite Detention' *IRRC* 87 (857) 15–38. Note the earlier Response of the United States to Request for Precautionary Measures 41 ILM (2002) 1015. And Human Rights Watch (2002) *The Geneva Conventions and Persons Held by US Forces* (NYC, HRW).

[501] See *Hamdi v Rumsfeld* 34 ILM (2004) 1166; *Hamdan v Rumsfeld* 44 ILM (2005) 1276; *Boumediene v Bush* (2008) 47 ILM 647.

[502] See Military Commission Act 2006 in 45 ILM 1246 (2006); Glaberson, W 'US Trials Are Thrown into Doubt' *Herald Tribune* (6 June 2007) 9.

[503] Anon 'The Guantanamo Six' *Economist* (16 Feb 2008) 44–45; AP 'Surprise Rebuke for Pentagon' *New Zealand Herald* (9 Aug 2008) A24.

[504] President Barack Obama's Executive Orders on Guantanamo Bay, Interrogation and Detention of Terror Suspects 48 ILM (2009) 394; Associated Press, 'Guantanamo Trials to Continue' *New Zealand Herald* (10 Oct 2009) A17.

G. Pirates and Terrorists

One area where the international community has achieved clarity is with regards to the illegality of pirates. The United Nations Convention on the Law of the Sea defines piracy as:

> [A]ny illegal acts of violence or detention, or any act of depredation, committed for private ends by the crew or the passengers of a private ship or a private aircraft, and directed on the high seas, against another ship or aircraft, or against persons or property on board such ship or aircraft; or against a ship, aircraft, persons or property in a place outside the jurisdiction of any State.[505]

Military warships or aircraft which have crews which have mutinied are also considered to be pirates.[506] The point of distinction with other forms of informal people using violence to achieve goals is that pirates are pursuing matters 'for private ends' in areas beyond national jurisdictions and are not under the authority of any State. As such, it has been clear since the middle of the twentieth century that any State may (through clearly marked military forces) seize the pirate ship or aircraft when it is operating beyond national boundaries and arrest the persons and seize the property on board.[507] These international rules have been supplemented by the concerns of the Security Council, who have, when dealing with acts like those off the Horn of Africa, called for the deployment of naval vessels and military aircraft for the seizure and disposition of boats, vessels and weapons used in the commission of piracy and armed robbery off Somalia.[508] Such calls have been supplemented by Regional Cooperation Agreements on Combating Piracy and Armed Robbery Against Ships.[509] This rapid increase in international attention has been due to the fact that since the end of the Cold War the problem of piracy had escalated to hundreds of attacks per year. However, of note, there is little dissent against such definitions of piracy or suggested responses to it.[510]

Although the international community has achieved a relative clarity on the topic of piracy, the same cannot be said of terrorism. This is despite the fact that acts done in times of international or non-intentional conflict, intended to spread terror amongst civilians, are prohibited. This point, which was first made in 1949 (as noted above), was reiterated in 1977 in Protocol II to the Geneva Conventions relating to the Protection of Victims of Non-International Armed Conflicts. This clearly stated that 'acts of terrorism' are absolutely prohibited as are 'acts or threats of violence the primary purpose of which is to spread terror among the civilian population'.[511]

In subsequent decades, especially after the Cold War, the unequivocal condemnation of terrorism as a direct threat to international peace and security has been repeatedly

[505] UNCLOS, Art 101. Participation must be voluntary, and may also involve incitement to be a pirate. These rules are based on Arts 15 and 16 of the Convention on the Law of the Sea 1958.

[506] UNCLOS, Art 102.

[507] UNCLOS, Arts 104, 105, 106 and 107. Note, a warship belongs to the armed forces of a State, has distinguishing marks, is under the command of an officer duly commissioned by that State whose name is recorded for that purpose by that State, and is manned by an a crew under regular armed forces discipline. Art 29.

[508] S/RES/1840 (2008, Oct 14); S/RES/1851 (2008, Dec 16); S/RES/1816 (2008, June 2); S/RES/1838 (2008, Oct 7); S/RES/1846 (2008, Dec 2); S/RES/1816.

[509] 44 ILM 826 (2005).

[510] Knight, W 'Pirates Ahoy' *New Scientist* (10 Dec 2005) 40–44; Bowcott, O 'Send Warships To Fight Pirates, Urge Union' *The Guardian* (23 June 2003) 9.

[511] Protocol II, Art 13(2) and 4(2)(d).

recognised by the Security Council in, inter alia, 1989,[512] 1992,[513] 1996,[514] 1998,[515] 1999,[516] 2001,[517] 2002,[518] 2003,[519] and 2004.[520] Such recognition has often been linked to bombing campaigns by terrorist groups which have targeted civilians, such as those in the new century in Columbia,[521] Iraq,[522] Turkey,[523] Spain,[524] Lebanon[525] and London.[526] The General Assembly has mirrored all of these initiatives in the Security Council, concurring that:

> [A]ll acts, methods and practices of terrorism in all its forms and manifestations as criminal and unjustifiable, wherever and by whomsoever committed . . . [irrespective of] the considerations of a political, philosophical, ideological, radical, ethnic, religious or other nature that may be invoked to justify them.[527]

Despite the stern nature of such resolutions, and the Security Council's creation of a Counter Terrorism Committee which keeps a watching eye on related international developments, 'terrorism' or 'terrorists' is a label which is light on legal certainty. It is not, however, bereft of all certainty. What is agreed is that when dealing with the international context, terrorists are non-governmental. That is, although in some instances terrorists may be sponsored by a State, they should not be. If a terrorist group is clearly linked to a sovereign State, the acts of the terrorist may be interpreted as acts of war. As such, it is a clear rule of international law that States should not 'organise, assist, foment, finance, incite or tolerate subversive, terrorist or armed activities directed towards the violent overthrow of the regime of another State, or interfere in civil strife of another State'.[528] This principle, emphasised by the Security Council,[529] has meant that they have had to call upon specific countries or authorities to condemn and/or cooperate in combating terrorism, such as with Libya, (which was placed under embargo for its destruction of Pan Am flight 103 over Scotland in 1988),[530]

512 S/RES/ 635 (1989, June 14).
513 S/RES/ 731 (1992, Jan 21).
514 S/RES/1089 (1996, Dec 13).
515 S/RES/1189 (1998, Aug 13).
516 S/RES/1269 (1999, Oct 19).
517 S/RES/1373 (2001, Sep 28); S/RES/1377 (2001, Nov 12).
518 S/RES/1438 (2002, Oct 14); S/RES/1440 (2002, Oct 24); S/RES/1450 (2002, Dec 13).
519 S/RES/1456 (2003).
520 S/RES/1535 (2004) Mar 26.
521 S/RES/1465 (2003).
522 S/RES/1511 (2003) Oct 16; S/RES/1546 (2004) June 8; S/RES/1618 (2005) Aug 4.
523 S/RES/1516 (2003) Nov 20.
524 S/RES/1530 (2004) Mar 11.
525 S/RES/1595 (2005) Apr 7.
526 S/RES/1611 (2005) July 7.
527 UNGA Resolution (2006) 60/43 Measures to Eliminate International Terrorism.
528 See the Declaration on the Principles of International Law 1970.
529 S/RES/1373 (2001, Sept 28) Note also UNGA Res 39/159. Inadmissibility of the Policy of State Terrorism (1984).
530 This was largely over the 1988 Lockerbie bombing that was only finally resolved through a trial for those accused of the bombing in the Netherlands of which their guilt led to personal payouts by the Libyan government: S/RES/731 (1992, Jan 21); S/RES/748 (1992, Mar 31); S/RES/1192 (1998, Aug 27); Agreement Between the Netherlands and United Kingdom Concerning a Scottish Trial in the Netherlands 38 ILM (1999) 926; ICJ Case Concerning Questions of Interpretation and Application of the 1971 Montreal Convention 37 ILM (1998) 587; *Rein v The Socialist People's Libyan Arab Jamahiriya* 38 ILM (1999) 447; Statements Calling on Libya to Cooperate in Investigations of Aerial Incidents at Lockerbie and in Niger 31 ILM (1992) 717; Anon 'Gaddafi's Confession?' *TIME* (18 Aug 2003) 5; Lederer, E 'Libya To Pay $17 million For Each Lockerbie Victim' *New Zealand Herald* (15 Aug 2003) B3; Henley, J 'Libya Agrees

Iraq,[531] Palestine,[532] Kosovo[533] and Sudan (which was also subject to an economic and travel embargo until it acceded to all of the relevant conventions for the suppression of terrorism).[534] In some instances, such as with Afghanistan, the Security Council from 1996 onwards, was greatly concerned that it was providing 'a fertile ground for terrorism and drug trafficking which destabilised the region and beyond'.[535] Thereafter until September 11, it was repeatedly requesting the Taliban to 'stop providing sanctuary and training for international terrorists and their organizations, and that all Afghan factions co-operate with efforts to bring indicted terrorists to justice'.[536] In particular, the Security Council repeatedly demanded that the Taliban turn over Osama bin Laden to the appropriate authorities in a country where he has been indicted, so that he could be brought to justice.[537] Following the terror attacks on 11 September 2001, which the Security Council recognised as unequivocal 'threats to international peace and security',[538] the failure of the Taliban to hand over Osama bin Laden became the pretext for invasion of Afghanistan.[539] Even since the invasion, the Security Council has kept up its pressure targeting the Al-Qaeda network and its associated terrorist groups. In doing so, since 2005, it has consistently targeted named individuals and their assets.[540]

Aside the agreement that terrorists are not State-related, there is little else when looking for generic rules. This is despite the fact that since the late 1960s there have been repeated attempts to define the term terrorism. For example, following the hostage-taking and execution of children in Beslan in 2004, Russia tried to have terrorism defined as, 'any act intended to cause death or serious injury to hostages with the purpose to provoke a state of terror, intimidate a population or compel a government or international organization to do or to abstain from doing any act'.

However, this definition was rejected after lobbying from several countries that deemed this definition an affront to the principle of national liberation.[541] Similar attempts to define attacks on civilians as the core of terrorism when the United Nations was reformed in 2005 met without resolution. This was despite the Security Council noting in 2005 that terrorism was increasingly linked to the 'indiscriminate targeting of different religions and cultures'.[542]

Payout for French Plane Bombing' *Guardian Weekly* (15 Jan 2004) 7. Note, after it agreed it was responsible and abandoned all of its linkages to terrorist groupings, the Security Council embargo was lifted. See S/RES/1506 (2003, Sept 12).

531 S/RES/687 (1991, Apr 3).

532 S/RES/1435 (2002, Sept 24).

533 S/RES/1160 (1998, Mar 31); S/RES/1199 (1998, Sept 23); S/RES/1202 (1998, Oct 15); S/RES/1345 (2001, Mar 21).

534 S/RES/1372 (2001, Sept 28); S/RES/1054 (1996, Apr 26); S/RES/1070 (1996, Aug 16); S/RES/1044 (1996, Jan 31); S/RES/1054 (1996, Apr 26).

535 S/RES/1076 (1996, Oct 22).

536 S/RES/1193 (1998, Aug 28); S/RES/1214 (1998, Dec 8); S/RES/1267 (1999, Oct 15); S/RES/1333 (2000, Dec 19).

537 S/RES/1267 (1999, Oct 15); S/RES/1333 (2000, Dec 19); S/RES/1390 (2002, Jan 28).

538 S/RES/1368 (2001, Sept 12).

539 S/RES/1368 (2001, Sept 12).

540 S/RES/1526 (2004 Jan 30); S/RES/1617 (2005 July 29); S/RES/1735 (2006 Dec 22); S/RES/1822 (2008, June 30).

541 Bosco, D 'An Indefinable Problem' *Bulletin of Atomic Scientist* (Jan 2006) 44–49.

542 S/RES/1624 (2005, Sept 14). Note also S/RES/1566 (2004, Oct 8).

The rejection by some other members of the international community of a definition that equates terrorism with the intentional targeting of civilians has been due to a belief that some acts of warfare, unlawful in conventional senses, may become lawful if the justification is sufficient. The problem is that there is no agreement on what, if any, are sufficient justifications.[543]

Despite the failure of international law to define terrorists in a generic sense, the international community has made considerable progress in defining them by the acts that they do. This process began in the 1960s, when certain types of acts were becoming of increasing concern to the international community. In some instances, some acts typically associated with terrorism which have failed to achieve international condemnation,[544] like assassination, appear to be coming into focus. For example, in 2009, for the first time, a Special Tribunal for Lebanon was created by the Security Council under Chapter VII of the United Nations Charter, and given jurisdiction over '[p]ersons responsible for the attack . . . resulting in the death of former Lebanese Prime Minister Rafik Hariri and in the death of other persons and certain attacks which preceded the assassination'.[545]

In other instances, the international community has galvanised much more quickly in issuing cohesive condemnations. Post World War II, such condemnations began following the explosion of aircraft mid-flight in 1955, the sinking of passenger vessels in 1961 and the first ever hijacking of an aircraft (from Florida to Cuba – by far the most popular destination for the hijacking terrorist during that decade) in the same year. The response was the 1963 (Tokyo) Convention on Offences and Certain Other Acts Committed on Board Aircraft.[546] This Convention was joined by supplementary conventions in 1970 for the Suppression of Unlawful Seizure of Aircraft[547] and the 1971 Convention for the Suppression of Unlawful Acts Against the Safety of Civil Aviation.[548] These Conventions were in direct response to what the Security Council saw as increasing 'acts of violence resulting in the loss of life of innocent individuals and the endangering of international civil aviation'.[549] The 1979 International Convention Against the Taking of Hostages followed a rash of hostage-taking during the 1970s.[550] The 1988 Protocol for the Suppression of Unlawful Acts of Violence at Airports Serving International Civil Aviation followed some high level attacks on

[543] Whittaker, D (ed) (2001) *The Terrorism Reader* (London, Routledge) 254–57; Hoffman, B (1998) *Inside Terrorism* (London, Indigo) 14; Higgins, R (1997) *Terrorism and International Law* (London, Routledge) 15.

[544] Belfield, R (2005) *Terminate With Extreme Prejudice* (London, Macmillan) xiv–xv, 4, 27, 33, 39, 53–54, 115–18, 133, 135–47, 222, 233. The American example was well explored by the ICJ. See the Case Concerning Military and Paramilitary Activities in and Against Nicaragua, 27 June 1986; General List No 70, Paras 116–18, 120, 255; Human Rights Watch (1993) *A License to Kill: Israeli Undercover Operations* (NYC, HRW); Fisk, R 'Sinister Precedent for Our Brave New World' *New Zealand Herald* (24 Mar 2004) B1; Reuters 'Sharon Makes It Clear: Israel Won't Kill Arafat' *New Zealand Herald* (29 Oct 2003) B2; Raynor, G 'Heat on MPs Over Link to Assassination' *New Zealand Herald* (20 Feb 2010) A24; Reuters 'Revelations Fuel Demand for CIA Probe' *New Zealand Herald* (15 July 2009) A15.

[545] See S/RES/1757. This is also reprinted in 48 ILM (2009) 1149. Also, S/RES/1595 (2005, Apr 7); S/RES/1636 (2005, Oct 31); S/RES/1644 (2005, Dec 15); S/RES/1664 (2006, Mar 29); S/RES/1748 (2007, Mar 27); S/RES/1757 (2007, May 30).

[546] The 1963 (Tokyo) Convention On Offences And Certain Other Acts Committed On Board Aircraft. Australian Treaty Series, 1970 No 14.

[547] 10 ILM (1971) 133; Australian Treaty Series 1972 No 16.

[548] Convention for the Suppression of Unlawful Acts Against the Safety of Civil Aviation 1971, UNTS No 14118, Vol 974, 178–184. Also, 10 ILM (1971) 1151.

[549] S/RES/286 (1970, Sept 9); S/RES/332 (1973, Apr 21); S/RES/337 (1973, Aug 15).

[550] The International Convention Against the Taking of Hostages, A/C6/34/L23, Dec 4, 1979. Also, 18 ILM (1979) 1456.

international civilian airports[551] (including by Israel, much to the ire of the Security Council)[552] and in the same year, the Convention for the Suppression of Unlawful Acts Against the Safety of Maritime Navigation[553] and the Protocol for the Suppression of Unlawful Acts Against the Safety of Fixed Platforms Located on the Continental Shelf were agreed. At the end of the 1990s, the 1997 Convention for the Suppression of Terrorist Bombings[554] was added with the 1999 International Convention for the Suppression of the Financing of Terrorism.[555] In 2005, the International Convention for the Suppression of Acts of Nuclear Terrorism[556] was added to the mix.

In all of the above instances, terrorism has been identified by specific acts rather than by specific types of people. As a starting point, all of the Conventions are of an international context, with the incidents either occurring in international spaces or the perpetuators or property involved being linked to States other than where the incidents occurred.[557] Moreover, in no case can the acts be justified by 'considerations of a political, philosophical, ideological, racial, ethnic, religious or other similar nature'.[558] All of the identified crimes are also linked to civilian – not military – contexts. Thus, the 1979 Hostage Convention specifically excluded hostage situations covered in the Geneva Conventions and their associated Protocols.[559] Likewise, the 1997 Convention did not apply to activities of armed forced as understood and governed by other rules of international law.[560] The 2005 Convention on Nuclear Terrorism also explained that the activities of armed forces of sovereign States were governed by other rules of international law, and not by that Convention.[561] The 1999 Financing Convention gave a clear insight into the overall focus by targeting those who fund:

> Any other act intended to cause death or serious bodily injury to a civilian, or to any other person not taking an active part in the hostilities in a situation of armed conflict, when the purpose of such act, by its nature or context, is to intimidate a population, or to compel a government or an international organization to do or to abstain from doing any act.[562]

After these considerations, each Convention came to focus on their exact context which was recognised as a 'grave concern'. This was the case for the unlawful acts of seizure or exercise of control of aircraft in flight,[563] the taking of hostages[564] or the

[551] For the Convention, see 27 ILM (1988) 627. For the background, see Statements on International Terrorism. 25 ILM (1986) 202.

[552] S/RES/262 (1968, Dec 31).

[553] 27 ILM (1988) 668.

[554] A/52/653 25, Nov 1997 37 ILM (1998) 249.

[555] International Convention for the Suppression of the Financing of Terrorism. This is found in UNGA Resolution (2000) 54/109.

[556] International Convention for the Suppression of Nuclear Terrorism 44 ILM (2005) 815.

[557] Reiterated in Hague 1970, Art 3; Airports 1971, Art 4; Hostages 1979, Art 13; Maritime Navigation 1988, Art 4; Bombing 1997, Art 3; Nuclear 2005, Art 3.

[558] This language is from Art 5 of the Terrorist Bombings Convention 1997. Note also the Preamble to this Convention and that of the Financing Convention. Finally, see UNGA Res 49/60 Measures to Eliminate International Terrorism (1994).

[559] Hostages 1979, Art 12.

[560] Bombings 1997, Art 19.

[561] Art 4.

[562] Financing 1999, Art 2(b).

[563] Hague 1970, Preamble. The Preamble from the 1971 Convention had very similar language. See also UNGA Res 2551 (XXIV); Forcible Diversion of Civil Aircraft in Flight (1969); UNGA Res (XXV); Aerial Hijacking or Interference with Civil Air Travel (1970).

[564] Hostages 1979, Preamble and Art 2.

jeopardising of maritime navigation safety[565] or of fixed platforms attached to the Continental Shelf.[566] In each area, a specific offence is recognised. For example, the 1963 Convention covered acts which jeopardise the safety of aircraft or of persons or property therein.[567] The 1970 Convention was similar to this, but the emphasis of the offence was upon seizing (or attempting to seize) the aircraft 'unlawfully by force or threat thereof'.[568] The 1971 Convention extended the ambit including the destruction of air safety equipment (typically for communication), destroying or damaging the aircraft itself or (with the first international reference to terror bombing):

> [P]laces or causes to be placed on an aircraft in service, by any means whatsoever, a device or substance which is likely to destroy that aircraft, or to cause damage to it which renders it incapable of flight, or . . . is likely to endanger its safety in flight.[569]

For the Maritime Navigation and Fixed Platforms to the Continental Shelf Conventions,[570] the primary offences are in seizing control of the ship (or attempting to or abetting), endangering its safe navigation, placing a device or substance on it likely to endanger it, and destroying navigational facilities which would thereby endanger it.[571] With regard to the international taking of hostages, any person (or their accomplices) who attempts to or succeeds in seizing, detaining or threatening to kill or injure another person (that is a hostage) in order to compel a third party, namely a State, international intergovernmental organisation, a natural or juridical person, or a group of persons, to do or abstain from doing any act as an explicit or implicit condition for the release of the hostage, commits the offence of 'hostage-taking'.[572] The 1997 Bombing Convention stipulated that anyone who either assists in or who directly or intentionally causes death or extensive destruction via the delivery, discharge or detonation of an explosive or similar device into a place of public use commits an offence against the Convention.[573] The 1999 Financing Convention classified anyone who participated, organised or contributed 'directly or indirectly, unlawfully and wilfully' in the collection of funds, with the knowledge that they are to be used, in full or in part, to carry out acts which constitute an offence against any of the earlier Conventions, commits an offence within the context of the Convention.[574] Finally, as if any explanation was necessary, it is a crime to 'possess, use, threaten or participate with an accomplice . . . with radioactive material or device[s] . . . aimed at causing death, injury or damage to the environment'.[575]

In all of the above Conventions, the goal is that countries which have links to where the incident happened, the property involved in the incident, or the people perpetuating it, should seek to establish the jurisdiction of the people involved.[576] States should

[565] Maritime Convention 1988, Preamble.
[566] Protocol for the Suppression of Unlawful Acts Against the Safety of Fixed Platforms Located on the Continental Shelf 1988.
[567] Tokyo 1963, Art 1.
[568] Hague 1970, Art 1.
[569] 1971, Art 11(c).
[570] Protocol on Fixed Platform 1988, Art 2.
[571] Maritime Navigation 1988, Art 3.
[572] Hostages 1979, Art 1.
[573] Terrorist Bombing Convention 1997, Art 2.
[574] Financing 1999, Art 2.
[575] Art 2.
[576] Tokyo 1963, Art 3.

cooperate and assist each other in investing the crimes and bringing those responsible to justice,[577] including via extradition, as appropriate,[578] to where they will face 'severe' punishments,[579] but done in accordance with the due process of law.[580] Moreover, the suspects were not meant to disappear. This was most evident with the Hostages Convention, which noted if any of the signatories to the Convention held alleged violators, they shall invite the ICRC to visit the detainee.[581] This was in broad accordance with the view the Security Council would take, namely, that all States, in their fight against terrorism, must comply with all of their obligations in accordance with international law and international human rights law and humanitarian law in particular.[582]

[577] Hague 1970, Arts 10 and 11; 1971, Arts 11–13; Hostages 1979, Arts 4, 7 and 11; Maritime Navigation 1988 Arts 12–15; Bombings 1997, Arts 10, 15 and 16; Financing 1999, Arts 8, 12, 18 and 19.

[578] Tokyo 1963, Art 16; Hague 1970, Preamble, Art 8; 1971, Art 8; Hostages 1979, Arts 9, 10, 12; Maritime Navigation 1988, Art 11; Bombings 1997, Arts 9, 11–14; Financing 1999, Arts 11, 13–16.

[579] Hague 1970, Arts 2, 7; 1971, Art 3; Hostages 1979, Art 8; Maritime Navigation 1988, Arts 5 and 10; Terrorist Bombings 1997, Arts 4 and 7; Financing 1999, Art 10.

[580] Tokyo 1963, Art 13; Hague 1970, Art 6; Airports 1971, Art 6; Hostages 1979, Arts 6 and 8(2); Maritime Navigation 1988, Art 10(2); Bombings 1997, Art 7; Financing, Arts 9 and 17.

[581] Hostages Convention, Arts 2–11, 14 and 15.

[582] S/RES/1457 (24 January 2003).

II

Captives

1. Beginnings

THIS CHAPTER IS about people, typically combatants, captured in battle. It is about what happens to their status as prisoners, about the possibilities of torture, assistance if they are wounded and what happens to their remains should they be killed. The theme that ties all of these considerations together is that all of the acts befall those who are, to one degree or another, captives of their enemies. As such, they are no longer masters of their own fate.

Humanity appears harsh towards captives from the beginning. The massacre of prisoners in warfare – as in societies which did not leave written records – involving common occurrence. The best alternative a captive could hope for was slavery. Slavery then, as now, is the status or condition of a person over whom any or all of the powers attaching to the right of ownership are exercised. Such a status is the antithesis of any ideal of the intrinsic dignity and worth of the human person or the goal that each individual is born free.[1] The only redeeming feature of being made a slave as a consequence of battle, was that they were at least left alive, if only for as long as their owner deemed desirable.

Being without rights or social significance of any kind meant that they could be used, or abused, as the owner thought fit. This meant that torture was also common in many early societies. A number of these societies, such as the Aztecs and the Incas with their insatiable demand for prisoners to sacrifice to their gods, shocked the Western standards of the time. Records suggest that sacrifices could consume thousands of victims in a single session, with Hernan Cortes (1485–1557) claiming that some 136,000 skulls of sacrificial victims were exposed near the great pyramid of Tenochtitlan. Whilst Cortes remained cool when he saw this being done to other Indian tribes, he could not maintain his composure after hearing of the death of at least 53 of his own men who had been taken prisoner, along with four of their horses, all of which had their hearts removed and their heads decapitated and placed on pikes facing the sun. Similarly, when European colonists came into conflict with some of the tribes of North American Indians, they were astounded at the tortures that they practiced such as putting hot stone on the soles of feet or running needles through eyes. The gouging of eyes and placing of red-hot embers in the sockets, various forms of mutilation and burning to death over an open fire are also recorded as the fate of hundreds, if not thousands, of opposing tribes and later colonists. Many of these tribes

[1] The definition is from the Slavery Convention, 60 LNTS 253, Art 1. Note also the definition of the International Criminal Court, Art 7.2(c). The commentary on slavery is from the preamble of the Supplementary Convention on the Abolition of Slavery, the Slave Trade, and Institutions and Practices Similar to Slavery, 226 UNTS 3.

when they conducted warfare were, as the second President of the United States, John Adams (1735–1826) noted, 'without faith or humanity' as they scalped men and butchered both women and children.[2] Similar atrocities were also recorded in other parts of the world, where a strange delight in the torture of other human beings appears to have developed. In some kingdoms in Africa during the nineteenth century, prisoners were sometimes sacrificed in batches of up to 2,000 per day.[3]

To complete such processes of domination, acts of violence against the bodies of dead enemies are also well recorded. Such acts appear to have been done to reflect the victors' desire to have some tangible sign of his bravery, to take away his opponents strength or to prolong the suffering of the dead in the afterlife. Whatever the reason, the practice is very long standing. For example, in Offnet Cave in Germany, a cache from 12,000 years ago of 34 skulls of men, women and children was found, brained with stone axes. This would appear to prove that the practice of head-hunting was already in vogue, and subsequent primitive societies would commonly indulge in, inter alia, headhunting, skinning, cannibalism, scalping and/or collection of specific body parts as trophies or the collection of the bodies for bargaining purposes.[4]

With regards to early societies which left written records, it appears the prospects for prisoners taken in war were also bleak in ancient Mesopotamia. The best case scenario to survive the conflict was to be taken as a slave, and the losers of conflict of early Mesopotamia appear to have been a source of supply for what quickly developed into the institution of slavery. Given that most records of the time only list women and children as spoil, and are conspicuously absent of males, it is tempting to assume the worst, and infer that many, if not all, males were executed. If a prisoner actually survived the conflict and the aftermath, their lives do not appear to be pleasant. Pictorial representations of the period, as far back as 2200 BCE, show captives being marched long distances, hands and elbows tied and all held in one long line via a neck stock. Many also appear to have been blinded so they could not run away, but were kept like animals to water the fields.[5]

The deliberate killing of the leaders of the opposition is a well represented theme which was frequently painted upon the walls of temples of Egypt. Thutmose II (reigned 1493–79 BCE) promised that he 'would not let live anyone among their males' of certain rebellious areas. This may have been carried out, as some campaign records note the killing of all males 'except one of the children of the chief'.[6] The overall

[2] Adams, noted in Maguire, P (2001) *Law and War: An American Story* (NYC, Columbia University Press) 20, 27–29.

[3] Cooley, L (2002) *Captives: Britain, Empire and the World 1600–1850* (London, Cape) 177; Scott, G (1940) *A History of Torture Throughout the Ages* (London, Torchstream) 24–25, 36, 41–43; Wood, M (2000) *Conquistadors* (London, BBC) 65, 76, 88; Pakenham, T (2003) *The Scramble for Africa* (London, Abacus) 301–303; Keegan, J (1993) *A History of Warfare* (London, Hutchinson) 106–13; Rowden, M (1974) *The Spanish Terror* (London, Constable) 121–24.

[4] Keeley, L (1996) *War Before Civilisation* (Oxford, Oxford University Press) 83–87, 100–101; Davie, M (1929) *The Evolution of War* (Boston, Yale University Press) 61, 65–75, 86–95, 136–46; Doyne, D (2001) *The First Armies* (London, Cassell) 53, 188–90; Pakenham, T (2003) *The Scramble for Africa* (London, Abacus) 446–47.

[5] Postgate, J (1996) *Early Mesopotamia: Society and Economy and the Dawn of History* (London, Routledge) 107, 254, 255; Kramer, S (1963) *The Sumerians: Their History, Culture and Character* (London, University of Chicago Press) 78–82, 81; Edwards, I (ed) (1971) *The Cambridge Ancient History: Early History of the Middle East*, 3rd edn, Vol 1(2) (Cambridge, Cambridge University Press) 357–58.

[6] Thutmose II in Breasted, J (ed) (1988) *Ancient Records of Egypt*, Vol II (London, Histories and Mysteries) 49, 50.

Egyptian practice was best summed up by Ramses III (1198–1167 BCE) who has his prisoners recorded as saying 'His Majesty . . . give[s] to us the breath that we breathe, the life which is in thy hands'.[7] Such life, in the hands of the Pharaohs was also consciously displayed as a sign of power, primarily in the representation of very long lines of prisoners of war, along with lavish descriptions of such captives. In some instances, such as with Tuthmosis III (reigned 1479–25 BCE), the leaders of a rebellion were executed by the king's own hand, and six of them were exposed at Thebes, whilst the seventh was hung on the walls of Napata as a grisly warning to other would-be rebels. Other Egyptian leaders took wider approaches, not separating the ringleaders from the followers, and swept them all up together, gathering thousands of slaves in single campaigns. Seti I (reigned 1294–79 BCE) recorded 'fill[ing] their storehouse [of the gods] with male and female slaves, the captivity of every country'.[8] This idea, of 'filling the storehouse' or bringing back to Egypt a victorious army overflowing with bound and submissive captives, soon to be slaves, is recorded by many other Pharaohs.[9]

The Egyptian tradition also leaves the first records of captured soldiers being beaten and tortured. Ramses II (1303–1213 BCE) recorded that he tortured prisoners so as to 'make them tell where the wretched chief of [the rebellion] is', whilst later records reveal that the success of the first recorded battle for substantial study, that of Kadesh in 1275 BCE, had victory secured for the Egyptians because two Hittite scouts were captured in advance, and tortured to reveal the location of the enemy camp.[10] Desecration of the dead followed suit. Pictorial representations of desecrated corpses, or body parts like hands or foreskins as trophies being collected from the dead enemies of the Egyptians can be traced to 2200 BCE. The troops of Pharaoh Merneptah (reigned 1212–1203 BCE) took more than 9,000 hands and penises as trophies in a battle with Libyan aggressors. To complete such desecrations, Egyptian philosophers writing around 1785 BCE would warn that the enemies of the king 'had no tomb' and their bodies would be 'tossed into the water'.[11]

What would happen to prisoners in Assyrian times appears to have depended on the willingness of the conqueror to collect slaves and on the acts of the prisoner. The records certainly suggest that in places, large numbers of prisoners of war were executed after

[7] Ramses III in Breasted, J (ed) (1988) *Ancient Records of Egypt*, Vol IV, 49. Note also Seti, I in the same work, Vol III, 54, 74, 78–79.

[8] Seti I in Breasted, J (ed) (1988) *Ancient Records of Egypt* Vol III at 42; Edwards, I (ed) (1973) *The Cambridge Ancient History of the Middle East and Aegean Region 1800–1380 BCE*, 3rd edn Vol II(1) (Cambridge, Cambridge University Press) 459.

[9] Breasted, J (ed) (1988) *Ancient Records of Egypt*, Inscription of Pepi-Nakht, Vol 1, at 144, 163; Ahmose, I, Vol II, 7–9; Thutmose III, Vol II, 165–66, 188, 198, 203, 236, 258, 263 and 308; Seti, I, Vol III, at 49–50; Amenhotep III, Vol II, at 356, 374; Ramses II, Vol III, 157; Ramses III, Vol IV,2 02. For secondary commentary, see Trigger, B (1999) *Ancient Egypt: A Social History* (Cambridge, Cambridge University Press) 315; Saggs, H (1989) *Civilisation Before Greece and Rome* (New Haven, Yale University Press) 42–43; Cohen, R (2000) *Amarna Diplomacy: The Beginnings of International Diplomacy* (Baltimore, John Hopkins University Press) 76; Edwards, I (ed) *The Cambridge Ancient History: History of the Middle East and Aegean Region 1800–1380 BCE*, 3rd edn, Vol II(1) (Cambridge, Cambridge University Press) 501–503.

[10] Ramses II in Breasted, J (ed) (1988) *Ancient Records of Egypt*, Vol III; Dawson, D (2001) *The First Armies* (London, Cassell) 140–41; Edwards, I (ed) (1975) *The Cambridge Ancient History. History of the Middle East and Aegean Region 1380–1000 BCE*, 3rd edn, Vol II(2) (Cambridge, Cambridge University Press) 226–28.

[11] See Asante, M (2000) *The Egyptian Philosophers* (Chicago, African Images) 64. For the Egyptian practices, see Ramses III in Breasted, J, (ed) (1988) *Ancient Records of Egypt*, Vol IV, at 31; Ramses II, Vol III, 248–249; Saggs, H (1989) *Civilisation Before Greece and Rome* (New Haven, Yale University Press) 189; Kern, B (2001) *Early Siege Warfare* (Indiana, Indiana University Press) 24; Dawson, D (2001) *The First Armies* (London, Cassell) 103, 139.

the battles.[12] The collection of thousands of defeated enemy and made into slaves is also well recorded by most of the Assyrian kings, with some, such as Shamshi-adad I (late eighteenth century BCE), recording that 'captive warriors were given to the soldiers of my land like grasshoppers'.[13] Sennacherib (705–681 BCE), may have held the Assyrian record with the reputed capture of some 208,000 prisoners following the capture of nearly 100 cities.[14] Lower ranking soldiers and their families who survived the Assyrians, once surrendered, were often transported en-masse, to remote parts of the Assyrian empire to start up new colonies under their new overlord, after they had, as Tiglath-Pileser III (reigned 725–727 BCE) suggested 'embraced his feet'.[15]

Survival as a slave or distant colonist could not be expected if the captured were directly involved in leading the wars against Assyria. These people could expect to be tortured, dismembered, killed and horrifically displayed in public.[16] For example, Sennacherib sometimes divided prisoners inside into those who lead rebellions (who were hung on stakes around the city); those who had 'sinned lightly' (who were carried away as slaves); and those who were not guilty of sin or contempt and were pardoned.[17] However, at points, the distinction between the ill-treatment of the ring-leader prisoners and those who were effectively just the foot soldiers blurs, as everyone in the opposition is recorded as killed, regardless of level of complicity in the rebellion. Within this mix, torture and amputation and other forms of mutilation, often by blinding and/or castration, as well as removing the fingers of archers, or the tongues of those who gave orders, are all recorded. The Assyrian king Shalmaneser I (1274–45 BCE) boasted of having blinded 14,000 enemy captives. Sennacherib noted how those he captured '[their] testicles I cut off, and tore out their privates like the seeds of cucumbers. Their hands I cut off'.[18]

The Assyrians also desecrated the dead. Tiglath Pileser I (1114–1076 BCE) repeatedly recorded the decapitation and stacking of the bodies or heads of the enemy dead or having the skins of flayed victims 'spread . . . upon the city wall'.[19] The composition of pyramids of heads, impalement and/or flaying the dead and using their skins for decoration, was utilised by many other Assyrian kings.[20] The Persians also had incidents of cruelty, with the public execution and torture of those who defied them.[21]

[12] Bury, J (ed) (1965) *The Cambridge Ancient History: The Assyrian Empire*, 1st edn, Vol III (Cambridge, Cambridge University Press) 91.

[13] Luckenbill, D (1989) *Ancient Records of Assyria and Babylonia*, Vol 1 (London, Histories and Mysteries) (hereafter Luckenbill *Ancient Records*). 259. Note also Shalmaneser, I in Vol 1, 40; Tilgath Pilsener, I in Vol 1, 74, 143; Esarhaddon in Vol II, 243, 417.

[14] Greene, J (2000) *Slavery in Ancient Egypt and Mesopotamia* (London, Watts) 33.

[15] Luckenbill, *Ancient Records*, Vol 1, 75.

[16] For the kings, see Assurnasirpal, in Luckenbill, *Ancient Records*, Vol 1, 145; Shalmaneser III in Vol 1, 212, 213, 215; Tiglath Pileser III, Vol 1, 279, 281, 284; Sargon, Vol II 27; Sennacherib, Vol II, 117.

[17] Luckenbill, *Ancient Records*, Vol II, 120, 127, 143 and 207.

[18] Luckenbill, *Ancient Records*, Vol II, 127, 155. Note also Tiglath Pileser III in Luckenbill, *Ancient Records*, Vol 1, 271; Ashurbanipal Vol 1, 145 and Vol II, 315; Saggs, H (1989) *Civilisation Before Greece and Rome* (New Haven, Yale University Press) 191; Edwards, I (ed) (1975) *The Cambridge Ancient History: History of the Middle East and Aegean Region 1380–1000* BCE, 3rd edn, Vol II(2) (Cambridge, Cambridge University Press) 280–81, 458.

[19] Luckenbill, *Ancient Records*, Vol 1, 74, 81, 143, 145, 150, 153 and 334. Also Vol II, 295, 324, 395, 398.

[20] Shalmaneser III (858–824), Tiglath Pileser III (ruled 745–727), Sargon II (ruled 722–705), Sennacherib (704–681) and Esarhaddon (ruled 681–669) in Luckenbill, D (1989) *Ancient Records*, Vol 1, 212, 213, 215, 279, 281, 284. Also Vol II, 117, 127, 207, 233.

[21] Herodotus in trans de Salincourt, A (2005) *The Histories* (Penguin, London) 3:159.

Despite the above examples, the idea that prisoners would be kept in order to later be exchanged within some sort of peace deal is well recorded in early history. Such exchanges, as recorded in a number of instances around 1800 BCE, involved each type of prisoner being given a different exchange rate.[22] By the time of Hammurabi (1750 BCE) the laws relating to the return of prisoners via ransom were remarkably clear. That is, prisoners, who may have been purchased by merchants, could get the merchant repaid via his estate, the temple, or the palace. Notably, the soldiers own property could not be used to pay the ransoming. As such, a type of social insurance existed for prisoners of war. This coincided with other social rights that soldiers possessed when held as prisoners of war taken in royal campaigns which protected their properties and families.[23] The Assyrians had a similar practice, with the exception that the first person expected to pay a ransom for a captured soldier, was the soldier himself. However, if the ransomed soldier could not raise sufficient money, the temple at which he worshipped was supposed to assist, or failing that, the landowner from whom the soldier had his land.[24]

The instruction within the Bible was that if the opposing forces refused peace and conflict was undertaken, then upon capture 'thou shalt smite every male thereof with the edge of the sword' but everything else – women, children, cattle 'and all that is in the city' shall be spoil for the victor.[25] This practice of killing male prisoners was recorded in some instances. If such captives were not killed, it was likely they would end up being sold in the slave market, blinded or ransomed.[26] The ransoming of prisoners appears to have been such an established practice of the period that Israelites were obliged to donate money to a fund used to ransom their captured country folk. Torture and/or extreme physical punishment, although not mentioned with regards to prisoners, was certainly part of the period. For example, Samson had his eyes gouged out by the Philistines, whilst after Jerusalem was captured in 586 BCE, Zedekiah was blinded before being carried off. The corpses of enemy soldiers also risked being desecrated. The bodies of Saul and Jonathan would end up impaled on the walls of the enemies and whilst the ancient Israelites would not replicate such practices, after David slew Goliath, he cut off his head, and took it to Jerusalem.[27]

2. The Greeks

One of the unique aspects of the Greek epoch was the development of medicine and its linkage to the battlefield. Medical treatment for battle injuries is as old as war itself. It is discussed in ancient Egyptian surgical texts from 3000 BCE. Over the coming centuries, progress in medical development was slow. With the Persians, the best medicine was prescribed in the form of a talisman or some charm from a prophetess. There was no

[22] Postgate, J (1996) *Early Mesopotamia: Society and Economy and the Dawn of History* (London, Routledge) 256.

[23] Hammurabi's Code, s 36. For the reprinted section of the code, see McNeill, W (ed) (1968) *Readings in World History: The Ancient Near East*, Vol II (New York, Oxford University Press) 198; VerSteeg, R (1999) *Early Mesopotamian Law* (Carolina, Carolina Academic Press) 84–85, 148.

[24] Reid, P (1984) *Prisoner of War* (London, Hamlyn) 16.

[25] Deuteronomy 20: 13–14.

[26] 2 Chronicles 25:11–12; Judges 16:19–21.

[27] 1 Samuel 17:54. Also, Snow, R (2005) *Battle* (London, DK) 18; Greene, J (2000) *Slavery in Ancient Egypt and Mesopotamia* (London, Watts) 52.

cure for infectious diseases, beyond portions of foxglove, sorrel, marjoram or hellebore. Mushrooms could provide potency and courage, whilst bleeding a man white was the only remedy for a snakebite. By the time of the Greeks, if battle injuries could be cured at all, they were, in general, incapacitating. Sword slashes were plastered over with heated resin from the umbrella pine. Deeper cuts were sewn up with catgut. Amputated stumps were cauterised with a piece of red-hot metal sizzling on the flesh. The specific Greek contribution to medicine and the battlefield was that under the guidance of foundation physicians like Hippocrates (c 460–377 BCE), who emphasised the importance of health before a battle, ranging from a good diet through to strict sanitation for the army. This healing of the wounded was an idea that was so well known by the time of Homer (840 BCE) that it was recognised that 'a healer is worth many other men when it comes to cutting out arrows and applying soothing drugs'.[28] However, in practice, it appears that there were very few men with medical skill. Only two men in the entire Greek army at Troy counted as specialist healers. Melelaus was lucky enough to have one of these men suck out the blood from his wound, but most others had to rely on the help of their helots or friends who would be 'appointed as doctors' on the spot to deal with the casualties of their wounded friends.[29] Fundamentally, the treatment of the wounded, however basic and limited this may have been, was only ever given to soldiers on the side of the victorious army, unless the wounded enemy had something of value that the victors wanted. As such, the enemy wounded could expect no treatment and were often killed when discovered. This was because the life of a vanquished enemy soldier was a precarious thing in the times of Greek antiquity. Their fate was entirely at the disposal of the victor.

Ideally, healthy prisoners would be taken and kept safe until they could be exchanged at a later date. In this regard, it was the Greeks who provided the first full treaties, such as the Peace of Nicias of 421 BCE, which contained provisions for the mutual exchange of prisoners.[30] However, such ideal situations are the exception and not the rule for this period of history. If Greeks were fighting non-Greeks, such as Persians, the chances of being taken prisoner were remote. The point, made by Plato, was that whilst Greeks should spare fellow Greeks in battle, they could legitimately enslave or massacre the 'alien and foreign'.[31] From such thinking it is possible to trace the rule of no-quarter given at the battle of Marathon in 490 BCE between the Athenian lead forces and the Persians. It was also seen at the battle of Thermopylae by the Persians against the Spartans in 480, and later in the same year, by the Athenians against the Persians at Salamis. In the last instance, when the 12,000 or so men in the Persian forces abandoned ships, assuming they survived the use of pitch-forks, arrows or stones thrown at men flailing in the water, and managed to swim to shore, they were killed by the watching Athenians who guarded the beaches.[32]

[28] Homer in trans Fagleo, R (1988) *The Iliad* (London, Penguin) 11.514–15, 11.833.

[29] Van Wees, H (2009) *Greek Warfare: Myths and Realities* (London, Duckworth) 146–47; Durschmied, E (2002) *From Armageddon to the Fall of Rome* (London, Hodder) 73; Strauss, B (2006) *The Trojan War* (NYC, Schuster) 53–54, 95, 120–21.

[30] 'The Peace of Nicias (421 BC)' in Ferguson, J (ed) (1978) *Political and Social Life in the Great Age of Athens: A Sourcebook* (London, Open University Press) 420–21. See also Thucydides in trans Warner, R (1972) *The History of the Peloponnessian War* (London, Penguin) 5.3.

[31] Plato, *The Republic* in Jowett, B (ed) (1931) *The Dialogues of Plato*, Vol III (Oxford, Oxford University Press) 470c.

[32] Straus, B (2005) *Salamis* (NYC, Arrow) 22, 203, 216, 218, 228, 249; Pritchet *The Greek State at War*, Vol 5, 203–205; Durschmied, E (2002) *From Armageddon to the Fall of Rome* (London, Hodder) 64, 73, 76–77 and 88.

The practice of killing the captured male combatants was not restricted to warfare with non-Greeks. The killing of all the men after a conflict was in the background of historical wars mentioned in the *Iliad*,[33] and also ran through the siege of Troy, of which Achilles slayed the unarmed Hector as he was leading prisoners from the field. In the Peloponnesian war (431–404 BCE), the killing of male prisoners directly after a battle was recorded at, inter alia, Torone, Thyrea, Lecythus, Melos and Argos. After the battle of Aegospotami alone, in 405 BCE when Lysander's fleet had defeated the Athenians, between 3,000 and 4,000 prisoners were executed. From such acts, reprisals against prisoners of war held by the opposing side often resulted. In addition, mercenaries who fought against forces of their own nationality, would almost certainly be killed if captured.[34]

The execution of all fighting males, and torture of many, by Alexander the Great (356–323 BCE) was noted after the sieges of Gaza and Tyre in 322 BCE after the defenders had rejected his terms for their safe surrender. Over 8,000 combatants were killed after Tyre was stormed, including 2,000 by crucifixion.[35] Despite such practices, one of the first clear instances that prisoners of war should not be executed after a conflict comes from this period, with one of his Alexander's generals who suggested to him that it was wrong to kill prisoners, as prisoners were men to be kept safe, and not criminals to be punished.[36] This view may have been a reflection of the contemporary Indian Code of Manu which suggested that, 'enemies captured in war are not to be killed but are to be treated as one own children'.[37]

The Ancient Greeks did not execute all of their prisoners, preferring to often make them into economically valuable slaves. However, exceptions to this policy existed, with some commanders refusing to enslave captured prisoners of war because of strategic reasons, such as they wished to make them allies. Alexander liked this approach. Alternately, commanders sometimes chose not to enslave defeated warriors because they were fellow Greeks. For example, Philip II of Macedonia (382–336) decreed that any prisoner taken in war who could recite Homer should be released. The Spartan commander Callicratidas who fought in the Peloponnesian wars, had earlier advocated a very similar policy,[38] and this was very much in line with the view of Plato that it was 'infinitely better' for Greeks not to enslave men from other Hellenic States.[39] Nevertheless, the fundamental point remained in practice, that discretion to free on enslave prisoners was clearly up to the commander.[40]

[33] *Illiad* 6.447–65.

[34] Thucydides 1.30, 3.35, 3.59, 3.68, 4.116, 4.122, 4.130, 4.57.3–4, 5.116. Also, Kagan, D (2003) *The Peloponnesian War* (NYC, Harper) 84, 244 and 249; Bury, J (ed) (1969) *The Cambridge Ancient History: Athens*, Vol V (Cambridge, Cambridge University Press) 89, 180 and 192.

[35] Arian in trans de Salincourt, A (1977) *The Campaigns of Alexander* (London, Penguin) 1.19.6; 2.27.7, 4.26.4.

[36] Xenophon in trans Dakyn, H *Agesilaus* (London, Dodo Press) Section I:21.

[37] Although they could be kept as a slave for one year. See *The Law Code of Manu* (London, Penguin, trans Olivelle, P, 1987). 48.

[38] Diodorus Siculus in trans Welles, T *Library of History* (Boston, Loeb) 13.76.2 and 17.84. Note also, Thucydides 2.67.4; Arrian 1.19.6, 4.26.4.

[39] Plato *The Republic* in Jowett, B (ed) (1931) *The Dialogues of Plato*, Vol III (Oxford, Oxford University Press) 165.

[40] Diodorus in trans Oldfather, C *The Library of History* (London, Penguin) 13.76.2; Xenophon in trans Warner, R (1968) *Hellenica* (Oxford, Oxford University Press) 2.1.19.

The incentives of capturing and selling prisoners, as opposed to killing captives were attractive. By the time of the *Illiad* around 800 BCE, the victors were quick to sell their captives to ransom brokers. The captured Trojan prince in Homer's *Illiad* was traded for valuables 'worth a hundred oxen' and was later ransomed by a friend 'for three times as much'.[41] Around 500 BCE clear inter-state rules for the ransoming of prisoners, with a rate of 200 drachmas being accepted as a standard rate of a captured hoplite throughout most of Greece. One hundred years later, it had fallen to 100 drachmas.[42] If these ransoms for prisoners could not be met, then it was common for the prisoners to be sold as slaves. Prisoners of war were turned into slaves by fellow-Greeks at least 34 times between the sixth and second century BCE.[43] This was an entrenched practice during the Peloponnesian War, with mass enslavements of soldiers and civilians following, inter alia, the fall of Eion, Scyros, Chaeronea, Mycenae and Zanacle.[44] Alexander continued this trend with mass enslavements (and sometimes massacres) at Gaza, Tyre and Thebes. With the last incident alone, some 30,000 prisoners were said to have been taken, which were sold into the slave market. This was always considered both a humane and economically attractive option suited to the demand for slaves in ancient Greece, of which at least two thirds were of non-Greek origin and directly acquired, originally, as prisoners of war.[45]

Once condemned as a slave, there was no guarantee that survival was assured. This period of history has a number of examples where prisoners of war were worked to death digging out minerals or breaking rocks. Most notably, over 1,000 Athenian prisoners of war were intentionally worked to death in the stone quarries of Syracuse in 413 BCE. Such men, once converted into slaves, also risked being tortured or mutilated. When Alexander captured Persepolis in 331 BCE, he found it full of his former soldiers who had been captured and mutilated. Specifically, 'some with feet, others with their hands and ears cut off, and branded with the characters of some barbarian letters . . . they resemble strange images, not human beings, and there was nothing that could be recognised in them except their voices.'[46] Alexander responded in kind.

Torture was the norm in this epoch. The Phoenicians, who gave the world crucifixion, preferred to bind the living face to face with the dead, as their favoured torture. The Buddhist emperor Asoka, retained torture during his supposedly enlightened reign, and the Greeks also practiced inflicting pain and mutilation upon the helpless. The Athenians were known to cut off the hands of captured enemy rowers, whilst other Greek commanders were known to blind their captives before returning them to their homes.[47]

[41] *Iliad* 21:76-9.

[42] The Laws of Gortyn in Botsford, G (ed) (1929) *Hellenic Civilisation: Records of Civilisation* (Columbia, Columbia University Press) 282; Ormerod, H (1987) *Piracy in the Ancient World* (NYC, Dorset) 146.

[43] Van Wees, H (2009) *Greek Warfare: Myths and Realities* (London, Duckworth) 26. For examples, see Diodorus 22.10.4, 14.112, 14.15.2-3; Bury, J (ed) (1969) *The Cambridge Ancient History*: *Athens*, Vol V (Cambridge, Cambridge University Press) 310–11.

[44] Thucydides 1.113, 1.98. Also, Diodorus 11.65.5.

[45] Rostovtzeff, R (1940) *The Social and Economic History of the Hellenistic World* (Oxford, Oxford University Press) 148, 204, 1258–62.

[46] Quintus Curtius in trans Yardley, J (1984) *The History of Alexander* (London, Penguin) Section 5.5.6.

[47] Quintus 4.2.15; Xenophon in trans Warner, R (1968) *Hellenica* (Oxford, Oxford University Press). Section 2.1.31–32; Kagan, D (2003) *The Peloponnesian War* (NYC, Harper) 321; Ferrill, A (1988) *The Origins of War* (London, Thames & Hudson) 139; Ormerod, H (1987) *Piracy in the Ancient World* (NYC, Dorset) 155; Reid, P (1984) *Prisoner of War* (London, Hamlyn) 17, 137; Farrington, K (2003) *A History of Punishment and Torture* (London, Hamlyn) 4.

Despite these barbaric acts, the Greeks also provided some notable humane actions pertaining to those who fell in battle, and were subsequently venerated. Although the Greeks were aware that not all civilisations respected the fallen in war, the Greeks tried to honour a higher standard. Herodotus (c 484–425 BCE) was amongst the first to recognise that 'to offer indignities to the dead was condemned by the laws of civilised warfare'.[48] It was for this reason that the actions of Achilles, by dragging the desecrated body of Hector behind his chariot around the besieged walls of Troy was condemned by Greeks, mortal and otherwise. Achilles then refused to return the body and Troy's king, Priam, had to brave a journey into the enemy camp to plead, on his knees, for the return of the mangled body of his son. This was a journey racked with personal and political cost, for to ask for the return of his son's body was to demonstrate that he did not control the battlefield, and such a failure could be taken as a symbol of defeat. Nevertheless, Priam had to act in such a way as Greek religion required that each man be given a proper burial and be remembered for his sacrifice. There was great shame to leave the dead on a battlefield and failure to retrieve them, as with the generals and their victory over the Persian fleet at Salamis in 480 BCE, could lead to public trial and condemnation. A similar situation occurred again around 406 BCE, where generals were brought to trial for failing to rescue (their own) survivors and the bodies of the dead of sunken triremes. As such, the Greeks would expend considerable effort to keep their dead from falling into enemy hands, or if necessary, they would ask for truces to retrieve the fallen or not pursue the fleeing enemy, as Alexander was known to do, so that the rites owed to the dead could be met.[49] The rule was well summed up by Plato:

> And is there not illiberality and avarice in robbing a corpse, and also a degree of meanness and womanishness in making an enemy of the dead body when the real enemy has flown away and left only his fighting gear behind him, – . . . we must abstain from spoiling the dead or hindering their burial . . . when a man dies gloriously in war, shall we not say, in the first place, that he is of the golden race?[50]

In accordance with such considerations, the Spartans would carefully bury their fallen warriors at the sites where they fell. Conversely, the Athenians would attempt to bring the bodies or the ashes of their fallen home, and without consideration of status, they would be buried on sides of the road leading to the Academy and their names inscribed on public casualty lists. Such acts were supplemented by the creation of monuments, designed to ensure remembrance, such as that built after the battle of Marathon in 490 BCE, to commemorate the 192 warriors who fell in the defence of freedom. Similarly, the armour which was recovered with the body of Masisttius (the recovery of the body itself had become a central focus of the battle) was placed in the temple of Athena on the Athenian Acropolis.[51] Sometimes these acts were bilateral. For example, at the end

[48] Rawlson, J (trans) (1909) *The History of Herodotus*, Vol I (London, Dent) 4:103. 9.79 and 11.120, *Illiad*, 7.84–91.

[49] Strauss, B (2006) *The Trojan War* (NYC, Schuster) 154–55, 159, 160, 164, 167; Hedreen, G (2004) *Capturing Troy* (USA, University of Michigan Press) 111–12; Kagan, D (2003) *The Peloponnesian War* (NYC, Harper) 134, 135, 278, 297, 459–66; Adcock, F (1959) *The Greek and Macedonian Art of War* (California, University of California Press) 7.

[50] Plato *The Republic* in Jowett, B (ed) (1931) *The Dialogues of Plato*, Vol III (Oxford, Oxford University Press) 165–66.

[51] Rice, E (1995) 'The Glorious Dead' in Rich, J and Shipley, G (eds) *War and Society in the Greek World* (London, Routledge) 224–57; Holland, T (2005) *Persian Fire* (London, Abacus) 199–200 and 294–95; VanWees, H (2009) *Greek Warfare: Myths and Realities* (London, Duckworth) 137; Garland, R (1985) *The Greek Way of Death* (London, Duckworth) 90.

of the war between Macedon and Athens, Philip II (382–336 BCE) as part of his generous peace settlement, returned the bones of the Athenians who had fought, lost and died at the battle of Chaeronea in 338 BCE. Similarly, Philip's son, Alexander, when he discovered the body of Darius, covered it with his own purple cloak, and sent it to Persepolis for burial.[52] However, a certain degree of pragmatism also entered into these attempts at venerating the dead. For example, when Philip II held one of the last, open casket, mass funerals, ever, Titus Livy (59 BCE–17AD) recorded:

> When they had seen bodies chopped to pieces by the Spanish sword, arms torn away, shoulders and all, or heads separated from bodies . . . or vitals laid open . . . they realised in a general panic with what weapons, and what men they had to fight.[53]

3. The Romans

'No-Quarter' is commonly traced to the Roman style of war known as *guerre mortelle* in which there would be no privilege of ransom and the conquered would be killed. This practice within Roman traditions, which was predicated on the assumption that if opposing forces refused to surrender, they could be slaughtered when beaten, dates back to the sixth century BCE. In Roman history before the birth of Christ, notable instances in which all the men were killed (and the women and children enslaved) were at Samnium in 311, Leontini in 213, Antipatrea in 200, Cauca in 151, Corinth in 146 and Capsa in 107.[54] When the Celts who invaded Italy in 102 were finally defeated, the historians suggested that over 100,000 men were slaughtered, with very few escaping. When Asculum fell in 89 BCE, all officers and leading men were scourged and beheaded. Similar practices were recorded with the cities of Gabara, Japha, Jotapata and Jerusalem during the Jewish uprising. In the last example, following the Jewish refusal to surrender, Titus Vespasianus (39–81) decided to publically crucify prisoners in the hope of encouraging a surrender of those inside. He eventually got to a rate of 500 crucifixions per day, before the city was stormed. Although even the Romans realised this was not a necessarily moral course of action, it was accepted because they believed military expediency necessitated it.[55] Further execution of prisoners who were rebelling against their Roman overlords occurred during the wars around the Danube in 172 AD. If necessary, they would adopt actions whereby no obligations to protect the surrendering were even created. For example, when besieging the town of Uspe in the Crimea in 49 BCE, the Romans refused the surrender of the town because they could not guard all of the prisoners who would have been taken. Due to the fact that the Romans felt it would have been barbarous to slaughter men who had surrendered, they refused to take the surrender and fought them to their deaths.[56]

[52] Bury, J (ed) (1969) *The Cambridge Ancient History. Macedon*, Vol VI (Cambridge, Cambridge University Press) 265, 386, 455.

[53] Livy in trans de Salincourt, A (1960) *The History of Rome* (London, Penguin) Book 31.34.4–6.

[54] Livy 1.53.2–3, 2: 97, 9.31.2–3, 24.30.4, 31.27.3–4; Sallust in trans Handford, R (1968) *The War With Jugurtha* (London, Penguin) 91.6–7; Appian Hisp 52.

[55] Josephus in trans Grant, M (1981) *The Jewish War* (London, Penguin) 3.133, 3.303, 3.336, 5.289, 5.450 and 6.404.

[56] Tacitus, in trans Wellesley, K (1975) *The Histories* (London, Penguin) 259; Cook, S (ed) (1969) *The Cambridge Ancient History. The Imperial Peace*, Vol VIII (Cambridge, Cambridge University Press) 358–59; Ellis, P (1990) *The Celtic Empire* (Guild, London) 124–25. Lendon, J (2005). *Soldiers and Ghosts, A History of Battle in Classical Antiquity*. (NYC, Yale University Press) 210, 235–36.

Death as a reprisal could also be expected for defeated opponents, if the opposing forces had been guilty of killing Roman prisoners. For example, around 353 BCE, the Tarquinienses killed 307 captured Roman prisoners of war in a sacrifice to their gods. In retaliation, after the Tarquinienses were defeated, all except 358 of their captured nobles were killed.[57] A second example was in 311 BCE, when the Samnites captured a Roman town in Samnium via a negotiated surrender and then, contrary to their promises, proceeded to torture and kill all of their Roman prisoners. When Romans retook the town, they killed every adult Samnite male.[58] A third example occurred at Ilurgeia in 206 BCE when Scipio Africanus (235–183 BCE) told his troops, prior to the wholesale massacre of the population: '[T]o avenge the atrocious slaughter of their comrades . . . by a severe example to ordain that no one should ever account a Roman citizen or soldier in any misfortune as fair game for ill treatment'.[59]

The killing of the captured was also likely to increase in certain types of conflict. Whilst being made a prisoner was possible in the Roman civil wars, as the armies were essentially fighting their colleagues, it was by no means certain. Cornelius Tacitus (56–117) recorded 'The roads were choked with heaps of dead . . . after all, in civil war, you cannot make money out of prisoners'.[60]

The ability to surrender was very unlikely when fighting conflicts against belligerents with no status. For example, with the slave uprisings in Italy (134, 104 and 73–71 BCE), death was assured for men who had exhausted their utility as slaves by rebelling. This was especially so since many slaves fought as if their freedom depended on it. With the final great slave uprising, as led by Spartacus (109–79 BCE) the last 6,000 prisoners who were captured, were denied any idea of a status that could even negotiate a surrender and when beaten, they were all crucified along the Appian Way from Capua to Rome. The former slaves reacted in kind. Thus, when Crixos, one of the generals of Spartacus was captured and executed, Spartacus responded by the killing of 300 Roman prisoners in retaliation. The other type of conflict in which the killing of prisoners could be expected was in fights against pirates. Crucifixion was also the standard practice for dealing with these men, with the only clemency being considered, being the cutting of their throats before they were nailed to the cross. Soldiers accused of treason, such as those defying Severus (145–211) were executed when their city of Byzantium opened its gates in 193. Soldiers in auxillary forces could also be killed en masse if their loyalty could not be relied upon, as occurred in the year 408, before Alaric's invasion of Rome.[61]

Before the prisoners were killed or sold as slaves, they were often brought back to Rome for public display. This practice was learnt by the Romans during their conflict with the Samnites, whereby the Romans who surrendered were forced to undergo humiliation by 'pass under the yoke' which was an arch formed by Samnite spears. The Romans adopted similar practices for large-scale public displays of the defeated who were brought back to Rome to be either sold or executed. The most obvious

[57] Livy 7.15.10 and 7.19.1–3.

[58] Livy 9.31.2–3.

[59] Livy 28.19.6–8, 28.20.6–7 and 28.19, 9–20.7.

[60] Tacitus in trans Wellesley, K (1975) *The Histories* (London, Penguin) 107.

[61] Strauss, B (2009) 'Spartacus' in Summer *Quarterly Journal of Military History* 38, 44–45; Cook, S (ed) (1966) *The Cambridge Ancient History*: *The Roman Republic*, Vol IX (Cambridge, Cambridge University Press) 331–32; Cook, S (ed) (1969) *The Cambridge Ancient History. The Imperial Crisis*, 1st edn, Vol XII (Cambridge, Cambridge University Press) 10–12; Champion, C (2004) *Roman Imperialism* (London, Blackwell) 155–57.

manifestation of this was with gladiators, who were often either taken directly as prisoners of war and sold as slaves, before being on-sold as gladiators. The competitions these people fought in were often supplemented by public executions of common criminals, and on occasion, captured enemy leaders. The deportation of captured enemy leaders to Rome for public torture and execution was what Diodorus, writing in the first century before Christ, called an 'ancestral custom'.[62] For example, Simon, Son of Giovas who was involved in the Jewish uprising was taken to a location near the forum which was 'the traditional place at Rome for the execution of those condemned to death for war crimes'.[63] Later examples in the fourth century saw Constantine I (272–337) throw Frankish kings and thousands of their followers to the beasts in the amphitheatre to the point where one contemporary noted that the animals became exhausted with so much slaughter. Attempted usurpers or Roman power were treated with equal brutality.[64]

The Romans were not unusual within this epoch for their killing of prisoners. In the Punic Wars, Hannibal (248–183 BCE) was reputed to have killed thousands of prisoners. In the East, with disasters such as that at Carrhae in 54 BCE, at least 4,000 seriously wounded Roman soldiers were slaughtered as soon as their position was overrun.[65] Other conflicts before the birth of Christ which involved the torture and massacre of Roman prisoners occurred in 406 with the Volsci, around 353 with the Tarquinienses and in 311 with the Samnites.[66] In some instances, Romans were taken prisoner for the explicit purpose of sacrifice. This was often in accordance with the practices of their opponents. For example, when the Hermunduri and Chatti, two Germanic tribes, fought a battle over the possession of a salt-producing river, with economic and religious significance to them both, each side took a vow to Mars and Mercury promising to sacrifice their foes to the gods if they were granted victory. The Chatti were beaten and then all of their captured warriors and horses were ritually executed. Such policies appear to have overflowed into their conflicts with the Romans. Thus, with the battle in the Teutoberg forest in 9 AD in which three entire legions disappeared, an estimated 1,500 Romans who surrendered (after 13,500 of their colleagues had been killed) were believed to have been sacrificed to the German gods, (although some may have been made into slaves). Similar practices were later recorded in the wars against some other German tribes, the Goths, the Visigoths and the Celts.[67]

The Romans did not kill every prisoner who had opposed them. At times, for reasons of strategy, they would allow their captives, being either notable individuals, or

[62] Tacitus in trans Wellesley, K (1975) *The Histories* (London, Penguin) 194–98; Dioddorus 19.101.3. Also Livy 9.24.14–15 and Elton, H (1997) *Warfare in Roman Europe* (Oxford, Oxford University Press) 196–98; Meijer, F (2004) *The Gladiators* (NYC, Dunne) 17, 28, 39, 42–47, 148–51; Ellis, P (1990) *The Celtic Empire* (London, Guild) 5–6.

[63] Josephus reprinted in Ayerst, D (ed) *Records of Christianity*, Vol I (London, Blackwell) 9.

[64] Elton, H (1997) *Warfare in Roman Europe* (Oxford, Oxford University Press) 175; Norwich, J (1988) *Byzantium: The Early Centuries* (London, Guild) 37.

[65] Goldsworthy, A (2003) *The Fall of Carthage* (London, Cassell) 211; Sampson, G (2008) *The Defeat of Rome in the East* (Philadelphia, Casemate) 138; Diodorus 13.62.1–4.

[66] Livy 4.58.3, 7.15.10 and 9.31.2–3.

[67] For the Germanic practices, see Ann 13.57 and Ceasar in trans Hammond C, (2008) *Gallic War*, (Oxford, Oxford World Classics) Vols VI, XIII–XXIII. Also, Tacitus in trans Wellesley, K (1975) *The Histories* (London, Penguin) 248–49; Barbero, A (2005) *The Day of the Barbarians* (London, Atlantic) 111; Jones, T (2006) *Barbarians: An Alternative Roman History* (London, BBC Books) 61–63; Wells, P (2003) *The Battle That Stopped Rome* (NYC, Norton) 43, 77, 134, 185–89; Cook, S (ed) (1971) *The Cambridge Ancient History: The Augustan Empire*, 1st edn, Vol X (Cambridge, Cambridge University Press) 845–47.

entire armies, to live in freedom. This policy was used by both Julius Caesar (100–44 BCE) and Scipio Africanus. With the last example, with the 10,000 soldiers who survived the capture of New Carthage, Scipio allowed them to return home with their property without being enslaved. He did this with the intention of encouraging surrenders at further Carthaginian towns.[68] It is possible that these acts were following those of Hannibal who was also inclined to use clemency towards Latin, as opposed to Roman, prisoners for strategic reasons.[69]

The Romans were the first to develop large scale military medicine centres that had the facilities to help their own wounded. Caesar spent several days after defeating the Helvetti in attending to numerous wounded and dead. In Italy in 43 BCE, Mark Antony (83–30 BCE) sent out his cavalry into the night to bring in his wounded left on the battlefield, and during his Parthian campaign, he went around to visit and speak to the wounded men in the days after a battle. In Dacia, Trajan on one occasion had his own clothes cut up into bandages to cope with the large number of wounded – and also help sagging morale in his army. Aside the theatrical aspect, Trajan did not need to cut up his own clothes as Roman regiments carried their own doctors, field hospitals, medical instruments, medicinal chemicals and plants needed to treat diseases and wounds. Roman medical doctors even developed a special device that could remove arrows without tearing the tissue they were embedded in. They also developed a surgical clamp that helped stop gangrene spreading. This medical information appears to have circulated freely between the Eastern and Western parts of the Roman Empire to such a degree that medical chronicles from the sixth to the twelfth century cover topics from the removal of arrow-heads through to fractured and broken bones from combat. The Byzantine emperor Maurice (439–602) explained the ethos in this area 'after the battle the general should give prompt attention to the wounded and see to the burying of the dead. Not only is this a religious duty, but it greatly helps the morale of the living.'[70]

The Byzantines actually went one step further and developed a well-organised medical service for the army. Part of this involved the mounted *deputati* whose task it was to evacuate the wounded during times of combat. The *deputati* received a special reward for each of those whose rescue they procured. However, despite being able to look after their own wounded, there are no records of them ever helping the wounded of the opposition. These people, it must be assumed, were either killed or left to die on the battlefield. Perhaps, if they were worth saving, medical attention may have been given to them, but only for the purpose of making them survive so they could be sold as a slave.[71]

The most common fate of a prisoner who survived combat with Romans was to be made into a slave. This policy was often followed because, as Horace (65–8 BCE) suggested 'it is unadvisable to kill a prisoner when he can be sold'.[72] With such thinking,

[68] Polybius 10.17.6; Diodorus 14.105.4; For Caesar, see Cicero *Ad Attic*, Vol IX 16.

[69] Livy in trans De Sekincourt (1972) *The War with Hannibal*, Vol XXII (Penguin) 108.

[70] Maurice in trans Dennis, G (1984) *Handbook of Byzantine Military Strategy* (Philadelphia, Philadelphia University Press) 75, 77; Goldsworthy, A (1998) *The Roman Army at War 100 BC–AD 200* (Oxford, Oxford University Press) 166–67; Haldon, J (2002) *Byzantium at War* (London, Osprey) 70; Wells, P (2003) *The Battle That Stopped Rome* (NYC, Norton) 99, 183–84.

[71] Hussey, J (ed) (1967) *The Cambridge Medieval History: The Byzantine Empire*, Vol IV(11) (Cambridge, Cambridge University Press) 43.

[72] Horace in trans Ruston, R (1929) *Epistles* (London, Loeb) 16.69.

the Romans took hundreds of thousands of prisoners, and came to base the economy of their empire on such labour.[73] The Carthaginians, and especially Hannibal, had done exactly the same, actually defying a number of his commanders who wanted to execute every captured Roman prisoner. In preventing the slaughter, he ordered 'we must not only win, [we must] also know how to use our victory well'.[74]

Enslaving, as opposed to executing captives was seen as an act of clemency. Following through with the Roman practice, entire populations of former soldiers and their civilian counterparts were enslaved after defeat. Some 69,000 slaves were taken from defeated populations between 297 and 293 BCE, as were a number of populations which fell before the Romans during the first Punic war such as the 250,000 who were reputedly taken at Agrigentum in 262. A further 25,000 were taken from Sicily the following year and an additional 20,000 from Africa in 256 BCE. When Panormus was taken in 254, 14,000 captives who could not afford to purchase their own freedom were sold into slavery. During the second Punic war, in 215 BCE, Rome sold all 5,000 inhabitants of the three towns that had earlier deserted to the Carthaginians when they were recaptured. A further 30,000 captives from southern Italy were sold as slaves in 209 BCE. A similar fate happened with the city of Antipatrea, which the Romans captured in 200 BCE, with the exception of all of the men of military age who were executed.[75] At other times, such as with the Roman capture of Capua, Rome was more discerning, enslaving only the aristocratic and middle classes. Apparently 150,000 were enslaved after the fall of Epirus around 167 BCE, whilst Caesar is reputed to have taken and sold over 90,000 slaves. Trajan claimed 50,000 at the end of the first Dacian war around 100 AD.[76] Before these captives were sold, it was possible they would be mutilated. In this regard, amongst others, Caesar, Scipio and Titus all cut off the hands of large number of prisoners from rebellious provinces.[77]

The final point in the above paragraph leads to the discussion of torture. The word 'torture' comes from the French *torture*, originating in the Latin *tortura* and ultimately deriving the past participle of *torquere* meaning 'to twist'. Torture, as a means to solicit information, was restricted in use to non-Roman citizens. In times of warfare, it was clearly a common practice. In this regard, Caesar left records of how messengers sent to try to reach him within his besieged compounds, were often captured and tortured in full view of the defenders so as to weaken their resolve. Similarly, other commentators of the period, such as Tacitus, record how in some instances, people were tortured to reveal specific information.[78] Nevertheless, some scholars of the period, such as Seneca (4 BCE–65 AD), began to question the practices of torture. He argued that the practices of cruelty against other humans, such as:

[73] Ceasar *Gallic War* 2.32–33 and 7.89; Livy 42.54.6.

[74] Livy in trans De Sekincourt (1972) *The War with Hannibal*, Book XXII (Penguin) 160–65. Also Books XXIII (38) and XXV (7); Goldsworthy, A (2003) *The Fall of Carthage* (London, Cassell) 189.

[75] Livy 31.27.3–4.

[76] Livy 23.37.12 and 26.16.11; Tactitus, Hist. 3.32–34; Diodorus 23.9.1 and 23.18.15; Polyb 1.19.15; Ceasar *Gallic War* 2.32–33, 7.89; Harris, W (1979) *War and Imperialism in Republican Rome* (Oxford, Oxford University Press) 54, 153–54.

[77] Livy 10.101.10; Josephus 5.455 and 8.44. See also Champion, C (2004) *Roman Imperialism* (London, Blackwell) 134; Ellis, P (1990) *The Celtic Empire* (London, Guild) 53.

[78] Caesar in trans Warrington, J (1955) *Caesar's War Commentaries* (London, Dent) 90–91, 95; Tacitus in trans Mattingly, H (1951) *Britain and Germany* (London, Penguin) 89.

> the pony [aka the rack], the cords, the cross, the rings of fire round half buried living bodies, the hook tugging . . . the varieties of fetters, the lacerated limbs and branded foreheads, the cases of savage animals [these were displays of] unbridled lunatic frenzy.[79]

Despite Seneca's arguments, the practices of torture continued unabated. Perhaps the best known example of this was crucifixion, such as the execution of Jesus Christ (c 5 BCE–30 AD) by this method which involved being flogged, nailed to a cross and taking over nine hours to die.[80] In this period of history, such gratuitous violence, even if not for the purposes of getting information, was part and parcel of the social fabric. The public displays at the Colosseum and the hundreds of subsidiary venues where humans were executed via crucifixion, burnt to death or torn apart by animals are testimony to this numbness to human suffering. The gladiators, which made the killing of other humans a sport, are also examples of an epoch in which extreme gratuitous violence against humans appears to have become part of the fabric of the State. Possibly mad emperors like Nero (37–68) not only filled the Colosseum with victims of those he disliked, he also, reputedly, had men and women nailed to posts, soaked in oil and set on fire to help provide light at parties. Death screams were part of the fun.[81] By the fourth century, following the concerns of some theologians like Tertullian (160–220) and later Augustine (354–430), who pointed out that those tortured will confess to anything, some limitations were being imposed.[82] However, this is not to suggest that what became the Holy Roman Empire prohibited torture. Rather, it just regulated parts of it. For example, although Constantine (272–337) banned crucifixion he approved the putting to death of slaves guilty of crimes as dubious as 'seduction' by burning or the pouring of molten lead down their throat.

Execution or slavery was not the only possible outcome for those captured by the Romans. If they were neutral in the conflicts, yet had somehow been ensnared in wide slave-making nets, they may have escaped this fate if an existing treaty protected them. This type of arrangement was practiced in the first treaty between Rome and Carthage (509 BCE) which contained provisions by which if citizens of either signatory to the treaty were captured in the conflict, they were to be released.[83] Alternately, and more commonly when dealing only with captured combatants, prisoners could be kept alive for purposes of ransom or for helping cement peace deals. For example, in addition to one-for-one swaps and extra prisoners being exchanged for two and a half pounds of silver per person at the end of the first Punic war, the Peace Treaty Between Rome and Carthage of 241 BCE, had Carthage agree to 'give up all Roman prisoners without ransom'.[84] Similarly, the second Peace Treaty between Rome and Carthage of 201 BC, obliged the Carthaginians to hand over all Roman prisoners of war and deserters 'who had fallen into their hands'.[85] Similar conditions were imposed on Philip V of

[79] Cooper, E (ed) (1995) *Seneca: Moral and Political Essays* (Cambridge, Cambridge University Press) 79. Also 96, 145, 155.

[80] Mark 15:34–37.

[81] Jones, T (2006) *Barbarians: An Alternative Roman History* (London, BBC Books) 110–11; Meijer, F (2004) *The Gladiators* (NYC, Dunne) 149–59.

[82] Fortin, E (ed) *Augustine: Political Writings* (Cambridge, Hackett) 147–48, 247.

[83] Treaty Between Rome and Cartage 509 BC in Lewis, N and Reinhold M (eds) *Roman Civilisation: Records* Vol 1 (Columbia, Columbia University Press) (henceforward Lewis, *Roman Civilisation*, 72).

[84] Peace Treaty between Rome and Carthage 241 BC in Lewis, *Roman Civilisation* Vol 1, 153. Also, Livy in trans De Selincourt, A (1972) *The War with Hannibal*, Book XXII (London, Penguin) 24.

[85] Peace Treaty with Carthage, 201 BC in Lewis, N, *Roman Civilisation*, Vol 1,171.

Macedon following his eventual loss to Rome.[86] The same pattern was followed with the defeat of the Aetolian League in 189 BCE[87] and with the Peace Treaty with Antiochus III of Syria in 188 BCE.[88] In other instances, even though no formal treaty was concluded, the return of Roman prisoners was expected as part of the peace process. For example, after Julian (310–363) had subdued his opponents in Gaul, some 20,000 Roman prisoners were released from their captivity.[89]

The point about all of the above treaties is that they were achieved when Rome won. When they were losing, or lost, repatriation via treaty was far from guaranteed. For example, following the Roman defeat to Hannibal at Cannae in 216 BCE, the Senate refused to ransom the Roman prisoners of war due to the 'greatness of the sum required, not wishing either to exhaust the treasury, on which they had already made a heavy draft to purchase slaves and arm them for service, or to furnish Hannibal with money'.[90]

In other instances, negotiations could take decades. For example, it was some 32 years before an agreement between Rome and Parthia was reached for the repatriation of some 10,000 men captured at Carrhae. Although a number of these men did return, rumour has it, that after being transported across the Parthian empire, some of these troops ended up as mercenaries fighting and settling on the border with China and never returned to Rome.[91] Some captured men, like Emperor Valerian (193–264) who was taken prisoner by the Persian king Saphur I in 260 AD, never returned to Rome, and lived out his days being the footstool for the Persian king. When he finally died, he was stuffed and mounted on a palace wall.[92] In other instances when the Romans were on the losing side, such as with their wars with Attila (406–453), the free repatriation of all Barbarian prisoners was agreed by treaty in 446, whilst the Roman prisoners had to purchase their freedom at the price of 12 pieces of gold, each.[93]

The one area where the Romans did attempt, sometimes, to reach a higher standard was with regards to their treatment of the dead, for as Cassiuis Dio (155–229) suggested 'the slain are deemed to no longer be foes, nor are hated and insult wreaked upon their bodies'.[94] It appears this was not only a Roman standard, as some of the Roman foes had also learnt to copy the Greek traditions in this area. Hannibal would allow truces to recover the dead, and after battles was known to bury his own soldiers and the dead enemy commanders with honour. The Persians came to acquire a similar reputation. However, such restraint appears rare as head-hunting was apparently a practice followed by Carthaginian, Celtic and Gaul warriors, with the later being

[86] Peace Treaty with Philip V 196 BC in Lewis, *Roman Civilisation*, Vol 1, 174.

[87] Peace Treaty with the Aetolian League 189 BC in Lewis, *Roman Civilisation*, Vol 1, 178.

[88] Peace Treaty with Antiochus III of Syria 188 BC in Lewis, *Roman Civilisation*, Vol 1, 184.

[89] Gwatkin, H (ed) (1957) *The Cambridge Medieval History. The Christian Roman Empire* (Cambridge, Cambridge University Press) 69–70.

[90] Livy, XXII.lx.2–4; lxi.1–3. Also, trans Warrington, J (1966) *Cicero Officers* (London, Dent) 163.

[91] Sampson, G (2008) *The Defeat of Rome in the East* (Philadelphia, Casemate) 182–85; Cook, S (ed) (1971) *The Cambridge Ancient History: The Augustan Empire*, 1st edn, Vol X (Cambridge, Cambridge University Press) 263.

[92] Norwich, J (1988) *Byzantium: The Early Centuries* (London, Guild) 63–64, 168; Cook, S (ed) (1969) *The Cambridge Ancient History: The Imperial Crisis*, 1st edn, Vol XII (Cambridge, Cambridge University Press) 135–38.

[93] Gibbon, E (1926) *The Decline and Fall of the Roman Empire*, Vol 1 (London, Methuen) 288–89. See also Vol III, 455–56.

[94] Oration 75.9. Cf 76.5. Also, Cicero in trans Keyes, C (1928) *De Legibus* (Loeb, Harvard) 447–57.

known for using the flensed heads of dead enemies as drinking vessels. Similarly, when Marcus Crassus (115–53 BCE) fell at the Roman disaster of Carrhae his head was dispatched as a trophy to King Orodes of Parthia (ruled 57–38 BCE) who is alleged to have poured molten gold into the mouth of Crassus, mocking his great wealth. This exact type of desecration of Roman leaders is also recorded in other instances with different enemies, such as when the Byzantine Emperor (d 811) fell to his Bulgar enemies, only to be decapitated, and his skull flensed and mounted in silver to act as a drinking cup for the victor.[95]

The ritual decapitation of slain enemies seems to have been fairly common amongst northern European peoples, but was especially associated with Gallic and Celtic tribes. Although head-hunting was recorded with some Roman legions, the Romans as a whole tried to hold themselves to a higher standard with regards to the treatment of both their own and enemy dead when on the battlefield. They originally attempted to retrieve and bring home their dead leaders, although as their wars became bigger, the Senate began to fear the impact upon public morale of large amounts of bodies being returned to Rome. Accordingly, they opted to have all but the famous disposed of where they fell. However, once they discovered that tombs and cemeteries were not regarded as sacrosanct by all of their enemies, they opted to cremate them. Even if they lost the battle, in time to come, Romans would return to where their dead fell and attempt to bury or burn them with honour whenever possible. The same standards did not always apply when back in Rome. For example, if the vanquished were taken as slaves and/or turned into gladiators or became criminals, when they died, the disposal options could range from feeding their corpses to animals, through to their ritualistic throwing of bodies into the Tiber – as a way to 'purify' society. Even emperors who had gone too far in the eyes of the people, risked being thrown into the river when they died. For example, after Heliogabalus (203–222) was killed, his body was carried in triumph through the city, horribly mutilated, then weighted down with stones and thrown from a bridge into the Tiber.[96]

4. The Early Middle Ages

Acts of clemency towards prisoners, such as that of King Alfred (849–899) when he allowed the Danes to go free to return to their homeland after finally defeating them, are quite rare in the Early Middle Ages. The pattern is much more one of no prisoners being taken, for example, the Byzantine history records some 7,000 resident (but suspect) Goth soldiers being trapped and burnt to death in the church near the Imperial palace in the year 400. In England, in 655, at the battle of Winwaed nearly all 30

[95] Livy in trans De Selincourt (1972) *The War with Hannibal*, Book XXIII (London, Penguin) 24; Diodorus 13.57.3–6, 13.58.3; Webster, G (1978) *Boudica: The British Revolt Against Rome AD 60* (London, Anchor Press) 81–82; Sampson, G (2008) *The Defeat of Rome in the East* (Philadelphia, Casemate) 143; Griffith, P (1995) *The Viking Art of War* (London, Greenhill) 36; Jones, T (2006) *Barbarians: An Alternative Roman History* (London, BBC Books) 196–97; Ellis, P (1990) *The Celtic Empire* (London, Guild) 20–21; Norwich, J (1991) *Byzantium: The Apogee* (NYC, Knoff) 8–9.

[96] Goldsworthy, A (1998) *The Roman Army at War 100 BC–AD 200* (Oxford, Oxford University Press) 271–75; Wells, P (2003) *The Battle That Stopped Rome* (NYC, Norton) 39; Robinson, P (2006) *Military Honour and the Conduct of War* (Routledge, London) 50; Contamine, P (1984); Meijer, F (2004) *The Gladiators* (NYC, Dunne) 184–187; Roche, R (1995) *The Norman Invasion of Ireland* (Dublin, Anvill) 134–35.

commanders of the Mercian army who surrendered were killed, whilst in 778 Charlemagne (742–814) had 4,500 pagan Saxon prisoners decapitated at Verden. Surrender to Vikings in 886 with the siege of Paris and again at St Lo in 890 was met by bad-faith and the execution or enslavement of those tricked into laying down their arms. Otto the Great (912–973) had all the chieftain leaders executed so as to prevent any future uprisings. Such executions were more likely if the captives did not have economic value and could not offer rich rewards via ransoms.[97] Such rewards could be achieved by the taking and selling of slaves, of which the Vikings were the most renowned of the period, through to more formal ransoming systems being agreed at the end of a conflict. The Byzantines had some experience of the latter, and combinations of repatriation and ransoming existed at various points with its intermittently warring neighbours. However, although a number of instances existed when thousands of captured Byzantine soldiers were ransomed and returned to the Empire, this was not always the case. For example, in 599, Maurice refused to ransom 12,000 of his own captured by the Avar Khagan (562–602), because he did not want to enrich his opponent or create an incentive in his soldiers to surrender because they would believe they would be rescued by him if they surrendered. His advice for dealing with enemy prisoners was:

> If some of the enemy are captured . . . if they are in nicely armed and in good physical condition, they should not be shown to the army but sent off secretly to some other place. But if they appear in miserable shape, make sure to show . . . the whole army; have the prisoners stripped and paraded around, and make them beg for their lives so that our men may think that all the enemy soldiers are that wretched.[98]

Khagan subsequently had all the Byzantine prisoners put death. The Byzantine emperor Romanus I (870–948) would later do the same to all of his Russian prisoners, due to the outrages they had committed against his civilian communities.

After the Battle of Hastings, the only living beings upon the battlefield were Normans. Men captured in this period may well have ended up as slaves, for the Domesday Book of 1086 recorded that 10 per cent of the population were enslaved and in some areas the figure was as high as 20 per cent. After Stephen (1096–1154) had captured Shrewsbury castle in 1139, he had 93 of the defenders executed. Captured archers were executed by Henry II (1133–89) in 1153 as were the Irish prisoners taken by Strongbow (1130–76) at Waterford in 1170. Crossbow men were killed by King John (1167–1216) at Rochester in 1215. No mercy to prisoners was shown in the English civil war at the battles of Lewes and Evesham in 1264 and 1265 between Henry III (1207–72) and Simon de Montfort (1208–65). The intention to refuse quarter was displayed prior to the conflict, with the Red Dragon flag, which made clear that no prisoners would be taken, being unveiled. Henry also killed prisoners who had

[97] McGlynn, S (2008) *By Sword and Fire: Cruelty and Atrocity in Medieval Warfare* (London, Weidenfeld) 66, 73, 74, 78–79, 92–94; Norwich, J (1988) *Byzantium: The Early Centuries* (London, Guild) 126, 294; Contamine, P (1984) *War in the Middle Ages* (Oxford, Blackwell) 37, 261.

[98] Maurice in trans Dennis, G (1984) *Handbook of Byzantine Military Strategy* (Philadelphia, Philadelphia University Press) 75. See also Norwich, J (1988) *Byzantium: The Early Centuries* (London, Guild) 275, 300; Griffith, P (1995) *The Viking Art of War* (London, Greenhill) 94; Wallace, J (1962) *The Barbarian West: The Early Middle Ages* (NYC, Harper) 103; Norwich, J (1991) *Byzantium: The Apogee* (NYC, Knopf) 72–74, 111, 152–53, 171, 223.

failed to surrender to him when he demanded surrender at the siege of Bedford. When the Flemish townspeople and peasants defeated the cream of French nobility at Courtrai in 1302, instead of seeking a fortune from ransoms, the order was 'kill all that has spurs on' and between 40 and 50 per cent of their captives were executed. The massacre of Scottish knights, by Edward, Prince of Wales was recorded before Bannockburn in 1314, and Robert the Bruce (1274–1329) and William Wallace (1272–1305) replied with a slaughter of common soldiers and fallen English knights.[99]

Despite these practices, the early part of the twelfth century had begun with attempts to bring some civility into these areas. The jurist Gratian had suggested as early as 1140 that with regards to warfare between Christians 'In victory mercy ought . . . to be shown to the captive, especially to him from whom one need fear no disturbance of the peace'.[100]

The key word in the quote above is 'ought'. That is, taking prisoners was an option, not an obligation in this period. Nevertheless, building on such thinking, a number of belligerents attempted to reach such higher standards. For example, in a battle in 1119 between Henry I (1068–1135) of England and Louis VI (1081–1137) of France, of some 900 knights involved, only three were killed, because of their armour, out of fear of God and chivalric brotherhood. Their desire to capture, not kill each other meant that bloodshed was minimal, although those not inside the knightly brotherhood could not expect mercy. Accompanying acts of clemency towards prisoners, which were freed unconditionally once the conflict had ended were also recorded at the siege of Rochester in 1215 and by Edward III (1312–77).[101] These approaches were buttressed by some of the first scholars of international law, such as Giovanni da Legnano (1320–83) who stated in 1360: 'I believe that quarter should be granted to one who humbles himself and does not try to resist, unless the grant of quarter gives reason for fearing a disturbance of the peace, in which case he must suffer.'[102]

Despite this recommendation, and with an average death rate of between 20 and 50 per cent of knights for defeated sides during the eleventh to fifteenth century, a number of instances were recorded, such as in the Hundred Years' War, when there was no-quarter offered. This was typically when the English would unfurl their Red Dragon flag, or the French would unfurl their *Oriflamme* – their red war banner, on which was written, *pavillon nomme sansquartier*. The *Oriflamme* implied that the mercy of the French had been entirely consumed and that no-one's life would be spared – just as flaming oil destroys everything that can be burnt. In practice, it did not preclude the possibility of taking prisoners. Nevertheless, it was a sign of intent, and crucially, that nothing, not even mercy, would stand in the way of victory. The rule of no-quarter could also be

[99] Gravett, C (1990) *Medieval Siege Warfare* (London, Osprey) 19; Morillo, S (1994) *Warfare Under the Anglo-Norman Kings* (Suffolk, Boydell) 178; McGlynn, S (2008) *By Sword and Fire: Cruelty and Atrocity in Medieval Warfare* (London, Weidenfeld) 97–100, 134, 136; Seward, D (2003) *The Hundred Years War* (London, Robinson) 53; Warner, P (2004) *Sieges of the Middle Ages* (Yorkshire, Pen and Sword) 97–98, 136–37; Nusbacher, A (2005) *1314: Bannockburn* (Gloucestershire, Tempus) 135, 154; Roche, R (1995) *The Norman Invasion of Ireland* (Dublin, Anvill) 157–59.

[100] Gratian *Decretum*, Part II, Cau xxiii, Q 1. Can iii.

[101] Keen, M (1965) *The Laws of War in the Late Middle Ages* (London, Routledge) 17; McGlynn, S (2008) *By Sword and Fire: Cruelty and Atrocity in Medieval Warfare* (London, Weidenfeld) 76; Prestwich, M (1995) *Armies and Warfare in the Middle Ages* (Yale University Press) 152, 236.

[102] Legnano, G (1360) in trans Brierly, J (1917) *Tractatus: De Bello, De Represalis et De Duello Classics of International Law* (Oxford, Clarendon) 224, 289.

implemented by the order of 'havoc' – 'and let slip the dogs of war' as William Shakespeare (1564–1616) would add.[103] Jean Froissart (1337–1405) recorded of the period:

> As for taking any prisoners, one can hardly get any of them to surrender but they will fight to the death saying that it is better to die a free Frisian than to be subject to a Lord or a Prince. And as for the prisoners that have already been taken, hardly any ransoms can be exacted, nor will their friends and relatives redeem them, but they leave them to die one after another in prison, nor otherwise will they ransom their people unless, having taken some of their enemies, they exchange them man for man. Yet if they think that none of their men are prisoners, they will certainly put all their prisoners to death.[104]

Practices developed of having 'scirmishers' whose speciality was not only stabbing the belly of the horses of knights, but cutting the throats of the wounded or piercing wounded knights with a special short dagger, called the *misericord*, or 'mercy' on account of the weapon being designed to slip between the plate armour of the wounded who lay on the field. Massacres of able-bodied men after they had surrendered are also common during the period. Bertrand du Guesclin (1320–80) ended quarrels over ransoms for about 1,000 English prisoners by having them all killed. When the English sacked Limoges in 1370, they cut the throats of over 3,000 French prisoners. Further massacres of prisoners were recorded in 1413 and most famously, in 1415 at Agincourt when Henry V (1387–1422), fearing a renewed attack, ordered the killing of nearly all of his prisoners. The result of this order was the deaths of three dukes, five counts, over 90 barons, 1,500 knights and between 4,000 and 5,000 gentlemen. In 1420, Henry had prisoners try to persuade their comrades still inside the castle to open the gates so he would spare their lives. They did not open the gates and he duly killed them after they eventually surrendered. The fact that their artillery had earlier scored a direct hit on his tent did not help a consideration of mercy. He was also known to have executed Scottish soldiers from Britain who fought for the French, and a trumpeter who had disrespectfully directed his blasts from the walls of Meaux towards him. The fall of Jargeau in 1429, after a storming lead by Joan of Arc (1412–31), saw a thorough sacking of which only 50 prisoners out of an original 700 who surrendered, survived. On at least one occasion, Joan of Arc also had an English prisoner beheaded in cold blood. John Talbot (1384–1453) was responsible in 1440 for the hanging of surrendered garrisons of captured castles. Likewise, when Pontoise fell in 1441, 500 defenders were put to the sword and only the garrison commander was kept alive to ransom back to England.[105]

It can be suggested that the practice of killing prisoners grew in direct response to the growing aversion of keeping them as slaves if they were of the same religious faith.

[103] Keen, M (1965) *The Laws of War in the Late Middle Ages* (London, Routledge) 104–106; Meron, T (1993) *Henry's Wars and Shakespeare's Laws* (Oxford, Oxford University Press) 163–73; Barber, R (ed) *The Life and Campaigns of the Black Prince: From Contemporary Accounts* (London, Folio) 42–43; McGlynn, S (2008) *By Sword and Fire: Cruelty and Atrocity in Medieval Warfare* (London, Weidenfeld) 125; Stacy, R (1994) 'The Age of Chivalry' in Howard (ed) *The Laws of War* (NY, Yale) 26, 33; Prestwich, M (1995) *Armies and Warfare in the Middle Ages* (Yale University Press) 314; Contamine, P (1984) *War in the Middle Ages* (Oxford, Blackmore) 104.

[104] Trans by Bayners, L *The Chronicles of Froissart* (NYC, Harvard University Press) xv, 295.

[105] Seward, D (2003) *The Hundred Years War* (London, Robinson) 45, 57, 66, 168–69, 173, 186, 240; Prestwich, M (1995) *Armies in the Middle Ages* (Yale University Press) 240, 332, 252; Cheyney, E (1962) *The Dawn of a New Era: 1250–1453* (NYC, Harper) 110–39, 164–66; Lucie-Smith, E (1976) *Joan of Arc* (London, Penguin) 133; Hemingway, A 'Like Apples Fallen in Autumn' *Military Heritage* (24 Feb 2008) 30; Curry, A 'Agincourt' *BBC History* (July 2005) 13–17.

The scholars of the period like Bartolus (1314–57) and Pierino Belli (1502–75)[106] confirmed this trend, as Hugo Grotius (1583–1645) would strongly reiterate centuries later.[107] The accompanying result was that as slavery ebbed away, the direct economic benefits with selling captives as slaves were lost. These benefits were quickly replaced by ransoming the same captives as free, but captured, men.[108] The way this system worked was that in theory, the captor had the option to make someone a prisoner. This was not an obligation, but there were often strong economic reasons to do so. Once taken prisoner, they could not be executed, unless they had committed treason against their captor or their life endangered the public weal. The way the system worked was when a soldier caught a prisoner, he was entitled to one third of the value. The other third would go to his feudal lord and a further third to his King. From such a process, a clear mechanism developed to protect the lives of captives for as Machiavelli (1469–1527) explained 'the unarmed rich man is a booty to the poor soldier'.[109]

In theory, every captive had a value. The rule of thumb was that the ransom should equate to about one year's gross income for the prisoner. This rule mean a peasant was normally worth a few pence, an archer about £2 and a scribe like Geoffrey Chaucer (1343–1400), £15. Some people captured on the battlefield, like Joan of Arc, were traded between different groups, before being sold to the English for 10,000 gold crowns. When Kings, such as the Byzantine Emperor Romanus IV (1030–71), David of Scotland (1085–1153), Richard of England (1157–99) or John of France (1319–64) were captured, the ransom demands were so enormous – such as the three million gold crowns for John, one million for Romanus, 100,000 marks for David and 150,000 marks for Richard – that they could only be paid for by extra taxation. Since most captives did not have their own treasury to pay for their release, the costs fell upon the captive or their family. On occasion, the Crown would help out with such payments if there was no other option. Evidence is scarce about the fate of prisoners who could not afford a ransom. Some, no doubt, were murdered to save having to feed them. Some were turned loose, and what may have been more common, they simply changed sides.[110]

In terms of conditions for holding such captives, it appears that the standards were as diverse as the captives who held the prisoners. Thus, whilst the French King John who was captured by the Black Prince would live out his day in royal splendor in England, Richard II who was imprisoned by Henry Bolingbroke (later crowned as Henry IV) died of starvation in the Tower of London around 1399. Such inhumane conditions were in keeping with the vast majority of prisons of the period which until

[106] Belli, P (1563) *A Treatise of Military Matters and Warfare* in trans Nutting, HC (1936) *Classics of International Law* (Oxford, Clarendon) 87–88, 115–16.

[107] Grotius, H (1904) *The Rights of War and Peace* (London, Dunne) 346–47.

[108] Contamine, P (1984) *War in the Middle Ages* (Oxford, Blackwell) 262, 266; France, J (1999) *Western Warfare in the Age of the Crusades 1000–1300* (London, UCL Press) 11, 137–38; Morillo, S (1994) *Warfare Under the Anglo-Norman Kings* (Suffolk) 21, 22.

[109] Machiavelli, N in trans Whitehorne (1990) *The Art of War* (Eastern Press, Connecticutt) 224.

[110] For the original discussion on this topic, see De Pisan, C (1408/09) in trans Byles, A (ed) (1932) *The Book of Fayttes of Armes and of Chyvalrye* (London, Oxford University Press) 217, 224–25, 264–65. For subsequent interpretations, see Keen, M (1965) *The Laws of War in the Late Middle Ages* (London, Routledge) 156–65, 179; Meron, T (1993) *Henry's Wars and Shakespeare's Laws* (Oxford, Oxford University Press) 66–68; Prestwich, M (1995) *Armies and Warfare in the Middle Ages* (Yale University Press) 107–109, 217, 224–25, 264–65; Seward, D (2003) *The Hundred Years War* (London, Robinson) 80, 93; Gillingham, J (1978) *Richard the Lionheart* (London, Weidenfeld) 217–40; Lucie-Smith, E (1976) *Joan of Arc* (London, Penguin) 210–12, 228.

the nineteenth century were as vile as any place that can be imagined. These man-made cell hells often amounted to a death sentence as those incarcerated perished by the thousands from disease, starvation, violence and lack of both sanitation and heat. This was despite the presumption that knights 'and above' would be held in relative comfort or else they would be justified in escaping.[111]

The use of torture appears to have become common during the Early Middle Ages. As the centuries evolved the boundaries blurred over the lawful infliction of pain on captives and the use of physical pain to resolve judicial questions. It was only in 1215 with the Fourth Council of the Lateran that 'judicial tests or ordeals by hot or cold water or hot iron bestow any blessing' were forbidden.[112] Before this time, restraints on torture, especially on enemies, were few and far between. The Vandals were particularly vicious with practices such as binding heads so tight they burst. Atilla the Hun (406–453) preferred more brutal methods, such as having those who betrayed him put to death, with a stake up their anus, being slowly pushed through their through the organs, until it came out their shoulder. The Byzantine leader Flavius Phocas who ruled from 602 to 610 introduced the gallows, rack, blinding and mutilations on a semi-industrial scale for both commoners and royalty alike. Irene (752–803), had the eyes of her own son put out to prevent her throne being usurped, whilst when Justinian was captured in 704, his nose was removed and his tongue was mutilated. After the battle of Lechfeld in 955 between the Magyars and the Saxons, Otto I (912–973) had the noses and ears of all the Magyar prisoners cut off. Similarly, after the battle of Balathista in 1014, Emperor Basil II (958–1025) blinded his 15,000 Bulgar prisoners, leaving one man in every 100 with one good eye so that he could lead his comrades home. King Alfred (849–899) was also known to blind his prisoners of war and the use of blinding became a common punishment after 1066 in England. The Norman Robert Guiscard (1015–85) took pleasure in blinding and removing the noses of enemies whilst the blinding, or mutilation by the removal of feet or/and hands of resistant, but captured garrisons, was not unusual for William the Conqueror (1027–87). This was especially so if the defeated had done certain outrageous acts, such as insulting him. Such acts of amputation of prisoners were common in this period, with men losing feet, hands, genitalia, eyes and other facial features. Richard the Lionheart captured 15 French knights in 1198, and in response to a French atrocity, had 14 of them blinded and the last one blinded in only one eye so he could guide the other 14 back. Roger Mortimer (1287–1300) had Edward II (1284–1327) killed with a red hot poker up his anus. Gold was poured down the throat of the blacksmith who betrayed Kildrummy castle in 1306, whilst the captured pagan Hungarian King Vazul was blinded and had boiling lead poured into his ears by Christian knights in 1031.[113]

[111] Hemingway, A 'Like Apples Fallen in Autumn' *Military Heritage* (Feb 2008) 24, 25; Seward, D (2003) *The Hundred Years War* (London, Robinson) 91–101; Meron, T (1993) *Henry's Wars and Shakespeare's Laws* (Oxford, Oxford University Press) 15; Stacy, R (1994) 'The Age of Chivalry' in Howard (ed) *The Laws of War* (NY, Yale University Press) 26, 37; Farrington, K (2003) *A History of Punishment and Torture* (London, Hamlyn) 88–89.

[112] Fourth Lateran Council 1215, Canon 18.

[113] Scott, G (1940) *A History of Torture Throughout the Ages* (London, Torchstream) 86–94; Man, J (2005) *Attila the Hun* (London) 160–61; Wood, H (2008) *The Battle of Hastings* (London, Atlantic) 16, 42; Donsbach, M 'A Pagan Uprising in Hungary' *Military History* (Nov 2005) 31–35; Laing, J (2000) *Warriors of the Dark Ages* (London, Sutton) 14, 75; Hussey, J (ed) (1966) *The Cambridge Medieval History. The Byzantine Empire*, Vol VI(I) (Cambridge, Cambridge University Press) 517–18; Norwich, J (1991) *Byzantium: The Apogee* (NYC, Knopf) 133, 136, 256, 262, 268–69, 273, 289, 356.

Mutilation of prisoners was known in the Hundred Years War with archers typically losing their fingers or thumbs when captured. In time to come, the soldiers who would fire the first arquebusiers would lose their hands when captured. Like other forms of mutilation common at the time, these acts were seen as a more merciful fate than death, as they were often designed to render the victim harmless or to scare the comrades of those not yet defeated. Frederick I Barbarosa (1152-89) was known to cut the right hand off prisoners. Similar examples were not unique to this epoch. For example, after Tedaldo fell in 1309 the Venetians lost nearly every man of their 6,000 garrison either in the battle or the executions which followed. The exception was the handful who were returned to Venice, blinded. This was unlike acts of physical torture designed to extract information of interest to the Crown, of which captives could find themselves being tortured under the personal oversight of, inter alia, Henry V (1387–1422), Edward IV (1442–83), or Henry VII (1457–1509).[114]

One of the worst forms of torture of this epoch dates back to Henry III around 1240, who introduced a new and novel punishment to bring the rebels in Wales, Scotland and Ireland under control. The torture known as 'hanging, drawing and quartering' would stay on the British statute books until 1814. This was a spectacularly gruesome and public form of torture and execution. It was reserved only for the most serious crimes, which were deemed more heinous than murder and other capital offences. The miscreant would be drawn on a hurdle, facing backwards to the place of execution. He would then be forced up a ladder, hung for a few moments to the jeers of the crowd, then cut down whilst still conscious. His penis and testicles would first be cut off and dangled in his face. A knife through his anus would deftly extract a few feet of bowel, which would be set alight before his eyes. Oblivion, in the stench and excruciating pain would be delayed as long as possible and would be followed by cutting up pieces of the carcass ('quartering') before it was dragged away by sledge. The head, arms, legs and torso would be boiled and preserved for exhibition in public places. This was the fate of many leading rebels, such as William Wallace (1272–1305) and the Welsh Prince Dafydd (1238–83). Phelim O'Neil (1603–53) met the same fate for the Irish rebellion against Cromwell.[115]

The tortures of the period also overlapped with the judicial systems of the time in which burnings, pressings, brandings and mutilations were common penalties for either civil or religious crimes. Sometimes these penalties overlapped with the wars of period, with some captives being tortured and then executed for disputes about theology. The Albigensian Crusades, like those against the Waldensians and the Knights Templar saw this policy at a macro level, whilst the burning of individuals like Joan of Arc saw this at a micro level.[116] However, it would be an exaggeration to stretch this

[114] Tanner J (ed) (1957) *The Cambridge Medieval History. Decline of Empire and Papacy*, Vol VII (Cambridge, Cambridge University Press) 29.

[115] Norwich, J (1988) *Byzantium: The Early Centuries* (London, Guild) 279, 298, 334, 375; Finucane, R (2004) *Soldiers of the Faith* (London, Phoenix) 191; Duffy, C (2003) *The '45* (London, Cassell) 538–39; Hobbes, N (2003) *Essential Militaria* (London, Atlantic) 33; Bradbury, J (1992) *The Medieval Siege* (Suffolk, Woodbridge) 53–54; Nusbacher, A (2005) *1314: Bannockburn* (Gloucestershire, Tempus) 1–2; Hemingway, A 'Like Apples Fallen in Autumn' *Military Heritage* (Feb 2008) 24, 25; O'Siochru, M (2008) *God's Executioner: Oliver Cromwell and the Conquest of Ireland* (London) 222–23.

[116] Farrington, K (2003) *A History of Punishment and Torture* (London, Hamlyn) 52–53; Scott, G (1940) *A History of Torture Throughout the Ages* (London, Torchstream) 56–59; Seward, D (2003) *The Hundred Years War* (London, Robinson) 154, 166.

point. Most of the people who were killed by torture from the Middle Ages to the Reformation were not prisoners of war, but citizens who fell foul of religious orthodoxy and/or their neighbours. In the Catholic context, with four decrees between 1204 and 1213 Pope Innocent III (1160–1216) empowered bishops to seek out heresy in named venues, rather than wait for it to manifest itself. From such instructions, special officials known as 'Inquisitors' were employed and the Inquisition began. The Inquisitors came to attack knowledge, books and people. In the last instance torture, which was only meant to be utilised within limits, was permissible from 1252 until 1816. Given that the crime of heresy was the ecclesiastical equivalent of treason, torture seemed appropriate. Pulleys, weights and water torture were the preferred methods over four continents. Exactly how many were killed or tortured is a matter of debate. Estimates from 1481 to 1517 alone suggest 13,000 were burnt alive and a further 17,000 were subjected to other forms of punishment. Other estimates suggest up to 135,000 people may have died from torture and other deprivations in prison due to the Inquisition.[117]

Dying slowly from the impacts of warfare or torture was an exceptionally easy thing to do in this period. Medical help had barely advanced since Antiquity, although hospitals – who would treat all patients – were beginning to appear. For example, one of the first hospitals in Jerusalem, set up by the Order of Saint John, before the first Crusade, was renowned for its equal treatment of Christians, Jews and Muslims. Nevertheless, even within these institutions, or whilst being treated on the battlefield, the chances of survival were a gamble. Thus, whilst Richard I (1157–91) died of his wounds after a clumsy extraction of an arrow from his shoulder, Edward I (1239–1307) was saved by a surgeon who cut away the morbid flesh around a deep wound. It appears that most military forces did not have large medical support units. Nevertheless, Richard I, whilst fighting Saladin in 1183, had a mule-drawn, four wheeled cart, which carried a wooden mast painted white with red spots. It also had his banner on it, which contained a red cross. It was a place of refuge for his wounded. Thereafter, a red painted cross appears to have been adopted by the Order of Saint John, or the Hospitallers, and gained some currency as a type of passport to allow people to safely cross battlefields. Moreover, in some instances during the Crusades, there are examples of chivalry where the enemy wounded were given medical attention.[118]

Although the combatants of the period could often do little to help the wounded, many of them did attempt to show respect to the dead. The Normans were leaving huge wooden crosses to remember their dead at battlefields as early as 777 AD, when such a monument was constructed at the Pass of Roncevalles in the Pyrenees to mark the spot where 25,000 of Charlemagne's Frankish army were killed by the Basques whilst withdrawing from Spain. Often this respect for the dead extended to the enemy. Noble behaviour in this area was notable in 1066 when William the Conqueror expelled one of his knights who struck at the body of the fallen English king, Harold Godwinson (1022–66), with his sword. Similar acts can be seen in the Hundred Years'

[117] Green, T (2007) *Inquisition. The Reign of Fear* (London, Macmillan) 8–10, 69–72; Scott, G (1940) *A History of Torture Throughout the Ages* (London, Torchstream) 81; Wood, M (2000) *Conquistadors* (London, BBC) 85, 109–10.

[118] Riley-Smith, J (1999) *Hospitallers: The History of the Order of Saint John* (London, Hambledon Press) 21, 37; Keen, M (1965) *The Laws of War in the Late Middle Ages* (London, Routledge) 110–11; Maalouf, A (2006) *The Crusades Through Arab Eyes* (Paris, Sagi) 74, 112–13.

War in that, although there were some instances of using the decapitated heads of knights as missiles for catapults, the conflict is more notable for the respect shown to the dead. At one end of the spectrum, when Henry V died overseas on campaign, his body was boiled and his bones removed and returned home. At the other end of the spectrum, a respect was often shown to the fallen enemies. After the battle of Crecy in 1346, Edward III sent out two knights and three heralds to identify the dead by their arms and two clerks to write down their names of those who could be identified. Fallen French nobility were treated with the greatest respect, being carefully removed from the battlefield and buried with honour. The Black Prince (1330–76) has a similar record on this matter, as did Henry V, who treated the 1,200 dead Frenchmen after the battle of Agincourt 'with full honors' before burying them all in five large pits.[119]

It is important to not be too romantic over this period as such restrained behaviour was not universal during the Middle Ages This was especially so when dealing with what were often closer to civil wars. For example, when the treasurer for England (Hugh de Cressingham, died 1297) was killed by the Scots at Stirling Bridge, he was flayed and his skin divided. William Wallace used to boast that the sheath of his sword was made of this skin. However, not all of the English dead were desecrated, as a number of the bodies of the knights were kept and returned to their families if they could afford the ransom price for their bodies. Of course, the body of William Wallace met an equally grim fate, as noted above. In wars between the English and the Scottish, the English and the Welsh, and even the English against the English, a practice of the hunting and presentation of heads of fallen warriors became well known. In the period after the battle of Evesham in 1265, the head of Simon de Montfort, gruesomely decorated with his genitals, was sent to Lady Mortimer. In their wars with the Welsh, the practice of head-hunting was encouraged by the paying of one shilling per head. More famous heads, like Llywelyn ap Gruffudd (1223–82) would end up decorating the Tower of London, whilst those of lesser enemies were hung around the streets of London. This practice of the desecration and public display of the dead would continue through to the War of the Roses.[120]

5. The Crusades

One of the most obvious features of Islam as it quickly spread across the Middle East and Europe was that many captives were not executed, but rather turned into slaves. The taking of most, if not all inhabitants of (Christian and non-Christian) cities as slaves following subjugation during the Muslim expansion was the rule with cities such as Damascus in 635, Antioch in 638, Alexandria in 642, the cities in Christian Armenia and then Cappadocia in 650. This tradition derived from the Quran which stipulated 'so, when ye meet in battle those who disbelieve, then let there be a striking off of

[119] Seward, D (2003) *The Hundred Years War* (London, Robinson) 49; Barber, R (ed) *The Life and Campaigns of the Black Prince: From Contemporary Accounts* (London, Folio) 45, 89; Ayton, A 'The Battle of Crecy' *BBC History* (July 2005) 18–19; Robinson, P (2006) *Military Honour and the Conduct of War* (London, Routledge) 70, 97; Warner, P (2004) *Sieges of the Middle Ages* (Yorkshire, Pen and Sword) 90; Contamine, P (1984) *War in the Middle Ages* (Oxford, Blackmore) 257–58.

[120] Taylor, J 'Springing A Trap at Stirling Bridge' *Military History* (June 2007) 58.

heads until, when ye have slaughtered them, then make the bond strong. Then grant either favour afterwards or ransom.'[121]

This passage suggested to some jurists such as Shaybani (749–805) that prisoners of war should not be killed, but ransomed or made into slaves. This was especially so if they were under 20 years of age. Nasir Al-Din Al-Tusi (1201–74) would add:

> So far as possible, taking prisoners is preferable to killing and has many advantages. You can keep prisoners as slaves or hostages to be exchanged or force the enemy to do as we want, whereas there is no advantage in killing. Above all, do not give the order to kill after a victory. Do not be fanatical and commit excesses of belligerence. After victory, an enemy should enjoy the same status as a subject or a protected slave.[122]

However, it was clear that making prisoners slaves was an option, not an obligation. In this regard, the jurisprudence was direct that the commanders of forces which held prisoners were advised they could immediately execute prisoners (especially if required 'for high Muslim interests'), take them for ransom, exchange them for Muslim prisoners, or enslave and sell them. Only with women and children, was there an expectation that if taken prisoner they would not be executed.[123] All four of these options can be found dating back to the beginnings of Islamic history. For example, following an abortive siege by the Meccans of Medina in 627, between 600 and 800 Jewish soldiers who were fighting for Muhammad were charged with collaboration with the enemy. They were then taken outside, and beheaded one by one. Their women and children were then sold into slavery and the money they fetched was divided amongst the Muslims. Later battles between the contending interpretations of Islam in 687 ended with the execution of all prisoners of war, irrespective of their ethnic identity.[124]

The exchange of prisoners between Byzantine and Muslim communities can be traced to, at least, the early part of the ninth century, although it may have occurred earlier. This was because the redeeming of captives was a religious imperative for many Muslim groups, and this formed the basis for what became well established routines between Islam and Byzantine. In particular, prisoner exchanges and ransoming were the subject of quite elaborate regulations. This was especially so in Spain. However, nothing quite as structured appears to have developed in the Middle East, where the Military Religious Orders attempted to act as intermediaries in matters of ransom. Most of the records in this area refer to redemptions and/or ransoms for captured elite members on both sides, but in time, rank and file combatants also benefited from such exchanges. For example the end of the third crusade was sealed with the Treaty of Jaffa of 1215 whereby both Saladin (1138–93) and Richard I agreed to return the prisoners they held of the other.[125] Similarly, the Fifth Crusade was marked by an exchange of prisoners, as was the sixth in 1229. Another large scale exchange occurred in 1250 with 3,000 Christian knights traded for 300 Muslim warriors, large areas of land and one million bezants. In particular, the Treaty Between

[121] Quran 47:4–5. Also, Ye'or, B (2002) *The Decline of Eastern Christianity Under Islam* (NJ, Dickinson University Press) 271–77.

[122] Tusi in Chaliand, G (ed) *The Art of War in World History* (California, California University Press) 445.

[123] Khadduri, M (1955) *War and Peace in the Law of Islam* (Baltimore, John Hopkins Press) 127–32.

[124] Karsh, E (2006) *Islamic Imperialism. A History* (NYC, Yale University Press) 13, 36–37.

[125] Treaty of Jaffa 1215 in Laffan, R (ed) (1929) *Select Historical Documents: 800–1492* (NY, Holt) 72. For the early exchanges, see Gibbon, E (1926) *The Decline and Fall of the Roman Empire*, Vol VI (London, Methuen) 48–49; Norwich, J (1991) *Byzantium: The Apogee* (NYC, Knopf) 14, 46–47.

Egypt and King Louis stated 'All prisoners of war made since the battle of Gaza [in 1244] shall be released and the territory of both Parties should be as it was before the Christians landed'.[126] Exchanges between the Knights of Saint John and the Corsairs of the Barbary coast for prisoners also occurred in 1541. Sometimes, leaders such as Saladin would practice clemency allowing defeated captives to go free, such as with the negotiated surrender of Jerusalem.[127]

Combatants of the period were also directly involved of the ransoming of captives of different religions. Such ransoming bore a strong similarity to the practice of ransoming in Europe, with both sides ransoming captured knights and even kings, such as with the ransoming of Raymond of Tripoli (1140–87) and Baldwin II (d 1131), who were returned for a king's ransom.[128] If a captive could not be ransomed, they could be sold as slaves. This practice was so established that at times there were so many Christian slaves in circulation in Muslim cities, that they became worth as little as the price of a pair of sandals.[129] The Muslims were not alone in their practice of making slaves of prisoners of war of opposing faiths, as the Christians did the same. This was direct contrast to the rules within Europe seeking to prohibit the enslavement of fellow Christians. In part, this view was reflected by the 1452 Papal bull, *Dum Diveras* of Pope Nicholas V (1397–1455) which proclaimed:

> We grant you [Kings of Spain and Portugal] by these present documents, with our Apostolic Authority, full and free permission to invade, search out, capture, and subjugate the Saracens and pagans and any other unbelievers and enemies of Christ wherever they may be, as well as their kingdoms, duchies, counties, principalities, and other property [. . .] and to reduce their persons into perpetual slavery.[130]

From such dictates, the taking of prisoners of war of different religious faiths and selling them into slavery was a practice followed not only by Muslim empires but also a number of Christian ones, as scholars like Pierino Belli (1502–75)[131] and Samuel Rachel (1628–91)[132] would approve. With such support, the practice of making prisoners of war into slaves well into the seventeenth century in the West, and even longer in the East.

Christians, Muslims and Mongolians all utilised captives for military tasks long before they got to the slave market. From being human shields, digging tunnels, through to being condemned as galley slaves, the life of the captive could be both

[126] The 1250 treaty in Ghunaimi, M (1968) *The Muslim Conception of International Law* (NYC, Columbia University Press) 49–50.

[127] Runciman, S (1954) *A History of the Crusades*, Vol 3 (Cambridge, Cambridge University Press) 187, 276; France, J (1999) *Western Warfare In the Age of the Crusades* (London, UCL Press) 228–29; Seward, D (1974) *The Monks of War* (Herts, Penguin) 79; Bradford, E (1962) *The Great Siege* (London, Reprint Society) 32.

[128] Runciman, S (1954) *A History of the Crusades*, Vol 1 (Cambridge, Cambridge University Press) 182. See also Vol 2, 46, 173, 395, 420; Seward, D (1974) *The Monks of War* (Herts, Penguin) 45, 55, 59.

[129] Khadduri, M (1955) *War and Peace in the Law of Islam* (Baltimore, John Hopkins Press) 127; Shaybani, [100]–[101]; Finucane, R (2004) *Soldiers of the Faith* (London, Phoenix) 109; McGlynn, S (2008) *By Sword and Fire: Cruelty and Atrocity in Medieval Warfare* (London, Weidenfeld) 104.

[130] 'Dum Diveras' in Davenport, F (1917) *European Treaties Bearing on the History of the United States and Its Dependencies to 1684* (Washington, Carnegie Institute) 12.

[131] Belli, P (1563) 'A Treatise of Military Matters and Warfare' in trans Nutting, H C (1936) *Classics of International Law* (Oxford, Clarendon) 96.

[132] Rachel, S (1676) *The Law of Nature and Nations* in trans Bate, J (1916) *Classics of International Law* (Oxford, Clarendon) 187.

harsh and short. Prisoners, Christian and otherwise, could be roasted alive, crucified or impaled if they were disrespectful to their overlords or shirked in their work. The only blessing of life as a slave was that life was often short. Heart attacks, ruptures, beatings and torture, malnutrition and insufficient water and food quickly killed them off. This was particularly so with galley slaves. Tens of thousands of men were killed like this, unless they were rescued as 15,000 such Christian slaves recaptured after the battle of Lepanto in 1571. Galley slaves were also used by European powers against Muslim forces, and against each other. In terms of enslaving Muslims, Malta's sea-going Knights of Saint John routinely preyed on Muslim vessels. This policy was so entrenched that there was an estimated 10,000 Muslim slaves in Malta in 1720. In terms of enslaving fellow Christians, the Spanish, who had 2,088 such men, including captured English, in their boats when the Spanish Armada set sail. Even into the century following, Oliver Cromwell (1599–1658) would ensnare hundreds of defeated Scots in the 1650s, dispatching them to the West Indies as slaves, as was the fate for captured rebels in subsequent decades in Britain and Ireland. In the latter instance, at least 12,000 Irish were sent to the West Indies as bonded labour. The European powers were also not above purchasing prisoners of war from other nations to serve as galley slaves. The French acquired large numbers of Balkan prisoners in 1690–92 during the Nine Years' War, to be bonded to their galleys.[133]

Although negotiated exchanges of prisoners, ransoms and even slavery, all helped to negate the option of putting captives to death, this execution option remained popular throughout the Crusading period. For example, with the siege of Antioch in 1097, several Muslim prisoners were beheaded to encourage the Crusaders and discourage the besieged. The Crusaders were also known to have a special trebuchet with which they could throw captured spies into besieged enemy castles. The largest instance of killing prisoners of war in this period involved Richard the Lionheart, who despite being known for his occasional clemency towards prisoners in Europe (including the archer who shot him), failed to apply the same constraints whilst in the Middle East. In particular, after the capitulation of Acre in 1190–91 Richard had 2,700 Muslim prisoners, including their wives and children, killed. The garrison had surrendered on the understanding they would be spared and ransomed. However, due to Saladin dragging out negotiations and Richard's lack of trust in prisoners who said they were willing to accept Christianity, combined with his desire to keep advancing through the Middle East (but being unable to with so many prisoners in train) he had them all beheaded. Massacres of Turkish garrisons by Crusaders were later recorded at Vidin and Rahova in 1396 and at Ortranto in 1481. All Ottoman prisoners were executed after the battle of Chiappino Vitelli in 1554. At the battle Lepanto in 1571, although some Christians were willing to take prisoners, thousands were killed whilst pleading for mercy. This was a particular problem with the Venetians who explicitly wanted

[133] France, J (1999) *Western Warfare In the Age of the Crusades* (London, UCL Press) 138; Cooley, L (2002) *Captives: Britain, Empire and the World 1600–1850* (London, Cape) 45, 61, 143; Lambert, F (2005) *The Barbary Wars* (NYC, Hill) 37–39; Finucane, R (2004) *Soldiers of the Faith* (London, Phoenix) 106, 110–11; Bradford, E (1962) *The Great Siege* (London, Reprint Society) 18–19, 32–37, 45–47, 75; Capponi, N (2006) *Victory of the West. The Battle of Lepanto* (London, Macmillan) 196–99, 202, 291; Earle, P (2004) *The Pirate Wars* (London, Methuen) 41–42, 48–51; Hanson, N (2003) *The Confident Hope of a Miracle. The True Story of the Spanish Armada* (London, Corgi) 162, 170–71; Bromley, J (1970) *The New Cambridge Modern History. The Rise of Great Britain and Russia*, Vol VI (Cambridge, Cambridge University Press) 562–63.

most, if not all, of their Muslim captives executed. It was only the actions of Pope Pius V (1504–72) who stopped this proposal, recognising it as being akin to murder, although the captured Turkish 'experts' were all executed after the victory.[134]

Acts of violence against prisoners were not the monopoly of the Christian forces. Following the battle of Mersivan in 1101 during the Northern Crusades, only the mounted Christian knights escaped alive. In 1119, Christian prisoners were used for archery practice, or their arms or legs were hacked off, and they were left for townspeople to kill. A Christian garrison, despite promises for their lives, were massacred upon surrendering Marash in 1150. Similar actions were again recorded in 1158 and 1179. After the battle of Hattin, although many Christian soldiers were made slaves, Saladin demanded that the military orders of the Templars and the Hospitallers, some 240 in all, were to be executed, unless they were willing to convert to Islam. To a man, they all refused. Saladin then ordered the same approach to be followed with all of these captured men of these military orders within his territories. Saladin's chronicler, Ibn Al-Athir (1160–1233) explained 'he had these particular men killed because they were the fiercest of all the Frankish warriors, and in this way he rid the Muslim people of them.'[135]

Further executions of Crusaders, often in contravention of promises that they could safely surrender, were recorded in 1237, 1241, 1266, 1271, 1285 and 1291 when both Tripoli and Acre were stormed. With the fall of Acre, 2,000 Christian men were slaughtered, despite promises to the contrary. When the island of Ruad was captured by Mamelukes in 1303 and its Templar garrison taken in chains to Cairo, they were all executed by arrows before an appreciative crowd. Apart from 300 nobles who were forced to pay exorbitant ransoms, 3,000 Christian prisoners were killed after their defeat at the battle of Nicopolis in 1396. Tamerlane (1336–1405) is reported to have used thousands of prisoners to dig trenches and act as sappers against their own forces, whilst elsewhere he slaughtered 100,000 Hindu prisoners outside of Delhi, when he feared (like Henry at Agincourt) that the enemy was regrouping and the prisoners might overwhelm their guards. In another instance, involving the surrender of 3,000 Christian soldiers, he decided to have them buried alive rather than break his word that he would not draw their blood when they surrendered. Following the battle of Tannenberg in 1410, which ended the Baltic Crusade, some 14,000 were taken prisoner, of which only a few of the highest value knights were allowed to live to be ransomed. The massacre of captured Venetian sailors in 1451 was recorded in the lead up to the fall of Constantinople. This was followed by the massacre of two garrisons at the small castles situated before Constantinople. A similar fate awaited sailors who tried to sail supplies into the besieged city, of which 260 Muslim prisoners were executed in reply. A little over 20 years later as the Muslim troops attempted to cross the Mediterranean and captured Otranto, at least 800 defenders who refused to convert to Islam were slaughtered. A similar amount of men, or slightly higher, were refused quarter by the Sultan when Methoni fell in 1500. Similarly, when parts of the

[134] Runciman, S (1954) *A History of the Crusades*, Vol 2 (Cambridge, Cambridge University Press) 24. See also Vol 3, 53; Gillingham, J (1978) *Richard the Lionheart* (London, Weidenfeld) 182–84; Finucane, R (2004) *Soldiers of the Faith* (London, Phoenix) 107; Capponi, N (2006) *Victory of the West. The Battle of Lepanto* (London, Macmillan) 12, 62, 76.

[135] Al-Athir in Chaliand, G (ed) *The Art of War in World History* (California, California University Press) 404.

fortresses of Malta in 1565 were over-run, it was common to issue orders of no-quarter to the Christians.[136]

The torture of, and by Crusaders was noted in a number of their conflicts of this period. In the Northern wars, around 1237, captured Crusaders were tortured and sacrificed to pagan gods, or burnt alive in their armour like chestnuts. Such acts were very common after the battle of Tannenberg in 1410 and again following the attack of Ivan the Terrible (1530–84) – one who was also known to torture his own citizens on a grand scale – on the Crusaders and their supporters in 1557.[137]

A number of Muslim forces were also known to utilise torture both within their societies and in their conflicts with others. Hajjaj ib Yusuf, who ruled from for 20 years (694–714) developed methods of torture of prisoners that involved applying hot wax to the skin of victims and pulling it off until the skin lacerated and then pouring salt and vinegar into the wounds, until death, after a very long period, ensued. Genghis Khan (1162–1227), killed captured leaders who defied him either by pouring molten silver into their eyes and ears or slowly crushing them to death before crowds of onlookers. The forces of Tamerlane were also well skilled in the arts of torture and slow executions. The skinning alive of prisoners who would not accept Islam is recorded as late as 1571. Some Crusading orders could also display remarkable cruelty which ranged from burying their enemies alive, through to burning their genitals off. In 1209, during the Albigensian Crusade, Simon de Montfort, took the castle, and with the garrison, he cut off the upper lip and the nose of each prisoner. He blinded them all except one, who he left with a single eye, to guide the victims to the next fortress he planned to besiege. These acts were supplemented by the French Inquisition which launched itself on the Albigensian heretics with the thumb screw, burnings, the boot and a rack to dislocate limbs. Men were spreadeagled and crushed by weights or filled with water through a funnel until they suffocated. Possibly the most excruciating torments were the wedges hammered under the finger nails, teeth wrenched out and the exposed nerves prodded. Thirty six of the Albigensian brethren died, whilst 123 confessed to the crime of spitting on the crucifix or, inter alia, homosexuality.[138]

Whilst some of the warriors of the period were indulging in great acts of cruelty, others were clearly aware of some limits when it came to questions like dealing with

[136] Runciman, S (1954) *A History of the Crusades*, Vol 2 (Cambridge, Cambridge University Press) 24, 460; McGlynn, S (2008) *By Sword and Fire: Cruelty and Atrocity in Medieval Warfare* (London, Weidenfeld) 106; Capponi, N (2006) *Victory of the West. The Battle of Lepanto* (London, Macmillan) 272, 303–304; Finucane, R (2004) *Soldiers of the Faith* (London, Phoenix) 25, 98; Seward, D (1974) *The Monks of War* (Herts, Penguin) 39–40, 58, 105, 122, 197, 230; France, J (1999) *Western Warfare In the Age of the Crusades* (London, UCL Press) 228; Finucane, R (2004) *Soldiers of the Faith* (London, Phoenix) 25, 98; France, J (1999) *Western Warfare In the Age of the Crusades* (London, UCL Press) 51, 227–29; Runciman, S (1965) *The Fall of Constantinople 1453* (Cambridge, Cambridge University Press) 66–67, 96, 108; Marozzi, J (2005) *Tamerlane: Sword of Islam* (London, Harper) 93, 264, 287, 289.

[137] Pavlov, A (2003) *Ivan the Terrible* (Essex, Pearson) 120–21, 127, 133, 157–59, 170 and 172; Seward, D (1974) *The Monks of War* (Herts, Penguin) 104, 116, 133.

[138] Karsh, E (2006) *Islamic Imperialism. A History* (NYC, Yale University Press) 34–35; Seward, D (1974) *The Monks of War* (Herts, Penguin) 203; France, J (1999) *Western Warfare In the Age of the Crusades* (London, UCL Press) 227–29; Bradford, E (1962) *The Great Siege* (London, Reprint Society) 65; Runciman, S (1965) *The Fall of Constantinople 1453* (Cambridge, Cambridge University Press) 43; Turnbull, S (2003) *Genghis Khan and the Mongol Conquests* (London, Osprey) 21, 75; Juvaini, A (1997) *Genghis Khan: The History of a World Conqueror* (Paris, Manchester UP/UNESCO) 51, 66, 168, 172; Marozzi, J (2005) *Tamerlane: Sword of Islam* (London, Harper) 308–309; Capponi, N (2006) *Victory of the West. The Battle of Lepanto* (London, Macmillan) 235; Finucane, R (2004) *Soldiers of the Faith* (London, Phoenix) 101–102; McGlynn, S (2008) *By Sword and Fire: Cruelty and Atrocity in Medieval Warfare* (London, Weidenfeld) 191.

the dead. In this regard, Christian armies of the Crusading period went to considerable effort to ensure their dead could receive a Christian burial. However, the same respect was rarely accorded to Muslim bodies, which would either be disposed of in whichever way was easiest or desecrated. Whilst some desecration involved the Muslim dead being gutted to search for swallowed valuables, more commonly, it involved head-hunting or the placement of the dead on pikes to terrorise their living opponents. This was notable at, inter alia, Nicea in 1097, Ascalon in 1153 and Tiberias in 1187. After the Crusader victory outside Antioch in 1098, some 500 Muslim heads were carried back to base and 200 were then shot over the wall of the besieged area. When Alhama in Spain in 1482 was recaptured by the Christian forces, they threw the bodies of the dead defenders over the walls, for the dogs to eat the rotting remains, whilst during the siege of Malta, the commander of the besieged Order of Saint John, had all of his Turkish prisoners executed, decapitated, and their heads used as cannonballs. It was recorded that this was done 'as a lesson in humanity'.[139] Cannibalism of enemy soldiers was recorded after the fall of Ma'arra 1098, during the siege of Antioch in 1098 (due to starvation) and also when Peter the Hermit (d 1115) urged his followers to make 'ritual meals' out of the dead Saracens, as a religious process to reach the promised land.[140] Extreme behaviour towards enemies of the Church with regards to defiling the dead was not restricted to Muslims. That is, during the Inquisition, it was decreed that the heretics who were burnt were to be incinerated to such a degree, that not even ashes should remain.[141]

The armies of Genghis Khan (1162–1227) displayed a similar contempt for dead enemies. Khan used to command his generals to make piles of the heads of the dead, divided by sex. Alternately, he would have the ears of the dead enemy soldiers collected so he could see the magnitude of his victories. In one battle alone in 1223, a Georgian army of over 40,000 soldiers was completely destroyed, and nine sacks of (right) human ears were collected.[142]

Following the desecration of his own uncle by enemy soldiers, Mohammad (570–632) banned the mutilation of the dead. Following suit, Abou Bekr (571–634), explicitly told his soldiers going out to fight enemies that 'see that none deals with treachery. You shall mutilate none.'[143] The scholar Abd al-Rahman al Awza'i (704–74), reiterated this rule against mutilation of the enemy dead.[144] Some subsequent Muslim leaders showed a clear respect for the dead, irrespective of side. For example, after Constantinople fell in 1453, Sultan Mehmet (1432–81) gave the body of the fallen emperor back to the Greeks for a Christian burial. However, such practices were far from universal as numbers of Islamic fighters desecrated the dead in both their own inter-faith wars and in their wars against others. In their inter-faith wars, the collection

[139] Bradford, E (1962) *The Great Siege* (London, Reprint Society) 140; France, J (1999) *Western Warfare in the Age of the Crusades 1000–1300* (London, UCL Press) 115; Runciman, S (1954) *A History of the Crusades*, Vol 1 (Cambridge, Cambridge University Press) 179, 228; Finucane, R (2004) *Soldiers of the Faith* (London, Phoenix) 102–105; McGlynn, S (2008) *By Sword and Fire: Cruelty and Atrocity in Medieval Warfare* (London, Weidenfeld) 107, 191; Seward, D (1974) *The Monks of War* (Herts, Penguin) 185.

[140] Finucane, R (2004) *Soldiers of the Faith* (London, Phoenix) 64–65, 102, 128; France, J (1999) *Western Warfare in the Age of the Crusades 1000–1300* (London, UCL Press) 227.

[141] Green, T (2007) *Inquisition. The Reign of Fear* (London, Macmillan) 272.

[142] Juvaini, A (1997) *Genghis Khan: The History of a World Conqueror* (Paris Manchester, UP/UNESCO) 178, 195, 270; Gabriel, R 'The Right Hand of Khan' *Military History* (May 2008)) 42–50.

[143] Reprinted in Islam and the League of Nations (Grotius Society Publication) V:126.

[144] Khadduri, M (1955) *War and Peace in the Law of Islam* (Baltimore, John Hopkins Press) 53, 106.

and transportation of the heads of the defeated contenders was renowned. For example, the last leader of the Umayyad dynasty had his head removed and sent to Abul Abbas (721–54), who reportedly fed his tongue to a cat. Even the longer dead were not spared. After one of the inter-faith battles, the Umayyad capiphs were exhumed and desecrated. In this regard, the corpse of Hisham (724–43) was discovered virtually intact. It was then crucified, given 120 lashes and burnt to ashes.[145]

The desecration of non-Muslim dead was also not known. Some Muslim warriors argued that decapitation of Christian dead was essential to ensure the Crusaders did not contaminate paradise. Accordingly, the taking of Christian heads as trophies was also not uncommon by Muslim forces. For example, some 1,000 Christian heads were taken and brought back to Aleppo in 1133, where Muslim leaders paid a bounty for them, whilst in 1153, the defenders of Ascalon hung the bodies of captured and killed Crusaders over the battlements in front of their enemies. Saladin (1138–93) displayed the heads of fallen knights during his siege of Tiberias in 1187, although he was careful with who he displayed, as he kept some corpses, such as that of Odo-Saint-Amaund – the Eighth Grand Master of the Knights Templar between 1171 and 1179 – for exchange of living Muslim prisoners. Tamerlane (1336–1405) left towers and pyramids built from the skulls of decapitated victims on every battlefield he fought, as a warning to anyone who dare oppose him. He also used the heads of fallen Christian soldiers as ammunition for catapults in 1402. Nevertheless, he did show a certain respect for enemy rulers, in that although he kept them in gold cages whilst they were alive, he did allow their bodies to be returned to their families when they died. Notable desecrations were also evident in centuries to come, such as those in 1565, when killed Christian knights were decapitated, and their headless trunks were nailed to cross beams of wood in mockery of the crucifixion and launched onto the surrounding waters to wash up at the base of the areas still holding out. Their heads were used as ammunition or attached to notes offering terms of surrender. Similar practices of desecration were known to continue by Turkish forces, at least until the siege of Belgrade in 1688.[146]

6. The Sixteenth and Seventeenth Centuries

The period that is commonly recognised as the Reformation is notable because many of the great scholars of international law, Francisco de Vitoria[147] (1492–1546) and Alberico Gentili (1552–1608), both argued that it was correct to give quarter to enemy soldiers (although perhaps not enemy leaders) who had surrendered and posed no physical threat.[148] Thomas More (1478–1535) broadly concurred, arguing that in an ideal situation after battles were concluded, prisoners should be taken, not throats

[145] Karsh, E (2006) *Islamic Imperialism. A History* (NYC, Yale University Press) 37, 39, 46, 47–49.

[146] Bradford, E (1962) *The Great Siege* (London, Reprint Society) 139; Capponi, N (2006) *Victory of the West. The Battle of Lepanto* (London, Macmillan) 144; McGlynn, S (2008) *By Sword and Fire: Cruelty and Atrocity in Medieval Warfare* (London, Weidenfeld) 105, 191; Seward, D (1974) *The Monks of War* (Herts, Penguin) 155, 185, 230; Marozzi, J (2005) *Tamerlane: Sword of Islam* (London, Harper) 5, 7; Runciman, S (1965) *The Fall of Constantinople 1453* (Cambridge, Cambridge University Press) 42. Finally, see s 16:126 of the Koran.

[147] Pagden, A (ed) *Vitoria: Political Writings* (Cambridge, Cambridge University Press) 320–22.

[148] Gentili, A (1612) *De Jure Belli Libri Tres* in *Classics of International Law*, 1933 edn (Oxford, Oxford University Press) 385, 477–81, 525. Cf Gentili, A (1661) *Hispanicae Advocationis Libri Duo* in *Classics of International Law*, 1904 edn (Oxford, Clarendon) 41.

cut.[149] Pierino Belli (1502–75) summed up this position well in 1563 when he suggested that 'nature admonishes us that it is humane to spare a captured enemy and not kill him . . . it is not right to treat a captured prisoner with cruelty'.[150]

In addition, from this era, the first clear instances whereby the sick or wounded were treated by both sides, irrespective of their original loyalty, appear towards the end of the sixteenth century. Thus, in 1599 Spain and the Dutch Republic concluded a formal convention, and by 1639 Spain and France had also agreed that sick and injured soldiers who fell into enemy hands should be placed under a special safeguard and repatriated with a minimum of formality.[151]

Despite the increasing overlapping of these views, it would be mistaken to suggest they represented the practice of warfare of the period from the Renaissance to the end of the Reformation. The execution of prisoners was recorded during the English War of the Roses, with the execution of perhaps 1,500 prisoners after the battle of Tewkesbury in 1471 on the orders of Edward IV (1442–83) being particularly notable.[152] Evidence of such acts surfaced in the twenty-first century, when a mass grave containing 40 bodies of men aged between 17 and 50, was uncovered at Towton. The majority of these fighters still retained the same execution marks on the back of their skulls.[153] Similar acts of killing prisoners are recorded in numerous other conflicts of the fifteenth and sixteenth centuries, after the captives had, inter alia, refused offers to surrender, used novel weapons (like arquebusiers) or had the misfortune to be fighting Swiss mercenaries, who refused to take prisoners as a matter of principle. The Turks often behaved in the same manner, seldom giving quarter to prisoners unless it was agreed well in advance. Even when terms were made, safety was by no means guaranteed. Thus, after the surrender by agreement of Buda in 1529, the garrison was massacred as it marched out. Other nations, like France, were on occasion equally merciless, such as when all of the prisoners were killed out of hand after the fall of Chateau le Compte near Hesdin in 1552.[154] Sometimes, such as with the Conquistadors in Mexico and Peru, prisoners were killed despite their fulfilling their ransom demands, simply because of changing interpretations of political expediency. Such problems continued as the Reformation gathered pace. Acts of no-quarter are recorded during the French religious wars and the Spanish wars against what became the Netherlands. As one example of the latter conflict, the Duke of Parma (1545–92) refused the surrender of soldiers at Sichem in 1578, hanging their commander and having all of the soldiers clubbed to death, as an example of what lay in store for others who defied both their political and spiritual masters. Such intolerance was not the monopoly of any one faith. Elsewhere, Martin Luther (1483–1546) would preach in 1525 when speaking of peasant uprisings 'I think all the peasants should perish . . . because the

[149] More, T and Logan, G (1975) *Utopia* (Cambridge, Cambridge University Press), 215.

[150] Belli, P (1563) in trans Nutting, H (1936) *A Treatise of Military Matters and Warfare* in *Classics of International Law* (Oxford, Clarendon) 85.

[151] See Parker, G (2002) *Empire, War and Faith in Early Modern Europe* (London, Penguin) 52.

[152] McGlynn, S (2008) *By Sword and Fire: Cruelty and Atrocity in Medieval Warfare* (London, Weidenfeld) 128–33.

[153] McGlynn, S (2008) *By Sword and Fire: Cruelty and Atrocity in Medieval Warfare* (London, Weidenfeld) 128–33; Anon (2010) 'Nasty, Brutish and Not That Short' *Economist* 18 December, 100–102.

[154] Potter, G (ed) (1969) *The New Cambridge Modern History. The Renaissance*, Vol 1 (Cambridge, Cambridge University Press) 284; Elton, G (ed) (1968) *The New Cambridge Modern History: The Reformation*, Vol II (Cambridge, Cambridge University Press) 484–86, 503.

peasants have taken up the sword without divining authority . . . no mercy, no toleration is due to the peasants; on them should fall the wrath of God and man . . . The peasants may be treated as mad dogs.'[155]

On the battlefields between the Catholics and the Protestants, acts of no-quarter were repaid in kind, by both the Dutch and Spanish, and also when the Spanish attempted to invade the British Isles. In the latter case, although most of the Spanish who washed up on the shores of England from their ill-fated Armada in 1588, survived, of the estimated 6,000 shipwrecked sailors who washed up on the shores of Ireland and Scotland only about 750 survived to be ransomed. Some 2,000 are believed to have drowned, with the remainder being captured and executed within minutes or days upon reaching land. On the Continent, the English slaughtered some 500 Spanish troops at Corunna in 1589, sparing only a few officers for ransom. The same policy occurred with the fall of the Spanish fort of Crozon in Brittany in 1594. There are also many instances in the Thirty Years War of the killing of prisoners in cold blood. Most of these atrocities occurred after a fortress had been stormed. In 1631, when Neubrandenburg was captured, the garrison of 3,000 was put to the sword. The garrisons' of Ingolstadt were massacred in 1633, Frankfurt in 1637 and Turin in 1640. All were massacred without mercy.[156]

Acts of no-quarter were not the only methods of regarding prisoners at this point. Charles I (1600–1649), reflecting some of the influential legal scholarship of his age, such as that of Richard Zouche (1590–1661)[157] proclaimed in 1640 that 'None shall kill an enemy who yields and throws down his arms'.[158] Likewise, the English command for war at sea from 1653 added: 'If in time of fight God shall deliver any of the enemy ships into our hands, special care is to be taken to save their men as the present state of our condition will permit.'[159]

Despite such proclamations, Charles was not feeling so generous when the English Civil War broke out and the soldiers of Parliament were initially tried for treason, after surrendering, for which they could be executed. When Parliament responded in kind, Charles changed his practices. Nevertheless, despite some prisoner exchanges, hundreds of captives, on both sides, were slaughtered without mercy at, inter alia, Torrington, Lincoln and Cirencester. These practices grew as Oliver Cromwell (1599–1658) stormed through Ireland. This was a particular issue for Irish Catholics, as the British Parliament had in 1644 explicitly stated that no quarter was to be offered to

[155] Luther in Reddaway, F (ed) (1930) *Select Documents in European History*, Vol II 1492–715 (London, Methuen) 55.

[156] Parker, G (2002) *Empire, War and Faith in Early Modern Europe* (London, Penguin) 148; Robinson, P (2006) *Military Honour and the Conduct of War* (London, Routledge) 101; Hanson, N (2003) *The Confident Hope of a Miracle. The True Story of the Spanish Armada* (London, Corgi) 211, 479–88, 492–97; Stradling, R (1992) *The Armada of Flanders* (Cambridge, Cambridge University Press) 40–45; Glover, M (1982) *The Velvet Glove. The Decline and Fall of Moderation in War* (London, Hodder) 99; Chamberlin, E (1979) *The Sack of Rome* (London, Batsford) 39; Anderson, M (1998) *War and Society in Europe of the Old Regime* (London, Sutton) 65; Childs, J (2001) *Warfare in the Seventeenth Century* (London, Cassell) 53, 58; Wood, M (2000) *Conquistadors* (London, BBC) 73, 114, 144; Hemming, J (1970) *The Conquest of the Incas* (Macmillan, London) 77–78, 80–85.

[157] Zouche believed it was only possible to kill prisoners of war in moments of great stress and when being attacked. See Zouche, R (1650) *An Exposition of Fecial Law and Procedure, or Of Law Between Nations and Questions Concerning the Same* (Baltimore Press, 1911) 116–17.

[158] Meron, T (1993) *Henry's Wars and Shakespeare's Laws* (Oxford, Oxford University Press) 151.

[159] 'English Line of Battle Orders 1653' in Symcox, G (1974) *War, Diplomacy and Imperialism* (NYC, Walker) 212.

such men captured 'taken in hostility against the Parliament'. Significantly, this order applied to the war in England, Wales and on the High Seas, but not in Ireland. Thereafter, many of the massacres of prisoners of war in the English Civil War, were Irish Catholics. In Eire, the massacre of prisoners predated the arrival of Cromwell. However, it was the acts of Cromwell in this war that are most renowned. For example, at Drogheda, Cromwell sent an ultimatum to surrender to the commanders 'to the end [that] effusion of blood may be prevented'. When this was refused, the besieged areas were stormed, whereupon he 'forbade [his men] to spare any that were in arms in the town, and I think that night they put to the sword about 2,000 soldiers'.[160] In other conflicts in Ireland, the process of executing prisoners was more regulated. For example, Cromwell explained to the English Parliament in 1648 that with storming of Tredah that: 'When they submitted, their officers were knocked on the head, and every tenth man of the soldiers killed, and the rest shipped to the Barbados.'[161]

Whilst these acts were the source of much criticism, some scholars, such as Samuel Rachel (1628–91) argued that the laws of war 'allows . . . the slaughter at any time of prisoners and those who have surrendered unconditionally'.[162] This was not an outrageous position, as conflicts of no-quarter continued to be recorded throughout the last parts of the seventeenth century, such as with the battle of Ligny between the French and the Prussians in 1689 and during the Jacobite uprising in Ireland in the same year.[163]

Although progress was slow on the issue of making the giving of quarter mandatory to defenceless prisoners, progress began to appear on the issue of torture. The roots of this progress can be traced to Michel de Montaigne (1533–92) who condemned the cruelty involved in torture and was also highly sceptical of confessions obtained under torture, pointing out that such confessions can be made up by the suspect just to escape the torture they were subjected to.[164] Montaigne's work was joined by Anton Praetorius (1560–1613) a German Calvinist pastor who spoke out against torture and the persecution of witches and Johann Graefe, who in 1624 published *Tribunal Reformation*, a case against torture. Although these works did little to slow the practice of torture during this period, it is notable that many of the worst tortures of this period occurred outside of times of war. The most notable manifestation of this was with the hunting of witches. The hunting of witches who were allegedly involved with *maleficia* (making pacts with the Devil for harmful purposes) swept through Protestant Europe in the sixteenth and seventeenth century. On the basis of biblical direction,[165] over this period perhaps 100,000 persons (which ranged between 75 and 90 per cent female depending on the country) were tried for witchcraft of which just under half were executed.

[160] Cromwell, noted in Carlton, C (1992) *Going to War: The Experience of the English Civil Wars* (London, Routledge) 174; See also O'Siochru, M (2008) *God's Executioner: Oliver Cromwell and the Conquest of Ireland* (London, Faber) 20, 42–49, 69–70, 79–84; Robertson, J (2006) *The Tyrannicide Brief* (London, Vintage) 86, 114, 229.

[161] Cromwell in Reddaway, F (ed) (1930) *Select Documents in European History 1492–1715*, Vol II (London, Methuen) 137.

[162] Rachel, S (1676) *The Law of Nature and Nations* in Scott, JB (ed) (1916) *The Classics of International Law* (Oxford, Clarendon) 183.

[163] Gebler, C (2005) *The Siege of Derry* (London, Abacus) 196, 203; Reid, P (1984) *Prisoners of War* (London, Hamlyn) 25.

[164] Scott, G (1940) *A History of Torture Throughout the Ages* (London, Torchstream) 135.

[165] Exodus 22:18: 'Thou shalt not suffer a witch to live.'

Before they were executed, confessions had to be secured. Accordingly, torture became increasingly important. Despite limits in terms of duration and pregnant women being exempt, pulleys, the rack, thumb screws, leg screws, head clamps and tourniquets were all the methods of choice. Water torture and sleep deprivation were also widely used. When such methods were used the conviction rates could be as high as 95 per cent. This is a remarkable figure when key parts of the crime they confessed to involved flight, metamorphosis into animals and various interactions with the devil.[166]

Acts of no-quarter and torture were also part and parcel of life for pirates on the high seas. With regards to the first issue, some pirates were known to fly red flags, although in time, the 'skull and crossbones' came to replace it, to signal that they would take no prisoners. This was designed to show a 'triad of interlocking symbols' namely, death, violence and limited time. The message was that immediate surrender was required or death was imminent.[167] Assuming that seafarers survived the storming of their vessel by pirates, (and although 'walking the plank' appears to be a theatrical creation), whipping, burning, the placing of burning matches under fingernails and other mutilations were common. In addition, men were pressed to death, nailed to the deck of their ship, hung by their digits till they separated, or had knotted cords, which were progressively tightened, tired around their heads. In other instances, those who would not reveal the location of treasure were placed in buckets of gunpowder and taunted with open flames. Of course, captured pirates could expect to be tortured as well, especially before trials. Records remain of men having their thumbs bound together and squeezed with a whipcord, or having weights placed upon them in official Press Yards.[168]

Torture was also of interest to the sovereigns of the period, although by the time of James I (1566–1625) torture was restricted, to people accused of treason. This meant that only the Sovereign or the Privy Council could approve it. When faced with the capture of the world's first modern terrorist who was proving reluctant to provide details of his accomplices, James ordered that 'the gentler tortures are to be first used unto him and so by degrees proceeding to the worst'. The 'gentler tortures' to which Guido (Guy) Fawkes and his accomplices were first given was manacles by which they were hung from the wall for hours or longer. The 'worst torture' was the rack which was housed in the Tower of London. The rack was a large open frame of oak, raised from the ground. The prisoner was laid on it with his back to the floor, his wrists and ankles attached by cords to rollers at either end. Levers were operated which stretched the prisoner, quite slowly, while he was urged to talk, as Guido did.[169] Despite such confessions, within a few decades, judicial torture had ended in Britain. This position became so well recognised that when prisoners were tortured by Royalist forces during the English Civil War, despite promises that he would not do such things, Charles I was eventually forced to stand trial and condemnation.[170] To ensure such mistakes were not

[166] Levack, B (1995) *The Witch Hunt in Early Modern Europe* (London, Longman) 21–26, 44, 49, 75–84.

[167] Earle, P (2004) *The Pirate Wars* (London, Methuen) 154; Cordingly, D (2006) *Under the Black Flag* (NYC, Random) 116–19.

[168] Cordingly, D (2006) *Under the Black Flag* (NYC, Random) 41, 127, 130–34; Earle, P (2004) *The Pirate Wars* (London, Methuen) 33, 106, 174–75.

[169] Fraser, A (1996) *The Gunpowder Plot* (London, BCA) 175–80; Hanson, N (2003) *The Confident Hope of a Miracle* (London, Corgi) 33.

[170] Robertson, J (2006) *The Tyrannicide Brief* (London, Vintage) 68, 174, 193, 211.

repeated, the English Bill of Rights of 1689, like the subsequent Constitution of the United States, came to prohibit 'cruel and unusual punishments'.[171]

Death and/or torture was not the outcome for all captives of this period. Prisoners could, as Hugo Grotius (1583–1645) recognised, be either ransomed or exchanged at the end of hostilities.[172] The ransoming of prisoners occurred in conflicts such as the English Civil War and Cromwell's invasion of Ireland. In this conflict, the ransoming of a common soldier was put at the rate of 18 shillings, increasing thereafter according to rank. When no money was available from central funds to release these men, many of the troops remained in captivity unless freed following the intervention by relatives and friends. The ransoming of prisoners occurred both within Europe and between Europe and the Middle East. Before 1650, ransoming captives held hundreds of miles away was a low priority for Britain. However, after 1642 the authorities put a levy on some imports to help pay ransoms for captives taken by Muslim Corsairs, over 3,000 were ransomed between 1677 and 1682. France and Spain which had two religious orders who were dedicated to redeeming their Christian subjects taken by Islamic forces. Likewise, the Church of England was active in this area from 1579. However, many had to wait years to be rescued, and many were never ransomed at all and had to try to survive life as slaves. In the mid seventeenth century, there was an annual death rate of 20 per cent for all European captives held in Tripoli.[173] Conditions were not that much better for captives held in Europe. For example, in the war between Spain and England, of the captured 240 English sailors taken by the Spanish in 1563, only 80 of them survived their captivity to eventually be ransomed and returned to England. Similarly, with the crewmen of the Spanish Armada who were lucky enough to land in England (and not Scotland or Ireland), the British Crown explicitly refused to pay for the upkeep of Spanish rank and file on English soil. The upkeep of such men fell to the individual captors, who hoped to keep their possessions alive for their eventual ransoming.[174]

By the end of the sixteenth century, the informal and often ad hoc regimes for ransom were being supplemented by more formal arrangements. For example, the ransom or exchange of prisoners was established between Spain and the Netherlands in 1599, with ransoms being set at one month's salary for each captive, or a free mutual exchange based on equivalent rank.[175] These options for ransoming which continued throughout the periods that many European nations were at war, were supplemented by a clear development whereby when wars were concluded, all prisoners were returned, without ransom. For example, the Peace of Westphalia concluded 'all prisoners on the one side and the other without any distinction of the gown or the sword, shall be released'.[176] Exactly the same obligation would follow in subsequent

[171] See Devastation and Torture During the Thirty Years War in Reddaway, F (ed) (1930) *Select Documents in European History* Vol II (London, Methuen) 1492–715: 129. Also, Macartney, C (ed) (1970) *The Habsburg and Hohenzollern Dynasties* (NYC, Harper) 21.

[172] Grotius, H (1625) *The Rights of War and Peace*, 1901 edn (London, Dunne) 410.

[173] Cooley, L (2002) *Captives: Britain, Empire and the World 1600–1850* (London, Cape) 50, 52–55, 76, 105.

[174] Rowdon, M (1974) *The Spanish Terror* (London, Constable) 227; O'Siochru, M (2008) *God's Executioner: Oliver Cromwell and the Conquest of Ireland* (London, Faber) 75–76.

[175] Parker, G (2002) *Empire, War and Faith in Early Modern Europe* (Penguin, London) 160, 164; Symcox, G (1974) *War, Diplomacy and Imperialism* (NYC, Walker) 151; Rowdon, M (1974) *The Spanish Terror* (London, Constable) 260–61.

[176] The Treaty of Westphalia 1648, Art CX.

peace treaties, such as those of Wehlau in 1657,[177] Nijmegen in 1678,[178] Ryswick in 1697[179] and Rastadt in 1714.[180] Similarly, the Peace Treaty between Persia and the Ottoman Empire of 1746 would stipulate 'all prisoners of war of the two contracting Parties shall be liberated and may not be bought or sold as slaves. These prisoners desiring to return to their homes shall not be impeded by either side.'[181]

In this age, if a common soldier died on active service, it was likely they would receive little or no acknowledgement for their sacrifice. It was also quite possible that they would have received no assistance if they were wounded in the process, as very few sovereigns believed it was their responsibility to look after their own wounded men, let alone the wounded of the other side. However, some sovereigns acted differently. For example, Charles the Bold (1433–1477) placed one surgeon in each army unit under this command. Henri IV (1533–1610), upon seeing his own wounded soldiers went one step further, and ordered 'the creation of a house to accommodate and dress the wounded, to treat and feed the poor soldiers wounded during the siege'. This was the first recorded army field hospital and was soon to be supplemented by the first field dressing stations. The Spanish included two hospital ships with 85 surgeons in their Armada which set sail to defeat England. Nevertheless, these actions were exceptions in this age. Thus, the English force of some 32,500 men who took part in the war of 1544 had no surgeons directly employed by the army. Mary Tudor (1516–58) was the first to leave an endowment for a hospital for poor, aged or disabled soldiers, whilst the first hospital for wounded seamen in Britain was established in 1580 by Francis Drake (1540–96) and his friends, not Elizabeth I (1533–1603) – although her government began to take this matter much more seriously when ex-soldiers returned home and effective demobilisation packages, including care of the sick and the wounded, had to be created to avoid social upheaval.

On the battlefield, this meant that looking after the wounded was seen as the responsibility of individual commanders, not the State. In some instances, the commanders took this responsibility to include the looking after of the wounded of the opposition. For example, the 1581 surrender document beween Alexander Farneze (1545–1592) and the town of Torunai stipulated:

> 'As for the wounded and sick who cannot go out at present due to their infirmity, our intention is that then they have recovered they shall enjoy the same benefits as their comrades and that they shall all be given passports and vehicles to take them out of danger'.

Similar provisions can be found in a large number of documents of surrender, particularly in those of Breda (1625 and 1637), Bois-le-Duc (1629), Mainz (1635), Turin (1640), Ypres (1658) and Strasbourg (1675). Moreover, when medical people were known to exist, this period was notable for the development of rules, as early as 1673, whereby captured medical personnel would be exchanged without ransom. Although such changes were becoming known it remained an option, not an obligation, for each commander. Thus, during the Thirty Years' War, few commanders seem to have had much time for their wounded, except on special occasions, such as in 1632

[177] Treaty of Wehlau 1657, Art II.
[178] The Peace of Nijmegen 1678, Art X.
[179] The Treaty of Ryswick 1697, Art IX.
[180] The Treaty of Rastadt 1714, Art XXXV.
[181] The Treaty Between Persia and the Ottoman Empire 1746, Art VII.

when Albrecht von Wallenstein (1583–1634) went around his defenders throwing handfuls of coins into the laps of the wounded, to encourage the rest.[182]

It is debatable how much merit was provided by medical assistance. The difficulty was that it was a very haphazard system in a period when medical knowledge and its application was minimal. For example, in 1684, William Phillips, the boatswain of HMS *Swallow* which was engaged against pirates, was wounded in the leg during a skirmish. There was no surgeon on board and it was decided that the ships carpenter was the most suitable man to tackle the job. The carpenter produced the biggest saw from his tool chest and went to work 'as though he were cutting a deal board in two and soon the leg was separated from the body of the patient'.[183] To cauterise the wound, the carpenter used his broadaxe, but he proved less skilled with this tool and burned more of the flesh than was necessary. Miraculously, Phillips survived the operation.[184]

The chances of survival of wounded soldiers were also directly linked to the limited medical knowledge of the time, and the ever evolving military technologies that quickly eclipsed their limited knowledge. This was particuarly so with the advent of gunpowder and its assocaited projectiles. Musket balls, two-thirds of an inch across, could do horrific damage. Moving far slower than modern bullets, they did not pass cleanly through the body, but bounced off bones and organs, dragging bits of dirt and clothing with them, in a sure-fire recipe for dangerous infection, of which surgeons had no idea how to cure. Thoracic and abdominal wounds were usually fatal. By the end of the sixteenth century, the standard treatment for gunshot wounds was cauterisation with burning oil, by using a mixture of egg yolk, rose oil and turpentine, and the tying of the severed arteries in an amputation with cord, rather than application of a red hot iron to the stump, of which the patients regularly died of shock. Hits on limbs usually required amputation and it was not uncommon to amputate limbs from 30 to 40 per cent of the wounded. There was a 25 per cent death rate following amputations due to gunpowder projectiles up until 1850.[185]

With respect to the dead, this period is notable because some fallen heroes were clearly being remembered. For example, Sir Roger Williams, (1539–95) a Protestant Welsh soldier of fortune, was buried 'with full military honours' in Saint Paul's Cathedral in 1595. Such respect, was only given the most high ranking soldiers of their own side. Thus, through until the end of the Napoleonic wars, if an officer was hurt, his name would be entered on a casualty list. This was not the same with the common soldiers, who were listed by number not name. The desecration of the enemy dead, especially the leaders, was also a practice of this period. This was despite the advocacy of scholars like Hugo Grotius who argued in 1625, that the burying of the dead, irrespective of

[182] Symcox, G (1974) *War, Diplomacy and Imperialism* (NYC, Walker) 151; Boissier, P (1978) *A History of the International Committee of the Red Cross: From Solferino to Tsushima* (Henry Dunant Institute, Geneva) 126–27.

[183] Cordingly, D (2006) *Under the Black Flag* (NYC, Random) 8.

[184] Nichol, J and Rennell, T (2009) *Medic* (London, Penguin) 7–10; Hanson, N (2003) *The Confident Hope of a Miracle. The True Story of the Spanish Armada* (London, Corgi) 353, 453, 540; Parker, G (1997) *The Thirty Years' War* (Routledge, London) 183; *Medic* (Penguin, London) 28–29; Neillands, R (2006) *The Wars of the Roses* (London, Phoenix) 79, 162; Elton, G (ed) (1968) *The New Cambridge Modern History: The Reformation*, Vol II (Cambridge, Cambridge University Press) 503–504.

[185] Moorehead, C (1998) *Dunant's Dream: War, Switzerland and the History of the Red Cross* (NYC, Carroll and Graf) 27–28; Kelly, J (2004) *Gunpowder* (London, Atlantic) 79; Bell, D (2007) *The First Total War: Napoleon's Europe and the Birth of Modern Warfare* (London, Bloomsbury) 40; Greenwood, J (2005) *Medics at War: Military Medicine from Colonial Times to the 21st Century* (Annapolis, Naval Institute Press) 30; Ponting, C (2005) *The Crimean War: The Truth Behind the Myth* (London, Pimlico) 193.

side, was 'a moral act, sanctioned by the unwritten laws of nature'.[186] Unfortunately, many of the combatants of this period disagreed. For example, after 'King' Philip of Metacom (1639–76), was killed near his New England home, the pious killers hacked his body to pieces and displayed it on trees and placed his head on permanent display at Plymouth colony, whilst his jawbone was used by preachers as proof of his blasphemy. Elsewhere, pirates were renowned for disemboweling captured officers, cutting out their hearts, soaking them in spirits and then eating them. Replying in kind, desecrations awaited the pirates when apprehended. The head of Blackbeard (1680–1718) was slung beneath the bowspirit of the sloop of the vessel belonging to the captain who killed him, whilst the body of Captain Kidd (1645–1701) was suspended on a gibbet at Tilbery Point on the lower reaches of the Thames. The ports of Britain were said to be decorated with such bodies, which were coated with tar after death, to help prevent the ravages of weather and discourage the crows and seagulls. Such punishment was not unusual for other forms of criminals for time to come, with the Murder Act of 1752 including the option of hanging corpses in chains in prominent public places. This was particularly so with high profile issues. Thus, following the trial and execution of those who were still alive and responsible for the death of his father, Charles II (1630–85) ordered the newly dead regicides to be fixed to poles about the entrance of Westminster Hall. One step further, the 1660 Act of Free and General Pardon that accompanied the restoration of Charles II, stipulated that the corpses of Oliver Cromwell and his primary accomplices, to be dug up and their skeletons hung from the gallows.[187]

7. The Eighteenth Century

By the early decades of the eighteenth century, it was possible for leading jurists like Cornelius van Bynkershoek (1673–1743) to suggest that 'the right of executing the vanquished has almost grown obsolete [nevertheless] the right might still be exercised if anyone wished to avail himself of it . . . against those who defend themselves too obstinately.'[188]

From such thinking, a number of conflicts of the period continue to reflect practices of no-quarter. For example, in 1716, the Austrian army, having defeated the larger invading Turkish force in a battle that heralded Austria's conquest of Hungary, put to the sword some 30,000 Turkish troops. A year earlier, following the failed Jacobite uprising in Scotland in 1715 there were at least 40 executions of prisoners, as examples of the rebels who failed. These executions were supplemented by thousands of prisoners who were sent to the colonies as slaves. Similarly, the uprising of Bonnie Prince Charlie (1720–88) in 1745 was met with the Crown treating his British soldiers (unlike his French who were treated as prisoners of war) as traitors, deserving of either death or slavery. However only 1,000 or so of the 3,000 prisoners were turned into slaves in the New World whilst hundreds of others died in captivity, awaiting to hear of

[186] Grotius, H (1625) *The Rights of War and Peace*, 1901 edn (London, Dunne) 213, 313.

[187] Farrington, K (2003) *A History of Punishment and Torture* (London, Hamlyn) 170; Earle, P (2004) *The Pirate Wars* (London, Methuen) 194; Cordingly, D (2006) *Under the Black Flag* (NYC, Random) xiv, 225–27, 230; Robertson, G (2006) *The Tyrannicide Brief* (London, Vintage) 43, 284, 341.

[188] Bynkershoek, C (1737) *Quaestionum Juris Publici Libri Duo* (Oxford, Clarendon,1930) 27, 29.

their fate. Further acts of no-quarter are notable during the War of Austrian Succession at Dettinen in 1743 and Bergen-op-Zoom in 1747. The Seven Years War (1756–63) saws several acts of no-quarter. In North America, a number of instances, one involving George Washington (1732–99), saw accusations and counter-accusations as Indian allies fell upon prisoners who were meant to be protected. Washington also had strong disagreements with his own Indian allies, because he would not hand over French prisoners who were wounded, who he knew would be scalped by the Indians. Some French commanders attempted to respond in the same way, but were not always successful in restraining their Indian allies from killing the wounded enemy prisoners, such as with the surrender of Fort Henry in 1757, where despite French assurances of the safety of the prisoners, the Indians stormed the hospital, killing and scalping over 200 men.

On the European continent, acts of no-quarter occurred at the battle of Zorndorf in 1758 and Kunersdorf in 1759. Alternately, hundreds of prisoners could be taken, only to be marched to death, as the Russians did to their Polish prisoners of war after their capture of Tarnopol in 1769. Eighteen years later in 1787, the Russians executed 26,000 prisoners out of hand in the Balkans.[189]

Supplementary practices of concern that occurred in this period, especially in some colonial contexts, involved the scalping and sometimes consumption of wounded men. This appears to have been an entrenched practice of many North American tribes. This became such a problem that after some skirmishes, the colonial forces had to secretly bury their dead so they would not be dug up and mutilated. Such practices were not only carried on by indigenous groups. For example discovering that some of their (European) soldiers had been scalped, some European authorities offered bounties for every Indian scalp delivered to them. Such practices of bounty paying for scalps continued until the nineteenth century in North America. Even notable British generals such as James Wolfe (1727–59) allowed his troops to scalp Indians and even Canadians dressed as Indians.[190] However, such practices were far from standard. This was especially the case on the Continent, where as early as 1726, some Prussian officers were threatening corporal punishment or execution to prevent the dead being plundered. This is because the desire to plunder the dead was causing some plunderers to execute the wounded. Frederick the Great (1712–68) would come to entrench this tradition, in his attempt to ensure the dead were given some respect.

By the middle of the eighteenth century, there was a clear humanitarian movement which was beginning to question some of the norms of this period, such as the option of being able to refuse to take prisoners. In this regard, jurists like Christian Wolff

[189] Black, J (1994) *European Warfare 1600–1815* (New Haven, Yale University Press) 231, 234–39; Duffy, C (2003) *The '45* (London, Cassell) 523–24, 527–28, 533, 537; Marston, D (2001) *The Seven Years' War* (London, Osprey) 53, 83; Bell, D (2007) *The First Total War: Napoleon's Europe and the Birth of Modern Warfare* (London, Bloomsbury) 48; Hymel, K 'Fort Necessity: George Washington's First Defeat' in *Military Heritage* (Feb 2008) 40, 41–42; Fregault, G (1969) *Canada: The War of Conquest* (Toronto, Oxford University Press) 151–56. Boatner, M (1969) *The Encyclopaedia of the American Revolution* (NYC, McKay) 541; Fowler, W (2005) *Empires at War* (NYC, Walker) 42, 103–104, 125–30.

[190] Fowler, W (2005) *Empires at War* (NYC, Walker) 29, 42, 44, 63, 72–73, 120–21; Boatner, M (1969) *The Encyclopaedia of the American Revolution* (NYC, McKay) 646, 688; Carr, C (2002) *The Lessons of Terror: A History of Warfare Against Civilians* (NY, Little) 111; Kiernan, V (1998) *Colonial Empires and Armies* (London, Sutton) 155.

(1679–1754)[191] and Emerich de Vattel (1714–67)[192] were notable, as was Samuel Johnson (1709–84), who also argued that it was wrong to kill prisoners who posed no risks to their captors.[193] Jean Jacques Rousseau (1712–78) added:

> War is not a relationship between men, but rather a relationship between States, in war individuals are enemies wholly by chance, not as men, not even as citizens, but only as soldiers; not as members of their country, but only as its defenders. . . . Since the aim of war is to subdue a hostile state, a combatant has the right to kill the defenders of that state while they are armed; but as soon as they lay down their arms to surrender, they cease to be either enemies or instruments of the enemy; they simply become men once more, and no one has any longer the right to take their lives . . . war gives no right to inflict any more destruction than is necessary for victory.[194]

The growing recognition that belligerents did not have the right to execute their prisoners was supplemented by the idea that torture was also an act worthy of prohibition. The strongest advocacy for this position came from Cesare Beccaria (1738–94) who argued that 'a man on the rack, in the convulsions of torture, has little in his power to declare the truth . . . the very means employed to distinguish the innocent from the guilty will most effectually destroy all difference between them'.[195]

Whilst some, like Denis Diderot (1713–84), came to argue for the terror value of torture,[196] more influential voices such as Voltaire (1694–1778) argued that torture was not only an 'idiotic barbarity' that destroyed the victim, but also came to 'horrify the spectator' whilst failing to deter illegal acts.[197] Immanuel Kant (1724–1804) added that torture 'dishonour[ed] humanity itself'.[198] From such arguments, and following the British lead in 1689, Frederick the Great abolished torture in Prussia in 1742. Torture was banned in what became Italy in 1786. The United States outlawed pressing in 1772, branding in 1779 and burning in 1790.[199]

The late seventeenth and early eighteenth centuries saw in Western Europe the first real attempts to develop some system of military and naval hospitals so as to give better care to sick and wounded servicemen. Hitherto, what facilities of this type existed were usually run by religious orders or charities. The English military finally introduced field hospitals in 1690, although ad hoc assistance was clearly available in the conflicts before this by imposing on the existing town medical facilities. In 1692, Queen Mary, moved by the suffering of her wounded sailors, converted the incomplete Royal Palace at Greenwich into a naval hospital. In 1705, the British navy commissioned five hospital ships and in 1794 they had the astonishingly named *Charon* (the ferryman of hell) attached to the fleet. A few years later, the most famous British naval vessel of all time, HMS *Victory*, would be added to this growing collection of hospital ships. The French

[191] 'It is not allowable to kill those captured in war . . . one ceases to be an enemy when he is in my power.' Wolff, C (1764) *Jus Gentium Methodo Scientifica Pertractatus,* 1934 edn (Oxford, Clarendon) 382, 421.

[192] 'Once your enemy has surrendered you have no longer any right over his life unless he gives it to you by some further attack, or unless he has previously rendered himself guilty toward you of a crime deserving death.' Vattel, E (1758) *The Law of Nations or the Principles of Natural Law* (Carnegie Institute, 1916) 284.

[193] Johnson, S (1820) *Collected Works*, Vol II (London, Heinemann) 368.

[194] *The Social Contract*, Book I, Ch 4.

[195] Beccaria, C (1974) in trans Davies, R (1993) On Crimes and Punishments' and Other Writings (Cambridge, Cambridge University Press) 32, 56.

[196] Mason, J (ed) *Diderot. Political Writings* (Cambridge, Cambridge University Press) 119.

[197] Williams, D (1994) *Voltaire. Political Writings* (Cambridge, Cambridge University Press) 172–73, 261.

[198] Kant, I in trans Gregor, M (1991) *The Metaphysics of Morals* (Cambridge University Press) 255.

[199] Farrington, K (2003) *A History of Punishment and Torture* (London, Hamlyn) 22–26, 32, 34, 36.

built over 50 military hospitals in 1708, and also devised the first systematic plans for the stage by stage evacuation of the wounded from the battlefields. This planning was so successful, that at the battle of Fontenoy in 1747, the French had 4,000 hospital beds and 1,200 carts to transport the wounded, prepared in advance of the battle. Similarly, but on a smaller scale, the Americans in their War of Independence, despite limited facilities (wheelbarrows were the typical method to transport wounded men) knowledge and medical equipment, were quick to organise both wagons to remove their wounded and field hospitals to treat them in.[200]

This growth of interest in looking after their own wounded, also flowed over to looking after the wounded on the opposite side. For example, Frederick the Great, whilst going to great lengths to ensure that, 'those who have staked their lives so often on behalf of the State' should be cared for in safety and by competent medical staff added 'think also of the poor wounded of the two armies. Especially have a paternal care for your own wounded and do not be inhuman to those of the enemy.'[201]

In accordance with such thinking, during the Austrian War of Independence, proposals made nine days before the battle of Dettingen of 1743, in which the sick of neither side were to be taken prisoner, and the wounded were not harassed, were respected. Two years later, Louis XV (1710–74) instructed his army surgeons to treat the enemy wounded as his own, stating that once they were wounded, they were no longer his enemies. This was evident at the battle of Fontenoy, noted above, when the French authorities were so quick to pick up wounded soldiers of all sides, that when the defeated armies returned to the field the following day to pick up their wounded, they discovered the French had already taken them and proceeded to treat them without discrimination. This was in accordance with the 1743 Agreement between the French and Allied forces in the Austrian War of Independence. Specifically, this landmark agreement specified:

> Care shall be taken of the wounded on both sides, their medicines and food shall be paid, their expenses shall be refunded on both sides; it shall be permitted to send them surgeons and their servants . . . the sick of neither side shall be taken prisoner, they shall remain in safety in the hospitals . . . they shall be returned . . . by the shortest possible route and without harassment or arrest. The same shall apply to the commissioners, chaplains, physicians, surgeons, apothecaries, medical orderlies, servants and other people belonging to the medical medical service, who many not be taken prisoner and shall likewise be returned.[202]

Against this rising tide of humanitarianism, the Seven Years War (1756–63) produced problems and responses of the like never seen before. The most obvious of these was the sheer scale of prisoners of war which were taken. That is, by 1762 there were over 26,000 French prisoners held in Britain and Ireland. These numbers were unprecedented and created previously unforeseen problems, complicated by a

[200] Greenwood, J (2005) *Medics at War: Military Medicine from Colonial Times to the 21st Century* (Annapolis, Naval Institute Press) 2; McCullough, D (2005) *1776. America and Britain at War* (London, Penguin) 35–36, 287; Boatner, M (1969) *The Encyclopaedia of the American Revolution* (NYC, McKay) 689; Lambert, A (2002) *War at Sea in the Age of Sail* (London, Cassell) 87; Anderson, M (1998) *War and Society in Europe of the Old Regime* (London, Sutton) 107; Downing, T (1991) *Civil War* (London, Gardner) 92; Kreiser, C 'Medic!' *Military History* (Nov 2005) 31–35.

[201] Luvaas, J (1999) *Frederick the Great on the Art of War* (NYC, De Capo) 147. Also, Frederick in Chaliand, G (ed) *The Art of War in World History* (California, California University Press) 607.

[202] The 1743 Agreement is reprinted in Boissier, P (1978) *A History of the International Committee of the Red Cross: From Solferino to Tsushima* (Henry Dunant Institute, Geneva) 158–59.

background of barbaric prison conditions which were considered the norm for this period. The result of these conditions could be horrific. The worst example of these problems from this period involved the so called 'Black Hole of Calcutta', where in 1756 Suraj-ud Dowla (1733–57) allegedly had confined 150 British prisoners into a room, barely 18 by 14 feet wide, with only two tiny windows for ventilation. The intense summer heat meant that by the next morning, only 23 men were left alive. Although by no means as immediate, the incarceration policies of some of the primary belligerents, such as Britain, were also a cause for concern. By 1759, it was estimated that there was a death rate of 25 per cent per year for prisoners of war who were not officers (as officers were paroled on land in relative comfort whilst common soldiers were kept in the hulks of old ships). This worked out to some 5,000 fatalities each year. Originally, the French King, who did not want his own soldiers to suffer such a fate, gave money so that his soldiers being held as prisoners in England could have a sufficient diet. However, when the French King withdrew this action, partly due to a belief it was not being handed out correctly, the conditions of French prisoners became so bad that another solution had to be found. This came in the form of a public appeal in England. From this thousands of pounds were raised for everything from clothing to medicines as the British came to represent themselves as not merely victorious, but also humane.[203]

When the American War of Independence began, Westminster refused to grant the American captives prisoner of war status, preferring to treat their captives as rebels, akin to common criminals. Although on occasion the American rebels were executed when captured, this was not a policy which saw mass executions taking place. American troops were not above similar actions, although these were typically seen as reprisals. In at least one instance, George Washington ordered an English officer to be executed as a reprisal for the killing of a militia officer. From such actions, both sides learnt to show restraint in this area. Whilst restraint was being made in this area, problems of inhumane incarceration started to proliferate. This was a particular problem for American prisoners, of which some 8,000 or so would die whilst being held in overcrowded, unheated barns, sheds or prison ships in Boston and New York harbours. To put this in context, more American soldiers died in captivity than died on the battlefield. The British government utilised such prison ships despite the protests of some of their own generals.[204]

In terms of developments in international law, the conclusion of the Seven Years War,[205] like the American War of Independence, was unremarkable as both ended, to quote the Paris Peace Treaty of 1783 with the reciprocal promise that 'all prisoners on

[203] Cooley, L (2002) *Captives: Britain, Empire and the World 1600–1850* (London, Cape) 102, 173, 212–13, 220, 254–56; Porch, D (2000) *Wars of Empire* (London, Cassell) 83.

[204] McCullough, D (2005) *1776. America and Britain at War* (London, Penguin) 181, 244; Boatner, M (1969) *The Encyclopedia of the American Revolution* (NYC, McKay) 495, 895, 1086; Best, G (1980) *Humanity in Warfare* (London, Weidenfeld) 168, 1174; Cooley, L (2002) *Captives: Britain, Empire and the World 1600–1850* (London, Cape) 212–13, 219, 221; Farrington, K (2003) *A History of Punishment and Torture* (London, Hamlyn) 96–97.

[205] 1763 Treaty of Paris, Art III. Note, this was to be done within six weeks and payment for debts taken out by prisoners. See also the similar clause in the Treaty of Hubertsburg 1763, Art VII. Note the problems in late, or never, repatriations from this conflict. See Cooley, L (2002) *Captives: Britain, Empire and the World 1600–1850* (London, Cape) 275–84; Fowler, W (2005) *Empires at War* (NYC, Walker) 225, 281; Marston, D (2001) *The Seven Years' War* (London, Osprey) 45.

both sides shall be set at liberty . . . with all convenient speed'.[206] The United States also came to conclude similar treaties with some of the Indian tribes within their borders.[207] What was novel was the agreement in 1785 between Prussia and the United States where, for the first time ever, it was agreed in advance that if the two sides should ever come into conflict, certain standards for prisoners of war would apply. The two sides pledged not to place prisoners in:

> [D]istant and inclement countries, or by crowding them into close and noxious places . . . [nor shall they be] . . . confined in dungeons, prison-ships, nor prisons, nor be put into irons, nor bound, nor otherwise restrained in the use of their limbs . . . the common men [shall] be disposed in cantonments, open and extensive enough for air and exercise, and lodged in barracks as roomy and good as are provided by the party in whose power they are for their own troops; that the officers shall also be daily furnished by the Party in whose power they are, with as many rations and of the same articles and quality as are allowed by them . . . [equivalent] . . . to officers of equal rank in their own army and all others shall be daily furnished by them with such ration as they allow to a common-soldier in their own service.

It was agreed that nominated commissaries would be allowed to see the prisoners as often as they pleased, and these commissaries could distribute whatever comforts which they may obtain. The commissary was also to be free to make reports in open letters to those who employed them.[208]

8. The Wars of the French Revolution

On 14 July 1789, when the revolutionaries of Paris stormed the Bastille, they completed their act by massacring its garrison. Soon after, this practice became commonplace. This was despite some clear attempts at humanity at the beginning of the revolution, by both sides. For example, Charles-Melchior Arthus, the Marquis de Bonchamps (1760–93) ordered the release of 5,000 republican prisoners, as a gesture of mercy. Likewise, the Declaration of 2 May 1792 by the French National Assembly recorded:

> [W]ishing . . . to regulate by the principles of justice and humanity, the treatment of such enemy soldiers as the fortunes of war may place within the powers of the French nation decrees, first, that prisoners of war are safeguarded by the Nation and under the special protection of the Law; second, that unjustifiable severities, or insults, or violence or homicidal assaults committed against prisoners of war will be punished by the same laws, in just the same way as if those excesses has been committed against Frenchmen . . . fifthly, that the upkeep of prisoners shall be provided from the revenues specially provided for the war, and shall be on the scale enjoyed by corresponding grades of French infantry in peacetime.[209]

Despite these intentions, French Royalist soldiers were executed in their thousands during the following two years, being shot, drowned in boats (between 2,800 and 4,600) or guillotined (another 1,896) after capture. When the revolution was threatened from abroad in 1793, the French parliament prohibited the ransoming of prisoners of war

[206] Treaty of Paris Between the United States and Great Britain 1783, Art 7.
[207] The Treaty With the Six Nations 1784, Art 1. See also Art V of the Treaty of Fort Jackson 1814.
[208] Treaty of Amity and Commerce Between His Majesty the King of Prussia, and the United States of America; 10 September 1785, Art 24.
[209] 'National Assembly' in Best, G (1980) *Humanity in Warfare* (London, Weidenfeld) 78–79. Also, Andress, D (2007) *The Terror: Civil War in the French Revolution* (NYC, Brown) 195, 245.

and ordered that they be shot as 'an example of the vengeance of an outraged nation'. Maximilien Robespierre (1758–94) defended this approach, by suggesting that those who make war on a people to prevent the progress of liberty or destroy the rights of man must be attacked 'as assassins and brigands' and therefore could not treated as 'an honourable adversary'. The results were that in 1794 alone, aside the prisoners of the opposing side in the French part to the civil conflict, some 8,000 Spanish prisoners were executed as well as many English from the international side of the conflict. The British replied in kind, with Edmund Burke (1729–97) arguing that 'the mode of civilized warfare will not be practiced . . . nor are the French entitled to expect it.'[210]

Away from their respective legislative bodies, the commanders on the ground tried to stay away from such rules, fearing their strict implementation would quickly come back to haunt them as reprisals. Although the French National Assembly revoked their no-quarter policy, some commanders, like Napoleon (1769–1821) nevertheless authorised the execution of between 2,000 and 4,000 Ottoman troops after the sack of Jaffa in 1799, on the grounds that he could not provide for such men – although when in a similar situation in 1796, he simply freed over 2,000 Austrian prisoners, as the British did with all of the French captives they came to hold in Egypt, repatriating them to France. At the battle of Austerlitz in 1805, until the last hour, the French refused to give any quarter. Little mercy was shown to French soldiers retreating from their ill-fated invasion of Russia in 1812, while at both Katzbach in 1813 and Waterloo in 1815 the Prussians clubbed and bayoneted any wounded French they came across.[211] The British record on this count appears much better, in that although such acts undoubtedly occurred during the wars with Napoleon, they appear quite isolated. Nevertheless, it would be wrong to assume that the British believed there was an absolute right to surrender, for as the Duke of Wellington (1769–1852) wrote 'I believe that it has always been understood that the defenders of a fortress stormed have no claim to quarter.'[212]

When the Napoleonic Wars reached Latin America, Jean Jacques Dessaline (1758–1806), in his attempts to subdue the French defenders on Haiti, hung over 500 French prisoners outside of Cap Haitien.[213] Similarly, in the decades that followed, the revolutionary forces of Simon Bolivar (1783–1830) were often refused quarter, whilst trying to grasp independence from their European overlords. In some instances, Bolivar's forces replied in kind, decapitating the prisoners of the captured Royalist forces. Similar actions occurred against Royalist prisoners taken in the conflicts over the vice-royalties of Rio de la Plata and Peru. The war for Spanish independence also saw the execution of rebel prisoners after battles were concluded, or alternately, prisoners of both sides were held in conditions so poor that heat and heavy labour quickly caused their deaths. Manuel Rosas (1793–1877) is credited with the death of perhaps 20,000 prisoners after the port of Buenos Aires was taken in 1838.[214]

[210] Bell, D (2007) *The First Total War: Napoleon's Europe and the Birth of Modern Warfare* (London, Bloomsbury) 141–42, 145, 182; Best, G (1980) *Humanity in Warfare* (London, Weidenfeld) 81; Griffith, P (1998) *The Art of War of Revolutionary France: 1789–1902* (London, Greenhill) 26, 76.

[211] Bell, D (2007) *The First Total War: Napoleon's Europe and the Birth of Modern Warfare* (London, Bloomsbury) 213; Rothenberg, G (2000) *The Napoleonic Wars* (London, Cassell) 53; Rothenberg, G (1980) *The Age of Warfare in the Age of Napoleon* (Bloomington, Indiana University Press) 89, 90–91; Black, J (1994) *European Warfare 1600–1815* (New Haven, Yale University Press) 231.

[212] Wellington, in Parker, G (2002) *Empire, War and Faith in Early Modern Europe* (Penguin, London) 155.

[213] Scheina, R (2003) *Latin America's Wars: The Age of the Caudillo, 1791–1899* (Washington, Brassey) 18.

[214] Scheina, R (2003) *Latin America's Wars: The Age of the Caudillo, 1791–1899* (Washington, Brassey) 29, 31, 33, 47, 67, 74–76, 125.

If a prisoner was taken, it was seen as a matter of honour to protect them. Thus, when Horatio Nelson (1758–1805) did not guarantee the safety of prisoners as he promised, his acts were strongly criticised in the House of Commons. This was an unfortunate mistake on Nelson's part, as he had a good record in this area. He was explicit in his belief that firing on a ship that had surrendered was a crime, and in practice, he had refused to allow captured prisoners of war on their ruined ships be cut free to die in the storms, despite the dangers to his own men in keeping the ruined ships.[215] Possibly the clearest articulation of what the British came to view as the rule in this area was not set down until 1820, after the Napoleonic wars had ended. In particular, their General Treaty for the Suppression of Piracy and the Slave Trade which they signed with the Arab Tribes stated:

> The putting men to death after they have given up their arms is an act of piracy and not of acknowledged war; and if any tribe should put to death any persons, either Muhammadans or others after they have given up their arms . . . the British will wage war on them . . . until they surrender those who performed the act.[216]

Although the British may have had a better record in the field for protecting the lives of surrendered prisoners, the same could not be said of their treatment of those who surrendered and who were placed in captivity. In part, this was due to the massive numbers of captured. That is, in 1799, there were just under 26,000 French prisoners in Britain whilst by 1814 the number was close to 200,000. These numbers filled every available place in the forts, prisons and hulks of old ships. There were dozens of these hulks moored off England and parts of Spain. By the end of 1814, some 30,000 French prisoners would die in English captivity, with 7,000 of these dying of malnutrition and disease on the hulks. The majority of the men on the hulks were soldiers or sailors, and not officers who were typically held on land and subject to parole and relatively good standards of captivity.[217]

Despite the poor holding standards for the majority of prisoners, a progress was evident in that both the French and British authorities agreed that both sides could, in principle, have both national commissioners and a 'protecting power' (which was the United States until they joined the conflict in 1812) who could visit all of the prisoners and supply additional provisions to the captive men. Agreements on minimal food and the rule that escape attempts could not be punished with execution were also concluded. Similar agreements were reached between the United States and Britain when they went to war in 1812. These rules also prohibited corporal punishment and fixed the daily food ration.[218]

[215] Clayton, T (2004) *Trafalgar: The Men, the Battle, the Storm* (London, Hodder) 33, 131, 209, 250, 279, 339.

[216] The 1820 General Treaty for Supressing Piracy in Hurewitz, T (ed) *Diplomacy in the Near and Middle East: A Documentary Record* (NYC, Columbia University Press) 88–89.

[217] Rothenberg, G (1980) *The Age of Warfare in the Age of Napoleon* (Bloomington, Indiana University Press) 90; Garrett, R (1981) *POW* (London, Charles) 55–56; Esdaile, C (2003) *The Peninsular War* (London, Penguin) 83.

[218] Before 1797 they could expect three quarters of a pound of beef, half a pound of bread and one quart of beer, after the agreement, they would get half a pound of beef per day, 26 ounces of bread, two ounces of cheese, half a pint of pease, one and a half fresh vegetables and one quart of beer: Glover, M (1982) *The Velvet Glove. The Decline of Moderation in War* (Auckland, Hodder) 176–77; Hickey, D (1995) *The War of 1812* (Chicago, University Press of Illinois) 86, 147, 177–78.

Such acts of humanity were not universal in this period. For example, during the siege of Genoa in 1800, one of Napoleon's generals, Andre Massena (1758–1817), allowed several thousand Austrian prisoners to starve to death in the prison hulks that were within the besieged area that was desperately short of food. However, it should be noted that Massena had asked the Austrians and British to feed the prisoners but they both refused to do so. A situation of greater brutality occurred when the Spanish government captured 17,000 French soldiers after the Battle of Bailen in 1808 and rather than repatriate the prisoners as they promised, they placed them on the desert island of Cabrera in the Balearics, where half of them died of exposure and malnutrition. In addition, some 25,000 of the 30,000 French soldiers taken prisoner following Napoleon's attack on Russia were dead, due to disease, maltreatment, lack of food and long distances marched on foot, well before they reached their prison camps.[219]

One area where there appears to have been relative progress, was with regards to torture. Aside the development of curiosities like the supposedly pain-free guillotine, torture itself, was banned throughout Europe between 1792 and 1851. This trend would appear to parallel the progressive outlawing of slavery on national, bilateral and international levels throughout the nineteenth century.[220] The no-torture rule also appears to have been adopted by a number of armies. For example, while in Egypt in 1798, Napoleon wrote that the:

> [B]arbarous custom of whipping men suspected of having important secrets to reveal must be abolished. It has always been recognized that this method of interrogation, by putting men to the torture, is useless. The wretches say whatever comes into their heads and whatever they think one wants to believe. Consequently, the Commander-in-Chief forbids the use of a method which is contrary to reason and humanity.[221]

Despite such dictates, the torture of prisoners continued in some theatres of the Napoleonic wars, such as when the French were captured by Spanish guerrillas. However, the acts carried out against these men often had little to do with extraction of information and more to do with sadism, with men being, inter alia, stoned to death, boiled in oil, sawn in half or buried up to their necks in the ground and being left to die of thirst. After these wars, despite assumptions to the contrary, torture reappeared with vengeance in the Greek War of Independence in 1821.[222]

[219] Rothenberg, G (1980) *The Age of Warfare in the Age of Napoleon* (Bloomington, Indiana University Press) 89; Glover, M (1982) *The Velvet Glove. The Decline of Moderation in War* (London, Hodder) 180; Zamoyski, A (2004) *1812: Napoleon's Fatal March on Moscow* (London, HarperCollins) 402–404, 442–45, 484–85, 512, 531–32 and 536.

[220] Whilst the first bilateral treaties to abolish the slave trade can be traced to 1818 with Britain and Spain, and supplementary bilateral treaties with Britain and other nations pepper the 1820s and 1830s, it was the 1841 Quintuple Treaty, which was signed by Britain, France, Russia, Prussia and Austria that the prevention of the slave trade, and condemnation of it as a form of piracy became an international concern. There were further bilateral treaties in the 1840s and 1860s. The international efforts were followed by the General Act of Berlin of 1885 and the General Act and Declaration of Brussels of 1890, both of which reflected international efforts to suppress the international slave trade.

[221] Howard, J (ed) (1961) *Napoleon Bonaparte, Letters and Documents of Napoleon, Volume I: The Rise to Power* (London, Cresset) 274.

[222] Cooley, L (2002) *Captives: Britain, Empire and the World 1600–1850* (London, Cape) 333; Hernon, I (2007) *Britain's Forgotten Wars. Colonial Campaigns in the 19th Century* (London, Sutton) 16; Lambert, A (2002) *War at Sea in the Age of Sail* (London, Cassell) 50, 54; Farrington, K (2003) *A History of Punishment and Torture* (London, Hamlyn) 112–17; Esdaile, C (2003) *The Peninsular War* (London, Penguin) 254–57; Howarth, D (1976) *The Greek Adventure* (London, Collins) 43.

In terms of repatriation of prisoners after the conflict had ended, the treaties of the Napoleonic wars were largely of the same ilk as those of the earlier centuries. As such, in addition to some public gestures by Napoleon to free a few token prisoners go to see their sick families or repatriating prisoners to make new allies, most prisoners were exchanged after, not during the conflict, without the need for ransoms to be paid. For example, the 1801 Treaty of London between the Britain and France agreed that 'the prisoners made respectively shall, immediately after the exchange of the ratifications of the definite treaty, be restored and without ransom, on paying reciprocally the debts which they may have individually contracted.'[223]

Similar examples can be seen between France and its various enemies in 1801,[224] 1802,[225] 1806[226] and 1808.[227] Such exchanges were not possible during the war because attempts to have exchanges were difficult to conclude, due to the massive inequities in amounts of prisoners held. This meant that soldiers could not be traded one-for-one, but rather, such as with the 1810 exchange, five to one, with 50,000 French being exchanged for 10,000 Brits. Only the Americans seemed to get a little further on this question, when they agreed a cartel with Britain after they went to war in 1812, for the exchange of prisoners, such as a general being worth 30 privates.[228]

Although such returns of soldiers at the end of conflicts were not, in themselves, novel, what was unique of this period was the first exchanges of badly wounded or sick prisoners, during the course of the conflicts despite the fact that there was no general cartel of exchange. Between 1803 and 1814, the British repatriated 17,607 – or 14 per cent – of their French prisoners. Most of these men had lost at least one limb and would not be able to fight again.[229] Alternately, the care of the enemy wounded could be agreed as one of the considerations for a capitulation agreement. For example, Article 9 of the Convention of Cintra 1808 for the Suspension of Arms, stated:

> All the sick and wounded, who cannot be embarked with the troops, are entrusted to the British army. They are to be taken care of, whilst they remain in this country, at the expence of the British Government . . . The English government will provide for their return to France.[230]

Similarly, with the 1809 Treaty of Schonbrunn, Napoleon directed that although the city of Baden was to be demilitarised, the baths of the city were to be made available

[223] Art X.

[224] The 1801 Treaty of Luneville which brought an end to hostilities between France and the Germanic Body, Art XV.

[225] The 1802 Treaty of Amiens, Art II. Note also the 1802 Treaty Between France and the Ottoman Empire, Art VIII.

[226] The Franco–Russian Peace Treaty of 1806, Art XI.

[227] Treaty of Tilsit, Art XXVI. Note also the 1808 Convention of Cintra by which the French who agreed to surrender their position were shipped back to France from Portugal.

[228] Rothenberg, G (1980) *The Age of Warfare in the Age of Napoleon* (Bloomington, Indiana University Press) 89; Zamoyski, A (2004) *1812: Napoleon's Fatal March on Moscow* (London, Harper) 21; Garrett, R (1981) *POW* (London, Charles) 49, 79; Hickey, D (1995) *The War of 1812* (Chicago, University Press Illinois) 86, 147, 177–78; Clayton, T (2004) *Trafalgar: The Men, the Battle, the Storm* (London, Hodder) 365.

[229] Glover, M (1982) *The Velvet Glove. The Decline of Moderation in War* (London, Hodder) 186–87.

[230] The Annual Register, or, A View of the History, Politics, and Literature for the Year 1808. Likewise, the Capitulation of the City and Fortress of Magdeburg on 8 November 1806 stipulated, 'the wounded officers and soldiers and patients will be able to remain in Magdeburg until their cure. They will be taken care of at the expense of the city'.

for 'the wounded and sick from the two armies . . . to use alike'.[231] This period also records a number of instances where the medical staff of one side were known to either assist enemy wounded or provide a truce to allow an enemy to attend to their own wounded. Whilst non-discrimination in the treatment of wounded was considered a customary practice in European conflicts at this time, it was not considered customary to allow medical personnel immunity on the battlefield. As such, they could be both fired on and/or made prisoners of war. Nevertheless, in some instances, the sanctity of medical staff was recognised. For example, the Agreement on the Capitulation of the City and Fortress of Magdeburg in 1806 stated 'surgeons . . . will not be considered like prisoners of war'.[232]

Such agreements were possible, as by the beginning of the nineteenth century many of the major belligerents of the period (but by no means all) had greatly expanded medical services and attached hospitals for their military units. The French army had 1,200 doctors for around 300,000 troops at this point, along with specialised 'flying hospitals' of special carts for transporting the wounded. However the success that came with these developments was still very limited, for surviving the conflict did not mean an end to the butchery. For example, Dominique-Jean Larrey (1766–1842), Napoleon's chief surgeon, (who treated the wounded on both sides), performed over 200 amputations in the night after the battle of Borodino in 1812. Eugene Labaume (1783–1849) described 'the interior of gullies' that criss-crossed the battlefield where:

> almost all of the wounded by a natural instinct had dragged themselves thither to seek protection . . . heaped on top of each other and swimming helplessly in the own blood, some called on passers-by to put them out of their misery.[233]

Every warship of this period had at least one or two surgeons. Napoleon gave thought to the location, provision and transport to and from the battlefield for his wounded soldiers, although the intentions in this area were not always met. Despite these developments, hospitals were not yet given a protected status. This was contrary to the advocacy of some like John Pringle (1707–82) and the creation of some cartels that made hospitals around the battlefield immune from attack in the seventeenth century. Accordingly, it was not unheard of for the places where the wounded were being held being overrun and the wounded being executed. Similar practices were recorded in some of the 'small wars' in the early part of the nineteenth century, during the opening years of the French revolution, as well as in some theatres of the Napoleonic wars, such as those in Spain or in Latin America. For example, Jean Jacques Dessaline (1758–1806), after taking the besieged Haitian fort of Le Cap in 1803, took all 800 wounded French soldiers out to sea and drowned them.[234]

[231] See the Military Convention in association with Art 12 of the 1809 Treaty of Schonbrunn in Axelrod, A (ed) (2001) *Encyclopedia of Historical Treaties and Alliances*, Vol I (NYC, Facts on File) 185, 187.

[232] Art VII of the Capitulation Agreement. Also, Best, G (1980) *Humanity in Warfare* (London, Weidenfeld) 126–27; Zamoyski, A (2004) *1812: Napoleon's Fatal March on Moscow* (London, HarperCollins) 221; Rothenberg, G (1980) *The Age of Warfare in the Age of Napoleon* (Bloomington, Indiana University Press) 229; Lambert, A (2002) *War at Sea in the Age of Sail* (London, Cassell) 168; Clayton, T (2004) *Trafalgar: The Men, the Battle, the Storm* (London, Hodder) 258–60.

[233] Labaume, quoted in Keegan, J (1993) *A History of Warfare* (London, Hutchinson) 9–10.

[234] Rothenberg, G (1980) *The Age of Warfare in the Age of Napoleon* (Bloomington, Indiana University Press) 226; Best, G (1980) *Humanity in Warfare* (London, Weidenfeld) 126–27; Hernon, I (2007) *Britain's Forgotten Wars. Colonial Campaigns in the 19th Century* (London, Sutton) 22, 33; Esdaile, C (2003) *The Peninsular War* (London, Penguin) 77; Black, J (1994) *European Warfare 1600–1815* (New Haven, Yale University Press) 231;

Even if a man was lucky enough to be given medical attention, the chances of surviving medical assistance were not great. For example, statistics of a British military hospital for 10 weeks in 1814 noted that one in five of those who underwent surgery to the head died; for operations to the thorax the proportion was one in 2.3; operations to the abdomen one in 4.3 and with amputations to arms or legs, one in 5.3. In large part this was due to the fact that medicine of this period, known as 'heroic', was positively harmful as medical practitioners bled and blistered their patients and subjected them to an assortment of emetics, cathartics and diuretics designed to purge the body of disease, replete with an arsenal of unsterile instruments. In addition, there were no anaesthetics beyond vinegar and sometimes turpentine. Amputations were often done so quickly and so poorly that even if the victim survived, they had to be revisited later. Thus, Nelson's arm was taken off so badly that he later had to have the stump re-opened and the nerve secured.[235]

The respect for the dead killed in these conflicts varied between country and rank. That is, whilst the high ranking officers like Nelson may have returned home after being killed in battle, pickled in a barrel of rum, to a high level State funeral, the same could not be said for his dead sailors. The sailors who died with him during the battle were simply weighted and thrown overboard. These actions were unlike those of the French who were making great efforts to remember their fallen from the time of their revolution forward, as the *Arc de Triomphe* came to symbolise. Across the channel, similar proposals for a monument to name all those who died at Waterloo received little support in Parliament, with remembrances for common soldiers being left to local churches or walls in public schools. Even their bodies were not treated with respect, with the best that most could hope for being a common grave. However, this was not always achieved, with desecration being a noted problem with some American dead in their 1812 war against Britain and some of their Indian allies, and also on some of the battlefields of Europe. For example, many of the dead from the Battle of Waterloo were later dug up and their bones were crushed and turned into fertiliser, whilst their teeth were used to make dentures.[236]

9. Between 1815 and 1861

Between the end of the Napoleonic wars and the beginning of the American Civil War, prisoners were taken, held and subsequently exchanged, without ransoms, at the end of conflicts, such as with, inter alia, Crimea,[237] China,[238] Italy[239] and the conflict

Best, G (1980) *Humanity in Warfare* (London, Weidenfeld) 126–27; Scheina, R (2003) *Latin America's Wars: The Age of the Caudillo, 1791–1899* (Washington, Brassey) 16.

[235] Lambert, A (2002) *War at Sea in the Age of Sail* (London, Cassell) 203; Greenwood, J (2005) *Medics at War: Military Medicine from Colonial Times to the 21st Century* (Annapolis, Naval Institute Press) 35; Hickey, D (1995) *The War of 1812* (Chicago, University Press of Illinois) 79; Rothenberg, G (1980) *The Age of Warfare in the Age of Napoleon* (Bloomington, Indiana University Press) 235–36; Bell, D (2007) *The First Total War: Napoleon's Europe and the Birth of Modern Warfare* (London, Bloomsbury) 38; Glover, M (1982) *The Velvet Glove. The Decline and Fall of Moderation in War* (London, Hodder) 111.

[236] Hickey, D (1995) *The War of 1812* (Chicago, University Press of Illinois) 139.

[237] The Treaty of Peace Between Great Britain, Austria, Turkey, France and Russia 1856 in Mowat, R (1918) *The Great European Treaties of the Nineteenth Century* (Oxford, Oxford University Press). See Art VI.

[238] The Treaty of Nanjing between Great Britain and China 1842, Art VIII.

[239] The Treaty of Peace Between Austria, France and Sardinia 1859 in Mowat, R (1918) *The Great European Treaties of the Nineteenth Century* (Oxford, Oxford University Press). See Art II at 226.

between Austria and Prussia.[240] The killing of prisoners was equally notable in a number of conflicts involving, amongst others, Mexico, Ceylon, Jamaica, Greece, China and India. In the Indian context, the reciprocal killing of British and Sikh wounded was noted in both the 1845 and 1847 conflicts. One British officer recalled in his memoirs of the Indian wars how 'fearfully savage' it was, as he was obliged to shoot 30 prisoners with his own hand when his native soldiers refused to do the butchers work. In the New Zealand wars between 1845 and 1872, the killing of wounded soldiers was not an uncommon practice on both sides. In numerical terms, the greatest massacre of surrendered Maori warriors, some 120 men, occurred in 1868 in what is known as the Ngatapa Massacre.[241] Further massacres of enemy wounded occurred by British soldiers in the Zulu war of 1879, with one instance where perhaps 500 wounded Zulu warriors were executed after their failed attack on Rourke's Drift.[242]

The execution of enemy wounded appears to have been the norm in the war between Paraguay and the Triple Alliance between 1864 and 1870, with no quarter being the rule in at least six major battles.[243] In the case of Mexico, as Texas broke free of the State, the Mexican authorities made clear at the outset that every colonist found taking part in the insurrection would be executed, as the surviving defenders of the Alamo, who also promised not to take prisoners, found out. A further 300 or so men who had surrendered were executed after the Goliad fell. The Texans responded in kind after the battle of San Jacinto, with the difference that they also killed the non-combatants, including the children who performed roles as musicians for the Mexican forces. During the Second Texas–Mexican War of 1836–44, 233 Texans, after they surrendered, were marched off to starvation and exposure. Likewise, when 193 Texans who had escaped from Mexican authorities were recaptured, 19 of the escapees were executed. Later executions of Texan prisoners followed the battle of Tabasco in 1844. When the United States joined the war in 1846, any deserters from Texas or the United States who had ended up fighting for Mexico, such as a number of Irish-Catholic soldiers, could also expect no mercy when captured. The upside to such acts in this conflict was that when the war ended, the United States and Mexico agreed in their 1848 treaty that when dealing with mutual prisoners in future conflicts:

> In order that the fate of prisoners of war be alleviated, all such practices as those of sending them into distant, inclement or unwholesome districts, or crowding them into close and noxious places, shall be studiously avoided. They shall not be confined to dungeons, prison-ships or prisons; nor be put in irons or bound or otherwise restrained in the use of their limbs. The officers shall enjoy on their paroles . . . and the common soldier shall be disposed in cantonments, open and extensive enough for air and exercise and lodged in barracks as roomy and good as are provided by the Party in whose power they are in for its own troops.[244]

[240] The Treaty of Peace Between Austria and Prussia 1866 in Mowat, R (1918) *The Great European Treaties of the Nineteenth Century* (Oxford, Oxford University Press). See Art III.

[241] Belich, J (1986) *The New Zealand Wars* (London, Penguin) 43, 94, 153, 228–29, 232, 266, 286.

[242] Saul, D (2005) *Zulu, The Heroism and Tragedy of the Zulu War of 1879* (London, Penguin) 184–85.

[243] Huffines, A (2005) *The Texas War of Independence* (London, Osprey) 37, 40, 44–45, 53–54, 59–60; Kiernan, V (1998) *Colonial Empires and Armies* (London, Sutton) 50, 161; Hernon, I (2007) *Britain's Forgotten Wars. Colonial Campaigns in the 19th Century* (London, Sutton) 156, 44, 76, 95–97, 383, 569–71; Saul, D (2002) *The Indian Mutiny* (London, Penguin) 328, 337–39; Howarth, D (1976) *The Greek Adventure* (London, Collins) 43.

[244] The Treaty of Guadalupe Hidalgo 1848, Art XXII(2).

It was also agreed that if future conflict were to break out between the United States and Mexico that, inter alia, hospitals 'and all persons connected with the same' would be respected.[245] Despite such novel steps, in practice, the prospects for wounded soldiers was often bleak, as medical military services dwindled. Thus, in 1854, Britain had only 163 surgical officers for all of its garrisons – throughout the entire world. Even if the medical facilities were in existence, in some parts of the world they became battlegrounds (such as in the Zulu wars), whilst in times of conflict they were often enmeshed in bureaucratic inefficiency, inertia and fundamental gaps in capacity in terms of everything from medicines, medical ability, evacuation transports and dedicated stretcher-bearers. These problems applied when armies were either besieged, such as at Vienna in 1848, or in the field, such as in the Crimean war of 1853–56. In the latter case it could take up to two days for the British to clear the field of their own wounded and at least a further day to collect any of the Russians still left alive after three days in the hot sun. Although heroic figures like Florence Nightingale (1820–1910) and her 200 nurses would arise from such wars, fundamental problems such as whether to treat enemy wounded remained. In some theatres, such as with the British in China, their treatment of enemy wounded was of great bemusement to the enemy, or, as was recorded of period, 'the Chinese cannot understand, and say, yours is a curious kind of warfare; you come and fire upon us and wound us and then pet and cure us.'[246]

Elsewhere, surgeons who treated enemy wounded risked imprisonment and possible execution.[247] This was particularly so in some of the conflicts of Latin America, where not only the enemy wounded, but also those who assisted them, were at risk. For example, during the Mexican wars of 1857 to 1860, both the physicians and the medical students who came to help the (enemy) wounded were executed upon capture.[248]

It was against such backgrounds in 1859 that a young Swiss national, Henry Dunant (1828–1910) was trying to secure a meeting with Napoleon III (1808–73) on commercial matters. Napoleon III was not an inhumane man. For example, he freed 40 Austrian surgeons after the battle of Montebello so that they could look after their wounded compatriots. However, when he did this, he was acting on an impulse that had little to do with contemporary customs. It was these very contemporary customs that Dunant stumbled upon in the immediate aftermath of the battle of Solferino. This battlefield, where Italy and France had waged a war against Austria, in addition to subsidiary troops from Algeria and Croatia, was one of the bloodiest battles of the nineteenth century. After 13 hours of fighting, 6,000 men were dead and 42,000 – mostly defeated Austrian soldiers – lay wounded. All 10 of the French medical staff were called away to duty elsewhere. Accordingly, the wounded had no water, food,

[245] The Treaty of Guadalupe Hidalgo 1848, Art XXII.

[246] Noted in Kiernan, V (1998) *Colonial Empires and Armies* (London, Sutton) 162. For the Vienna example, see Keates, J (2006) *The Siege of Vienna* (London, Pimlico) 352–53. Saul, D (2005) *Zulu, The Heroism and Tragedy of the Zulu War of 1879* (London, Penguin) 159–60.

[247] McCoubrey, H (1995) 'Before Geneva Law' *International Review of the Red Cross* 304: 69–80; Forsythe, D (2005) *The Humanitarians: The International Committee of the Red Cross* (Cambridge, Cambridge University Press) 18; Ponting, C (2005) *The Crimean War: The Truth Behind the Myth* (London, Pimlico) 106, 193, 195–204; Greenwood, J (2005) *Medics at War: Military Medicine from Colonial Times to the 21st Century* (Annapolis, Naval Institute Press) 17–18, 20–27.

[248] Scheina, R (2003) *Latin America's Wars: The Age of the Caudillo, 1791–1899* (Washington, Brassey) 34, 253, 299, 347.

medical attention, shelter, help or comfort of any kind. There was a hospital, but it was miles away and there was no transport. Some of the wounded had to wait six days before food or even water reached them. Dunant, who refused to make a distinction between the wounded, threw himself into trying to alleviate the human suffering surrounding him. He also persuaded the French to allow the captured Austrian doctors to continue with their work and treat the wounded. From these experiences, Dunant went on to write the book, *A Memory of Solferino*, that would make him famous. The most important part of the book suggested: 'Would it not be possible in time of peace to form relief societies with the aim of providing care for the wounded in time of war, by zealous volunteers properly qualified for such work?'.[249]

In addition to receiving little assistance on the battlefield if wounded, it was equally likely that the victims would not be respected when dead. This was notable after the Battle of San Jacinto in 1836, when Texans walked casually amongst the Mexican corpses, pulling out the gold and silver teeth of their fallen enemy. However, by 1862 in the wars against the Sioux, American authorities were clearly prohibiting the desecration of dead enemy warriors, even if some individual American soldiers wanted to replicate the practices of their enemies. The Sioux behaviour at this point of history was not unique with regards to essentially European powers fighting in non-European contexts. For example, in the Zulu wars, there are a number of instances when all the killed British soldiers were stripped of their red coats and mutilated. Small scale examples can be seen with the decapitated torso of British Major-General Charles Gordon (1833–85), which was used to dip the points of the spears of the victors in his blood (along with the desecration of all the other killed defenders). Large-scale desecration can be seen in New Zealand in the trade of tattooed Maori heads. In the New Zealand instance, with the arrival of Europeans, the Maori tribes were eager to acquire their firearms which gave them a military advantage over their neighbours. Although the desecration of the dead, including their consumption, was a regular feature of Maori warfare of this period, a number of tribes worked out that Europeans would pay for tattooed Maori heads that could be sold as curios, artworks or as museum specimens in Europe and America. Accordingly, a number of tribes carried out raids to acquire more heads to trade. The peak years of the trade in heads were from 1820 to 1831, during the so-called 'musket wars'. The international trade was stopped in 1831 when the Governor of New South Wales issued a proclamation banning the trade in heads out of New Zealand. In 1840 when New Zealand became a British colony, the export trade virtually ended, although occasional small-scale trade continued for several years.[250]

[249] Dunant, H (1862) *A Memory of Solferino* 2004 edn (Geneva, ICRC) 7. The battle figures come from Moorehead, C (1998) *Dunant's Dream: War, Switzerland and the History of the Red Cross* (NYC, Carroll and Graf) 3–8, 26; Bennett, A (2006) *The Geneva Convention: The Hidden Origins of the Red Cross* (Gloucestershire, Sutton) 10–14.

[250] Crosby, R (1999) *The Musket Wars* (Auckland, Reed) 12, 16–17, 24, 28–32, 43, 53, 64, 72–75, 81; Saul, D (2005) *Zulu, The Heroism and Tragedy of the Zulu War of 1879* (London, Penguin); 151–52, 157, 182–83; Hernon, I (2007) *Britain's Forgotten Wars. Colonial Campaigns in the 19th Century* (London, Sutton) 295, 537; Green, D (2008) *Armies of God* (London, Arrow) 221–22; Kiernan, V (1998) *Colonial Empires and Armies* (London, Sutton) 75; Cooley, L (2002) *Captives: Britain, Empire and the World 1600–1850* (London, Cape) 161; Capdevilla, L (2006) *War Dead: Western Societies and the Casualties of War* (Edinburgh, Edinburgh University Press) 39–40, 42; Maguire, P (2001) *Law and War: An American Story* (NYC, Columbia University Press) 30–31; Hanson, N (2005) *The Unknown Soldier* (London, Doubleday) 330; Pakenham, T (1991) *The Scramble for Africa* (London, Abacus) 69–70, 266–72.

10. The American Civil War

There were occasional reports of troops killing prisoners in the American Civil War. Most of these featured irregular forces which did not respect rules such as those propagated in the Lieber Code of 1863, also known as Instructions for the Government of Armies of the United States in the Field, which recognised a general, but not absolute, right of surrender.[251] Irregular forces were responsible for one of the worst aspects in this area in 1863 when in Lawrence, Kansas, 150 of the male inhabitants were killed in cold blood. When irregulars, such as those involved in similar activities were captured and executed, Northern prisoners of war were killed in reprisal. Prisoners of war who had black coloured skin also faced the possibility of execution upon capture. At least 100 were killed in 1864 at the Battle of Saltville when they attempted to surrender and a further 100 at Fort Pillow on the Mississippi suffered exactly the same fate. If black soldiers were successful in surrendering, they still faced the prospect of being used as human shields. Captured snipers of both sides also faced difficulties in trying to surrender, due to perceptions that these men killed for the sake of killing and rarely for strategic advantage.[252]

Far greater numbers died in the American Civil War due to incarceration than due to acts of no-quarter. What began as a humane affair with adequate accommodation and fair exchanges, degenerated with the progression of the war and exchanges stopped. The exchanges stopped due to the North having the upper hand in numbers and the South not being willing to consider black and white soldiers as equal in terms of exchange. An estimated 30,218 Union prisoner died whilst in captivity, out of an overall total of 194,743 Union captives. The Andersonville prison in the South, which was meant to hold 10,000 men ended up holding 32,899. The prison had a 29 per cent mortality rate. After the war, the commander of Andersonville, Henry Wirz (1823–65) was hung after being convicted of murdering 13 inmates. This was notable, as the Union had explicitly ruled out amnesties for anyone in the civil war who had been 'engaged in any way in treating other than lawfully as prisoners of war persons found in the United States services'.[253] The death rate of Southern prisoners incarcerated in the Union were higher than the South when viewed in percentage terms. The overall mortality rates for the prisons in the South was 12 per cent and for the North 15 per cent. The highest death rate of any prison camp throughout the civil war was 77 per cent at Rock Island in Illinois. In terms of bodies, of the 214,865 Southern prisoners held, 25,976 died whilst in captivity. These figures are particularly surprising given that not only did the North have more material resources to allocate prisoners, they also had a greater legal overview of the situation with the Lieber Code. This Code had made clear that the prisoners were the responsibility of the government and that captivity was not to involve 'intentional suffering or indignity'[254] and prisoners had to

[251] Lieber Code, Arts 60, 61, 62, 63, 66. Soldiers wearing enemy uniforms could be shot, and a commander could kill his prisoners if they were 'in great straits' and their own salvation made it necessary.

[252] Stout, H (2006) *Upon the Altar of the Nation: A Moral History of the Civil War* (NYC, Viking) 161–62, 301, 319, 359; Robinson, P (2006) *Military Honour and the Conduct of War* (London, Routledge) 129.

[253] The 1865 Proclamation of Amnesty in Axelrod, A (ed) (2001) *Encyclopedia of Historical Treaties and Alliances*, Vol I (NYC, Facts on File) 272. See Art 1; Stout, H (2006) *Upon the Altar of the Nation: A Moral History of the Civil War* (NYC, Viking) 294–301.

[254] Lieber Code, Art 75.

be fed 'plain and wholesome food, whenever practicable'.[255] Although work for the prisoners was possible, this was to be according to their 'rank and condition'.[256] They were not to be shot if they attempted to escape and were recaptured.[257] Finally, in a remarkably modern reflection on the use of torture, the Code when dealing with the topic of interrogation, stated:

> Honourable men, when captured, will abstain from giving to the enemy information concerning their own army, and the modern law of war permits no longer the use of any violence against prisoners in order to extort the desired information or to punish them for having given false information . . . military necessity does not admit cruelty – that is, [the use] of torture to extort confessions.[258]

Dealing with the wounded in the American Civil War reflected the European standards of the time in terms of both technology and practice. The technology side was influenced by the fact that warfare was beginning to evolve quickly, and with it, the types of wounds inflicted on the human body changed. For example, the projectile of choice for most infantry in the later half of the nineteenth century, were so-called 'minie balls' which although being able to shoot eight times the range of the older flintlocks, flattened on impact, smashing tissue, organs and bones. These produced injuries previously unforeseen. At the same time, developments like shrapnel replaced earlier technologies that often had worse implications for the victims. Thus, in naval warfare, burns and fragment wounds became commonplace as ironclad fighting meant wounds from splinters, became fewer.

In terms of practice, the highlight was that as the war was progressing, both sides agreed to an exchange of severely wounded and sick prisoners in 1864. The Lieber Code, which proclaimed the neutrality of military hospitals and not making medical personnel prisoners of war added that '[e]very captured wounded enemy shall be medically treated, according to the ability of the medical staff.'[259]

One of the lowlights of the American Civil War was that commanders could refuse flags of truce to allow the collection of the wounded from the battlefield. For example, after the Battle of Cold Harbor in 1864, Ulysses Grant (1822–85) sent a note to Robert Lee (1807–70) asking for an agreement that neither side would shoot at stretcher parties sent out for the dead and wounded. As he had no dead or wounded outside his own lines, Lee refused and instead demanded a formal truce, which would have been akin to Grant admitting defeat. Initially Grant refused, but after two days relented. By that time all but two of the wounded on the battlefield had expired. In addition, even if the men were retrieved, the medical facilities they were evacuated to were often of a very low quality. For example, at the outset of the conflict, despite both sides having medical departments dating back to 1818, there were no evacuation or hospitalisation plans, only a few ambulances, no trained ambulance attendees and no medical control over the volunteer unit surgeons or the evaluations. Men asked to help stretcher-bearers, duly deserted under the guise of transporting men to the rear. The cumulative result was that in the first two years, the wounded could end up stuck on a battlefield for days. This meant that at the beginning of the civil war, between 10 and 25 per cent

[255] Lieber Code, Art 76.
[256] Lieber Code, Art 76.
[257] Lieber Code, Arts 74, 77, 78.
[258] Lieber Code, Arts 16, 80.
[259] Lieber Code, Arts 35, 53, 79.

were expected to die when wounded. From such situations, the American equivalent of Florence Nightingale – Clara Barton (1821–1912) and the other 20,000 nurses in the American civil war, would emerge, popularising modern nursing, military medicine and the care for the wounded behind the lines. In the front lines, medical officers were at the forefront of some of the action, of which 29 medical officers were killed in action, 10 died of wounds, 35 were wounded, and 297 died of diseases. This was out of a total of 2,109 surgeons and 3,882 assistants who were directly involved in the conflict.[260]

The first military cemetery in the United States was created in 1847, to show respect for those who died in the Texas War of Independence. By the time their civil war broke out, the principle of respecting the dead was an idea embraced by both sides. This process was assisted by the fact that this was the first major conflict in which soldiers felt the need to wear some sort of personal identification badge in the event that they were killed or wounded in battle. To prevent them remaining anonymous, soldiers were given a small parchment tag, on one side of which was written 'I am . . .' as well as details of their company, regiment, division and corps. Such identification methods also helped facilitate the repatriation of bodies from the battlefields, which became an active practice during and after the conflict, although in practice, it was the wealthy and known who were brought home. For example, when the body of George Armstrong Custer (1839–76) was retrieved after the 1874 Battle of Little Bighorn, the same did not happen for the men who fell by his side. Moreover, despite the attempts at identification, almost half of all the graves in the American Civil War bear the legend 'unknown'. This problem was multiplied by the fact that there appears to have been a difference in the treatment of the dead of the victorious, as opposed to the dead of the losing, side. For example, after the Battle of Franklin in 1864, the Confederates laid their own soldiers out in two man graves covered with blankets and when their identity was known, markers were placed at the heads of graves. The dead opposition, however, were placed in a common mass grave.[261]

11. From 1863 to 1914

A. The Wounded

At the same time that the American Civil War was grinding on one side of the Atlantic, Henry Dunant's work was becoming a massive hit on the other side of the Atlantic. This point coincided with rapid advances in the science of medicine, whereby the discovery of practices such as sterilisation and anti-septic dressing meant that the wounded were gaining greater odds with respect to the chances of surviving if wounded. With such a

[260] Greenwood, J (2005) *Medics at War: Military Medicine from Colonial Times to the 21st Century* (Annapolis, Naval Institute Press) 16–18, 20–27; Stout, H (2006) *Upon the Altar of the Nation: A Moral History of the Civil War* (NYC, Viking) 161, 346–47; Robinson, P (2006) *Military Honour and the Conduct of War* (London, Routledge) 123, 129.

[261] Stout, H (2006) *Upon the Altar of the Nation: A Moral History of the Civil War* (NYC, Viking) 120–21, 195; Swift, E (2003) *Where They Lay* (NY, Bantam) 6–7; Robinson, P (2006) *Military Honour and the Conduct of War* (London, Routledge) 123; Troiani, D'Personal Identification Badges' *Military History* (Aug 2008) 20–23; Capdevilla, L (2006) *War Dead: Western Societies and the Casualties of War* (Edinburgh, Edinburgh University Press) 22–23, 43; Huffines, A (2005) *The Texas War of Independence* (London, Osprey) 77.

background and the help of a few others, most notably Gustave Moynier (1826–1910), Dunant began to publicise his ideas and in 1863 what became known as the International Committee of the Red Cross (ICRC) was formed.

The first topic the ICRC addressed, following on directly from Dunant's experiences at Solferino, was the plight of wounded soldiers. Accordingly, at their first formal meeting, they proposed three principles. These were that all belligerent nations should be able to care for their wounded, that the people attending the wounded should wear 'a uniform distinctive sign, a white armlet with a red cross' and that the people wearing the Red Cross, like the transports they used and the hospitals in which this work was done, were to be considered to be absolutely neutral in times of conflict.[262] Although these ideas were viewed with great suspicion by some military figures and even Florence Nightingale, others like Queen Augusta of Prussia (1811–90) and Napoleon III (1808–73) came to support them and, along with 14 other countries, sent delegates to conclude what became the 1864 Convention for the Amelioration of the Condition of the Wounded in Armies in the Field.[263]

The 1864 Convention provided five fundamental principles which were to govern international humanitarian law on the question of wounded soldiers and those who cared for them. The first, contained in the opening article, was that:

> Ambulances and military hospitals shall be recognized as neutral, and as such, protected and respected by the belligerents as long as they accommodate wounded and sick. Neutrality shall end if the said ambulances or hospitals should be held by a military force.[264]

The second was that:

> Persons employed in hospitals and ambulances, comprising the staff for superintendence, medical service, administration, transport of wounded, as well as chaplains, shall participate in the benefit of neutrality, whilst so employed, and so long as there remain any wounded to bring in or to succour.[265]

The third principle, although other complimentary 'distinctive emblems' have been identified subsequently, as a compliment to Switzerland with the twist that their heraldic emblem of a red cross on a white ground being reversed, it was agreed that both the protected people and the places they worked within, would be identified by wearing or displaying a Red Cross which was to help guarantee their identification and neutrality.[266] Their neutrality meant that not only should they not be targeted, they should also not be captured and held as prisoners of war unless needed for medical

[262] Resolutions from the 1863 Geneva Conference in ICRC (1995) *The Humanitarian Endeavour* (Geneva, ICRC) 135.

[263] 22 Stat 940; Treaty Series 377. For the history of this period, see Bennett, A (2006) *The Geneva Convention: The Hidden Origins of the Red Cross* (Gloucestershire, Sutton) 28, 35, 36, 42, 60–66; Moorehead, C (1998) *Dunant's Dream: War, Switzerland and the History of the Red Cross* (NYC, Carroll and Graf) 26.

[264] 1864, Art 1. Also, Oxford Manual, Art 35.

[265] 1864, Art 2. Also, Oxford Manual, Art 13.

[266] 1864, Art 7. Other distinctive emblems include the red crescent or red lion and sun on a white background. In 2006, the Red Crystal was added to the list of options. See Protocol Additional to the Geneva Conventions of 12 August 1949, Relating to the Adoption of an Additional Distinctive Emblem. 45 ILM 555 (2006). For other reiterations of this, see the 1899 Hague Declaration, Art 23(f), 1907 Art 23(f); Geneva I (1949), Art 38 and Geneva II (1949), Arts 4, 42. Also, 1977 Protocol I, Art 38; Slim, H (1989) 'Protection of the Red Cross Emblem' *IRRC* 272: 420–37; Bouvier, A (1989) 'Special Aspects of the Use of the Red Cross or Red Crescent Emblem' *IRRC* 272: 438–58; Sandoz, Y (1989) 'The Red Cross and Red Crescent Emblems: What Is At Stake' *IRRC* 272:405–40).

work on other prisoners.[267] The genius of achieving neutrality for the medics and the areas they worked in came with the fourth, fundamental, point. This was that 'wounded or sick soldiers shall be entertained and taken care of, to whatever nation they may belong'.[268] The final principle of note was that wounded soldiers who were held as prisoners of war, once healed, if they were incapable of serving again, should be repatriated back to their own countries on the proviso that they would never again serve in a combat role.[269]

These principles, especially in terms of respect for the Red Cross on the battlefield and non-discrimination in terms of treatment of the wounded, were largely followed in the decades that followed in the Prussian wars against Austria and Denmark. When the conflicts moved to include Russia and Turkey in the 1870s, there were questions over the neutrality and status of the Red Cross as the Turkish armies showed a complete contempt for the Geneva Convention, stripping, massacring and mutilating the enemy wounded. Medical units were also fired upon despite the red cross flag they bore. In addition, there were questions over how seriously commanders took the issue of sick and wounded troops in general. For example, the conflicts in Egypt in 1882 were separated between British commanders trying to help the wounded, and British commanders trying to kill them. Alternately, commanders could be simply callous, and not value such considerations as helping the wounded, no matter what side they were on. For example, when Lord Herbert Kitchener (1850–1916) took an army of nearly 10,000 to the Sudan in 1896, he could only be bothered to include five medical officers. In the Boer War a few years later he drastically cut back medical supplies when it suited him. Conversely, the Boers were known to have dealt well with the wounded of both sides, including in at least one instance when they left behind their own doctors to attend wounded British soldiers before departing.[270]

Although the laws and practices of assisting the wounded on land were clearly evolving, the same could not be said for helping the wounded and/or defenceless at sea. This topic was a clear oversight of the drafters of the 1864 regime, as was demonstrated two years later in 1866 with the war between Prussia and Austria, when a number of ships fought and were sunk at the battle of Lisa. The problem was that the 1864 principles only applied to land warfare, and the victorious sailors had no obligation (or intention) to save the opposing men from drowning or being left to the elements. This lacuna, which was a constant source of concern to the ICRC delegates throughout the last decades of the nineteenth century, was not resolved until 1907. That is, the topic of searching and assisting shipwrecked sailors was not mentioned in the 1899 Convention (III) for the Adaptation to Maritime Warfare of the Principles of the Geneva Convention of 22 August 1864, as Convention III was more concerned with the status of hospital ships in times of maritime conflict. However, in 1907, Article 16

[267] 1864, Art 3.

[268] 1864, Article 6. For the problems of acting in a non-discriminatory way in practice, see Bennett, A (2006) *The Geneva Convention: The Hidden Origins of the Red Cross* (Gloucestershire, Sutton) 72–73, 110–20; Nichol, J and Rennell, T (2009) *Medic* (London, Penguin) 193, 194, 201.

[269] 1864, Art 6. See also Art 74 of the Oxford Manual.

[270] Resolutions from the 1875, 1867, 1884, 1892 and 1902 ICRC Conferences in ICRC (1995) *The Humanitarian Endeavour* (ICRC, Geneva) 139, 141, 149; Moorehead, C (1998) *Dunant's Dream: War, Switzerland and the History of the Red Cross* (NYC, Carroll and Graf) 63, 139; Tucker, S (1996) *The European Powers in the First World War* (New York, Garland) 471; Pakenham, T (2003) *The Scramble for Africa* (London, Abacus) 95–97, 138–40.

of Convention (X) for the Adaptation to Maritime Warfare of the Principles of the Geneva Convention stipulated 'after every engagement, the two belligerents, so far as military interests permit, shall take steps to look for the shipwrecked, sick, and wounded, and to protect them, as well as the dead, against pillage and ill-treatment.'[271]

The other topic which was not immediately addressed was that of hospital ships. Although, hospital ships had been in existence for hundreds of years, the 1864 Convention was limited to land warfare. Moreover, some countries believed military hospital ships should be available for capture. These uncertainties meant that when hospital ships were utilised in conflicts such as the 1898 American–Spanish war, both sides had to agree before the conflict not to target these vessels.[272] It was not until Part III of the 1899 Hague Convention, which adapted Maritime Warfare to the Principles of the 1864 Geneva Convention, stipulated in its first article:

> Military hospital ships, that is to say, ships constructed or assigned by States specially and solely for the purpose of assisting the wounded, sick or shipwrecked, and the names of which shall have been communicated to the belligerent Powers at the beginning or during the course of hostilities, and in any case before they are employed, shall be respected and cannot be captured while hostilities last.[273]

B. Prisoners

Aside the question of *franc-tireurs*, as discussed in chapter one on combatants, the 1870–71 war between France and Germany was relatively civilised when it came to the question of dealing with the wounded and prisoners of war. The war saw the parole of French officers (but not enlisted men) and the swift repatriation of men when the conflict ended was clear in the Treaty of Peace Between France and Germany 1871.[274]

What was not particular civilised was the Paris uprising in 1871 which directly followed the war. This was the ICRC's first experience with civil war, where Henry Dunant tried to get the Communards to promise to abide by the 1864 Geneva Convention. Although they did promise, they went on to shoot a government doctor, Abbe Allard, a member of the French Red Cross society, who went before the firing squad wearing his Red Cross armband. The Government troops responded by massacring every prisoner they seized. From then on, the conflict went from atrocity, to reprisals to counter-reprisals. Dunant was left trying to secure the safety of a few key individuals, whilst he could not stop the killing thousands of Communards after they had been defeated, with tens of thousands of others being deported to French colonies. This approach was significantly harder than in the 1848 uprising, when 1,500 French workers were killed in the fighting, and only 468 were deported to Algeria. It was,

[271] Resolutions from the 1867, 1869, 1892 and 1897 ICRC Conferences in ICRC (1995) *The Humanitarian Endeavour* (Geneva, ICRC) 137, 145, 147. Also, Bennett, A (2006) *The Geneva Convention: The Hidden Origins of the Red Cross* (Gloucestershire, Sutton) 74; Moorehead, C (1998) *Dunant's Dream: War, Switzerland and the History of the Red Cross* (NYC, Carroll and Graf) 56.

[272] Bennett, A (2006) *The Geneva Convention: The Hidden Origins of the Red Cross* (Gloucestershire, Sutton) 104, 108, 167.

[273] They must be 'respected and protected' at all times, and the other side must have been notified of their existence and travel plans. See 1907 Maritime, Arts 1–3.

[274] The 1871 Treaty of Peace Between France and Germany in Mowat, R (1918) *The Great European Treaties of the Nineteenth Century* (Oxford, Oxford University Press) Art VI; Howard, M (2002) *The Franco-Prussian War* (London, Routledge) 116, 222.

however, more in accordance with the Prussians during their 1848 uprising, where one in every 10 prisoners was executed.[275]

Such developments made a number of pivotal figures within the ICRC suggest that their mandate to help should go beyond helping the wounded, to also helping prisoners – irrespective of the nature of the conflict – as they can be equally vulnerable. Accordingly, they turned their attention to the creation of an international instrument, despite the reservations of both Britain and Austria, for the protection of prisoners of war. The emperor of Austria, Franz Josef (1848–1916) cautioned that 'to secure to prisoners of war great comforts and indulgences would be to hold out an inducement to cowardly or effeminate soldiers to escape the dangers and hardships of war by surrendering themselves to the enemy.'[276]

Despite these concerns, on the initiative of Alexander II (1818–81) of Russia, the delegates of 15 European States met in Brussels in the middle of 1874 to examine the draft of an international agreement concerning the laws and customs of war submitted to them by the Russian Government. Although the conference adopted the draft with minor alterations, not all the governments were willing to accept it as a binding convention and it was not ratified. The project nevertheless formed an important step in the movement for the codification of the laws of war, as this was the first time a substantive international attempt to codify the rules on warfare with regards to prisoners was made. This was supplemented six years later with the scholarly *Manual of the Laws and Customs of War*, which was concluded at Oxford in 1880. The Brussels Declaration and the Oxford Manual formed the basis of the two Hague Conventions and the Regulations annexed to them, which were adopted in 1899 and 1907. Although only 17 States ratified the 1899 Convention, the provisions of the two Conventions, soon became considered as embodying rules of customary international law. As such they were also binding on states which were/are not formally parties to them. This was especially so by the time of the Second World War.[277] Due to this sequence of events and the way they are all linked together, the following discussion on prisoners of war will draw from all of the developments of 1874, 1880, 1899 and 1907.

The 1874 Project of an International Declaration concerning the Laws and Customs of War, prohibited the declaring that no quarter would be given on a battlefield. Accordingly, the killing of an enemy who had laid down his arms and surrendered was 'murder'.[278] The Declaration recognised that the maintenance of prisoners was the responsibility of the government 'in whose hands the prisoners of war had fallen'.[279]

[275] Horne, A (2004) *The Terrible Year: The Paris Commune, 1871* (London, Phoenix) 92–95, 126, 137, 140; Rapport, M (2009) *1848: Year of Revolution* (London, Abacus) 206–208, 347; Moorehead, C (1998) *Dunant's Dream: War, Switzerland and the History of the Red Cross* (NYC, Carroll and Graf) 81, 125; Bennett, A (2006) *The Geneva Convention: The Hidden Origins of the Red Cross* (Gloucestershire, Sutton) at 130–36.

[276] Josef noted in Best, G (1980) *Humanity in Warfare* (London, Weidenfeld) 157; Moorehead, C (1998) *Dunant's Dream: War, Switzerland and the History of the Red Cross* (NYC, Carroll and Graf), 126–28; Bennett, A (2006) *The Geneva Convention: The Hidden Origins of the Red Cross* (Gloucestershire, Sutton) 151.

[277] In 1946 the Nüremberg Tribunal stated with regard to the Hague Convention on land warfare of 1907, 'the rules of land warfare expressed in the Convention undoubtedly represented an advance over existing International Law at the time of their adoption . . . but by 1939 these rules . . . were recognized by all civilized nations and were regarded as being declaratory of the laws and customs of war'. This comment is reprinted in 41 *American Journal of International Law* (1947) 248–49. Note, this explanation is from Schindler, D (1988) *The Laws of Armed Conflicts* (the Netherlands, Nihjoff,) 69–93.

[278] 1874, Art 13(b), (d).

[279] 1874, Arts 27 and 33.

That is, prisoners of war were deemed to be in the power of the Government not in that of the individuals or corps who captured them. Prisoners of war could be made to work, but they could not be 'compelled in any way to take any part whatever in carrying on the operations of the war'.[280] Although the Government had the right to control acts of insubordination 'as necessary', such captives 'must be humanely treated'.[281] It went on, 'as a general principle, prisoners of war shall be treated as regards food and clothing, on the same footing as the troops of the Government which captured them'.[282] Although arms could be used in attempting to stop escapes, prisoners who escaped but were recaptured were only liable to 'disciplinary punishment or subject to stricter surveillance'.[283] The rule that a prisoner would only be bound to give their name, rank and serial number was clearly iterated.[284] The importance of considerations of safety when confining prisoners was recognised as was the value of prisoner exchanges and parole.[285]

Following the absolute failure of many of these goals on respect for prisoners of war in the 1875–78 Russo–Turkish war,[286] the 1880 *Oxford Manual of Laws of War on Land*, reiterated all of the salient points from the 1863 Convention[287] and the 1874 Declaration.[288] In addition, the Manual added two points. First, the confinement of prisoners of war was not in the nature of a penalty for crime nor was it an act of vengeance.[289] Second, the importance of termination of captivity was highlighted 'as a matter of right, at the conclusion of peace; but their liberation is then regulated by agreement between the belligerents'.[290]

A good example of this approach to repatriation occurred soon after with the 1896 Treaty of Addis Ababa whereby Italy and Ethiopia came to peace, with the promise that both sides would release their prisoners. Notably, for the first time, this treaty included the agreement from the Ethiopians that they would accept a detachment from the Italian Red Cross to meet with the prisoners and assist in this process.[291]

In 1899, the international community agreed the Hague Convention. The second part of this dealt with the Laws and Customs of War on Land (Hague II), of which 17 articles, for the first time in international law (as opposed to the soft document noted above), dealt with prisoners of war. These articles, which were largely based upon the documents of 1874 and 1880, emphasised the points of, inter alia, the right

[280] 1874, Art 26.
[281] 1874, Art 23.
[282] 1874, Art 27.
[283] 1874, Art 28.
[284] 1874 Declaration, Art 29. For a discussion of this requirement, see Geiss, R (2005) 'Name, Rank, Date of Birth, Serial Number and the Right to Remain Silent' in *International Review of the Red Cross*, Vol 87, No 860, 45–76.
[285] 1874, Arts 31–33.
[286] Moorehead, C (1998) *Dunant's Dream: War, Switzerland and the History of the Red Cross* (NYC, Carroll and Graf) at 132–35; Bennett, A (2006) *The Geneva Convention: The Hidden Origins of the Red Cross* (Gloucestershire, Sutton) at 163.
[287] Oxford Manual, Art 10.
[288] The right to surrender is in Art 9. The point that they are in the power of the government, not the troops who capture them, is in Art 61. The obligation of humane treatment is in Art 63. Standards at a minimum soldiers and prisoners being treated alike in terms of food and clothing, is in Art 69. Safety in housing is in Art 66. Escape is in Arts 67 and 68. Work is in Arts 71 and 72. Exchange is in Art 75, and parole can be found in Arts 76– 78. Torture is in Arts 65 and 70.
[289] 1880, Art 21.
[290] 1880, Art 73.
[291] The 1896 Treaty of Addis Ababa, Agreement on Prisoners, Art II.

to surrender,[292] humane treatment,[293] governmental control over prisoners,[294] respect for the 'distinctive badges of the Geneva Convention',[295] the treatment of wounded without distinction,[296] the neutrality of hospitals,[297] feeding and clothing prisoners at least on par between soldiers and prisoners,[298] parole,[299] 'name, rank and serial number'[300] and speedy repatriation upon the end of the conflict.[301] Although it was agreed that prisoners could be put to work, it was added that 'their tasks shall not be excessive, and shall have nothing to do with the military operations'.[302] Prisoners who escaped but were recaptured could be disciplined, but not executed.[303] What was new was that the 1899 Declaration recognised that:

> Relief Societies for prisoners of war, which are regularly constituted in accordance with the law of the country with the object of serving as the intermediary for charity, shall receive from the belligerents for themselves and their duly accredited agents every facility, within the bounds of military requirements and Administrative Regulations, for the effective accomplishment of their humane task. Delegates of these Societies may be admitted to the places of interment for the distribution of relief, as also to the halting places of repatriated prisoners, if furnished with a personal permit by the military authorities, and on giving an engagement in writing to comply with all their Regulations for order and police.[304]

It was also agreed that a bureau for information relative to prisoners of war would be instituted, on the commencement of hostilities in each of the belligerent States, and, when necessary, in the neutral countries on whose territory belligerents had been received. This Bureau was to answer all inquiries about prisoners of war, and was to be furnished by the various services concerned with all the necessary information to enable it to keep an individual return for each prisoner of war.[305]

With such developments in mind, in some parts of the world the humanitarian ideals with regards to prisoners were clearly becoming operative. This was clearly evidenced in the wars of Japan and China (1894–95) and Japan and Russia (1904–1905). The Japanese, who were the victors in both instances, displayed exemplary respect for the 1864 Convention in addition to showing a clear humanity towards prisoners of war. The Japanese went so far as to pay their Russian prisoners a salary that was double the amount paid to Japanese soldiers of the same rank, as well as providing them with better food and conditions than their own army possessed. Accordingly, in both conflicts, the death rate of the tens of thousands of prisoners taken was very low.[306]

[292] 1899, Art 23.
[293] 1899, Art 4.
[294] 1899, Art 4.
[295] 1899, Art 23(f).
[296] 1899, Art 21.
[297] 1899, Art 27.
[298] 1899, Art 7.
[299] 1899, Art 10.
[300] 1899, Art 9.
[301] 1899, Art 20.
[302] 1899, Art 6.
[303] 1899, Art 8.
[304] 1899, Art 15.
[305] 1899, Art 14.
[306] Moorehead, C (1998) *Dunant's Dream: War, Switzerland and the History of the Red Cross* (NYC, Carroll and Graf) at 156; Barenblatt, D (2004) *A Plague Upon Humanity* (NYC, Harper) 860, 101–102; Garrett, R (1981) *POW* (London, Charles) 100.

The 'immediate' repatriation of prisoners was then followed in both the 1895 Treaty of Shimonoseki[307] and the 1905 Treaty of Portsmouth.[308]

Despite the Japanese examples, the other conflicts at the end of the nineteenth and beginning of the twentieth century showed only a scant regard for the emerging ideals of humanitarian concerns with prisoners, and the nascent ICRC had very little impact on any of the conflicts which were often without pity. A young Winston Churchill (1874–1965) wrote in 1897 of the wars in Afghanistan, that these were 'wars without quarter . . . they kill and mutilate everyone they catch, and we do not hesitate to finish their wounded off'.[309]

The following year after the battle of Omdurman, Lord Herbert Kitchener after organising the looking after of the few dozen of his own wounded allowed one Muslim doctor to attend the estimated 16,000 wounded Dervishes, who had charged head-first into the technology, and machine guns in particular, of modernity. The result was that thousands of men were left to die on the battlefield.[310] The victory of the Ethiopian forces over the Italians in 1896 also saw extreme acts, with only 1,700 men ever returning out of a defeated force of 10,596 at the battle of Adowa in 1896. This battle ended with large-scale executions of prisoners, followed by the forced marching of 500 miles of the 1,900 survivors of which 200 died en-route.[311] The forces of the United States were known to have executed prisoners following their conquest of Cuba in the Spanish American war of 1898. During the Philippine–American war of 1899–1902, following an attack upon his men by disguised insurgents, the American commander, General Jacob Smith (1840–1918), ordered; 'I want no prisoners. I wish you to kill and burn, the more you kill and burn the better it will please me.'[312]

Although Smith would subsequently face a court martial for this order, the practice was far from unusual at this point in time. The failure to give quarter was also a clear feature in the Boxer Rebellion by most sides to the conflict, with the Germans within the European contingent being particularly notable. In Latin America, the mercenaries who attempted to invade Cuba, and parts of Mexico and Central America, were often executed upon capture throughout the nineteenth century. Insurgents who fought against the newly minted Latin American governments in Bolivia, Columbia and Mexico, met the same fate if captured. No-quarter was a common event in war of the Triple Alliance (1864–70), which saw Brazil, Argentina and Uruguay opposing Paraguay. The same practice was followed in the wars of Dominican independence from Haiti (1849), as it was (initially) to revolutionaries in their attempts to free Cuba from Spanish rule towards the end of the nineteenth century. When the Cuban revolutionaries gained the upper hand, they reversed this practice, killing a number of Spanish prisoners. This was despite the efforts of the United States, which had joined the conflict in 1898, to prevent such actions.[313]

[307] The 1895 Treaty of Shimonoseki, Art 9.

[308] The 1905 Treaty of Portsmouth, Art XIII.

[309] Churchill in Kiernan, V (1998) *Colonial Empires and Armies* (London, Sutton) 70.

[310] Green, D (2008) *Armies of God* (London, Arrow) 297–99; Robinson, P (2006) *Military Honour and the Conduct of War* (London, Routledge) 156.

[311] Pakenham, T (2003) *The Scramble for Africa* (London, Abacus) 485–86.

[312] Smith, noted in Maguire, P (2001) *Law and War: An American Story* (NYC, Columbia University Press) 59–60.

[313] Scheina, R (2003) *Latin America's Wars: The Age of the Caudillo, 1791–1899* (Washington, Brassey) 162, 171, 175, 177, 193, 229, 265, 276, 299, 325, 331, 345, 353 and 424.

The killing of prisoners was also implemented by the Germans in East and Southwest Africa as they used ultimate force to suppress rebellions. Similar problems occurred with the Boer Wars, especially the second one of 1899–1902. In the latter instance, although both sides had pledged to abide by the 1864 and 1899 Conventions, the killing of prisoners by both the Boers and the British, in a series of reprisals and counter-reprisals occurred. This was especially so when the Boers captured black prisoners. Even with the prisoners that were taken, the conditions of captivity, such as keeping men in the open without medical care, were often atrocious. When these conditions were made public, the British authorities made a public display of rejecting such practices. Accordingly, they were known to release men they could not feed, even though they knew they would probably regroup and fight again, and they made a distinct effort to stop the killing of prisoners. As such, six officers (five Australians and one Englishman) were court-martialled for multiple murders of Boer prisoners. Two of these men, Lieutenants 'Breaker' Morant (1864–1902) and Peter Handcock (1868–1902), were executed for this offence on the direct orders of Kitchener.[314] Following the end of such conflicts, in accordance with the now established practices, the prisoners were returned without ransom. This was clear in both the 1898 Treaty of Peace Between the United States and Spain,[315] and the 1902 Treaty of Vereeniging[316] which ended the Boer War.

With regards to the problem of torture, although such acts were notable against non-Chinese in the Boxer Rebellion, it was expected that Europeans would not indulge in such practices, although the problem was recorded with American troops in both the Philippines in 1900 and Haiti in 1915. However, these were isolated non-sanctioned incidents. This was unlike the torturing to death of several anarchists in 1892 by Spanish authorities which resulted in an international outcry.[317]

Initiatives in the area of dealing with the dead were driven by the ICRC repeatedly during the 1860s. In particular, they emphasised the importance of the identification of victims, notification of the names of the dead and clear prohibitions on desecration.[318] In accordance with such work, the 1880 Oxford Manual would suggest that preventing the desecration of the dead and establishing and sharing the identity of the dead was customary best practice.[319] This was an easy point to conclude as in addition to the ICRC work, the respect for the dead at the national, and even bilateral level, was being incorporated into peace treaties at the ends of conflicts, by which the fallen would be respected. For example, the 1871 treaty of peace between France and

[314] Hull, I (2005) *Absolute Destruction: Military Culture and the Practices of War in Imperial Germany* (Ithaca, Cornell University Press) 19, 20, 26, 135, 145–47; Preston, D (2000) *The Boxer Rebellion* (NYC, Berkeley Books) 99, 114, 116, 143, 159, 303; Totten, S (2004) *Century of Genocide* (London, Routledge) 25–29; Pakenham, T (1991) *The Boer War* (London, Cardinal) 538–39; Robinson, P (2006) *Military Honour and the Conduct of War* (London, Routledge) 155.

[315] The 1898 Treaty of Peace Between the United States and Spain, Arts V and VI.

[316] The 1902 Treaty of Vereeniging, Art II.

[317] Boot, M (2002) *The Savage Wars of Peace: Small Wars and the Rise of American Power* (NYC, Basic) 100, 113, 171; Preston, D (2000) *The Boxer Rebellion* (NYC, Berkeley Books) 76; Beevor, A (1982) *The Spanish Civil War* (London, Cassel) 25.

[318] Resolutions from the 1867, 1869 and 1884 ICRC Conferences in ICRC (1995) *The Humanitarian Endeavour* (Geneva, ICRC) 137, 139, 141; Moorehead, C (1998) *Dunant's Dream: War, Switzerland and the History of the Red Cross* (NYC, Carroll and Graf) 63.

[319] 1880, Arts 19 and 20.

Germany had the two governments agree to 'reciprocally engage to respect and preserve the Tombs of soldiers buried in their respective territories'.[320]

Similar obligations were hoisted on the Chinese with the 1901 Peace Agreement between the Great Powers and China which ended the Boxer uprising. In addition, by the turn of the century, belligerents, such as Japan and Russia in their conflict of 1904–1905, were sharing accurate information on the dead who had fallen.[321]

The Second Peace Conference at the Hague in 1907 modified some parts of the 1899 Convention. However, the Laws and Customs of War on Land (Hague IV), on the question of prisoners of war were largely unchanged. As such, the basic rules on, inter alia, the right to surrender,[322] humane treatment,[323] governmental authority,[324] safety in captivity,[325] rules on work,[326] freedom of religion,[327] free access to mail and parcel deliveries,[328] at least equal treatment on board, lodging and clothing between prisoners and captors,[329] parole,[330] the role of relief societies,[331] inquiry offices,[332] escape,[333] non-discrimination in treating the wounded,[334] the neutrality of hospitals,[335] no torture,[336] and speedy repatriation upon the end of the conflict remained the same.[337] There were also clear obligations to search for and prevent the desecration of the dead, keep clear records of the dead, and both notify and share with the opposition all of the applicable information.[338]

12. The First World War

A. Prisoners

Although the need to update the 1907 rules was being advocated by the ICRC in 1912,[339] and the Balkan wars of 1912–13 showed that the rules were far from univer-

320 The Definitive Treaty of Peace Between France and Germany 1871 in Mowat, R (1918) *The Great European Treaties of the Nineteenth Century* (Oxford, Oxford University Press) Art XVI, 285.

321 Boxer Peace Agreement, Art IV. Also, Moorehead, C (1998) *Dunant's Dream: War, Switzerland and the History of the Red Cross* (NYC, Carroll and Graf) at 157.

322 1907, Art 23.

323 1907, Art 4.

324 1907, Art 4.

325 1907, Arts 5 and 7.

326 1907, Art 6.

327 1907, Art 18.

328 1907, Art 16.

329 1907, Art 7.

330 1907, Arts 10–12.

331 1907, Art 15.

332 1907, Art 14.

333 1907, Art 8.

334 1907, Art 21.

335 1907, Art 5 and 27.

336 1907,Art 9.

337 1907, Art 20.

338 1907 Convention for the Adaptation to Maritime War, Arts 16 and 17. Also, Art 19 on the Land rules.

339 This conference resolved to assist POWs by the creation of a 'special commission' within the National Societies, to be given the task of collecting and sending to the ICRC relief supplies for combatants in captivity. Resolutions from the 1912 Conference in ICRC (1995) *The Humanitarian Endeavour* (Geneva, ICRC) 153.

sally adhered to, it was the 1907 Convention that governed the belligerents in the First World War.[340]

Despite the incidents that occurred in many of the so-called colonial conflicts between 1864 and 1914, by the time the First World War broke, the primary belligerents appear to have incorporated these values. For example, with regard to the issue of prisoners, the *War Book of German General Staff* stipulated:

> The State regards [prisoners] as persons who have simply done their duty . . . they are protected against unjustifiable severities, ill treatment and unworthy handling . . . war captivity is no longer an act of grace on the part of the victor but a right of the defenceless . . . prisoners can only be put to death in case of overwhelming necessity . . . or for purposes of reprisal.[341]

Despite such clarity, the practice of killing prisoners and wounded soldiers was 'widespread and commonplace' by both sides between 1914 and 1918. Machine gunners, those using mortars, flamethrowers and especially snipers all had difficulty surrendering. Such killings may even have been routine in certain battles, such as the Somme where orders have surfaced such as those by British General Claud Jacob (1863–1948) in 1916 urging that no prisoners should be taken. It is equally possible that a blind eye was turned to the killing of some German sailors by the British authorities in the acts undertaken by some of the Commanders of the Q-ships. Similar allegations surround some U-boat captains, with these men being involved in the killing of survivors of ships. When this issue of firing on the lifeboats of a sinking ship by German sailors was addressed in the case of Lieutenants Dithmar and Boldt in the Leipzig trials in 1921, the court held:

> The firing on the boats was an offence against the law of nations. In war on land the killing of unarmed enemies is not allowed . . . similarly, in war at sea, the killing of shipwrecked people, who have taken refuge in life boats, is forbidden [unless the inmates of the boats are still trying to fight].[342]

A much greater death rate for prisoners occurred once they were incarcerated. Of the British and French soldiers in German captivity about 3 per cent died. This was unlike the 2.11 million Habsburg prisoners of war in Russian camps of which 9.24 per cent died and another 9 per cent went missing. Of the 158,000 German soldiers in Russian hands, 9.97 per cent died and 33 per cent went missing, although many of these eventually made it home through the chaos of the Russian civil war. The total mortality rate for Russian prisoners of war in Germans hands was 5.06 per cent, although this

340 Best, G (1980) *Humanity in Warfare* (London, Weidenfeld) 217; Forsythe, D (2005) *The Humanitarians: The International Committee of the Red Cross* (Cambridge, Cambridge University Press) 30; Kramer, A (2007) *Dynamic of Destruction: Culture and Mass Killing in the First World War* (Oxford, Oxford University Press) 136, 139; For the exchange of prisoners at the end of the conflict, see the 1913 Treaty of Bucharest, Art IX.

341 Grossgeneralstab (1915) in trans Morgan, T (2005) *War Book of the German General Staff* (Pennsylvania, Stackpole Books) 22–23, 28–29.

342 German War Trials, Judgment in the Case of Lieutenants Dithmar and Boldt, 1922 *AJIL* 16(4): 708–24. For some of the complimentary allegations in this area, see, for the Jacob order, Ferguson, N (2006) *The War of the World* (London, Allen Lane) 128. Also, Ferguson, N (2006) 'Prisoner Taking and Prisoner Killing' in Kassimeris, G (ed) *The Barbarisation of Warfare* (London, Hurst) 126, 133–37; Kramer, A (2007) *Dynamic of Destruction: Culture and Mass Killing in the First World War* (Oxford, Oxford University Press) 63; Bourke, J (2000) *An Intimate History of Killing* (London, Granta) 182–83, 189, 210, 242; Coles, A (1986) *Slaughter at Sea: The Truth Behind a Naval War Crime* (London, Hale). Also, Bridgland, T (1999) *Sea Killers In Disguise* (Yorkshire, Pen and Sword) 20–37.

may be an underestimate due to the problem that the blockade created and views by Kaiser Wilhelm II (1859–1941) that Russian prisoners 'should be left to starve', despite official positions to the contrary.[343] The problem for the Russian prisoners, was that unlike the British and the French, they had no regular source of Red Cross food parcels, of which the ICRC dispatched some 33 million to Germany for the prisoners of the Western Allies, or roughly one parcel per fortnight per man. Italian prisoners of war held in Austro-Hungary captivity suffered a mortality rate of 19.91 per cent, but only 5.68 per cent when held by Germany. The Serbs, who managed to allow thousands of the prisoners they held die, suffered a death rate of 6.07 per cent when held by the Germans, but almost 29 per cent for the Romanians. Lack of food was also a problem with Italian prisoners, although it should be noted that the Italian State tried to stop the sending of food parcels to its own prisoners, to prevent their own men seeing surrendering as an attractive option. Turkey also had a very poor record for looking after prisoners of war. Captured officers were treated reasonably, but the food was poor. For standard soldiers the situation was different. Of the 3,700 British and 9,300 Indians captured in April 1915, 2,600 British and 2,500 Indians died in captivity. Although the British and the Turks met in 1917 to remedy some of the conditions that lead to these deaths, it is doubtful if these were ever implemented before the war ended. These failures were an important factor in the British seeking war crimes trials for the leaders of the Ottoman Empire.[344] Accordingly, Article 215 of the Sevres Treaty had Turkey promise 'to facilitate the establishing of criminal acts punishable by the penalties referred to in . . . the present Treaty and committed by Turks against the persons of prisoners of war or Allied nationals during the war.'[345]

Although the proposed war crimes tribunals for Turkey never took place, over half of the trials held at Leipzig following the First World War had to do with the maltreatment of prisoners of war. When the trials concluded, German camp commanders Emil Muller,[346] and Karl Heynen,[347] as well as the prison guard Robert Neumann,[348] had all been convicted of ill-treatment (mainly in the forms of hitting prisoners) and insults to British prisoners of war. The sentences these men received varied between six months and two years in jail.

It may be that the death toll for prisoners could have been much greater in the First World War had it not been for the moderating influences of independent countries acting as Protective Powers and the ICRC operations between Germany, Britain and France. In the first instance, before they joined the conflict, since the United States was looking after the diplomatic interests of both Britain and Germany, it was suggested that it should also undertake the protection of prisoners. Accordingly, both Germany and Britain agreed to unannounced visits by the Protecting Power in 1915. When the

[343] Wilhelm is noted in Beevor, A (1998) *Stalingrad* (London, Penguin) 59.

[344] Kramer, A (2007) *Dynamic of Destruction: Culture and Mass Killing in the First World War* (Oxford, Oxford University Press) 63, 65–67, 142, 223; Bass, G (2000) *Stay the Hand of Vengeance: The Politics of War Crimes Tribunals* (Princeton University Press) 114; Moynihan, M (1978) *Black Bread and Barbed Wire: Prisoners in the First World War* (London, Cooper) 3–35, 159–88; Tucker, S (1996) *The European Powers in the First World War* (New York, Garland) 571; de Zayas, A (1989) *The Wehrmacht War Crimes Bureau, 1939–1945* (Nebraska, Nebraska University Press) 10; Moorehead C (1998) *Dunant's Dream: War, Switzerland and the History of the Red Cross* (NYC, Carroll and Graf) 192–94, 199.

[345] Sevres, Art 215(c).

[346] German War Trials. Judgment in the Case of Emil Muller, 1922 *AJIL* 16(4): 684–96.

[347] German War Trials. Judgment in the Case of Karl Heynen, 1922 *AJIL* 16(4): 674–84.

[348] German War Trials. Judgment in the Case of Robert Neumann, 1922 *AJIL* 16(4): 696–704.

United States joined the conflict, Switzerland became the Protecting Power, and a series of independent visits to prisoner of war camps to ensure that standards were being met, were undertaken.

The ICRC, which had never been officially designated a role in dealing with prisoners of war, also became actively involved forming the International Prisoner of War Agency on 21 August 1914 for the exchange of information on, and supplies to, prisoners of war. The fact that Switzerland was neutral and pressure from a number of national Red Cross societies meant that the ICRC gained access to many prisoner of war camps and managed to conduct a total of 524 visits to Prisoner of War camps in France, Britain, Germany, Tunisia, Morocco, Austria-Hungary, Italy, Russia, Egypt, India, Burma, Bulgaria, Rumania, Macedonia, Poland, Bohemia and even Japan. The ICRC also compiled a list of 4,895,000 index cards of prisoners held by all sides to the conflict, and forwarded 1,884,914 individual parcels and 1,813 wagonloads of collective relief supplies. These supplies were often directed to places which the ICRC found in need of assistance. The assistance came from the ICRC visits, which in addition to the provision of adequate food, also checked inter alia, hygiene and the state of the prisoners' quarters. After each visit to a prisoner of war camp the ICRC drew up a report containing their findings and comments. These reports were then sent to the detaining power of the prisoners of war – so that it could take steps to improve the conditions of detention – and to the captives' power of origin. At this stage, the ICRC reports were publically available and not dealt with discretely. In general, these reports showed that German camps for the British, the British for the German and French were not as bad as feared, but the French camps could do better. The ICRC also had a moderating influence on the practice of the prevention of reprisals against prisoners, via a secret agreement between France and Germany in 1916 on this topic.[349]

The final issue of note that arose with the First World War was what to do with the 6.5 million captives held in Europe at the end of the conflict. Many of these men were not released until the Treaties of Versailles and Sevres were concluded in 1919 and 1920. Although these treaties required the 'greatest rapidity' with repatriation, prisoners could take up to two years to trickle home.[350] In other instances, such as with the 1921 Treaty of Friendship Between Russia and Turkey, well after hostilities had ended, the Soviets' 'under[took] to return, at her own expense within three months, to the north-east frontier of Turkey, all Turkish prisoners of war'.[351]

One novelty of this period was Article 220 of the Versailles Treaty, which gave an un unprecedented freedom of choice to prisoners. This stated:

> Prisoners of war or other German nationals who do not desire to be repatriated may be excluded from repatriation; but the Allied and Associated Governments reserve to themselves the right either to repatriate them or to take them to a neutral country or to allow them to reside in their own territories.

[349] Tucker, S (1996) *The European Powers in the First World War* (New York, Garland) 591; Forsythe, D (2005) *The Humanitarians: The International Committee of the Red Cross* (Cambridge, Cambridge University Press) 31; Moorehead, C (1998) *Dunant's Dream: War, Switzerland and the History of the Red Cross* (NYC, Carroll and Graf) at 117, 190–-91, 203; Glover, M (1982) *The Velvet Glove. The Decline of Moderation in War* (London, Hodder) 210.

[350] Versailles, Art 215. The Arts on the prisoner exchanges go to 224.

[351] Art XIII of the 1921 Treaty of Friendship Between Russia and Turkey in Axelrod, A (ed) *Encyclopedia of Historical Treaties and Alliances*, Vol II (NYC, Facts on File) 514.

This freedom to choose had not been replicated in the 1918 Treaty of Brest-Litovsk which had concluded hostilities between Germany and the new Soviet Government. In this instance, the difficulty was not the commitment of both to release prisoners of war to their homeland,[352] but that neither the Allies (once they had defeated Germany, despite the creation of an Inter-Allied Armistice Commission to help) nor the new Soviet government felt much responsibility for the Russian captives. Accordingly, tens of thousands of these men attempted to wander home through the pandemics of 1919 and the turmoil of the Russian civil war, whilst others remained incarcerated (on both sides) as collateral for war debts. This was not resolved until the Treaty of Rapallo of 1922 between Germany and Soviet Russia, of which both sides renounced payments of the expenses incurred for the holding of prisoners of war of the other. This finally allowed any of the remaining prisoners to be released.[353] However, even if the Russian prisoners did finally manage to make it home, many of the officers were shot on arrival by the new Bolshevik overlords who viewed all former soldiers of the Czar with extreme suspicion. Such acts appear consistent with what appears to have been relatively common practice of denying the right to surrender to the enemy during the Russian civil war, although Allied prisoners of wars (as opposed to White Russians) were relatively well treated, if only for propaganda purposes.[354]

B. Wounded

The leaps and bounds of the technological methods, from flame throwers to chemical weapons, to kill other human beings were remarkable in the decades leading up to 1914. However, some changes in technology, actually reduced the amount of pain and injury caused on the battlefield, such as high velocity bullets which tended to produce cleaner wounds. Most of the new methods presented vast challenges to the medical personnel of the day, who responded with their own developments in technologies, including blood transfusions, understanding and treatment of shock, reconstructive and plastic surgery, and diagnostic use of x-ray machines. The end result of this clash of technologies was that the overall death rate by the end of 1918 for soldiers who were wounded was 8.1 per cent. This figure fell from a wound mortality rate of 28 per cent in the first two years of the conflict. In addition to the new technologies, a number of new practices were implemented which assisted in reducing the mortality rate. In particular, dedicated men were tasked with the removal of the wounded from the front line. Stretcher bearers were particularly vulnerable in this conflict, and it is noteworthy that the British Army's Royal Army Medical Corps, is the only component of the British Army to have had two members awarded double Victoria Crosses for their work as stretcher bearers. Similarly, the Medal of Honor was given to two American stretcher bearers in 1918, for the recovery of wounded officers in no-man's land. In addition to the stretcher bearers, medical officers were increasingly close to the front

[352] Art VIII.

[353] The Treaty of Rapallo, in Axelrod, A (ed) *Encyclopedia of Historical Treaties and Alliances*, Vol II (NYC, Facts on File) 570.

[354] For the Commission, see Versailles, Art 215; Bessel, R (1995) *Germany After the First World War* (Oxford, Oxford University Press) 86–91; Challinger, M (2010) *ANZACs in Arkhangel* (Melbourne, Hardie) 122–23, 152; Moorehead, C (1998) *Dunant's Dream: War, Switzerland and the History of the Red Cross* (NYC, Carroll and Graf), at 266–74; Garrett, R (1981) *POW* (London, Charles) 134–35, 180–81.

lines. These men were largely the ones responsible for taking the wounded from the stretcher bearers and were situated within 250 yards of the fighting. Motorised ambulance services then took casualties to treatment centres with trained staff. The Americans also began to experiment with various aircraft, painted with Red Crosses, for patient evacuation. Nevertheless, in this conflict, the average time to a field hospital was between 12 and 48 hours.

In addition, at various points during this conflict in a number of cases, sick and/or badly wounded prisoners were repatriated or sent to Switzerland. The bilateral exchange occurred between France and Germany, for 100 men each, in 1916; whilst a total of 67,726 sick prisoners of war were transferred to hospitals in neutral Switzerland. Captured medics were also repatriated. This happened first in 1915, when nearly 4,000 French and almost 1,000 German medical staff were repatriated, and again in 1916 when 2,970 French medical staff were exchanged for 1,150 German medical staff. Similar exchanges also occurred with the repatriation of Austro-Hungarian medical personnel.[355]

Although there was a type of progress in the above considerations, progress was retarded with the issue of the neutrality of hospital ships. In this regard, despite the reiteration of this rule in 1907,[356] and the 1913 *Oxford Manual of the Laws of Naval War*,[357] a number of nations, such as the United States decided to keep their hospital ships in American waters until close to the end of the First World War. This was due to a fear that the German government would not abide by the Hague Convention on their protection. This thinking was due to the fact that Germany had been practicing unrestrained submarine warfare towards hospital ships. This situation first arose in early 1915 when attempts were made to torpedo the British hospital ship *Asturias*. The following year, the Russian hospital ships *Portugal* and *Vperiod* were torpedoed, as were the British hospital ships, the *Britannic* and *Breamer Castle*. These were joined by the *Glocester Castle* and *Salta* in 1917. The following year, the British hospital ships *Rewa*, *Glenart Castle*, and *Guildford Castle* were torpedoed, along with the Australian hospital ship of *Baron Call*. Two further attacks on the *Llandovery Castle* and *Dover Castle* caused particular outrage. The sinking of the *Llandovery Castle*, and machine gunning of its lifeboats, killed 234 people. The sinking of the *Dover Castle* killed another six. The commander of the vessel that sunk the hospital ship *Dover Castle*, Karl Neumann, was clearly following orders, which had been made publicly available to the British, that in certain war zones, only specifically named hospital ships, notified to the Germans six weeks in advance and travelling via specific routes, would be safe. This was done as a reprisal because the Germans believed the British were using hospital ships for military purposes. Accordingly, since reprisals against hospital ships were not explicitly prohibited and the Germans had notified what they were intending to do, Neumann was acquitted.[358] This was unlike Lieutenants Dithmar and Boldt, who were convicted

[355] Durand, A (1984) *A History of the International Committee of the Red Cross: From Sarajevo to Hiroshima* (Dunant Institute, Geneva) 53–54; Tucker, S (1996) *The European Powers in the First World War* (New York, Garland) 471; Greenwood, J (2005) *Medics at War: Military Medicine from Colonial Times to the 21st Century* (Annapolis, Naval Institute Press) 35, 52, 63, 67, 73; Junod, M (1982) *Warriors Without Weapons* (Geneva, ICRC) 43.

[356] Hague 1907; Maritime, Art 16. Note also Art 4 of the 1907 Convention (XI) Relative to Certain Restrictions With Regard to the Exercise of the Right of Capture in Naval War.

[357] Arts 41 and 42.

[358] German War Trials. Judgment in the Case of Karl Neumann, 1922 *AJIL* 16(4): 704–709.

for the sinking of the *Llandovery Castle* and each received four years in jail. This hospital ship was sunk outside of the restricted war zone without orders from high command to do so. The defence was that they 'would torpedo a hospital ship with all of its characteristic markings, in the expectation of being able to prove it was being used for improper purposes (of which it was not)'.[359]

C. Defenceless

Although the instances of sinking hospital ships was dealt with in war trials after the First World War, the problem of sinking non-military ships and not helping the survivors was not. In large part this was due to the nature of submarine warfare and a long-held fear that submariners could practice a type of odious warfare, because they could strike without detection. Such practices were initially seen as repugnant and closer to piracy than rules that civilised countries would follow. This meant that although most of the major belligerents of the period had submarines in their naval yards in 1914 (Britain had 56 and Germany had 28), British Admiral William Henderson (1845–1931) could state confidently in 1914 that 'no country in this world would ever use such a vicious and petty form of warfare.'[360]

It was expected that submariners would conduct warfare by the prevailing norms, known as the Prize or Cruiser Rules. The rules, that were clear throughout the nineteenth century, were that the captor had to ensure that the crew and passengers were taken about the captors vessel, or put in lifeboats with sufficient food, water and navigational equipment to ensure safe passage to the nearest port. The rules, as laid down at the beginning of the twentieth century in the 1909 London Declaration Concerning the Laws of Naval Warfare explained that neutral merchant vessels under national convoy, were, prima facie exempt from interference, although in certain situations they could be searched so as to ensure that they were they were not shipping contraband, troops or other forms of listed assistance to the enemy. Failure to allow the search could involve the condemnation of the vessels. In principle, even if they were found to be involved in contraband, or failed to stop, they were meant to be taken into a port 'for the determination there of all questions concerning the validity of the capture'.[361] However, if this operation would 'involve danger to the safety of the warship or to the success of the operations in which she is engaged at the time' then the vessel could be destroyed. Before this could be done, the rule was clear that 'all persons on board must be placed in safety'.[362] The 1913 *Oxford Manual of the Laws of Naval War* reiterated these rules.[363] In the case of submarines, these rules were very important, because submarines could rarely take prizes, and therefore, more often than not, they had no alternative but to sink them. In theory, before a vessel could be

[359] German War Trials, Judgment in the Case of Lieutenants Dithmar and Boldt 1922 *AJIL* 16(4): 708–24; Durand, A (1984) *A History of the International Committee of the Red Cross: From Sarajevo to Hiroshima* (Dunant Institute, Geneva) 62–63.

[360] Henderson in Hobbes, N (2004) *Essential Militaria* (London, Atlantic) 118. Also, Harris, B (1997) *The Navy Times Book of Submarines. A Political, Social and Military History* (NYC, Berkley) 8, 27–31, 80, 91 and 135; Tucker, S (1996) *The European Powers in the First World War* (New York, Garland) 301.

[361] London Declaration 1909, Art 48. The earlier part is from Arts 61 and 63.

[362] London Declaration 1909, Arts 49 and 50.

[363] 1913 Oxford Manual. See Arts 17(2) and 104.

sunk, the submarine had to allow the crews and passengers of the doomed ships enough warning and time enough to get into lifeboats.[364]

In the beginning of the conflict, Germany abided by such rules. For example, on 20 October 1914, the British merchant steamer *Glitra* was sunk by a U-boat. However, before this was torpedoed, the *Glitra* was boarded by German sailors, verified as being within the British registry, and then the crew were ordered into lifeboats before the ship was sunk. The submarine then towed the lifeboats close inshore to a safe position. Similarly, the captains of German high-sea raiders, which operated against merchant vessels far from home were often very courteous, acting to protect the crews and passengers on vessels claimed as prizes. For example, the light cruiser *Emden,* under the command of captain Karl von Muller (1873–1923) captured and sunk 23 merchant vessels without the loss of a single life.

Two factors helped Germany move away from implementing the Prize Rules. First, the British deployed what was known as 'Q-ships' which were disguised merchantmen which would waiting for the submarine to come to the surface to search them, and then the Q-ship would quickly strike their colours, and attack. This method resulted in the sinking of 13 U-Boats. It also resulted in the Germans moving away from the Prize Rules. As such, they decided to stop their practice of surfacing to warn a vessel that they were going to be sunk, as it put the submarines at too great a risk of being attacked by armed vessels disguised as merchant vessels.[365]

The second factor was that as the Allied Blockade around occupied Europe began to tighten, Germany gave notice, in early 1915, that a war zone was being declared around the United Kingdom and Ireland. This amounted to a warning that any ship within the specified areas was liable to be sunk without warning. To neutral objections this was intolerable, to which Germany replied that neutrals ought to have found the British blockade also intolerable. The first merchant vessel of note which was sunk in the middle of 1915 without warning to those aboard after this policy was announced was the *Lusitania.* The sinking of the *Lusitania,* which was listed as an armed merchant vessel and may have been carrying munitions, resulted in the death of 1,201 civilians, including 128 Americans. Despite public outcry, this was followed by the sinking of the *Arabic* in August of the same year, in which a further 40 civilians were killed. Fearing that the United States might join the war because of this action, the German government issued what became known as the 'Arabic pledge' which stated that Germany would warn non-military ships 30 minutes before they sank them to make sure the passengers and crew got away safely. They broke this pledge on 24 March 1916 when the French ship *Sussex* was torpedoed without warning. Once more, Germany promised in what was known as the 'Sussex pledge' that passenger ships would not be targeted; that merchant ships would not be sunk until the presence of lite boats had been established; and that merchant ships would not be sunk without provision for the safety of passengers and crew.[366] Seven months later in early 1917, the Sussex pledge was rescinded and Germany announced it would practice unrestricted submarine warfare.

364 Boot, M (2006) *War Made New. Technology, Warfare and the Course of History* (NYC, Gotham) 190.

365 Bridgland, T (1999) *Sea Killers In Disguise* (Yorkshire, Pen and Sword) 11; Harris, B (1997) *The Navy Times Book of Submarines. A Political, Social and Military History* (NYC, Berkley) 176; Ireland, B (2002) *War at Sea: 1914–45* (London, Cassell) 42–45, 68.

366 See the 1916 Letter of German Secretary of State in Naval War College (1945) *International Law Documents* (Washington, Government Printer) 52.

This was done because the Germans had become convinced they could defeat the Allies by this practice. In fact, this decision helped bring about their own defeat, as it helped convince the United States into the First World War. Notably, President Woodrow Wilson (1856–1924), in his War Address to Congress in 1917, explaining why the United States should join the conflict said that Germany had 'put aside all restraints of law or humanity' in their practice of submarine warfare, sweeping aside 'every restriction'. Specifically:

> Vessels of every kind, whatever their flag, character or cargo, cargo destination, or errand, have been ruthlessly sent to the bottom without warning, without thought of help or mercy for those on board vessels of friendly neutrals. Even hospital ships carrying relief to the sorely bereaved and stricken people of Belgium . . . were sunk with the same reckless lack of compassion . . . German warfare is . . . warfare against mankind. It is warfare against all nations.[367]

Whether the German actions were 'warfare against mankind' is a question of debate. What is not debatable is that by the end of the First World War, Germany had managed to condemn thousands of civilians and seafarers of non-military vessels to their death by acting in direct contradiction to the Prize Rules. By 11 November 1918, German submarines would sink 6,394 Allied merchantmen that would lead to the direct deaths of an estimated 14,661 merchant seafarers in the process. The majority of these deaths were not by the explosion of the torpedo, but exposure to the elements when they were abandoned on the oceans after their vessels sunk.[368]

When the war ended, it was envisaged that Grand Admiral Alfred von Tirpitz (1849–1930) and six of his admirals would stand trial at Leipzig for their unrestricted submarine warfare. However, this never occurred, as his name was deleted when the trial started to get watered down, due to a fear of possible uncontrollable rebellions in Germany. Accordingly, the focus came to be upon the weapon, rather than the way it was utilised. Thus, some leaders at Versailles, like Lloyd George (1863–1945) and the American secretary for the navy, Josephus Daniels (1862–1948) argued that submarines should be compared to chemical weapons, and absolutely prohibited. However, theirs was a minority view, and the decision was made to regulate, not restrict the weapon that had caused so much damage. Accordingly, submarines were listed in the Treaty of Versailles as a prohibited weapon for Germany and 'the construction or acquisition of any submarine, even for commercial purposes, [was] forbidden in Germany'.[369]

[367] Wilson in Birley, R (ed) (1944) *Speeches and Documents in American History*, Vol IV (Oxford, Oxford University Press) 27, 29.

[368] Friel, I (2003) *Maritime History of Britain and Ireland* (London, The British Museum Press) 245–50; Tucker, S (1996) *The European Powers in the First World War* (New York, Garland) 571, 665–66; Kramer, A (2007) *Dynamic of Destruction: Culture and Mass Killing in the First World War* (Oxford, Oxford University Press) 225; Harris, B (1997) *The Navy Times Book of Submarines. A Political, Social and Military History* (NYC, Berkley) 168–69.

[369] Versailles, Arts 181 and 191. For commentary, see MacMillan, M (2002) *Peacemakers: Six Months That Changed the World* (London, Murray) 188; Bessel, R (1995) *Germany After the First World War* (Oxford, Oxford University Press) 86; Bass, G (2000) *Stay the Hand of Vengeance: The Politics of War Crimes Tribunals* (Princeton University Press) 78, 80.

D. The Dead

These principles of dealing with the dead agreed before 1914 were broadly adhered to in the First World War, with aspects like graves registration operating on both sides by 1915. This is not to suggest that abuse of the dead did not occur. Although the Allied-used propaganda that the Germans were boiling down the corpses of soldiers for use to distill glycerine for munitions was completely fabricated, the pillaging of the dead, by both sides, was not uncommon, nor the usage of bodies for trenching materials. Intentional acts of desecration were very difficult to prove, as the nature of warfare was now of such a ferocity that bodies were destroyed, if not evaporated. For example, of the French soldiers killed in the first four months of World War I, 90 to 95 per cent were never identified. This small sample went on to form part of the 3 million men, or one in three of all killed in this conflict, who were without known graves. For French soldiers alone, the reports of missing men would fill 228 volumes, each of 400 pages. Similarly, almost half of the British dead, 499,000, were listed as missing in action, of whom 173,000 were never identified. These figures are despite over 100,000 bodies being discovered since the conflict, with an average of 60 bodies per year still being discovered in France and Belgium in the twenty-first century.[370] The only clear cases of desecration appear to have followed with the Russian civil war and the destruction of the bodies of soldiers and commanders of the White Army. This went so far as digging up the corpses of dead White army commanders, dragging them around and then setting fire to them on rubbish dumps. However, this was probably not a sanctioned policy, as the remains of a number of executed White generals were given full respect and buried in the Kremlin wall.[371]

After the First World War ended, in terms or repatriation and remembrance of the dead, two major developments took place. First, the various governments came together to respect the dead in a manner, and scale, which had previously been unforeseen. In this regard, within the Treaty of Versailles, the signatories agreed to share all the information they had on enemy dead and respect and maintain the graves of the soldiers and sailors buried in their respective territories. Furthermore they agreed, as far as possible, to give every facility for giving effect to requests that the bodies of their soldiers and sailors may be transferred between countries.[372] Similar obligations were also included in the 1920 Serves peace treaty with Turkey, with the notable difference with Turkey being that the land for the cemeteries of Allied soldiers was to be transferred to the British, French and Italian Governments.[373] However, not all nations, notably France and the United States, wished their fallen soldiers to remain buried in foreign lands or official cemeteries. Within France, between 1921 and 1923, 240,000 bodies were exhumed and taken home to parents all over the country. The United States also repatriated some 45,000 American dead from Europe, if the families of the deceased so wished. The United States also authorised, through a private agency

[370] Hanson, N (2005) *The Unknown Soldier* (London, Doubleday) ii, 43–44, 102–103, 149, 170–71 and 283; Capdevilla, L (2006) *War Dead: Western Societies and the Casualties of War* (Edinburgh, Edinburgh University Press) 24, 28, 53; Knightley, P (1975) *The First Casualty* (London, Pan) 105; Lichfield, J 'Major War Find Threatened By Motorway' *New Zealand Herald*, (12 Nov 2003) B2.

[371] Mawdsley, E (2000) *The Russian Civil War* (Edinburgh, Birlinn) 21,195; Amis, M (2003) *Koba the Dread* (London, Vintage) 57, 58.

[372] Versailles, Arts 225 and 226.

[373] Sevres, Art 228.

(as they had no diplomatic relations with the Soviet Union) for the remains of 68 of their soldiers buried in Russia to be returned. The French later did the same. In some instances, countries would repatriate or move a single, 'unknown soldier' back to a place of prestige, such as those transferred to be reinterred beneath the *Arc de Triomphe* or at Westminster Abbey. These key State mausoleums were supplemented by memorials which sprang up in individual areas. In Britain alone, over 50,000 memorials were created, listing the names of those who had fallen. Conversely, the *Neue Wache* which was made from a reconverted building in Germany to commemorate the dead, had only an oculus, without the great lists of names.[374]

13. Between the Wars

A. Prisoners

In Latin America, the execution of prisoners in the first half of the century was not unheard of. This was especially so if they were considered 'rebels' and therefore devoid of legal standing. In the uprising involving Peru in 1932, over 1,000 males who were assumed to be guilty of fighting against the establishment were executed.[375]

Similarly, in the case of the Russian civil war both sides often refused quarter to surrendering opposition. The Soviets only expressly ordered the stopping of the execution of captured opponents in the middle of 1919 – as a way to encourage the desertion of enemy soldiers. However, when the Whites achieved some military victories, official circulars were issued which suggested that the enemy must be 'exterminated on the spot, to be annihilated like mad dogs' and the killing of White officers and soldiers, *en masse*, continued despite orders to the contrary. Similarly, when the Soviets and Polish forces clashed throughout 1920, the execution of prisoners by both sides appears to have been a common practice. When they were taken alive, prisoners of war, common criminals and 'class enemies' were all mixed together in what became known as *Gulags* or what the Western world knew as 'concentration camps'.[376]

In theory, the ICRC could have helped moderate some of the excesses of these early Soviet conflicts. This was especially so since the Russian Red Cross Society had been in existence in Russia since 1867 and the ICRC had maintained a delegate in Russia from the beginning of the First World War. However, the relationship between the ICRC and the Soviet Union soon after the revolution in 1917 deteriorated, when the ICRC was seen as a proxy for capitalist Switzerland and the Russian Red Cross as a home for wealthy aristocrats. Despite such suspicions, the Soviets initially decided not to distance themselves too far from the ICRC which had received remarkable standing

[374] Hanson, N (2005) *The Unknown Soldier* (London, Doubleday) i, 305, 417; Capdevilla, L (2006) *War Dead: Western Societies and the Casualties of War* (Edinburgh, Edinburgh University Press) 54, 57–58; Robinson, P (2006) *Military Honour and the Conduct of War* (London, Routledge) 152; Challinger, M (2010) *ANZACs in Arkhangel* (Melbourne, Hardie) 212–14.

[375] Scheina, R (2003) *Latin America's War. The Age of the Professional Soldier, 1900–2001*, Vol II (NYC, Brassey) 15, 19, 137.

[376] Courtois, S et al (1999) *The Black Book of Communism. Crimes, Terror, Repression* (Massachusetts, Harvard University Press) 73–74; Bullock, D (2008) *The Russian Civil War* (London, Osprey) 38–39, 68, 79, 81, 84, 101, 122, 286; Ferguson, N (2006) *The War of the World* (London, Allen Lane) 154–56; Zamoyski, A (2007); Warsaw 1920 (London, Harper) 31, 60, 105; Applebaum, A (2003) *Gulag. A History* (London, Penguin) 31.

within the new League of Nations (even though the Soviets were not yet members). In particular, Article 25 of the Covenant stated:

> The Members of the League agree to encourage and promote the establishment and co-operation of duly authorised voluntary national Red Cross organisations having as purposes the improvement of health, the prevention of disease and the mitigation of suffering throughout the world.

Accordingly, rather than disband the Russian Red Cross, the Soviets 'reorganised' the organisation, despite ICRC concerns that national societies should be 'freely accepted and not imposed by the State'.[377] Nevertheless, between 1921 and 1923 the ICRC, which sought to help alleviate suffering in civil as well as international wars, was allowed to visit all political detainees in the Soviet Union. However, by the mid 1920s, as ICRC criticism of some of the Soviet policies began to build, all such visits were stopped.[378]

Aside the political reasons of the Soviets not wishing to have external criticism of their country, the prevention of independent visits to prisoners in the Soviet Union appears to have coincided with the Soviet growing interest in torture. Torture was probably prevalent during the civil war, with instances of Bolsheviks hammering nails into the shoulders of captured officers, one nail for each star they possessed. Conversely, White Army Commander Ungern Sternberg (1886–1921) fed captured Soviet prisoners into the engine of his train. In Moscow, despite pronouncements that torture was prohibited, the *Cheka*, Lenin's Secret Police, perfected the art of skinning prisoners alive. Sadistic amputations of Polish officers were recorded during the Soviet war with Poland in 1920.[379] In the following decade, torture by physical beatings appears to have reintroduced as the necessity to get confessions as proof of conspiracies against the new State increased. This increase was not surprising as Stalin sent out a memo to regional State police chiefs in 1939 explicitly confirming that the use of physical pressure or prisoners was permitted but:

> [O]nly with respect to such overt enemies of the people who take advantage of humane interrogation methods in order to shamelessly refuse to give away conspirators, who for months don't testify and try to impede the unmasking of those conspirators who are still free.[380]

With such people, Stalin advised his interrogators that the best way to get confessions was 'beat, beat and beat again'.[381] Nevertheless, in 1939, torture via physical beatings appeared to have, again, been officially prohibited. In its place, methods such as sleep deprivation, prolonged standing and beatings with instruments, such as small sandbags or rubber truncheons, which did not leave marks were introduced. Nikita Khrushchev

377 Resolutions from the 1921 ICRC Conference in ICRC (1995) *The Humanitarian Endeavour* (Geneva, ICRC) 155.

378 Resolutions from the 1921 and 1923 ICRC Conferences in ICRC (1995) *The Humanitarian Endeavour* (Geneva, ICRC) 153, 155; Applebaum, A (2003) *Gulag. A History* (London, Penguin) 134–38; Forsythe, D (2005) *The Humanitarians: The International Committee of the Red Cross* (Cambridge, Cambridge University Press) 34; Moorehead, C (1998) *Dunant's Dream: War, Switzerland and the History of the Red Cross* (NYC, Carroll and Graf) 331–38.

379 Othen, C (2008) *Franco's International Brigades* (Wiltshire, Reportage) 135; Zamoyski, A (2007); Warsaw 1920 (London, Harper) 31.

380 Stalin, in Applebaum, A (2003) *Gulag. A History* (London, Penguin) 143.

381 Stalin in Amis, M (2003) *Koba the Dread* (London, Vintage) 112.

(1894–1971) later explained these acts had to be performed to make sure prisoners pleaded guilty to crimes they did not commit.[382]

Against a background of the First World War and the Russian civil war, the ICRC began to suggest that the Hague Regulations of 1899 and 1907, as they dealt with prisoners of war, needed to be updated. The eventual result of this work in 1929 was the (Geneva) Convention Relative to the Treatment of Prisoners of War.[383] The 1929 Convention with over 80 substantive articles did not replace, but rather complimented, the Hague Conventions of 1899 and 1907 and their 17 articles related to prisoners of war. Accordingly, all the existing rules were reiterated.[384] Some topics, whilst reiterated, were slightly expanded. For example, on the topic of torture:

> No coercion may be used on prisoners to secure information [related] to the condition of their army or country. Prisoners who refuse to answer may not be threatened, insulted, or exposed to unpleasant or disadvantageous treatment of any kind whatever.[385]

Aside some oddities of the period such as the attempts at the racial segregation of troops,[386] the most important innovations in the 1929 Convention consisted in the prohibition of reprisals,[387] collective penalties,[388] limits on punishments (with the general principle that punishments between the captor's forces and prisoners of war should, at a minimum, be comparable),[389] standards for prisoner camps, (especially in terms of space and hygiene)[390] location of camps (especially outside of combat zones),[391] medical facilities for prisoners,[392] how far prisoners could be transported on foot, per day (a general rule of 20 kilometres per day),[393] the organisation and limitations of prisoners' non-military related work[394] and rules for transport. Thus, Article 7 stipulated, 'Prisoners shall not be unnecessarily exposed to danger while awaiting evacuation from a fighting zone.'

The 1929 Convention also gave prisoners due process rights,[395] prisoner representatives,[396] and attempted to further enhance the influence exercised by protecting

[382] Applebaum, A (2003) *Gulag. A History* (London, Penguin) 143–45; Amis, M (2003) *Koba the Dread* (London, Vintage) 61–62.

[383] Resolutions from the 1921 and 1923 ICRC Conferences in ICRC (1995) *The Humanitarian Endeavour* (Geneva, ICRC) 155, 159.

[384] Including, inter alia, the right to surrender, humane treatment (Art 2), the authority and responsibility of the capturing states (also Art 2), escape (Arts 48 and 51), food and clothing at a minimum on par with the soldiers of the capturing State (Art 12), freedom of religion, mail and newly added sport (Arts 16, 17, 36–40), relief societies (Arts 8, 78, 79), repatriation – prima facie, with the 'least possible delay after the conclusion of peace' (Art 75).

[385] 1929, Art 5.

[386] 1929, Art 9.

[387] 1929, Art 2. For a discussion of this, see Kalshoven, F (2005) *Belligerent Reprisals* (Leiden, Nijhoff) 69–82.

[388] 1929, Art 11.

[389] 1929, Arts 46, 55– 58. On the possibility of death sentences, see Arts 101 and 107.

[390] 1929, Arts 10 and 13. Which should be comparable to those given to the captors combatants.

[391] 1929, Art 9.

[392] 1929, Arts 14 and 15.

[393] 1929, Art 7.

[394] The 1929 Convention set down appropriate rest days and the bottom line that the prisoners should not be made to work harder than comparable civilians in the same areas (Art 30). It expanded the list of labour which was not permitted in general (that for which they are physically unfit (Art 29) or the work is unhealthy or dangerous (Art 32). Rules for pay for the work were also clarified (Art 34). On military work, see Art 31. On considerations of rank, see Art 21.

[395] 1929, Arts 60–62.

[396] 1929, Arts 42–43.

Powers. That is, the 1929 Convention stipulated that to further the goals of the Convention, each side could send missions to the others prisoner of war camps[397] if agreement between the two sides was reached. If there was disagreement, discussions on matter of concern could take place in a neutral third country, which could be assisted by the ICRC. The ICRC was also recognised for the work they did as a bureau of information.[398]

The 1929 Prisoner of War Convention was signed and ratified by the United Kingdom, the United States and Germany. It was signed, but not ratified by Japan. This was a surprise, as up until this point, Japan had displayed an exemplary respect for the Red Cross. However, in 1942 Japan sent a telegram to Geneva stating 'we agree to operate the Geneva Convention under conditions of reciprocity and *mutatis mutandis*'.[399] In addition, the 1929 Convention was neither signed nor ratified by the Soviet Union. However, both Japan and the Russian Federation, had signed and ratified the 1907 Hague Convention on the Laws and Customs of War on Land, and a few months after the beginning of the Second World War, the Soviet Government adopted the 1907 Hague Convention as its predecessor had done. The Soviets also adopted the 1929 Convention for the Amelioration of the Condition on the Wounded and Sick in Armed Forces in the Field.

Spain was also a signatory to the 1929 Convention on Prisoners of War, although the extent to which this convention had a moderating influence on their civil war is a matter of debate. The execution and/or torture of Republican soldiers, both Spanish and those of the International Brigades, was a common feature both during and after the conflict ended. These acts were followed by swift reprisals with the killing of the prisoners held by the Republic. Exactly how many were killed in such incidents is unknown, although it is possible that the figures run into the tens, if not hundreds, of thousands. There appear to have been large scale executions of prisoners after the fall of some key areas such as with Catalonia and Badajoz. In other instances, it was simply impossible to know how many prisoners were being held, by whom, and where. For instance, in Barcelona in early 1937, the ICRC delegate noted,

> In addition to the more or less legal arrests, many people are arrested unofficially, but there is no way of ascertaining this, as they are held in the secret prisons of the revolutionary committees where, usually, all trace of them is lost so that it is generally impossible to know whether they are still alive. The number of detainees in Catalonia may be estimated at 6,000 to 8,000, half of them in government prisons, the other half in secret ones.[400]

Prison conditions during and after the Spanish civil war are also believed to have been as poor as some of the worst examples from the Second World War. These conditions may have been mitigated to a degree by the influence of the ICRC, of

[397] 1929, Art 86.

[398] 1929, Arts 79, 87 and 88.

[399] See United Nations War Crimes Commission, Trial of General Tanaka Hisakasu (1946) *Law Reports of Trials of War Criminals*, Vol VI (London, HMSO) 66; Kosuge, M (2003) 'The Non-Religious Red Cross Emblem and Japan' *IRRC* 85: 75–93; Junod, M (1982) *Warriors Without Weapons* (Geneva, ICRC) 260; Maga, T (2000) *Judgement at Tokyo* (Kentucky University Press) 28, 53.

[400] ICRC Delegate, reprinted in Durand, A (1984) *A History of the International Committee of the Red Cross: From Sarajevo to Hiroshima* (Dunant Institute, Geneva); Durand, A (1984) *A History of the International Committee of the Red Cross: From Sarajevo to Hiroshima* (Dunant Institute, Geneva) 341; Beevor, A (1982) *The Spanish Civil War* (London, Cassell) 51, 73, 76, 82, 248–49, 310, 367; Othen, C (2008) *Franco's International Brigades* (Wiltshire, Reportage) 52–54, 74–75, 207; Knightley, P (1975) *The First Casualty* (London, Pan) 201–202.

which both the Republican and Nationalist sides agreed to admit into their prisons, of which they had visited 89,000 prisoners held by both sides, by the end of 1938. However, once the war ended, so did the ICRC visits. This was the point that international oversight was needed more than ever as by 1939 at least 200,000 Republican prisoners of war were being held by the victorious Nationalist forces. By 1944, more than 100,000 of these prisoners had been executed or died in prison as a result of appalling conditions.[401]

B. Wounded

The 1929 Convention on Prisoners of War was supplemented by the 1929 Convention for the Amelioration of the Condition of the Wounded and Sick in Armies in the Field.[402] This convention largely reiterated the basic rules from 1864, 1899 and 1907. Accordingly, the first article of the 1929 Convention stipulated all wounded service personnel were to be 'treated with humanity and cared for medically, without distinction of nationality, by the belligerent in whose power they may be'.

In addition, the repatriation of wounded prisoners, the sanctity of the Red Cross and the neutrality of hospitals, medical staff and medical transports was underlined. What was not resolved in the 1929 convention, despite the recommendations of the ICRC, was the clear recognition that aircraft marked with Red Crosses would receive the same guarantees of neutrality as either land or water based ambulances. This issue was not resolved prior to the Second World War. This was despite the final act of the 1929 Geneva Conference, calling for resolution of this outstanding issue 'in the near future'.[403] However, the practice of the wars in both Ethiopia and Spain in the 1930s saw hospitals, on occasion, being targeted.[404] In the case of the Spanish civil war, the ICRC received protests from both sides against the bombing of medical convoys and hospitals. In the Ethiopian case, the targetting of Red Cross vehicles was further complicated by the fact that Italy was barely cooperating with the ICRC during this conflict, and that Ethiopia was not a signatory to either of the 1929 Convention on prisoners of war or the 1929 Convention dealing with wounded soldiers in the field.[405]

[401] Moorehead, C (1998) *Dunant's Dream: War, Switzerland and the History of the Red Cross* (NYC, Carroll and Graf) 319, 327; Junod, M (1982) *Warriors Without Weapons* (Geneva, ICRC) 115; Best, G (2002) *War and Law Since 1945* (Oxford, Oxford University Press) 83; Beevor, A (1982) *The Spanish Civil War* (London, Cassell) 392–95.

[402] 118 LNTS 303.

[403] See Artis 6–8, 17, 28, 69,70, 73, 74, 112–14 and 117. One notable addition was Art 30, which facilitated enquiries for violations of its provisions. Note also Art 18 of the 1929 Convention; For the ICRC push in this area – see Resolutions from the 1925 ICRC Conference in ICRC (1995) *The Humanitarian Endeavour* (Geneva, ICRC) 159.

[404] Nichol, J and Rennell, T (2009) *Medic* (London, Penguin) 37; Beevor, A (1982) *The Spanish Civil War* (London, Cassel) 109; Junod, M (1982) *Warriors Without Weapons* (Geneva, ICRC) 30, 35, 40, 54; Moorehead, C (1998) *Dunant's Dream: War, Switzerland and the History of the Red Cross* (NYC, Carroll and Graf) 307–309. Cf Knightley, P (1975) *The First Casualty* (London, Pan) 186.

[405] Durand, A (1984) *A History of the International Committee of the Red Cross: From Sarajevo to Hiroshima.* (Dunant Institute, Geneva) 298–299.

C. Defenceless

The question of dealing with defenceless combatants between the wars was dealt with in two areas. The first involved the targeting of pilots who had bailed out of their aircraft via parachutes. The chivalrous response to this practice, which only began towards the very end of the First World War (when parachutes were finally deployed to pilots), was seen as one whereby the pilots without defence should not be shot at. Of course, whilst this may have been true in some instances, it should be remembered that the tactical characteristics of the single seater fighter in the First World War made it advisable to shoot an opponent from behind, or if possible, to dive on him without warning. Although there were certainly instances of long and skilfully conducted duels between equal opponents, the majority of kills achieved by the major aces were at the expense of fledgling pilots, barely able to control their planes. Thus, the average life expectancy of a new airman on the western front was somewhere between three and six weeks.[406] Nevertheless, on the question of parachuting to safety, attempts to codify this rule were made in 1923 with the Hague Rules of Air Warfare. Article XX proscribed, '[w]hen an aircraft has been disabled, the occupants when endeavouring to escape by means of parachute must not be attacked in the course of their descent.'

However, the Hague Rules never came into force, and despite the strong feelings of chivalry around this issue, there was no legal prohibition on targeting defenceless airmen before or during the Second World War.

The second issue of dealing with defenceless persons after the First World War was with regards to submarine warfare. As noted above, the topic of submarines abandoning the Prize Rules was initially dealt with by focusing on the weapon, rather than the way it was used. This approach followed through with the 1922 Washington disarmament conference. The resultant treaty from this conference was drawn up in express reaction to the German submarine practices in the First World War, and was intended to 'make more effective the rules adopted by civilized nations for the protection of the lives of neutrals and non-combatants at sea in time of war'.[407]

Although it was agreed that merchant vessels could be stopped and inspected by submarines, it was added they 'must not be destroyed unless the crew and passengers have been first placed in safety'.[408] Moreover, 'if a submarine cannot capture a merchant vessel in conformity with these rules the existing law of nations requires it to desist from attack and from seizure and to permit the merchant vessel to proceed unmolested'.[409] Finally, it was agreed that in 'desiring to ensure the enforcement of the humane rules with respect to attacks upon and the seizure and destruction of merchant ships' that:

> Any person in the service of any Power who shall violate any of those rules, whether or not such person is under orders of a governmental superior, shall be deemed to have violated the laws of war and shall be liable to trial and punishment as if for an act of piracy and may be brought to trial before the civil or military authorities of any Power within the jurisdiction of which he may be found.[410]

[406] O'Connell, R (1989) *Of Arms and Men: A History of War, Weapons and Aggression* (Oxford, Oxford University Press) 263.
[407] Preamble.
[408] Art 1(1).
[409] Art 1(2).
[410] Art 3.

Although this 1922 treaty was never ratified, the London Treaty of 1930 (for the Limitation and Reduction of Naval Armaments) which was accepted by many countries, including Germany, again declared that submarines must conform to the same rules as surface warships.[411] It was added:

> In particular, except in the case of persistent refusal to stop on being duly summoned, or of active resistance to visit or search, a warship, whether surface vessel or submarine, may not sink or render incapable of navigation a merchant vessel without having first placed passengers, crew and ship's papers in a place of safety. For this purpose the ship's boats are not regarded as a place of safety unless the safety of the passengers and crew is assured, in the existing sea and weather conditions, by the proximity of land, or the presence of another vessel which is in a position to take them on board.[412]

These provisions were incorporated verbatim into the London protocol of 6 November 1936. Prior to the Second World War, Germany and the Soviet Union acceded to this protocol, as did the United Kingdom, France, Italy and Japan. However, before this 1936 Protocol was tested in the Second World War, there was one further agreement of note. This was the Nyon Agreement of 14 September 1937.[413] The background to this Agreement was the flow of arms, to both sides, during the Spanish civil war. In seeking to stem this flow, especially to the side of the Republic, unidentified groups (which were most likely Italian) began direct attacks on merchant shipping, irrespective of their flag and began sinking them without warning. Some 26 merchant vessels (including eight flagged to Britain) were sunk in 1937 alone. To help keep up the charade of who was sinking them, the submarines abandoned the survivors of the torpedoed ships to their fate. The British government in particular, wished to have an agreement that officers engaging in such hostilities, even when acting under sovereign orders, should be treated as pirates, tried and punished. In many regards the British were successful, as the Nyon Agreement came to reflect many of their goals. The Agreement was recorded as being created because of 'attacks . . . repeatedly committed in the Mediterranean by submarines against merchant ships not belonging to either of the conflicting Spanish Parties'. These attacks were recognised as:

> [V]iolations of the rules of international law referred to . . . [in] the 1930 Treaty of London . . . with regard to the sinking of merchant ships [such acts were] . . . contrary to the most elementary dictates of humanity, [and] should be justly treated as acts of piracy.[414]

The Parties to the Nyon Agreement agreed to counter-attack, and if possible, destroy, any submarine (which was not connected to either of the Parties involved in the conflict) acting contrary to the rules to 1930 Treaty of London.[415]

[411] 1930 Naval Disarmament Conference, Art 22(1).

[412] 1930 Naval Disarmament Conference, Art 22(2).

[413] The Nyon Agreement, 181 LNTS 137 in Hudson, R (ed) (1950) *International Legislation*, Vol VII, 1935–37 (NY, Oceana) 831.

[414] Preamble, Nyon Agreement.

[415] Art 2, Nyon Agreement. Note also the Agreement supplementary to The Nyon Agreement, 181 LNTS 137. For commentary, Ronzitti, N (1981) *The Law of Naval Warfare* (Amsterdam, Nijhoff) 485–92; Beevor, A (1982) *The Spanish Civil War* (London, Cassell) 297, 299.

D. The Dead

After the First World War, the ICRC came to take an increased interest in dealing with the dead. From the work they conducted from 1925 onwards, clear proposals from enhanced forms of identification discs through to greater information sharing in order to reduce the number of persons reporting missing in wartime, came into existence. The ICRC also emphasised that greater respect needed to be made in this area and recognised the religious practices of the deceased should be achieved wherever possible.[416] Many of these goals were incorporated into the 1929 Convention for the Amelioration of the Condition of the Wounded and Sick in Armies in the Field. This convention obliged its signatories to communicate to each other reciprocally, as soon as possible, the names of the dead, collected or discovered, together with any indications which may assist in their identification. To assist this they were to hand over death certificates and one of the identity tags (the second to remain with the body). They were also obliged to ensure 'that the dead are honourably interred, that their graves are respected and marked so that they may always be found.'[417]

To help with this process, graves registration services were to be created to render eventual exhumations possible and to ensure the identification of bodies whatever may be the subsequent site of the grave. The accompanying convention of 1929 on Prisoners of War added, 'Belligerents shall see that prisoners of war dying in captivity are honorably buried and that the graves bear all due information, are respected and properly maintained.'[418] Good practice in this area was supplemented in the specific agreements to protect and maintain the then existing war graves from the First World War.[419]

14. The Second World War

A. Executing Prisoners

For China and Japan, the Second World War began in the middle of 1937 as Japanese troops restarted their original incursion (with the initial entry being in 1931) into China. From the outset, incidents of no-quarter on the part of both sides, appear common. However, the Japanese seem to have gone to greater lengths in this area. On 5 August 1937, an under-secretary in the Army Ministry issued a decree stating, 'It is inappropriate to act strictly in accordance with the various stipulations in Treaties and Practices Governing Land Warfare and Other Laws of War.'[420] Four months later on the 13th of December, the Japanese authorities promulgated orders that, 'all prisoners of war are to be executed. Method of execution: Divide the prisoners into groups of a dozen. Shoot to kill separately.'[421]

[416] Resolutions from the 1925 ICRC Conference in ICRC (1995) *The Humanitarian Endeavour* (Geneva, ICRC) 159.

[417] 1929, Art 4.

[418] 1929, Art 76.

[419] Agreement Concerning War Graves 1935, 167 LNTS 141; Convention Concerning the Transfer to the French State of the Property in Sites of British Monuments, BTS No 24 (1939) Cmd 6003 in Hudson, R (ed) (1950) *International Legislation*, Vol VIII, 1938–41 (NY, Oceana) 222.

[420] Decree, in Burleigh, M (2010) *Moral Combat. A History of World War II* (London, Harper) 18.

[421] Order, reprinted in Chang, I (1997) *The Rape of Nanking* (Sydney, Penguin) 41.

The Japanese media covered such killings like sporting events. One notorious issue involved the recording of a competition between two sub-lieutenants on who would be the first to behead 100 Chinese with blows from their swords. The Japanese did not acknowledge that a state of war existed with China; as such the captives could not be classified as prisoners of war, and therefore they refused ICRC requests to assist Chinese prisoners. Prosecutors at the Tokyo War Crimes Trial suggest as many as one million Chinese prisoners may have been killed by the Japanese in this conflict, although later estimates put this figure at about 400,000.[422] Such killing of prisoners also continued after the end of the Second World War, as China descended into a viscous civil war, before the Communists emerged victorious.[423]

Japanese soldiers behaved in comparable, but not as numerically great, ways in other theatres of the Second World War. For example, 50 British officers were bayoneted to death on Christmas Day in 1941. At least four separate massacres occurred on New Britain Island, when more than140 Australians were executed and British soldiers were known to have been tortured and executed in Burma. A further 200 or so Australian and Indian prisoners of war were believed to be executed following some of the battles surrounding Singapore. French soldiers, including one general, were forced to dig their own graves and were then beheaded on what became Vietnam, as late as March 1945. After the Battle of Midway, none of the American aviators who had crashed into the ocean but were fished out by the Japanese made it back to shore. Some Japanese submarines and surface raiders also appear to have operated a policy of sinking ships and then eliminating the crews. This process claimed the crews of at least nine different vessels. In addition, when dealing with Allied Airmen who had to parachute out over Japan, the Japanese authorities treated many of these men as criminals who were executed, rather than as prisoners of war. Thus, following the Doolittle raid, a Japanese military tribunal (despite protests from Nazi Germany) sentenced those captured to death 'for indiscriminate attacks on civilians'. Three were executed by firing squad, but five had their sentences commuted to life imprisonment. This practice, which was worsened by the fact that most of the defendants were not told they were being tried, were given no defence council and could not defend themselves, call witnesses or even understand the court documents which were all in Japanese. Such trials and executions continued, even in the immediate aftermath of the Japanese surrender.[424] This was in direct contradiction to the Japanese instrument of surrender, by which the Japanese authorities promised, with regards to the prisoners of war they held to 'provide for their protection, care, maintenance, and immediate transportation to places as directed'.[425]

[422] Hastings, M (2008) *Nemesis: The Battle for Japan* (London, Harper) 53, 226–27; Moorehead, C (1998) *Dunant's Dream: War, Switzerland and the History of the Red Cross* (NYC, Carroll and Graf) 365; Chang, I (1997) *The Rape of Nanking* (Sydney, Penguin) 42–46, 56; Brackman, A (1990) *The Other Nuremberg: The Tokyo War Crimes Trials* (Glasgow, Fontana) 187–90, 203; Barber, L (1999) *The Last War of Empires: Japan and the Pacific War* (Auckland, Bateman) 74.

[423] Rummel, R (1996) *Death by Government* (London, Transaction) 125.

[424] Lamont-Brown, R (2002) *Ships from Hell. Japanese War Crimes on the High Seas* (London, Sutton) 78–104, 108–14, 131; Brackman, A (1990) *The Other Nuremberg: The Tokyo War Crimes Trials* (Glasgow, Fontana) 44–45, 47, 292–93, 358, 366; MacArthur, B (2005) *Surviving the Sword: Prisoners of the Japanese* (London, Time) 15; Owen, F (1960) *The Fall of Singapore* (London, Penguin) 132–33, 188–89; Hastings, M (2008) *Nemesis: The Battle for Japan* (London, Harper) 349, 398; Hough, R (2003) *The Longest Battle. The War at Sea 1939–45* (London, Cassell) 197.

[425] Art 5 of the Japanese Instrument of Surrender in Axelrod, A (ed) *Encyclopedia of Historical Treaties and Alliances*, Vol II (NYC, Facts on File) 619.

German soldiers were also responsible for the execution of Allied soldiers. The execution of at least 300 Polish prisoners as insurgents – after the German commander had ordered them to remove their uniforms – occurred in 1939, after a particularly intense fight following the invasion of Poland. Some 98 British prisoners were executed in 1940 during the retreat to Dunkirk. In the same year, in Northern France and later near Lyon between 1,500 to 3,000 French colonial troops from Senegal were massacred. Some American soldiers were executed in the Italian campaign and during the battle for Normandy campaign, at least 195 soldiers, of which 187 were Canadian, were executed in the first days of the invasion by various SS regiments. A further 129 were executed in the Ardennes and 44 in Northern France in the same year. These atrocities were added to with the massacre of Italian soldiers on the island of Cephalonia, which occurred after the Italians had changed side. After a 10 day battle, some 10,700 surrendered. Five thousand of these men were immediately executed. Those who survived the original massacre, after being given starvation rations, were shipped to Germany, but all three of the transport vessels hit mines and sunk. Those who jumped overboard were machine gunned in the water. In all, 9,406 soldiers were wrongfully killed. On the high seas, aside some similar reports of U-boats machine-gunning survivors, the most notable instance involved the German submarine U-852, which sunk the SS *Peleus*. The sinking vessel left a large amount of debris, amongst which were a number of survivors clinging to rafts and wreckage. This wreckage would have betrayed the presence of the U-852 to aircraft and vessels patrolling the area, so the commander of the submarine decided to destroy the wreckage – and those clinging to it.[426] In other instances, such as with Allied airmen who parachuted out over German held territory, although these men were not executed (this was proposed by Goebbels following the bombing of Dresden, but objected to by Goering) the more common approach was laid down by Heinrich Himmler (1900–1945) by which they would not be protected by German forces when lynched by angry civilians.[427] Himmler explained that the bombing of civilian populations was 'an act of terrorism' and therefore, if downed aircrew fall in the vicinity of civilians, that, 'it is not the task of the police to interfere in clashes between German and the English and American terror flyers who have baled out . . . the German people are only treating child murderers as they deserve.'[428]

Unlike the above instances, at least two examples involved systematic attempts by the Nazis to comprehensively execute specific classes of prisoners. Although Hitler may have intended to go much further in his massacring of prisoners as the war drew to a close, the only instances where he put this in practice was with regard to the so called 'Commando' and 'Commissar' orders. In the first example, following the initial

[426] Burleigh, M (2010) *Moral Combat. A History of World War II* (London, Harper) 121; Holland, J (2008) *Italy's Sorrow: A Year of War, 1944–1945* (London, St Martins) 60, 390, 423; Jackson, R (2004); Dunkirk (London, Cassel). 92–93, 97; Scheck, R (2006) *Hitler's African Victims: The German Army Massacres of Black French Soldiers* (New York, Cambridge University Press) 24, 29, 45–53; Beevor, D (2009) *D-Day. The Battle for Normandy* (London, Viking) 55, 160, 180, 186, 377; Lord Russell of Liverpool (2002) *Scourge of the Swastika: A Short History of Nazi War Crimes*, 2nd edn (London, Greenhill) 26–27; Hough, R (2003) *The Longest Battle. The War at Sea 1939–45* (London, Cassell) 56–57; White, D (2006) *Bitter Ocean* (London, Headline) 149.

[427] Neillands, R (2002) *The Bomber War* (London, Murray) 142; Lambert, M (2005) *Night After Night: New Zealanders in Bomber Command* (Auckland, Harper) 314, 396–99; Lord Russell of Liverpool (2002) *Scourge of the Swastika: A Short History of Nazi War Crimes*, 2nd edn (London, Greenhill) 40–41.

[428] Himmler's Order & Note in Lord Russell of Liverpool (2002) *Scourge of the Swastika: A Short History of Nazi War Crimes*, 2nd edn (London, Greenhill) 39.

successes of Allied Commandoes, Hitler issued an order, which applied only to this particular class of soldier, and not those who are captured in the 'course of normal hostilities'. The basis of this order was Hitler's assertion that these commandoes were not in uniform and were not taking prisoners. Accordingly, as a type of reprisal, Hitler ordered:

> For this reason . . . they will be ruthlessly mowed down by German troops in combat wherever they appear . . . even when it is outwardly a matter of soldiers in uniform . . . [they are] . . . to be exterminated to the last man in battle or when in flight. Even should these individuals . . . surrender . . . all quarter is to be denied them on principle.[429]

The Commando Order was widely carried out in areas of German occupation, whereby despite being in uniform, over 200 special forces soldiers captured behind enemy lines were shot under the terms of this order. Only Erwin Rommel (1891–1944) and Alfred Jodl (1890–1946) refused to carry it out.[430]

The second example involved the deliberate execution of the Political Commissars who accompanied, fought with, and helped instill morale in the Soviet troops. According to testimony from Nuremberg, these troops were regarded as 'thoroughly bolshevised or as active representatives of Bolshevist ideology'.[431] As it was, the killing of Soviet prisoners already occurred, especially if they were Jewish, during both the heat of battle and its aftermath. It is possible up to 600,000 Soviet soldiers were executed by the Germans and their Allies with their invasion of the Soviet Union. Thousands were also sent to concentration camps for extermination, with a process that began on 1 September 1941 when the first experiment of killing human beings with gas, was carried out on 600 Soviet prisoners. These were not the last Soviet prisoners to be directly executed in concentration camps, of which at least 20,000 died in Auschwitz alone. Hitler supplemented this process with his so-called Commissar (or 'Keitel') Order of 6 June 1941 which ordered the execution, as soon as captured or if already held in camps, of all Political Commissars.[432] Although these soldiers fought in uniform next to their comrades, Hitler believed them to be particularly dangerous and in need of annihilation. Some commanders, such as Alfred Rosenberg (1893–1946) objected to the order. Others, like Lieutenant-Colonel Henning von Tresckow (1901–44 – later a driving force in the plans to kill Hitler) commented 'if international law is to be broken, then the Russians, not we, should do it first'. The vast majority of other commanders did not object.[433]

[429] The Commando Order was reprinted in UN War Crimes Commission, Law Reports of the Trials of War Criminals, The Trial of Nickolaus Von Falkenhorst. Case No 61, Vol XI (1949, HMSO, London) 21.

[430] Gilbert, A (2006) *POW: Allied Prisoners in Europe* (London, Murray) 18, 89; Lord Russell of Liverpool (2002) *Scourge of the Swastika: A Short History of Nazi War Crimes*, 2nd edn (London, Greenhill) 28–39; Davidson, E (1966) *The Trial of the Germans: 22 Defendants at Nuremberg* (NY, Macmillan) 344, 349; Owen, J (2006) *Nuremberg: Evil on Trial* (Kent, Headline) 269; Beevor, A (2002) *Berlin: The Downfall 1945* (London, Penguin) 294.

[431] Testimony of Lahousen in Owen, J (2006) *Nuremberg: Evil on Trial* (Kent, Headline) 55.

[432] Directive for the Treatment of Political Commissars in Lord Russell of Liverpool (2002) *Scourge of the Swastika: A Short History of Nazi War Crimes*, 2nd edn (London, Greenhill) 53. Also, Keitel Order in Davidson, E (1966) *The Trial of the Germans: 22 Defendants at Nuremberg* (NY, Macmillan) 336 Kershaw, I (2008) *Hitler* (London, Allen) 600–603.

[433] Megargee, G (2007) *War of Annihilation: Combat and Genocide on the Eastern Front, 1941* (Boulder, Rowman) 38–39, 59, 116, 141; Whitlock, F 'Horrific Discovery' in *WWII History* (November 2008) 49, 55; Beevor, A (1998) *Stalingrad* (London, Penguin) 59; Lord Russell of Liverpool (2002) *Scourge of the Swastika: A Short History of Nazi War Crimes*, 2nd edn (London, Greenhill) 48; Owen, J (2006) *Nuremberg: Evil on Trial*

The forces of the Axis were not alone in killing prisoners of war. In the middle of 1944 when German prisoners were arriving in the United States at a rate of 50,000 captives per month, after three years of war, the United States only held 1,990 Japanese prisoners. These figures reflected a strong desire by most Japanese combatants not to be taken prisoner. The Japanese Field Army Service Code of January 1941 stated: 'You shall not undergo the shame of being taken alive. You shall not bequeath a sullied name . . . after exerting all your powers, spiritually and physically, calmly face death rejoicing in the eternal cause for which you strive.'[434]

Such attitudes lead to extreme results. Many Japanese pilots disdained wearing parachutes in combat because they did not want the shame of being captured. This was assisted by the fact that Japan had no effective air-sea rescue to retrieve its own ditched airmen. Accordingly, hundreds were simply left to perish in the Pacific. Similarly, those on the ground fought with a near insane ferocity and determination not to be captured. Of the 22,000 Japanese soldiers present at the beginning of the Battle of Iwo Jima, only 1,083 survived to be taken prisoner. Of the 30,000 Japanese troops that defended Saipan, less than 1,000 remained alive at end of the battle. Likewise, of the 1,700 prisoners taken in Burma, 150,000 Japanese soldiers were killed. Even those who were captured were difficult to keep alive both physically and mentally. That is, the disgrace of being a prisoner of war was so great that they did not want to receive loving messages or packets from Japan. In at least two instances, Japanese prisoners attempted to rectify their situation by making suicidal escape attempts. Thus, 46 Japanese prisoners were killed when they tried to break out of a camp in New Zealand, whilst 251 died, along with four guards, during a similar incident at Cowrah in New South Wales. With such attitudes, it is not surprising that the line between executions and assisted suicide would often be difficult to draw.

It would appear that a number of Allied servicemen were happy to help them in their goal not to be taken prisoner, as many appear to have been shot if they tried to surrender.[435] The situation was not helped by certain American field commanders, such Colonel Puller (1898–1971), who told his men upon their reoccupation of the Philippines 'you will take no prisoners, you will kill every yellow-son-of-a-bitch, and that's it.'[436]

It is possible this approach was embedded by some naval commanders. When the Japanese vessel the *Rakuyo Maru* was sunk, carrying over 1,000 Allied prisoners of war, the commander of one of the submarines was preparing to kill the survivors, when it became apparent that one of the men struggling in the water was blond, and the order was aborted. There are also recorded instances where Japanese sailors were left in the water and American commanders declined to rescue them after sinking their vessels. After the battle of Leyte Gulf, Admiral William Halsey (1882–1959) told his destroyers

(Kent, Headline) 100–103, 204; Ferguson, N (2006) *The War of the World* (London, Allen Lane) 442–44; Merridale, C (2005) *Ivan's War: The Red Army 1939–1945* (London, Faber) 111; Rees, L (1999) *War of the Century: When Hitler Fought Stalin* (London, BBC) 51; Kershaw, I (2008) *Hitler* (London, Allen) 600–603.

434 Noted in MacArthur, B (2005) *Surviving the Sword: Prisoners of the Japanese* (London, Time) 13; Also, Hastings, M (2008) *Nemesis: The Battle for Japan* (London, Harper) 7, 57.

435 Hastings, M (2008) *Nemesis: The Battle for Japan* (London, Harper) 39, 200–201; Rees, L (2001) *Horror of the East* (London, BBC) 90; Moorehead, C (1998) *Dunant's Dream: War, Switzerland and the History of the Red Cross* (NYC, Carroll and Graf) 471.

436 Puller in Hastings, M (2008) *Nemesis: The Battle for Japan* (London, Harper) 123. Note also, Bourke, J (2000) *An Intimate History of Killing* (London, Granta) 183–85.

not to be over-zealous about their rescue activities. He stated: 'Bring in cooperative flotsam for an intelligence sample. Non-cooperators would probably like to join their ancestors and should be accommodated [in this wish].'[437]

It is also recorded elsewhere that the day after the Battle of the Bismarck Sea, American and Australian planes systematically searched for Japanese survivors and shot up every lifeboat they found. Similarly, the commander of the American submarine *Wahoo*, after sinking a Japanese troop transport, spent an hour killing hundreds of survivors with deck guns, an act for which he was apparently decorated.[438]

The killing of German prisoners appears to have occurred in, inter alia, France in 1940, Crete in 1941, at some points during the conflict in North African and during the Italian campaign. In the last instance, 74 Italian and two German prisoners were executed by men of the United States 45th Infantry Division at Biscari in Sicily on 14 July 1943. There was also instances during the Normandy invasion, in which German soldiers were executed in cold blood. Although some Allied commanders, such as General Maxwell Taylor (1901–1987) may have advised this approach, others, such as General Harry Crerar (1888–1965), issued strong orders against committing excesses to avenge dead comrades. However, in other instances, the evidence would seem to suggest that certain commanders did authorise the deliberate execution of prisoners who were wounded or simply vulnerable. According to the author Stephen E Ambrose (1936–2002), of the roughly 1,000 United States combat veterans that he had interviewed, roughly one third told him they had seen American troops kill German prisoners.[439] In addition, French Resistance Fighters (similar to their Soviet and Yugoslavian counterparts) were known to execute both wounded and captured German prisoners on a number of instances. Ironically, this was because the Germans refused to treat them as lawful combatants. The irony was, if they were lawful combatants they would have known that such reprisals against prisoners had been illegal since 1929.[440] Italian Resistance Fighters would also execute, rather than hold, prisoners. The foremost example of this was their decision to execute Benito Mussolini (1887–1945), as 'the necessary conclusion of a historical era . . . to free the Italian people',[441] rather than detain him as a prisoner of war, which he clearly was.

Such approaches may have also been common with warfare at sea. A number of instances whereby no attempt was made to rescue the crews of seeking vessels was recorded, as well as possible instances where the survivors were machine gunned. This appears to have occurred with the British submarine *Torbay*, which allegedly machine

[437] Halsey, noted in Hastings, M (2008) *Nemesis: The Battle for Japan* (London, Harper) 173–74. Also, 158, 186, 288, 431; MacArthur, B (2005) *Surviving the Sword: Prisoners of the Japanese* (London, Time) 342; Davidson, E (1966) *The Trial of the Germans: 22 Defendants at Nuremberg* (NY, Macmillan) 421.

[438] O'Connell, R (1989) *Of Arms and Men: A History of War, Weapons and Aggression* (Oxford, Oxford University Press) 291–92.

[439] Ambrose is noted in Weingartner, J (2008) 'Americans, Germans and War Crimes' 94(4) *Journal of American History* 32, 38. See also de Zayas, A (1989) *The Wehrmacht War Crimes Bureau, 1939–1945* (Nebraska, Nebraska University Press) 147, 148, 160–63, 245, 250; Holland, J (2008) *Italy's Sorrow: A Year of War, 1944–1945* (London, St Martins) 390, 423; Beevor, D (2009) *D-Day. The Battle for Normandy* (London, Viking) 24. Also, 67, 68, 103, 107, 121, 158, 181, 220–21, 231, 253, 260, 266, 349, 393, 423; Burleigh, M (2010) *Moral Combat. A History of World War II* (London, Harper) 378–81.

[440] Kalshoven, F (2005) *Belligerent Reprisals* (Leiden, Nijhoff) 197–200; Keegan, J (1993) *A History of Warfare* (London, Hutchinson) 54–55.

[441] 'The Execution of Mussolini in Delzell', C (ed) (1970) *Mediterranean Fascism 1919–1945* (NYC, Harper) 254.

gunned German survivors in the Mediterranean near Crete in 1941. At Narvik, when all 10 German destroyers were sunk there were accusations of the British shooting at the survivors. This was especially with the case of the vessel the *Erich Giese*, although other British boats in the area did pick up survivors.[442]

The Soviet forces were also implicated in the direct massacre of captured Germans in a number of instances from 1941 onwards. In such times they may have been killed because they could not be transported, because of insufficient food, or simply because they were fascists. Members of the SS, the field police, Luftwaffe pilots and panzer crews were all at high risk of being killed when captured. This was especially with Soviet aligned soldiers who had chosen, even when press-ganged, to fight for the Nazis. Polish troops of the Red Army were reknowned for not taking prisoners. Apparently, at the beginning of December of 1941 Stalin had stated that all German prisoners, wounded or not, should be shot immediately upon capture. However, this may have been general propaganda as the specific order was never produced, although a number of Commissars who ordered the execution of German soldiers clearly believed it did exist. Conversely, the Soviets issued a number of specific orders not to kill their prisoners. For example, Stalin's order Number 55 stipulated, '[I]f German soldiers and officers give themselves up, the Red Army must take them prisoner and spare their lives.'[443] This order was deemed necessary to enhance the flow of prisoners and thus deplete the German forces, increase the flow of information taken from prisoners and enhance the reputation of the Soviet forces.[444]

Although the Soviets may have exercised some restraint in the cold-blooded execution of German prisoners, they did not adopt the same policy with regard to the political prisoners they already held which were often liquidated in large numbers as they retreated. The Soviet Secret Police killed before retreating, inter alia, 11,000 political prisoners in the Ukraine and the Baltic states.[445] The other cold-blooded execution of note involved the massacre of Polish officers in the Katyn forest. Although only 4,143 Polish bodies were ever recovered, it is likely that the number may have been as high as 14,700. At the Nuremburg trials, the Russians attempted to blame the massacre on the Germans, but the Germans prepared a defence, and the case was dropped. This implicit finding that the Wehrmacht was not guilty of the killings left little doubt as to who was really responsible. It appears to have been part of a much greater plot, in which up to 25,000 Polish officers, in total, were executed by the Soviets, soon after the shared occupation with Nazi Germany. Such practices were not unknown to the Soviets, who in 1937, had purged 36,671 of their own officers. However, the topic of the Katyn massacre remains a matter of strong debate in Russia,

[442] de Zayas, A (1989) *The Wehrmacht War Crimes Bureau, 1939–1945* (Nebraska, Nebraska University Press) 250–53; Lord Russell of Liverpool (2002) *Scourge of the Swastika: A Short History of Nazi War Crimes*, 2nd edn (London, Greenhill) 75–76; Davidson, E (1966) *The Trial of the Germans: 22 Defendants at Nuremberg* (NY, Macmillan) 414.

[443] Order, noted in Beevor, A (1998) *Stalingrad* (London, Penguin) 308.

[444] de Zayas, A (1989) *The Wehrmacht War Crimes Bureau, 1939–1945* (Nebraska, Nebraska University Press) 164–79. Note, this may have been done in secret. There is no complete record of Stalin's speeches from the 6th and 7th 1941; Beevor, A (1998) *Stalingrad* (London, Penguin) 60, 357, 384–85; Beevor, A (2002) *Berlin: The Downfall 1945* (London, Penguin) 46, 65, 112–14, 132, 397.

[445] de Zayas, A (1989) *The Wehrmacht War Crimes Bureau, 1939–1945* (Nebraska, Nebraska University Press) 210–11, 221–26, 240–44.

and as of 2010, was still classified as a State secret, despite former President Boris Yeltsin (1931–2007) admitting Soviet responsibility for the massacre in 1991.[446]

B. Killing Prisoners by Methods of Incarceration

One of the most obvious differences between the Soviets, Germans and Japanese, as opposed to the Western Allies, in the Second World War, was that their treatment of prisoners was considerably different when it came to issues of captivity. Only in the last instance did prisoners have a good chance of surviving until the end of the conflict. The same could not be said for prisoners of the others. This is not to suggest that the Western Allies were without fault. Aside a rather unpleasant instance of tit-for-tat non-lethal reprisals (which were prohibited by the 1929 Convention but Churchill avoided the classification suggesting the reciprocal shackling was done 'to stand up to a bully like Hitler')[447] the British holding of prisoners appears relatively good. The Americans also appear to have acted to high standards on this issue. Thus, the accidental suffocating of 140 German prisoners in United States hands in March 1945 had the Americans report the matter immediately to the Protecting Power and Dwight Eisenhower (1890–1969) personally promising the German High Command a full investigation and punishment of those responsible. In addition, the use of torture appears to be relatively rare, as it seems the Allies preferred to use more subtle methods of collecting information, such as direct interrogation, hidden microphones and agents disguised as prisoners. However, this may not be the full story and very basic torture via starvation and beatings may have been administered to some Nazi prisoners.[448] Such standards were not always followed by the other Western Allies. The Poles, despite their relatively short war with Germany still managed to achieve at least one alleged atrocity with the killing of some 230 prisoners via a forced march for 11 days. The worst atrocities committed by the Allies in this area was probably by the French, who came to hold 600,000 men after the conflict ended. This was at the same point that Switzerland was told it was no longer required as a Protecting Power, as Germany had ceased to exist. Without such oversight, many of the French camps developed very harsh conditions, with only minimal medicine or communication with the outside world. By the end of September 1945, at least 40,000 men were not fit for work and another 150,000 were unfit due to malnutrition. It is suggested that as many as 80,000 prisoners may have died because of the French brutality, with perhaps 20,000 of these killed by the clearing of minefields.[449]

[446] Anon 'Unburied Dead' *Economist* (13 February 2010) 47; Anon (2008) 'Dead Leaves in the Wind' in *Economist* (19 June, 2008) 65; Davies, N (2003) *Rising '44: The Battle for Warsaw* (London, Pan) 44, 129; Applebaum, A (2003) *Gulag. A History* (London, Penguin) 390; de Zayas, A (1989) *The Wehrmacht War Crimes Bureau, 1939–1945* (Nebraska, Nebraska University Press) 229; Merridale, C (2005) *Ivan's War: The Red Army 1939–1945* (London, Faber) 64–66; Davidson, E (1966) *The Trial of the Germans: 22 Defendants at Nuremberg* (NY, Macmillan) 72–74; Owen, J (2006) *Nuremberg: Evil on Trial* (Kent, Headline) 120; Courtois, S, et al (1999) *The Black Book of Communism. Crimes, Terror, Repression* (Massachusetts, Harvard University Press) 366–69.

[447] Churchill, W (1957) *Great War Speeches* (London, Transworld) 170; Geneva Convention 1929, Art 2(3). Note, this issue was resolved by the quiet mediation of the ICRC; Kalshoven, F (2005) *Belligerent Reprisals* (Leiden, Nijhoff) 178–84.

[448] Reuters (2005) 'Nazis Tortured By British After World War II' *New Zealand Herald*, 19 December 2005 B3; Garrett, R (1981) *POW* (London, Charles) 165–67; Gilbert, A (2006) *POW: Allied Prisoners in Europe* (London, Murray) 53.

[449] de Zayas, A (1989) *The Wehrmacht War Crimes Bureau, 1939–1945* (Nebraska, Nebraska University Press) 86, 94; Moorehead, C (1998) *Dunant's Dream: War, Switzerland and the History of the Red Cross* (NYC, Carroll and Graf) 534, 537–38.

Twenty-seven per cent, some 35,756 men out of a total of 132,134 Allied prisoners (not counting Chinese, who probably suffered a higher percentage), died whilst being held in Japanese captivity. Although there are some examples of compassion within some Japanese camps, the overall practices of transport, work and food suggest that their overall policies of dealing with captive prisoners were the antithesis of humanitarian considerations.[450]

Japanese reports suggest that 10,800 of the 50,000 prisoners of war which they transported by sea, died at sea. However, the correct figure may be double this. More Allied prisoners under Japanese control died via transport than any other cause of death. Whilst some of these men died due to conditions of over-crowding, extreme heat and lack of water, most died because the vessels they were travelling on were not marked as carrying prisoners of war. Allied submarines operating in the Pacific had no way of identifying the transports carrying prisoners of war. This was, thus, deliberately exposing them to danger despite the rules of the 1929 Convention on this question. However, ICRC proposals to ensure that transports carrying prisoners should be explicitly neutralised, could not be agreed. This failure meant that by the time the Second World War was over, thousands of prisoners had died in transit via bombings or torpedoes which had been fired by their own side. Although the Allies were aware through intelligence that some convoys were transporting prisoners, they adopted a view that the destruction of the enemy must take priority over the attempts to safeguard prisoner lives. The results of the Japanese indifference and the Allied determination meant that at least 25 of the 45 shiploads of prisoners were sunk. When the vessels were torpedoed, it was put at a 50–50 chance that the prisoners would be released, and even if they were, it was unlikely they would be picked up by Japanese vessels. Accordingly, the death rates were very high. Thus, when the *Rakuyo Maru*, with 1,248 prisoners on board was hit, 971 of the prisoners were killed. Only 72 prisoners of over 1,000 survived the sinking of the *Kachidoki Maru*, whilst 1,782 of some 1,800 American prisoners of war went down with the *Arisan Maru*. When the *Montevideo Maru* was sunk of Papua New Guinea, 840 Australian prisoners of war and 160 civilians died, whilst 900 out of 1,800 on board the *Lisbon Maru* drowned after it was torpedoed. A similar problem also occurred in Germany towards the end of the war when the *Thielbek* was sunk by the Allies who did not know it was holding 2,800 prisoners of war. Due to the fact that the German authorities refused to help the prisoners, only 50 survived. A similar fate met the prisoners on board the accompanying vessel the *Cap Arcona*, of the 6,400 prisoners on board this vessel 4,250 of them drowned.[451]

Where the Japanese had an even greater control over the fate of their prisoners was in the areas of nutrition, medicine and work. Starvation may have been an intentional, if not a reckless, policy in some instances. This was because the calorie intake required for the health of an Allied prisoner was typically much higher than that required for a Japanese soldier, and attempts at parity, as demanded by the 1907 Hague and 1929 Geneva Conventions, resulted in Allied prisoners being denied the food levels they required. Attempts by the Allied governments in conjunction with the ICRC to rectify

[450] Hastings, M (2008) *Nemesis: The Battle for Japan* (London, Harper) 374, 395; Barber, L (1999) *The Last War of Empires: Japan and the Pacific War* (Auckland, Bateman) 144–51.

[451] Lamont-Brown, R (2002) *Ships from Hell. Japanese War Crimes on the High Seas* (London, Sutton) 21, 25, 29, 41, 64–65, 116, 118; MacArthur, B (2005) *Surviving the Sword: Prisoners of the Japanese* (London, Time) 325, 332, 340–41; Hastings, M (2008) *Nemesis: The Battle for Japan* (London, Harper) 298–99, 374, 395.

part of this problem with a steady and reliable supply of food parcels failed, as the Japanese refused neutral ships into their waters and attempts to create a transfer of such food parcels to Japanese ships came to an end after one of them, the *Awa Maru*, was torpedoed. Nevertheless, three relief shipments of food parcels did reach Japan during the Second World War. However, the way that these were distributed remains a mystery, for whilst some camps received over 20 parcels per prisoner, others received less than one sixteenth of a single parcel per prisoner.[452]

Although the Japanese allowed a few ICRC visits to some camps in Japan, they did not permit any such visits in their occupied territories. An inkling of the type of problem first emerged in Manchuria in 1931, where the ICRC delegate only managed to gain access to the hospitals of the Chinese Red Cross, whilst his attempts to find out anything about the Chinese prisoners of war were fruitless. This same problem reappeared after the Japanese attacked the United States and the Commonwealth. With virtually no Japanese prisoners in Allied hands, the whole idea of reciprocity was irrelevant. The one exception to this was an ICRC appointment in Shanghai, who was allowed to visit Hong Kong. Outside of these areas, there was virtually no mail, no list of names and very little relief provided to the camps. There was no official ICRC delegates in Singapore, Java, Sumatra, Borneo, Burma, Manila or Bangkok. In one instance, one ICRC delegate, Dr Matthaeus Vischer who was in Borneo when it was captured by the Japanese, died with 25 others, after allegedly confessing to being involved in an 'anti-Japanese plot'.[453] Some camps in Japan where the high level prisoners were held did receive restricted ICRC visits towards the end of the war. But even at this stage, the ICRC was mislead, for whilst they believed there to be 43 prisoner of war camps in Japan, in fact, there were 103 camps and 34,000 prisoners were being held, not the 27,000, as declared.[454]

Many of the camps were run on extremely authoritarian methods that ran counter to both the Hague and Geneva Conventions. The Japanese tortured their Chinese prisoners of war and civilians in their occupied territories. Beatings, slashings, burnings and water torture of Allied prisoners also appears to have been not uncommon with some Japanese prisoner of war camps. More than 3,000 prisoners of war (and Chinese civilians) were used as guinea pigs in biological and medical experiments. Attempts to escape were typically met with the death of the escapee and also a number of their fellow prisoners as a collective penalty. Tens of thousands of prisoners were treated like slaves who laboured in the copper and zinc mines of Japan and Taiwan, as well as on roads, railways and airfields in Burma, Thailand, the Spice Islands and the Philippines. In some instances, they were also used as pathfinders through minefields. The 258 miles of the Burma railway took the labour of 330,000 men, including some 60,500 prisoners of war. The death rate for prisoners was 28.9 per cent for the Australian (1,060 men) and 60 per cent for the British (2,036 men). Such hard labour

[452] Miller, D (2008) *Mercy Ship. The Untold Story of Prisoner of War Exchanges* (NYC, Continuum) 130–31; Junod, M (1982) *Warriors Without Weapons* (Geneva, ICRC) 264–65; MacArthur, B (2005) *Surviving the Sword: Prisoners of the Japanese* (London, Time) 202, 219–36, 257; Moorehead, C (1998) *Dunant's Dream: War, Switzerland and the History of the Red Cross* (NYC, Carroll and Graf) 480, 479.

[453] Moorehead, C (1998) *Dunant's Dream: War, Switzerland and the History of the Red Cross* (NYC, Carroll and Graf) 82, 495–96.

[454] Moorehead, C (1998) *Dunant's Dream: War, Switzerland and the History of the Red Cross* (NYC, Carroll and Graf) 474–75, 485, 487–88; Junod, M (1982) *Warriors Without Weapons* (Geneva, ICRC) 253, 267–68, 277; Garrett, R (1981) *POW* (London, Charles) 184–85.

was supplemented with various 'death marches' such as that of Bataan in 1942 and Sandakan in 1945. In the first instance, approximately 16,000 American and Philippine prisoners of war out of a total of 70,000 died (of which about 600 were American) in a six day march of 75 miles in temperatures of 90 degrees fahrenheite. In the second instance, some 2,400 Allied prisoners and 3,600 Indonesian civilian slave labourers held captive in Northern Borneo were marched from Sandakan to Ranau. By the end of the war, the only survivors of these prisoners were six men who had escaped en-route. This is widely considered to be the single worst atrocity suffered by Australian servicemen during the Second World War.[455]

Four per cent of the western Allied soldiers held by the Germans or Italians during the Second World War died whilst they were in captivity. Hundreds of these prisoners died when their transports were sunk by British submarines, although large numbers were saved by the courage of their German captors doing what they could to help them. Between 2,500 and 3,500 such men also died because of lack of food, medicine, brutality, forced marches and being bombed by their own air forces, as the Third Reich disintegrated and the prisoners were marched away from advancing armies from late 1944 until the war in Europe ended. Some prisoner of war camps were also bombed by their own air forces as a result of Hitler's order that camps containing Allied airmen should be placed in the residential districts of large cities, as a way to obtain the protection of the civilian inhabitants. Aside these instances, the situation was probably helped by the independent oversight of the prisoners of war of the western allies by 340 ICRC delegates who visited 11,170 prisoner of war camps over the course of the war. The exception to this was when the prisoners were sent to concentration camps, at which point they disappeared from ICRC view. Likewise, spies of the western Allies who were captured by the Nazis were often subjected to primitive forms of torture, such as beatings or having their nails pulled out, before being executed. However, most of the conventional prisoners were independently watched by the ICRC in terms of, inter alia, the work they did and the food they were given. In terms of work, although some prisoners of the Western Allies were used in war zones, it was much more common to put them to work in mines, industry, forestry or agriculture. Although failure to work could lead to severe discipline, it appears rare that these prisoners were worked to death, as occurred in Japan. The food question was dealt with by a good supply of provisions from the Germans and Italians, in addition to the 90 million five kilogram parcels provided by the Red Cross. Thus, although for soldiers the calorie target for prisoners (3,300 per day) was revised down (to a minimum of 2,000), this was still substantially above what comparable prisoners got whilst in Japanese hands.[456]

[455] MacArthur, B (2005) *Surviving the Sword: Prisoners of the Japanese* (London, Time) 29, 35, 48–49, 57, 69–70, 75, 89, 102, 111, 137, 158, 193; Rees, L (2001) *Horror of the East* (London, BBC) 76, 83–89; Brackman, A (1990) *The Other Nuremberg: The Tokyo War Crimes Trials* (Glasgow, Fontana) 45–47, 216, 271–72, 278–88; Maga, T (2000) *Judgement at Tokyo* (Kentucky University Press) 108–109; Chang, I (1997) *The Rape of Nanking* (Sydney, Penguin) 87–88; Nichol, J and Rennell, T (2009) *Medic* (London, Penguin) 81–82.

[456] Moorehead, C (1998) *Dunant's Dream: War, Switzerland and the History of the Red Cross* (NYC, Carroll and Graf) 378–79, 383, 390; Owen, J (2006) *Nuremberg: Evil on Trial* (Kent, Headline) 99; Gilbert, A (2006) *POW: Allied Prisoners in Europe* (London, Murray) 49, 51, 60–64, 86–87, 101–106, 144–45, 153; Nichol, J (2003) *The Last Escape. The Untold Story of Allies Prisoner of War in Germany 1944–45* (London, Penguin) 402–403; Lord Russell of Liverpool (2002) *Scourge of the Swastika: A Short History of Nazi War Crimes*, 2nd edn (London, Greenhill) 38; Bugnion, F (1997) 'ICRC Action During WWII' *IRRC* 317: 156–77; Miller, D (2008) *Mercy Ship. The Untold Story of Prisoner of War Exchanges* (NYC, Continuum) 73, 77; Garrett, R (1981) *POW* (London, Charles) 122, 163; Bailey, F (2009) *Forgotten Voices of the Secret War* (London, Ebury) 111, 176, 195;

The greatest atrocity against prisoners of war of the western Allies whilst in captivity had more to do with the direct instructions of Hitler, in direct contravention of the 1907 and 1929 instruments to kill prisoners of war who attempted to escape. The most famous of these incidents followed the 'great escape' of 76 prisoners on 25 March 1944 from Stalag Luft 3 at Sagan. Seventy three were recaptured and 50 of these men were shot in small groups and their bodies cremated to prevent any post-mortem examinations. Officially, they were killed 'while trying to escape'. Previously, if escapees were caught out of uniform and without their identity tags, they may have been sent to concentration camps or executed, as the Germans argued this divested them of prisoner of war status. This was especially so with prisoners of war who were not American or Commonwealth citizens, under Hitler's 'Operation Bullet'. This followed the loss of between 31,000 and 70,000 French prisoners of war who had escaped and made their way back to France. However, with the Stalag Luft 3 escape, Hitler extended this policy, to cover the execution of prisoners of the western Allies.[457]

The Nazis captured some 5.7 million Red Army soldiers during the course of the Second World War. Approximately 3.3 million of these men died in German camps from disease, exposure, starvation and ill-treatment. These deaths were assisted because the prisoners did not receive assistance from a Protecting Power, the ICRC or other humanitarian organisations. There was also only minimal adherence to the most basic of the 1907 Hague standards. The transport of Soviet prisoners during the opening months of the war with Germany was extreme. In some cases, between 25 and 70 per cent of the prisoners died through a combination of exposure, hunger and thirst whilst being moved away from the war zone. Thousands more died whilst awaiting transport. As was testified at Nuremberg:

> [T]he enormous crowds of prisoners of war remained in the theatre of operation, without proper care – care in the sense of prisoner of war conventions – with regard to housing, food, medical care; and many of them died . . . Epidemics broke out, and cannibalism – human beings driven by hunger devouring one another – manifested itself.[458]

The idea that the Russian prisoners had to be given adequate food was described by German high officials as 'misplaced humanitarianism' and the Nazi officials set their calorie target below survival levels. Thus, the minimum ration set down for Russian prisoners for a 28 day period was 6 kilos of bread, 400 grams of meat, 600 grams of sugar and 400 grams of fat. The situation was so extreme, that in some camps at the end of 1941, death rates were being recorded of 1 per cent per day. Between 21 October and 30 October, 45,690 prisoners died in occupied Poland, or an average of close to 4,600 men per day. In November, another 83,000 died. By the end of November, the death rates in some camps was around 2 per cent per day. On average, about 6,000 Soviet prisoners died every day between the start of the campaign in the middle of 1941 and the end of January 1942. This only began to change towards the end of 1941, when they stopped open-roof train transports and forced marches as the Nazis realised they were killing off large potential labour pools. However, surviving

Schoenbrum, D (1980) *Soldiers of the Night. The Story of the French Resistance* (New York, Dutton); Gilbert, A (2006) *POW: Allied Prisoners in Europe* (London, Murray) 64.

[457] Viven, R (2006) *The Unfree French: Life Under Occupation* (London, Penguin) 189, 192, 197; Gilbert, A (2006) *POW: Allied Prisoners in Europe* (London, Murray) 29–31, 71, 272; Lambert, M (2005) *Night After Night: New Zealanders in Bomber Command* (Auckland, Harper) 334–37, 392–93.

[458] Testimony of Lahousen in Owen, J (2006) *Nuremberg: Evil on Trial* (Kent, Headline) 55.

to be used for labour for everything from clearing minefields, building fortifications, or work in the armaments industry, through to being used as pack animals to drag food and ammunition in the snow, did not add greatly to their longevity. Soviet prisoners were also known to have been tortured. Attitudes degenerated to such an extent that Field Marshal Wilhelm Keitel (1882–1946) suggested that Russian prisoners should be tattooed on the buttocks, so as to assist identification if they escaped. When told that this was illegal and the Russians would then tattoo German prisoners on the forehead, he desisted.[459]

The Soviet reaction to Keitel's suggestion reflected their intention to reply to German barbarism in kind. In part, this was due to two considerations. The first was the existing Soviet practice of dealing with prisoners in their *Gulags*. The second was Stalin's dislike of humanitarianism in his war with Germany.

The distinction between *Gulags* and prisoner of war camps for enemy soldiers was never clear and the conditions and food standards in both institutions were very similar. Although *Gulags* were designed to utilise the labour of their captives, they were also exceptionally effective at killing them via their transport methods, overwork and starvation. The Soviets had already shown this in their management of the 230,000 prisoners they captured when they invaded Poland in 1939. Only 82,000 of these prisoners were still alive when Hitler invaded Russia two years later. Six months after Germany invaded the Soviet Union, death rates in the *Gulags* in 1942 were the highest on record. One in four prisoners died in the *Gulag* system in 1942 (some 352,560 human beings). In the first few months of 1943, the death rate of German prisoners of war was near to 60 per cent and some 570,000 men are listed as having died in captivity from hunger, disease or untreated wounds. Food was critically short with prisoners getting about one third fewer calories than was issued in the late 1930s. The totals may have been higher, as those fit to work were put into all sorts of labour that ranged from burying the diseased dead through to clearing minefields. The Soviets were known to torture captured German prisoners. In one camp near Smolensk, 200 died per day from starvation, typhus, dysentery or freezing to death. Of the 91,000 German troops who surrendered at Stalingrad, more than 50,000 died of disease and exposure within a month. By 1945, 95 per cent of the non-commissioned officers and ordinary soldiers from Stalingrad were dead, along with 55 per cent of the junior officers. By the time the war ended between the Soviets and Germany on 8 May 1945 at least one million of the 3.3 million German prisoners captured, were dead. Such problems were also replicated with the large numbers of Japanese prisoners who fell into Soviet hands as the war drew to a close. An estimated 68,000 of the 600,000 Japanese prisoners taken at the end of the war also died of starvation. A further 46,000 of the Japanese prisoners were so damaged by the labour that they had had to perform that they were impacted for life.[460]

[459] For Hitler's directive on this area, see Trevor-Roper, H (1964) *Hitler's War Directives 1939–1945* (London, Pan) 156; Directive 36; Megargee, G (2007) *War of Annihilation: Combat and Genocide on the Eastern Front, 1941* (Boulder, Rowman) 40, 61–62, 90–91, 117–19; Merridale, C (2005) *Ivan's War: The Red Army 1939–1945* (London, Faber) 123–24; Rees, L (1999) *War of the Century: When Hitler Fought Stalin* (London, BBC) 57–60; Beevor, A (1998) *Stalingrad* (London, Penguin) 59, 257, 350; Lord Russell of Liverpool (2002) *Scourge of the Swastika: A Short History of Nazi War Crimes*, 2nd edn (London, Greenhill) 52, 58–61; Davidson, E (1966) *The Trial of the Germans: 22 Defendants at Nuremberg* (NY, Macmillan) 83, 334, 493.

[460] de Zayas, A (1989) *The Wehrmacht War Crimes Bureau, 1939–1945* (Nebraska, Nebraska University Press) 164–68; Rees, L (1999) *War of the Century: When Hitler Fought Stalin* (London, BBC) 166–67, 180,

Stalin disdained efforts at humanitarianism in this area. The ICRC had no visiting rights to prisoner of war camps during the conflict. Although the Soviets had come to adopt the 1907 Hague Convention (but not the 1929 Geneva Convention) when they had proposed to Germany that they would follow the 1907 rules, if the Germans did the same, Hitler decided not to answer their suggestion. Conversely, when Bulgaria, as Germany's Protecting Power, requested Red Cross visits to the Soviet prisoner of war camps, their requests were refused. The Soviets also refused to release lists of captured prisoners to either Germany or the ICRC. The Germans replied in kind, refusing to allow ICRC visits to their prisoner of war camps for Soviet soldiers and refused to hand over lists of who was captured. These positions did not alter during the conflict. This is not to suggest that records were not kept. In fact, the Germans kept individual records, with the majority of them ending up in the archives of the NKVD after the war. Nevertheless, during the conflict, this impasse with regards to fundamental considerations relating to prisoners of war suited both leaders who willingly entered into a conflict with little restraint, which was unlike the Soviet war with Finland or the German war with the Western Allies. In August of 1941, Stalin even went so far as to declare that all captured officers were 'malicious traitors' whose families were subject to arrest. Given that his own son had been captured, he had his son's wife arrested. When the Nazi's tried to negotiate an exchange, Stalin refused saying 'I have no son called Yakov'.[461] The following month, an appeal by the Germans for postal services solicited the following reply from the Soviets:

> There are no Russian prisoners of war. The Russian soldier fights till death. If he chooses to become a prisoner, he is automatically excluded from the Russian community. We are not interested in a postal service only for Germans.[462]

The other notable problem that the Soviet's created for their prisoners was to do with their repatriation. This problem became so pressing that the United Nations General Assembly was calling, as late as the end of 1950, for the repatriation of all prisoners of war taken between 1939 and 1945, by the end of 1951. For many countries, this goal had been achieved relatively quickly.[463] For example, the Italians had attempted to release all of their prisoners of war upon the armistice being agreed, whilst Germany

186–87; Applebaum, A (2003) *Gulag. A History* (London, Penguin) 277, 390; Moorehead, C (1998) *Dunant's Dream: War, Switzerland and the History of the Red Cross* (NYC, Carroll and Graf) 687; Beevor, A (2002) *Berlin: The Downfall 1945* (London, Penguin); Beevor, A (1998) *Stalingrad* (London, Penguin) 78–79, 406–409; Lord Russell of Liverpool (2002) *Scourge of the Swastika: A Short History of Nazi War Crimes*, 2nd edn (London, Greenhill) 60–61; *Kamibayashi v Japan (War Claims of Former Japanese Prisoners of the Soviet Union)* 29 ILM (1990) 391; Courtois, S et al (1999) *The Black Book of Communism. Crimes, Terror, Repression* (Massachusetts, Harvard University Press) 379–80.

[461] Yakov got himself killed running at the perimeter fence in a concentration camp. See Amis, M (2003) *Koba the Dread* (London, Vintage) 165.

[462] Noted in Tolstoy, N (1977) *Victims of Yalta* (London, Hodder) 34. Also, Rees, L (1999) *War of the Century: When Hitler Fought Stalin* (London, BBC) 223. For the facts and figures, see de Zayas, A (1989) *The Wehrmacht War Crimes Bureau, 1939–1945* (Nebraska, Nebraska University Press) 85–88; Junod, M (1982) *Warriors Without Weapons* (Geneva, ICRC) 219; Moorehead, C (1998) *Dunant's Dream: War, Switzerland and the History of the Red Cross* (NYC, Carroll and Graf) 397; Beevor, A (1998) *Stalingrad* (London, Penguin) 60; Applebaum, A (2003) *Gulag. A History* (London, Penguin) 376, 392–93; Amis, M (2003) *Koba the Dread* (London, Vintage) 64, 67, 71–72; Forsythe, D (2005) *The Humanitarians: The International Committee of the Red Cross* (Cambridge, Cambridge University Press) 43.

[463] UNGA Resolution 427 (V) Measures for the Peaceful Solution of the Problem of Prisoners of War (1950).

generally disgorged prisoners as the country collapsed, with prisoners of war being released at a rate of 22,000 a day in the British zone of Northern Germany alone, days after the German surrender. Other countries were not as quick in releasing their prisoners of war. The Commonwealth and American forces repatriated the Japanese prisoners within two years. Conversely, the Soviets took between three and 13 years. Although the Soviet Union repatriated a group of 225,000 prisoners, mostly sick or injured privates, as early as June 1945, thousands were still inside Russia in 1955 and were only released when political needs such as the Hungarian elections, dictated. Others, such as the estimated 70,000 Italian prisoners of war taken on the Russian Front, an estimated 22,000 died en route to the camps, and a further 38,000 perished in captivity, with only 10,000 ever making it home – and thousands still simply listed as missing – years after the conflict had ended.[464]

For the Soviets, the repatriation question was not only to do with the prisoners that they held, but also the prisoners of Soviet interest, that others held. These included the Soviet or Russian citizens who had fought for Germany, the Russian prisoners of war who had decided to swap sides (one in five of the men in German uniforms in Normandy in 1944), partisans in occupied countries (but were not communist partisans) and entire Cossack divisions stationed in Italy. The Western Allies agreed to Stalin's demands for the repatriation of all of these men. Accordingly, Article 1 of the 1945 Yalta Agreement on Prisoners of War between the United States, Britain and the Soviet Union stipulated:

> All Soviet citizens liberated by the forces operating under British command and all British subjects liberated by the forces operating under Soviet command will, without delay after their liberation, be separated from enemy prisoners of war and will be maintained separately . . . until they have been handed over to the Soviet or British authorities.[465]

The Soviet's had managed to achieve this agreement because they (the Soviets) had come into the possession of over 100,000 western Allied prisoners and civilians. By such collateral, the provision noted above facilitated the exchange of perhaps two million Russians, who were handed over to Stalin in the years 1945 to 1947, in exchange for the 100,000 or so of the Allied prisoners and associated civilians. This act was not prohibited by the 1929 Geneva Convention as it did not contain provisions regarding the return of unwilling citizens or soldiers.[466] Although the Yalta agreement was only meant to cover Soviet citizens, thousands of Russians who never had or wanted Soviet citizenship, along with many others in occupied countries, including some 200,000 German civilians, were caught in the net. This was despite the fact that they, and perhaps 40 per cent of the total two million who were transferred, did not want to be sent to the Soviet Union. Such reticence was not surprising given the fate that awaited

[464] de Zayas, A (1989) *The Wehrmacht War Crimes Bureau, 1939–1945* (Nebraska, Nebraska University Press) 210; Moorehead, C (1998) *Dunant's Dream: War, Switzerland and the History of the Red Cross* (NYC, Carroll and Graf) 399, 501; 'Conditions of an Armistice With Italy, 1943' in Hudson, J (1978) *International Legislation*, Vol IX (New York, Oceana) 51; Applebaum, A (2003) *Gulag. A History* (London, Penguin) 393; Beevor, A (1998) *Stalingrad* (London, Penguin) 430–31; Burleigh, M (2010) *Moral Combat. A History of World War II* (London, Harper) 316.

[465] Reprinted in Szkopiak, Z (1986) *The Yalta Agreements: Documents Prior To, During and After the Crimea Conference 1945* (London, Polish Government in Exile) 34.

[466] Note however, that many of the Russians who fought for Hitler wore German uniforms, and as such, should have been considered under the authority of Germany and not, therefore, so easily tradable amongst the victors. The Yalta agreement ignored this fact, seeing through the uniforms and seeing only nationalities.

them. Rough figures suggest that assuming they actually made it back to Russia and were not executed straight away, as many were, then 20 per cent of those repatriated received a death sentence or 25 years in a *Gulag*. A further 15 to 20 per cent received sentences in the range of five to 10 years. Ten per cent were given *Gulag* sentences of less than six years. Thirty-five per cent more were given work sentences, but were allowed to live in their homes whilst completing their sentences.[467]

C. Wounded

By the time of the Second World War, the chances of survival if wounded were getting much better as only 4.5 per cent of the wounded who reached hospitals did not survive. The chances of survival were being increased by the development of new technologies and refined practices on the battlefield. In terms of new technologies, drugs based on sulfonamide were developed in the 1930s which controlled some infections and the discovery of penicillin in 1944 was beyond massive. For example, the death rate from pneumonia fell from 24 per cent to 6 per cent for American troops between the First and Second World Wars. Penicillin alone is credited with creating a fundamental difference that allowed the Allied troops to survive and recover from wounds and illnesses which decimated German soldiers.

In terms of refined practices, there are some instances in the Second World War which reflected perfectly how the laws pertaining to the treatment of the wounded should be implemented, with medical units stuck in the middle of a conflict which could sweep around them whilst both they, their wounded, and their facilities, would remain unmolested. Clear examples of this are recorded in the conflict in North Africa, with some New Zealand medical facilities being stuck between the advances and retreats of both sides, but being left alone by the Germans when it was seen that the New Zealand doctors were treating the German and Allies wounded equally.[468] Further evidence of the belligerents working relatively well in this area can be seen from the exchanges of wounded prisoners that took place. The first exchange for 1,229 British and Commonwealth prisoners of war occurred in 1942 with Italy. Three smaller exchanges returned a further 1,916 wounded and/or sick prisoners from the Commonwealth, in exchange for 9,114 Italians. The following year four exchanges took place between Germany and Britain including 5,195 British, Commonwealth and American soldiers for 5,765 Germans. The vast majority of these men were sick

[467] Tolstoy, N (1977) *Victims of Yalta* (London, Hodder) 236–37, 250–51, 260, 306–307, 316, 409; Davies, N (2003) *Rising '44: The Battle for Warsaw* (London, Pan) 467; Applebaum, A (2003) *Gulag. A History* (London, Penguin) 392–96; Olson, L (2003) *For Your Freedom and Ours* (London, Heinemann) 210–13, 225; Amis, M (2003) *Koba the Dread* (London, Vintage) 211; Davies, N (2003) *Rising '44: The Battle for Warsaw* (London, Pan) 49; Beevor, D (2009) *D-Day. The Battle for Normandy* (London, Viking) 38; Davidson, E (1966) *The Trial of the Germans: 22 Defendants at Nuremberg* (NY, Macmillan) 83.

[468] Stout, D (1956) *New Zealand Medical Services in the Middle East and Italy* (Wellington, Government Printer) 198–99, 206, 243, 277. For other examples, see Barnett, G 'Caring for the Casualties' in *WWII History* (November 2008) 40, 46; Beevor, A (2009) *D-Day. The Battle for Normandy* (London, Viking) 289; Greenwood, J (2005) *Medics at War: Military Medicine from Colonial Times to the 21st Century* (Annapolis, Naval Institute Press) 61; Miller, D (2008) *Mercy Ship. The Untold Story of Prisoner of War Exchanges* (NYC, Continuum) 8–9; Viven, R (2006) *The Unfree French: Life Under Occupation* (London, Penguin) 192, 197; de Zayas, A (1989) *The Wehrmacht War Crimes Bureau, 1939–1945* (Nebraska, Nebraska University Press) 115–16; Moorehead, C (1998) *Dunant's Dream: War, Switzerland and the History of the Red Cross* (NYC, Carroll and Graf) 185; Nichol, J and Rennell, T (2009) *Medic* (London, Penguin) 42–43, 255, 273.

and/or wounded. A further, 1,000 were exchanged in May 1944, 2,560 in September, and a last exchange was concluded in January 1945 for 2,500 men.[469]

Whilst these are far from the only examples of the system actually working, there are also multiple examples pushing in the opposite direction, with the targeting of medics, medical transports and hospitals. In terms of medics being targets, in total, 2,265 American medical personnel were killed in action. On Iwo Jima, the percentage of casualties among the Medical Corps was greater than the proportion of losses among the marines. These losses appear to be consistent with overall Japanese practices in the Pacific, where Red Cross insignias were treated as desirable targets. Some 1,474 medical personnel died in this Pacific theatre, of which 858 were killed in action.[470]

The targeting of medical transports was also a problem. The targeting of vehicle ambulances was a problem which occurred, inter alia, during the Italian invasion of Ethiopia and the Japanese invasion of China, as well as during the Second World War on the Eastern and Western fronts. In the Far East, records have emerged of British Secret Service Agents systematically attacking convoys of wounded Japanese soldiers.[471] The targeting of air-ambulances was also a particular problem. This was regrettable as aero-medical evacuations were improving life expectancy for wounded soldiers, by getting soldiers to hospitals in one hour, for a trip that previously took 24 hours via ambulances and trains. The Americans were using helicopters for medical evacuations from late 1944 in the Pacific. However, international rules for the neutrality of medical aircraft had not, at this point, been agreed. Accordingly, the British would not accept the Red Cross markings on German planes seeking to rescue fliers who bailed out over the English Channel and a number of these were subsequently shot up. The German Admiralty accepted their shooting at these planes without protest as no specific international agreement on the status of these planes had ever been reached. Conversely, when the British experimented with Red Cross marked planes, these were not harassed by the Germans.[472]

Perhaps from the trials following the First World War and the reiteration of the rules in 1929, the Germans learnt not to target hospital ships. This point was made strongly at Nuremberg, with assertions that not one Allied Red Cross ship was sunk by the Germans between 1939 and 1945. This may have been an exaggeration, as Churchill alleged that British hospital ships were targeted during the retreat from Dunkirk. In addition, the *Maid of Kent* was sunk and the British Hospital Ship *Aba* was bombed, but not sunk, during the Crete campaign, as were a number of other British ships that had stopped to pick up survivors of sinking ships. At least one clearly marked Red Cross

[469] Miller, D (2008) *Mercy Ship. The Untold Story of Prisoner of War Exchanges* (NYC, Continuum) 17–20, 56–64; Gilbert, A (2006) *POW: Allied Prisoners in Europe* (London, Murray) 225.

[470] Beevor, A (2009) *D-Day. The Battle for Normandy* (London, Viking) 293, 378; Barnett, G 'Caring for the Casualties' in *WWII History* (November 2008) 40, 46; Littleton, M (2005); *DOC: Heroic Stories of Medics, Corpsmen and Surgeons in Combat* (Zennith, Minnesota) 4; Greenwood, J (2005) *Medics at War: Military Medicine from Colonial Times to the 21st Century* (Annapolis, Naval Institute Press) 93, 102, 106.

[471] de Zayas, A (1989) *The Wehrmacht War Crimes Bureau, 1939–1945* (Nebraska, Nebraska University Press) 104; Moorehead, C (1998) *Dunant's Dream: War, Switzerland and the History of the Red Cross* (NYC, Carroll and Graf) 363; Beevor, A (2009) *D-Day. The Battle for Normandy* (London, Viking) 294, 474; Bailey, F (2009) *Forgotten Voices of the Secret War* (London, Ebury) 315; Stout, D (1956) *New Zealand Medical Services in the Middle East and Italy* (Wellington, Government Printer) 257.

[472] Davidson, E (1966) *The Trial of the Germans: 22 Defendants at Nuremberg* (NY, Macmillan) 399; Stout, D (1956) *New Zealand Medical Services in the Middle East and Italy* (Wellington, Government Printer) 63, 349, 433; Knightley, P (1975) *The First Casualty* (London, Pan) 236.

sponsored ship was sunk by Italian fighters, trying to deliver food supplies into Greece. In addition, well marked Red Cross ships like the *Padua* fell victim to a mine off Marseilles in 1943, the SS *Talamba* was sunk off Sicily as was the *Embla* which was bombed and sunk in 1944. However, it should also be noted that in at least one instance, an Italian Red Cross plane purposefully got between Allied soldiers in lifeboats and German fighter aircraft that wanted to attack the defenceless during the battle for Crete.[473] The Japanese sunk the Australian hospital ship *Centaur* in 1943 and of the 332 medical personnel and crew aboard, 268 died. It may be that this sinking was a reprisal for the destruction of a Japanese field hospital in New Guinea by Australian troops. Finally, kamikaze attacks in late April 1945 on the American Hospital ship *Comfort* resulted in the deaths of 29 service personnel, including six nurses. Japanese forces were also accused of targetting Red Cross ships in their conflict in China, althoug the Japanese also asserted that the Chinese forces were targetting their hospitals on land and their hospital ships. They later asserted that American forces behaved in the same way, bombing, torpedoing and machine gunning their hospital ships. In their reply, the American authorites pointed out that such attacks only occurred when the hospital ships were insufficiently marked and therefore unidentifiable, as hospital ships.[474]

With regard to the hospital ships of the Axis, the Soviet Union refused to recognise any such vessels flying under a German flag. Accordingly, in 1941 they bombarded the *Alexander von Humboldt* and the *Pitea*. Later, in early 1945, the hospital ship *General von Steuben* was torpedoed after leaving Pillau with 2,680 wounded aboard, of which almost all were drowned. In addition, the British refused to recognise small German hospital ships (unlike the Americans, who recognised them all, as the Convention set no size limits) and felt free to attack these. By the middle of 1943 the nine small Italian hospital ships had been bombarded. In terms of larger German vessels, the *Tubingen*, a recognised hospital ship, was sunk, allegedly by mistake, at the end 1944. The *Deuchland*, which was poorly marked as a hospital ship, but was carrying prisoners of war and wounded when it was sunk in a British air attack in 1945 caused a great loss of life. At this point, reprisals were considered against Allied hospital ships, but decided against.[475] In the Pacific, the Americans managed to sink the Japanese Red Cross ship the *Awa Maru*, which had been given a safe passage by the Americans to carry Red Cross supplies to Japan for Allied Prisoners of War. The Submarine commander was court martialled, for which he was given a 'letter of admonition' for his negligence. Although the United States apologised to Japan over the *Awa Maru* incident, it is legitimate to wonder how far the Red Cross symbol was respected in the campaigns in the Pacific. For example, Rear Admiral Robert Carney (1895–1990) recorded:

[473] Nichol, J and Rennell, T (2009) *Medic* (London, Penguin) 104; Clark, A (2001) *The Fall of Crete* (London, Cassel) 175; Junod, M (1982) *Warriors Without Weapons* (Geneva, ICRC) 202; Miller, D (2008) *Mercy Ship. The Untold Story of Prisoner of War Exchanges* (NYC, Continuum) 82; Churchill, W (1957) *Great War Speeches* (London, Transworld) 19; Nichol, J and Rennell, T (2009) *Medic* (London, Penguin) 40–41; Clark, A (2001) *The Fall of Crete* (London, Cassell) 110, 118–19; Stout, D (1956) *New Zealand Medical Services in the Middle East and Italy* (Wellington, Government Printer) 166.

[474] Smith, A (1992) *Three Minutes of Time – the Torpedoing of the Australian Hospital Ship Centaur* (Queensland, Tasman Press) 17–20; Barnett, G 'Caring for the Casualties' in *WWII History* (November 2008) 40, 45; Knightley, P (1975) *The First Casualty* (London, Pan) 293; Durand, A (1984) *A History of the International Committee of the Red Cross: From Sarajevo to Hiroshima* (Dunant Institute, Geneva) 380–83, 537.

[475] de Zayas, A (1989) *The Wehrmacht War Crimes Bureau, 1939–1945* (Nebraska, Nebraska University Press) 108, 261, 262; Beevor, A (2002) *Berlin: The Downfall 1945* (London, Penguin) 88.

> We ran afoul of Japanese hospital ships, some were sunk, some couldn't be identified, some were adjacent to proper military targets and suffered as a result . . . it would seem to be an unnecessary refinement to worry too much over these incidents.[476]

Hospitals appear to have been viewed as legitimate targets for some Soviet forces. The worst incident occurred on 29 December 1941 when a German field hospital was overrun at Feodosia on the Crimean coast and about 160 German wounded were killed. Hundreds were also killed when the hospital at Grischino was overrun in 1943. During the siege of Stalingrad, the patients at the hospital of Gumrak were machine gunned. Similarly, as the Soviet forces advanced through Eastern Europe, there were a number of instances involving either the deliberate, or reckless, targeting of clearly marked Red Cross areas. A notable example of this occurred during the Battle for Berlin, when the S-Bahn and U-Bahn tunnels were blown up by Soviet forces. This act killed up to 15,000 people, as water, up to a metre and half high, swept through the tunnels, including many 'hospital' sections. Italian partisans were known to intentionally burn hospitals to the ground with all of the wounded soldiers inside.[477]

The Japanese were also known to attack hospitals. Their attack on Alexandra Barracks Hospital in Singapore, after it was alleged they had been fired upon, ended in 323 people, including 230 patients, being bayoneted to death. General Tomoyuki Yamashita (1885–1946) had the commander responsible for the Alexandra atrocity executed. Nevertheless, other notable atrocities were recorded, such as the Japanese over-running and executing patients and medics alike in the hospitals of the Salesian Mission and St Stephen's College in Hong Kong. Aid stations which were over-run with patients and medics executed were recorded at Saipan, Burma and with some of the battles around Singapore.[478] The Germans were involved in a number of instances when the Red Cross areas of the Western allies were attacked in Crete, North Africa, Italy, France, and with the Warsaw uprising.[479] Reciprocal allegations were also made against the Western Allies. However, when Germany and the Western Allies were fighting each other, it appears that relatively successful lines of communication between the opposing forces were opened and issues involving the targeting of hospitals was investigated and reports made and returned. Sometimes, when it realised a mistake had been made and a hospital had been inadvertently targeted, the wrong-doing side would communicate and confess their mistake before the other side even knew of the event.[480]

[476] Carney in Hastings, M (2008) *Nemesis: The Battle for Japan* (London, Harper) 186; Miller, D (2008) *Mercy Ship. The Untold Story of Prisoner of War Exchanges* (NYC, Continuum) 130–42; Davidson, E (1966) *The Trial of the Germans: 22 Defendants at Nuremberg* (NY, Macmillan) 396–97.

[477] de Zayas, A (1989) *The Wehrmacht War Crimes Bureau, 1939–1945* (Nebraska, Nebraska University Press) 180–91; Beevor, A (2002) *Berlin: The Downfall 1945* (London, Penguin) 339, 371; Beevor, A (1998) *Stalingrad* (London, Penguin) 60–66, 339, 363, 384; Tolstoy, N (1977) *Victims of Yalta* (London, Hodder) 155.

[478] Littleton, M (2005) *DOC* (Minnesota, Zennith) 41–42; Hastings, M (2008) *Nemesis: The Battle for Japan* (London, Harper) 82; Nichol, J and Rennell, T (2009) *Medic* (London, Penguin) 62–71; MacArthur, B (2005) *Surviving the Sword: Prisoners of the Japanese* (London, Time) 14; Owen, F (1960) *The Fall of Singapore* (London, Penguin) 130–31, 202–203.

[479] Stout, D (1956) *New Zealand Medical Services in the Middle East and Italy* (Wellington, Government Printer) 166–167; Greenwood, J (2005) *Medics at War: Military Medicine from Colonial Times to the 21st Century* (Annapolis, Naval Institute Press) 90; Barnett, G (2008) 'Caring for the Casualties' in *WWII History* (November) 40, 45; Nichol, J and Rennell, T (2009) *Medic* (London, Penguin) 95; Davies, N (2003) *Rising '44: The Battle for Warsaw* (London, Pan) 354.

[480] de Zayas, A (1989) *The Wehrmacht War Crimes Bureau, 1939–1945* (Nebraska, Nebraska University Press) 85–87; Stout, D (1956) *New Zealand Medical Services in the Middle East and Italy* (Wellington, Government

D. Defenceless

The targeting of aircrews whilst in descent was seen, initially, by the Germans as a war crime in the Second World War. However, by the time of the Battle of Britain, the Germans commonly fired on British pilots knowing that by the afternoon, the recovered British pilots could be airborne again. Although the British authorities forbade the shooting of German pilots who parachuted (as they would be captured within a matter of minutes upon arrival), many British pilots seem to have taken this as an invitation to give the enemy everything they could before they could escape the cockpit. The end result was that as the war progressed, a number of pilots of most, if not all, of the belligerents took opportunities to shoot at defenceless pilots stuck in slowly descending parachutes. Only those with degrees of chivalry acted otherwise, or when there was uncertainty over what nationality the pilot was floating beneath the parachute, made shooting at unknown men unwise.[481]

The question of merchant sailors being torpedoed without warning and being left to fend for themselves on the high seas produced exactly the same result in the Second World War as had occurred in the First World War. Germany, despite publicly arguing that such weapons should be done way in a multilateral process, began rebuilding U-boats in secret in 1932. By the end of May 1945, they had constructed 1,153 submarines. Although the Germans possessed such weapons, it was hoped that the indiscriminate sinking of merchant shipping that had occurred in the First World War would not be repeated due to the international instruments of 1922, 1930, 1936 and 1937 which had all reinstated the humanitarian aspects of the Prize Rules. However, these steps were directly challenged by the new radio technologies which allowed a merchant ship to call for help as soon as a submarine appeared, as many merchant navies were instructed to do. In addition, the Defence of Merchant Shipping Handbook of 1938 stated 'no British merchant vessel should ever tamely surrender to a submarine, but should do her utmost to escape.'[482]

The advent of such dictates, coupled with the new radio technologies, ensured that complying with the Prize Rules, restated or not, could be near suicide for any submarine commander when dealing with merchant vessels flying under the flags of opposing countries. This was not necessarily the case for more conventional warships, such as the *Graf Spee*, which managed to sink nine merchant ships, and only opened fire with machine guns aimed at the bridge of one (the *Trevanion*), when she tried to radio a location and distress message. As such, Captain Hans Langsdorff (1894–1939) strictly adhered to the rules of mercantile warfare at the time and saved all of the crew members of these ships and not a life was lost in these sinkings. The other clear example of chivalrous behaviour over helping defenceless sailors came from the Japanese, who after their air force had sunk the *Prince of Wales* and the *Repulse*, pulled back and signaled to the supporting destroyers 'we have completed our task. You may carry on.'

Printer) 116–17, 129, 147, 174, 345; Beevor, A (2009) *D-Day. The Battle for Normandy* (London, Viking) 173.

[481] de Zayas, A (1989) *The Wehrmacht War Crimes Bureau, 1939–1945* (Nebraska, Nebraska University Press) 148; Olson, L (2003) *For Your Freedom and Ours* (London, Heinemann) 134–35; Knightley, P (1975) *The First Casualty* (London, Pan) 236; Lambert, M (2005) *Night After Night: New Zealanders in Bomber Command* (Auckland, Harper) 214; Bourke, J (2000) *An Intimate History of Killing* (London, Granta) 63–64.

[482] Handbook, noted in Kalshoven, F (2005) *Belligerent Reprisals* (Leiden, Nijhoff) 127.

Accordingly, the destroyers were able to pull alongside the sinking vessels and take off the wounded or those floundering in the ocean. Through this act, nearly 800 out of 1,300 officers and men were saved.[483]

For submarines, the history was different. This was displayed when the Second World War began with a loud explosion at 9 pm on the very first day that war was declared. This explosion was caused by the submarine U-30 which was stationed 250 miles northwest of Ireland. Without warning, the U-30 sunk the liner *Athenia*, which was mistaken as an armed merchant vessel. Prior to firing, no opportunity was provided to the ship's crew or passengers to be first delivered to a place of safety. One hundred and twelve people were killed out of 1,417 passengers on board. Hitler had not ordered this and the act was originally explained by the Nazis as British propaganda designed to inflame world opinion against Germany.[484] In fact, at the outset of the war despite advising that 'danger zones' were being created around England, Hitler had committed himself to observing Prize Rules, 'for the time being'.[485] He added, at the end of September 1939 that 'attacks on passenger steamers, or large vessels which obviously carry passengers in considerable numbers in addition to cargo, [are] forbidden'.[486]

By the end of September, he cancelled any restrictions on naval warfare against France and Britain. He added that 'merchant ships and troopships definitely established as being hostile may be attacked without warning'. 'Hostile' was taken to include 'ships sailing without lights in waters around England'. In addition, 'merchantmen which use their radio transmitters after being stopped will be fired upon'. But the restraints on passenger ships were reiterated, although one month later, this was weakened when he authorised his navy to 'attack passenger ships in convoy or proceeding without lights'.[487] The year ended with his approval of War Order No 154, which stated:

> Do not rescue any men; do not take them along; and do not take care of any boats of the ship. Weather conditions and proximity of land are of no consequence. Concern yourself only with the safety of your own boat and with efforts to achieve additional successes as soon as possible. We must be hard in this war. The enemy started the war in order to destroy us, and thus nothing else matters.[488]

By the end of the following year, 1940, Hitler, in his attempt to crush all English imports, declared that 'the sinking of merchantmen is more important than attack on enemy warships'.[489] This followed his decision to allow his U-boats to target neutral as well as enemy shipping if found within the war zone.[490] In reply, Churchill stated:

[483] Owen, F (1960) *The Fall of Singapore* (London, Penguin) 62.

[484] Vandiver, F (2003) *1001 Things Everyone Should Know About World War II* (NYC, Broadway) 14; Hitler's Speech to the Reichstag, 1935 in Keith, K (ed) *International Affairs*, Vol II (Oxford, Oxford University Press) 33; Harris, B (1997) *The Navy Times Book of Submarines. A Political, Social and Military History* (NYC, Berkley) 272; Grove, E (2002) *German Capital Ships and Raiders in World War II* (London, Routledge) 54–59.

[485] Trevor-Roper, H (1964) *Hitler's War Directives 1939–1945* (London, Pan) 41, Directive 1 and 2.

[486] Trevor-Roper, H (1964) *Hitler's War Directives 1939–1945* (London, Pan) 45, Directive 4.

[487] Trevor-Roper, H (1964) *Hitler's War Directives 1939–1945* (London, Pan) 52, Directives 5 and 7.

[488] Order 154 in Harris, B (1997) *The Navy Times Book of Submarines. A Political, Social and Military History* (NYC, Berkley) 274.

[489] Trevor-Roper, H (1964) *Hitler's War Directives 1939–1945* (London, Pan) 103, Directive 23.

[490] Lord Russell of Liverpool (2002) *Scourge of the Swastika: A Short History of Nazi War Crimes*, 2nd edn (London, Greenhill) 68; Hough, R (2003) *The Longest Battle. The War at Sea 1939–45* (London, Cassell).

> U-boat warfare, as conducted by Germany is entirely contrary to international agreements freely subscribed to by Germany only a few years ago. There is no effective blockade, but only a merciless murder and marauding over wide, indiscriminate areas utterly beyond the control of German sea power.[491]

Despite the tirades of Hitler and the accusations of Churchill, some German U-Boat commanders behaved with chivalry, stopping the lifeboats of the merchant ships they torpedoed, whenever possible, to ensure the survivors had a compass, bread and water. However, this practice was stopped following the sinking of the *Laconia* on 12 September 1942 off the coast of West Africa. This vessel was carrying some 80 civilians, 328 Allied soldiers and about 1,800 Italian prisoners of war. When it was sinking, it became apparent that the prisoners were trying to survive in shark infested waters. The U-boat commander radioed for instructions on how to proceed and was told to assist in the recovery of the shipwrecked and also dispatched three other submarines to assist. Admiral Karl Doenitz (1891–1980) also broadcast in English that any Allied vessels assisting would not be attacked. The U-boats then linked together, underneath a large Red Cross flag so as to clearly identify their rescue work, and attempted to help the survivors. However, the flag and broadcast did not deter an attack by Allied aircraft, which forced the U-boats to dive, cutting free the life rafts and leaving the rescued on the decks of the submarines to their fate. The result was only 450 of the 1,800 Italian prisoners were saved and less than half of the other passengers made it to shore. Soon after this incident Donitz' issued what was known as the Laconia Order. This stated:

> No attempt of any kind must be made at rescuing members of ships sunk, and this includes picking up persons in the water and putting them in lifeboats, righting capsized lifeboats, and handing over food and water. Rescue runs counter to the most primitive demands of warfare for the destruction of enemy ships and crews . . . Shipwrecked [are] only to be rescued in case their information is important for the boat.[492]

This non-rescue rule was most clearly stated by Hitler when he told the Japanese ambassador (who represented a side whose submarines appear to have had minimal interest in sinking merchant vessels, preferring to focus on warships, but came to adopt the policy of slaughtering crew who survived torpedo attacks) that in his war with the Allies 'merchant shipping will be sunk without warning with the intention of killing as many of the crew as possible . . . we are fighting for our existence and cannot therefore take a humanitarian point of view'.[493]

The result of this policy was the death of thousands of seafarers, both military and non-military, who were left without pity, to fend for survival on the open ocean. In terms of war effort, U-boats sank nearly 14.7 million tons of allied shipping. This amounted to 2,828 ships (around two-thirds of the total allied tonnage lost). The

[491] Churchill, W (1957) *Great War Speeches* (London, Transworld) 101.

[492] The Laconia Order in Davidson, E (1966) *The Trial of the Germans: 22 Defendants at Nuremberg* (NY, Macmillan) 406; Hough, R (2003) *The Longest Battle. The War at Sea 1939–45* (London, Cassell) 56; White, D (2006) *Bitter Ocean* (London, Headline) 74–76.

[493] Hitler, noted in Harris, B (1997) *The Navy Times Book of Submarines. A Political, Social and Military History* (NYC, Berkley) 294, 302–303; Lord Russell of Liverpool (2002) *Scourge of the Swastika: A Short History of Nazi War Crimes*, 2nd edn (London, Greenhill) 66–68. Also, Naval Operations Staff Memo in Davidson, E (1966) *The Trial of the Germans: 22 Defendants at Nuremberg* (NY, Macmillan) 396; Brackman, A (1990) *The Other Nuremberg: The Tokyo War Crimes Trials* (Glasgow, Fontana) 398.

United Kingdom alone suffered the loss of 11.7 million tons, which was 54 per cent of the total Merchant Navy fleet at the outbreak of the Second World War. In 1942, U-boats sunk a total of 1,006 Allied merchant ships. This was just a fraction beneath the figure that was believed necessary to cripple the convoy chain to Britain. It was also a loss rate which was more than three times greater than ships were being built. In human terms, more than 36,200 Allied sailors, airmen and servicemen and women went to their deaths in the Second World War as the oceans claimed their military vessels. An additional 36,000 merchant ship sailors were also lost between being killed in the explosions which sunk their ships, or to succumbing to isolation, exposure or starvation in open lifeboats or rafts. Often the seafarers in lifeboats of rafts could not be picked up, because rescuing boats became easy targets for the U-boats or marauding aircraft. However, Allied rescue attempts were often made, for both Allied and Axis seafarers.[494]

The Allies were not above the unrestrained sinking of merchant vessels and leaving the sailors to their fate. With the Axis attempts to supply their forces in North Africa, some 1,324 merchant vessels were sunk, leading to the death of over 11,400 Italian seamen. The Soviets also were known to target vessels of mixed usage. The greatest killing in the history of submarine warfare was in late January 1945, when a Soviet submarine sunk the German liner *Wilhelm Gustloff*. This vessel had over 8,000 soldiers and refugees on board, of which fewer than 1,000 survived the attack.[495] Of course, the *Wilhelm* was a legitimate target, as it was carrying combatants. This was unlike much of the practice adopted by the United States during its war in the Pacific, in one of the greatest ironies in debates about armed conflict of the twentieth century. That is, the United States mirrored the behaviour of the Germans of unrestrained submarine warfare, which they condemned and which drew them into the First World War, in the Second World War against the Japanese. It took the United States all of six hours after the attack on Pearl Harbour to order 'unrestricted air and submarine warfare against Japan'.[496]

In this area, no single class of warship did as much as the submarine to defeat Japan at sea. By August 1945, the Japanese merchant navy had ceased to exist. Sixty-three per cent of it had been sent to the bottom of the ocean by American submarines. In human terms, during the course of the Second World War, 116,000 of 122,000 seamen serving Japan's pre-war merchant fleet were killed or wounded. Admiral Chester Nimitz (1885–1966), the Commander of the Pacific fleet, went on to testify at Nuremberg that it was customary for United States submarines to attack Japanese merchant vessels without warning and 'US submarines did not rescue survivors if undue additional hazard to the submarine resulted or the submarine would thereby be prevented from accomplishing its further mission'.[497]

[494] White, D (2006) *Bitter Ocean* (London, Headline) 2, 17, 26, 69, 177, 186–90; Hough, R (2003) *The Longest Battle. The War at Sea 1939–45* (London, Cassell) 225, 254, 268; Hope, R (1990) *A New History of British Shipping* (London, Murray) 356.

[495] Harris, B (1997) *The Navy Times Book of Submarines. A Political, Social and Military History* (NYC, Berkley) 339; Ireland, B (2002) *War at Sea: 1914–45* (London, Cassell) 211.

[496] Ireland, B (2002) *War at Sea: 1914–45* (London, Cassel) 155.

[497] Nimitz in Harris, B (1997) *The Navy Times Book of Submarines. A Political, Social and Military History* (NYC, Berkley) 341; Hastings, M (2008) *Nemesis: The Battle for Japan* (London, Harper) 288–89; Hough, R (2003) *The Longest Battle. The War at Sea 1939–45* (London, Cassel) 277.

E. The Dead

The desecration of the dead in the Second World War was a multifaceted problem. At its most extreme, some prisoners were taken from some of the concentration camps such as Buchenwald because of their tattoos, so they could be killed and their skin could be made into household objects such as lampshades and photo albums. In other instances, prisoners were turned into soap or decapitated for the purpose of shrinking their skulls into items of decoration. The German Reich also profited from the corpses in their possession. Gold from teeth was melted down and handed to the Reichsbank in ingots. Human hair was spun into thread and turned into felt for the war industry, and presumably it was also used in the manufacture of ropes and mattresses. Human ash was also used as a fertilizer and a filling material for insulation and in the building of roads and paths. Even the ashes of the people that were not utilised for profit were treated without respect, being scattered into surrounding fields, ponds and rivers.[498]

The enforced disappearances of people and their remains via concealed burials was a common method of warfare used by the Germans when dealing with Partisans. 'Enforced disappearances' were (and remain) the arrest, detention, abduction or any other form of deprivation of liberty by agents of the State or by persons or groups of persons acting with the authorisation, support or acquiescence of the State, followed by a refusal to acknowledge the deprivation of liberty or by concealment of the fate or whereabouts of the disappeared person. Such acts place detained people outside the protection of the law. Here, it was not so much that the dead were desecrated, as much as they were hidden, and their fate was never known. Such uncertainties of the fate and final resting place of the dead can be a clear impediment to the founding of peace, after the conflicts have ended. It is probable that the German policy in this area was following the precedents of the Spanish Civil War, where despite the mutual and common practice of desecration of the dead, the Nationalist's went one step further, with the denial of death certificates for killed insurgents. This appears to have been used as a method to refuse their enemy any status as a member of a national community. By not allowing deaths to be officially registered, the Nationalists persecuted the living, denying them their widowhood, their right to mourn and symbolically banished the dead from the nation.[499] Hitler's variation of this occurred his *Nacht und Nebel* or the Night and Fog Decree whereby suspected underground agents and others would vanish without a trace into the night and fog. Field Marshall Keitel issued a letter which explained the purpose of the policy of enforced disappearances that would plague humanity in a number of conflicts in coming decades:

> Efficient and enduring intimidation can only be achieved either by capital punishment or by measures by which the relatives of the criminals do not know the fate of the criminal. The prisoners are, in future, to be transported to Germany secretly, and further treatment of the offenders will take place here; these measures will have a deterrent effect because . . . the

[498] Owen, J (2006) *Nuremberg: Evil on Trial* (Kent, Headline) 65, 93–95, 119; Steinbacher, S (2005) *Auschwitz* (London, Penguin) 103; Whitlock, F 'Horrific Discovery' in *WWII History* (November 2008) 49, 50; Beevor, A (2002) *Berlin: The Downfall 1945* (London, Penguin) 94–95; Capdevilla, L (2006) *War Dead: Western Societies and the Casualties of War* (Edinburgh, Edinburgh University Press) 106.

[499] Beevor, A (1982) *The Spanish Civil War* (London, Cassel) 101; Othen, C (2008) *Franco's International Brigades* (Wiltshire, Reportage) 197–98; Capdevilla, L (2006) *War Dead: Western Societies and the Casualties of War* (Edinburgh, Edinburgh University Press) 87.

> prisoners will vanish without a trace [and] no information may be given as to their whereabouts or their fate.[500]

The Partisans replied in reciprocal ways making public displays of dead enemies, as the publically displayed bodies of Benito Mussolini and 15 others, including his mistress, came to show. This display was sufficient to persuade Hitler that his own body should be burned once he died so as to prevent its subsequent display in Moscow. Although the Allies may not have actually done such a primitive act, the Allies were not above reproach on this question. For example, a denial of a proper burial to Nazis condemned at the Nuremburg War Crimes tribunal was achieved by ensuring that after they were executed and cremated, their ashes were not scattered with any form of ritual respect, but as a mark of disapproval and disdain. Similarly, most of the remains of Hitler and Eva Braun, after originally being buried in 1946 were exhumed and burnt in 1970. The exception was with regards to Hitler's lower jaw bone and part of a skull with a bullet hole in it, which found their way to Moscow.[501]

The mutilation of enemy dead was not uncommon in the Soviet–Nazi war. Mutilations of German dead may also have occurred in the battle of Crete, although these acts were probably done by Partisans and not regular soldiers. The Japanese treatment of enemy war dead was one of the focuses of some of the war crimes trials of the Far East. In these trials, cannibalism was an issue which was dealt with, as was, inter alia, the failure to give honourable burials to executed prisoners of war. The cannibalism appears to have been linked to food shortages, although comparable acts of cannibalism by Australian troops may have been the result of bets or dares. Such acts were the complete antithesis of the Australian cremation of the dead Japanese submariners who died in their attack on Sydney harbour. The Australians returned the ashes of these men to Japan. This act received large and positive media coverage in Japan during the war, due to the reverence that the Japanese give to the departed. As an overlap of such considerations, the extent of Japanese atrocities in this area may need to be questioned as this appears to be one area where some restraints operated. For example, with the Allied prisoners in Thailand and Burma, of the 40,000 who died in captivity, only 1.2 per cent remained unidentified and proper funeral practices appear to have been respected. This was completely unlike the deaths of the local labourers. In terms of desecrating dead enemy combatants it appears that it was more the American soldiers in the Pacific who developed the habit of collecting and dealing in the remains of fallen Japanese soldiers. This was not surprising as dead Japanese soldiers were often left to the elements, or if bulldozers were about, they were pushed into pits. From such remains, body parts were taken and used for, inter alia, unauthorised private possession, public displays or gifted to public institutions. Some of these human remains of Japanese soldiers were held in institutions in the United States well into the twenty-first century.[502]

[500] Capdevilla, L (2006) *War Dead: Western Societies and the Casualties of War* (Edinburgh, Edinburgh University Press) 32, 89, 94. Also, Lord Russell of Liverpool (2002) *Scourge of the Swastika: A Short History of Nazi War Crimes*, 2nd edn (London, Greenhill) 91.

[501] Holland, J (2008) *Italy's Sorrow: A Year of War, 1944–1945* (London, St Martins) 523; Beevor, A (2002) *Berlin: The Downfall 1945* (London, Penguin) 357; Kershaw, I (2008) *Hitler* (London, Allen) 958.

[502] Hastings, M (2008) *Nemesis: The Battle for Japan* (London, Harper) 82, 280, 286, 345; Maguire, P (2001) *Law and War: An American Story* (NYC, Columbia University Press) 132–33; Knightley, P (1975) *The First Casualty* (London, Pan) 149, 293; *Associated Press* (2009) 'Japanese War Bones Being Kept By University' *New Zealand Herald* (22 August 2009, A25); Capdevilla, L (2006) *War Dead: Western Societies and the Casualties of War*

Aside the example noted above of Australia, the bodies of Japanese soldiers were rarely returned to Japan and the Japanese have learnt to live with their memory with the *Yasukuni Shrine* which is situated in Tokyo. This shrine which is dedicated to the spirits of over 2,466,000 soldiers who died fighting on behalf of the Emperor remains highly controversial whenever it is visited by dignatories. This is unlike the shrines built for the Allied soldiers who fought against them, many of which, such as the Dutch, British and Anzacs left their men in the countries they fell. This was unlike the Americans and French who would continue to go to great lengths to repatriate all of their fallen soldiers. The extent that repatriation, let alone burial with a body, has been possible has often been limited by the bodies that have never been found in the Second World War. For example between 10 and 15 per cent of all French soldiers killed in the Second World War remain either missing or unidentified. Likewise, some 78,000 American bodies were never recovered from this conflict, whilst over 20,000 Allied airmen are without known graves.[503]

15. After the Second World War

A. Trials

It was clear from the outset that the tribunals that were created after the Second World War, were going to examine the maltreatment of prisoners as a central concern. Article 6 from the Constitution of the International Military Tribunal stipulated that crimes coming within the jurisdiction of the Tribunal for which there would be individual responsibility, were, inter alia: 'War Crimes: namely, violations of the laws or customs of war. Such violations shall include, but not be limited to, . . . murder or ill-treatment of prisoners of war or persons on the seas.' Similarly, the Allied surrender terms for Japan stipulated that the trial of all war criminals would occur 'including those who have visited cruelties upon our prisoners'.[504]

From such a basis, a number of German commanders, including, amongst others, Nikolaus Von Falkenhorst (1885–1968),[505] Anton Dostler (1891–1945)[506] and Eric Raeder (1876–1960) were all convicted under the Nuremberg trials for having executed Allied commandos.[507] Nuremberg also saw the conviction of German commanders who

(Edinburgh, Edinburgh University Press) 80–81; Bourke, J (2000) *An Intimate History of Killing* (London, Granta) 37–43; de Zayas, A (1989) *The Wehrmacht War Crimes Bureau, 1939–1945* (Nebraska, Nebraska University Press) 157; Rees, L (1999) *War of the Century: When Hitler Fought Stalin* (London, BBC) 118; Beevor, A (1998) *Stalingrad* (London, Penguin) 36; Clark, A (2001) *The Fall of Crete* (London, Cassel) 83; Maga, T (2000) *Judgement at Tokyo* (Kentucky University Press) 90–104, 111; Rees, L (2001) *Horror of the East* (London, BBC) 93–95.

[503] Capdevilla, L (2006) *War Dead: Western Societies and the Casualties of War* (Edinburgh, Edinburgh University Press) 28, 67; Swift, E (2003) *Where They Lay* (NY, Bantam) 6–7; Lambert, M (2005) *Night After Night: New Zealanders in Bomber Command* (Auckland, Harper) 80–81.

[504] Surrender Terms in Brackman, A (1990) *The Other Nuremberg: The Tokyo War Crimes Trials* (Glasgow, Fontana) 35.

[505] UN War Crimes Commission, (1949) Law Reports of the Trials of War Criminals, The Trial of Nickolaus Von Falkenhorst, Case No 61, Vol XI (London, HMSO) 18.

[506] United Nations War Crimes Commission, (1949) The Dostler Case, Case Number 2 in *Law Reports of Trials of War Criminals*, Vol I (London, HMSO) 23.

[507] Davidson, E (1966) *The Trial of the Germans: 22 Defendants at Nuremberg* (NY, Macmillan) 381, 386. See also UN War Crimes Commission (1946) The Trial of Karl Golkel, Case No 30 in *Law Reports of the Trials of War Criminals*, Vol V 40.

argued that they had to kill their prisoners due to military necessity.[508] Those responsible for the massacre of American soldiers in the Ardennes, were also brought to justice in the case of Valentin Bersin, *et al*, as part of the Dachau trials under the auspice of the United States, of whom 43 of the SS soldiers involved were given the death sentence and the other 30 were given long prison sentences.[509] Likewise, those responsible for the machine gunning of the survivors of the *Pegasus* were convicted and sentenced to death.[510] Multiple defendants were also brought to justice for not protecting Allied aircrew who had been forced to parachute into Germany from angry civilians.[511] For the Laconia order, Admirals Doenitz and Raeder were forced to face the Nurermburg Tribunal as this order was, the Allies asserted, in 'breach of the international law of submarine warfare'.[512] Doenitz did not deny his order or that it was contrary to all of the rules that had been re-established between the wars. His defence was that the Allies practiced exactly the same type of warfare. This was successful and he avoided conviction on this count.[513] When dealing with escaping prisoners, the Nuremberg judgements held that although the shooting of prisoners when necessary and in the actual act of escape was lawful,[514] divesting prisoners of their protected status because they were not in their uniforms[515] or the mass killing as occurred with the Sagan escape, was not lawful.[516] The question of whether it was lawful to move prisoners of war in the face of what the Germans believed to be a worsening and forthcoming combat zone was examined in the Berger trial in 1949. The Court found that this action was not illegal, as long as the moving did not put

[508] UN War Crimes Commission (1948) The Trial of Gunther Thiele, Case No 14 in *Law Reports of the Trials of War Criminals*, Vol III (London, HMSO) 56.

[509] War Crimes Office (1948) Case Number 6-24 (*US v Valentin Bersin et al*). This is discussed in Owen, J (2006) *Nuremberg: Evil on Trial* (Kent, Headline) 106–107 and Lord Russell of Liverpool (2002) *Scourge of the Swastika: A Short History of Nazi War Crimes*, 2nd edn (London, Greenhill) 26–27.

[510] Including the ship's engineering officer, Hans Lenz, who was sentenced to life imprisonment; the ship's doctor, Walter Weisspfennig who was executed as was the second in command August Hoffmann. An enlisted engineer, Wolfgang Schwender was sentenced to seven years imprisonment; Owen, J (2006) *Nuremberg: Evil on Trial* (Kent, Headline) 240–41; Davidson, E (1966) *The Trial of the Germans: 22 Defendants at Nuremberg* (NY, Macmillan) 410–12.

[511] UN War Crimes Commission (1948) The Trial of Erich Heyer. Case No 8 in *Law Reports of the Trials of War Criminals*, Vol I (London, HMSO) 89; UN War Crimes Commission (1948) The Trial of Albert Bury. Case No 16 in *Law Reports of the Trials of War Criminals*, Vol III (London, HMSO) 60; UN War Crimes Commission (1949) The Trial of Peter Back. Case No 15 in *Law Reports of the Trials of War Criminals*, Vol III (London, HMSO) 60; UN War Crimes Commission (1948) The Trial of Anton Schosser et al. Case No 17 in *Law Reports of the Trials of War Criminals*, Vol III (London, HMSO) 65; United Nations War Crimes Commission, Trial of Karl Buck and Ten Others. Case Number 29 in *Law Reports of Trials of War Criminals*, Vol V (London, HMSO); Neillands, R (2002) *The Bomber War* (London, Murray) 369. Cf Davidson, E (1966) *The Trial of the Germans: 22 Defendants at Nuremberg* (NY, Macmillan) 83–84, 322, 339.

[512] Proceedings of the Trial of the Major War Criminals Before the International Military Tribunal, Vol 22 (1947) 138–40.

[513] Owen, J (2006) *Nuremberg: Evil on Trial* (Kent, Headline) 241; Gellately, R (2007) *The Nuremberg Interviews* (London, Pimlico). 8–9.

[514] United Nations War Crimes Commission (1949) Trial of Albert Wagner, Case No 75 in *Law Reports of Trials of War Criminals*, Vol V (London, HMSO) 118; and Trial of Richard Bruns, Case No 12, Vol III (London, HMSO); (1947) The Trial of Karl Amberger, Case No 7, Vol I (London, HMSO) 82; (1948) The Trial of Kurt Meyer, Case No 22, Vol IV (London, HMSO) 97; (1948) The Trial of Karl Rauer. Case No 23, Vol IV (London, HMSO) 113; (1949) The Trial of Franz Schonfeld, Case No 66, Vol XI (London, HMSO) 64.

[515] United Nations War Crimes Commission (1945) The Almelo Trial, Case No 3 in *Law Reports of Trials of War Criminals*, Vol I (London, HMSO) 35.

[516] United Nations War Crimes Commission (1947) Trial of Max Wielden and 17 Others. Case No 62 in *Law Reports of Trials of War Criminals*, Vol XI (London, HMSO). Note also the case of Goering, in Owen, J (2006) *Nuremberg: Evil on Trial* (Kent, Headline) 164–65.

the prisoners under greater danger.[517] On the question of torture, the practice of torture of prisoners of war, resistance fighters and/or civilians was held to be illegal in all settings,[518] for as the trial of Herman Klinge (1909–1946) explained; 'torture . . . [wa]s a war crime due to being directly contra to the dictates of humanity and any meaningful public conscience.'[519]

Very similar judgements were reached in the Tokyo War Crimes Trials. In this setting, a number of Class A, but mostly Class B defendants who were indicted for war crimes, including, inter alia, General Tanaka Hisakasu (1889–1947) who was tried for executing allied airmen and Vice Admiral Koso Abe (1892–1947) who had personally supervised the beheading of nine American prisoners of war. Admiral Shigetaro Shimada (1883–1976) was also found guilty for having units under his command that massacred prisoners. General Heitaro Kimura (1888–1948) was executed for being the commander who approved the brutalisation of labour for the Burma railway, as were the Generals Kenji Doihara (1883–1948) and Seishiro Itagaki (1885–1948) for being responsible for prisoner of war camps in Java, Sumatra, Malaya, Borneo and elsewhere. Masaharu Homma (1887–1946) paid with his life for the Bataan death march. General Masao Baba (1892–1947) and Captain Susumi Hoshijima were held responsible for the Sandakan death marches. General Kenryo Sato (1895–1975) was convicted for approving the directives on transport involving prisoners of war, as was Admiral Takasumi Oka, (1890–1973) for issuing the directives allowing the extreme conditions that Allied prisoners of war were transported over the ocean. These 'higher level' trials were supplemented by the prosecutions of hundreds of local commanders and/or their soldiers who were involved in similar war crimes. For example, in the Australian section of these trials, 922 men were tried and 641 were found guilty. Of 148 sentenced to death, 137 were actually executed.[520]

B. The 1949 Geneva Conventions

In the wake of what happened in the Second World War, the international community reassembled in Geneva in 1949 to renew and update the international commitments with regards to the three areas at hand. These were Convention (I) for the Amelioration of the Condition of the Wounded and Sick in Armed Forces in the Field, Convention (II) for the Amelioration of the Condition of Wounded, Sick and Shipwrecked Members of Armed Forces at Sea, and Convention (III) relative to the Treatment of Prisoners of War. By 2010, together with Geneva IV, the total number of State Parties to these conventions was 194, making the Geneva Conventions universally applicable.

[517] This case can be found in Trials of War criminals before the Nuremberg Military Tribunals under Control Council Law (1952) No 10, Vol XIII (Washington DC, US Government Printing Office) 17.

[518] United Nations War Crimes Commission, Trial of Richard Bruns. Case No 12 in *Law Reports of Trials of War Criminals*, Vol III (London, HMSO). Also, (1948) The Trial of Ernst Flesch. Case No 36, Vol VI (London, HMSO) 116.

[519] United Nations War Crimes Commission (1948) Trial of Karl-Han Hermann Klinge. Case No 11 in *Law Reports of Trials of War Criminals*, Vol III (London, HMSO).

[520] United Nations War Crimes Commission (1946) Trial of General Tanaka Hisakasu in *Law Reports of Trials of War Criminals*, Vol VI (London, HMSO) 66; UN War Crimes Commission (1948) The Trial of Harukei Isayama. Case No 32 in *Law Reports of the Trials of War Criminals*, Vol VI (London, HMSO) 60. Also, Maga, T (2000) *Judgement at Tokyo* (Kentucky University Press) 113, 120–29, 158; Brackman, A (1990) *The Other Nuremberg: The Tokyo War Crimes Trials* (Glasgow, Fontana) 454–64.

(i) Prisoners

Geneva III was a clear reflection of what happened to prisoners of war between 1939 and 1945. In addressing such concerns, it became a more substantial document than its 1929 predecessor, containing a total of 143 articles whereas the 1929 Convention had only 97. It also went further in that it was deemed to cover all situations, as such whether the war was internal or external, or if one side did not accept its terms, it still applied.[521] A large number of the 1929 rules were clearly reiterated. The rules prohibiting reprisals against prisoners, the prisoner being under the authority of the capturing government and information exchange were all underlined.[522] The importance of adequate food, medicine and clothing were added to with important differences such as the habitual diet of the prisoner and making sure that those who performed labour got adequate provisions.[523] The goal of keeping the prisoners in good health was added to with the goal that food provisions should also 'prevent loss of weight or the development of nutritional deficiencies'.[524] Rules on transferring prisoners added that it should be done with regard to considerations of safety and adequate food and water being provided.[525] The conditions and places of captivity were more precisely defined in terms of being safe, adequate (in terms of warmth and insulation) and hygienic. Additional rules were added on placement, visibility/marking of camps to prevent their inadvertent bombardment and the provision of air-raid shelters was added.[526] Rules with regard to the labour of prisoners of war were added which ranged from their minimum rates of pay through to the refinement of what appropriate work specifically.[527] For example; 'the removal of mines or similar devices shall be considered as dangerous [prohibited] labour.'[528]

The existing rules were slightly advanced on freedom of religion and the encouragement of sport and intellectual diversions, as well as good, adequate and free access to mail, parcel and other forms of communication. Rules for the distribution of collective relief parcels were elaborated.[529] The principle that it was possible to punish a prisoner for an attempted escape but not execute them upon their recapture was reiterated.[530] Geneva III also focused on the judicial proceedings instituted against

[521] 1949, Art 3.

[522] Geneva III, 1949, Arts 12, 13(3), 42, 69, 70, 91–93, 122–23.

[523] 1949, Art 27.

[524] 1949, Art 26.

[525] 1949, Arts 15, 30, 31, 46–49.

[526] 1949, Arts 15, 19, 22, 23, 25, 29.

[527] The principle that prisoners 'may be required to work for the benefit of the captor's government, according to their rank and condition' was recognised continued throughout the 1949 Convention (Art 49) along with a general recognition that officers are to be given preference for supervision positions (also Art 49). The 1949 Convention (in addition to emphasising safety of the work, adequate training and clothing, the work must not humiliate, and they must be fit enough for it, Art 51, 52 and 55) went further, stipulating that in addition to routine camp administration and maintenance, prisoners could be 'compelled' to work in the non-military related areas of agriculture; industries connected with the production or the extraction of raw materials, and manufacturing industries (with the exception of metallurgical, machinery and chemical industries) public works and building operations which have no military character or purpose; transport and handling of stores; commercial business, and arts and crafts; domestic service; and/or public utility services having no military character or purpose (Art 50). The issue of minimum pay is dealt with in Art 62.

[528] 1949, Art 52.

[529] 1949, Arts 34–38, 71, 72, 76; Annex III, Regulations Concerning Collective Relief.

[530] Successful escapes were defined in Art 91 of the 1949 Convention.

prisoners of which the importance of due process, judicial systems 'which are recognized as indispensable by civilized peoples'[531] was emphasised and although the death penalty was retained, broad limitations on penalties, which could not be 'inhumane, brutal or dangerous', collective or exceed those given to the armed forces of the detaining Power, were agreed.[532] The right to (essentially) complain without threat of punishment, through a nominated person, about internment conditions was re-emphasised.[533] Despite the initial protests of the Soviets, French and British, the Convention also clearly stated the principle that prisoners of war would be released and repatriated without delay after the cessation of active hostilities.[534]

Geneva III emphasised that each side could send missions to the others prisoner of war camps, if agreement between the two sides was reached. If there was disagreement, discussions on matter of concern could take place in a neutral third country, which could be assisted by the ICRC. If the Parties could not resolve the issues, a neutral State or impartial organisation, such as the ICRC, could be utilised to make sure the provisions of the Convention were being applied.[535] This approach was consistent with giving the ICRC a bigger humanitarian role for the protection of prisoners of war and for their relief. Article 125 stated that although recognising that the Detaining Powers may instigate, 'measures which [it] may consider essential to ensure their security or to meet any other reasonable need' the representatives of . . . relief societies, . . . shall receive . . . all necessary facilities for visiting the prisoners, for distributing relief supplies and material.' In this regard; 'the special position of the International Committee of the Red Cross in this field shall be recognized and respected at all times.'[536]

Article 126 added that the ICRC, in addition to representatives or delegates of the Protecting Powers, had:

> [P]ermission to go to all places where prisoners of war may be, particularly to places of internment, imprisonment and labour, and shall have access to all premises occupied by prisoners of war . . . [and] to be able to interview the prisoners . . . without witnesses . . . with only very limited restrictions.

The 1949 Convention made clear, that a bottom line was that all prisoners, without distinction, were to receive humane treatment and were not to be subject to violence to life and person, in particular murder of all kinds, mutilation, cruel treatment and torture.[537] Causing the death or seriously endangering the health of a prisoner of war was not only prohibited, it was to 'be regarded as a serious breach of the present Convention'.[538]

The question of torture was also addressed in both Geneva III and Geneva IV (the latter, dealing with civilians). Both Conventions state in Article 3, in similar wording, that in a non-international armed conflict; 'Persons taking no active part in the hostilities, including members of armed forces who have laid down their arms . . . shall in all circumstances be treated humanely'.[539] The Fourth Convention, dealing with civilians, added that there must not be any:

531 1949, Art 3(d).
532 1949, Arts 20, 21, 39, 41, 45, 63, 66, 82, 84, 87, 88, 90, 99, 100–102, 105–107.
533 1949, Arts 78 and 79.
534 1949, Art 118; Best, G (2002) *War and Law Since 1945* (Oxford, Oxford University Press) 141.
535 1949; Arts 8 and 10.
536 Note also Art 9.
537 1949, Arts 3, 13 and 15.
538 1949, Art 13.
539 Note Art 5 of GC IV.

> Violence to life and person, in particular murder of all kinds, mutilation, cruel treatment and torture [or] outrages upon personal dignity, in particular humiliating and degrading treatment . . . No physical or moral coercion shall be exercised against protected persons, in particular to obtain information from them or from third parties.[540]

These rules on prohibiting the torture of civilians were supplemented by the 1948 Universal Declaration of Human Rights[541] and the International Covenant on Civil and Political Rights which also concurred[542] that 'no-one shall be subjected to torture or to cruel, inhuman or degrading treatment or punishment'.[543] The 1955 United Nations Standard Minimum Rules for the Treatment of Prisoners also helped buttress this area as they set standards on, inter alia, accommodation, clothing, bedding, food, exercise, medical and discipline standards. Of note, they prohibited punishment by placement in a dark cell, close confinement, or reduction of diet without medical approval. It went on to stipulate that hand cuffs, irons, chains or strait jackets could never be used as a punishment but only for safety, transit, medical reasons and so on.[544] With regards to prisoners of war, Geneva III, although iterating the necessity of prisoners to supply serial number and identity card, emphasised that; '[n]o physical or mental torture, nor any other form of coercion, may be inflicted on prisoners of war to secure from them information of any kind whatever.'[545]

Finally, Convention III clearly linked certain abuses of prisoners as types of war-crimes, by which the signatories agreed to undertake legislation to deal with any 'grave breaches' of the Convention, promising to bring any such offenders to justice and not absolving itself (or any other Party) of liability. It defined 'grave breaches' as those:

> [C]ommitted against persons or property protected by the Convention: wilful killing, torture or inhuman treatment, including biological experiments, wilfully causing great suffering or serious injury to body or health, compelling a prisoner of war to serve in the forces of the hostile Power, or wilfully depriving a prisoner of war of the rights of fair and regular trial prescribed in this Convention.[546]

Such matters were to be investigated in a manner agreed by the Parties to the conflict, or an agreed upon umpire.[547]

(ii) Wounded and Defenceless

Geneva Conventions I and II dealt with the question of wounded or sick members of armed forces on land and at sea. The developments with these conventions were not as great as with Convention III, although a great clarity was applied as the 1949 Conventions took the widest possible view of belligerents in need of assistance.[548] Thus

[540] 1949, GC IV, Art 31.

[541] Universal Declaration, Art 5.

[542] GA Res 2200A (XXI), 21 UN GAOR Supp (No 16) at 52, UN Doc A/6316 (1966), 999 UNTS 171, Art 7. Note also Art 10.

[543] Universal Declaration of Human Rights, GA Res. 217A (III), UN Doc A/810 at 71 (1948), Art 5.

[544] As approved by ECOSOC Res 663 C (XXIV) July 1957.

[545] 1949, Art 17.

[546] 1949, Art 130. See also Arts 129 and 131.

[547] 1949, Art 132.

[548] The 1949 Conventions on sick and wounded cover traditional armed forces, militia, volunteer corps, organised resistance movements (which meet the 1907 Hague 4 requirements) civilian persons who accompany the armed forces without actually being members thereof, members of merchant marine and the

the rules were taken to apply, even if a state of war was not recognised by one of the belligerents, whether both sides are signatories to the Convention or not, and irrespective of whether the land is fully or partly occupied. Likewise, the minimum rules for armed conflict not of an international character occurring in the territory of one of the High Contracting Parties, were, with respect to the wounded and sick, that they be treated humanely by being 'collected and cared for' and 'protected in all circumstances'.[549] With regards to the defenceless in the ocean, Article 18 of Geneva II stipulated: 'After each engagement, Parties to the conflict shall, without delay, take all possible measures to search for and collect the shipwrecked, wounded and sick, to protect them against pillage and ill-treatment, to ensure their adequate care.'

The rule on the wounded or the sick being assisted, without distinction, irrespective of nationality or side was re-emphasised.[550] Convention I underlined that 'any attempts upon their lives, or violence to their persons, shall be strictly prohibited'.[551] Reprisals against such peoples were also, once more, strictly prohibited.[552] Rules for the establishment of Mixed Medical Commissions, which can work together on deciding which unwell prisoners should be repatriated were refined,[553] along with the standing rule that civilian local communities on land or at sea (with non-military vessels) may be called upon to assist in this process, and helping the wounded generally, must be done without fear of retribution.[554] The rule on the complete neutrality of (clearly identifiable) medical personnel doing their job of looking after the sick or wounded being 'respected and protected in all circumstances' was reiterated, along with the prima facie rule that these people cannot be made prisoners of war unless required to look after wounded or sick prisoners.[555] The same neutrality for fixed and mobile medical units was reiterated as it was for hospital ships, although in the later instance, the possibilities of inspection and restricted routes and operation methods were also recognised.[556] A clear development was Article 36 which stated:

> Medical aircraft, that is to say, aircraft exclusively employed for the removal of wounded and sick and for the transport of medical personnel and equipment, shall not be attacked, but shall be respected by the belligerents, while flying at heights, times and on routes specifically agreed upon between the belligerents concerned.

crews of civil aircraft of the Parties to the conflict, and inhabitants of a non-occupied territory, who on the approach of the enemy, spontaneously take up arms to resist the invading forces. See Art 13 in both the Land and Sea Conventions.

[549] Geneva I, Arts 2 and 12 1949; Geneva II, Arts 2, 3 and 7.

[550] Geneva I, Arts 3 and 12; Geneva II, Arts 12 and 30. Note also s 3(2) of Geneva Convention III.

[551] Geneva I, Art 12; Geneva II, Art 12.

[552] Geneva I, Art 46; Geneva II, Art 47.

[553] 1949, Arts 112–114; Annex I, Model Agreement Concerning Direct Repatriation And Accommodation In Neutral Countries Of Wounded And Sick Prisoners Of War. Also, Annex II, Regulations Concerning Mixed Medical Commissions.

[554] Geneva I, 1949 Art 4 and Geneva II, Art 21.

[555] Geneva I, Arts 24–27. For Geneva II, see Art 36. In addition, front line medics also require special identify cards. These are assisted by the model card set out in the 1949 Land Convention. See Art 40. Note the rules for medical units attached to the military, if they are not acting outside their humanitarian duties and threatening the enemy They must still be warned first before attacked; 1949, Wounded. Land, Art 21; Art 22 sets down a series of instances which cannot abrogate Art 19. Of note, that they are armed or escorted, or act in their own, of that of their wounded, self-defence. Similar points are listed in the 1949 Wounded Sea. Arts 34 and 35. The 1949 Convention for Wounded and Sick at Sea was built on the 1907 Convention on this point. See Art 8 of the 1907 Document.

[556] Geneva II, Arts 14, 22, 29 and 31. For Geneva I, see Art 20, 30. For the rules on signage, see Art 29 for Geneva II and Arts 19–22 and 24 of Geneva I.

Thus, clearly marked medical aircraft could be used, but it was added, not to fly over enemy territory unless permission was given. Such aircraft were also obliged to 'obey every summons to land' for inspection and examination in enemy-occupied territory. The neutrality of hospitals was also strongly underlined in 1949. In part, this may have been because the bombing of hospitals was a problem that was happening (in the first Indian-Pakistani conflict, along with the capture of combatants and denial of prisoner of war status) as the Geneva Conventions were being negotiated.[557] It was strongly restated that hospitals are protected areas in times of conflict. This protection is to be facilitated by making sure that they are not situated so close to the front lines that their safety is imperilled. The belligerents may exchange information on where their clearly marked hospitals are located so that they are visible to the enemy land, air and/or naval forces, in order to obviate the possibility of any hostile action. The availability for investigation by Special Commissions in accordance with the Convention, to help avoid them becoming areas of conflict was also added. A Draft Agreement Relating to Hospital Zones, in terms of what was permitted in them so as to make them clearly as non-military as possible was annexed to the 1949 Convention. This contained the primary rule, that: 'In no circumstances may hospital zones be the object of attack. They shall be protected and respected at all times by the Parties to the conflict.'[558]

When the topic of the dead soldiers and civilians of opposing forces came up, there was a surprising congruence amongst the Geneva Conventions. Each regime agreed on the importance of looking for the dead, retrieving the bodies, establishing the identity of the dead person, preventing pillage and showing respecting for the dead combatants whether on land, sea or as prisoners of war.[559] Similar obligations were established for civilians who died whilst under occupation. In this last area, there were clear obligations on recording the death, clearly marking the graves and as a show of respect, honour and ensuring that the funerals were carried out accordance with the rites of the deceased. Even if cremation was necessary for hygienic reasons, the ashes were to be retained and returned to the family of the deceased.[560]

Finally it was agreed that with Geneva I and II that:

> Grave breaches . . . shall be those involving any of the following acts, if committed against persons or property protected by the Convention: wilful killing, torture or inhuman treatment, including biological experiments, wilfully causing great suffering or serious injury to body or health . . . not justified by military necessity and carried out unlawfully and wantonly.[561]

As with Geneva Convention III, all Parties were obliged to take action against grave breaches of the conventions. This also involved preventing breaches and making enquiries into breaches of the Convention, possibly with the assistance of a neutral country or the ICRC, and prosecuting those involved with grave breaches.[562]

[557] See Rey-Schirr, C (1998) 'The ICRC's Activities on the Indian Subcontinent Following Partition' *IRRC* 323: 267, 272–91.

[558] Geneva I, Annex 1, Art 11. Note also Arts 6, 7, 8 and 9. For the Arts of importance in Geneva I on this topic, see 19 and 23.

[559] See Arts 15 and 17 of Geneva I. See Art 16, 18 and 20 of Geneva II, and Arts 120 and 121 of Geneva III.

[560] Geneva IV, Artis 129 and 130. Also Froidevaux, S (2002) 'Religious Ritual and Death' *IRRC* 848: 785–801.

[561] Geneva I, Art 50; Geneva II, Art 51.

[562] Geneva I, Artis 8, 10, 49, 51 and 52; 1949, Wounded Sea, Arts 8, 10, 11, 50, 52 and 53.

16. Between 1949 and 1977

The only major international conflict of note that caught the attention of the Security Council before the revisions to the 1949 Geneva Conventions were concluded and the 1977 Additional Protocols were introduced, was the conflict between India and Pakistan in 1971. During this conflict, the Security Council demanded all of the belligerents to 'apply in full the [Geneva Conventions of 1949] provisions as regards the protection of the wounded, sick and prisoners of war'[563] and a negotiated settlement was required for the eventual exchange of prisoners of war, many of whom India accused of war crimes.[564] Outside of this one conflict, the Security Council was silent on this topic. This silence was because in all of the primary conflicts of this period, either one of the permanent members of the Security Council, or one of their close allies, was involved in the fight. As such, via the weight of the veto, topics of prisoners, torture and/or dealing with the wounded and dead, were largely invisible at the highest international levels for the decades following the Second World War.

A. Indo-China

The period between the adoption of the new Geneva Conventions in 1949 and their next update in 1977 was a period of several particularly vicious international and civil wars. The first of these of note was the French–Indo-China war. This raged from the end of the Second World War until 1954, during which time the new Geneva conventions were completed. However, one would be mistaken to assume that it had much influence on this conflict as both sides displayed remarkably inhumane practices. For example, the French were notable for their use of torture in Indo-China via methods which included, inter alia, casual blows, beatings with weapons, water torture and mutilation. Reciprocally, the Viet Mihn dealt with the wounded, prisoners and the dead in ways that were far from progressive. In the first instance, the Viet Minh, despite showing humanity in some instances allowing wounded soldiers to be collected and hospitals left in peace, would also target military hospitals and routinely targeted Red Cross aircraft that attempted to come into land to remove wounded soldiers at strategic locations like Dien Bien Phu. In the second instance, when this location fell, some 10,000 French troops were taken prisoner. These men, including some 4,500 wounded were made to take part in a forced march to camps with limited food and medical supplies. Coupled with harsh treatment, the Viet Mihn succeeded in killing at least 4,100 of these prisoners. Uncertainty is still rife with these statistics as the Viet Mihn refused to provide official lists of casualties or accept lists from the French for confirmation until it suited their purposes. To complete the practice of a lack of humanity, rather than return the bones of fallen French soldiers, they decided to retain the remains of the dead French soldiers and sell them back at a profit to their former enemies.[565]

[563] S/RES/307 (1971, Dec 21).

[564] Bangladesh, Pakistan and India Agreement on the Repatriation of Prisoners of War and Civilian Internees, 13 ILM (1974) 501–505. Also, Agreement on the Repatriation of Prisoners, 12 ILM (1973) 1081.

[565] Windrow, M (2005) *The Last Valley* (London, Cassel) 101, 389, 416, 420–43, 451, 616, 622–25, 647; Rochester, S (2007) *Honor Bound. American Prisoners of War in Southeast Asia 1961–1973* (Annapolis, Naval Press) 16, 21.

B. Korea

One of the few positive features of the Korean war was that the death rate for soldiers evacuated from the battlefield and taken to a medical centre fell to 2.5 per cent. This achievement was because of, inter alia, the wide use of antibiotics, new practices of vascular surgery and much faster evacuation methods, namely, the helicopter. Some 21,658 United Nations soldiers would be evacuated in this way. In terms of time management this meant that at the beginning of the Korean war, only 40 per cent of wounded could expect to reach a hospital the same day. By the end of the war, this had risen to 85 per cent.[566] However, these advances had to be balanced by the practices of the North Korean forces. In this regard, the Red Cross brassard appears to have had little protection for medics in the field during the Korean conflict, with aid stations and regimental stations also being considered prime targets. When Seoul fell North Korean troops entered the university hospital and shot or bayoneted 150 wounded South Korean soldiers. The only redeeming acts in this area occurred just before the 1953 Armistice which concluded when 694 United Nations prisoners who were sick and wounded were exchanged for 6,670 comparable North Korean and Chinese troops.[567]

The North Koreans also paid very little regard to the new, or old, laws on prisoners of war. At the outset of the conflict, despite the United Nations forces expressing a willingness to comply with the Geneva Conventions, the North was silent when asked. However, they later made a declaration to the effect that their forces would abide by the principles of the new Geneva Conventions. It would appear that this declaration was never conveyed to their soldiers as prisoners of North Korea were repeatedly executed when being taken from the battlefield, wounded or not. Unsurprisingly, as the atrocities against the United Nations forces became apparent, the United Nations forces, Americans included, replied in kind. This was especially so with civilian prisoners with suspected communist sympathies. United Nations prisoners taken from the front often had to endure forced marches with minimal food or assistance and, being unmarked, they were often bombed by their own forces. Somewhere between 1,000 and 2,300 men would die on such marches. The camps they were marched to often had inadequate shelter, food and medical attention, at least until China entered the war and began to organise proper prisoner of war camps. However, these Chinese attempts were often of limited success. For example, when partisans attempted to release some 1,700 prisoners in North Korea in 1951, they found that once they had entered into the camp, only 400 of the prisoners were even capable of moving. Although these men were taken away, those who remained were later massacred by Chinese troops. The United Nations troops also came face-to-face with torture in both the Korean wars suffering torture which included castration, the cutting out of tongues and the gouging out of eyes. In addition, the North Koreans and Chinese came to utilise interrogation methods that leave deep psychological wounds but few scars such as sleep deprivation, bright light, temperature and food control, isolation and pain inflicted from stress positions, such as forced standing. Such tactics created dependency

[566] Greenwood, J (2005) *Medics at War: Military Medicine from Colonial Times to the 21st Century* (Annapolis, Naval Institute Press) 8, 99, 104, 123, 125 and 127; Barnett, G 'Caring for the Casualties' *WWII History* (November 2008) 40, 43; Nichol, J and Rennell, T (2009) *Medic* (London, Penguin) 32, 107–108, 127.

[567] Chinnery, P (2000) *Korean Atrocity. Forgotten War Crimes 1950–1953* (Maryland, Naval Institute Press) 3, 20, 91, 120, 161, 198.

and dread on those being tortured. The impact of these tortures was that 70 per cent of American prisoners cooperated with the Chinese and North Koreans.[568]

Collectively, it is possible that up to 57,000 victims, including some 10,233 American soldiers met their deaths at the hands of North Korean or Chinese soldiers after they had surrendered but before they made it to a prison camp. Of those who made it into a camp, an estimated 92,500 prisoners, including 16,000 United Nations troops, died whilst being held. In percentage terms, 38 per cent of American prisoners of war died in North Korean captivity – 2,730 out of a total of 7,190. These numbers could have been greatly reduced had the ICRC been able to utilise its influence as it had successfully in some previous conflicts. However, China refused this because they believed the ICRC was nothing but a 'capitalist spy organisation' trying to use its special privileges to obtain 'strategic intelligence'.[569] Accordingly, although some left-wing British journalists were allowed to visit some of the model camps, there was no independent oversight of the holding on the United Nations troops.[570] The problems that the less than desirable countries of North Korea and China represented at this time were not only problematic to prisoners of war captured under the United Nations flag. That is, a large number of North Korean and Chinese prisoners of war did not want to be repatriated to the country they fought for. The solution to this problem was eventually dealt within the Korean War Armistice. Article III stated:

> Within sixty days after this Armistice Agreement becomes effective, each side shall, without offering any hindrance, directly repatriate and hand over in groups all those prisoners of war in its custody who insist on repatriation to the side to which they belonged at the time of capture.[571]

From this option, four out of five Chinese prisoners and three out of five North Korean prisoners – some 14,325 men or 22 per cent of the total prisoners taken, did not want to be repatriated to their own countries of origin. In terms of the United Nations prisoners, of the non-Korean prisoners, only 22 (21 American and 1 British) elected not to return home. The North Koreans and Chinese only accepted this outcome when the free will and choice of the prisoners became the paramount consideration which was independently verified.[572]

[568] Otterman, M (2007) *American Torture. From the Cold War to Abu Ghraid and Beyond* (London, Pluto) 33; Chinnery, P (2000) *Korean Atrocity. Forgotten War Crimes 1950–1953* (Maryland, Naval Institute Press) 22, 26, 89, 183; Reuters (2008) 'Guantanamo Confession Tactics Copied from Chinese' *New Zealand Herald*, (4 July 2008) A14; Knightley, P (1975) *The First Casualty* (London, Pan) 343–44.

[569] Moorehead, C (1998) *Dunant's Dream: War, Switzerland and the History of the Red Cross* (NYC, Carroll and Graf) 570.

[570] Chinnery, P (2000) *Korean Atrocity. Forgotten War Crimes 1950–1953* (Maryland, Naval Institute Press) 8, 10, 13, 17, 20, 22, 24–26, 32, 36, 45, 52, 57, 70, 79, 88–89, 94, 96, 102, 111, 117, 126, 129, 132, 138, 145, 154, 155, 159, 168, 204, 206; Harclerode, P (2002) *Fighting Dirty* (London, Cassel) 179; Reid, P (1984) *Prisoners of War* (London, Hamlyn) 28–29; Knightley, P (1975) *The First Casualty* (London, Pan) 351; Moorehead, C (1998) *Dunant's Dream: War, Switzerland and the History of the Red Cross* (NYC, Carroll and Graf) 578. Note the ICRC 1952 Conference Resolutions in ICRC (1995) *The Humanitarian Endeavour* (Geneva, ICRC) 171

[571] Art III:51 of the Korean War Armistice in Axelrod, A (ed) (2001) *Encyclopedia of Historical Treaties and Alliances*, Vol II (NYC, Facts on File) 731. Note, many of the principles were derived from UNGA Resolution 610 (VII) Korea (1952).

[572] Bailey, S (1994) *The United Nations Council and Human Rights* (Basingstoke, Macmillan) 61–65; S Reid, P (1984) *Prisoners of War* (London, Hamlyn) 39, 47; Mayda, J (1953) 'The Korean Repatriation Problem and International Law' in *American Journal of International Law* 47, 414.

The final point of note in this conflict was the way the dead were dealt with. The North Korean forces collected the dead and stored them for their tradable value. This was relatively easy to achieve due to the high numbers of soldiers missing in action. At the time of the ceasefire for the Korean war, there were 7,956 unaccounted United Nations soldiers, including 944 men from the United States. The United Nations forces, keen to find out the fate of these men and retrieve their bodies, demanded, and North Korea agreed, to the right for graves registration teams to enter North Korea to recover the remains of United Nations soldiers. However, entry was later refused and the work was done by the North Koreans who returned some remains in 1954. A further 16 sets of human remains were returned to the United States in 1990 and a further 30 sets in 1992. By the mid 1990s a total of 162 sets of human remains, since 1954, had been returned and in all instances the returns coincided with political goals. For example, in 1994 the North Korean demanded and received US$2 million for the return of a few more sets of bones.[573]

C. From Algeria to Israel

The Algerian conflict of 1952 to 1962 between France and the local insurgency was particularly nasty. Prisoners were routinely executed and tortured. This was not particularly unusual in the 1950s and 1960s, as torture was a manifest problem in other countries, such as Greece and Britain's colony of Kenya.[574] The execution and/or torture of prisoners was also common in the wars of Latin America following the Second World War. For example, during the Cuban revolution, dozens of rebels were executed after capture, and Fidel Castro (b 1926) only survived after being captured, when an army officer refused to obey orders to execute them after they had surrendered. Those who were taken alive were often tortured, and then the corpse of the suspected guerrilla or sympathiser was left at some prominent intersection in the city.[575]

In the Algerian conflict, the extent of the torture appears to have surpassed other examples from the period. This was despite the French government publicly announcing that interrogations were to be conducted without physical violence and that 'every offence against human dignity' was 'vigorously forbidden'. Unofficially, in the detention centres special schools were developed to deliver 'humane torture' that did not leave marks, such as water torture or electric shocks. Such acts were not meant to be witnessed by non-military personnel and the administration of the acts was meant to be overseen by an officer who was not a sadist. After the torture, the French army would often display the bodies of the captured along public highways or on military vehicles. Alternately, the bodies would be hidden, so that the tortures committed on them could not be discovered. These practices, which the victorious Algerian authorities went on to practice after the French left, were uncovered by the ICRC which – remarkably – was

[573] Chinnery, P (2000) *Korean Atrocity. Forgotten War Crimes 1950–1953* (Maryland, Naval Institute Press) 210, 211, 213, 263; Rochester, S (2007) *Honor Bound. American Prisoners of War in Southeast Asia 1961–1973* (Annapolis, Naval Press) 22; Swift, E (2003) *Where They Lay* (NY, Bantam) 6–7.

[574] Elkins, C (2005) *Britain's Gulag. The Brutal End of Empire in Kenya* (London, Pimlico) 65–70, 79–87, 96–97, 206–11, 226–27, 249; Anderson, D (2006) 'Surrogates of the State: Collaboration and Atrocity in Kenya's Mau Mau War' in Kassimeris, G (ed) *The Barbarisation of Warfare* (London, Hurst) 159–74; Moorehead, C (1998) *Dunant's Dream: War, Switzerland and the History of the Red Cross* (NYC, Carroll and Graf) 612–15.

[575] Scheina, R (2003) *Latin America's War The Age of the Professional Soldier, 1900–2001*, Vol II (NYC, Brassey) 215, 220, 221, 223.

allowed to visit the detention centres. However, the ICRC reports of these visits were leaked to the press. Soon after, what Jean-Paul Sartre (1905–80) called 'a plague infecting our whole era' lead to a fundamental loss of heart and effort on the part of the French, leading directly to their decision to withdraw from their former colony.[576]

What a number of countries did learn from the Algerian experience, was not that torture was bad, but that ICRC oversight was not necessarily a good thing if you wished to abuse your own citizens and your enemies. Accordingly, the pattern began to emerge whereby countries increasingly restricted, or out-rightly banned, ICRC access. With the communist countries, this process began around the time of the Korean war and was linked to, inter alia, issues such as the recognition of the Republic of China. After the Bay of Pigs in Cuba in 1961, the doors were closed to the ICRC. This closing of doors coincided with the execution of over 100 of the failed invaders. The other 1,113 prisoners were later traded back to the United States for US$53 million in food and medicine. Similarly, although the Soviets did consider allowing the use of the ICRC as independent inspectors in the Cuban Missile crisis, ICRC access to places of detention in Russia or other parts of the Soviet Bloc were refused until the early 1980s and the onset of the Gorbachev era. Doors also closed to the ICRC with non-Soviet countries that were political allies of the west, but had appalling human rights records, such as Argentina, Chile, Greece, Indonesia and Peru.

Other countries which were involved in debates about torture, such as Britain, acted differently. Britain had moved away from blunt forms of torture and had come to utilise the 'enhanced techniques' that the Soviets and Chinese had pioneered. The techniques involved prisoners being forced to stand on the tips of their toes against the wall, having powerfully loud music played at them and/or being deprived of sleep, food and drink. These techniques were challenged at the European Court of Human Rights. The Court found that these acts, even if used cumulatively, were not acts of torture as 'they did not occasion suffering of the particular intensity and cruelty implied by the word torture as so understood'. Nevertheless, these acts were recognised as inhumane and degrading, and were thus prohibited.[577] The other area in which Britain acted differently, was that although they refused to recognise the IRA captives as prisoners of war (despite their hunger strikes) they did place these captives in a special prison and gave them visits by the ICRC – which the IRA did not like because it made the British look good. However, the British did not look so good when it appeared they were operating a policy of taking no prisoners, or at least, making it very hard to surrender, when they got the upper-hand in a number of military operations against the IRA.[578]

[576] Horne, A (2006) *A Savage War of Peace: Algeria 1954–1962* (NYC, New York Review Books) 18–20, 101–102, 172–73, 195–205, 212–13, 232–34; Fisk, R (2006) *The Great War for Civilisation: The Conquest of the Middle East* (London, Harper) 641, 708, 718; Branche, R 'Torture of terrorists? Use of Torture' in a "War Against Terrorism": Justifications, Methods and Effects: the Case of France in Algeria, 1954–1962' in (2007) *International Review of the Red Cross*, 867, 34–56; Moorehead, C (1998) *Dunant's Dream: War, Switzerland and the History of the Red Cross* (NYC, Carroll and Graf) 586–97; Knightley, P (1975) *The First Casualty* (London, Pan) 365; Forsythe, D (2005) *The Humanitarians: The International Committee of the Red Cross* (Cambridge, Cambridge University Press) 60; Capdevilla, L (2006) *War Dead: Western Societies and the Casualties of War* (Edinburgh, Edinburgh University Press) 96.

[577] *Ireland v UK* EHRR. 25. For some of the earlier tortures, see Moloney, E (2002) *A Secret History of the IRA* (London, Penguin) 109, 133.

[578] Burleigh, M (2008) *Blood and Rage. A Cultural History of Terrorism* (London, Harper) 325–28; Moloney, E (2002) *A Secret History of the IRA* (London, Penguin) 12, 144, 177, 189–216; Forsythe, D (2005) *The Humanitarians: The International Committee of the Red Cross* (Cambridge, Cambridge University Press) 60.

Despite the European ruling on torture, this collection of practices became entrenched in other countries having to deal with informal combatants, such as Israel, which also came to utilise sleep deprivation, hooding, loud noises, shaking and so on. These practices were only brought into public view when a number of inmates subjected to such practices died and the techniques were examined by the Supreme Court of Israel. This body agreed that such methods should be prohibited, but the prohibition was not absolute and it depended upon the merits of each case.[579] Nevertheless, Israel, like Britain, has continuously allowed ICRC access to its detainees. Thus, in 2009, some 24,604 detainees were visited in 103 institutions within Israel. This is unlike the situation with some captured Israeli combatants, where ICRC access has been denied. This has been despite Security Council resolutions calling on all of the Parties in the region within the inter-related conflicts to abide by international humanitarian law and allow ICRC access.[580]

A number of exchanges of prisoners whereby one or two Israeli captives are exchanged for hundreds of opposition fighters, has become a practice which has appeared in every decade since the 1950s. In addition, Israel and some of its neighbours have developed the practice whereby the bodies of the dead are also traded. This policy, which can be seen in the 1974 agreement between Israel and Syria,[581] became a practice also utilised by non-State forces, with live prisoners held by Israel being exchanged for the bodies of dead Israeli soldiers. For example, in 2004, 436 living prisoners and the bodies of 59 insurgent fighters were exchanged for the bodies of three Israeli soldiers. In 2008, two Israeli bodies were exchanged for an undisclosed number of Palestinian and Lebanese prisoners and 'dozens of bodies' of Lebanese Hizbollah guerillas.[582]

D. Vietnam

The forces of North Vietnam refused to even consider the prima facie application of the basic rules for prisoners, torture, wounded or the dead until towards the end of the United States involvement in this conflict in 1972–73. The Viet Cong were heirs to the Viet Mihn. As such, they were particularly well schooled and seasoned in all of these questions and knew when to play by the rules, such as with the Sino-Vietnamese war

[579] Supreme Court of Israel, Judgement Concerning the Legality of the General Security Service's Interrogation Methods 38 ILM (1999) 1471; Fisk, R (2006) *The Great War for Civilisation: The Conquest of the Middle East* (London, Harper) 531–32; Otterman, M (2007) *American Torture. From the Cold War to Abu Ghraid and Beyond* (London, Pluto) 12, 29–31, 51, 108; Human Rights Watch (1994) *Torture and Ill-Treatment in the Occupied Territories* (NYC, HRW) 2–16; Human Rights Watch (1992) *Israeli Interrogation Methods Under Fire After Death of Detained Palestinian* (NYC, HRW); Human Rights Watch (1997) *Human Rights Under the Palestinian Authorities* (NYC, HRW) 17–25; Human Rights Watch (1991) *Prison Conditions in Israel and the Occupied Territories* (NYC, HRW) 12–17.

[580] S/RES/237 (1967, June 14); S/RES/316 (1972, June 26); S/RES/317 (1972, July 21); S/RES/436 (1978, Oct 6); S/RES/542 (1983, Nov 23); S/RES/564 (1985, May 31).

[581] Agreement on Disengagement Between Israeli and Syrian Forces 13 ILM (1974) 880.

[582] Reuters 'Military Admits Stealing Body Parts' *New Zealand Herald*, (22 Dec 2009) A17; Blomfield, A 'Freedom May Be In Sight' *New Zealand Herald* (25 Nov 2009) A16; Moore, M (2004) 'Soldier's Burial Ends a Father's Mission' *Guardian Weekly* (5 Feb 2004) 32; Reuters 'Prisoner Swap for Dead POWs' *New Zealand Herald*, (3 June 2008) B4; Reuters 'Mourners Vow Revenge After Deal' *New Zealand Herald*, (17 July 2008) A12; Reuters 'Prisoner Swap Frees Notorious Killer' (*New Zealand Herald* (1 July 2008) A12; Reuters 'Exchange of Prisoners to Go Ahead' *New Zealand Herald*, (27 Jan 2004) B2.

of 1979, which was fought in strict accordance with Geneva I and III. This was the exact opposite of their conflict with South Vietnam and the United States which was not fought in accordance with Geneva I or III. This was because the Viet Cong argued that Geneva III did not apply in this conflict, as a large number of American captives, especially pilots, were criminals and not prisoners of war. This was unlike the behaviour of the governments of the United States and South Vietnam who, in an attempt to ensure that their captives were held in full compliance with Geneva III, allowed ICRC visits to combatants who fulfilled the criteria of combatant by, inter alia, carrying their weapons in the open. There were no comparable ICRC visits in North Vietnam until the end of the conflict.[583]

Prior to 1970, the killing of prisoners by South Vietnamese forces or their American allies, via either intention and/or recklessness was not an uncommon occurrence. The Viet Cong responded in exactly the same manner. Between 1961 and 1964 American prisoners suffered a 50 per cent death rate due to executions as reprisals, failed escape attempts and maltreatments ranging from torture through to years in solitary confinement. Conditions for prisoners held in the jungles of South Vietnam were worse than those of the pilots shot down over North Vietnam. Approximately 20 per cent of those captured in the South perished in captivity, compared to only five per cent in the North. In terms of torture, although Ho Chi Minh (1890–1969) officially banned it, the Viet Cong still managed to beat, twist, drop and suffocate American prisoners of war. In return, captured combatants and interred civilians of North Vietnam suffered, inter alia, non-sanctioned bare knuckle beatings, water torture and possible ejection from airborne helicopters. The taking of Viet Cong prisoners was, in itself, unlikely as a combination of giving no prisoner of war status to non-uniformed combatants, and the ill-treatment of the captured appear to have coincided. This assertion can be gleaned from official statistics. For example, between the beginning of 1966 and the end of 1972, a total of 37,451 prisoners of war were logged. In comparison, during the Korean war, over 170,000 enemy prisoners were captured over a three-year period. Even if they were taken into custody, in Vietnam their protection was often minimal. This was because the South Vietnamese forces, who the captives of the Americans were often handed over to, showed little restraint and openly used threats, physical suffering and mental or psychological torture. The use of torture via water or electricity, was particularly popular.[584]

The North Vietnamese did not provide a list of the prisoners they held until 1973. Although the occasional Red Cross parcel and/or letter from their families reached some of these men, the North Vietnamese authorities denied for most of the conflict that they even held such prisoners. The handing over of the list of prisoners in 1973

[583] Letter of the International Committee of the Red Cross, 4 ILM (1965) 1171; Application of Geneva Conventions in Vietnam, 5 ILM (1965) 124; Forsythe, D (2005) *The Humanitarians: The International Committee of the Red Cross* (Cambridge, Cambridge University Press) 54, 77; Bugnion, F (1995) 'From the End of the Second World War to the Dawn of the Third Millennium: The Activities of the Red Cross During the Cold War' *IRRC* 305: 207–24.

[584] Rochester, S (2007) *Honor Bound. American Prisoners of War in Southeast Asia 1961–1973* (Annapolis, Naval Press) 12, 35, 59, 60, 65, 141–51, 157, 164, 209–210, 216, 228, 230, 243, 248, 254, 264, 305, 344, 363, 460, 485–93; Brenner, S (ed) (2006) *Vietnam War Crimes* (NYC, Greenhaven) 27; Sheehan, N (1998) *A Bright Shining Lie* (London, Pimlico) 102–107, 114–16; Tucker, S (1998) *The Encyclopaedia of the Vietnam War* (Oxford, Oxford University Press) 348, 395; Otterman, M (2007) *American Torture. From the Cold War to Abu Ghraid and Beyond* (London, Pluto) 58–72; Greiner, B (2010) *War Without Frontiers. The USA in Vietnam* (NYC, Vintage) 76–79, 105–107, 156–58, 163–64.

coincided with the Paris Peace Accords of the same year. At this, the ICRC was finally allowed to visit all of the places where all of the detainees were held. From these lists, the ICRC visits and the promise to return all detainees, both 'regular and irregular' some 591 prisoners of war and 25 associated civilians were returned to the United States. These prisoners were the lucky ones. This was particularly so when considering the combatants who were captured in the non-declared conflicts such as those involving Laos, of whom only nine out of at least 300 missing ever returned. Moreover, after the Americans had left, once North Vietnam finally conquered the South, hundreds of thousands, if not over one million people, were rounded up and placed in 're-education' camps. Some of these captives were not released until the late 1980s. In Laos, tens of thousands may have perished in such camps which were once more off-limits to the ICRC.[585]

The treatment of the wounded during the Vietnam war should have been viewed as a success story, as the death rate of wounded soldiers who made it to hospitals was only 2.6 per cent. In large part this was due to the ever-increasing speed with which this was achieved, via air ambulances which got wounded soldiers from the front line to the hospital, on average, in under two hours.[586] However, such progress was not universal as the medics in the front lines, the medical transports and even the hospitals were all targeted at various points in the conflict. Specifically, 1,300 medics and 690 medical corpsmen were killed in action, as were 208 pilots and crew in Red Cross marked helicopters, of which 199 air ambulances were lost. A further 1,653 other air ambulances were hit by hostile fire. At one point in 1968, the death rate of medics was so high, it was anticipated there would be no medics left alive in any of the combat units by the end of their tours of duty. Fixed medical facilities of the United States and South Vietnam were subject to rocket and mortar attacks. However, the bombing and shelling of hospitals of the Viet Cong and North Vietnamese was also recorded as being a somewhat common occurrence.[587]

The final consideration here has to do with the dead. The defilement of enemy dead and/or the collection of body parts as trophies appears to have been a common occurrence by all sides. One American colonel was known for wanting the hearts cut out of the dead Viet Cong to feed his dogs. Conversely, the Viet Cong were known to assassinate civilian opponents, disembowel and decapitate them in full view of a village to demonstrate their primacy in a given area. At the other end of the scale was the problem of the missing, presumed dead. By the time the United States left Vietnam, there were 2,583 service personnel who were unaccounted for. Due to such numbers, a key part of the Paris Peace Accords stipulated that:

[585] United States and the Democratic Republic of Vietnam, Agreement on Ending the War and Restoring Peace in Vietnam and the Protocol on the Return of Captured Military Personnel 12 ILM (1973) 63 Art 9; United States and the Democratic Republic of Vietnam, Agreement on Ending the War and Restoring Peace in Vietnam 12 ILM (1973) 48 Chapter III, Art 8. Also, Protocol on the Return of Captured Military Personnel 12 ILM (1973) 63.

[586] The point about 'average' needs to be underlined, as evacuations depended on each battle. During the Falklands War the wounded were sometimes stuck without evacuation for up to 26 hours.

[587] Nichol, J and Rennell, T (2009) *Medic* (London, Penguin) 6–7; Greenwood, J (2005) *Medics at War: Military Medicine from Colonial Times to the 21st Century* (Annapolis, Naval Institute Press) 139, 140; Glasser, R (2006) *Wounded* (NYC, Braziller) 29–30; Nichol, J and Rennell, T (2009) *Medic* (London, Penguin) 189; Tucker, S (1998) *The Encyclopaedia of the Vietnam War* (Oxford, Oxford University Press) 263; Knightley, P (1975) *The First Casualty* (London, Pan) 396.

> The Parties shall help each other to get information about those military personnel and foreign civilians of the parties missing in action, to determine the location and take care of the graves of the dead so as to facilitate the exhumation and repatriation of the remains, and to take any such other measures as may be required to get information about those still considered missing in action.[588]

From this obligation a Four Party Joint Military Commission was designed to obtain information about missing persons and determine the location of the dead. The Hanoi government created an independent agency which devoted itself to finding the missing in action American troops – but not the 300,000 Vietnamese missing in action from the war. From these searches, in 1980, Hanoi handed over 161 sets of bones. These bones bore traces of chemical preservatives, suggesting that the remains had been warehoused with the purpose of using them for political leverage. However, as the relationship between the United States and communist Vietnam began to thaw, a further 200 sets of remains were returned during the late 1980s. The latter searches and retrievals of American remains was often done with the assistance of American teams who were allowed to deepen their searches in the 1990s. The Communists also handed back remaining bodies to the French who had died during the war in Indo-China, nearly 40 years earlier.[589]

17. The 1977 Additional Protocols

In 1977, after three years of negotiations, the Protocol Additional to the Geneva Conventions of 1949, and relating to the Protection of Victims of International Armed Conflicts (Protocol I) was concluded. By 2010, this Protocol with 102 articles which dealt with everything from civilians to combatants had 170 State Parties. Although not as widely adhered to as the 1949 Conventions, the Protocols reflect a 'trend towards a similarly wide acceptance'.[590]

Protocol I was accompanied by Protocol II, which contained 28 articles, expanding the obligations contained in common Article 3 of the 1949 Geneva Convention, dealing with the protection of victims related to Non-International Armed Conflict.[591]

[588] Paris Peace Accords, Art 8(b). Also, United States and the Democratic Republic of Vietnam, Agreement on Ending the War and Restoring Peace in Vietnam and the Protocol on the Return of Captured Military Personnel 12 ILM (1973) 63 Art 9. On the issue of desecration, see Bourke, J (2000) *An Intimate History of Killing* (London, Granta) 15, 39, 42–43. Also, Greiner, B (2010) *War Without Frontiers. The USA in Vietnam* (NYC, Vintage) 170–73, 222–24.

[589] Swift, E (2003) *Where They Lay* (NY, Bantam) 6–7, 128; Capdevilla, L (2006) *War Dead: Western Societies and the Casualties of War* (Edinburgh, Edinburgh University Press) 66, 87; Tucker, S (1998) *The Encyclopaedia of the Vietnam War* (Oxford, Oxford University Press) 29–30, 179; Knightley, P (1975) *The First Casualty* (London, Pan) 387; Brenner, S (ed) (2006) *Vietnam War Crimes* (NYC, Greenhaven) 28–29; Rochester, S (2007) *Honor Bound. American Prisoners of War in Southeast Asia 1961–1973* (Annapolis, Naval Press) 282–83, 290–91, 588–89.

[590] UNGA Resolution (2006) 61/30 Status of the Protocols Additional to the Geneva Conventions of 1949.

[591] Protocol II which developed and supplemented Art 3 common to the Geneva Conventions of 1949 was designed to apply to all armed conflicts which are not covered Protocol I 'and which take place in the territory of a High Contracting Party between its armed forces and dissident armed forces or other organized armed groups which, under responsible command, exercise such control over a part of its territory as to enable them to carry out sustained and concerted military operations and to implement this Protocol. Protocol II did not apply to situations of internal disturbances and tensions, such as riots, isolated and sporadic acts of violence and other acts of a similar nature, as not being armed conflicts'. See Art 1.

With regards to prisoners of war, although most of the focus was on fighters who could, and could not claim prisoner of war status, Protocol I went right back to basics and restated the most fundamental rule. Namely 'it is prohibited to order that there shall be no survivors, to threaten an adversary therewith or to conduct hostilities on this basis'.[592] Protocol II, added a similar fundamental rule, in that although it did not deal with questions of prisoner of war status, it was nevertheless stipulated:

> All persons who . . . have ceased to take part in hostilities, whether or not their liberty has been restricted, are entitled to respect for their person, honour and convictions and religious practices. They shall in all circumstances be treated humanely, without any adverse distinction. It is prohibited to order that there shall be no survivors.[593]

Protocol I added that that when persons entitled to protection as prisoners of war had fallen into the power of an adverse Party under unusual conditions of combat which prevented their evacuation, they must be released and all feasible precautions must be taken to ensure their safety.[594] The other development from Protocol I was that it was agreed that it was a grave breach of the Protocol to be involved in the 'unjustifiable delay in the repatriation of prisoners of war'.[595]

Torture, which had become a topic of interest with both the General Assembly[596] and the Security Council, with particular regard to the apartheid regime of South Africa (which also practiced enforced disappearances)[597] was also addressed in the Additional Protocols. Protocol I, emphasised as a fundamental guarantee of the instrument that 'persons who are in the power of a Party to the conflict' (assuming they are not already given greater protection) would be 'treated humanely in all circumstances'. Accordingly, corporal punishment, mutilation and 'torture of all kinds, whether physical *or mental*' (my italics) was explicitly prohibited.[598] Protocol II, added that 'cruel treatment such as torture, mutilation or any form of corporal punishment' is prohibited at all times and in all places.[599] The importance of the Protecting Power and the ICRC was again emphasised in Protocol I with Parties being obliged to grant the ICRC access (if there was no Protecting Power) 'within their power' to enable them 'to carry out the humanitarian functions assigned to [them]'.[600] In Protocol II, although the importance of 'relief actions for the civilian population which are of an exclusively humanitarian and impartial nature' was recognised, it was clear that any such action could only 'be undertaken subject to the consent of the High Contracting Party concerned'. Outside of this point, there was no substantial recognition of the potential role of the ICRC. This

[592] 1977, Protocol 1, Art 40.
[593] 1977, Protocol II, Art 4.
[594] 1977, Protocol 1, Art 40(3).
[595] 1977, Protocol 1, Art 85(4)(b).
[596] The UNGA Declaration on the Protection of All Persons From Being Subjected to Torture and Other Cruel, Inhuman or Degrading Treatment of Punishment, UNGA Res 3452 (XXX) Dec 9, 1975. Importantly, 'exceptional circumstances such as a state of war or a threat of war, internal political instability or any other public emergency may not be invoked as a justification of torture or other cruel, inhuman or degrading treatment or punishment'. Art 3.
[597] S/RES/417 (1977, Oct 31). The 'established practice' of torture in apartheid lead South Africa between 1960 and 1990, was a combination of forms of suffocation, electric shock, enforced posture and forms of psychological torture. See Truth and Reconciliation Commission (2003) *South Africa Report* (Cape Town, TRC) 618–29.
[598] 1977 Protocol 1, Art 75 (2)(i).
[599] 1977 Protocol II, Art 4.2(a).
[600] 1977 Protocol 1, Arts 5, 81.

was consistent with Article 3 which was common to the four 1949 Geneva Conventions, which dealt with non-international armed conflicts and situations of internal violence. In these situations, the ICRC is encouraged to offer its services to visit detainees. However, the countries involved are by no means obliged to accept such offers.

The 1977 Protocols expanded their scope with considerations of persons who were *hors de combat*.[601] The best example of this expansion was with occupants of aircraft who were not airborne troops. Specifically 'no person parachuting from an aircraft in distress shall be made the object of attack during his descent'.[602]

With regard to more traditional settings, such as dealing with the wounded, sick and/or shipwrecked, the obligation to help, without discrimination, was strongly reiterated in both Protocol I and II 'to the fullest extent practicable and with the least possible delay'.[603] Protocol II, dealing with non-international conflicts, was particularly clear:

> All the wounded, sick and shipwrecked, whether or not they have taken part in the armed conflict, shall be respected and protected. In all circumstances they shall be treated humanely and shall receive to the fullest extent practicable and with the least possible delay, the medical care and attention required by their condition. There shall be no distinction among them founded on any grounds other than medical ones.[604]

The obligation to help was buttressed by the strong obligation to search for the sick, wounded or shipwrecked and collect them up after a conflict 'without delay' so far as military conditions permit.[605] The neutrality of (clearly identifiable) medics and other medical staff was reiterated in both Protocols along with the prima facie rule that they should not be made prisoners of war unless absolutely necessary to care for prisoners.[606] Similarly: 'fixed establishments and mobile medical units of the Medical Service may in no circumstances be attacked, but shall at all times be respected and protected by the Parties to the conflict.'[607]

The rule of not targeting Red Cross transport mechanisms explicitly included carefully marked medical aircraft which could not be used for military purposes.[608] So as to ensure the good faith of both sides with such transport mechanisms, the importance of notifying the opposition in advance if flying over their territory and stopping for inspection if required was iterated. It was added that failure to respond to calls to stop for inspection was deemed 'an act harmful to the enemy'.[609] Attacking the

[601] According to the 1977 Protocol 1, Art 40(2) a person is *hors de combat* if they are non-hostile and do not attempt to escape and: (a) he is in the power of an adverse Party; (b) he clearly expresses an intention to surrender; or (c) he has been rendered unconscious or is otherwise incapacitated by wounds or sickness, and therefore is incapable of defending himself.

[602] 1977 Protocol 1, Art 42(1). Moreover, upon reaching the ground in territory controlled by an adverse Party, a person who has parachuted from an aircraft in distress shall be given an opportunity to surrender before being made the object of attack, unless it is apparent that he is engaging in a hostile act.

[603] 1977 Protocol 1, 8(1), 9(1) and 10(2). See also Art 20 on reprisals.

[604] Art 7.

[605] 1977 Protocol II, Art 8.

[606] 1977 Protocol 1, Arts 12(3) and 15, 16 and 18; Protocol II, Arts 9 and 10.

[607] Medical transports are defined in the 1977 Protocol 1. See Arts 8 (7)–(10), 12, 18, 21. For hospital ships, Arts 22 and 23. Note the importance of conveying information of whereabouts. Also, Protocol II, Art 11.

[608] 1977 Protocol 1 Arts 24 and 28.

[609] 1977 Protocol 1 Art 23. Also, Arts 25–27, 29–31. Note, these aircraft may be requested to land to be inspected. If they refuse, and are forced to land in enemy territory, the sick and wounded shall become prisoners of war. However, if it is voluntary, and the aircraft is meeting its humanitarian objectives and act-

protected people, in terms of either those who were *hors de combat* or those trying to help them (including their transport methods and fixed locations) was recognised as a grave breach of Protocol 1.[610]

With regards to dealing with the dead, the obligation to search for the dead as soon as possible after a conflict and decently dispose of them was recognised in both Protocols.[611] Although the extension of the principle of respect by preventing despoliation was important for its linkages into non-international wars, it was the recognition in Protocol I that the general principle in this area was 'prompted mainly by the right of families to know the fate of their relatives'.[612]

This was the first time, all of the obligations in this area were clearly linked to the interests of the relatives of the deceased. As such, additional considerations such as facilitated access to gravesites were agreed, and most notably, the obligation to 'Facilitate [the] return of the remains of the deceased and of personal effects to the home country upon its request or, unless that country objects, upon the request of the next of kin'.[613]

18. Towards the End of the Cold War

The Khmer Rouge ruled over Cambodia between 17 April 1975 and 6 January 1979. In this instance, there was never any question of applying the Hague or Geneva Conventions, let alone the Protocols that were concluded during the height of this regime. Soldiers of the original regime which was defeated could expect execution, not prisoner of war status. The ICRC was expelled from the country and torture became part and parcel of the regime. In some camps such as Tuol Sleng or S-21, only 2–5 per cent of the prisoners who entered the camp survived the barbarity and tortures that claimed some 15,000 victims. Even the dead were denied any form of respect, with the Khmer Rouge going so far as to forbid cremations (the preferred method of disposal for Buddhists) in their attempt to break the values of the past, insisting that the dead be left in the mud.[614] Although the Khmer Rouge did not respect international humanitarian law, when they were overthrown, it was brought to them through the Extraordinary Chambers in the Courts of Cambodia.[615] These Chambers were designed to bring to trial senior leaders of the Khmer Rouge and those who were most responsible for the crimes and serious violations of international humanitarian law and custom, and international conventions as recognised by Cambodia at the time the

ing within the rules, then following inspection the aircraft shall be authorised to continue the flight without delay. Note the good practice in this area with regards to hospital ships in the 1982 Falklands War whereby both the United Kingdom and Argentina agreed to establish was known as the 'Red Cross Box' on the high seas to the North of the islands. This enabled hospital ships from both sides to hold position and exchange wounded soldiers throughout the conflict.

610 1977 Protocol I, Art 85.

611 1977 Protocol II, Art 8.

612 1977 Protocol I, Art 32.

613 1977 Protocol 1, Art 34 (2)(c).

614 Kiernan, B (2002) *The Poll Pot Regime* (New Haven, Yale University Press) 48–49, 55, 225, 232; Courtois, S, et al (1999) *The Black Book of Communism. Crimes, Terror, Repression* (Massachusetts, Harvard University Press) 582, 604–605, 613–615; Forsythe, D (2005) *The Humanitarians: The International Committee of the Red Cross* (Cambridge, Cambridge University Press) 79.

615 See the Law on the Establishment of the Extraordinary Chambers, with inclusion of amendments as promulgated on 27 October 2004 (NS/RKM/1004/006).

Khmer Rouge took power. These conventions covered crimes of war, as derived from the commission of grave breaches of the Geneva Conventions of 1949, such as, inter alia, crimes of war against prisoners of war or crimes against humanity, of which torture was a crime in both contexts. Accordingly, the man who ran S-21, Guek Eav Kaing (also known as 'Duch') (b 1949) would be the first to appear before the Extraordinary Chambers. After his promotion from Deputy-Secretary to Chairman and Secretary of S-21 in March 1976, Duch allegedly continued to personally oversee the interrogation of the most important prisoners and to be ultimately responsible for this entire institution. For these acts, Duch was indicted for crimes against humanity and grave breaches of the Geneva Conventions of 1949.[616]

Four other regimes had a similar time period, overlapping part of the 1970s, the creation of the Additional Protocols, and a few years after. The first of these was during the Indonesian occupation of East Timor during which between 1974 and 1999 approximately 18,600 unlawful killings and enforced disappearances occurred. Some 70 per cent of these were perpetuated by the Indonesian security forces, including East Timorese auxiliaries. There were also 25,000 reported cases of torture in this time period. This torture was particularly blunt, involving the victims being beaten, whipped or cut.[617] Similar practices also occurred in Guatemala and El Salvador where torture, extra-judicial executions and disappearances were common occurrences. Even the targetting of hospitals and execution of medical workers was recorded in El Salvador's civil war.[618] In Peru, torture and enforced disappearances were standard practices against the Shining Path insurgents. In this regard, between 1987 and 1990 some 884 people disappeared in Peru after being taken into military bases for interrogation. At this point of history, this was more disappearances than in any other country in the world. These disappearances were supplemented, in some instances, with a policy of executions. For example, when Shining Path prisoners rioted at two institutions in 1986, the recapturing of the prisons was sealed with the killing, after the prisoners had surrendered, of between 300 and 1,000 men. The Shining Path then reciprocated in kind when it captured government soldiers.[619]

The other three pro-western countries where torture was a particular problem during this period were Chad, Chile and Argentina. In the first instance, Hissene Habre (b 1942) who ruled Chad from 1982 until 1990 was allegedly responsible for the torture and murder of 40,000 of his own citizens.[620] Forcing Senegal, where Habre has been residing since fleeing Chad, to prosecute him in accordance with their obligations under

[616] Extraordinary Chambers in the Courts of Cambodia: Provisional Detention Order Against Kaing Guek Eav 46 ILM (2007) 911. Within the Chambers, see Case File No 001/18-07-2007/ECCC-TC. For the law in question, see the Law on the Establishment of the Extraordinary Chambers, with inclusion of amendments as promulgated on 27 October 2004 (NS/RKM/1004/006), Arts 5 and 6.

[617] Commission for Reception, Truth and Reconciliation Timor-Leste (2005) *Chega!* (CRTP, Faber) 54–72, 65–107.

[618] Historical Clarification Commission (1999) *The Guatemala Memory of Silence* (Guatemala) 80–93; Report of the United Nations Truth Commission on El Salvador, S/25500 (1 April 1993) 87–91, 101–10.

[619] The Peruvian Truth and Reconciliation Commission (2003) *Final Report* (Lima) 36, 46, 54; Strong, S (1992) *Shining Path* (NYC, Fontana) 132–43, 146–47; Scheina, R (2003) *Latin America's War. The Age of the Professional Soldier, 1900–2001*, Vol II (NYC, Brassey) 367–70.

[620] Allegedly, Habre was responsible for over 40,000 political murders. See Human Rights Watch (2006) *The Trial of Hissene Habre* (NYC, HRW) 7–14, 17–23; Human Rights Watch (2006) *The Case Against Hissene Habre* (NYC, HRW) 3–9; Human Rights Watch (2005) *Chad: The Victims of Hissene Habre Still Awaiting Justice* (NYC, HRW).

the Torture Convention, has been the subject of international dispute with International Court of Justice.[621] In the second instance, under the regime of Augusto Pinochet (1915–2006), the *Chilean Commission for Truth and Reconciliation* concluded that 1,198 people were 'forcibly taken and disappeared'. The second commission on the events within Chile, the *National Corporation for Reparation and Reconciliation* put the figure higher at 3,129 – although the breakdown of how victims of both sides died, included death being delivered by more than just enforced disappearances.[622] The figures in Chile were smaller than the 8,960 cases of 'forced disappearances' that the Argentine *National Commission on Disappearance* recorded.[623] This act of making a person 'disappear' was the most common method of repression adopted by the secret security services of Argentina in their war against left-wing insurgents. That is, someone would be captured, usually by an anonymous member of the security services, from which there would be a systematic denial from all levels of the state security or legal bodies of any knowledge about them. The detained were tortured, killed and their bodies disposed of in any way other than allowing its location and identity to be confirmed. Relatives or lawyers would be repeatedly told that these people were not being held in official custody. In the seven years of military dictatorship, only one *habeas corpus* writ was filed successfully.[624]

In addition to murder and enforced disappearances, both Chile and Argentina were plagued by the practice of torture. In Argentina, thousands of people who disappeared and others who survived, were tortured in one of 365 secret torture centres where suspects were submitted to beatings, electrocutions and 'an immense display of the most degrading and indescribable acts of degradation'.[625] Similarly, under the dictatorship in Chile, an estimated 30,000 Chilean (and non-Chilean) citizens were subjected to torture. Moreover, these two countries, in addition to Brazil, Bolivia and Paraguay developed the first systematic practice of a secret trade in prisoners to different, cross-border interrogation centres, through what was known as Operation Condor.[626] In all of these instances, ICRC access to places of detention was only re-established after most, if not all, of the damage had been done. Thus, in Chile, the ICRC was restricted in its access to military detention centres from the time of the coup in 1973 until 1989, whilst in Argentina, renewed access was not granted until three years after the coup. Augusto Pinochet narrowly avoided indictment for crimes against humanity which turned primarily on 94 counts of torture of Spanish citizens who were resident in Chile at the time of his tenure, through a complex series of cases in Britain at their House of Lords[627] and High Court.[628]

621 See the ICJ deliberations in 2009 on the Case of Questions Relating to the Obligation to Prosecute of Extradite (*Belgium v Senegal*).

622 Human Rights Watch (2003) *The Discreet Path to Justice? Chile, Thirty Years After the Military Coup* (NYC, HRW).

623 Judgement on Human Rights Violations By Former Military Leaders, 26 ILM (1987) 317; Capdevilla, L (2006) *War Dead: Western Societies and the Casualties of War* (Edinburgh, Edinburgh University Press) 99, 101.

624 The National Commission of Argentina on Disappeared People (1986) *Nuncas Mas* (London, Faber) x–xv, 10–11, 215–41.

625 The National Commission of Argentina on Disappeared People (1986) *Nuncas Mas* (London, Faber) 18–51, 60–63; Judgement on Human Rights Violations By Former Military Leaders, 26 ILM (1987) 317.

626 See the Report of the Chilean National Commission on Truth and Reconciliation (2002) reprinted by the United States Institute of Peace, Washington) 997–1010; Dinges, J (2005) *The Condor Years* (NYC, New Press) 14, 64–67, 99–100.

627 37 ILM (1998) 1302. Also, 38 ILM (1999) 432 (on bias of the Judge, due to Amnesty links).

628 38 ILM (1999) 70. Also, 38 ILM (2000) 135.

In the Soviet–Afghanistan war of 1979 to 1989, the killing of prisoners, by both sides, was common. With the insurgents, often there was a perfunctory trial and if they were found to be communists they would be executed. Hundreds, if not thousands, of Soviet soldiers died from such processes. One of the leaders of the Afghani insurgency, Ahmad Shah Massoud (1953–2001) explained when asked why no Soviet soldiers were in his prisons: 'hatred for the Russians is just too great. Many mujahedin have lost their families or homes through communist terror. Their first reaction when coming across a Russian is to kill him.'[629] In some instances, the killing of prisoners was done with gratuitous violence, such as by skinning their captives alive and leaving them to suffer excruciating deaths. However, around 400 prisoners were kept alive (most of whom converted to Islam to save their lives). Although the Soviet authorities argued that there were no missing Soviet soldiers at the end of the conflict, dozens of these men began to turn up in the 1990s in Afghanistan and Pakistan, when some of these men tried to be repatriated.[630]

During the conflict, the Soviet forces replied in kind, torturing and executing hundreds of captured Mujhadeen. If combatants were lucky enough to be taken alive as a prisoner, the chances of any type of ICRC oversight of basic prisoner of war rights was remarkably slim, as the Afghan government and its Soviet allies refused to allow ICRC access or help with prisoner exchanges (of which only a few ad hoc instances occurred). Although the Mujhadeen allowed some limited ICRC access to prisoners they transferred to their camps in Pakistan, such visits were minimal and could do little to improve conditions that were far from adequate. This war also saw forms of blunt torture such as electric shocks, near strangulation, beatings, kicking, biting, hair pulling, exposure to the elements and deprivation of food, water and sleep. The torture and execution of prisoners continued in the civil war that continued when the Soviet Union left the country in 1989.[631]

The Iranian revolution of 1979 also saw high degrees of ferocity against each other's combatants. After the change of administration, and before the ICRC gained access to the jails, a large number of former Shah soldiers and sympathisers were convicted and executed for fighting against the revolution and/or because of their crimes of 'corruption on earth' and 'a battle against God'.[632] Iraq would follow suit, also executing tens of thousands of their own dissidents, with little restraint.[633] Soon after, Iran and Iraq locked heads and did not break away for eight years. Although Iran and Iraq had both signed the Geneva III, neither side strictly abided by their international obligations which ended up causing distress for the 100,000 Iraqi and 50,000 Iranian prisoners who only had limited ICRC visits. Moreover, repatriation of many of these

[629] Massoud in Coll, S (2005) *Ghost Wars* (London, Penguin) 117.

[630] Feifer, G (2009) *The Great Gamble, The Soviet War in Afghanistan* (NYC, Harper) 108–109, 181, 187, 201, 262–94.

[631] Feifer, G (2009) *The Great Gamble, The Soviet War in Afghanistan* (NYC, Harper) 147–49, 172–73; Human Rights Watch (1988) *Violations of the Laws of War in Afghanistan By All Parties to the Conflict* (NYC, HRW) 2, 3, 40–47, 51–57, 63–68; Human Rights Watch (1991) *The Forgotten War* (NYC, HRW) 5–7; Fisk, R (2006) *The Great War for Civilisation: The Conquest of the Middle East* (London, Harper) 214.

[632] Fisk, R (2006) *The Great War for Civilisation: The Conquest of the Middle East* (London, Harper) 127, 129–31, 135.

[633] Fisk, R (2006) *The Great War for Civilisation: The Conquest of the Middle East* (London, Harper) at 159, 186, 212, 244, 280, 336–37, 339; Totten, S (2004) *Century of Genocide* (London, Routledge) 376–78; Human Rights Watch (2003) *Iraq: The Mass Grave of Al-Mahawil: The Truth Uncovered* (NYC, HRW) 4–8; Human Rights Watch (1992) *Unquiet Graves: The Search for the Disappeared in Iraqi Kurdistan* (NYC, HRW) 3–15.

prisoners, despite strong dictates of the Security Council, did not end until over a decade after the conflict ended. Iraq continued these poor practices with their invasion of Kuwait in 1990, refusing to allow ICRC access. This approach was consistent with the Iraqi treatment of enemy soldiers in 1991 and 2003 who were subject to public exposure, used as shields, and tortured.[634] Although there were questions about the failures of Coalition forces to pass on information about Iraqi dead after the first Gulf war ended, there were no substantive concerns pertaining to the treatment or repatriation of the 70,000 Iraqi prisoners of war. This was unlike more than 600 Kuwaiti prisoners taken by Iraq who never returned from Iraq.[635] Accordingly, the Security Council, was forced to request Iraq to, inter alia, 'immediately release under the auspices of the International Committee of the Red Cross . . . or Red Crescent societies or return the remains of any deceased Kuwaiti and third State nationals'.[636]

19. The 1984 Convention Against Torture

All of the above conflicts helped strengthen international opinion that stronger rules in some areas were required. This was most obvious with regards to torture. This need was due to what the ICRC saw as an 'alarming degree' in which torture had become practiced in many countries. Accordingly, they recommended a specific convention on the prohibition of torture and all of its forms.[637] The eventual result of such concerns was the United Nations Convention against Torture and Other Cruel, Inhuman or Degrading Treatment or Punishment. By 2010 there were 146 State Parties to this Convention, and it (like its associated Protocol) has received continual support and overview from the General Assembly, who have consistently attempted to draw to international attention, situations of torture in times of war and times of peace.

Torture was defined in the Convention Against Torture as:

> [A]ny act by which severe pain or suffering, whether physical or mental, is intentionally inflicted on a person for such purposes as obtaining from him or a third person information or a confession, punishing him for an act he or a third person has committed or is suspected of having committed, or intimidating or coercing him or a third person, or for any reason based on discrimination of any kind, when such pain or suffering is inflicted by or at the instigation of or with the consent or acquiescence of a public official or other person acting in an official capacity. It does not include pain or suffering arising only from, inherent in or incidental to lawful sanctions.[638]

In the twenty-first century, the most common and prevalent form of torture worldwide in both developed and under-developed countries was beating. Professional torturers in

[634] Department of Defence Report to Congress on the Conduct of the Persian Gulf War, 31 ILM (1992) 612, 630; Bin, A (1998) *Desert Storm. A Forgotten War* (Westport, Prager) 48, 117; Human Rights Watch (1991) *POWs, Wounded and Killed Soldiers* (NYC, HRW) 10–15; Forsythe, D (2005) *The Humanitarians: The International Committee of the Red Cross* (Cambridge, Cambridge University Press) 103, 106; Dombey, D 'Iran and UK Seek to Calm Row Over Captives' *Financial Times* (31 March 2007) A7.

[635] See Department of Defence Report to Congress on the Conduct of the Persian Gulf War, 31 ILM (1992) 612. Also, S/RES/ 686 (1991, Mar 2); Fisk, R (2006) *The Great War for Civilisation: The Conquest of the Middle East* (London, Harper) 810, 850–51, 853.

[636] S/RES/ 686 (1991, Mar 2). Also, S/RES/1284 (1999, Dec 17).

[637] ICRC 1971 and 1981 Conference Resolutions in ICRC (1995) *The Humanitarian Endeavour* (Geneva, ICRC) 181 and 183.

[638] Torture Convention, Art 1.

some countries used what were noted above as 'enhanced techniques' that can be directly traced to the practices of the 50 years before this Convention was created. These techniques, such as electric shock, asphyxiation, heat, cold, noise, and sleep deprivation which leave little physical evidence of impact but may cause long term psychological damage, have retained their attraction to those who wish to inflict gratuitous pain on other human beings. In addition to damaging the victim via the violation of one of the most fundamental of all human rights, such acts also damage the torturer, the culture of the society that surrounds them and often produce information of a dubious quality.[639]

Nevertheless, many countries, such as the United States view 'enhanced techniques' as legitimate interrogation methods and not as torture if they do not cause *severe* mental or physical pain.[640]

The broad obligation of the 1984 Convention was that each Party was to ensure that torture was prohibited within its territory and to take effective legislative, administrative, judicial or other measures to prevent such acts in any territory under its jurisdiction.[641] The prohibition against torture was found to exist in both times of conflict and times of peace. Thus: 'No exceptional circumstances whatsoever, whether a state of war or a threat or war, internal political instability or any other public emergency, may be invoked as a justification of torture.'[642] Exceptional circumstances has subsequently been interpreted to include combatting terrorism. Thus, even in extreme situations, fundamental human rights still exist, and therefore torture can never be justified in the opinion of the General Assembly.[643]

It was agreed with the Convention in Article 3(1) that,'No State Party shall expel, return ("refouler") or extradite a person to another State where there are substantial grounds for believing that he would be in danger of being subjected to torture.' The term which is usually utilised with regards to the expulsion, return or extradition of a captive to a place of torture is 'rendition'. In law, rendition is a 'surrender' or 'handing over' of persons or property, particularly from one jurisdiction to another. For criminal suspects, extradition is the most common type of rendition. Rendition can also be seen as the act of handing over, after the request for extradition has taken place. Extraordinary or irregular rendition is distinct from both deportation and extradition, being inherently illegal as it may be used to avoid international obligations such as those under the Convention Against Torture. This is because suspects are taken to countries where torture during interrogation remains common, thus circumventing the protections the captives would enjoy in nations who abide by the terms of the Convention. Suspects who are illegally rendered are also denied due process because they are often arrested without charge (so as to avoid a paper trail of where they are and to prevent claims of *habeas corpus*), and deprived of legal counsel, visits or oversight by the ICRC. This act of disappearing makes the practice of torture very easy to achieve.

[639] Robbins, I 'We Have Ways . . .' *New Scientist* (20 Nov 2004) 44–53; Editor 'Modern Barbarity' *New Scientist* (23 Feb 2008) 3, 44–45; Aldhous, P 'The Grim Aftermath of Torture' *New Scientist* (24 Feb 2007) 13; Vinar, M (2007) 'Civilization and Torture' *IRRC* 137–53; Reyes, H (2007) ' The Worst Scars' 867 *IRRC* 124–36; McDonald, P (1993) *Make Em Talk: Principles of Military Intelligence* (London, Paladin) 17–21.

[640] Otterman, M (2007) *American Torture. From the Cold War to Abu Ghraid and Beyond* (London, Pluto) 109.

[641] UNCAT, Art 2.1.

[642] UNCAT, Art 2.2.

[643] UNGA Resolution (2010) 64/153 Torture and Other Cruel, Inhuman or Degrading Treatment of Punishment; UNGA Resolution (2010) 64/168 Protection of Human Rights and Fundamental Freedoms While Countering Terrorism; 63/185 (2009); 61/153 (2007); 60/148 (2006).

Under the Convention, if the victim, location or perpetuator of the torture is from a given State, that State should seek jurisdiction over the offences of torture in question. Moreover, they should take the alleged perpetrator into custody, and although it is not obligatory, should – in essence – look favourably upon extraditing the perpetuator in question if they are from another country. If this is not done, then at the very least, they should assist other States looking into such matters and stringently investigate – and deal with as appropriate, all proven violations of the Convention.[644] The Parties to this Convention also agreed to provide reports to a Committee which was established under the Convention to examine issues of concern related to the regime, investigate allegations of systematic torture and hear complaints from individuals about violations of the Convention by a Party.[645]

Following the conclusion of the United Nations Convention Against Torture, the General Assembly passed two 'basic principle' documents for the humane treatment of all prisoners,[646] and two notable regional conventions on torture were also adopted. These were the Inter-American Convention to Prevent and Punish Torture[647] and the European Convention for the Prevention of Torture and Inhuman or Degrading Treatment or Punishment.[648] The European Convention was supplemented by the European Prison rules, which contained a number of explicit prohibitions which could be construed as torture, such as placement in a dark cell, use of chains and irons and so on.[649] The fundamental difference between the United Nations Convention and the regional instruments, and the European one in particular, was the facilitation of independent inspections into places of incarceration so as to ensure compliance with the rules.[650] Due to such differences, and recognising that independent inspections must be facilitated if torture is to be prevented, Costa Rica proposed that an Optional Protocol be added to the Convention on Torture – the eventual Optional Protocol to the Convention Against Torture.[651]

By 2010 there were 50 State Parties to the Optional Protocol which came into force in 2006. The Protocol was predicated on the objective: '[t]o establish a system of regular visits undertaken by independent international and national bodies to places where people are deprived of their liberty, in order to prevent torture and other cruel, inhuman or degrading treatment or punishment.'[652]

[644] Torture Convention, Arts 4–12.

[645] UNCAT, Arts 17–22.

[646] The Body of Principles for the Protection of All Persons under Any Form of Detention or Imprisonment, (GA Res 43/173, annex, 43 UN GAOR Supp (No 49) at 298, UN Doc A/43/49 (1988)) which set down a number of principles to achieve so as to treat prisoners in a 'humane manner' and the Basic Principles for the Treatment of Prisoners (GA Res. 45/111, annex, 45 UN GAOR Supp (No 49A) at 200, UN Doc A/45/49 (1990)) which begins with the principle that, 'all prisoners shall be treated with the respect due to their inherent dignity and value as human beings' and, prima facie, retain most of their human rights.

[647] Adopted at the 15th Session of the General Assembly of the OAS Dec 1985. It came into force on 28 February 1987. Note, this had a slightly wider definition of torture. Like the UNCAT, it too, explicitly applied in times of war. See Arts 2 and 5.

[648] 27 ILM (1988) 1152.

[649] European Prison Rules 1987, Recommendation No R. (87); Committee of Ministers for Europe, Feb 12, 1987. See Arts 37 and 39.

[650] European Convention for the Prevention of Torture 1987, Chapter 1, Arts 1–3. Note also Art 94 of the Inter-American Commission on Human Rights.

[651] E/CN.4/2002/WG.11/CRP.1, 17 Jan 2002.

[652] Art 1.

20. From the 1990s into the Twenty-first Century

A. The Wars in the former Yugoslavia

The 1990s saw the Security Council calling for the strict application of Geneva III in a number of conflicts.[653] This call was most obvious in the wars of the former Yugoslavia in which the killing of prisoners of war appears to have relatively common. The most extreme instance of this occurred with the fall of Srebrenica where an estimated 7,475 Muslim men would die after surrendering or through the practice of no-quarter.[654] This was despite direct calls from the Security Council to Serbia to allow the ICRC to visit all places of detention related to the storming of safe areas.[655] However, most of the men killed after the fall of Srebrenica, never made it to a detention centre. Radovan Karadzic (b 1945), the former President of the Republika Srpska is currently on trial for allegedly ordering this massacre.[656] His trial for this event has been supplemented by some of the soldiers involved in the incident. These soldiers range from Radislav Krystic (b 1948)[657] who was one of the commanders involved in the massacre, Momir Nikolic (b 1955)[658] an assistant commander, through to some of those who formed the firing squads for the massacre, such as Drazen Erdemovic (b 1971).[659] Others convicted for the wilful killing – or failure to prevent the killing of – prisoners elsewhere included, inter alia, Mile Mrksic (b 1947), Miroslav Radic, (b 1962),[660] Mrda Darko (b 1959),[661] Ranko Cesic (b 1964)[662] and Slavko Dokmanovic (b 1949). The latter was charged for taking men from a hospital and executing them.[663]

A number of prisoner of war camps gained notoriety during the wars in the former Yugoslavia. On the Serb side, these included, inter alia, Manjaca, Sremska Mitrovica, Stajicevo, Omarska, Trnopolje and Keraterm. There were over 3,700 prisoners (many who were detained because they were male and of the opposing ethnicity, not because they had been captured carrying arms) held at Manjaca, where there were significant beatings and killings of prisoners. Sremska-Mitrovica prison held between 3,000 and 4,000 non-Serb (mostly Croatian) prisoners of war and/or males of opposing ethnicities. Murder, torture and rape also occurred in this prison. At least 25 prisoners were killed in front of witnesses, but the actual number is believed to be much higher. The

[653] See eg, Western Sahara S/RES/1056 (1996, May 29); S/RES/1084 (1996, Nov 27); S/RES/1429 (2002, July 30); Ethiopia and Eritrea S/RES/1369 (2001, Sep 14); S/RES/1398 (2002, Mar 15); S/RES/1430 (2002, Aug 14); Angola (S/RES/1008 (1995, Aug 7); S/RES/1045 (1996, Feb 8); S/RES/1055 (1996, May 8); Tajikistan (S/RES/968 (1994, Dec 16); S/RES/999 (1995, June 16); S/RES/1061 (1996, June 14); S/RES/1089 (1996, Dec 13).

[654] Drakulic, S (2004) *They Would Never Hurt a Fly. War Criminals on Trial in the Hague* (London, Abacus) 95–106, 146; Human Rights Watch (1995) *The Fall of Srebrenica and the Failure of the United Nations Peacekeeping* (NYC, HRW) 7–14; Human Rights Watch (2005) *Safe Areas for Srebenica's Most Wanted* (NYC, HRW).

[655] S/RES/1010 (1995, Aug 10); S/RES/1019 (1995, Nov 9).

[656] See Black, I (2003) 'Karadzic Ordered Killing of Muslim Captives' *Guardian Weekly* (27 Nov) 5.

[657] Radislav Krstic, IT-98-33.

[658] Momir Nikolic, IT-02-60/1.

[659] Drazan Erdemovic, IT-96-22.

[660] Mrksic et al, IT-95-13/1.

[661] Mrda Darko, IT-02-59.

[662] Ranko Cesic, IT-95-10/1.

[663] Slavko Dokmanovic, IT-95-13a. For the attack on the patients of the hospital, see Forsythe, D (2005) *The Humanitarians: The International Committee of the Red Cross* (Cambridge, Cambridge University Press) 110; Stephen, C (2004) *Judgement Day. The Trial of Slobodan Milosevic* (London, Atlantic) 65.

Stajićevo camp also held between 1,500 and 6,500 Croatian prisoners of war and civilians. The Omarska camp held between 3,000 and 5,000 individuals. These men were subject to beatings, torture, insanitary conditions and chronic shortages of food. Many of these events were possible because although the ICRC was given access to some camps, from which improvements began to register quite quickly, they did not even know of the existence of some other camps, like Omarska, which were hidden and only discovered by journalists. It was from such discoveries that the Security Council demanded that 'unimpeded and continuous access' to these places be granted 'immediately to the International Committee of the Red Cross and other relevant international organizations and that all detainees therein receive humane treatment, including adequate food, shelter and medical care'.[664] However, before the ICRC could achieve its humanitarian goals, terrible atrocities were committed. The view of the International Court of Justice on such camps was that in addition to being involved in unlawful killings: 'Members of the protected group were systematically victims of massive mistreatment, beatings, rape and torture causing serious bodily and mental harm, during the conflict and, in particular, in the detention camps.'[665]

On the opposing side, the Celebici prison camp was utilised by the Bosnian authorities to hold Serbian prisoners of war. Although the exact number of detainees at Celebici is not known, there is strong evidence that murder, torture, sexual assaults, beatings and otherwise cruel and inhuman treatment occurred in this facility, despite their original high standards and allowance of ICRC visits (which were later restricted, much to the ire of the Security Council).[666] Finally, the Lapunsnik camp in central Kosovo, which was used to hold Serbian and other non-Albanian prisoners, gained notoriety in the war of 1999. This notoriety was supplemented by the alleged execution of prisoners (by both Serbian and Kosovo forces).[667]

Against this background of concern and atrocities, it was no surprise that the Statute for the International Criminal Tribunal for the Former Yugoslavia stipulated that war crimes against prisoners of war, including with regards to executions and torture, was to be a central focus of their work.[668] From such a focus, a number of convictions have occurred. These have included, inter alia, the commander, deputy commander and a particularly sadistic guards from the Celebici camp (Delalic, Landzo and Mucic) who were all convicted of murder, torture and inhumane treatment.[669] Zlatko Aleksovski (b 1960),[670] commander of the prison facility at Kaonik which held non-Croatian prisoners, was convicted for excessive and cruel interrogation, forced labour of prisoners including digging trenches, and using prisoners as human shields. Dusco Sikirica

[664] S/RES/770 (1992, Aug 13); S/RES/770 (1992, Aug 13); S/RES/1010 (1995, Aug 10).

[665] ICJ (2007) *Application of the Convention on the Prevention and Punishment of the Crime of Genocide* (*Bosnia v Serbia*) 72.

[666] S/RES/1009 (1995, Aug 10).

[667] Del Ponte, C (2008) *Confrontations with Humanity's Worst Criminals and the Culture of Impunity* (NYC, Other Press) 273–304; Glenny, M (1996) *The Fall of Yugoslavia* (London, Penguin) 203, 207, 210; Stephen, C (2004) *Judgement Day. The Trial of Slobodan Milosevic* (London, Atlantic) 20–24; Human Rights Watch (1994) *Bosnia-Hercegovina: Sarajevo* (NYC, HRW) 17–24; Anon (1999) 'The Balkan Conflict and Respect for International Humanitarian Law' *IRRC* 834: 408–11.

[668] Statute for the International Criminal Tribunal for the Former Yugoslavia, Arts 2(b), 2(e), 5(f), and 8(2).

[669] *Prosecutor v Hazim Delic, Esad Lanzo & Zdravko Mucic* The Hague Oct 9 2001, PIS/628e. Also, 40 ILM (2001) 626.

[670] *Prosecutor v Aleksovski* The Hague 24 March 2000, CC/PIS/481-e.

(b 1964) et al, as commanders and superiors at the Keraterm camp were convicted of inhumane conditions inflicted on the prisoners in terms of inadequate food, clothing and medical assistance.[671] Predbrag Banovic (b 1968) a guard at the Keraterm camp, received eight years in jail for the murder of five prisoners as a result of his participation in beatings. He also beat 27 detainees using various weapons including baseball bats, truncheons, cables and iron balls. Two of the detainees in question were shot. He also participated in the confinement in inhumane conditions, harassment, humiliation and psychological abuse of non-Serbs.[672] Miroslav Kvocka (b 1957), Dragoljub Prcac (b 1937), Milojica Kos (b 1963), Mlado Radic (b 1952) and Zoran Zigic (b 1958) as police officers, prison guards and associated staff were convicted for, inter alia, the deaths and torture of non-Serbian prisoners that occurred in the Omarska and Keraterm prisoner of war camps as well as the Omarska police station.[673] Similarly, Haradin Bala (b 1957) was convicted for the murder and torture of inmates at Llapushnik prison camp.[674] Milorad Krnojelac (b 1962),[675] the commander of the Foca Kazneno-Popravni Dom camp was found guilty of murder, torture and beatings as well as perpetuating inhumane living conditions in terms of hygiene, heating, medicine and food.[676] Goran Jelisic[677] (b 1968), a Bosnian Serb, was sentenced to 40 years for executing 13 prisoners, some at a police station, and others at a prison camp, but it is likely he executed many more; whilst Dusko Tadic (b 1955), a prison guard at Omarska, was found guilty of assault upon prisoners.[678] Milan Simic (b 1960) was given a sentence of five years for kicking a prisoner in the genitals, firing a gun over his head, and threatening to cut off his penis while brandishing a knife.[679] Likewise, Stevan Todorovic (b 1957) was convicted of crimes against humanity due to, inter alia, his beatings of captives.[680]

Although there were a series of prisoner exchanges during the conflict, when the war ended, the vast majority of the prisoners of war were exchanged as part of the 1995 Dayton Peace Agreement. These exchanges were assisted by an exchange of information on all prisoners held and unrestricted ICRC visits to detainees, so they could not only assess the individuals, but also learn the individuals' choice of place of repatriation.[681] A very similar process was followed with the Agreement for Peace and Self-Government in Kosovo.[682] Finally, the repatriation of the dead was recognised as an important part of the final peace agreement in the former Yugoslavia.[683]

[671] Sentencing Judgement in the Case of Sikirica, Dosen & Kolundzija, CC/PIS/635e. Also available at http://www.un.org/icty.org .

[672] Banovic, IT-02-65/1.

[673] Kvocka et al, IT-98-30/1.

[674] Bala et al, IT-03-66.

[675] *Prosecutor v Krnojelac*, 43 ILM (2004) 286.

[676] *Prosector v Krnojelac*, The Hague 15 March 2002, JL/PIS/663-e. Also, IT-97-25.

[677] Goran Jelisic, IT-95-10; Drakulic, S (2004) *They Would Never Hurt a Fly. War Criminals on Trial in the Hague* (London, Abacus) 59–73.

[678] *Prosecutor v Tadic*, 36 ILM (1997) 908.

[679] *Prosecutor v Milan Simic*, The Hague Oct 17 2002, JL/PIS/704-e.

[680] *The Todorovic Case*, The Hague 31 July 2001, JL/PIS/608e. Also, *Prosecutor v Naletilic & Martinovic*, The Hague 31 March 2003, CC/PIS/742e; *Prosecutor v Hazim Delic, Esad Lanzo & Zdravko Mucic*, The Hague 9 Oct 2001, PIS/628e. Also, Drakulic, S (2004) *They Would Never Hurt a Fly. War Criminals on Trial in the Hague* (London, Abacus) 18–22.

[681] 1995 Dayton Peace Agreement, Annex 1A, Art IX.

[682] 1999 Interim Agreement for Peace and Self-Government in Kosovo, Art 1:10. Also, Chapter VII.

[683] 1995 Dayton Peace Agreement, Annex 1A, Art IX.

B. Dirty Wars and the War on Terror

Although the wars in the former Yugoslavia had more than their fair share of atrocities, the conflicts ended up resembling conventional conflicts with relatively defined belligerents holding large swathes of territory. This was far from the case in many other conflicts of the 1990s and the new century, where warfare tended to engage more informal combatants and unrestrained types of conflict. For example, during the 1990s and the first decade of the new century, enforced disappearances became standard practices of warfare or 'counter-terrorism' within, inter alia, Algeria (at least 7,000 people in the 1990s),[684] China,[685] Thailand,[686] Sri Lanka[687] and Nepal.[688] By 2010 there were over 41,000 registered cases of disappearances in Columbia since 1990. This practice in Columbia is linked to an overall disintegration of humanitarian law, with Columbian insurgents attacking medical workers and health facilities, because 'the laws of war were inappropriate for the Columbian context'.[689] Conversely, as in 2008, the Columbia authorities were sending our military rescue missions beneath the (unauthorised) cover of the Red Cross.[690]

The belligerents fighting the Russian forces in the conflicts in Chechnya are also reknowned for their attacks on civilian populations. They are also known to have executed six ICRC workers in 1996, as well as capturing hospitals, such as that in Budennovsk, and taking 1,600 people hostage. The Russian forces responded with equal ferocity. Orders for no-quarter for some such insurgents were issued by former Russian President Vladimir Putin (b 1952) in 2006. Conversely, the Chechen insurgents were known to refuse attempts to surrender from certain Russian military personnel, such as pilots who had been shot down. Enforced disappearances (largely conducted by Russian forces) were in the range of 3,000 to 5,000 people in the period 1999 to 2005. Hostage taking and torture, by both sides, supplemented these acts, along with a practice of holding and exchanging some corpses for political purposes. Even ICRC convoys, suspected of carrying Chechen soldiers and ammunition (which would nullify their neutrality) were also targeted.[691] Similarly, Red Cross ambulances in Lebanon

[684] Human Rights Watch (2003) *Truth and Justice on Hold: The New State Commission on Disappearances* (NYC, HRW) 10–22; Human Rights Watch (2003) *Time for Reckoning: Enforced Disappearances in Algeria* (NYC, HRW).

[685] Human Rights Watch (2009) *Enforced Disappearances in the Wake of Xinjiang's Protests* (NYC, HRW) 2–14.

[686] Human Rights Watch (2007) *No-One is Safe* (NYC, HRW) 23–35; Human Rights Watch (2007) *Enforced Disappearances In Thailand's Southern Border* (NYC, HRW) 17–28.

[687] Human Rights Watch (2008) *Disappearances and Abductions in Sri Lanka* (NYC, HRW) 7–16; Human Rights Watch (2007) *Return to War: Human Rights Under Siege* (NYC, HRW) 7–9, 24–37.

[688] Human Rights Watch (2008) Waiting For Justice (NYC, HRW) 13–17, 23–39; Human Rights Watch (2005) *Disappearances in Nepal* (NYC, HRW) 4–7, 34, 38, 40–42; Human Rights Watch (2004) *Between a Rock and a Hard Place: Civilians Struggle to Survive in Nepal's Civil War* (NYC, HRW) 25–60.

[689] Human Rights Watch (2001) *Columbia: Beyond Negotiation: International Humanitarian Law and its Application to the Conduct of the FARC* (NYC, HRW) 14–15.

[690] See Jenatsch, T (1998) 'The ICRC As A Humanitarian Mediator in the Colombian Conflict Possibilities and Limits' *IRRC* (323): 303–18.

[691] Gilligan, E (2010) *Terror in Chechnya* (New Jersey, Princeton University Press) 3, 27–28, 47, 60–64, 70–71, 77–97, 128, 188–89; Human Rights Watch (2010) *Russia, the European Court on Human Rights and Chechnya* (NYC, HRW) 1–14, 29–35; Human Rights Watch (2006) *Widespread Torture in Chechen Republic* (NYC, HRW) 12–18, 23–25, 32–36; Human Rights Watch (2005) *Disappearances in Chechnya* (NYC, HRW) 2–7; Human Rights Watch (2002) *Continued Disappearances in Chechnya* (NYC, HRW); Human Rights Watch (2002) *Swept Under: Torture, Forced Disappearances and Extrajudicial Killings in Chechnya* (NYC, HRW) 23–45; Human Rights Watch (2001) *Russia/Chechnya: The Dirty War in Chechnya* (NYC, HRW) 3–7; Human Rights Watch (2000) *Russia/Chechnya: Civilian Killings in Grozny* (NYC, HRW) 12–15; Human Rights Watch (2000)

during the conflict with Israel in 2006 were attacked by Israeli forces, whilst Israeli hospitals were hit by the rockets of insurgents.[692]

The similarities between some of the dirty wars of the 1990s and the so-called 'wars on terror' that engaged the United States and her associated allies, are striking. The opponents of the United States lead forces in both Afghanistan and Iraq that have little regard for the laws of war when it comes to dealing with the opposition, who are not perceived to possess a right to surrender. Rather, the decision on whether to kill, release or exchange prisoners rests with the Imam or deputy Imam. Accordingly, many captives have been tortured, executed and then mutilated. Many of these acts are filmed for public release. In addition, despite remarkable advances in medicine, technology (body armour), and evacuation whereby only one American soldier in 16 was dying due to their wounds, medics, medical transports, and even the ICRC have been seen as fair targets. The ICRC headquarters in Baghdad was bombed in 2003 (with the bomb being delivered in an ambulance) and some of its members were targeted because they were seen to be helping people. In the eyes of some insurgents, in the wake of the United States invasion, any help was seen as contributing to the legitimacy of the American invasion. Similarly, at least one Red Cross worker and five workers from Doctors Without Borders were executed in Afghanistan in 2004. A further eight doctors and nurses were added to this tally in 2010.[693]

The response of the United States and its allies in Afghanistan and Iraq against the belligerents who show minimal respect for the laws of war with regards to either civilians or military captives, has – been less than commendable. This has been with regard to their general treatment as prisoners, with problems ranging from extreme solitary confinement for prolonged periods amounting to years, through to the practice of torture. The practice of torture by United States forces in the so-called 'war on terror' can be divided into the acts that were not sanctioned, acts that were sanctioned and systematic attempts to avoid the obligations of the Torture Convention. In the first instance, physical, psychological and/or sexual abuse was committed by soldiers of the United States together with additional governmental agencies, including some of those from Britain, at a number of holding locations, of which Abu Ghraib, was the most notable. The ICRC, which uncovered this problem a year before it was made public, was of the opinion that what happened in these places amounted to torture. When these practices were made public, the White House condemned the acts and 17 soldiers were removed from duty before 11 of them were charged and convicted with dereliction

Russia/Chechnya: 'No Happiness Remains' (NYC, HRW) 6–13; Human Rights Watch (2000) *Russia/Chechnya: A Day of Slaughter* (NYC, HRW) 2–7; Human Rights Watch (2000) *Arbitrary Detention, Torture and Exhortation in Chechnya* (NYC, HRW); Myers, S (2006) 'Putin Order Death for Killers' *New York Times* (June 29) A9.

692 Human Rights Watch (2006) *The Hoax That Wasn't* (NYC, HRW) 1–10.

693 AP 'Medics Killed in Afghanistan' *New Zealand Herald*, (August 9 2010) A12; Geddes, L 'Pill to Turn Soldiers Into Super-Survivors' (*New Scientist*, 30 Jan 2010) 13; Filkins, D ((2009) *The Forever War* (NYC, Vintage) 91–92, 182, 187, 221; Anon 'Shock Waves Shake Up Soldiers' *New Scientist*, (2 Feb 2008) 4; Reuters (2009) 'Taleban Code of Conduct' *New Zealand Herald*, (31 July 2009) A12; Moorehead, C (1998) *Dunant's Dream: War, Switzerland and the History of the Red Cross* (NYC, Carroll and Graf) 619, 675, 682; Forsythe, D (2005) *The Humanitarians: The International Committee of the Red Cross* (Cambridge, Cambridge University Press) 98–99, 112, 141; Red Cross (1997) 'Dec 17, 1996: Six Red Cross Staff Assassinated in Chechnya' *IRRC* 317: 135. See *Independent* (2003) 'Suicide Bomb: Red Cross Pullout Looms' *New Zealand Herald* (29 Oct 29 2003) B1; Nichol, J and Rennell, T (2009) *Medic* (London, Penguin) 6–7; Greenwood, J (2005) *Medics at War* (Annapolis, Naval Institute Press) 139, 140; Glasser, R (2006) *Wounded* (NYC, Braziller) 29–30; Howard, M 'Iraqi Soldiers Massacred' *Guardian Weekly* (29 Oct 29 2004) 1.

of duty, maltreatment and aggravated assault and battery. The United States admitted that many of the acts at Abu Ghraib went significantly beyond the interrogation methods they had approved. Whether these were a 'few bad apples' or the problem of very blunt forms of torture was significantly larger than admitted, is a matter of debate. This is especially due to the poor conditions in which prisoners were collected, transported and held following the initial stages of the invasions of Afghanistan and Iraq, as a result of which hundreds of prisoners may have died. This is more so since the ICRC did not gain access to all the places of detention in these countries until 2009. That is, although the United States voluntarily (remembering that the United States position was that the detainees were not prisoners of war under Geneva III, and therefore not allowed ICRC visits as of right) allowed the ICRC into high-level places like Guantanamo as early as 2002, it was only following criticism at the United Nations Human Rights Committee in 2008 and the election of a new president, that the ICRC gained access to all places of detention at the end of the decade.[694]

The greatest abuses prior to 2009 probably occurred when prisoners were rendered from one country to another. This process of extraordinary rendition was first authorised in 1995 by Bill Clinton (b 1946). It remained on the books and was then greatly enhanced in 2001 after which perhaps tens of thousands were captured and transferred around the world. As noted above, this practice which grew out of Operation Condor in Latin America, by the twenty-first century, was being used by China, Egypt, India, Iran, Russia, Sudan and Zimbabwe – as well as the United States. In other instances, it appears that the United States authorities turned a blind eye to the acts of torture committed by their allies, such as the (Coalition approved) Iraqi military forces, who appear to have routinely beat, burnt and electrocuted detainees. The United States defences to the charge that they were transferring prisoners to places where torture was likely, was that they would not transfer prisoners to places they knew they would be tortured and to ensure this they requested 'diplomatic assurances' from the places of destination, that torture would not occur. The value of these assurances, especially when taken from a country with entrenched problems of the practice of torture, are questionable.[695] Accordingly, the General Assembly of the United Nations urged:

[694] Observations of the United Nations Human Rights Committee With Regards to the Second and Third Reports by the United States of America, 47 ILM (2008) 586; Rose, D (2004) *Guantanamo* (London, Faber) 16–17, 52–53, 89–91; Anon 'Under Duress' (*Economist*, 13 February 2010) 53; Reuters 'Red Cross Given Access to Terrorist Detainees' *New Zealand Herald* (24 August 2009) A14; Forsythe, D (2005) *The Humanitarians: The International Committee of the Red Cross* (Cambridge, Cambridge University Press) 130–41, 148–49; Human Rights Watch (2008) *Locked Up Alone: Detention Conditions at Guantanamo* (NYC, HRW) 7–10, 15–19; Ross, J (2007) 'Black Letter Abuse: the US Legal Response to Torture Since 9/11' 867 *IRRC* 234–56; Human Rights Watch (2005) *Getting Away With Torture?* (NYC, HRW) 3–9; Dehghanpisheh, B 'The Death Convoys of Afghanistan' *Newsweek*, (26 August 2002) 12–19; Ripley, A 'The Rules of Interrogation' *TIME* (17 May 2004) 27–30; Barry, J 'Abuse in Iraq' *Newsweek* (17 May 2004) 24–29.

[695] Associated Press 'Catalogue of Terror, Torture' *New Zealand Herald* (25 October 2010) A17; Human Rights Watch (2008) *Not the Way Forward* (NYC, HRW) 14–25, 34–43; Commission on Human Rights (2006) Situation of Detainees at Guantanamo Bay 45 ILM 716; Human Rights Watch (2007) *The Stamp of Guantanamo* (NYC, HRW) 2, 6, 9, 14–20; Human Rights Watch (2006) *Ghost Prisoners* (NYC, HRW) 1–4, 7–14; Human Rights Watch (2005) *Still at Risk: Diplomatic Assurances* (NYC, HRW) 7–10; Human Rights Watch (2004) *Empty Promises: Diplomatic Assurances* (NYC, HRW) 3–8; Borelli, S (2005) 'Casting Light on the Legal Black Hole: International law and Detentions Abroad in the "War on Terror"' 857 IRRC 110–34; Human Rights Watch (2010) *Cruel Britannia* (NYC, HRW) 14–23, 34–45; Human Rights Watch (2008) *CIA Renditions to Jordan* (NYC, HRW) 1–8, 24–18, 23–38; Human Rights Watch (2005) *Cairo to Kabul to Guantanamo* (NYC, HRW) 8–13; Hirsh, M (2005) 'All Aboard Air CIA' (Newsweek, Feb 28) 32–33; Human Rights Watch (2004) *The United States 'Disappeared'* (NYC, HRW) 11, 20–23.

> States not to expel, return ('refouler'), extradite or in any other way transfer a person to another State where there are substantial grounds for believing that the person would be in danger of being subjected to torture, and recognises that diplomatic assurances, where used, do not release States from their obligations under international human rights, humanitarian and refugee law, in particular the principle of non-refoulment.[696]

Soon after his inauguration, President Barack Obama (1961) signed an Executive Order opposing rendition torture and establishing a task force to provide recommendations about processes to prevent rendition torture.

Although the Bush administration condemned the acts that happened at Abu Ghraib, it defended the use of 'stress and duress' techniques. As seen above, these techniques had been actively utilised by security forces throughout the latter half of the twentieth century by, inter alia, the Soviet Union, China, Nicaragua, North Korea, Iran, Iraq, the United Kingdom and Israel.[697]

The Bush administration (2001–2009) allowed the utilisation of 'stress and duress' (or 'no blood no foul') techniques. These were permitted because many of those held in the custody of the United States were not believed to be lawful combatants. For those not entitled to combatant status, although they were to be treated 'humanely' in 'a manner consistent' with the Geneva conventions, they were not to be given the same rights that prisoners of war were entitled to. Alberto Gonzales (b 1955), the Attorney General of the Bush Administration, described the 'war against terrorism' as 'a new kind of war' and 'a new paradigm' that showed Geneva's 'strict limitations on questioning of enemy prisoners' to be 'obsolete' and even 'quaint'.[698] The stress and duress techniques were also authorised due to a belief that they were not torture. The official position was that acts only constituted torture if the physical pain rose to the level of death, organ failure or the permanent impairment of a significant bodily function. If it were mental, to constitute torture, it must result in significant psychological harm of a duration of months or years.

As Geneva III was deemed 'quaint', three new categories of interrogation were unveiled. If the detainees were uncooperative, interrogators were meant to start at Category I, which comprised of techniques utilising yelling and deception. If Category I produced no result, the interrogator could move to Category II. Category II included 12 techniques aimed at humiliation and sensory deprivation. Stress positions, like standing for a maximum of four hours; isolation for up to 30 days; deprivation of light and auditory stimuli, and hooding during transportation and questioning. Interrogations could go on for 24 hours, deprivation of sleep could be enforced (restricting captives to four hours per 24 hour period, for an unlimited amount of days) and all religious and comfort items could be removed. Clothing could be removed and forced grooming (such as the removal of beards) could be enforced. Individual phobias, such as the fear of dogs, could also be used to induce stress. Finally, Category III methods, only to be used for exceptionally resistant individuals, could be utilised. These included 'mild,

[696] UNGA Resolution (2009) 63/166 Torture and Other Cruel, Inhuman or Degrading Treatment or Punishment; UNGA Resolution (2009) 63/185 Protection of Human Rights and Fundamental Freedoms While Countering Terrorism. Also (2007) 61/171; 58/174 (2004); 58/164 (2004).

[697] Human Rights Watch (2004) *'Stress and Duress' Techniques Used Worldwide* (NYC, HRW) 7–10, 23–34, 65–73; Blum, W (2003) *Rogue State: A Guide to the World's Only Superpower* (Zed, London) 49–57; Fisk, R (2006) *The Great War for Civilisation: The Conquest of the Middle East* (London, Harper) 120–21, 123, 137, 190, 358.

[698] Gonzales memo, in Sands, P (2009) *Torture Team* (London, Penguin) 39, 51.

non-injurious physical contact' like grabbing, poking and pushing; convincing the detainees that death or severe pain was imminent for him or his family; or exposure to cold weather and water such as keeping a prisoner naked at a constant temperature of 10 degrees and constantly dousing him with cold water. The final option under Category III involved the use of a wet towel and dripping water (also known as 'waterboarding') to induce the misperception of suffocation. This technique involved prisoners being bound to a board, head slightly lowered below the feet, plastic is wrapped over their face and water poured over them or their head as they are lowered into a bath. The gag reflex is automatic as they think they are drowning and few can endure it for more than a few minutes. One prisoner was subjected to water-boarding at least 183 times. Water-boarding was permissible until 2007. All of these stress and duress tactics were used on detainees in Afghanistan, Iraq and Guantanamo Bay. This was especially so if the captured were classified as illegal combatants, unlike high profile belligerents, like Saddam Hussein (1937–2006), who were entitled to none of the protections of Geneva III.[699]

The view of the United States that they were not committing acts of torture was the opposite to the view of the ICRC and independent international experts acting under the auspices of the various conventions concerned with torture, who concluded that these practices, especially Category II and III, when used cumulatively, were torture.[700] All of these enhanced methods came to an end in 2009 when President Obama was elected. They were cancelled because of the inhumanity of the techniques, the negative effect they were having on the conflicts the United States was involved in, and because there was no scientific evidence suggesting that they were either reliable or helpful in the gathering of intelligence.[701]

21. The Developments in the Twenty-first Century

In 1998 when the International Criminal Court was formed, the denial of quarter and the killing of prisoners, in conflicts of either an international or non-international

[699] Sands, P (2009) *Torture Team* (London, Penguin) 5–7, 15, 62, 74, 90, 100–103, 161, 167, 169, 184, 206–209; Editor, 'Modern Barbarity' New Scientist (23 Feb 2008) 3; Rose, D (2004) *Guantanamo* (London, Faber) 90–91; Verkalik, R 'Ex-Soldier Breaks Ranks on Torture' *New Zealand Herald*, (18 Nov 2009) A21; Famer, B 'Former Prisoners at Bagram Tell of Torture' *New Zealand Herald*, (26 June 2009) A21; Reuters 'Call to Ban Torture Music' *New Zealand Herald* (21 May 2009) A20; Hess, P 'Rice Gave Approval for Water Torture' *New Zealand Herald* (24 April 2009) A15; AP 'CIA Kept Prisoners Awake for 11 Days' *New Zealand Herald*, (11 May 2009) A16; Editor 'The Pentagon and the Torture Report' *Herald Tribune*, (19 Dec 2008) A8; Reuters 'Bush Vetoes Anti-torture Legislation' *New Zealand Herald* (10 March 2008) B2; Whitaker, I 'The Torture Files' *The Independent on Sunday* (4 Dec 2005) 42; Human Rights Watch (2006) *No Blood, No Foul* (NYC, HRW) 3–8, 12–18, 21–45; Human Rights Watch (2004) *Interrogation Techniques for Guantanamo Detainees* (NYC, HRW); Goldenberg, S 'US Forces Taught Torture Techniques' *Guardian* (14 May 2004) 5; Reuters 'CIA Ditches Water Torture' *New Zealand Herald*, (17 Sept 2007) B2.

[700] Commission on Human Rights (2006) *Situation of Detainees at Guantanamo Bay* 45 ILM 716; Human Rights Watch (2004) *Guantanamo: Detainee Accounts* (NYC, HRW) 12–23, 27–34; Reuters 'US Treatment of al Qaeda Captives Constituted Torture' *New Zealand Herald* (17 Mar 2009) A13; Anon 'Detainee Panel Slammed' *New Scientist* (1 Aug 2009) 4; Sevastopulo, D 'Red Cross Study Reignites Dispute Over US Torture' *Financial Times* (1 Dec 2004) A1.

[701] President Barack Obama's Executive Orders on Guantanamo Bay, Interrogation and Detention of Terror Suspects 48 ILM (2009) 394; Bond, M 'Obama Turns to Science in Quest to Clean Up Interrogation Methods' *New Scientist* (5 Sept 2009) 14; Editor 'The Dark Pursuit of Justice' *Economist* (11 Aug 2009) 20–21; Independent 'CIA Probe But Rendition Goes On' *New Zealand Herald* (26 Aug 2009) A14.

character, was recognised as a war crime.[702] So too was 'intentionally directing attacks against buildings dedicated to . . . hospitals and places where the sick and wounded are collected, provided they are not military objectives',[703] or against 'material, medical units and transport, and personnel using the distinctive emblems of the Geneva Conventions in conformity with international law'.[704] Enforced disappearances, when done as part of a widespread or systematic attack directed against any civilian population, were recognised as crimes against humanity.[705] Torture was also recognised as a crime against humanity and/or a crime of war in both international or non-international conflicts. It was defined as:

> [T]he intentional infliction of severe pain or suffering, whether physical or mental, upon a person in the custody or under the control of the accused; except that torture shall not include pain or suffering arising only from, inherent in or incidental to, lawful sanctions.[706]

The crime of torture would come to be recognised in indictments from the International Criminal Court for the Sudan in the cases of Ahmad Muhammad Harun ('Ahmad Harun' – the former minister of the Interior of the Government of Sudan) and Ali Muhammad Ali Abd-Al-Rahman ('Ali Kushayb' – alleged leader of the Militia/Janjaweed)[707] as well as Omar Hassan Ahmad Al Bashir, the president of Sudan (b 1993).[708] These indictments were particularly welcomed, as torture had grown to plague-like proportions in a number of African conflicts such as with Liberia,[709] Sierra Leone (in which some combatants developed the practice of amputation as signature wounds imposed on civilians) and Uganda. In the last instance, combatants aligned with the Lord's Resistance Army commonly removed people from their tongues, ears and lips if they were involved in the election processes, or removed their legs if they were doing prohibited acts such as cycling, due to a fear they may be informers.[710]

The final development of note in the twenty-first century has been the increased focus upon the dead and other victims of enforced disappearance. The progress in this area began when the International Commission on Missing Persons (ICMP) was established at the initiative of Bill Clinton in 1996 at the G-7 Summit in Lyon, France. Its primary role was, and remains, to ensure the cooperation of governments in locating and identifying those who have disappeared during armed conflict or as a result of human rights violations. Since November 2001, ICMP has led the way in using DNA as a first step in the identification of large numbers of persons missing from armed conflict. By the new century, it was working, at the invitation of national

[702] See Art 8(b)(xii) and e(x).

[703] ICC 8(b)(xxiv) and 8(e)(ii).

[704] ICC 8(b)(vii), (xxiv) and 8(e)(ii).

[705] See Art 7(1)(i). For the purpose of the International Criminal Court, 'enforced disappearance of persons' means the arrest, detention or abduction of persons by, or with the authorisation, support or acquiescence of, a State or a political organisation, followed by a refusal to acknowledge that deprivation of freedom or to give information on the fate or whereabouts of those persons, with the intention of removing them from the protection of the law for a prolonged period of time.

[706] ICC, Art 7.2(e). Also, Art 8.

[707] ICC-02/05-01/07.

[708] ICC-02/05-01/09.

[709] Human Rights Watch (1990) *Liberia: A Human Rights Disaster* (NYC, HRW) 6, 9; AP, 'Son's Grisly Role in Liberia's War' *New Zealand Herald* (1 Nov 2008) A29.

[710] Slim, H (2008) *Killing Civilians* (NYC, Columbia University Press) 59, 198, 236–37.

governments, in Iraq, Chile, Columbia and parts of the former Yugoslavia. In the last instance, the ICMP has been able to identify 15,510 people who were missing from the conflicts and whose mortal remains were found in hidden graves.[711]

Supplementing the work of the IMCP in dealing with the aftermath of conflicts, has been the repeated calls of the General Assembly in times of armed conflict to prevent people going 'missing'[712] and the International Convention for the Protection of All Persons from Enforced Disappearance, in dealing with practices utilised during conflict. The Convention, which followed the General Assembly keeping this issue on the international agenda since 1992 (and supporting subsequently) was finally concluded at the end of the first decade of the new century.[713] When this treaty comes into force it will fill one of the clear gaps that developed with the question of dealing with the dead and their living loved ones, post the Second World War. The convention is built upon two foundations. The first is that no person should be subjected to enforced disappearance. Accordingly, it was agreed that no one would be subjected to enforced disappearance or secret detention. This rule has no exceptions whatsoever. A state of war or a threat of war, internal political instability or any other public emergency, may not be invoked as a justification for enforced disappearance.[714] The second foundation is the right of any family members/partners to know the truth about the circumstances of an enforced disappearance and the fate of the disappeared person, and their right to freedom to seek, receive and impart information to this end. To achieve these goals each Party agreed to take appropriate measures to investigate acts of alleged enforced disappearance and ensure it is recognised as an extremely serious offence within their criminal laws. Extradition and cross-border cooperation in the investigation and prosecution of the listed crime was also encouraged, and a Committee on Enforced Disappearances is to be established to carry out the functions provided for under the Convention.[715]

[711] The International Commission on Missing Persons (2010) *The Facts* (Sarajevo, Bosnia) 3, 4, 7.

[712] UNGA Resolution (2009) 63/183 Missing Persons. Also, (2007) 61/155.

[713] UNGA Resolution 41/133 Declaration on the Protection of all Persons from Enforced Disappearance (1992). UNGA Resolution (2010) 64/167 International Convention for the Protection of All Persons from Enforced Disappearance. Also, (2009) 63/186.

[714] Arts 1 and 17.

[715] See Part II of the Convention, from Arts 26 onwards.

Conclusion

For the purposes of this first volume, I set myself seven questions by which to assess whether there was 'progress' (or not) in the way that humanity has dealt with the issues of combatants and captives over the last 5,000 years of warfare. With regards to the topic of combatants, the questions were:

> *Can armies be restricted in numbers?*
> *Who can fight – in terms of age, sex and nationality?*
> *Can people be forced to fight?*
> *Must the combatants be formal, and identifiable?*

On the first question, it was well recognised that in an ideal world, there would be no armed forces because fighting would not be necessary. As a second-best alternative, if fighting must be done, it would be best achieved by a very small number of combatants, representing the many. History is full of examples of this type of warfare, where the champions, ideally the leaders of one side, fought the leaders of others. However, rarely did the losing side accept defeat if their champion fell, and in reality, few leaders wanted to risk their own necks when they could get their soldiers to do it for them. As a third-best alternative, if fighting must be done by beyond one combatant, it would be ideal to limit the numbers involved. This alternative has never been taken seriously. Rather, the focus of humanity on the question of combatants over the last 5,000 years has been upon who can be a 'lawful' combatant and the form that that combatant may take. These questions are very important as the giving or denial of combatant status ultimately affects the ability of belligerents to surrender. It can also, depending on how the equation is cut, make warfare more dangerous to both the belligerents and the non-combatants who they may seek to hide behind.

Early history on the question of who could be a combatant was in part dictated by the types of weapons used. This meant that as they were typically heavy, warfare was restricted to males above a certain size, usually well into their late teenage years. There were women leaders, and occasionally combatants too, but these were few in number. The armies, which were largely conscript, were beginning to standardise around 1,000 years before Christ, but so too were the practices of informal warfare, in the forms of insurgents disguised as non-combatants, pirates and a flow of mercenaries. All of these 'other' types of combatants were condemned, in one way or another, due to lacking courage, virtue and/or integrity – although as required, most belligerents were willing to utilise informal methods, to achieve their goals. This was particularly the case with mercenaries. These patterns held sway until the rise of the Republic of Rome, when there was a clear movement towards standardised armed forces, made up of men via large-scale conscription, based and with minimal reliance on mercenaries and a strong disdain for informal types of combatants. Although the Empire came to defeat the first systematic attempts of conscientious objectors, it failed to beat off its marauding enemies, despite having to build a foundation of mercenaries to defend themselves. Soon after, when the western Roman empire fell, so too did many of these values of formalised combatants.

As Western Europe emerged into the Feudal era, the principles of large-scale conscription of men, when necessary, came with it. Uniforms also began to emerge from this period, as combatants sought to distinguish themselves clearly on the battlefield. However, the other side of the feudal system and its development of generations of warriors, in an age without strong State controls, was the creation of large-scale mercenary bands, who fought for whoever paid their wages. Controlling these bands was increasingly hard, given that many States benefited from this system. Moreover, States began to actively experiment with privateers, whereby they learnt to condemn piracy on the one hand, but endorse privateers on the other, provided the privateer flew under the sovereign's flag, and the sovereign received a good share of the booty.

From the Reformation through to the Enlightenment, the State gained control of the use of force under its auspice. In doing so, it increasingly controlled, formalised and uniformed the armed forces under their control. These forces, which were beginning to reach sizes in excess of 100,000 bodies, were obtained from various forms of conscription. Although some women were involved in warfare, it was an overwhelmingly male occupation, and most of the males were adults, although in many instances those under the age of 18 were supplementary to many military forces. States in this epoch also came to adopt standard approaches against pirates, informal combatants who tried to fight out of uniform (who were dealt with strictly), and learnt how to tolerate those within their societies who did not want to fight for them. Even the use of foreign soldiers were being improved, as the trade was becoming more of buying regiments from one country to another, rather than a free flow of individuals in search of the highest bidder. Yet even by the middle of the nineteenth century, this was an uncommon practice. The pursuit and eradication of pirates became an international concern. Moreover, to avoid any ongoing ambiguities in this area, privateering was abolished. Collectively, all of these policies were beginning to solidify, so that the combatant was one who was under State control, could be recognised from a distance by distinctive emblems which could identify him as a combatant, carried his weapon openly and obeyed the laws of warfare.

Many of the above rules became codified in international contexts towards the end of the nineteenth century, and the implementation of them between the American Civil War and the end of the Second World War, only served to continue this momentum. For example, in all theatres of this period, informal combatants, despite growing in attractiveness to many of the belligerents, were not given combatant status which allowed them to be made prisoners of war, and therefore risked execution as they were captured. However, in this epoch it was also clear that trends were beginning to change. For example, the rise of the informal combatant, as a type of belligerent who actively used violence, and either directly or recklessly targeted civilians within their own society with the purpose of creating terror, grew with speed out of the end of the nineteenth century. The culmination of this problem resulted in international attempts to control terrorism during the final years of the League of Nations. Other changes involved the active involvement of women in the efforts of war. In this regard, although women began to enter into the field of combat in slowly growing numbers, it was in their direct supplementary support that the growth was exponential.

In this period, although it was men who were meant to do the fighting, boys continued to find their ways into the front line. By the end of the Second World War, at least one regime had come to mobilise children as young as 12 for its final defences. Soldiers of foreign lands were increasingly common in the Second World War, but this was not perceived as a major difficulty, and individuals from all around the world came to volunteer for one side or the other. On the question of conscription, the approaches between countries split, with the tolerant democracies learning, often with reluctance, to live with conscientious objectors, whilst the intolerant totalitarian regimes, did not tolerate such dissent.

Between the end of the Second World War and the twenty-first century, the situation which appeared to be solidifying in many areas, began to unravel, and the hopes of progress with them. This is not to suggest that this last epoch did not see some achievements. Most notably, the international community, after witnessing an increasing trend of utilising children under the age of 15 as primary, not supplementary, combatants, moved to prohibit this trend. Other areas, such as with women as combatants, have seen a continuation of earlier trends, where women combatants enter onto the battlefield, although these remain a minority, albeit a growing one, in both formal and informal wars. The questions of conscription progressed no further than the decades before it, with each country developing the approach that suits it. That is, the right to object to killing was not made into a recognised human right.

Attempts to deal with informal combatants reflected mixed success. On the one hand, whilst piracy came to be, again, condemned, the condemnations of terrorist activities have ended up becoming very act specific. That is, the international community, despite repeatedly condemning terrorism, has been unable to define terrorist acts in an all encompassing way, such as with the deliberate targeting of civilians. Rather, a collection of much more limited treaties have evolved where terrorism is being defined in relation to specific acts, such as, inter alia, hijacking aeroplanes. The other area where success has been elusive has been with the lowering of standards of what makes a formal combatant, with particular regard to the requirement of being clearly identifiable. In this regard, the practices post 1945 for insurgents, guerrillas, death squads and terrorists have all been separate from the formal requirements that defined lawful combatants for the previous 300 years. The revised laws in 1977 supported this trend. Finally, since the 1970s, attempts have been made to deal with mercenaries, but the willingness to actually resolve these issues, despite three attempts to control the flow of soldiers of foreign lands and repeated recognition of the problem that these people can cause, have all failed, as soldiers from foreign lands continue to be reclassified under all sorts of euphemisms.

In short, on the area of combatants, it is difficult to be optimistic or suggest that great progress in any area has been made after 5,000 years of warfare. Whilst the clear rules on child soldiers are commendable, the lack of international rules on conscription are regrettable. The move towards equality with women on the battlefield, as a reflection of a very long-standing practice, is a type of progress when viewed from deliberations about equality. The ambiguity of rules on formal requirements for combatants, terrorism and soldiers of foreign lands do not, at this point in history, give any cause for optimism or assertions of progress.

The second half of this book dealt with the topic of captives. The three questions at play in this section were:

What happens to combatants when captured as prisoners of war?
Can they be tortured, or helped when wounded?
And what happens to their remains when dead?

In these areas, the evidence suggests death was often the assured end for captives caught in pre-literate societies. These deaths were often accompanied by extreme acts of torture whilst alive, and mutilation once dead. By the time that written records were available in ancient Mesopotamia, death for captives was by no means a certainty. The first prisoner of war exchange, after a conflict, can be traced to 1800 BCE. By the time of Greece, philosophers were speaking of the desirability of not always killing prisoners of their own ethnicity, although in practice, this was not applied. Death after capture or via incarceration was well recorded in this period. The Roman period had the same rule – that it was the captives' choice to decide whether prisoners would, or would not be taken. Typically, the best case outcome that a captive had, was to be made into a slave. Prisoner exchanges rarely occurred in this epoch, as most wars were not equal draws, but had winners and losers. Assistance for the sick and wounded of opposing sides was highly unlikely. Torture was endemic, but more as part of the fabric of society than as the infliction of gratuitous cruelty on other humans. The crucifixion of Christ is a good example of this epoch. Unsurprisingly, the Dark Ages offered little light or improvement in any of these practices, with the lack of quarter in times of battle, lack of assistance for enemy sick or wounded, torture and desecration of the dead, being much more the rule, than the exception, for the period. The Middle Ages, as exemplified by the Crusades, largely followed suit, although there were some clear acts of chivalry in this period. Nevertheless, slavery was the best outcome that most of the captured could hope for, if they were lucky enough to survive the battle. In addition, torture became ingrained into the religious contexts of western society with it becoming a highly visible and operational approach until the end of the Reformation.

The progress of humanity over the question of dealing with the remains of fallen enemy was also patchy for most of this period. Despite the initial practices, as evidenced from early Antiquity, the Greeks came to show a relatively high level of sophistication in this area, which the Romans tried to emulate. Early Islam did the same. How successful they were is a matter of debate, as all of the conflicts, in addition to many of the wars throughout Europe up until the Enlightenment, are peppered with instances of desecration and abuse of enemy dead. They are also, however, salted with instances of respect. By the turn of the nineteenth century, the respect for fallen leaders was becoming apparent, although the same could not be said for common soldiers.

The Enlightenment saw the first instances of hospitals and medical officers being, sometimes, respected in times of battle. This era also saw a clear reaction against the practices of torture. Similarly, this period saw the option of letting captives live, rather than be executed, be adopted with much greater frequency. By this stage, it was more likely that prisoners had a better chance to surrender and live through the process, than in the past. Moreover, they were not going to be turned into slaves and sold. This was a monumental breakthrough, as armies by this point were numbering in the tens, if not hundreds, of thousands of men. However, the sheer size of these armies meant that the standards in which the prisoners were held were often shocking, and deaths from incarceration often came to outnumber deaths on the battlefield. By the beginning of the nineteenth century, the creation of the first bilateral treaties on standards for incarceration, and the allowance of independent inspectors to visit captives and provide assistance, began to rectify these problems.

The end of the nineteenth century saw the first clear manifestations of a 'right' to surrender. It also saw the rise of medical practices and facilities, that could actually start to help the wounded and sick, irrespective of side. The sanctity of those trying to help these wounded and the places that they worked in was increasingly understood and accepted. The recognition that it was possible to sink enemy merchant vessels was predicated on the assumption that the seafarers upon them must first be placed into positions of safety. The collection, identification and respect for the dead of all sides was also recognised as best practice within the customs of war at this point. The laws, which emerged to formalise all of these norms in 1864, 1899 and 1907, solidified all of these progresses. They also underlined the accepted custom by this point, that torture was prohibited and the captive was obliged to give over nothing more than their name, rank and serial number. Whilst all of these rules were far from adhered to in the series of 'small wars' that occurred at the turn of the twentieth century, they were largely accepted as the norm by the time of the First World War. This is not to suggest that acts of no-quarter or targeting medical facilities such as hospital ships did not occur. Rather, that when these acts did occur, they were recognised as wrongful (or at least, nothing to be proud about) and their breach was the exception, not the rule. The same could not be said for the sinking of merchant vessels and the abandonment of these seafarers to their fate, in which this rule all but disappeared beneath the waves. These rules were reiterated after the First World War. The war was also the first to confront the problem of 'missing in action' whereby the military technology did not simply kill the opposition, it could do so with such force that the remains of the dead could actually disappear.

The period between the First and Second World Wars saw further attempts to strengthen the positions of both those who were wounded and those who were prisoners. The rules on helping the shipwrecked were also reiterated. The difficulty was not that these new rules were not implemented in the civil wars that raged through this period, but that only some of these rules were adopted by the primary belligerents in the Second World War. In this regard, the execution of prisoners was recorded in most theatres of conflict, in which commanders were often nonchalant in respect to their obligations. However, only in the case of Nazi Germany, did this, in some instances, turn into a high level authorised policy. These deaths were supplemented by extremely poor conditions of transport and incarceration of prisoners in the conflicts with the Soviet Union, Japan and Nazi Germany, which all had no, or very limited access of independent oversight by groups such as the ICRC to help ensure compliance. Where the ICRC had access, such as with the western theatres of this conflict, it is clear that great progress was made in helping to ensure the survival and humane treatment of captives. Where the western Allies appear to have slipped was with their attacks on hospital ships and their lack of regard with the helping of the shipwrecked. In this regard, their practice was much closer to that of their enemies, although in the latter instance, the attack and abandonment of those on the high seas was a policy which, without equivocation, expressly ignored the reformulated rules.

After the war, through a combination of trials and revisiting of the rules, the norms of taking and keeping prisoners, helping the wounded and not torturing were all expanded and reiterated. However, in the conflicts that followed, there was often minimal adherence to these rules. This was especially so in Indo-China, where the conflicts were largely conducted outside of ICRC oversight. Moreover, torture and enforced disappearances, although never officially sanctioned, became of plague-like proportions from Algeria to Zimbabwe. Attempts to seriously open this blind eye to the causation of intentional human suffering were only taken in 1984 and thereafter, as the obligation not to torture was linked with mechanisms to allow visitations to ensure that it was not occurring. In the decade that followed, the explicit outlawing of enforced disappearances was agreed. This followed the additional protocols to the laws of war in 1977, and the formation of the International Criminal Court at the end of the twentieth century. Exactly how far the additions of 1977, 1984, 1998 and 2009 will go is a matter of debate. That is, although the rules on most of the questions at issue are clear, the practice of the vast majority of conflicts, especially those involving at least one non-conventional opponent, tended to reflect practices where the only thing that has clearly changed is the military technology and the devising of ways to avoid the obligations that have been agreed internationally. That is, the development of practices such as rendition or the authorisation of stress and duress techniques, reflect a desire to avoid the clear humane limits that were slowly becoming the norm. As isolated examples, these do not reflect progress.

The point that a country was trying to avoid an international norm that was attempting to set humane standards is critical. It is critical because on practically all of the issues at hand, it is now very clear what is acceptable behaviour when dealing with captives, and what is not. In many regards it has been clear for over a century, although every few decades it has been necessary to keep filling in the loopholes that have been exploited in times of conflict. Nevertheless, humanity, as manifested through the sections of the laws of war on captives, the wounded, torture and the dead – is now clear about where the lines of civilised behaviour are agreed. Accordingly, it is possible to suggest that progress is being made in this area, as humanity now agrees where the limits are. Of course, there is a long way to go, especially in terms of compliance with these limits and goals. Non-compliance with what is now accepted as the norm remains common in many contemporary conflicts. However, the tentative steps evolving out of international criminal law from the 1990s merit a small degree of optimism. This is especially so when weighed against the impunity that has largely covered these questions for the last 2,500 years. We now agree what is wrong, and we are now, slowly, moving towards stamping out these problems. We are far from the end of journey, but at least now, we have all the pieces in place, and we are on the right track.

Index